The Structure of Argument

NINTH EDITION

The Structure of
ARGUMENT

Annette T. Rottenberg

Donna Haisty Winchell

Clemson University

bedford/st.martin's
Macmillan Learning

Boston | New York

For Bedford/St. Martin's

Vice President, Editorial, Macmillan Learning Humanities: Edwin Hill
Senior Program Director for English: Leasa Burton
Program Manager: John E. Sullivan, III
Marketing Manager: Joy Fisher Williams
Director of Content Development: Jane Knetzger
Developmental Editor: Alicia Young
Senior Content Project Manager: Kerri A. Cardone
Senior Workflow Project Manager: Lisa McDowell
Production Supervisor: Robert Cherry
Media Project Manager: Rand Thomas
Editorial Services: Lumina Datamatics, Inc
Composition: Lumina Datamatics, Inc.
Text Permissions Researcher: Elaine Kosta, Lumina Datamatics, Inc.
Photo Researcher: Richard Fox, Lumina Datamatics, Inc.
Permissions Editor: Angela Boehler
Permissions Assistants: Claire Paschal, Allison Ziebka
Design Director, Content Management: Diana Blume
Text Design: Lisa Buckley
Cover Design: William Boardman
Cover Art/Cover Photo: Ragnar Schmuck / Getty Images
Printing and Binding: LSC Harrisonburg

Manufactured in the United States of America.

2   1   0   9   8   7
f   e   d   c   b   a

For information, write: Bedford/St. Martin's, 75 Arlington Street, Boston, MA 02116

ISBN   978- 1-319-05662-9

Acknowledgments

Text acknowledgments and copyrights appear at the back of the book on pages 475–478, which constitute an extension of the copyright page. Art acknowledgments and copyrights appear on the same page as the art selections they cover.

Acknowledgments and copyrights appear on the same page as the text and art selections they cover; these acknowledgments and copyrights constitute an extension of the copyright page.

Preface

Purpose

One look at today's headlines is all it takes to see that every American citizen needs to be able to think critically about what is going on in the nation and in the world. Biased reporting slants the news, and it is hard even to discern what is fact. More than ever, people of conscience need to be able to take a stand and articulate a position.

College has long been a place where values and beliefs are tested. Exposure to new ideas and new perspectives is a part of coming of age. A course in argumentation is a place where students can learn the tools to critically examine the ideas they come in contact with. It is also a place where they can learn to construct their own arguments in defense of what they believe.

In order to get our students really thinking critically about argument, we have to get them to slow down and practice the art of critical reading—and listening. We have to provide timely, accessible readings, we have to get them to analyze sustained argumentative discourse, and we have to give them a vocabulary to be able to talk about it. The vocabulary we use in this text incorporates Aristotle's ancient rhetoric, the stasis theory questions, Carl Rogers's notion of common ground, and Stephen Toulmin's three principal elements of argument: claim, support, and assumption (warrant). In addition, we present the concepts of definition, language, and logic as critical tools for understanding and responding to arguments.

We also have to get our students to write sustained argumentative discourse. They have to learn to apply their knowledge of claim, support, and warrant. They have to learn to define key terms and to recognize, write, and support claims of fact, value, and policy, or, in the language of stasis theory, they have to be able to consider Questions of Fact, Questions of Definition, Questions of Quality, and Questions of Policy. They have to understand that successful arguments require a blend of *logos*, *pathos*, and *ethos*.

They have to appreciate the significance of audience as a practical matter. In the rhetorical or audience-centered approach to argument, to which we subscribe in this text, success is defined as acceptance of the claim by an audience. Arguers in the real world recognize intuitively that their primary goal is not to demonstrate the purity of their logic, but to win the adherence of their audiences.

To do so, students must read critically and think critically about what others have to say. The Internet has redefined what research means to our students. A large part of the challenge is not to find sources but to eliminate the thousands of questionable ones. Faced with the temptation to cut and paste instead of read and understand, students need more help than ever with accurate and fair use of sources. We provide that help in the context of an increasingly digital world.

Organization

Part One of *The Structure of Argument* begins with an introduction to Aristotelian, Rogerian, and Toulmin approaches to argumentation and to stasis theory. Next, it addresses the critical reading of written as well as visual and multimodal arguments. It then provides instruction on writing responses to arguments and writing arguments, particularly in an academic context. Part One is rich in selections that both illustrate various arguments and offer practice for student analysis.

Part Two devotes one chapter apiece to the chief structure of argument—claim, support, and assumption (warrant). Straightforward explanations simplify these concepts for students, and examples are drawn from everyday print and online sources—essays, articles, graphics, reviews, editorials, and advertisements—by both student and professional writers.

Part Three details important matters of reading and writing effective argument: definition, language, and logic. Chapter 9 teaches students the importance of defining key terms as well as the nature of the extended definition essay. Chapter 10 deals with the power of word choice, and Chapter 11 covers the various logical fallacies as well as how to identify and avoid logical errors in arguments.

The first three parts of the book—comprising Chapters 1 through 11—include four unique feature boxes to enhance and reinforce the text. "Writer's Guide" boxes give practical advice on how to write effective arguments and response essays; "Strategies" boxes provide more in-depth information on important skills such as prereading and annotating texts. "Essentials" boxes summarize and reinforce basic argument concepts, and "Research Skills" boxes explain a variety of academic research tasks

Coverage of traditional rhetorical issues such as audience and purpose spans all chapters, helping students grasp the importance of clear communication in a variety of situations. And student essays, with documented sources, serve as models for effective writing and proper form. This ninth edition of *The Structure of Argument* shows students how to apply concepts of rhetoric and logic to spoken, visual, online, and other multimedia arguments. Throughout the text, an abundance of visual arguments—including ads, photographs, screen shots, and graphics—provide visual examples and opportunities for analysis.

Part Four takes up the process of planning, writing, and documenting arguments based on independent research. Chapter 12 focuses on planning and research, including how to narrow a topic as well as how to find and evaluate sources. Chapter 13 addresses drafting and revising written arguments as well as oral presentations. Chapter 14 covers documentation and provides two sample research papers, one employing the Modern Language Association (MLA) documentation system and the other employing the American Psychological Association (APA) documentation style.

Part Five, "Debating the Issues," includes a pair of readings related to each of five current debatable topics: student evaluation of faculty, gender-neutral bathrooms, trigger warnings, princess culture, and paying college athletes. Each pair illustrates contrasting opinions on the same issue and is followed up with discussion questions and writing suggestions.

For instructors who want to apply current events to their argument course, see our blog, "Argument in the Headlines." In our regularly updated posts, we use argument concepts to frame issues in the news, helping students relate the text and the course to their everyday lives. Students are encouraged to visit the blog at the end of each chapter. You can find the blog at **blogs.bedfordstmartins.com /bits**.

New to This Edition

In this edition, a new Chapter 5 focuses early in the text on how to write arguments, particularly in an academic context. This new chapter provides a clearer distinction between writing arguments generally and writing researched arguments, which is the focus of Chapters 12-14. It also makes it possible to make a clearer distinction between analyzing argument (Chapter 4) and writing argument (Chapter 5).

An introduction to stasis theory has been added to Chapter 1. This instruction is intended to help students further understand how logical questions can be used as a means of invention and to structure arguments effectively.

The concept of the warrant has always been a difficult one for students. In this edition we use the term *assumption* to make the concept more accessible.

As is the case with each edition of *The Structure of Argument*, we have updated readings throughout to keep information current and subjects interesting. In this ninth edition, over one-third of the readings are new. In the Debating the Issues section, new issues include the value of student evaluations of faculty, the pros and cons of gender-neutral bathrooms, and wisdom of providing trigger warnings in college classes.

Acknowledgments

This book has profited by the critiques and suggestions of instructors who responded to a questionnaire: John Adrian, University of Virginia; Patricia Andujo, Azusa Pacific University; Carol Bledsoe, Florida Gulf Coast University; Rebecca Briley, Midway University; Joe Davis, North Iowa Area Community College; Hedda Fish, San Diego State University; Deanna Gabrielson, Morehead State University; Steve Holland, Community College; Jeffrey Hotz, East Stroudsburg University; Tammy Jabin, Chemeketa Community College; Jess Koski, Hibbing Community College; Mark Meritt, University of San Francisco; Steven Mohr, Terra State Community College; Daniel Powell, Florida State College at Jacksonville; Jennifer Roscher, De Anza College; Kent Ross, Northeastern Junior College; and Guy Shebat, Youngstown State University. We also thank those reviewers who chose to remain anonymous.

We are grateful to those at Bedford/St. Martin's and Macmillan Learning who have helped in numerous ways large and small: John Sullivan, Leasa Burton, Jennifer Prince, Kalina Ingham, Jennifer Kennett, Angie Boehler, Richard Fox, Kerri Cardone, and, most especially, Alicia Young.

We're all in. As always.

Bedford/St. Martin's is as passionately committed to the discipline of English as ever, working hard to provide support and services that make it easier for you to teach your course your way.

Find **community support** at the Bedford/St. Martin's English Community (community.macmillan.com), where you can follow our *Bits* blog for new teaching ideas, download titles from our professional resource series, and review projects in the pipeline.

Choose **curriculum solutions** that offer flexible custom options, combining our carefully developed print and digital resources, acclaimed works from Macmillan's trade imprints, and your own course or program materials to provide the exact resources your students need.

Rely on **outstanding service** from your Bedford/St. Martin's sales representative and editorial team. Contact us or visit macmillanlearning.com to learn more about any of the options below.

Choose from Alternative Formats of *The Structure of Argument*

Bedford/St. Martin's offers a range of formats. Choose what works best for you and your students:

- *Popular e-Book formats* For details of our e-Book partners, visit **macmillanlearning.com/ebooks**.

Select Value Packages

Add value to your text by packaging any Bedford/St. Martin's, such as Writer's Help 2.0 or *LaunchPad Solo for Readers and Writers*, with *The Structure of Argument* at a significant discount. Contact your sales representative for more information.

LaunchPad Solo for Readers and Writers allows students to work on what they need help with the most. At home or in class, students learn at their own pace, with instruction tailored to each student's unique needs. *LaunchPad Solo for Readers and Writers* features:

- **Pre-built units that support a learning arc.** Each easy-to-assign unit is comprised of a pre-test check, multimedia instruction and assessment, and a post-test that assesses what students have learned about critical reading, writing process, using sources, grammar, style, and mechanics. Dedicated units also offer help for multilingual writers.
- **Diagnostics that help establish a baseline for instruction**. Assign diagnostics to identify areas of strength and for improvement and to help students plan a course of study. Use visual reports to track performance by topic, class, and student as well as improvement over time.
- **A video introduction to many topics.** Introductions offer an overview of the unit's topic, and many include a brief, accessible video to illustrate the concepts at hand.

- **Twenty-five reading selections with comprehension quizzes.** Assign a range of classic and contemporary essays each of which includes a label indicating Lexile level to help you scaffold instruction in critical reading.
- **Adaptive quizzing for targeted learning.** Most units include Learning-Curve, game-like adaptive quizzing that focuses on the areas in which each student needs the most help.

Order ISBN 978-1-319-19264-8 to package *LaunchPad Solo for Readers and Writers* with *The Structure of Argument* at a significant discount. Students who rent or buy a used book can purchase access and instructors may request free access at **macmillanlearning.com/readwrite**.

Writer's Help 2.0 is a powerful online writing resource that helps students find answers, whether they are searching for writing advice on their own or as part of an assignment.

- **Smart search.** Built on research with more than 1,600 student writers, the smart search in Writer's Help provides reliable results even when students use novice terms, such as *flow* and *unstuck*.
- **Trusted content from our best-selling handbooks.** Choose *Writer's Help 2.0, Hacker Version,* or *Writer's Help 2.0, Lunsford Version,* and ensure that students have clear advice and examples for all of their writing questions.
- **Diagnostics that help establish a baseline for instruction.** Assign diagnostics to identify areas of strength and areas for improvement and to help students plan a course of study. Use visual reports to track performance by topic, class, and student as well as improvement over time.
- **Adaptive exercises that engage students.** Writer's Help 2.0 includes LearningCurve, game-like online quizzing that adapts to what students already know and helps them focus on what they need to learn.

Student access is packaged with *The Structure of Argument* at a significant discount. Order ISBN 978-1-319-19261-7 for *Writer's Help 2.0, Hacker Version,* or ISBN 978-1-319-19267-9 for *Writer's Help 2.0, Lunsford Version,* to ensure your students have easy access to online writing support. Students who rent or buy a used book can purchase access and instructors may request free access at **macmillanlearning.com/writershelp2**.

Instructor Resources

You have a lot to do in your course. We want to make it easy for you to find the support you need—and to get it quickly.

Resources for Teaching The Structure of Argument is available as a PDF that can be downloaded from macmillanlearning.com. Visit the instructor resources tab for *The Structure of Argument*. In addition to chapter overviews and teaching tips, the instructor's manual includes sample syllabi, classroom activities, additional research assignments, discussion questions, teaching tips and ideas, and classroom activities.

How This Book Supports WPA Outcomes for First-Year Composition

In 2014, the Council of Writing Program Administrators updated its desired outcomes for first-year composition courses. The following chart provides information on how *The Structure of Argument* helps students build proficiency and achieve the learning outcomes that writing programs across the country use to assess their students' work.

Rhetorical Knowledge

Learn and use key rhetorical concepts through analyzing and composing a variety of texts.	The organization of *The Structure of Argument* supports students' understanding of rhetorical strategy. **Part One** (Chapters 1–5) introduces students to the Aristotelian, Rogerian, and Toulmin approaches to argumentation and to stasis theory. Next, it addresses the critical reading of written as well as visual and multimodal arguments. It then provides instruction on writing analytical responses to arguments and writing arguments, particularly in an academic context. **Part Two** (Chapters 6–8) devotes one chapter apiece to the chief The Structure of Argument: claim, support, and assumption. **Part Three** (Chapters 9–11) details important matters of reading and writing effective argument: definition, language, and logic. **Part Four** (Chapters 12–14) takes up the process of planning, writing, and documenting arguments based on independent research. Coverage of traditional rhetorical issues such as audience and purpose spans all chapters, helping students grasp the importance of clear communication in a variety of rhetorical situations.
Gain experience reading and composing in several genres to understand how genre conventions shape and are shaped by readers' and writers' practices and purposes.	The **68 readings** in the book span a variety of topics and disciplines. Each selection features apparatus that gives students practice analyzing and writing for a variety of purposes and in a range of styles. Throughout the text chapters, **Writers' Guides**, **Research Skills** boxes, end-of-chapter **Assignments**, and **post-reading questions** prompt students to compose different kinds of arguments and responses.
Develop facility in responding to a variety of situations and contexts calling for purposeful shifts in voice, tone, level of formality, design, medium, and/or structure.	**Chapter introductions** for Chapters 1 through 11 explain how each rhetorical element and strategy helps to achieve an author's purpose. Throughout the text, **post-reading questions** call attention to the form and function of different arguments.
Understand and use a variety of technologies to address a range of audiences.	**Chapter 3** shows students how arguments can be made using a variety of multimodal contexts, including photographs, print advertisements, political cartoons, graphics, commercials, speeches, debates, broadcast news, print news, social media, and interactive Web sites.

Match the capacities of different environments (e.g., print and electronic) to varying rhetorical situations.	**Chapter 3** shows students how a variety of print and electronic environments can be used to build persuasive arguments.

Critical Thinking, Reading, and Composing

Use composing and reading for inquiry, learning, critical thinking, and communicating in various rhetorical contexts.	**Part 1** guides students through the process of understanding how arguments function, reading them critically, analyzing them in writing, and composing them effectively. In particular, **Chapters 3 and 4** focus on critical reading of different kinds of arguments, and **Part Four** provides guidance on researching and crafting effective arguments using inquiry and critical thinking.
Read a diverse range of texts, attending especially to relationships between assertion and evidence, to patterns of organization, to the interplay between verbal and nonverbal elements, and to how these features function for different audiences and situations.	Throughout the text, diverse selections illustrate different rhetorical elements, and post-reading questions prompt students to analyze the relationship between assertion and evidence. Further, **Chapter 3** shows students how to analyze the relationship between verbal and nonverbal elements of multimodal texts. **Chapter 6** explores different kinds of claims, and **Chapter 7** offers instruction on how to effectively support assertions.
Locate and evaluate (for credibility, sufficiency, accuracy, timeliness, bias and so on) primary and secondary research materials, including journal articles and essays, books, scholarly and professionally established and maintained databases or archives, and informal electronic networks and internet sources.	**Chapter 12** offers practical instruction for locating and evaluating primary and secondary research materials, and **Chapter 13** illustrates best practices for reviewing research.
Use strategies — such as interpretation, synthesis, response, critique, and design/redesign — to compose texts that integrate the writer's ideas with those from appropriate sources.	The questions and prompts that accompany each reading ask students to interpret, respond, and critique the writer's choices, thereby engaging in academic conversation. **Chapter 13** helps students compose texts that integrate the writer's ideas with those from appropriate sources.

Processes

Develop a writing project through multiple drafts.	**Chapter 12** illustrates best practices for planning and research, and **Chapters 13 and 14** take students through the process of drafting, revising, and presenting effective arguments.
Develop flexible strategies for reading, drafting, reviewing, collaborating, revising, rewriting, rereading, and editing.	**Part Four** offers strategies for reading, drafting, reviewing, revising, and rewriting arguments.

Use composing processes and tools as a means to discover and reconsider ideas.	Throughout each chapter, the text emphasizes the importance of rereading and rewriting to discover and reconsider ideas. In particular, **Chapter 2** provides strategies for evaluating arguments and ideas, and **Chapter 13** reemphasizes evaluation as part of the writing process.
Experience the collaborative and social aspects of writing processes.	**Writer's Guides** and **Research Skills boxes** throughout the text provide insights into the writing and research processes that can be used as prompts for discussion of the writing process.
Learn to give and to act on productive feedback to works in progress.	**Post-reading questions**, as well as the **Writer's Guides**, **Research Skills boxes, and end-of-chapter Assignments** in Chapters 1 through 11, can be used as prompts for peer feedback.
Adapt composing processes for a variety of technologies and modalities.	**Chapter 3** shows students how a variety of technologies and modalities can be used to build persuasive arguments.
Reflect on the development of composing practices and how those practices influence their work.	**Post-reading questions** and **end-of-chapter Assignments** often encourage students to reflect on their knowledge, assumptions, and writing habits.

Knowledge of Conventions

Develop knowledge of linguistic structures, including grammar, punctuation, and spelling, through practice in composing and revising	**Chapter 9** teaches the importance of defining key terms to build effective arguments. **Chapter 10** focuses on language, drawing students' attention to the rhetorical effectiveness of connotation, slanting, concrete and abstract language, clichés, and figurative language. **Chapter 11** helps students to understand logical linguistic structures. **LearningCurve activities** (available in *LaunchPad Solo for Readers and Writers*) provide extensive practice with grammar, punctuation, and spelling.
Understand why genre conventions for structure, paragraphing, tone, and mechanics vary	The text's overarching emphasis on rhetorical context and situation in the text chapters fosters critical thinking about genre conventions. In particular, **Chapter 2** teaches students how to read arguments for content and structure, and **chapter introductions** for Chapters 1 through 11 explain how each element of argument serves a writer's purpose.
Gain experience negotiating variations in genre conventions	The variety of formats and genres represented in the **68 selections** gives students plenty of experience negotiating variations in genre conventions. Post-reading questions encourage students to apply the rhetorical strategies to real-world genres and situations.

Learn common formats and/or design features for different kinds of texts	Annotated selections throughout the text, including student essays, impart awareness of common formats and/or design features for difference kinds of texts, and **Chapter 14** provides specific instruction on formatting and design, including **MLA**- and **APA**-style student research papers with annotations highlighting the genre conventions.
Explore the concepts of intellectual property (such as fair use and copyright) that motivate documentation conventions	**Chapter 13** teaches students how to avoid plagiarism, and **Chapter 14** on documenting sources raises issues of different documentation conventions, specifically MLA and APA formats.
Practice applying citation conventions systematically in their own work	**Chapter 13** offers detailed guidance on avoiding plagiarism, and **Chapter 14** shows students how to apply citation conventions of MLA and APA styles in their own writing.

Brief Contents

Contents

A conservative columnist reports that despite Americans' assumption that, in health as in other areas, the United States is Number 1, the health of our citizens rates lower than many other industrialized nations.

A journalist for a health newsletter explains how, with in vitro fertilization, it is now possible to screen embryos for certain diseases before they are implanted.

2 Critical Reading of Written Arguments   42

A lawyer and journalist defends tattoos as a form of artistic expression.

An American of Indian descent feels a sense of solidarity with foreigners going through immigration screening at the airport.

A travel editor compares Spirit, a villain of an airline, and Southwest, a hero.

An editor focuses on the son of a shooting victim as he pleads for some middle ground in the gun debate.

A freelance journalist argues that homosexual practice and identity are a choice but regrets that she could not admit her choice in the matter when she came out to her family.

3   Critical Reading of Multimodal Arguments   69

4 Writing Argument Analysis 118

5   Writing Arguments   145

PART TWO   Analyzing the Elements   161

6   Claims   163

PART THREE   Using the Elements   245

PART FOUR   Researching and Crafting Arguments   341

12   Planning and Research   343

The nation's largest philanthropy devoted exclusively to health and health care warns about the risks we take if we do not reverse our nation's epidemic of childhood obesity.

A newspaper's editorial board argues for balance between what students will eat and what they are served as a California law governing school lunches is reexamined.

13 Drafting, Revising, and Presenting Arguments   376

14   Documenting Sources   399

PART FIVE   Debating the Issues   437

The Structure of Argument

Understanding ARGUMENT

Approaches to Argument

S ocial networking sites have changed the nature of human discourse. They provide an easy means of staying in touch with people all over the world, a means of sharing the most trivial or the most exciting news. You can tell your friends you are headed to the gym, or you can tell them you are headed for a breakup. You can debate in real time about your politics or your sports teams. You can reestablish old relationships and establish new ones. You can share pictures of your family or your cat's most recent antics.

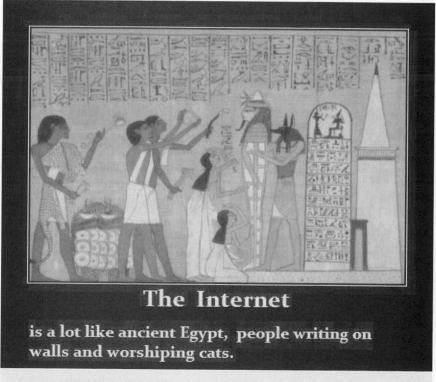

The Internet

is a lot like ancient Egypt, people writing on walls and worshiping cats.

FIGURE 1.1 Meme comparing the Internet to ancient Egypt.

Through social networking, we have the means of presenting a public persona like never before. Some of you may not want to "friend" your parents because of the public persona you project online. You may not want prospective employers to see some of the comments or pictures you post on Facebook. Some college students use LinkedIn for their professional contacts and Facebook or another social networking site for their personal contacts.

The very language of social networking captures its public nature. If someone writes on a wall, the message is intentionally made public. Facebook users can control who their "friends" are, but in practice a "friend" is anyone to whom you are willing to give access to your page. These are the people who can see the writing on your wall, for good or ill.

In writing online, as in other writing that you do, you have to be aware of your audience. You also have to be aware of the context, or rhetorical situation, of what you write and what you read. Consider the Internet meme, one of our newest forms of communication, and how it depends on context for its humor. An Internet meme is a bit of culture in the form of an idea, image, or behavior spread electronically through the culture with the speed of a virus. Use the following questions to analyze the rhetorical situation in Figure 1.2.

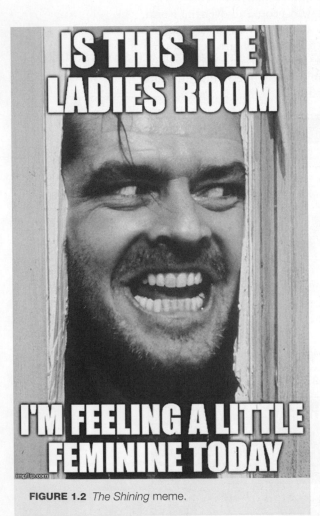

FIGURE 1.2 *The Shining* meme.

Reading and Discussion Questions

1. Examine Figure 1.2. Even if you are not familiar with the film *The Shining*, how would you describe the expression on Jack Nicholson's face in the picture? If you were on the other side of the bathroom door that he is breaking down (with an ax), how might you be feeling?

2. What is the connection between the picture and the words added to it? What political controversy is the meme making a comment? What is the meme saying about that controversy?

A picture and a few words can be good for a laugh. However, they can go further to make a serious statement. Even a simple visual can present an argument. For example, consider Figure 1.3. The vandalized sign makes a point different from what was originally intended.

FIGURE 1.3 Vandalized sign.
JIM LO SCALZO/EPA/Redux

Reading and Discussion Questions

1. Look at Figure 1.3. What do you think the sign might have said before it was vandalized?

2. What makes it clear that the vandalism was not random?

3. What point was someone trying to make in changing the sign in the way he or she did? How does the sign reflect the social and political situation in which the change was made?

Electronic media have added a whole new dimension to the study of rhetorical situations, but the theoretical study of rhetoric has been around since the time of the Greek philosopher Aristotle, who defined rhetoric as all available means of persuasion. The means of persuasion available have expanded from the oral argument of the law court of ancient Greece to include documents transmitted electronically, e-mail, Twitter, pictures, audio, video, and mixed media. This textbook will explore the forms that argument takes in the twenty-first century and, as the title suggests, its elements.

What Is Argument?

In this book, we use the term **argument** to represent forms of discourse that attempt to persuade readers or listeners to accept a position on a controversial issue.

In argument, as in all forms of communication, a person (the writer or speaker) presents a text *about* something (the subject) and *for* someone (the audience). These three main components can be viewed as a triangle:

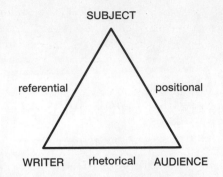

The legs that connect each of the components represent the three main relationships that we study in argument. The relationship between writer and subject is the **referential relationship**. That between writer and audience is the **rhetorical relationship**.[1] The third leg of the triangle, that connecting subject and audience, considers the reader's notions about an issue, or his or her position on an issue. Thus we have labeled that leg of the triangle the **positional relationship**.

Dating back to 400 B.C.E., with the work of Aristotle and other Greek philosophers, the study of argument has evolved over the centuries as scholars continually examine what makes an argument most effective. Although they may use different words and emphasize different ideas, the approaches to argument given in this book—those of Aristotle as well as those of American psychologist Carl Rogers and British philosopher Stephen Toulmin—share important similarities and overlapping concepts, and the basic relationships in the communication triangle are evident in all three. However, even though the basic relationships among writer, audience, and subject remain in place, today's world presents both arguers and audiences with new challenges and new opportunities in creating and understanding argument texts.

Most of the argumentative writing presented in this book will deal with matters of public controversy, an area traditionally associated with the study of argument. As the word *public* suggests, these matters concern us as members of a community. In the arguments you will examine, human beings are engaged in explaining and defending their own actions and beliefs and opposing or compromising with those of others. They do this for at least two reasons:

1. to justify what they do and think, both to themselves and to their audiences
2. to solve problems and make decisions.

In the arguments you will write in this course, you will be doing the same.

---

[1] The terms *rhetorical* and *referential* come from James Moffett, *Teaching the Universe of Discourse* (Boston: Houghton Mifflin, 1968), p. 18. He illustrates the two with a grid crossing *rhetorical* and *referential*.

Aristotelian Rhetoric

Aristotle wrote a treatise on argument that has influenced its study and practice for well over two thousand years. He used the term **logos** to refer to logical appeals and the term **pathos** to refer to emotional appeals. He believed that in an ideal world, logic alone would be enough to persuade. He acknowledged, however, that in the less-than-ideal real world, effective arguments depend not only on *logos* and *pathos* but also on the writer's or speaker's credibility, which he called **ethos**. Together, *ethos*, *logos*, and *pathos* were the primary focus of Aristotle's *Rhetoric*. The writer-audience leg of the communications triangle—the **rhetorical** component—is named for Aristotle's work.

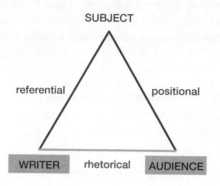

Ethos

Aristotle considered *ethos* to be the most important element in the arguer's ability to persuade the audience to accept a claim. He named intelligence, character, and goodwill as the attributes that produce credibility. Today we might describe these qualities somewhat differently, but the criteria for judging a writer's credibility remain essentially the same:

- Writers must convince their audience that they are knowledgeable and as well informed as possible about the subject.
- Writers must persuade their audience that they are not only truthful in the presentation of evidence but also morally upright and dependable.
- Writers must show that as arguers with good intentions, they have considered the interests and needs of others as well as their own.

A reputation for intelligence, character, and goodwill is not often earned overnight. And it can be lost more quickly than it is gained. Once writers or speakers have betrayed an audience's belief in their character or judgment, they may find it difficult to persuade that audience to accept subsequent claims, no matter how sound the data and reasoning are. Witness the fall from grace of those like Ryan Lochte and Oscar Pistorius, athletes who lost some of the esteem in which they were formerly held. Former president Bill Clinton is unusual in that he has regained much of the esteem he lost when his fidelity to his wife was called into question.

Logos

Logos refers to the logic of an argument: the evidence or proof that supports a writer's claim. Aristotle taught that there are two types of proof to offer in support of an argument: the example and the enthymeme. In simplest terms, this meant induction and deduction. **Induction** is the process of generalizing from specifics (examples). Aristotle was less concerned with providing a large number of examples than with providing one particularly apt one. **Deduction** is the process of applying a generalization to a specific instance.

An **enthymeme** is a variation on the syllogism, the foundation of deductive reasoning. In a **syllogism**, a major premise and a minor premise lead to a logical conclusion.

Syllogism:

Major premise: All mammals are warm blooded.

Minor premise: Dolphins are mammals.

Conclusion: Dolphins are warm blooded.

Because premises in a syllogism are generally certain, the conclusions are rarely disputable. Aristotle defined an enthymeme as a syllogism in which the conclusion is probable, but not certain, because it deals with human affairs, not scientific fact.

Aristotle's Enthymeme:

Major premise: Mass murderers are narcissists.

Minor premise: Seung-Hui Cho was a mass murderer.

Conclusion: Seung-Hui Cho was a narcissist.

Today we use the term **enthymeme** to refer to a syllogism in which one of the premises is *implied* rather than stated outright.

Modern Enthymeme:

Major premise (implied): Bombs that detonate are lethal.

Minor premise: The bomb is going to detonate in one minute!

Conclusion: Let's get out of here!

Pathos

Pathos is appeal to the emotions. An audience can be moved by the logic of an argument alone, but more often emotional appeal combines with logic and ethical appeal to sway the audience. Appeals to the emotions and values of an audience are an appropriate form of persuasion unless (1) they are irrelevant to the argument or draw attention from the issues being argued or (2) they are

RESEARCH SKILL › Using Databases

What is the first step you should take when you need to do some research?

If your response is to go to *Google*, the answer is yes and no. In your daily life, if you need to look up some factual information, you can find it quickly on *Google* or another similar search engine. For most assignments for your classes, the answer is no.

For one thing, remember that *Google* finds any reference to your search term and doesn't discriminate based on quality. Anyone can post on the Internet, so there is no control over accuracy. You will also be inundated with far more sources than you could ever look at.

If you had checked *Google* for information about Aristotle when this book went to press, you would have found these numbers:

"Aristotle" — 23,800,000 results
"Aristotle" and "argument" — 70,000 results
"Aristotle's argument" — 530,000 results
"Aristotle" and "rhetoric" — 603,000 results
"Aristotle's rhetoric" — 164,000 results

Wikipedia will be near the top of the list for many subjects, but you shouldn't plan to use *Wikipedia* as a source for college work. It lacks the authority your professors will expect.

Where, then, should you start? At the library, by prowling the shelves? Don't rule out electronic sources. Instead, find out what databases your school has access to and which of those databases are most appropriate for your research.

For example, a good general database for academic subjects is Academic OneFile. There, a search for information about Aristotle yields these results:

"Aristotle" — subject search 1,503 results
keyword search 12,749 results
"Aristotle" and "argument" — 5 results (subject)
247 results (keyword)
"Aristotle" and "rhetoric" — 67 results (subject)
261 results (keyword)

As you can see, by the end of this search you are reaching a manageable number of sources to explore. Even with 55 results, a quick look at the titles will eliminate some and let you know which ones are worth investigating.

The numbers refer to articles in academic journals, generally the ones most widely accepted by college faculty.

You will learn more about finding sources in Chapter 12.

---

used to conceal another purpose. The most popular emotional appeals are to pity and to fear. A picture of a starving child in Africa is a legitimate emotional appeal unless the picture leads donors to send money that goes largely to administrative costs and not to the children who need help. It is legitimate to arouse fear of the consequences of texting while driving if the descriptions are accurate. It is not legitimate to scare a family into buying an insurance policy they cannot afford by appealing to their fear of ruinous medical bills if the insurance would not provide the promised relief.

An argument becomes personal when it hits close to home. We can sometimes look objectively at society's problems until our own children are threatened or our own livelihood is in jeopardy. Then emotion enters the picture and often outweighs logic.

Some individuals and groups are quick to take advantage of human willingness to show compassion to others. Our emotional response to an event like the Orlando nightclub shootings is to contribute to those who have suffered loss or injury. In our emotional vulnerability, though, unfortunately, we have to guard against those who are only out for personal gain and may collect gifts that will never reach the victims.

Ancient Rhetoric Today

How can we apply the teachings of Aristotle in the digital age? We can use the same vocabulary and study the same writer-subject-audience relationships, but we must also take into account the many cultural and technological changes that have occurred in the past two thousand years.

Writers — but more commonly speakers — in Aristotle's world of the fourth century B.C.E. were very limited in audience and in subject matter. As far as the rhetorical relationship is concerned, inventions like the printing press, and later the telegraph, gave writers access to a wider and wider range of audiences; more recent developments such as blogs, Facebook, and Twitter have increased exponentially the audiences a writer can reach. Moreover, today's audiences have more access to background information about authors, enabling readers to consider a writer's *ethos* for themselves. In addition, readers are more active participants in today's rhetorical relationships: They are encouraged to think critically about and respond to the arguments they encounter, and they can do so instantly and publicly in online forums.

The amount of information available at the click of a mouse has also exploded. That means that the relationship between writer and subject — the referential relationship — has also changed with the times. Technological advances have raised expectations about what an arguer should know about a subject. Living in the information age as we do, writers must be able to find, understand, evaluate, and manage information from a seemingly endless range of sources — and then synthesize that information into a coherent argument.

Technology has also greatly influenced the audience-subject relationship. In the limited world of ancient Greece, it was relatively easy to predict what an audience would know about a subject. There was more of a shared worldview than has existed in more recent times. In ancient Greece, rigid rules dictated the organization of a speech, and the examples were drawn from well-known narratives, true or fictional. Today it is much more difficult for a writer to place himself or herself in someone else's position and try to see a subject from that person's point of view. And, just as writers do, readers also have more access to information than ever before. Readers, therefore, can — and do — form opinions based on their own chosen sources, which may contradict the evidence presented by the writer.

ARGUMENT ESSENTIALS

Aristotelian Rhetoric

Three means of appealing to an audience:

- *Ethos* — appeal based on the writer's or speaker's credibility
- *Logos* — logical appeal
- *Pathos* — emotional appeal

Two types of proof:

- Inductive reasoning — drawing a conclusion based on examples
- Deductive reasoning — drawing a conclusion based on probability

READING ARGUMENT

Seeing Aristotelian Rhetoric

The essay that follows was written a few weeks after the death of twenty students and six adults in the school shooting at Sandy Hook Elementary School in Newtown, Connecticut. It has been annotated to show key features of Aristotelian rhetoric used by the author.

In Gun Control Debate, Logic Goes out the Window
RICHARD J. DAVIS

President Obama has decided to move ahead with a variety of gun control measures, and Sen. Dianne Feinstein has proposed a new assault weapons ban. While Washington debates new proposals on gun control, attention also needs to focus on obstacles to effective enforcement of existing gun laws, including the ban imposed by Congress on the Bureau of Alcohol, Tobacco, Firearms and Explosives creating a federal database of firearms transactions.

> Davis will focus on one obstacle to enforcement of existing gun laws, the ban on creating a federal database.

A discussion of the origin of that ban, which was initially enacted in response to a proposal made when I served as the assistant Treasury secretary overseeing the bureau, is useful to a better understanding of the dynamics of the debate over specific gun control proposals. Sadly, both then and now, logic often loses out.

> *Ethos:* Davis establishes his credibility.
>
> Thesis: Logic lost out in the past, and it is losing out now.

Early in 1978, the proposal we developed was relatively simple: Manufacturers, wholesalers, and retailers would file reports of sales of firearms with the bureau, but to avoid the argument that the bureau was impermissibly creating a national registry of gun owners, retailers would not be required to list the name of the retail purchaser.

The rationale for creating a centralized firearms transaction database was twofold. First, it would speed up the ability to trace guns found at crime scenes, since even with the less sophisticated technology then available, such traces would still be able to be done virtually instantaneously.

> *Logos*: Major premise: Speeding up the tracing of guns would be beneficial to society.
> Minor premise: A federal database would speed up the tracing of guns.
> Conclusion: A federal database would be beneficial.

5   Second, and even more significant, it would allow the bureau to analyze the flow of firearms to identify potential diversions to the illegal gun market. For example, if a hundred handguns a week were going to one dealer in a small town in Virginia, that would suggest the possibility that guns were being sold illegally by that dealer to individuals smuggling them to New York

> Major premise: Allowing the bureau to analyze the flow of firearms would be beneficial.
> Minor premise: A federal

Richard J. Davis was the Assistant Secretary of the Treasury for Enforcement and Operations during the Carter administration (1977–1981). He is now a lawyer in New York. The article appeared on cnn.com on January 25, 2013.

database would enable the bureau to analyze the flow of firearms. Conclusion: A federal database would be beneficial.

Ethos: He admits his naiveté and his mistake.

Faulty logic used by opposition (see page 319).

Either/or fallacy: Either we stop it all, or we do nothing (see page 319).

Response to faulty logic uses induction: Examples of laws that work, although not 100% of the time, lead to the conclusion that gun laws would also save lives and be worth enacting.

Deduction based on induction from examples.

or other states. By allowing this kind of analysis, the bureau could target investigative resources on dealers mostly likely to be violating the law.

Proceeding with what can only be described as youthful naiveté, the day the proposed regulations were published, I convened a briefing for interested parties, including the NRA and other anti-gun control groups. After all, none of these proposals would in any way alter the rules relating to gun ownership.

The hope was that understanding the limited nature of the proposal would mute their opposition. I was very wrong. We had to withdraw the proposals, and Congress punitively reduced the bureau's budget and ultimately banned it from creating such firearms transaction databases.

The opposition to the proposed regulations was intense, with opponents writing hundreds of thousands of often angry letters, both to Treasury and to members of Congress. Little of the opposition, however, focused on the actual proposals themselves.

One common thread to the opposition was the "slippery slope argument," which argued that the regulation would create a centralized list of all gun owners' names — which it would not have done — or would lead to the creation of such a list, which would then enable the government to seize everyone's weapons and put us on a path to dictatorship.

After all, it was argued, this is what the Nazis had done.   10

Another often-used argument was that what we were proposing would not stop all criminals from securing or using firearms, and therefore it was not something worth doing.

Arguments like these prevent an honest discussion of any proposal to address the problem of gun violence in America. The assumption that any regulation of firearms sets us on the path to confiscation of weapons is not only ludicrous on its face, it ignores all political reality. And, if the test for any proposal is whether it totally solves the problem being addressed, then no action would be taken addressing so many of society's important issues.

Why require the use of seat belts if wearing a seat belt does not always save a life in an accident? Why prohibit people from carrying guns onto planes if it doesn't eliminate all risk of hijacking? Why prohibit providing assistance to terrorists if it doesn't stop all terrorist acts? Why require tests for the issuance of driver's licenses if it doesn't stop all accidents?

We require these regulations because they address problems that need to be addressed and because if these regulations can save some lives, they are steps worth taking. So it should be with the gun debate.

No proposal, or set of proposals, will ever stop all gun crime. But the 1978   15
proposals could have stopped some illegal sales of guns by renegade dealers.

And things like forced waiting periods for gun purchases, requiring background checks for firearms buyers at gun shows, and a ban on assault weapons would certainly save some lives.

Maybe it is thousands of lives over time; maybe it is hundreds. But isn't every life saved worth it? Would it not have been worth it if even some of the lives lost at Sandy Hook could have been saved because the shooter did not have an assault weapon?

Gun control is not the total answer to the problem of mass shootings, but it plainly needs to be part of any meaningful response. Let's hope that this time the debate on gun control will be a more sensible one.

Examples

Pathos: emotional appeal

Returns to his thesis idea that logic should not lose out

Practice: Aristotelian Rhetoric

Examine the print advertisement shown on page 14, and answer the questions below.

Reading and Discussion Questions

1. How did the creators of this ad use an unusual point of view to achieve humor?
2. Look carefully at all of the visual elements of the ad. How are they used in subtle and not-so-subtle ways to advance the ad's theme? What is that theme?
3. Look closely at all of the text and consider how it too advances theme.
4. Does the ad make use of *logos, ethos, pathos,* or a combination of these types of appeal? Explain.
5. How do similar ads that you have seen related to animals in need of a home use *pathos* differently?

A Person Is the Best Thing to Happen to a Shelter Pet
THE SHELTER PET PROJECT

The Humane Society of the United States, Maddie's Fund®, and the Ad Council.

Practice: Aristotelian Rhetoric

Applying the comments on the Richard J. Davis essay on pages 11-13 as a model, analyze the following blog post using Aristotle's terminology. Then answer the questions at the end of the essay.

I Am Adam Lanza's Mother
LIZA LONG

Three days before 20-year-old Adam Lanza killed his mother, then opened fire on a classroom full of Connecticut kindergartners, my 13-year-old son Michael (name changed) missed his bus because he was wearing the wrong color pants.

"I can wear these pants," he said, his tone increasingly belligerent, the black-hole pupils of his eyes swallowing the blue irises.

"They are navy blue," I told him. "Your school's dress code says black or khaki pants only."

"They told me I could wear these," he insisted. "You're a stupid bitch. I can wear whatever pants I want to. This is America. I have rights!"

5   "You can't wear whatever pants you want to," I said, my tone affable, reasonable. "And you definitely cannot call me a stupid bitch. You're grounded from electronics for the rest of the day. Now get in the car, and I will take you to school."

I live with a son who is mentally ill. I love my son. But he terrifies me.

A few weeks ago, Michael pulled a knife and threatened to kill me and then himself after I asked him to return his overdue library books. His 7- and 9-year-old siblings knew the safety plan — they ran to the car and locked the doors before I even asked them to. I managed to get the knife from Michael, then methodically collected all the sharp objects in the house into a single Tupperware container that now travels with me. Through it all, he continued to scream insults at me and threaten to kill or hurt me.

That conflict ended with three burly police officers and a paramedic wrestling my son onto a gurney for an expensive ambulance ride to the local emergency room. The mental hospital didn't have any beds that day, and Michael calmed down nicely in the ER, so they sent us home with a prescription for Zyprexa and a follow-up visit with a local pediatric psychiatrist.

We still don't know what's wrong with Michael. Autism spectrum, ADHD, Oppositional Defiant or Intermittent Explosive Disorder have all been tossed around at various meetings with probation officers and social workers and counselors and teachers and school administrators. He's been on a slew of antipsychotic and mood altering pharmaceuticals, a Russian novel of behavioral plans. Nothing seems to work.

Liza Long, from Boise, Idaho, is an author, musician, and mother of four who blogs under the name Anarchist Soccer Mom. This particular post, which appeared originally on her blog and then on December 16, 2012, on thebluereview .com, quickly went viral in the wake of the Newtown school shooting. Her son has since that time been diagnosed with bipolar disorder and received the proper medication, and in 2016 was making plans for college.

10   At the start of seventh grade, Michael was accepted to an accelerated program for highly gifted math and science students. His IQ is off the charts. When he's in a good mood, he will gladly bend your ear on subjects ranging from Greek mythology to the differences between Einsteinian and Newtonian physics to Doctor Who. He's in a good mood most of the time. But when he's not, watch out. And it's impossible to predict what will set him off.

Several weeks into his new junior high school, Michael began exhibiting increasingly odd and threatening behaviors at school. We decided to transfer him to the district's most restrictive behavioral program, a contained school environment where children who can't function in normal classrooms can access their right to free public babysitting from 7:30–1:50 Monday through Friday until they turn 18.

The morning of the pants incident, Michael continued to argue with me on the drive. He would occasionally apologize and seem remorseful. Right before we turned into his school parking lot, he said, "Look, Mom, I'm really sorry. Can I have video games back today?"

"No way," I told him. "You cannot act the way you acted this morning and think you can get your electronic privileges back that quickly."

His face turned cold, and his eyes were full of calculated rage. "Then I'm going to kill myself," he said. "I'm going to jump out of this car right now and kill myself."

15   That was it. After the knife incident, I told him that if he ever said those words again, I would take him straight to the mental hospital, no ifs, ands, or buts. I did not respond, except to pull the car into the opposite lane, turning left instead of right.

"Where are you taking me?" he said, suddenly worried. "Where are we going?"

"You know where we are going," I replied.

"No! You can't do that to me! You're sending me to hell! You're sending me straight to hell!"

I pulled up in front of the hospital, frantically waving for one of the clinicians who happened to be standing outside. "Call the police," I said. "Hurry."

20   Michael was in a full-blown fit by then, screaming and hitting. I hugged him close so he couldn't escape from the car. He bit me several times and repeatedly jabbed his elbows into my rib cage. I'm still stronger than he is, but I won't be for much longer.

The police came quickly and carried my son screaming and kicking into the bowels of the hospital. I started to shake, and tears filled my eyes as I filled out the paperwork—"Were there any difficulties with . . . at what age did your child . . . were there any problems with . . . has your child ever experienced . . . does your child have . . ."

At least we have health insurance now. I recently accepted a position with a local college, giving up my freelance career because when you have a kid like this, you need benefits. You'll do anything for benefits. No individual insurance plan will cover this kind of thing.

For days, my son insisted that I was lying—that I made the whole thing up so that I could get rid of him. The first day, when I called to check up on him, he said, "I hate you. And I'm going to get my revenge as soon as I get out of here."

By day three, he was my calm, sweet boy again, all apologies and promises to get better. I've heard those promises for years. I don't believe them anymore.

25   On the intake form, under the question, "What are your expectations for treatment?" I wrote, "I need help."

And I do. This problem is too big for me to handle on my own. Sometimes there are no good options. So you just pray for grace and trust that in hindsight, it will all make sense.

I am sharing this story because I am Adam Lanza's mother. I am Dylan Klebold's and Eric Harris's mother. I am James Holmes's mother. I am Jared Loughner's mother. I am Seung-Hui Cho's mother. And these boys — and their mothers — need help. In the wake of another horrific national tragedy, it's easy to talk about guns. But it's time to talk about mental illness.

According to *Mother Jones*, since 1982, 61 mass murders involving firearms have occurred throughout the country. Of these, 43 of the killers were white males, and only one was a woman. *Mother Jones* focused on whether the killers obtained their guns legally (most did). But this highly visible sign of mental illness should lead us to consider how many people in the U.S. live in fear, like I do.

When I asked my son's social worker about my options, he said that the only thing I could do was to get Michael charged with a crime. "If he's back in the system, they'll create a paper trail," he said. "That's the only way you're ever going to get anything done. No one will pay attention to you unless you've got charges."

30   I don't believe my son belongs in jail. The chaotic environment exacerbates Michael's

sensitivity to sensory stimuli and doesn't deal with the underlying pathology. But it seems like the United States is using prison as the solution of choice for mentally ill people. According to Human Rights Watch, the number of mentally ill inmates in U.S. prisons quadrupled from 2000 to 2006, and it continues to rise — in fact, the rate of inmate mental illness is five times greater (56 percent) than in the non-incarcerated population.

With state-run treatment centers and hospitals shuttered, prison is now the last resort for the mentally ill — Rikers Island, the LA County Jail, and Cook County Jail in Illinois housed the nation's largest treatment centers in 2011.

No one wants to send a 13-year-old genius who loves Harry Potter and his snuggle animal collection to jail. But our society, with its stigma on mental illness and its broken healthcare system, does not provide us with other options. Then another tortured soul shoots up a fast food restaurant. A mall. A kindergarten classroom. And we wring our hands and say, "Something must be done."

I agree that something must be done. It's time for a meaningful, nation-wide conversation about mental health. That's the only way our nation can ever truly heal.

God help me. God help Michael. God help us all.

Reading and Discussion Questions

1. Why is the essay called "I Am Adam Lanza's Mother"? (After all, she isn't.) What is her purpose in telling her story?
2. Where in the essay does Long most clearly state her thesis?
3. What type of appeal is Long using when she recounts the details of Michael's violence and threats of violence?
4. Where does she make use of logical appeal?

5. Does Long come across as a credible person? In other words, what sort of ethos does the essay convey?

6. Research the online responses to Long's blog post, and formulate your own response.

Stasis Theory

Another concept from the classical age of Greek and Roman rhetoric that can still be applied to arguments today is that of **stasis theory**. Aristotle and another Greek philosopher, Hermagoras, wrote about stasis theory, and their ideas were refined by the Roman philosophers Cicero, Quintilian, and Hermogenes. Stasis theory provided citizens preparing a legal case a means of exploring the case and of achieving stasis, or arriving at agreement as to the point at issue.

The Stasis Questions

Consider first how a series of questions could provide a structured way of thinking about an alleged crime:

- **Questions of Fact or Conjecture:** What happened? Did the accused do it?
- **Questions of Definition:** What crime was it?
- **Questions of Quality:** Was it right or wrong? Was it justified? What was the motivation?
- **Questions of Procedure:** What should be done about it? What is the proper court to hear the case?

These questions have been recast into more general questions that can be applied to any issue about which there is disagreement. It is important to achieve stasis in order to argue effectively because you have to know precisely what is at issue. For example, the term "gun control" is so broad that it is necessary to define the term before trying to argue for or against it. If one party is arguing in favor of taking all guns away from all American citizens, that party will not agree with someone who is arguing that "controlling" guns means enforcing stricter laws about the types of guns that can be sold or about the waiting period for buying a gun. There is a difference between which guns are controlled and how gun ownership is controlled that will make formal debate about the issue pointless until some definitions are clarified. A starting point could be to decide, for example, whether or not American citizens should be allowed to own semiautomatic weapons, but even then, the definition of "semiautomatic" would have to be agreed upon.

The stasis questions are frequently used in writing courses as a means of exploring a subject. Different textbooks and different scholars word the questions a bit differently, and some list four questions, while others list five. This list of four is fairly standard as a set of questions for exploring argumentative topics:

- **Questions of Fact:** What are the facts of the issue?
- **Questions of Definition:** What is the meaning or nature of the issue?
- **Questions of Quality:** What is the seriousness or value of the issue?
- **Questions of Policy:** What is the plan of action about the issue?

READING ARGUMENT

Seeing Stasis Theory

Used as a means of invention, the stasis questions can generate a wealth of information. You will most likely use only a portion of the ideas generated by the invention exercise, but you may also discover ideas that you might not have thought about otherwise.

Take a subject like the American Electoral College, and see what ideas might come to mind in working through the questions:

- **Questions of Fact: What are the facts about the Electoral College?**
  On September 6, 1878, the Constitutional Convention approved a proposal to create a group of Electors to select the president and vice president of the new United States. Each of the fifty states has a number of Electors equal to its number of members of Congress, and the District of Columbia has the same number of Electors as the least populous state. There are now 538 Electors. Since the 1880s, all states except Maine and Nebraska pledge all of their Electors to the presidential candidate who wins the most popular votes in that state. A majority of 270 electoral votes is needed to elect the president. When Americans cast their votes every four years, they are actually voting not for a candidate but for Electors representing that candidate.

  What has happened in some recent elections? In 2012, Barack Obama defeated Mitt Romney, winning 332 electoral votes to Romney's 206, and winning 65,446,032 popular votes to Romney's 60,589,084. Obama won the popular vote in 26 states and the District of Columbia, and Romney won the popular vote in 24 states.

  In 2000, George W. Bush defeated Al Gore, Jr., winning 271 electoral votes to Gore's 266, and winning 50,456,062 popular votes to Gore's 50,996,582.

  Electoral votes are not cast until December after a presidential election in November. Each state sends a Certificate of Votes recording how the Electors voted to the Senate, where the votes are counted on the sixth of January. There is no Constitutional requirement that Electors vote according to the popular vote, but some states require their Electors to do so, making it binding by state law or by pledges to the political parties. No Elector has ever been prosecuted for failing to vote as pledged.

- **Questions of Definition: What is the meaning or nature of the Electoral College?**

  The Electoral College is not a place but a process — the process by which the president and vice president of the United State are chosen. The Constitution refers to Electors but not to a college of Electors. The concept was written into federal law in 1845 as a "college of Electors." The Electoral College was originally a compromise between the election of a president by a vote in Congress and election by a popular vote of qualified citizens. The question of what constituted qualified citizens was complicated in the eighteenth century by the existence of slavery in some states. Technically, a vote for Clinton or Trump, Bush or Gore was not a vote for any of those individuals but a vote for an Elector chosen to vote for one of them. The Electors from each state do not meet as a group until December after a presidential election in November.

- **Questions of Quality: What is the seriousness or value of the Electoral College?**

  Some question whether in the twentieth century the Electoral College is preferable to popular vote as the method of choosing president and vice president. Is a procedure fair if it is possible for a candidate to win the popular vote but not win the election because of Electoral College votes? The writers of the Constitution felt that a small group of Electors would make a wiser political decision than the general public. Small states also feared the power of larger states. Would states with a small number of popular votes be largely ignored if popular vote were used? Are some states currently disadvantaged by the winner-take-all system in 48 states that can make almost 50 percent of voters feel that their votes are wasted because all of that state's electoral votes go to the candidate who wins the majority of the popular vote?

- **Questions of Policy: What is the plan of action about the issue?**

  Should the Electoral College be abolished? Should it be replaced by popular vote? Should the Electoral College continue to exist, but the winner-take-all method of distributing electoral votes be abolished?

Practice: Stasis Theory

Using the analysis of the Electoral College above as a guide, apply the four stasis questions to one of the following topics. Push yourself to write more than a sentence or two in response to each question. What you write can be a combination of questions and statements.

> Medical marijuana
> Late-term abortion
> Hazing
> Open carry
> Body cameras for police
> Good Samaritan laws

Stasis Theory Claims

The stasis questions can help lead to decisions regarding what to say about a topic. Each of the four questions leads most directly to a certain type of claim, or thesis statement, and a certain type of argument.

Questions of Fact	lead to	**Claims of Fact**	and	**Analysis.**
Questions of Definition	lead to	**Claims of Definition**	or	**Definition Arguments.**
Questions of Quality	lead to	**Claims of Value**	or	**Evaluation Arguments.**
Questions of Policy	lead to	**Claims of Policy**	or	**Proposal Arguments.**

Keep in mind that many arguments are not a pure form of any of these types of argument. Establishing facts and definitions is often a part of building a sound evaluation or proposal argument. Evaluation is often a part of establishing the need for a proposed change.

In the next section, on the Toulmin Method, you will read more about claims of fact, value, and policy, and the whole of Chapter 5 is devoted to the writing of these three types of claims. Chapter 8 discusses the need for clear definition in any argument and those topics that may require an entire essay of definition.

Rogerian Argument

Carl Rogers was a twentieth-century humanistic psychologist who translated his ideas about therapy into communication theory. As a therapist, he believed that the experience of two people meeting and speaking honestly to each other would have a healing effect. In later years, he became convinced that the same principles of nondirective, nonconfrontational therapy that emphasized attentive listening could work not only for couples and small groups but also for large groups, even nations, to create more harmonious relationships.

Such nonconfrontational communication between individuals or among groups is hampered, Rogers believed, by the fact that there is no longer anything approaching a shared worldview. In the past, those like Copernicus and Galileo who saw reality differently were often condemned or even killed. Rogers wrote, "Although society has often come around eventually to agree with its dissidents . . . there is no doubt that this insistence upon a known and certain universe has been part of the cement that holds a culture together."[2] In the Rogerian approach to argumentation, effective communication requires both understanding another's reality and respecting it.

Rogers's approach to communication is based on the idea of mutual elements or **common ground**. A writer or speaker and an audience who have very different opinions on a highly charged emotional issue need a common

---

[2] "Do We Need 'a' Reality?" *A Way of Being* (New York: Houghton Mifflin, 1980), p. 103.

ground on which to meet if any productive communication is going to take place. In the midst of all of their differences, they have to find a starting point on which they agree. In 1977, Maxine Hairston summed up five steps for using Rogerian argumentation that incorporate the two essentials of the approach — being able to (1) summarize another's position with understanding and clarity and (2) locate common ground between two different positions:

1. Give a brief, objective statement of the issue under discussion.
2. Summarize in impartial language what you perceive the case for the opposition to be; the summary should demonstrate that you understand their interests and concerns and should avoid any hint of hostility.
3. Make an objective statement of your own side of the issue, listing your concerns and interests but avoiding loaded language or any hint of moral superiority.
4. Outline what common ground or mutual concerns you and the other person or group seem to share; if you see irreconcilable interests, specify what they are.
5. Outline the solution you propose, pointing out what both sides may gain from it.[3]

Rogerian argument places more emphasis on the relationship between audience and subject than other rhetorical theories do. It emphasizes the audience's view of the subject and places it in juxtaposition to the writer's. Understanding another's ideas with the clarity and lack of a judgmental attitude that Rogers proposed requires taking on, temporarily, that other's point of view — walking a mile in his shoes — and seeing the subject with his eyes.

As shown on the communications triangle below, the Rogerian approach seeks to find common ground between the writer's and audience's relationship to the subject.

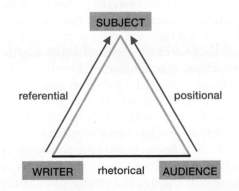

In an essay written using the Rogerian approach to argumentation, the thesis or claim will be one that reconciles opposing positions — at least as far as

---

[3] Maxine Hairston, "Carl Rogers's Alternative to Traditional Rhetoric," *College Composition and Communication*, December 1976, pp. 375–76.

that is possible with the sorts of emotionally charged subjects that call for a nonconfrontational approach in the first place.

Consider the example of management and striking union members. The situation can quickly degenerate into shouting matches and violence with little progress toward resolution. The union can make demands, which the management turns down, and the shouting matches begin again. Rogers would advocate the seemingly simple method of the two sides listening to each other with understanding. Management has to be able to explain the union's position in a way that the union members feel is fair before it can present its own. And then the reverse. This approach is time consuming, but it can keep the discussion from dissolving into anger and impasse. The resolution — parallel to the thesis of an essay employing the Rogerian method — will most likely be a compromise between the two positions.

In writing an essay using the Rogerian method, the test of the writer's *ethos*, or ethics, is how fairly she sums up her opponent's views. A common tactic for unethical writers is to attack an opponent for something he never said. This puts the opponent in the position of trying to defend a position that he does not believe and sidetracks the whole argument — which is exactly what the unscrupulous writer is trying to do.

ARGUMENT ESSENTIALS
Rogerian Argument

- Presents opponent's views accurately and objectively.
- Presents writer's views fairly and objectively.
- Explains what common ground exists between the two positions.
- Thesis statement presents a compromise between the two positions.

READING ARGUMENT

Seeing Rogerian Argument

The essay that follows has been annotated to show the key features of Rogerian argument used by the authors.

Katie Couric and the Celebrity Medicine Syndrome
JULIA BELLUZ AND STEVEN J. HOFFMAN

An email with the subject line "OMG" recently came from one of our mothers, and it contained chilling information about the HPV vaccine. "200 people have died from it," Mom claimed, "and it does not even last long enough to prevent cervical cancer."

Her source was not her doctor, a new study or the Food and Drug Administration. Her information came from a recent episode of Katie Couric's

First three paragraphs show dangers of celebrities as medical spokespeople.

Julia Belluz is a health journalist. Steven J. Hoffman is Scientific Director of the Canadian Institutes of Health Research's Institute of Population and Public Health and CIHR's lead for global health. Their article appeared in the December 18, 2013, edition of the *Los Angeles Times*.

ABC talk show about "all sides" of the "HPV controversy."[4] Since then, most of the alarmist vaccine claims made in the episode have been debunked. But Mom remains a victim of celebrity medicine: She heard a warning from someone famous, believed it and spread the misinformation.

Unfortunately, Mom is not alone. Celebrities have crept into our medicine cabinets and kitchens, influencing what pills we pop, tests we order, and foods we fear. More often than not, their advice and products are dubious. "Then why do so many people believe them?" Mom asked.

This time, we have an answer. One of us — Hoffman — just published a review of research on celebrity in the December 18 issue of the *British Medical Journal*. It addresses this question.

The review draws on studies from a range of disciplines and synthesizes key narratives on celebrity followership. The conclusion? Our brains, psyches, and societies appear to be hardwired to trust celebrities, whether on anti-vaccine antics or miracle medicines.

Economics tells us that we use celebrity endorsements as signals or shortcuts for judging qualities such as validity or relevance. So when Bill Clinton recommends veganism, his approval elevates animal-free eating, even though his expertise lies more with foreign policy than nutrition.

The halo theory from marketing studies explains how celebrities' success in one area — say, acting — makes people presume they are competent in unrelated areas — say, medicine. This influences how we interpret their health messages no matter how nonsensical, and may explain why Gwyneth Paltrow has become a credible advisor on vitamin D deficiency, even though she didn't go to medical school nor is she a health expert.

Classical conditioning suggests that we learn to psychologically associate unrelated stimuli in a way that exposure to them achieves similar responses. This means warm feelings toward celebrities are stirred up in us by the things they pitch. It's no surprise, then, that PepsiCo paid Beyoncé $50 million to promote its products.

Neuroscience studies also help explain why these endorsements work on us. Brain scans have demonstrated that images of celebrities increase activity in our medial orbitofrontal cortices, the region responsible for forming positive associations. So if you're an Angelina Jolie fan, seeing her image lights up this part of the brain, making you more likely to think highly about

5

---

[4] In a "For the Record" box accompanying this article, the *LA Times* notes, "[Couric's] show reported that there have been more than 200 claims filed, including 11 from families who believe the vaccine caused their children's deaths." – EDS.

(Margin notes:)

Alarmist claims made on the show are spread by victims who believe the claims.

Medical advice from celebrities is dubious.

Hoffman's review of studies shows *why* we trust celebrities anyway.

Explanation based on economics

Explanation based on marketing studies

Explanation based on psychology

Explanation based on neuroscience

whatever she is promoting, even when it's something extreme like a double mastectomy to prevent breast cancer.

10   Reason should help us overcome an illogical addiction to celebrity health advice. Questioning prescriptions from prominent people and asking about the evidence behind them could save us time, money, and harm. But, as the science shows, celebrity influence is not rational.

> One solution: Use logic and don't trust celebrities. But trusting celebrities is not rational.

The first step to addressing celebrity medicine is recognizing that it is a human vulnerability and a serious public health challenge. Doing that can empower us to think twice before we take advice from the stars.

We should also use these new insights to rethink how we promote healthy living and evidence-based decision-making. Actress and anti-vaccine activist Jenny McCarthy may be their arch-nemesis, but doctors and public health practitioners can learn from her. Making vaccines, exercise, and oral hygiene as attractive as celebrities would be more valuable than any million-dollar endorsement deal and more effective than any detox diet. It might also save Mom from putting her most sacred asset — her health — into the well-manicured hands of famous people.

> Second solution: Listen to the celebrities. But learn from them what they are good at — attracting attention.

> Compromise: Learn from celebrities not about health but about how to promote health.

Practice: Rogerian Argument

Use a Rogerian approach to analyze the following essay. Use the comments on the preceding essay as a model. Then answer the questions that appear at the end of the essay.

Teaching Trigger Warnings: What Pundits Don't Understand about the Year's Most Controversial Higher-Ed Debate
SARAH SELTZER

When Kyla Bender-Baird was an undergraduate a decade ago, a gender studies lecture she was attending ended with an incident she'll never forget: a visiting professor played a rape victim's graphic 911 call. Then the class was dismissed and, she says, everyone went home dazed and had "messed-up dreams" that night.

Although the professor apologized at the next session for failing to place the record-ing in appropriate context and give students adequate time to process it, Bender-Baird kept the incident in mind when she became a PhD candidate at the CUNY Graduate Center, teaching sociology courses to undergraduates. Now, she includes a note at the end of her syllabus that reads, in part:

> It is my goal in this class to create a safe environment in which we examine our assumptions . . . Discomfort can be part of the learning process as we

Sarah Seltzer is a journalist, essayist, and fiction writer in New York. This essay appeared on May 27, 2015, on flavorwire.com.

are challenged to shift our paradigms. I invite you to sit with this discomfort. However, if the discomfort starts to turn to distress, I want you to take care of yourself. You can withdraw from an activity or even leave the classroom.

Since Bender-Baird added this text to her syllabus, only one student has walked out of her class, simply slipping out when she opened a discussion about "reclaiming the N-word." Whether the student felt triggered by the word or simply couldn't bear having the same conversation yet again, the incident ended there.

5   Bender-Baird doesn't use the label "trigger warning" for her disclaimer, since it's unobtrusively placed at the end of her list of resources and segues into contact information for the counseling center. Yet it falls under the umbrella of cautionary notes encompassed by that loaded phrase, which has increasingly become the chief symbol of a tug-of-war on American campuses. "Trigger warning" — arising from PTSD psychology and popularized in feminist spaces on the Internet — refers to an advance notice for any content, usually violent, that might prompt a flashback, panic attack, or episode for survivors of trauma.

Intellectual heavyweights have decried trigger warnings in widely circulated pieces. In a *New York Times* op-ed published in March, Judith Shulevitz bemoaned the focus on "safety" on campus: "While keeping college-level discussions 'safe' may feel good to the hypersensitive, it's bad for them and for everyone else," she wrote. Much of the academic Internet seemed to agree, particularly after the publication of an op-ed by four Columbia University students arguing that Ovid's

Metamorphoses was triggering and that classes needed to respect diverse identities. The backlash was intense on all sides of the political spectrum: right-wing columnist Kathleen Parker called students "swaddled," while feminist Lori Horvitz worried they were "coddled." Biology professor Jerry A. Coyne said the students' request smacked of "Big Brotherhood" and "cocooning." The real world doesn't come with trigger warnings, he said. On the other side, radical writers like Malcolm Harris have argued that the real problem is the Western canon itself: "Why should students have to endure gender- and race-based contempt from their required reading list?" he asks.

The debate has mostly been framed as students vs. faculty, hand-holding vs. freedom, political correctness vs. mind-expanding curricula. But educators who choose to utilize these warnings in their classrooms often see more nuance in the issue. "We have to take [students demanding trigger warnings] seriously . . . because being more acutely aware of how students are responding to challenging material is just better and more responsible pedagogy," wrote Aaron R. Hanlon last week. Faculty in this camp say that they're committed to academic and intellectual freedom, but also to honoring students' experiences, in particular the often silent presence of rape survivors — a trauma-prone group — among the college-aged population. Rather than debating whether to teach troubling material, as much of the anti-trigger warning contingent fears, they say they've moved on to asking how to do so in a respectful way.

Trigger warnings arose out of the psychological concept of Post-Traumatic Stress Disorder "triggers" — experiences or events that cause a trauma survivor to re-experience an incident, go into avoidance mode, or "numb out." While the theory evolved in the wake of the Vietnam War, the use of "trigger warnings" is very much a result of the feminist Internet, and the atmosphere of the 21st-century political climate. In a recent piece about trigger warnings, Jeet Heer noted that today's students are products of a post-9/11, War on Terror mentality. "PTSD is, in a crucial sense, a theory of memory: It posits that for certain people the memory of a trauma always exists, lying just below the surface," he wrote. "A theory of this sort will naturally lead to a heightened vigilance." Heer failed to mention the growing media and government attention to the campus rape epidemic, but that, too, is part of the trauma-saturated cultural picture in 2015.

Though, in recent years, "trigger" has become one of those frequently used terms that begin to lose meaning, understanding PTSD helps us understand why a classroom setting can be so fraught for some. "People who go through a trauma, the main thing they're reacting to is a loss of control," says NYC psychotherapist Bea Arthur (no relation to the *Golden Girls* actress). "Any other opposing force is going to be hard to accept, especially if it's an authority figure."

10   Caroline Heldman, a professor in Occidental University's politics department, learned about trigger warnings the hard way the better part of a decade ago, when students began experiencing PTSD-related episodes in her classes. "There were a few instances where students would break down crying and I'd have to suspend the class for the day so someone could get immediate mental health care," she says. In a sense, Heldman says, she introduced trigger warnings in order to keep the long tail of trauma outside the doors of learning rather than ushering it in.

"Trigger warnings allow me to have a conversation, to say, 'This is not a class about your personal life,'" Heldman told me. "This actually helps to make the class more academic. And it has the benefit of letting students prepare for what might come."

From a trauma-suffering student's perspective, the opportunity for preparation is key. "What happens if I'm warned that something has images of domestic violence or abuse in advance? I have five seconds to take a deep breath, to say to myself, ok, this is not real," grad student Angela Bennett-Segler wrote in a blog post that several friends in academia flagged for me. "I never shy away. Why? Because stories are powerful. Because they empowered me."

Haylin Belay is a brand-new graduate of Columbia University who has been diagnosed with PTSD. She says she seeks out individual accommodations from professors, checking in intermittently if she thinks material is going to be triggering. "It's far less disruptive," says the anthropology major. "In those classes, I'm able to participate more fully." She notes that when these systems are deployed most effectively — via a private back-and-forth with a professor, in communications ranging from frequent to rare — other students aren't affected at all, since their curriculum isn't disrupted. As for whether such a system is tenable in the real world, beyond the university setting, Belay compares it to an experience she had at a recent health education job, where she politely asked her supervisor to steer her away from discussions on the topic of rape and was accommodated.

Some instructors, particularly those who are survivors of rape or other trauma, also benefit from warnings, hoping they'll create a larger culture of compassion. "Part of the reason I give warnings is that I hope that they'll give me a few seconds of prep time, as well," one friend, a poet who teaches graduate-level writing and preferred to remain anonymous, told me. "It sucks to read through an essay and just abruptly read a student's usage of rape as an analogy for, like, soccer." Indeed, when professors inveigh against trigger warnings by complaining that they give students too much power over the classroom, they are glossing over this potential dynamic of students re-traumatizing professors.

15   A close reading of the text of actual trigger warnings, or similar disclaimers, on college syllabi reveals little in the way of coddling. In fact, most of these statements put the onus directly on students to deal with trauma, while acknowledging that professors understand the material might be unpleasant. "Over the course of the semester, we will be examining topics that may be emotionally triggering for trauma survivors," Heldman's syllabus reads in part. "If you are a trauma survivor, please develop a self-care plan for the semester so that you can effectively engage the course material and participate in class." According to Heldman," It doesn't infantilize students, but treats them like they can handle information and process it. It makes me very comfortable introducing content I might otherwise be leery of introducing." It also reminds students that others in the classroom may be suffering from any number of causes, she says, preparing them to enter the real world with more empathy.

Dr. Mo Pareles, a postdoctoral fellow in Medieval Literature at Northwestern University, uses a similarly straightforward disclaimer for her Medieval Humans and Beasts class: "I will not give trigger warnings, except to say here that the literature in this course contains a good deal of nontrivial sexism, racism, violence, and so

forth," it reads. "However, although shock value is certainly a legitimate pedagogical tool, nothing is included in the syllabus for that purpose."

"There is so much violence and bigotry in the material I teach that I can't really catalog it all," Pareles explained to me. "So this trigger warning is my way of saying that being upset is a valid reaction to some of what you'll encounter."

Compare these warnings to the standard spoken introduction that Josh Lambert, a visiting assistant professor of English at University of Massachusetts–Amherst, has used in Holocaust-related courses, and you'll find something similar. Lambert sent me his old notes, which read in part: "We'll be dealing with some harsh images and subjects. These are topics about which many people are understandably sensitive, and yet in this class I specifically want to deal with some texts that are excessive, or strange, or humorous, or difficult to take, or offensive," he told his students. "We should be respectful of everyone in the room, and keep in mind that some people in the room lost relatives in the Holocaust."

When it comes to the Holocaust, a gentle heads up may sound like common sense rather than censoriousness. The struggle taking place on campuses now is, in part, a way of asking faculty to see rape and racialized or gendered violence on a continuum with such self-evidently difficult topics. Unfortunately, outside of activist circles, where such questions are ceaselessly analyzed, many faculty members or students might not even recognize the depiction of rape in art or literature they assign – as in the Columbia students' complaint that *The Metamorphoses* was taught without any explanation that it depicted rape. Conversely, students who think themselves fluent in the language of social justice might not understand why reading a book containing a depraved sexual assault isn't endorsing that depravity. This is exactly where more dialogue between professors and students might help, not hurt.

20   "Students who don't distinguish between conversations about racism and actual racism, for instance, are probably misunderstanding what 'triggers' actually are," says Carrie Nelson, a writer who worked as a TA in film classes at the New School when she was a graduate student. "Professors should teach students the nuances that distinguish feeling triggered and feeling uncomfortable or offended. But, of course, that involves a degree of extra work that underpaid university professors — rightfully — may not want to put in."

Columbia graduate Belay cites an example of a professor who gives the same lecture twice, once with potentially disturbing accompanying slides and once without, as a particularly thoughtful response to student needs. Regardless of whether faculty members are willing to go to such lengths, she says, "We're not asking for syllabi to be rewritten or classes to be struck from the curriculum. I find that just as alarming an as other people do. We're asking for accommodations." By understanding PTSD in the classroom as a disability, Belay makes a huge distinction between hurtful topics and triggering topics. She notes that students have said troubling things about subjects like welfare in classes she's attended — a potentially uncomfortable moment, but not necessarily a triggering one. When she was upset by comments like that, she had a voice to counter them. She contrasts this with the experience of actually having a PTSD reaction, when a student might feel paralyzed and unable to speak at all, and might disengage entirely.

When you read the warnings used by these teachers, it seems that they might achieve two goals: giving traumatized students time to prepare, but also asking all students to willingly engage. This second idea attempts to explicitly avoid the trigger warning "slippery slope" that concerns so many thinkers. The bottom of that slope is a passel of squeamish, conservative, or immature students gleefully manipulating the idea of triggers as a way of shirking intellectual growth—how far is the distance from, "I can't read Ovid because it depicts rape" to, "I can't read Sappho because it's gay"? Opening class by saying, "It's up to you to come up with a plan to handle upsetting stuff," might actually dissuade any students acting in bad faith from trying to use the concept of triggers to take over the classroom.

Moments of overreach are likely inevitable in any environment where entitled students roam — though, again, not always in precisely the way outside observers might assume. Faculty members relayed anecdotes to me including an objection to the word "breast" because it might offend breast cancer survivors, and another situation in which the lone male in a classroom said his position as such made him uncomfortable hearing the word "rape." Students who act in bad faith will probably do so no matter what. Still, this kind of "we can't read Gatsby" incident, strewn throughout every comment section of every article on the subject, explains many educators' understandable fear that the culture of trigger warnings will lead to a chilling atmosphere on campus.

Students and faculty who use trigger warnings acknowledge legitimate concerns about the state of academia — while maintaining that thinking about how to teach with sensitivity is very different from squelching autonomy. "Online, the conversation got ugly," says Bender-Baird. "Trigger warnings became the depository for a lot of things that are going wrong in academia, like corporatization and the expansion of administrative control over classrooms. The students and their emotional and psychological needs get completely lost in the conversation." By the same token, Pareles says, it's crucial to discuss "the erosion of academic freedom and the marketing of college as a consumer item," where students' demands are justified by their (or their family's) enormous investment. Yet to use those issues as a way to avoid the trigger question entirely, she says, means that faculty are ironically insulating themselves from painful material — namely, the real-world power dynamics involved in trauma.

25   If presented in a careful way, these warnings (as most often worded) can do the opposite of babying students; they open up the lines of communication between students and professors, ask students to take responsibility for their own reactions, and prevent disingenuous students from making every class discussion a venue for airing their own alleged grievances. As for situations in which students are demanding trigger warnings or asking administrators to make them mandatory, not a single person I spoke to, student or professor, supports administrative interference on this matter. They simply say that professors — whether through content warnings or in some other way — should let students know that they're approachable and responsive

and understand the existence of trauma in the population they teach. In this kind of environment, perhaps some outlandish curricular demands would be handled in one office-hours conversation rather than in the national news.

Similarly, the phrase "trigger warning" itself — whose meaning in the culture has morphed from vocabulary specific to the realm of therapy to an overused symbol of an "oversensitive" cadre — might be more distracting than useful. Faculty might be better off folding content notes into resource sections on syllabi, or into their introductory notes, without employing the term. Alternately, Belay says, rather than mandating trigger warnings, universities could systematically enable students with PTSD to communicate with professors via backchannels, making the entire process more streamlined and less public.

Whatever the individual solutions are, at least grappling with the subject beyond the pro/con debate might lead to growth and new approaches to teaching. "To be honest, I feel that the debate on trigger warnings is actually a blind," Pareles says. "No one is going to be forced to use trigger warnings, but thinking about them forces the question: How much do people who have not experienced sexual assault, racism, transphobia, and so on have to consider how profoundly these experiences continue to harm people in their own community?"

Reading and Discussion Questions

1. How does Seltzer define trigger warnings?
2. What are some of the positions that others have taken on the issue of trigger warnings?

3. In what sense is Seltzer's essay an example of Rogerian argument? What compromise does she offer?

4. How does Seltzer support her opinion about trigger warnings?

The Toulmin Model

Although Aristotle and Rogers, centuries and worlds apart, have both made significant contributions to rhetorical theory, we made the decision to organize this text around an argumentative model that we believe is more helpful in reading and writing arguments in a systematic manner: the Toulmin Model. The late Stephen Toulmin provided the vocabulary about argumentation that gives this book its structure.[5]

Toulmin's model, proposed in 1958 in *The Uses of Argument*, was designed to analyze courtroom arguments. Only after his model had been introduced to rhetoricians by Wayne Brockriede and Douglas Ehninger did he discuss its rhetorical implications in *Introduction to Reasoning* (1979). Of the six key terms in Toulmin's model, we draw heavily on three: claim, support, and assumption (also sometimes called a warrant).

The Toulmin model addresses all three legs of the communication triangle, connecting writer, subject, and audience.

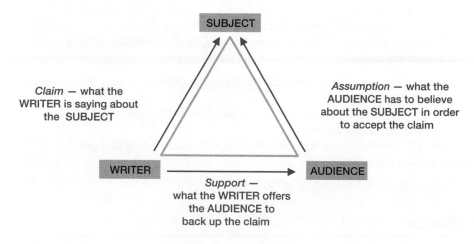

The Claim

The **claim** (also called a proposition) answers the question "What are you trying to prove?" It will generally appear as the thesis statement of an essay, although in some arguments it may not be stated directly. There are three

---

[5] Stephen Toulmin, *The Uses of Argument* (Cambridge: Cambridge University Press, 1958).

principal kinds of claims (discussed more fully in Chapter 6): claims of fact, of value, and of policy. **Claims of fact** assert that a condition has existed, exists, or will exist and are based on facts or data that the audience will accept as being objectively verifiable.

- The diagnosis of autism is now far more common than it was twenty years ago.
- Fast foods are contributing significantly to today's epidemic of childhood obesity.
- Climate change will affect the coastlines of all continents.

All these claims must be supported by data. Although the last example is an inference or an educated guess about the future, a reader will probably find the prediction credible if the data seem authoritative.

Claims of value attempt to prove that some things are more or less desirable than others. They express approval or disapproval of standards of taste and morality. Advertisements and reviews of cultural events are one common source of value claims, but such claims emerge whenever people argue about what is good or bad, beautiful or ugly.

- *Homeland* does an excellent job of depicting bipolar disorder.
- Abortion is wrong under any circumstances.
- The right to privacy is more important than the need to increase security at airports.

Claims of policy assert that specific policies should be instituted as solutions to problems. The expression *should, must,* or *ought to* usually appears in the statement.

- The Electoral College should be replaced by popular vote as the means of electing a president.
- Attempts at making air travel more secure must not put in jeopardy the passengers' right to privacy.
- Existing laws governing gun ownership should be more stringently enforced.

Policy claims call for analysis of both fact and value.

Practice

1. Classify each of the following as a claim of fact, value, or policy.
   a. Solar power could supply 20 percent of the energy needs now satisfied by fossil fuel and nuclear power.
   b. Violence on television produces violent behavior in children who watch more than four hours a day.
   c. Both intelligent design and evolutionary theory should be taught in the public schools.
   d. Some forms of cancer are caused by viruses.

e. Dogs are smarter than cats.

f. The money that our government spends on foreign aid would be better spent solving domestic problems like unemployment and homelessness.

g. Wherever the number of illegal aliens increases, the crime rate also increases.

h. Movie sequels are generally inferior to their originals.

i. Tom Hanks is a more versatile actor than Tom Cruise.

j. Adopted children who are of a different ethnic background than their adoptive parents should be raised with an understanding of the culture of their biological parents.

k. Average yearly temperatures in North America are already being affected by climate change.

l. Human activity is the primary cause of climate change.

2. Which claims listed above would be most difficult to support?

3. What type or types of evidence would it take to build a convincing case for each claim?

The Support

Support consists of the materials that the arguer uses to convince an audience that his or her claim is sound. These materials include evidence and motivational appeals to needs and values. The **evidence** or data consists of facts, statistics, and testimony from experts. The **appeals to needs and values** are the ones that the arguer makes to the values and attitudes of the audience to win support for the claim. These appeals (also known as *emotional* or *motivational* appeals) are the reasons that move an audience to accept a belief or adopt a course of action. (See Chapter 7 for a detailed discussion of support.)

The Assumption

Certain **assumptions** underlie all the claims we make. In the Toulmin model, the term *warrant* is often used for such an assumption, a belief or principle that is taken for granted. It may be stated or unstated. If the arguer believes that the audience shares the assumption, there may be no need to express it. But if the audience seems doubtful or hostile, the arguer may decide to state the assumption to emphasize its importance or argue for its validity. The assumption, stated or not, enables the reader to make the same connection between the support and the claim that the author does. In other words, you have to accept the assumption in order to accept the author's claim based on the evidence provided.

Claim: The popular vote should replace the Electoral College as the means of electing the president.

Support: The popular vote gives each voter one vote for president.

Assumption: The president should be elected by a system that gives each voter one vote.

Claim: A picture ID should be required for eligibility to vote.

Support: Picture IDs would cut down on voter fraud.

Assumption: A requirement that cuts down on voter fraud should be implemented.

Claim: In the United States, 1 in 68 children has an autism spectrum disorder.

Support: That number is based on the latest report from the Centers for Disease Control.

Assumption: The latest report from the Centers for Disease Control is a reliable source of information on the incidence of autism spectrum disorders in the United States.

Claim: The 2013 movie *Evil Dead* is a much better movie than the original 1981 *The Evil Dead*.

Support: The new movie is much more realistic.

Assumption: A more realistic movie is better than one that is less realistic.

One more important characteristic of the assumption deserves mention. In most cases, the assumption is a more general statement of belief than the claim. It can, therefore, support many claims, not only the one in a particular argument. For example, the assumption that being safe is worth a small loss of privacy expresses a broad assumption or belief that we take for granted and that can underlie claims about many other practices in American society. (For more on assumptions, see Chapter 8.)

Toulmin and the Syllogism

You will see some similarities between Toulmin's three-part structure of claim, support, and assumption and the classical deductive syllogism articulated by Aristotle. In fact, a comparison of the two may help in understanding the assumption.

The syllogism is useful for laying out the basic elements of an argument, and it lends itself more readily to simple arguments. It is a formula that consists of three elements: (1) the major premise, (2) the minor premise, and (3) the conclusion, which follows logically from the two premises. The following syllogism summarizes a familiar argument.

Major premise: Advertising of things harmful to our health should be legally banned.

Minor premise: Cigarettes are harmful to our health.

Conclusion: Therefore, advertising of cigarettes should be legally banned.

Cast in the form of the Toulmin model, the argument looks like this:

Claim: Advertising of cigarettes should be legally banned.

Support (Evidence): Cigarettes are harmful to our health.

Assumption: Advertising of things harmful to our health should be legally banned.

Or in diagram form:

```
       SUPPORT  ─────────────────┐         ┌──▶  CLAIM
   Cigarettes are harmful        │         │  Advertising of cigarettes
       to our health.            │         │  should be legally banned.
                                 │
                      ASSUMPTION
              Advertising of things harmful to our
                health should be legally banned.
```

In both the syllogism and the Toulmin model, the principal elements of the argument are expressed in three statements. You can see that the claim in the Toulmin model is the conclusion in the syllogism — that is, the proposition that you are trying to prove. The evidence (support) in the Toulmin model corresponds to the minor premise in the syllogism. And the assumption in the Toulmin model resembles the major premise of the syllogism.

While the syllogism is essentially static, with all three parts logically locked into place, the Toulmin model suggests that an argument is a *movement* from support to claim by way of the warrant (assumption), which acts as a bridge. Toulmin introduced the concept of warrant by asking, "How do you get there?" (His first two questions, introducing the claim and support, were "What are you trying to prove?" and "What have you got to go on?")

ARGUMENT ESSENTIALS
The Toulmin Model

Claim — the proposition that the author is trying to prove. The claim may appear as the thesis statement of an essay but may be implied rather than stated directly.

- *Claims of fact* assert that a condition has existed, exists, or will exist and are based on facts or data that the audience will accept as being objectively verifiable.
- *Claims of value* attempt to prove that some things are more or less desirable than others; they express approval or disapproval of standards of taste and morality.
- *Claims of policy* assert that specific plans or courses of action should be instituted as solutions to problems.

Support — the materials used by the arguer to convince an audience that his or her claim is sound; those materials include evidence and motivational appeals.

Assumption — an inference; a belief or principle that is taken for granted in an argument.

READING ARGUMENT

Seeing the Toulmin Model

The following essay has been annotated to show the key features of the Toulmin model used by the author.

In Health, We're Not No. 1
ROBERT J. SAMUELSON

Claim of value

Support: testimony from experts

Support: statistics

Support: statistics and motivational appeal

Support: statistics and motivational appeal

It turns out that being American is bad for your health, relatively speaking.

Anyone interested in health care ought to digest the findings of a massive new report from the National Research Council and the Institute of Medicine, which compared Americans' health with that of people in other advanced countries. After spending 18 months examining statistics and studies, the panel reached a damning conclusion: The United States ranks below most advanced countries.

Consider. Life expectancy at birth is 78.2 years in the United States, lower than the 79.5-year average for the wealthy countries belonging to the Organization for Economic Cooperation and Development (OECD); Japan's life expectancy is 83. Among 17 advanced countries, the United States has the highest level of diabetes. For 21 diseases, U.S. death rates were higher in 15 (including heart and lung diseases) than the average for these same countries.

Here, in somewhat clunky language, is the report's sobering summary:

"The U.S. health disadvantage is more pronounced among socio-economically disadvantaged groups, but even advantaged Americans [described as "white, insured, college-educated"] appear to fare worse than their counterparts in England and some other countries."   5

What to make of this?

The report's most important contribution is to show that much of the U.S. "health disadvantage" doesn't reflect an inadequate health-care system but lifestyle choices, personal behaviors, and social pathologies. The gap in life expectancy is concentrated in Americans under 50. Among men, nearly 60 percent of the gap results from more homicides (often gun-related), car accidents (often alcohol-related), and other accidents (often drug-related) than in comparable nations. For children under 5, car accidents, drowning, and fire are the largest causes of death.

Teen pregnancy is another big problem. Among girls 15 to 19, the pregnancy rate is about 3.5 times the average of other advanced societies. "Adolescent motherhood affects two generations, children and mothers," the report notes. Adolescent mothers often don't finish high school. "Their children face a greater risk of poor child care, weak maternal attachments,

Robert J. Samuelson, a contributing editor at *Newsweek,* has written a column for the *Washington Post* since 1977. This essay was posted on washingtonpost.com on January 16, 2013.

[and] poverty." Similarly, the incidence of AIDS in America is nearly nine times the OECD average.

The health-care system can't cure these ills, which are social problems with health consequences. Those who expect the introduction of the main elements of the Affordable Care Act ("Obamacare") in 2014 to improve Americans' health dramatically are likely to be disappointed. The lack of insurance is a problem, but it is not the main health problem, in part because the uninsured already receive much uncompensated care.

10   To be fair: Some of these social problems show progress. America's slippage is mostly relative to better outcomes elsewhere. Since 1980, the U.S. murder rate has dropped by roughly half (but remains higher than in many peer countries); traffic deaths per miles traveled have fallen by more than half since 1975 (though decreases abroad are greater); teen birth rates have fallen to a seven-decade low (but are higher than in most wealthy nations); and U.S. life expectancy is rising (but more slowly than elsewhere).

Support: statistics

Nor does the new report exonerate the U.S. health-care system from blame for the "health disadvantage." Despite enormous spending, the system is "deeply fragmented across thousands of health systems and payers . . . creating inefficiencies and coordination problems."

Support: fact

Much specialized care is of high quality; recovery rates for hospitalized U.S. stroke and heart attack victims are higher than in many wealthy nations. Cancer treatment is superior. But primary care is weak. Only 12 percent of U.S. doctors are general practitioners compared with 18 percent in Germany, 30 percent in Britain, and 49 percent in France. In 2009, Americans visited doctor's offices an average of 3.9 times; the OECD average is 6.5 times. Patients may not get needed care; one study found that Americans "receive only 50 percent of recommended" treatments.

Support: facts and statistics

The report's authors searched in vain for an overarching explanation for the peculiar determinants of Americans' health. But it missed the most obvious possibility: This is America. The late sociologist Seymour Martin Lipset argued that American "exceptionalism" is a double-edged sword. Values we admire also inspire behaviors we deplore. The emphasis on individual autonomy and achievement may aid a dynamic economy — and also feed crime and drug use.

Support: motivational appeal

Similar tendencies affect health care. The love of freedom and disdain for authority may encourage teen pregnancy and bad diets. The competitive nature of society may spawn stress that hurts the health of even the well-to-do. The suspicion of concentrated power may foster a fragmented delivery system.

Assumption: Americans' health is bad because of American values.

Commendable ambitiousness may push doctors toward specialization with its higher income and status.

Ever optimistic, Americans deny conflicts and choices. We excel at   15
self-delusion. Asked by pollsters to rate their own health, Americans say — despite much contrary evidence — that they're in better shape than almost anyone. We think we're No. 1 even if we aren't.

Practice: The Toulmin Model

Analyze the following article using Toulmin's three key terms: claim, support, and assumption. Use the above Robert J. Samuelson essay as a model. Then answer the questions that appear at the end.

Embryo Selection May Help Prevent Some Inherited Disorders
STEVEN REINBERG

When a 27-year-old woman wanted to have a baby using in vitro fertilization, there was one major problem — she was a carrier of Gerstmann-Straussler-Sheinker syndrome.

This rare, degenerative neurological condition is usually diagnosed in mid-life and is always fatal. Not wanting to risk having her child become a victim of the syndrome, she turned to a technique that tests embryos for certain mutated genes and only uses those embryos that don't carry the mutation for implantation.

"This disease was found in five generations in this family, and we stopped passing these bad genes to the next generation," said study co-author Svetlana Rechitsky, laboratory director at the Reproductive Genetics Institute in Chicago.

According to Dr. Ilan Tur-Kaspa, lead researcher and president and medical director of the Institute for Human Reproduction in Chicago, "These new cases can be prevented now by pre-implantation genetic diagnosis." Although this is the first report on using this method for a so-called prion disorder, it could also help prevent diseases like Huntington's and familial forms of Alzheimer's disease, he said.

Prion diseases involve abnormal foldings   5
of the prion protein in the brain. The most commonly known one, which is not inherited, is bovine spongiform encephalopathy, or "mad cow" disease.

The report was published online February 3 in the journal *JAMA Neurology*.

The process started with a simple in vitro fertilization procedure. Eggs from the woman were removed and fertilized. Then came the tricky part.

Doctors removed single cells from the embryos, and because the syndrome is caused by a single gene mutation, they looked at DNA to find embryos that didn't have the mutated gene.

"We can identify which embryo is healthy, and which embryo has the bad gene," Rechitsky explained.

Steven Reinberg is a senior staff reporter for healthday.com, where this article appeared on February 3, 2014.

10   Two of the disease-free embryos were implanted, and the woman had twins delivered by cesarean section a little more than 33 weeks later. The remaining normal embryos were frozen for later use.

    At 27 months, the twins had normal communication, social, and emotional skills, the researchers reported.

    One expert noted the importance of the finding.

    "Most of the genetic disorders identified by pre-implantation genetic diagnosis are caused by either single genes — such as cystic fibrosis, Huntington's disease, sickle cell anemia, Down syndrome, Trisomy 18 (Edwards syndrome) and chromosomal translocations — and most have no treatment or cure," said Christine Metz, director of Maternal-Fetal Medicine Research at the Feinstein Institute for Medical Research in Manhasset, New York. "Thus, it is important for young parents to know and understand their risks for inherited diseases prior to conception."

    In addition, pre-implantation genetic diagnosis is beginning to be used to reduce the transmission of mutant cancer genes, such as the BRCA1/BRCA2 genes, which are tied to breast cancer, and the MLH1, MSH2, and APC genes that are linked to colon cancer, she said.

15   "Over several generations, we can hope to improve human health by reducing the transmission of several hereditary disorders," Metz said.

    Rechitsky acknowledged that some people have ethical problems with the potential for this technology to be used to tailor babies to parents' desires. However, in the 25 years they have been doing the procedure it hasn't been a problem, she said.

    "We had the first successful pregnancy in 1990," Rechitsky said. "Over the years, we have performed over 4,000 procedures for single-gene disorders. It has become a more widely accepted approach to prevent hereditary disease," she explained.

    As to tailoring babies, "we have never ever had any requests like this," she said. Moreover, many of the things parents might want to select for like intelligence, involve many genes, not just one. "We don't know even how to approach this," she noted.

    Dr. Avner Hershlag, chief of the Center for Human Reproduction at North Shore University Hospital in Manhasset, New York, said, "Like any sophisticated technique, reproductive technology can be abused. There are ethical issues."

20   Hershlag said that "the most ethical approach is that it should be used for identifying disease only, and for selecting embryos that are free of disease. I don't want it to ever head into that murky, questionable line between what is right and what is wrong. It is absolutely right to diagnose a disease in an embryo and to use embryos that don't have disease."

Reading and Discussion Questions

1. How does the procedure that Reinberg describes stop the inheritance of diseases?
2. Why might some people find the procedure unethical? What is Dr. Hershlag's defense against that charge?

3. Is Reinberg's claim in the article the same as the claim that Dr. Hershlag is making?

4. What types of support for his claim does Reinberg offer?

5. What assumption must a reader be willing to accept in order to accept Reinberg's claim?

Assignments for Understanding Approaches to Argument

Reading and Discussion Questions

1. How are the traditional (Aristotelian) and the Toulmin approaches to argumentation different? How are they similar?

2. Do you believe that presidential debates are good examples of argumentation? Explain.

3. What are some of the controversial issues in the field of your major or a major that you are considering? Analyze one or more of them using Toulmin's terms: claim, support, and assumption.

4. When you write essays and reports for your classes, how do you establish your credibility? In contrast, how do students lose their credibility with the instructors who read their work?

5. What are some situations you have been in — or have read or heard about — in which people's opinions were so far apart that the best you could hope for was compromise rather than total victory for one side or the other?

Writing Suggestions

1. Write an essay in which you support your opinion about whether a federal registry of firearms transactions should be created.

2. Write an essay in which you discuss how technological advances have changed an audience's ability to evaluate a speaker's *ethos*.

3. Write an essay in which you discuss how both Aristotelian and Rogerian argument are useful in contemporary politics.

4. Write an essay in which you identify some of the issues about which it is most difficult to achieve common ground, and explain why.

5. Write an essay in which you explain why different underlying assumptions make it so difficult to reach a compromise on the issue of gun control.

RESEARCH ASSIGNMENT

1. Every library will have access to different databases for student use. Find a list of the databases available to you, and do a search for articles about how

Carl Rogers's theories about therapy relate to argument. You will have to try different combinations of search terms to find the best information. Write down what you discover about sources available to you.

2. What are two specialized databases that might be a starting point for information related to your major or a major that you might choose?

---

bits To see what you are learning about argumentation applied to the latest world and national news, read our Bits blog, "Argument and the Headlines," at **blogs.bedfordstmartins.com/bits**.

Critical Reading of Written Arguments

Consider the cardboard sign shown in Figure 2.1. It is a brief message — "Jesus had two dads" — but the point is clear. These four words make a statement in favor of same-sex marriage. They also suggest that there is nothing immoral about it because it was Jesus's heritage. This brief statement carries a lot of meaning because of the context within which it is understood.

An argument can be summed up on a sign, in a tweet, in an ad, or on a bumper sticker. Think of the contexts that give meaning to these statements from bumper stickers. Some are funny; all have a point to make.

I don't brake for protesters.

Against abortion? Then don't have one.

From Seneca Falls to Selma to Stonewall

WE TRANSFORM AMERICA

Gun nuts are keeping us

from controlling nuts with guns.

A full response to any argument means more than understanding the message. It also means evaluating, deciding whether the message is successful, and then determining *how* it succeeds or fails in persuading us. In making these judgments about the arguments of others, we learn how to deliver our own. We try to avoid what we perceive to be flaws in another's arguments, and we adapt the strategies that produce clear, honest, forceful arguments.

Critical reading is essential for mastery of most college subjects, but its importance for reading and writing about argument, where meaning is often complex and multilayered, cannot be overestimated. The ability to read arguments critically is essential to advanced academic work — even in science and math — since it requires the debate of multifaceted issues rather than the memorization of facts. Just as important, learning to read arguments critically helps you develop the ability to *write* effective arguments—a process valued at the university, in the professional world, and in public life.

Prereading

You will frequently confront texts dealing with subjects unfamiliar to you, and you should have a plan of action for prereading them, that is, for getting an overview of a piece before you read. As the Strategies box demonstrates, the most important things to understand about a text before you read it include the title, purpose, author, and target audience.

Following the Strategies box are two essays. The first includes annotations demonstrating the prereading steps. The second is part of a Practice exercise in which you can employ the prereading strategies yourself.

FIGURE 2.1 Signs can contain brief arguments.
Courtesy of Elias Kass /http://www.flickr.com/photos/eliaspunch/3032732765/

Strategies for Prereading

1. **Pay attention to the title.** The title may state the purpose of the argument in specific terms. It may also use a particular style of language — such as humorous, inflammatory, or somber — to set the tone for the argument.

2. **Understand the kind of text you are reading.** Where and when was it published? Is it a response to another text, or perhaps to an event? Certainly if it is argumentative writing, it is at least a response to a perceived problem. Was there something specific that led an author to write about this subject in this way at this particular time? What background about the subject are you familiar with?

3. **Learn about the author.** As a rule, the more information you know about an author, the easier and more productive your reading will be. You should learn to read in a way that enables you to discover not just meaning in the text itself but information about the author's point of view, background, motives, and ideology. Such understanding comes not only from close analysis of a text but also from (a) background reading on the author and/or the subject and (b) discussion with your classmates and instructors on the material.

4. **Imagine the context in which the author was writing and the target audience.** Was it a specific or general audience? Does the text come from a journal that publishes primarily conservative or liberal writers? What values and ideals that are shared by the author and the audience most likely agree with the argument? How might these values help make sense of the context? What sort of audience might be most strongly opposed to the argument, and why?

READING ARGUMENT

Seeing Prereading

The following is a screenshot of a blog post. It has been annotated to show the key strategies for prereading a written text.

On Pins and Needles Defending Artistic Expression
CAROL ROSE

Context and audience: The article was posted on Boston.com, the free portion of an electronic component of the *Boston Globe*. The site probably has a wide and diverse readership, although the nature of this blog probably draws a segment of the readership interested in politics.

Kind of text: The article appears to be part of a regular blog on privacy, freedom, and legal issues.

Title: The words *pins* and *needles* imply discomfort. The word *defending* signals that the author will take the side of artistic expression. The date of the article is given below the title.

Author: As the executive director of the Massachusetts ACLU, Rose probably leans toward a liberal point of view. (See "About the author" overlay at top right.)

About the author
Carol Rose is executive director of the American Civil Liberties Union of Massachusetts. A lawyer and journalist, Carol has spent her career working for and writing about human rights and civil liberties, both in the United States and abroad. More »

On Liberty
Carol Rose analyzes privacy, freedoms, and the law

« Back to front page

On pins and needles defending artistic expression

Posted by Carol Rose, On Liberty April 8, 2010 03:48 PM   Print | Comments (10)

Stroll down any Massachusetts street on a sunny day and you are will see a lot of bare skin adorned with some nifty (and some not-so-nice) tattoos.

Once the emblem of American GI's and Japanese yakuzas, tattoos have become ubiquitous among the under-30 crowd. It's the rare person who hasn't fallen under the spell of the needle and dye. Even the trend-setting Institute for Contemporary Art in Boston is opening an exhibit next week featuring Mexican tattoo artist, Dr. Lakra.

Carol Rose is a lawyer and journalist and serves as executive director of the American Civil Liberties Union of Massachusetts. She posted this article on the On Liberty column of boston.com on April 8, 2010.

But did you know that tattooing was recently illegal in Massachusetts and many other states? It's true. It took a lawsuit by the ACLU in 2000 to strike down restrictions on tattoo artists in Massachusetts, thus ensuring that this ancient form of self-expression is no longer criminalized in our Commonwealth.

On April 15 at 7 p.m., the ICA will feature a conversation about the case with ACLU attorney Sarah Wunsch, who was co-counsel with Harvey Schwartz in litigating the challenge to the Massachusetts law banning tattooing.

To some people, such legal victories seem only skin deep. But on closer examination, the right to tattoo is part and parcel of our right to artistic expression.

The art of "body art" goes back literally thousands of years. Tattooed mummies have been found in all parts of the world, including Egypt, Libya, Asia and South America. A five thousand year old man, nick-named "otzi the ice man" by the people who dug him up, reportedly bore 57 tattoos -- although they may have simply been scars from arthritis (apparently it can be hard to tell the difference after 5,000 years).

The first tattoo shop in New York was set up in 1846 and came to Boston soon thereafter. Soldiers from both sides in the civil war revived the ancient tradition of wearing tattoos as a sign of military prowess. Today, surveys show that more than one-third of Americans under age 30 have tattoos, and the numbers are growing.

Despite the historical persistence of tattooing, however, the law on tattooing as free expression isn't a slam-dunk. States have some right to ensure the sanitary operation of tattoo parlors and courts are still sorting out the hard cases, such as whether employers can require employees to cover tattoos. But our nation nonetheless has made progress in defense of tattooing as a fundamental form of artistic expression. Even South Carolina and Oklahoma -- two hold-out states -- recently passed laws legalizing tattooing as skin art.

Personally, I am content to let the Mother Nature etch her motif into my tender hide without additional help from dye and needles. But even I can't resist the fascination with tattooing as an ancient and compelling form of human expression. As the ICA enticement for its upcoming show attests: "From cave walls to touch screens, no surface is off limits to the creativity of artists and designers. What about the most accessible surface of all, our own bodies?"

This blog is not written or edited by Boston.com or the Boston Globe.
The author is solely responsible for the content.

Context and audience: Although posted on Boston.com, the Web site clarifies that it is independent from the site's content.

Practice: Prereading

Before you read the article on page 46, consider these questions:

1. Think about the title. Skim the first paragraph. Where is the piece set?
2. When and where was the piece published? How is the publication's purpose described?
3. What do you learn from the biographical information that provides background for the episode in the airport?
4. Does the article seem targeted to a specific or a general audience?

I Belong Here

AMIN AHMAD

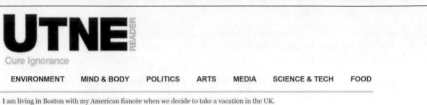

ENVIRONMENT   MIND & BODY   POLITICS   ARTS   MEDIA   SCIENCE & TECH   FOOD

I am living in Boston with my American fiancée when we decide to take a vacation in the UK. Standing in the customs queue at a London airport, we compare passports. Hers is sleek and clean, whereas my Indian passport resembles a small, tattered Bible. My photograph is pasted in, and spelling mistakes are corrected in Wite-Out.

My passport tells the story of my immigrant life: my student and work visas; all the entry and exit stamps as I traveled between India and the United States. Soon my fiancée and I will be married, and I'll have a brand-new U.S. passport in which to write the next chapter of my life.

When we reach the British immigration official, she gives my fiancée's passport a quick look and is done. Then she fingers the worn cardboard cover of mine, sighs, and says, "Would you please step this way for an immigration check."

The official gestures to a wooden bench where an old Sikh man in a saffron turban and a huddled Bangladeshi family sit.

I'm not like them, I want to say to the official. *I live in Boston.* But all the official sees is a brown face and an Indian passport. My fiancée says she will sit with me. The official shrugs.

Sitting on the hard wooden bench, I watch each white person clear immigration in seconds and am filled with hopelessness; the British, who ruled my country for decades and taught me the English that I speak, have always had the power to keep me out of their country.

Next to me the old Sikh man is crying silently. He smells of wood smoke and tobacco and reminds me of an uncle. The Bangladeshi family looks like an obscure branch of my own. A wave of solidarity washes through me, and I go from hopelessness to calm resignation. It feels right somehow to be sitting with these people. I belong here.

My fiancée tugs at my sleeve. The official is waving my passport at me. "I knew everything would be OK," my fiancée says, smiling a big, confident, American smile.

But I am angry. I don't want to enter the UK anymore. Let them keep their damn country. My place is here, with *my* people. I could sit on this bench all day with them.

But of course I don't. My fiancée is already walking away. I follow her and collect my passport, with its red entry stamp. At the exit doors I glance back at the bench and see the Bangladeshi family, glassy-eyed with fear, and the old Sikh man, still crying.

From the *Sun*, January 2010. Reprinted by the permission of the author.

From *The Sun*, January 2010. Reprinted by permission of the author, Amin Ahmad.

Amin Ahmad was born in Calcutta, India; lived for a time in Boston; and now divides his time between New York and Washington, DC. His work has appeared in *The Harvard Review*, *The New England Review*, *Narrative*, *The Sun*, and *Utne Reader*. As A. X. Ahmad, he writes novels. This essay appeared in *The Sun* magazine (January 2010), which, according to its editors, "for more than 30 years has used personal essays, short stories, interviews, poetry, and photographs 'to invoke the splendor and heartache of being human.'" It was reprinted in *Utne Reader* (May–June 2010).

Reading and Discussion Questions

1. How and why are Ahmad and his fiancée treated differently at the airport?
2. With whom does he identify rather than with his fiancée?
3. Where does he mean he belongs when he says, "I belong here"?
4. What is ironic about the fiancée's statement, "I knew everything would be okay"? Why does he specifically refer to her *American* smile?
5. What is Ahmad's argument?

Reading for Content and Structure

The next step in the critical reading process is comprehension—understanding what an author is trying to prove. Comprehending academic arguments can be difficult because they are often complex and often challenge accepted notions. Academic writing also sometimes assumes that readers already have a great deal of knowledge about a subject and therefore can require further research for comprehension.

Readers sometimes fail to comprehend a text they disagree with or that is new to them, especially in dealing with essays or books making controversial, value-laden arguments. Some research even shows that readers will sometimes remember only those parts of texts that match their points of view.[1] The study of argument does not require you to accept points of view you find morally or otherwise reprehensible, but to engage with these views, no matter how strange or repugnant they might seem, on your own terms.

Reading arguments critically requires you to at least temporarily suspend notions of absolute "right" and "wrong" and to intellectually inhabit gray areas that do not allow for simple "yes" and "no" answers. Of course, even in these areas, significant decisions about such things as ethics, values, politics, and the law must be made, and in studying argument you shouldn't fall into the trap of simple relativism: the idea that all answers to a given problem are equally correct at all times. We must make decisions about arguments with the understanding that reasonable people can disagree on the validity of ideas. Read others' arguments carefully, and consider how their ideas can contribute to or complicate your own. Remember Carl Rogers's approach (see Chapter 1) and look for common ground between your beliefs and those of the author. Also recognize that what appears to be a final solution will always be open to further negotiation as new participants, new historical circumstances, and new ideologies become involved in the debate.

---

[1] See, for example, Patrick J. Slattery, "The Argumentative, Multiple-Source Paper: College Students Reading, Thinking, and Writing about Multiple Points of View," *Journal of Teaching Writing*, 10, Fall/Winter 1991, pp. 181–99.

Working with the Text

Here are some suggestions about how to approach reading an argument. Remember: Your instructors will have considerations like these in mind when reading your written arguments, so they can help you with writing as well as reading an argument.

1. **Skim the reading for the main idea and overall structure.**
   - Are there subheadings or other divisions?
   - If it is a book, how are the chapters organized?
   - What is the claim or thesis statement that the piece is supporting? It will usually be in the first or second paragraph of an essay or in the introduction or first chapter of a book, but it may come at the end of the reading.
2. **Pay attention to topic sentences.** The topic sentence is usually the first sentence in a paragraph, but not always. It is the general statement that controls the details and examples in the paragraph.
3. **Don't overlook language signposts, usually transitional words and phrases:** *but, however, yet, nevertheless, moreover, for example, at first glance, more important, the first reason, next,* and so on.
4. **Consider any visuals** that are included with the text. Do they provide evidence to support the written argument? Do they set a mood or enhance the argument in other ways? (For help examining visuals, see Chapter 3.)

The best way to read a difficult text is with pen, pencil, and highlighter in hand. If it is an online text, it is worth printing a copy to hold the text in hand and **annotate** it, or mark it up. Scrolling from page to page on the computer screen does not let you see the structure of a piece as well as spreading the pages out in front of you does.

Strategies for Annotating a Text

One purpose of annotating a text is to comprehend it more fully. Another is to prepare to write about it.

1. **If you use a highlighter as you read a text, use it sparingly.** You might consider a more targeted approach to highlighting, focusing only on thesis statements and topic sentences, for example.
2. **More useful: Make marginal notes,** perhaps underlining the portion of the text to which each note refers. Some of the most useful marginal notes will be those that summarize key ideas in your own words. Such paraphrases force you to understand the text well enough to reword its ideas, and reading the marginal notes is a quick way to review the text when you do not have time to reread all of it.
3. **Make notes on both what a piece of writing says and how it says it.** Notations about how

a piece is written can focus on structural devices such as topic sentences, transitional words or phrases, and the repetition of ideas or sentence structure.

4. **Interrogate the text as you read.** Make note of surprising or interesting points, and don't be afraid to question or disagree with a point made by the author.

5. **Note similarities** that you see between the text you are reading and others you have read or between the text and your own experience.

READING ARGUMENT

Seeing Content and Structure

The following article has been annotated by a student reader to show its content and structure. After reading the article, answer the questions at the end.

A Tale of Two Airlines
CHRISTOPHER ELLIOTT

In travel, as in life, there are heroes and villains. There's good and evil. And there's Southwest Airlines and Spirit Airlines.

Sets up a clear comparison/ contrast structure.

Both are no-frills discount carriers, and both are success stories in the economic sense. But that's where the similarities end.

Similarities exist, but he will focus on differences.

Spirit is known for its preponderance of fees, the risqué tone of some of its ads (as in the naughty "MILF" acronym for its "Many Islands, Low Fares" sale), and a take-it-or-leave-it attitude toward customer service. Southwest has a reputation for inclusive fares (one of the few airlines left that don't charge extra for a checked bag), a Texas-style hospitality (concerts on planes), and its famous customer-focused way.

A brief contrast sets up Spirit as the villain and Southwest as the hero.

A look at these airlines offers a window into the relationship between air carriers and their customers, revealing why the modern flying experience can be so infuriating.

5   For Southwest—the Dallas carrier founded in 1971—customer service is part of its corporate DNA. Consider what happened to Robert Siegel. The retired engineer and his wife, Ruth, were scheduled to fly from West Palm Beach to Philadelphia when Ruth was diagnosed with lung cancer; her doctor

Southwest: Examples of excellent customer service

Christopher Elliott is an author, columnist, consumer advocate, and founder and publisher of elliott.org, a consumer advocate site. This article is from his Insider column in the December 2012/January 2013 issue of *National Geographic Traveler*.

ordered her to cancel the trip. Even though the tickets were nonrefundable, Siegel requested an exception. "Within one week, a complete credit had been posted to my credit card," he says.

What's wrong with that?

Southwest routinely waives its requirements in the interests of "Customer Service." (It also has an annoying habit of uppercasing key words, like "People.") Several years ago, one of its pilots even held the plane for a passenger so that he could make his grandson's funeral. It doesn't punish customers with ticket change fees or price its less restricted tickets so that only business travelers on an expense account can afford them. It's not perfect, of course. Southwest's prices can sometimes be significantly higher than the competition's. And its one-class service is too egalitarian for many business travelers.

Spirit: Customers treated like cargo

Spirit Airlines styles itself as the anti-Southwest. The airline, based in the suburbs of Fort Lauderdale, has its roots in the trucking business, which may explain a lot: Its customers often complain that they are treated like cargo. Seems Spirit wouldn't have it any other way.

Spirit often does the exact opposite of what Southwest would. When Vietnam vet Jerry Meekins was told his esophageal cancer was terminal and advised by his doctor to cancel his flight from Florida to Atlantic City, the airline refused a refund request. Only after veterans groups intervened did the carrier cave, and only reluctantly. In an effort to not set a precedent, CEO Ben Baldanza said he personally would pay for the refund, not his airline.

Spirit has many fees . . .

And Spirit does love fees. Fully one-third of its ticket revenue comes from fees (compared with 7.5 percent for Southwest). Spirit argues that its passengers just crave low fares, and that all of the extras are optional. But some passengers complain that the fees aren't adequately disclosed and that some are ridiculous (a $100 charge to carry—that's right, carry—a bag on a plane if you didn't prepay a lower fee online). Where Southwest's employees have a reputation for being sociable, Spirit's can be on the surly side. Baldanza once

Wow!

inadvertently replied directly by e-mail to a passenger this way: "Let him tell the world how bad we are. He's never flown us before anyway and will be back when we save him a penny."

. . . but the fares are low.

Baldanza has a point, and it's one that drives consumers (and consumer   10 advocates) crazy: If you can navigate the maze of fees, restrictions, and Spirit's $9 Fare Club ($60 per year, with automatic reenrollment whether you fly or not), you can travel for impressively low fares. And stockholders love their shares of SAVE (Spirit's ticker symbol) about as much as they do Southwest's (aptly, LUV).

Each airline likes its role.

I'd say Spirit enjoys playing the villain as much as Southwest likes being the hero. Spirit certainly hasn't suffered for it financially. These two airlines represent one of travel's most enduring paradoxes: that companies offering poor customer service can succeed as well as those offering good customer service. Spirit's success defies an easy explanation, unless you have a degree in psychology. Spirit taps into the very human need to snag a deal. But understanding what makes us tick and the way we can be manipulated points to a better future for every traveler. See, Southwest and Spirit are not the only examples of travel's curious yin and yang. Whether you're staying at a hotel, renting a car, or taking a cruise, you've faced the same kinds of choices between companies. At the beginning of 2013, many of these companies find themselves at a crossroads, wondering which path to take: the embrace of a LUV or the thriftiness of a SAVE. Both clearly work in the short term. But Southwest operates on the principle that, eventually, customers will catch on.

Then again, maybe not. If people continue to fall for the ultralow, lots-of-strings-attached rates, then the treatment of passengers like cargo might continue indefinitely. Travelers must consider more than the price when they book their ticket or make arrangements to take a cruise or rent a car. They have to take a company's service reputation into account, too. Reward the heroes of the travel industry with your business. Otherwise, the villains win.

Customers have a choice.

Thesis statement

Reading and Discussion Questions

1. The essay is a contrast between the two airlines. What specific aspects of the two does Elliott contrast?
2. What thesis or claim is Elliott supporting? What point does he make beyond the ways in which the two airlines differ? Is his essay based on a claim of fact, value, or policy?
3. What types of support does Elliott offer?

Summarizing

One skill required by the Rogerian approach to communication is the ability to summarize another's ideas fairly and objectively, just as in more confrontational forms of argumentation a writer or speaker cannot build a successful case on a misunderstanding or misinterpretation of an opponent's position. At least, such a case will not hold up under careful scrutiny. The ability to summarize is also a basic research skill used in writing research papers, as discussed in Chapter 12. Summarizing is the cornerstone on which all other critical reading and writing tasks are built.

A summary can be either referential or rhetorical. A **referential summary** focuses on an author's ideas about the subject. A **rhetorical summary** summarizes the text in terms of rhetorical or structural choices the author made.

RESEARCH SKILL ▸ Summarizing

When summarizing long or difficult texts, try some of the following strategies to help you comprehend the essential points of the text.

1. **Reread the introduction and conclusion after you have read the text once or twice.** These two sections should complement each other and offer clues to the most significant issues of the text.

2. **For a difficult text, you may want to list all the subheadings (if they are used) or the topic sentence of each paragraph.** These significant guideposts will map the piece as a whole: What do they tell you about the central ideas and the main argument the author is making?

3. **Remember that when you summarize, you must put another's words into your own (and cite the original text as well),** so do not simply let a list of the subheadings or chapter titles stand as your summary. They likely won't make sense when put together in paragraph form, but they will provide you with valuable ideas regarding the central points of the text.

4. **Remember that summarizing also requires attention to overall meanings and not only to specific details.** Therefore, avoid including many specific examples or concrete details from the text you are summarizing, and try to let your reader know what these examples and details add up to. As you write the summary, remember that it should

   - be shorter than the original
   - be objective instead of stating opinions
   - identify the author and the work
   - use present tense
   - summarize the main points of the whole work or passage, not just part of it.

(See Chapter 1 for a full discussion of the rhetorical approach.) The following examples are summaries of the article on page 49.

Referential (Content) Summary

According to Christopher Elliott in his article "A Tale of Two Airlines," both Southwest Airlines and Spirit Airlines are successful discount carriers, but where Spirit is a "villain," Southwest is a "hero." Where Spirit has a lot of fees, risqué ads, and poor customer service, Southwest does not charge extra for checked bags, is welcoming, and takes pride in its famous customer service, even waiving its own regulations in special circumstances to help a customer. Spirit originated as a trucking line and still treats customers "like cargo." Each airline seems to like the role it plays. A customer can save money flying Spirit because of its low fares, but as long as fliers are willing to be treated like cargo to save money, they will be rewarding the villains instead of the heroes of the travel industry.

Rhetorical (Structure) Summary

In his article "A Tale of Two Airlines," Christopher Elliott *contrasts* two airlines: Southwest and Spirit. He *points out* that both are successful airlines, but then *focuses* on how the two differ in fees, tone, and customer service.

Strategies for Writing Rhetorical Summaries

These approaches are not mutually exclusive, so you may get some repetition in the answers to questions like the following; but overall, the questions provide a means of discovering what to say about an author's rhetorical strategies. Not every question will apply to every reading.

Aristotelian Rhetoric

- Does the author make use of examples?
- Does he make use of deductive reasoning, showing how a generalization applies to a specific case?
- Does he make use of logical appeal? emotional appeal? appeal based on his own credibility? a combination of these types of appeal?

Rogerian Argument

- Does the author sum up an opposing point of view fairly and accurately?
- Does she attempt to establish common ground between conflicting positions?
- Does she present a compromise between the competing positions?

The Toulmin Model

- Does the author support a claim of fact? a claim of value? a claim of policy?
- Does he support his claim with facts? with statistics?
- Does he support his claim with appeals to the needs and values of his audience?
- Does he support his claim with expert opinion?

Elliott *provides examples* of how Southwest goes out of its way to provide excellent customer service, even waiving its own regulations in exceptional circumstances while Spirit refuses to make exceptions. Elliott *explains* that Spirit's treatment of its customers reflects its origins as a trucking business. He *warns* that as long as customers reward Spirit by choosing its low fares in spite of its bad customer service, the villains in the world of commercial airlines will win.

READING ARGUMENT

Practice: Summarizing

The following article has been annotated to show major rhetorical approaches the author employed. Read it, and then answer the questions that appear at the end of the article.

Gun Debate: Where Is the Middle Ground?

MALLORY SIMON

<table>
<tr><td>Opening example</td><td>

Amardeep Kaleka will never forget the moment when his father laid on the ground and prayed.

Satwant Singh Kaleka had been shot five times while wrestling a gunman in a Sikh temple in Oak Creek, Wisconsin. His turban was knocked off, and two kids and a priest crawled up beside him. Together, they prayed.

Amardeep Kaleka went to the temple and stared at that spot.

His father did not survive. He died along with five others.

"It felt like he was praying and putting something into the zeitgeist and imprinting it," he told CNN. His son hoped it would lead to a changing tide on gun violence.
</td></tr>
</table>

5

Opening example

Amardeep Kaleka will never forget the moment when his father laid on the ground and prayed.

Satwant Singh Kaleka had been shot five times while wrestling a gunman in a Sikh temple in Oak Creek, Wisconsin. His turban was knocked off, and two kids and a priest crawled up beside him. Together, they prayed.

Amardeep Kaleka went to the temple and stared at that spot.

His father did not survive. He died along with five others.

"It felt like he was praying and putting something into the zeitgeist and imprinting it," he told CNN. His son hoped it would lead to a changing tide on gun violence.

Emotional appeal

As he began his meditation that day, Amardeep made a vow: He would do whatever he could to ensure nobody ever went through what his family had.

"It just came over me that you can't stay silent," he said. "You can't continue to allow violence like this to happen haphazardly at a church, at a school, any place."

That was August 2012.

Related example

Four months later, 20 children and six adults were gunned down in Newtown, Connecticut.

That school massacre has led many people, including Kaleka, 33, to question where we go from here as a country. Or if we will ever get there at all.

It led him to stand up at a gathering here on Thursday, CNN's *Guns Under Fire: An AC360° Town Hall Special*, and ask a panel of advocates with polar opposite views if they could agree on anything. If there was actually any middle ground.

Looking for common ground

"After meeting with so many senators, so many gun proponents and gun control advocates, it seems like they're recycling the same jargon all the time," he said, explaining his reason for the question. "So I was just hoping, let's get to the common ground."

The panel included National Rifle Association board members, the president of the Brady Campaign to End Gun Violence, law enforcement representatives, and other participants voicing viewpoints across the spectrum.

10

Mallory Simon works for CNN as a writer and editor for all of CNN's digital, television, and social platforms. This piece appeared on cnn.com on January 31, 2013.

Was there a consensus?

15   Sort of.

"There's a lot of common ground," Sandra Froman, a member of the NRA board of directors and a former president of the group, said at the town hall. "We don't want people who are insane to have guns, we don't want terrorists to have guns. Part of this national dialogue is coming together."

> *Expert representing one position: There is common ground.*

So everyone agreed: Something has to happen. The devil is in the details.

> *Common ground*

"I think the common ground clearly exists from a policy standpoint when talking about background checks," said Dan Gross, president of the Brady Campaign to End Gun Violence.

> *Expert representing another position: There is common ground.*

But it isn't that simple. It never is when it comes to gun control.

20   "The NRA is not against background checks," Froman said. "We support making sure they are enforced. We're not supporting more background checks of law-abiding citizens."

Her remarks signaled a slight change in the NRA's stance.

In a heated back and forth, the two debated whether it was truly harmful to force everyone who wants to purchase a gun—whether at a gun store, a gun show, or in a private sale—to go through a background check.

Froman talked about how the current background check system was broken, noting that an "instant check" in Colorado can actually take about 10 days.

> *Example*

"We have to get it working before we add any more checks," she said, noting that requiring everyone to undergo a check would take a lot of resources and money.

> *Logical appeal*

25   Philadelphia Police Commissioner Charles Ramsey spoke from his experience, saying whatever it took, whatever the price tag, it would be worth it to stem the violence.

> *Expert opinion*

"Please, don't worry about the cost. I'll spend the money," he said, a line that drew massive applause from the crowd at George Washington University. "It's a much greater cost than human lives. We have to do something. The status quo is not acceptable."

> *Appeal to the need for security*

When Kaleka, the son of one of the Sikh shooting victims, rose to ask his question about finding a middle ground, he wasn't just talking about policy. He also meant in our collective way of thinking. A filmmaker, Kaleka has made a documentary about violence in America. There are too many facets to the problem, he says.

"It's a culture of violence. And that has to do with guns, that has to do with mental illness, it has to do with stigmatizing people, it has to do with the media, everything about our culture."

> *Deductive reasoning*

Many appeared to think he was right.

"Everybody's got to step up on this," Ramsey said. "That's prosecutors, the   30
courts, everyone. If we're serious about this, it can't just be a series of laws that
are passed."

Much of the discussion inside the town hall went beyond politics and
legislation. One heated debate focused on whether armed guards should be
posted at schools.

That's a proposal that's been discussed by former congressman Asa
Hutchinson.

Emotional appeal/appeal to
needs and values

"What is more important than the education and the safety of those
children?" he asked, noting that if malls have armed security, so should schools.
"I believe an armed security presence is very important."

It's an idea that Veronique Pozner thinks about. Her son Noah was killed
in the shooting at Sandy Hook Elementary in Newtown.

Example

"I think there might be a certain power in deterrence," she said. "In the   35
case of Newtown, it's clear that the perpetrator did choose the path of least
resistance, the most vulnerable defenseless victims. He didn't head for the high
school where he could have been tackled."

Appeal to need for security

While she said she wasn't sure an armed guard would have saved her son, she
did say it made her feel more comfortable dropping off her other children at the
new school for Sandy Hook children, a building that does have armed guards.

Colin Goddard, who survived the Virginia Tech shooting, said he
understood the desire to protect children, but he didn't understand why
arming guards is the go-to solution.

Logical appeal

"I just don't understand why the first idea put forth is something that
might help at the last second," he said, to massive applause from the audience.
"We can do things in advance to keep a dangerous person and a gun from
coming together in the first place."

Deductive reasoning

That's the conversation that usually leads to a debate about mental health.
It is an area President Barack Obama has pledged resources to; he and many
others hope to keep guns out of the hands of the mentally ill.

The difficulty comes in figuring out who poses a threat.   40

"We look at behavior and what's going on in the person's life, the social
dynamics and what are the personality issues that make that person think
acting out dangerously is a way to handle their problems," said Mary Ellen
O'Toole, a former FBI special agent and criminal profiler.

Expert opinion

Froman, the NRA board member, said she'd like to see more sharing of
resources to ensure a database of the mentally ill would prevent them from
having access to guns.

A possible compromise

But Liza Long, whose blog post *I Am Adam Lanza's Mom* went viral after the Newtown shooting, said perhaps we were thinking about this all wrong. What if it wasn't just about identifying threats, but actually making a change.

"We spend a lot of time talking about keeping guns out of the wrong hands," she said. "What if we could put those resources to making people less dangerous."

45   For Kaleka, at the end of the day, progress on enforcing background checks would be a step in the right direction.

A positive move on which different sides might agree

He recognizes that no solution will make everyone happy. But he wishes every advocate, no matter their point of view, would think about the issue as if they were in his shoes.

"When you are a survivor or a victim or someone close to you dies, it's everyday you think about it," he said. "Gun advocates or scholars or people making money about it, they probably think about it 10 percent of how much we think about it. We go to the bathroom and think about it. We take a cold shower one day, and we start to cry. We wake up in the middle of the night with night sweats, and we have to live with it. Every breath is taken with some thought of violence and safety."

Emotional appeal, pathos (appeal based on Kaleka's credibility)

He thinks it is time the country does the same: that its citizens think about the issue with every breath.

"I can never go another moment in my life without thinking about it. My wife, my brother, my mother, the people of Newtown, they will not go a moment for the rest of their life without thinking about it," he said. "Personally I think the tide is changing, the zeitgeist is moving towards justice. Hopefully, once we stop the fear mongering on both sides we can finally get to the point of what makes sense."

Need to work toward common ground

50   His greatest hope: That the will to do something about the violence does not die along with those who never had to.

Emotional appeal

Reading and Discussion Questions

1. Which of the three approaches to argument—Aristotelian rhetoric, Rogerian argument, or the Toulmin Model—seems the one best suited to use in discussing this particular essay? Why?

2. Is there information about the essay that you got from the other two approaches that complements what you learned through that primary approach? that contradicts it?

Writing Assignments

1. Use what you learned from the annotations on "Gun Debate: Where Is the Middle Ground?" to write a one-paragraph rhetorical summary of the essay. Remember that a rhetorical summary focuses on choices that the author made, not just on the ideas.

2. Write a one-paragraph referential summary of the essay, focusing on content rather than rhetorical choice.

Practice: Summarizing

Read and annotate the following article, using the Christopher Elliot article on pages 49–51 and the Mallory Simon article on pages 54–57 as models. Then answer the questions that appear at the end of the article.

The Gay Option
STEPHANIE FAIRYINGTON

I came out to my mother in a letter. I was 28. "I was born this way," I wrote, following with the most shattering high note of self-loathing I can think of: "If there were a straight pill," I lamented, "I'd swallow it faster than you can say the word *gay*."

I didn't mean either of these things. I said them because I knew they would elicit pity and absolve my mother of the belief that her parenting was to blame for my same-sex attractions. It worked. Five years later, my mother continues to talk about my lesbianism as if it were a genetic defect like Down syndrome—a parallel she's actually drawn—because clearly, in her mind, no one would choose such a detestable and challenging state of being.

This is not a message I'm proud to have sent. Contrary to how I actually feel about my sexuality, it suggests that I'm drowning in a sea of self-disgust, desperately grasping for a heterosexual lifeboat to sail my way out of it. But would my mother have been as sympathetic and tolerant if she thought I had a choice in

the matter? Would conservative allies support us if they believed we could help it?

If the answer is no, and I believe it is, what does it say about our self-worth and status in society if we, as gay people, must practice a politics of pity to secure our place in the world? It says, for one, that we don't have a place at the table. It says that we are tolerated, but not accepted. It says, ultimately, that it's time to change our rhetoric.

Until homosexuality is cast and understood   5 as a valid choice, rather than a biological affliction, we will never rise above our current status. We will remain Mother Nature's mistake, tolerable (to some) because our condition is her fault, not ours.

By choice, I don't mean that one can choose one's sexual propensities any more than one can

Stephanie Fairyington is the cofounder and editor of *The Slant* and a freelance journalist in New York. A version of this article appeared in the Winter 2010 issue of *Dissent* as "Choice as Strategy: Homosexuality and the Politics of Pity"; the excerpt here appeared in *Utne Reader*, May–June 2010.

choose one's personality. What I mean is that it's a choice to act on every desire we have, and that acting on our same-sex attractions is just as valid as pursuing a passion for the Christian faith or Judaism or any other spiritual, intellectual, emotional, or physical craving that does not infringe on the rights of others. And it should be respected as such.

As a firm Kinsey 6 — with 6 being the gayest ranking on sexologist Alfred Kinsey's 1-to-6 scale of sexual orientation — I understand the resistance to putting *choice* and *homosexuality* in the same sentence. My same-sex attractions were awakened in me at such a young age that they felt as much a part of me as my limbs. In the late 1990s, when I was coming out, had someone told me that I had chosen my deepest, most tender and passionate affections, it would have been like telling me that I had chosen the arms and legs I have.

But I have plenty of desires, like throwing my fists in the faces of conservative Republicans, which for one reason or another, I don't act on; my desire for women is not one of them. Biology is not destiny, and I am the architect of my own life, as is everyone. My point is not to challenge or even enter the debate about whether or not some combination of nature and nurture contributes to the formation of an inclination toward one's own sex. My point is that most inquiries into the origins of homosexuality are suspect, and their service to us is limited, if not perilous.

A politics of *choice* would be one that regards same-sex desire enough to announce it as a conscious decision rather than a predetermined abnormality. No matter how bumpy the ride or long the journey, *choice* as a political strategy is the only ride out of Freaksville.

Forty years ago, gay activists had a similar view, taking their cues from radical lesbian feminists who believed that heterosexuality and homosexuality were products of culture, not nature. "In the absence of oppression and social control," writes historian John D'Emilio, gay liberationists believed that "sexuality would be polymorphous" — fluid, in other words. Back then they talked about "sexual preference," which implies choice, as opposed to "sexual orientation," which does not.

It wasn't until the 1970s that the mental health establishment and its gay allies put forth the view that homosexuality is a permanent psychological condition and debunked the notion that it was a mental illness in need of a cure. Then came the 1980s and 1990s and a slew of shoddy and inconclusive scientific research on the biological origins of gayness, reinforcing the belief that sexuality is predestined. Both psychological and medical discourses formed today's dominant paradigm, which insists that sexuality is inborn and immutable.

The LGBT activists who have helped construct this sexual framework are neither lazy nor naive in their thinking, as D'Emilio points out in his essay "Born Gay?," a crisp case against the politics of biological determinism. As a political strategy, it has helped reap enormous benefits, from antidiscrimination legislation to adoption rights in some states and civil unions in others. The reasons this model of sexuality is politically expedient and effective are threefold.

First, if sexuality is understood as predestined and therefore fixed, it poses less of a challenge to the hetero monolith than does a shifting spectrum of desire. It protects straight people, in other words, from the threat of homosexuality. Second, by presenting homosexuality as a biological fact as firm and absolute as race or sex, gay activists have formed an identity the law can recognize and can follow in the footsteps of civil rights legislation. Third, it's conceptually easier to understand sexuality as a permanent trait rather than the complex, ever-morphing mess that it often is.

But for all the success this politics has had, in the end, it's not only shortsighted but rife with limitations—and dangers. As lesbian activist Joan Nestle told me, it's not good politics to cling to the "born gay" edict because "the use of biological 'abnormalities' was used by the Nazis when they measured the nostril thickness of imprisoned Jews to prove they were an inferior race; and when colonizers measured the brains of Africans to make a case for their enslavement; and when doctors at the turn of the century used the argument that the light weight of women's brains proved their inferiority to men. I do not want to enter into this sad history of biological dehumanization as the basis for gay rights."

15   All the studies that gay sympathizers and activists invoke to justify our right to same-sex love cast homosexuality as a loud hiccup at the dinner table of normality. As such, we're put on par with other undesirable deviations from nature's norm, taunting eugenics with the keys to eliminating us. This is the ugly underbelly of our biology-centered claims to human rights.

The typical conservative assault on homosexuality casts it as a sinful choice that can be unchosen through a commitment to God and reparative therapy. And the left usually slams into this simplistic polemic by taking up the opposite stance: Homosexuality is not a choice, and because we can't help it, it's not sinful.

By affirming that homosexual practice and identity *are* a choice, we can attach an addendum—it's a good choice—and open the possibility of a more nuanced argument, one that dismantles the logic of the very premise that whom we choose to love marks us as sinful and immoral and interrogates the assumption that heterosexuality is somehow better for the individual and society as a whole.

In my conservative Republican family, signs already point to a kind of readiness to engage homosexuality as a legitimate decision. Recently, I called my mother in California to throw out my "born-gay-pity-me" garbage. She didn't swallow my pill of choice with ease, but managed to cough up an exasperated, "Well, whatever makes you happy." That's one down and a nation to go.

Reading and Discussion Questions

1. At the beginning of paragraph 2, Fairyington says, "I didn't mean either of these things." To what two things is she referring? How does that relate to her title?

2. Five years later, how does she feel about the way she came out to her mother?

3. What does she mean when she says that homosexuality should be "cast and understood as a valid choice" (para. 5)? Isn't current thought that homosexuality is not a choice?

4. What two views of homosexuality is Fairyington contrasting? Where does she best sum up the contrast? Is the essay primarily a comparison and contrast essay?

5. Analyze the places in the essay where Fairyington discusses sexuality in political terms. What point is she trying to make?

Writing Assignments

1. Write a one-paragraph rhetorical summary of "The Gay Option."
2. Write a one-paragraph referential summary of the essay.

Evaluation

An **evaluation** builds on a summary by incorporating not only the argument's main point but also the reader's reaction to it. In Chapter 4, we will look more closely at how to build an effective response to an argument; in this section, we will briefly consider how to read not just with an ear for comprehension but also with a critical eye. Your overall goal is to make a careful judgment of the extent to which an argument has succeeded in making a point.

When you set out to evaluate a work, keep two points in mind:

- An argument that you disagree with is not necessarily wrong.
- An argument written by a published author or so-called expert is not necessarily right.

Critically evaluating an argument means not simply reading a text and agreeing or disagreeing with it, but doing serious analytical work that addresses multiple viewpoints before deciding on the argument's effectiveness.

Strategies for Evaluating Arguments

1. **Disagree with the author if you feel confident of the support for your view,** but first read the whole argument to see if your questions have been answered. Be cautious about concluding that the author hasn't proved his or her point.

2. **Talk about the material with classmates or others** who have read it, especially those who have responded to the text differently than you did. Consider their points of view. Defending or modifying your evaluation may mean going back to the text and finding clues that you may have overlooked.

3. **Consider the strengths of the argument,** and examine the useful methods of argumentation, the points that are successfully made (and those which help the reader to better understand the argument), and what makes sense about the author's argument.

continued

4. **Consider the weaknesses of the argument,** and locate instances of faulty reasoning, unsupported statements, and the limitations of the author's assumptions about the world (the assumptions that underlie the argument).

5. **Consider how effective the title of the reading is** and whether it accurately sums up a critical point of the essay. Come up with an alternative title that would suit the reading better, and be prepared to defend this alternative title.

6. **Evaluate the organizational structure of the essay.** The author should lead you from idea to idea in a logical progression, and each section should relate to the ones before and after it and to the central argument in significant ways. Determine whether the writer could have organized things more clearly, logically, or efficiently.

7. **Notice how the author follows through on the main claim, or thesis, of the argument.** The author should stick with this thesis and not waver throughout the text. If the thesis does waver, there could be a reason for the shift in the argument, or perhaps the author is being inconsistent. The conclusion should drive home the central argument.

8. **Evaluate the vocabulary and style the author uses.** Is it too simple or complicated? Are key terms and concepts defined? When considering style and vocabulary, keep in mind the audience the author was initially writing for.

ARGUMENT ESSENTIALS

Examining Written Arguments

The following steps will help you understand any written argument.

1. **Preread the article** to gain background information on the title, author, purpose, and audience.

2. **Read the article for content and structure.**
   - Pay attention to the organization and how the argument is shaped.
   - Read actively: Mark up the text and ask questions as you read.
   - Look for visuals that may enhance the argument.
   - Summarize the main point of the argument in your own words.
   - Referential summaries focus on content.
   - Rhetorical summaries focus on strategy.

3. **Evaluate the argument's effectiveness.**
   - Keep an open mind to opposing views.
   - Objectively consider the argument's strengths and weaknesses.
   - Consider the appropriateness of the title.
   - Determine how effective the argument's organization is.
   - Decide how well the argument supports its main claim or thesis.
   - Evaluate the use of language and the definitions of key terms.

READING ARGUMENT

Seeing Evaluation

The following article has been annotated by a student reader to demonstrate reading for content and structure as well as critical evaluation. The article is followed by a student response essay.

The Internet Is a Surveillance State
BRUCE SCHNEIER

I'm going to start with three data points.

One: Some of the Chinese military hackers who were implicated in a broad set of attacks against the U.S. government and corporations were identified because they accessed Facebook from the same network infrastructure they used to carry out their attacks.

Two: Hector Monsegur, one of the leaders of the LulzSac hacker movement, was identified and arrested last year by the FBI. Although he practiced good computer security and used an anonymous relay service to protect his identity, he slipped up.

> Examples: All 3 got caught because of the Internet. But isn't this a good thing?

And three: Paula Broadwell, who had an affair with CIA director David Petraeus, similarly took extensive precautions to hide her identity. She never logged in to her anonymous e-mail service from her home network. Instead, she used hotel and other public networks when she e-mailed him. The FBI correlated hotel registration data from several different hotels—and hers was the common name.

5   The Internet is a surveillance state. Whether we admit it to ourselves or not, and whether we like it or not, we're being tracked all the time. Google tracks us, both on its pages and on other pages it has access to. Facebook does the same; it even tracks non-Facebook users. Apple tracks us on our iPhones and iPads. One reporter used a tool called Collusion to track who was tracking him; 105 companies tracked his Internet use during one 36-hour period.

> Thesis *
>
> Examples

Increasingly, what we do on the Internet is being combined with other data about us. Unmasking Broadwell's identity involved correlating her Internet activity with her hotel stays. Everything we do now involves computers,

> Topic sentence
> Internet activity is combined with other sources.

Bruce Schneier is the Chief Technology Officer of Resilient, an IBM company, a fellow at Harvard's Berkman Klein Center for Internet and Society, and author of *Liars and Outliers: Enabling the Trust Society Needs to Survive* (2012) and *Data and Goliath: The Hidden Battles to Collect Your Data and Control Your World* (2015). This article appeared on cnn.com on March 16, 2013.

and computers produce data as a natural by-product. Everything is now being saved and correlated, and many big-data companies make money by building up intimate profiles of our lives from a variety of sources.

Facebook, for example, correlates your online behavior with your purchasing habits offline. And there's more. There's location data from your cell phone, there's a record of your movements from closed-circuit TVs.

Repeats thesis
Reference to 1984
Topic sentence:
Counter measures

This is ubiquitous surveillance: All of us being watched, all the time, and that data being stored forever. This is what a surveillance state looks like, and it's efficient beyond the wildest dreams of George Orwell.

Sure, we can take measures to prevent this. We can limit what we search on Google from our iPhones, and instead use computer web browsers that allow us to delete cookies. We can use an alias on Facebook. We can turn our cell phones off and spend cash. But increasingly, none of it matters.

But (transition):
They don't work.

There are simply too many ways to be tracked. The Internet, e-mail, cell   10
phones, web browsers, social networking sites, search engines: these have become necessities, and it's fanciful to expect people to simply refuse to use them just because they don't like the spying, especially since the full extent of such spying is deliberately hidden from us and there are few alternatives being marketed by companies that don't spy.

Topic sentence

This isn't something the free market can fix. We consumers have no choice in the matter. All the major companies that provide us with Internet services are interested in tracking us. Visit a website and it will almost certainly know who you are; there are lots of ways to be tracked without cookies. Cellphone companies routinely undo the web's privacy protection. One experiment at Carnegie Mellon took real-time videos of students on campus and was able to identify one-third of them by comparing their photos with publicly available tagged Facebook photos.

Examples

Topic sentence

Maintaining privacy on the Internet is nearly impossible. If you forget even once to enable your protections, or click on the wrong link, or type the wrong thing, you've permanently attached your name to whatever anonymous service you're using. Monsegur slipped up once, and the FBI got him. If the director of the CIA can't maintain his privacy on the Internet, we've got no hope.

Example

Topic sentence

In today's world, governments and corporations are working together to keep things that way. Governments are happy to use the data corporations collect—occasionally demanding that they collect more and save it longer—to spy on us. And corporations are happy to buy data from governments. Together the powerful spy on the powerless, and they're not going to give up their positions of power, despite what the people want.

What do the people
want?

Fixing this requires strong government will, but they're just as <u>punch-drunk on data</u> as the corporations. <u>Slap-on-the-wrist</u> fines notwithstanding, no one is agitating for better privacy laws.

Language a bit over-the-top? Exaggeration?

15   <u>So, we're done.</u> Welcome to a world where Google knows exactly what sort of porn you all like, and more about your interests than your spouse does. Welcome to a world where your cell phone company knows exactly where you are all the time. Welcome to the end of private conversations, because increasingly your conversations are conducted by e-mail, text, or social networking sites.

And welcome to a world where all of this, and everything else that you do or is done on a computer, is saved, correlated, studied, passed around from company to company without your knowledge or consent; and where the government accesses it at will without a warrant.

Argument assumes that data mining is a bad thing — is it? And we have hardly fought against it.

Welcome to an Internet without privacy, and we've ended up here with hardly a fight.

Giving Up Our Privacy: Is It Worth It?
WHITNEY CRAMER

Whitney Cramer
ENGL 203-017
Dr. Winchell
September 15, 2017

Giving Up Our Privacy: Is It Worth It?

The Internet is many things to many people. It provides a quick way to find information, an easy way to shop from the comfort of home or dorm room, and a way to stay in touch with friends and family. Most of us would probably not think of the Internet as a means of surveillance—that is, until we read Bruce Schneier's essay "The Internet Is a Surveillance State," posted to cnn.com on March 16, 2013. Primarily through his use of examples, Schneier builds a convincing case that by using the Internet, we have given up our privacy without even a fight, but he fails to acknowledge what some of his other examples reveal: that there are times when we *want* the Internet to be a surveillance state.

Schneier opens his essay with examples of three people who have been caught in indiscretions at least and in crimes at most by means of the Internet. Chinese hackers who targeted the American government and corporations were caught because they accessed Facebook on the same network. Hector Monsegur, another hacker, was caught by the FBI when he made one mistake and revealed his identity. Paula Broadwell's affair with the director of the CIA was discovered because she emailed him using public networks. But aren't these exactly the types of crimes and indiscretions that we should want revealed? Schneier writes, "If the director of the CIA can't maintain his privacy on the Internet, we've got no hope." But do we want the director of the CIA to use his Internet privacy to hide his wrongdoing?

Part of the reason we have no hope is that governments and corporations have joined forces to track us. Schneier cites Google, Apple, and Facebook as examples of companies that track users. Facebook, for example, combines what it knows about your online activity with information about your offline buying habits. Governments use what corporations collect, and corporations use what the government collects, for a price. Perhaps most unsettling, cell phones and closed-circuit TV's can be used to track your movements. Big Brother knows where you are and what you are doing (Schneier).

Schneier gives examples of things we can do to protect our privacy, but he admits that none of them matter. We could turn off our cell phones and our computers, but we have become so used to them that we would rather give up our privacy than give up our electronics. We could limit what we search, use aliases, and use cash rather than credit, but since the spying is not obvious, it is easy to ignore. And there is the other side of the issue—the good that Internet surveillance does. In spite of his opening examples, Schneier fails to acknowledge that for those who are doing no wrong, Internet surveillance may be annoying, but it may be worth the loss of privacy to protect the innocent against those who use the Internet to commit crimes.

Work Cited

Schneier, Bruce. "The Internet Is a Surveillance State." *CNN .com*, 16 Mar. 2013, http://www.cnn.com/2013/03/16/opinion/ schneier-internet-surveillance/index.html. Reprinted in *Elements of Argument: A Text and Reader*, 12th ed., edited by Annette T. Rottenberg and Donna Haisty Winchell, Bedford/St. Martin's, 2018, pp. 63–65.

Assignments for Critical Reading of Written Arguments

Reading and Discussion Questions

1. The chapter opens with some examples of bumper stickers as argument. What are some bumper stickers that you have seen, and what points were they making?

2. Protest signs also make arguments in just a few words. What examples have you seen? You can find numerous examples on *Google* or *Flickr*.

3. Where an essay or an image is published can, in itself, make a statement. Are you aware of certain publications that have a political bias? Consider how even advertisements are geared for the target audience of any given magazine. Locate two ads for the same product or type of product but published in different magazines. How are the ads targeted to the different target audiences?

4. Where do you in your daily life read written arguments? Where in newspapers, for example, are arguments published? Where do you find them online?

5. Locate a print or online editorial. Use what you have learned in this chapter to examine it for content, structure, and rhetorical strategies.

Writing Suggestions

1. Choose a print or online editorial, and write an essay analyzing the author's rhetorical strategies.

2. Choose two editorials or argumentative essays on different sides of the same issue and write an essay comparing the authors' rhetorical strategies.

RESEARCH ASSIGNMENT **Summarizing**

Do a database search to find a long magazine or journal article (at least 1,200 words) on a topic that interests you: sports, politics, the environment, entertainment, education, or the like.

1. Use the advice in this chapter to preread and then read the article. If possible, print it out and mark up the text.

2. On a separate sheet of paper, list each of the article's subheadings or main ideas, and then summarize each section's point in your own words.

3. Follow the Research Skill box on page 52 and the Strategy box on page 61 to write a paragraph that briefly and objectively summarizes the article. Your paragraph may be either referential (p. 52) or rhetorical (p. 52) — you should be able to identify which type of summary you are writing and explain what makes it so.

bits   To see what you are learning about argumentation applied to the latest world and national news, read our *Bits* blog, "Argument and the Headlines," at **blogs.bedfordstmartins.com/bits**.

Critical Reading of Multimodal Arguments

Of course, not all public arguments are written. In addition to the critical reading skills discussed in Chapter 2, special scrutiny is needed when listening to and viewing arguments in other media. We use the term **multimodal** in the title of this chapter because now we turn to arguments that use words in combination with another medium or that use a mode other than the printed word to get a message across — pictures, audio, video, and digital media.

Visual Rhetoric

In reading written arguments, we used three steps to help uncover the essential elements of claim, support, and assumption:

- Prereading
- Reading for content and structure
- Evaluation

The same general principles apply in looking at visual rhetoric, but we will change them a bit. With the visual, structure is more closely related to rhetorical strategy than to content, so we have broken that one step into two.

- **Prereading.** With a visual, prereading includes noticing who took or otherwise created the picture or graphic, but often more important are the context and purpose. It may also be relevant where the visual was published, if it was, and when. Print ads, especially, are targeted for a particular audience. The same ad, in different versions, often appears in different publications. With a political cartoon, the political context is critical to understanding the humor. Graphics are meant to convey information about a particular issue.
- **Reading for content.** To "read" a visual means to see what is there — pictures and text. Published images are usually carefully planned to convey a message by means of who or what is shown.

■ **Reading for rhetorical strategies.** As a viewer, consider the composition of the visual. Why did the photographer place things where he or she did? Why are some objects in sharp focus and others not? Why, in an ad, is the text a certain size and placed in a certain location? How does the eye move about the ad? Why is the logo where it is? the product? In a cartoon, what does the physical appearance suggest about the characters? In a graphic, what data are being highlighted?

■ **Evaluation.** Consider how effective the visual is in achieving its purpose. How does a photograph make you feel? Does an ad make you want to purchase a product? Does the cartoon make you consider a new perspective? Does a graphic aid your understanding of a complex issue?

Not every visual image makes a statement or presents an argument. Some, however, do so in a way that the printed word alone cannot. If an image arouses emotion in you or brings to mind a controversial issue, it is making some kind of statement to you. What statement, for example, does Figure 3.1 make to you?

The reading strategies given above are general guidelines for all visuals. The following pages discuss additional considerations for specific types of visuals: photographs, print advertisements, political cartoons, and graphics.

Photographs

You've probably seen powerful still images in photographic journalism: soldiers in battle, destruction by weather disasters, beautiful natural landscapes, inhumane living conditions, the great mushroom clouds of early atomic explosions. These photographs and thousands of others encapsulate arguments of fact, value, and policy: *The tornado devastated the town. The Grand Canyon is our most stupendous national monument. We must not allow human beings to live like this.* Sometimes captions are used to help get the photograph's message across.

FIGURE 3.1 Homeless Family. Bruce Ayres/Getty Images

READING ARGUMENT

Examining Photographs

The next two pictures gained wide circulation in the aftermath of Hurricane Katrina in 2005. They seemed innocuous enough when seen without commentary, except to show the extent of the flooding. The text accompanying the pictures, however, shows the bias of those who described the pictures. The wording produced such a response that *Yahoo!* offered this statement:

> Yahoo! News regrets that these photos and captions, viewed together, may have suggested a racial bias on our part. We remain committed to bringing our readers the full collection of photos as transmitted by our wire service partners.[1]

Looting
DAVE MARTIN

A young man walks through chest-deep water after looting a grocery store in New Orleans on Tuesday, August 30, 2005. DAVE MARTIN/AP Images

---

[1] The Yahoo! News statement can be found at http://news.yahoo.com/page/photostatement.

Finding
CHRIS GRAYTHEN

Two residents wade through chest-deep flood water after finding bread and soda from a local grocery store after Hurricane Katrina came through New Orleans, Louisiana. Chris Graythen/ Getty Images

Practice: Examining Photographs

Look at the images that follow on pages 73–74, and then answer the questions on page 75.

Los Angeles Airport Police Remove the Camouflaged Gun Case That Caused the Evacuation

RICK LOOMIS

Rick Loomis/Getty Images

Rio Olympics Refugees

CHARLIE RIEDEL

AP Photo/Charlie Riedel

Hey Mister! Hands Off My Sister!
DINENDRA HARIA

Dinendra Haria/REX Features via AP Images

Texting and Driving
MICHAEL KRASOWITZ

Michael Krasowitz/Getty Images

Reading and Discussion Questions

1. Look at Rick Loomis's photograph "Los Angeles Airport police remove the camouflaged gun case . . . ." The photo shows passengers returning to the Tom Bradley International Terminal at Los Angeles Airport after it was temporarily evacuated because of a suspicious package. The package turned out to be the gun in a camouflaged case that a police officer is holding. Loomis, from the *Los Angeles Times*, could have photographed the event at a number of different moments and from a number of perspectives—and probably did. What details about this particular image are noteworthy? To what people or objects is your attention drawn? Why might Loomis have composed the shot in the way that he did? What is significant about the people who appear in the picture?

2. Charlie Riedel's photograph "Rio Olympics Refugees" was taken on August 3, 2016, after the opening ceremony of the Olympics in Rio de Janeiro. Notice the sign saying "ROT." That abbreviation stands for Refugee Olympic Team. What do you know about the Refugee Olympic Team that participated in the 2016 Olympics? In other words, what is the specific context of this picture that makes these athletes different from all other athletes at the Games? How would you describe the looks on the faces of the athletes? Why might Riedel have focused this shot on these particular members of the team at this moment?

3. Dinendra Haria took the picture called "Hey Mister? Hands Off My Sister!" at a "Wear what you want" beach party protest in London on August 25, 2016. What were the women in London protesting? Why is what the two women are wearing significant? What is the sign in front of them referring to? What is the message on the sign behind them on the right? What might explain the expression on the face of the woman on the left?

4. Look at the picture titled "Texting and Driving" on page 74. The photographer's intent seems fairly clear in this photo. What is in focus? What isn't? Why?

5. What argument is this photo making?

Print Advertisements

In 1947, one analyst summed up the goals of the advertiser, which are still very relevant today:

1. attract attention
2. arouse interest
3. stimulate desire
4. create conviction
5. get action[2]

---

[2] J. V. Lund, *Newspaper Advertising* (New York: Prentice Hall, 1947), p. 83.

ARGUMENT ESSENTIALS
Visual Rhetoric

Use these four steps as basic guidelines for analyzing visual rhetoric:

- **Preread.** Consider who created the visual, what the context was, and whether and where it was published.
- **Read for content.** With visual rhetoric, this means "reading" both the pictures and the text.
- **Read for rhetorical strategies.** Consider the placement and focus of text and visuals. In general, what draws your eye?
- **Evaluate.** How does the image make you feel? What mood does it create? Is it effective in achieving its goal?

Alluring photographs from advertisers — car companies, animal-rights groups, restaurants, sporting goods manufacturers, clothiers, jewelers, movie studios — promise to fulfill our dreams of pleasure. On a very different scale, animal-rights groups show photographs of brutally mistreated dogs and cats; children's rights advocates publish pictures of sick and starving children in desolate refugee camps.

But photographs are not the only visual images used by advertisers. Other kinds of illustrations — as well as signs and symbols, which over the years have acquired connotations, or suggestive significance — are also used as instruments of persuasion. The flag or bald eagle, the shamrock, the crown, the cross, the hammer and sickle, the rainbow, and the swastika can all rouse strong feelings for or against the ideas they represent. These symbols may be defined as abbreviated claims of value. They summarize the moral, religious, and political principles by which groups of people live and often die. In commercial advertisements, we recognize symbols that aren't likely to enlist our deepest loyalties but, nevertheless, have impact on our daily lives: the apple with a bite in it, the golden arches, the Prudential rock, the Nike swoosh, and a thousand others.

In fact, a closer look at commercial and political advertising, which is heavily dependent on visual argument and is something we are all familiar with, provides a useful introduction to this complex subject. We know that advertisements, with or without pictures, are short arguments, often lacking fully developed support, whose claims of policy urge us to take an action: Buy this product or service; vote for this candidate or issue. The claim may not be directly expressed, but it will be clearly implicit. In print, on television, or on the Internet, the visual representation of objects, carefully chosen to appeal to a particular audience, can be as important as, if not more important than, any verbal text.

Consider these questions as you analyze print advertisements:

1. Who is the sponsor?
2. What does the sponsor want me to do or believe?
3. Is there sufficient text to answer questions I may have about the claim?
4. Are the visual elements more prominent than the text? If so, why?
5. Does the arrangement of elements in the message tell me what the sponsor considers most important? If so, what is the significance of this choice?
6. Does the visual image lead me to entertain unrealistic expectations? (Can using this shampoo make my hair look like that shining cascade on the model? Does the picture of the candidate for governor, shown answering questions in a classroom of eager, smiling youngsters, mean that he has a viable plan for educational reform?)

READING ARGUMENT

Examining Print Advertisements

The print advertisement below has been annotated with careful attention paid to the questions listed on page 76. The ad is followed by a brief analysis that shows prereading, reading for content, reading for rhetorical strategies, and evaluation.

Stop Climate Change before It Changes You
WORLD WILDLIFE FUND

Frightening visual more prominent than text; intended to show that humans are threatened by climate change

No evidence to support claim

Claim (that humans will turn into fish if we don't stop climate change) is exaggerated.

Message is clear: Stop Climate Change.

Sponsor is WWF: World Wildlife Fund.

Analysis

The advertisement is for the WWF, or World Wildlife Fund, a nonprofit environmental organization. The ad appeared in Belgium in 2008.

The creepy-looking visual is more prominent than the text. The front and top of the person's head are well lit, to show that a human face has turned into a fish face. The message here is that we could all be living under water if the sea level rises. The text is brief and direct: "Stop Climate Change before It Changes You." The text is located at the bottom of the ad, and it reinforces the image's message: that humans are threatened by climate change. The friendly-looking panda and WWF logo are small and are placed at the very bottom of the ad.

The ad is certainly attention-getting, and you really need to look at it for a minute to figure out what is going on. However, the human with a fish face is quite unrealistic, and the scare tactic used in the ad seems too heavy-handed. This ad may work for readers who already believe that climate change must be stopped. In that case, the ad is simply reinforcing readers' existing worldview as a way to generate support for the WWF. But the ad would probably be less effective in convincing more conservative readers because it lacks any evidence to support the claim that climate change is threatening the human species.

Practice: Examining Print Advertisements

Practice your analytical skills by applying the four steps — prereading, reading for content, reading for rhetorical strategies, and evaluation — to the following ad. Be sure to keep in mind the questions on page 76.

It Only Takes a Moment to Make a Moment
AD COUNCIL

Political Cartoons

Knowing the context of a political cartoon is essential to both understanding it and appreciating its humor. These cartoons age quickly. You can go back to historical cartoons and appreciate them only if you know the context in which they were created. If today's political cartoons are not created and published quickly, they will have lost their currency and their humor. Remember that if the cartoon is an argument, it has a claim. Consider what the claim is and how the artist used both drawing and text to articulate that claim. Often the picture will provide the support. Since political cartoons are generally judgmental, there will be an assumption on which that judgment is based; puzzling out that assumption may help you understand the cartoon.

READING ARGUMENT

Examining Political Cartoons

You would probably assume that the following cartoon was published during the 2016 presidential election. It could have been, but it happens that it was published instead on November 8, 1993. Consider why the cartoon makes some people think of the 2016 election. You have a woman waiting to vote, but from the feet dangling below the curtain of the voting booth, you surmise that the voter before her has committed suicide by hanging himself. Notice, by the way, that the other man and woman pictured don't seem to even notice. The cartoon was published in the *New Yorker*, so it could have been a comment on the heated gubernatorial race ending that month in nearby New Jersey between incumbent Jim Florio and Christine Todd Whitman. The argument seems to be that some people would rather die, literally, than choose any of the available candidates, which may be a bit of an exaggeration, but during the presidential race in 2016 between Hillary Rodham Clinton and Donald Trump, quite a few voters would rather have died, figuratively, than vote for either. This is a rare instance where a cartoon from an earlier time fits a more recent context.

PETER STEINER

Peter Steiner The New Yorker Collection/The Cartoon Bank

Practice: Examining Cartoons

Analyze the cartoon on page 81, which has a different focus from this. It will help if you think what assumption is behind it. The context of this cartoon was the waning days of President Obama's second term, when Republicans were trying to block his appointment of a new Supreme Court justice.

If One Political Party or the Other . . .
DAVID SIPRESS

"*If one political party or the other doesn't give in soon, there are going to be only two branches of government.*"

David Sipress The New Yorker Collection/The Cartoon Bank

Graphics

Graphics are charts, graphs, diagrams, and other visuals that provide an alternative to presenting information as text. They can offer a concise, efficient way of getting information across easily and quickly. A bar graph can show at a glance if sales are higher or lower in the fourth quarter than in the third. A pie chart can make clear how much of the national budget is spent on defense. A map can show emerging centers of population growth.

Different types of graphics serve different purposes. It's important to read accurately the type of graphic you are examining. Always look at the title of the graphic, which should be descriptive, and for labels and keys that will help you understand the information being presented. Color will often serve to make contrasts more striking and simply to make the graphic more visually appealing. Of course, you should always take note of who created or sponsored the graphic as you consider what argument it is making.

READING ARGUMENT

Examining Graphics

The following graphic on tobacco has been annotated for you.

Tobacco's Shifting Burden

theworld.org

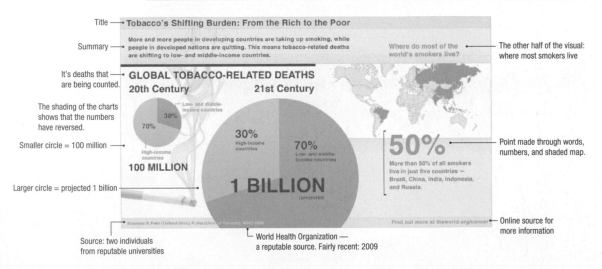

PRI/theworld.org: Kim Ducharme, Sonia Narang

Practice: Examining Graphics

Analyze this graphic sponsored by the Union of Concerned Scientists (ucsusa
.org), and answer the questions that follow.

Where Your Gas Money Goes
UNION OF CONCERNED SCIENTISTS

Where Your Gas Money Goes

$50.00 fill-up

Oil companies make
huge profits from your
pain at the pump.

Keep the profits
in your pocket by investing
in fuel efficiency.

$19.61 Private and Publicly Traded
Oil Companies

$13.63 Government-Owned
Oil Companies

$7.00 Taxes

$4.87 Refining

$4.08 Distribution and Marketing

$0.81 Gas Stations

© Union of Concerned Scientists 2013
Source: UCS Report, Where Your Gas Money Goes
For more information, visit www.ucsusa.org/gasmoney

Union of Concerned Scientists

Reading and Discussion Questions

1. "Read" the graphic. What is it saying?
2. The ad was sponsored by the Union of Concerned Scientists. What might you speculate about that group? What does your research reveal about it?
3. Does the group have a purpose in the ad beyond explaining where your gas money goes? If so, what is it?
4. What are some conclusions you can draw from the ad?

Audiovisual Rhetoric

Where in our daily lives do we see examples of argumentation that go beyond print? We see it on the television news and on talk shows that deal with politics. We hear news and opinions on the radio, and we hear political speeches and debates.

Audiovisual rhetoric includes all that the human voice adds, from a regional dialect to a tinge of nervousness; television includes all that the visual dimension adds, from body language to hair style. And, of course, in television commercials we see most of the features of print ads with the addition of sound and motion.

- **Prereading.** Prereading an argumentative speech or a debate that you are going to hear delivered orally means knowing the affiliation of the speaker or debaters and what biases you might expect from each. It also means knowing as much as possible about the topic or topics to be discussed. Prereading broadcast news or talk shows means noticing the network or station and acknowledging any known biases that suggests. With some news organizations, it won't take long for a liberal or conservative bias to become obvious. The sponsors of a show may be relevant. For talk shows, a practical part of prereading is finding out who the guests will be. That information is often available online in advance. What are the affiliations of the various guests and of the host? For commercials, prereading means determining what company's or organization's ad it is—and sometimes that's hard to tell.
- **Watching or listening for content.** Aside from the regional dialect or the tinge of nervousness, the body language or the hairstyle, what is being said? Televised news will incorporate photographs, video, and graphics along with the script. By way of all that, what are viewers being told? As you hear different speakers on a talk show or in a debate, can you start to recognize their positions on the issues? With commercials, what is being sold?
- **Watching or listening for rhetorical strategies.** How are you being "told" or "sold"? As you listen to a speaker or a debater, are you aware of any errors in logic? Does the speaker or debater support his or her claims?

Are there unspoken assumptions with which you do not agree? If news is not the objective reporting of facts that it should be, how is bias revealed? Is the news slanted for a particular audience? In analyzing commercials for rhetorical strategies, consider (1) all of the questions you considered in analyzing print ads and (2) any others that will reveal how an ad with speech, music, and special effects might appeal to a viewer logically, emotionally, and ethically.

- **Evaluation.** How effective is a speaker or debater in building a convincing case for the intended audience? How effective is "the news" in delivering the news? How effective is the talk show in presenting a legitimate exchange of opinions and not a shouting match? How effective is the commercial in selling a product or service?

Television Commercials

Television commercials have come of age since their first appearance in 1941 with an ad for Bulova watches. The cost of that ad? Nine dollars. Of course, we all know what a big business commercials are today. The cost of a thirty-second commercial during the Super Bowl hit four million dollars in 2013.

Television commercials can be analyzed much like print ads.

- **Prereading.** Preview a commercial, or watch it to get the general idea before breaking it down into component parts for analysis. Consider the context, including the intended audience, at what time of day the ad airs, and during what shows or types of shows it airs.
- **Reading for content.** Consider text and visuals, as you did with print ads, but also consider the action in the commercial and to what extent sound adds to its overall appeal.
- **Reading for rhetorical strategies.** Consider what audience the commercial targets and how it appeals to that audience.
- **Evaluating.** How effective is the commercial at achieving its purpose?

READING ARGUMENT

Examining Television Commercials

In 2012, Toyota changed its slogan to "Let's Go Places," replacing "Moving Forward," which had been its slogan since 2004, and did a series of commercials around the new theme. The new tagline was introduced on December 31, 2012, in launching the redesigned 2013 Avalon sedan. The stills presented here show the approach the company took in one of them. Look at the images and read the analysis that accompanies each one to understand how Toyota employed audiovisual rhetoric in its commercial.

Let's Go Places
TOYOTA

Voiceover: *Let's go places.*

This is one of numerous shots that show Toyotas moving through different types of landscape — mountains, residential neighborhoods, snowy woods, and so on. These are some of the physical places we can go to. The varied landscape suggests that wherever you go, you can do it in a Toyota. Different locales appeal to different viewers, depending on where they live or where they would like to travel. The first series of rapid shots shows the landscape but not the car. A second shows the landscape as seen from behind the car. The movement of the camera from in front of the car to behind it gives the impression of the car outracing the camera in the rush to go places.

Voiceover: *Not just the ones you can find on a map. But the ones you can find in your heart!*

The ad goes for emotional appeals, including shots of familiar points in the lives of everyday people. Some of them are common events like a trip out for ice cream with the family or a camping trip to the lake, and some are major events like going to the prom, bringing a new baby home, or being in a wedding.

Voiceover: *Let's go beyond everything we know and embrace everything we don't. And once we have reached our destination, let's keep going, because inspiration does not favor those that sit still. It dances with the daring and rewards the courageous with ideas that excite, challenge, and even inspire.*

Race-equipped vehicle with stunt driver on closed course. Do not attempt.

With these words, the focus shifts to Toyota's tough four-wheel drive vehicles to show how they can function in rough terrain. Toyotas are even shown painted like race cars. One vehicle "dances with the daring" by launching off a ramp into the air. The whole ad campaign stresses moving instead of sitting still. The text tells us that our destination is beyond everything we know and suggests new, tougher challenges, like making the car fly through the air. The music, "It's My Life" by Tim Myers, builds from soft piano notes at the beginning to a crescendo as the car takes to the air. This portion of the ad goes beyond the comfort of earlier familiar scenes to appeal to the daredevil in most of us.

Voiceover: *Ideas that take you to a place that you never imagined. Ideas big enough and powerful enough to make the heart skip a beat and in some cases even two. Toyota. Let's go places.*

The Tundra CrewMax 5.7L V8 is towing far beyond its published towing capacity in a one-time, short-distance event. Never tow beyond a vehicle's published towing capacity. Always consult Owner's Manual.

By the end of the ad, Toyota is appealing to viewers' pride in America. One place that you probably would not have imagined a Toyota going is the "parade route" along which the retired space shuttle *Endeavour* was pulled from Los Angeles International Airport to a downtown museum. The words "Born in America" across the front of the Toyota Tundra stress that although Toyota is a Japanese automaker, the Tundra is made in San Antonio. And the places that the shuttle has been advance the idea of humankind's ultimate journeys. The shuttle dwarfs all around it, just as its destinations dwarf most of our dreams of places we would like to go. However, the ad encourages its viewers not to place limits on themselves when they dream. A final shot of a globe reinforces the notion that there is no place, on this planet at least, that one cannot go in a Toyota.

Speeches and Debates

Good speeches on controversial issues are some of the best examples of argument. Unlike the brief sound bites that we hear on the evening news or in response to a microphone thrust in a politician's face as she leaves a building, a carefully prepared speech is the closest we come in the twenty-first century to the rhetoric that Aristotle taught. Of course, those in the highest offices have speechwriters, but whoever writes public addresses for candidates or governmental officials must be skilled at blending *logos*, *ethos*, and *pathos* to move an audience to act or at least to change an opinion.

Candidates also prepare carefully for debates, but the success of the debate depends largely on the moderator. A weak moderator might allow each candidate to deliver set speeches no matter what the question or allow the whole event to become a verbal sparring match, which can be entertaining but may not clarify the candidates' positions on a wide range of issues. A strong moderator can hold the candidates to a clear response and rebuttal format that covers a lot of ground in a short time.

Listening to a speech—or reading one—requires focus on the ideas to the exclusion of the distraction of physical appearance. It requires listening for claim and support. It requires keeping in mind the audience for whom the speech is or was intended. You will learn more in Chapter 10 about making language serve the needs of argument. For now, consider how well speeches fit the contexts in which they were delivered and how convincing you find their arguments to be.

READING ARGUMENT

Examining Speeches

The following speech was delivered by Senator Elizabeth Warren in 2015. It has been annotated for you.

Remarks at the Edward M. Kennedy Institute for the United States Senate, September 27, 2015

SENATOR ELIZABETH WARREN

Paul Zimmerman/Getty Images

Opens with praise for Kennedy, for whom the Institute is named. Reveals her respect for him and for the commitment to the people of Massachusetts that she shares with him. Use of pathos, or emotional appeal.

Thank you. I'm grateful to be here at the Edward M. Kennedy Institute for the United States Senate. This place is a fitting tribute to our champion, Ted Kennedy. A man of courage, compassion, and commitment, who taught us what public service is all about. Not a day goes by that we don't miss his passion, his enthusiasm, and—most of all—his dedication to all of our working families.

As the Senior Senator from Massachusetts, I have the great honor of sitting at Senator Kennedy's desk—right over there. The original, back in Washington, is a little more dented and scratched, but it has something very special in the drawer. Ted Kennedy carved his name in it. When I sit at my desk, sometimes when I'm waiting to speak or to vote, I open the drawer and run my thumb across his name. It reminds me of the high expectations of the people of Massachusetts, and I try, every day, to live up to the legacy he left behind.

Historical background for her subject, treatment of blacks in America. More use of pathos.

Senator Kennedy took office just over fifty years ago, in the midst of one of the great moral and political debates in American history—the debate over the Civil Rights Act. In his first speech on the floor of the Senate, just four months after his brother's assassination, he stood up to support equal rights for all Americans. He ended that speech with a powerful personal message about what the civil rights struggle meant to the late President Kennedy:

His heart and soul are in this bill. If his life and death had a meaning, it was that we should not hate but love one another; we should use our powers not to create conditions of oppression that lead to violence, but conditions of freedom that lead to peace.

A plea for peace and unity

"We should use our powers not to create conditions of oppression that lead to violence, but conditions of freedom that lead to peace." That's what I'd like to talk about today.

5   A half-century ago, when Senator Kennedy spoke of the Civil Rights Act, entrenched, racist power did everything it could to sustain oppression of African Americans, and violence was its first tool. Lynchings, terrorism, intimidation. The 16th Street Baptist Church. Medgar Evers. Emmett Till. When Alabama Governor George Wallace stood before the nation and declared during his 1963 inaugural address that he would defend "segregation now, segregation tomorrow, segregation forever," he made clear that the state would stand with those who used violence.

Examples of historical violence and discrimination against blacks in America

But violence was not the only tool. African Americans were effectively stripped of citizenship when they were denied the right to vote. The tools varied—literacy tests, poll taxes, moral character tests, grandfather clauses—but the results were the same. They were denied basic rights of citizenship and the chance to participate in self-government.

The third tool of oppression was to deliberately deny millions of African Americans economic opportunities solely because of the color of their skin.

Warren starts using the three aspects of black treatment that will organize her remarks: three tools used against blacks–violence, voting, and economic injustice.

I have often spoken about how America built a great middle class. Coming out of the Great Depression, from the 1930s to the late 1970s, as GDP went up, wages went up for most Americans. But there's a dark underbelly to that story. While median family income in America was growing—for both white and African-American families—African-American incomes were only a fraction of white incomes. In the mid-1950s, the median income for African-American families was just a little more than half the income of white families.

And the problem went beyond just income. Look at housing: For most middle class families in America, buying a home is the number one way to build wealth. It's a retirement plan–pay off the house and live on Social Security. An investment option—mortgage the house to start a business. It's a way to help the kids get through college, a safety net if someone gets really sick, and, if all goes well and Grandma and Grandpa can hang on to the house until they die, it's a way to give the next generation a boost—extra money to move the family up the ladder.

10   For much of the 20th century, that's how it worked for generation after generation of white Americans—but not black Americans. Entire legal

Contrasts economic opportunities for blacks and whites. Logos, or logical appeal.

structures were created to prevent African Americans from building economic security through home ownership. Legally-enforced segregation. Restrictive deeds. Redlining. Land contracts. Coming out of the Great Depression, America built a middle class, but systematic discrimination kept most African-American families from being part of it.

State-sanctioned discrimination wasn't limited to homeownership. The government enforced discrimination in public accommodations, discrimination in schools, discrimination in credit—it was a long and spiteful list.

Economic justice is not—and has never been—sufficient to ensure racial justice. Owning a home won't stop someone from burning a cross on the front lawn. Admission to a school won't prevent a beating on the sidewalk outside. But when Dr. King led hundreds of thousands of people to march on Washington, he talked about an end to violence, access to voting AND economic opportunity. As Dr. King once wrote, "the inseparable twin of racial injustice was economic injustice."

The tools of oppression were woven together, and the civil rights struggle was fought against that oppression wherever it was found—against violence, against the denial of voting rights, and against economic injustice.

The battles were bitter and sometimes deadly. Fire hoses turned on peaceful protestors. Police officers setting their dogs to attack black students. Bloody Sunday at the Edmund Pettus Bridge.

But the civil rights movement pushed this country in a new direction.   15

- The federal government cracked down on state-sponsored violence. Presidents Eisenhower, Kennedy and Johnson all called out the National Guard, and, in doing so, declared that everyone had a right to equal protection under the law, guaranteed by the Constitution. Congress protected the rights of all citizens to vote with the Voting Rights Act.
- And economic opportunities opened up when Congress passed civil rights laws that protected equal access to employment, public accommodations, and housing.

In the same way that the tools of oppression were woven together, a package of civil rights laws came together to protect black people from violence, to ensure access to the ballot box, and to build economic opportunity. Or to say it another way, these laws made three powerful declarations: Black lives matter. Black citizens matter. Black families matter.

Fifty years later, we have made real progress toward creating the conditions of freedom—but we have not made ENOUGH progress.

Fifty years later, violence against African Americans has not disappeared. Consider law enforcement. The vast majority of police officers sign up so they can protect their communities. They are part of an honorable profession that

King referred to the end of all three: violence, voting discrimination, and lack of economic opportunity. Use of authority, and a combination of logos and pathos.

Repetition used effectively for emphasis. The three are reiterated.

Emphasis through use of parallel structure, repetition

Warren's claim

takes risks every day to keep us safe. We know that. But we also know—and say—the names of those whose lives have been treated with callous indifference. Sandra Bland. Freddie Gray. Michael Brown. We've seen sickening videos of unarmed, black Americans cut down by bullets, choked to death while gasping for air—their lives ended by those who are sworn to protect them. Peaceful, unarmed protestors have been beaten. Journalists have been jailed. And, in some cities, white vigilantes with weapons freely walk the streets. And it's not just about law enforcement either. Just look to the terrorism this summer at Emanuel AME Church. We must be honest: Fifty years after John Kennedy and Martin Luther King, Jr. spoke out, violence against African Americans has not disappeared.

> 1. Examples of how fifty years later, there is still violence

And what about voting rights? Two years ago, five conservative justices on the Supreme Court gutted the Voting Rights Act, opening the floodgates ever wider for measures designed to suppress minority voting. Today, the specific tools of oppression have changed—voter ID laws, racial gerrymandering, and mass disfranchisement through a criminal justice system that disproportionately incarcerates black citizens. The tools have changed, but black voters are still deliberately cut out of the political process.

> 2. Examples of today's discrimination

20   Violence. Voting. And what about economic injustice? Research shows that the legal changes in the civil rights era created new employment and housing opportunities. In the 1960s and the 1970s, African-American men and women began to close the wage gap with white workers, giving millions of black families hope that they might build real wealth.

> 3. Examples of today's economic injustice

But then, Republicans' trickle-down economic theory arrived. Just as this country was taking the first steps toward economic justice, the Republicans pushed a theory that meant helping the richest people and the most powerful corporations get richer and more powerful. I'll just do one statistic on this: From 1980 to 2012, GDP continued to rise, but how much of the income growth went to the 90% of America—everyone outside the top 10%—black, white, Latino? None. Zero. Nothing. 100% of all the new income produced in this country over the past 30 years has gone to the top ten percent.

Today, 90% of Americans see no real wage growth. For African-Americans, who were so far behind earlier in the 20th century, this means that since the 1980s they have been hit particularly hard. In January of this year, African-American unemployment was 10.3%—more than twice the rate of white unemployment. And, after beginning to make progress during the civil rights era to close the wealth gap between black and white families, in the 1980s the wealth gap exploded, so that from 1984 to 2009, the wealth gap between black and white families tripled.

> Effective use of statistics—logos.

The 2008 housing collapse destroyed trillions in family wealth across the country, but the crash hit African-Americans like a punch in the gut. Because middle class black families' wealth was disproportionately tied up in homeownership and not other forms of savings, these families were hit harder by the housing collapse. But they also got hit harder because of discriminatory lending practices—yes, discriminatory lending practices in the 21st century. Recently several big banks and other mortgage lenders paid hundreds of millions in fines, admitting that they illegally steered black and Latino borrowers into more expensive mortgages than white borrowers who had similar credit. Tom Perez, who at the time was the Assistant Attorney General for Civil Rights, called it a "racial surtax." And it's still happening—earlier this month, the National Fair Housing alliance filed a discrimination complaint against real estate agents in Mississippi after an investigation showed those agents consistently steering white buyers away from interracial neighborhoods and black buyers away from affluent ones. Another investigation showed similar results across our nation's cities. Housing discrimination alive and well in 2015.

Violence, voting, economic justice.

We have made important strides forward. But we are not done yet. And now, it is our time.   25

I speak today with the full knowledge that I have not personally experienced and can never truly understand the fear, the oppression, and the pain that confronts African Americans every day. But none of us can ignore what is happening in this country. Not when our black friends, family, neighbors literally fear dying in the streets.

Listen to the brave, powerful voices of today's new generation of civil rights leaders. Incredible voices. Listen to them say: "If I die in police custody, know that I did not commit suicide." Watch them march through the streets, "hands up don't shoot"—not to incite a riot, but to fight for their lives. To fight for their lives.

This is the reality all of us must confront, as uncomfortable and ugly as that reality may be. It comes to us to once again affirm that black lives matter, that black citizens matter, that black families matter.

Once again, the task begins with safeguarding our communities from violence. We have made progress, but it is a tragedy when any American cannot trust those who have sworn to protect and serve. This pervasive and persistent distrust isn't based on myths. It is grounded in the reality of unjustified violence.

Policing must become a truly community endeavor—not in just a few cities, but everywhere. Police forces should look like, and come from, the   30 neighborhoods they serve. They should reach out to support and defend the community—working with people in neighborhoods before problems arise. All police forces—not just some—must be trained to de-escalate and to avoid the likelihood of violence. Body cameras can help us know what happens when someone is hurt.

We honor the bravery and sacrifice that our law enforcement officers show every day on the job—and the noble intentions of the vast majority of those who take up the difficult job of keeping us safe. But police are not occupying armies. This is America, not a war zone—and policing practices in all cities—not just some—need to reflect that.

Next, voting.

It's time to call out the recent flurry of new state law restrictions for what they are: an all-out campaign by Republicans to take away the right to vote from poor and black and Latino American citizens who probably won't vote for them. The push to restrict voting is nothing more than a naked grab to win elections that they can't win if every citizen votes.

Two years ago the Supreme Court eviscerated critical parts of the Voting Rights Act. Congress could easily fix this, and Democrats in the Senate have called for restoration of voting rights. Now it is time for Republicans to step up to support a restoration of the Voting Rights Act—or to stand before the American people and explain why they have abandoned America's most cherished liberty, the right to vote.

35   And while we're at it, we need to update the rules around voting. Voting should be simple. Voter registration should be automatic. Get a driver's license, get registered automatically. Nonviolent, law-abiding citizens should not lose the right to vote because of a prior conviction. Election Day should be a holiday, so no one has to choose between a paycheck and a vote. Early voting and vote by mail would give fast food and retail workers who don't get holidays off a chance to proudly cast their votes. The hidden discrimination that comes with purging voter rolls and short-staffing polling places must stop. The right to vote remains essential to protect all other rights, and no candidate for president or for any other elected office—Republican or Democrat—should be elected if they will not pledge to support full, meaningful voting rights.

Finally, economic justice. Our task will not be complete until we ensure that every family—regardless of race—has a fighting chance to build an economic future for themselves and their families. We need less talk and more action about reducing unemployment, ending wage stagnation and closing the income gap between white and nonwhite workers.

Solutions to voting discrimination

Specific suggestions for change

Solutions to economic injustice

And one more issue, dear to my heart: It's time to come down hard on predatory practices that allow financial institutions to systematically strip wealth out of communities of color. One of the ugly consequences of bank deregulation was that there was no cop on the beat when too many financial institutions figured out that they could make great money by tricking, trapping, and defrauding targeted families. Now we have a Consumer Financial Protection Bureau, and we need to make sure it stays strong and independent so that it can do its job and make credit markets work for black families, Latino families, white families—all families.

Yes, there's work to do.

Back in March, I met an elderly man at the First Baptist Church in Montgomery, Alabama. We were having coffee and donuts in the church basement before the service started. He told me that more than 50 years earlier—in May of 1961—he had spent 11 hours in that same basement, along with hundreds of people, while a mob outside threatened to burn down the church because it was a sanctuary for civil rights workers. Dr. King called Attorney General Bobby Kennedy, desperately asking for help. The Attorney General promised to send the Army, but the closest military base was several hours away. So the members of the church and the civil rights workers waited in the sweltering basement, crowded together, listening to the mob outside and hoping the U.S. Army would arrive in time.

After the church service, I asked Congressman John Lewis about that   40
night. He had been right there in that church back in 1961 while the mob gathered outside. He had been in the room during the calls to the Attorney General. I asked if he had been afraid that the Army wouldn't make it in time. He said that he was "never, ever afraid. You come to that point where you lose all sense of fear." And then he said something I'll never forget. He said that his parents didn't want him to get involved in civil rights. They didn't want him to "cause trouble." But he had done it anyway. He told me: "Sometimes it is important to cause necessary trouble."

The first civil rights battles were hard fought. But they established that Black Lives Matter. That Black Citizens Matter. That Black Families Matter. Half a century later, we have made real progress, but we have not made ENOUGH progress. As Senator Kennedy said in his first floor speech, "This is not a political issue. It is a moral issue, to be resolved through political means." So it comes to us to continue the fight, to make, as John Lewis said, the "necessary trouble" until we can truly say that in America, every citizen enjoys the conditions of freedom.

Thank you.

Marginal annotations:

Extended example/personal anecdote

Closes with memorable quotation

Reiterates her claim

Broadcast News

News shows were originally designed to present, in brief, the facts of what was happening around the country and around the world. The advent of twenty-four-hour news channels, however, has increasingly led to a need to fill time by talking about rather than presenting the news. Analysis of the news is crucial to understanding the events that shape our world, and hearing different perspectives can help enlighten the listening and reading public. Any subject, however, can become the subject of debate if at least two people have different opinions on it, and television networks seem never to be at a loss to find at least one advocate for any position.

From news shows that go well beyond reporting the news to expressing opinions about it, it is only a small step to political commentary shows that from their inception were meant to be a sounding board for different opinions on contemporary politics. Some of these shows have been around for decades. *Meet the Press* is the longest-running television series in the history of American broadcasting; it has been on the air for more than sixty years. The most intelligent and responsible programs usually consist of a panel of experts — politicians, journalists, scholars — led by a neutral moderator (or one who, at least, allows guests to express their views). Other examples of these programs are *Face the Nation* with Bob Schieffer, *This Week* with George Stephanopoulos, *Fox News Sunday* with Chris Wallace, and *State of the Union* with Candy Crowley.

More clearly biased news shows include the conservative *Hannity* and the liberal *The Rachel Maddow Show*. A variation on these are some very popular political comedy shows like *The Daily Show* with Trevor Noah, *Full Frontal* with Samantha Bee, and *Last Week Tonight* with John Oliver. Radio also has its share of news and call-in hosts who are known for their political bias, such as conservative Rush Limbaugh and liberal Stephanie Miller.

Whatever the merits or shortcomings of individual programs, significant general differences exist between arguments on radio and television and arguments in the print media. These differences include the degree of organization and development and the risk of personal attacks.

First, contributions to a panel discussion must be delivered in fragments, usually no longer than a single paragraph, weakened by time constraints, interruptions, overlapping speech, memory gaps, and real or feigned displays of derision, impatience, and disbelief by critical panelists. Even on the best programs, the result is a lack of both coherence — or connections between ideas — and solid evidence that requires development. Too often we are treated to conclusions with little indication of how they were arrived at.

Second, listeners and viewers of all spoken arguments are in danger of evaluating them according to criteria that are largely absent from evaluation of written texts. It is true that writers may adopt a persona or a literary disguise, which the tone of the essay will reflect. But many readers will not be able to identify it or recognize their own response to it. Listeners and viewers, however, can hardly avoid being affected by characteristics that are clearly definable: a speaker's voice, delivery, bodily mannerisms, dress, and physical appearance. In addition, listeners may be adversely influenced by clumsy speech containing more slang, colloquialisms, and grammar and usage errors than written texts that have had the benefit of revision.

But if listeners allow consideration of physical attributes to influence their judgment of what the speaker is trying to prove, they are guilty of evaluating the speaker rather than the argument. This is true whether the evaluation is favorable or unfavorable. (See p. 318 for a discussion of this fallacy.)

Strategies for Critical Listening

Listening is hearing with attention. It is a skill that can be learned and improved. Here are some of the characteristics of critical listening most appropriate to understanding and responding to arguments.

1. **Concentrate.** If you are distracted, you cannot go back as you do with the written word to clarify a point or recover a connection. As you listen, try to avoid being distracted by facts alone. Look for the overall patterns of the speech. Take notes using an outline of the material being covered.

2. **Pay attention to the claim and support.** Avoid focusing on the speaker's appearance and delivery. Research shows that listeners are likely to give greater attention to the dramatic elements of speeches than to the logical ones. But you can enjoy the sound, the appearance, and the drama of a spoken argument without allowing these elements to overwhelm what is essential to the development of a claim.

3. **Avoid premature judgments about what is actually said.** Good listeners try not to allow their prejudices to prevent careful evaluation of the argument. This doesn't mean accepting everything or even most of what you hear. This precaution is especially relevant when the speakers and their views are well known and the listener has already formed an opinion about them, favorable or unfavorable.

READING ARGUMENT

Examining Broadcast News

One way to detect bias in the news is to see how different networks report on the same news story. The transcript on pages 99–101 is a response from CNN to President Obama's decision to support same-sex marriage. It has been annotated to show bias in the comments.

Coverage of Obama's Announcement in Support of Gay Marriage
CNN CORRESPONDENTS

Brooke Baldwin: We're talking about this news here with a number of folks in Washington, D.C.

I want to bring in John King, because, John King, as we listen to this and we sort of let that statement reverberate, this is an election year. Talk to me about the timing of this. Obviously, this is great news for folks who support gay marriage. But certainly you talk about those independent voters who are so, so key come November, and obviously folks on Mitt Romney's team, how does this play with them?

> Emphasizes the positive, but also questions the effect on the election

John King, CNN Chief National Correspondent: Well, it's a gamble for the president. And we should say up front it's a bold, personal choice for the president to decide to do this publicly.

> Favorable slant

You used the word as you brought me into the conversation — *historic*. If you go back and show those pictures from ABC News just a moment ago, not only is this a political leader making this statement, Brooke. It's the president of the United States. It's the first president of the United States — he's sitting in the White House, those two flags over his shoulder, the seal of the United States of America and the American flag — this is the first American president sitting in the White House to say, I think same-sex couples should be able to marry, not just have legal unions, but able to marry.

> Appeal to patriotism. Obama is seen against a backdrop of national symbols.

5   And the president acknowledged the use of the term marriage. That's one of the reasons he's been hung up on this. You hear him talking about his daughters. You hear him talking about young Americans when he goes to college campuses. The president knows pretty well that young Americans are with him on this issue.

They're ahead of him on this issue even. They have pressured him. Gay Americans have supported him, the gay and lesbian community which is supporting him financially and otherwise, politically supports him. The question is, how does it play out in what we know is a very, very close, competitive election?

> Focuses on those who support Obama, emphasizing the positive

And even the president's own political team will tell you, there are risks here. Number one, this will energize evangelical Christians who might have some doubts about Mitt Romney. They have just seen the president of the United States sitting in the White House endorsing something they very, very much oppose on moral and religious grounds.

> What Obama has to lose

Objective look at election math

So this will help Mitt Romney energize his base. The question is, does it cost the president? If you get addition from young voters, addition from gay and lesbians who might have been disappointed and stayed home if the president didn't go this far, if you get that addition on the Democratic side, do you also get subtraction?

Are there conservative Democrats who say, sorry, Mr. President, I'm not with you on this one? Critically to me, Brooke, in this calculation, African-Americans and Latinos. Many Latinos who are Catholics. They go to Catholic Church, where their priest tells them every Sunday homosexuality isn't just wrong, it's evil. That's what their priest tells them. It's evil.

A lot of African-American preachers in the Southern Baptist—Southern   10
churches across this country, but particularly in Virginia, North Carolina, states the president carried last time, say the same thing.

Baldwin: Right.

Presents the risk in a positive light

King: And this is a—this is a big risk by this president. And give him credit for taking the risk. Many politicians duck from risks, but what we will watch play out now in the weeks and months ahead is how it works on turnout and the addition and subtraction, which politics in the end is about math.

Baldwin: I want to get back to you, John King, because I have more questions.

But I do want to go straight to the White House to Jessica Yellin, because, Jessica, I'm just curious, what kind of backstory do we have on this particular interview? I was mentioning to Wolf I read that this thing was put together, what, yesterday, yesterday afternoon, that they flew Robin Roberts up to Washington and then back to New York—or they will be. Tell me what you know about how this whole thing came together.

Jessica Yellin, CNN Chief White House Correspondent: Well, I know that this   15
wasn't the White House's plan to roll that—this out this week.

The president's campaign was planning to unveil their first positive ad campaign this week and start making their case for reelection. He was unveiling the congressional to-do list, which was supposed to be focused on pressing Congress on some of their major initiatives that the campaign wanted to focus on.

And then because of the vice president's comments, because of Arne Duncan, the education secretary's comment, it sort of forced the president's hand. And as you say, they put together an interview with Robin Roberts, as we understand it from sources, yesterday.

And she came up to do that interview quickly today. I understand that on ABC, while we have been on, Robin Roberts reported that she pressed the president on whether he was angry with the vice president and with Arne Duncan because of their comments. And the president laughed it off, saying no.

You know, from a number of people I have spoken with outside the White House, activists on this issue, Brooke, it was their sense that they believed the president, the White House was going to come to this position before the election. I don't know if that is true, but it was their view that he was.

20   This simply forced it to happen sooner and not on a time frame of their own choosing.

His hand was forced, but he was going to take a stand before the elections anyway.

Practice: Examining Broadcast News

Locate online a broadcast response to Obama's announcement in support of same-sex marriage that has a negative bias. Annotate a transcript of it, using the previous transcript and its annotations as a model.

ARGUMENT ESSENTIALS
Audiovisual Rhetoric

Use these four steps as basic guidelines for analyzing audiovisual rhetoric:

- **Preread.** Notice a television or radio show's network or station and its sponsors, and consider any possible bias. Consider the organization or company behind a commercial and the affiliations of a speaker.

- **Watch or listen for content.** Consider what you are being told when you listen to the news. Consider what product, service, candidate, or idea a speaker or a commercial is encouraging you to accept.

- **Watch or listen for rhetorical strategies.** Consider if and how any bias is being revealed. With speeches or debates, consider how the speaker is trying to appeal to a specific audience. With commercials, consider the questions used in analyzing visual rhetoric plus any added by sound, motion, and special effects.

- **Evaluate.** Consider how effective a news show is in delivering the news in a fair manner or how effective a talk show is in allowing varied opinions to be heard. Consider whether a speaker's content and strategies are appropriate for his or her audience. Consider how effective a commercial is in selling its product, service, candidate, or idea.

Online Environments

Many of us spend a good part of our lives online. What role does argumentation play in our digital lives? Any of us can get into an argument online, but can argument in online environments be studied as a rhetorical act? How does our study of writer, subject, and audience apply when our audience can range from our best friend to someone we may never meet face-to-face? How do claim, support, and assumption apply to a Web site or a blog? How do *logos*, *ethos*, and *pathos* apply when we can communicate online behind a mask of anonymity? The prose may be informal—at times, it is the digital world's own unique shorthand—but an online argument is still grounded in the theories of Aristotle, Hermagoras, Rogers, and Toulmin that are the focus of this book.

What the online world can also offer us that books, newspapers, and even television and radio can't—except for an occasional call-in show—is interactivity, and hyperlinks literally let us decide what direction our reading of a text will take.

- **Prereading.** In the context of electronic environments, prereading can be seen as familiarizing yourself with a new way of interacting. If you have never used Tumblr or Twitter, prereading is the step where you learn what exactly Tumblr or Twitter *is* and how to use it. You might sample a few blog posts to see if the blog covers topics of interest to you. You might explore a Web site to see who sponsors it and what it has to offer.
- **Reading for content.** This step is most relevant to blogs, forums, visual lectures, and Web sites—all of which you read or watch because you need the information or simply have an interest in the subject, and all of which are more fully developed than most Facebook posts. With social networking sites, the content is about as free of structure as a stream-of-consciousness novel. Facebook asks, "What's on Your Mind?" and millions of people type an answer. Social networking sites are your window into the lives of others; therefore, much of the content is the content of their lives, plus their views on what is happening in the world around them.
- **Online interaction.** Online environments let readers participate in ways that a static text cannot. On a social network, you can post a question, or you can tell all of your friends what your day has been like. You can comment on a blog or start your own. You can click from link to link to link in an endless chain of connections, controlling the twists and turns of your search. *Interactivity* is one of the two features that have helped the Internet revolutionize communication. The other is *hypertextuality*, or the ability to read different levels of a text by means of hyperlinks. There is no single linear way to read a Web site.
- **Evaluation.** Evaluation of online communication has to take place in the context of its purpose. Much of it is informal and certainly not polished prose. At the other extreme are Web sites that businesses depend on for their success, which must be professional in their design and content.

Networking Sites

In educational settings, closed networks are a means of linking students within one class or across several for the purpose of managing learning and providing a place to exchange ideas. Your school may use Blackboard, Angel, or Moodle as a convenient place to make announcements, explain assignments, and get students communicating with one another. Such systems allow the teacher or students to post to a class listserv and respond to one another.

On a much larger scale, the term *World Wide Web* is apt in that it is like a spider web. At any given juncture, there are multiple ways to branch off, and the strands of the web form a structure that is unbelievably complex and intricate. Online social networks are like that too. You may have Facebook friends whom you came to know — or at least to share some part of your life with — because you had a single friend in common or because of a common interest. They may be people that you might never have even struck up a conversation with in person, but your web branches in many directions for many different reasons. Sometimes that social web brings you together online with people with political and social views very different from your own. (They could be some of your best friends.) And since people like to share online the latest meme or the latest attack on President Obama or the latest dig at the NRA, you may find yourself on opposite sides of a computer screen from people whose views are diametrically opposed to your own. And then the debate begins.

ARGUMENT ESSENTIALS
Online Environments

Prereading. Familiarize yourself with the particular online environment that is new to you. Explore what it has to offer in content and in function.

Reading for content. Social networking sites provide primarily a source of information about your "friends" and their responses to the world around them. Blogs, forums, visual lectures, and Web sites may be worth exploring for information you might need or simply have an interest in.

Online interaction. Online environments let readers participate in ways that a static text cannot. Interactivity is one of the two features that have helped the Internet revolutionize communication. The other is hypertextuality, or the ability to read different levels of a text by means of hyperlinks.

Evaluation. Evaluation of online communication has to take place in the context of its purpose.

READING ARGUMENT

Examining Networking Sites

The social media exchange on pages 104–105 shows how even friends can find themselves at odds over a controversial issue. Read the text and analysis, and answer the questions that follow.

"Peaceful" Act of Compassion
WILLIAM WHARTON

William Wharton

William Wharton
June 21, 2013

Another "peaceful" act of compassion from the religion of "peace"!

REUTERS / Alamy

**Taliban behead boy aged 10 over "spying":
Two children killed after taking food from police.**
June 21, 2013
www.dailymail.co.uk
- Killed as a warning to villagers not to cooperate with Afghan government
- The boys named Khan and Hameedullah were killed on Sunday
- Their bodies and severed heads were left in their village

Sam Lane

Sam Lane
June 21, 2013

Unfortunately, Bill, stories like this just foster hate.

William Wharton
June 21, 2013

I don't hate Muslims. My son's best friend is a Muslim and I love that child like my own. But her religion teaches things that facilitate such actions as these.

Sam Lane
June 21, 2013

Kinda like the Old Testament?

William Wharton
June 21, 2013

Sam, you know as well as I that such a comparison is utterly false.

Sam Lane

Sam Lane

June 21, 2013

I really don't. Crazy stuff in Old Testament that we are told to do. But we know not to. Most Muslims don't kill people. And even if Muslims are the enemy . . .
Matthew 4:44 and Romans 12:17-21.

Analysis

William's sarcasm reveals his actual opinion:

Claim: Islam is not a religion of peace.

Support: The Muslims who killed these children had no compassion.

Assumption: A religion of peace does not kill children with no compassion.

Or

Major premise: A religion of peace does not kill children with no compassion.

Minor premise: These Muslims killed these children with no compassion.

Conclusion: Islam is not a religion of peace.

William's claim in the first example and conclusion in the second example are valid only if the particular Muslims who killed the children were acting in a way representative of the teachings of their religion. To prove that this is the case, William offers the example of his son's best friend, whose religion "teaches things that facilitate such actions as these." Whether or not you accept William's judgment of Islam depends largely on whether your own experience plus your knowledge of Islam convinces you that what these individuals did was in keeping with the dictates of their religion.

Sam's reasoning could be put into a syllogism in this way:

Major premise: There is crazy stuff in the Old Testament that we are told to do.

Minor premise: We know not to do crazy stuff.

Conclusion: We do not do crazy stuff that the Old Testament tells us to do.

Reading and Discussion Questions

1. Is Sam's conclusion valid?
2. How different is Sam's reasoning about Christianity from William's reasoning about Islam?
3. Is there any validity to Sam's comparing the actions of Taliban members to the teachings of the Old Testament?

Online News and Blogs

Online news sites and their less formal cousins — blogs — serve a different purpose than social networking sites do. News sites and blogs are primarily informational, although the major sites contain advertisements, and some blogs come closer to serving the function of a diary for their authors. As with their print and broadcast counterparts, news sites and especially blogs can be politically or socially biased. Many blogs have specific agendas that can be easily uncovered in the "About Us" section.

What blogs and news sites share with social networking sites is the ability for audience members to join the conversation by responding to content. Whether you are reading or writing comments in public forums such as these, remember that the most useful and worthwhile posts are both brief and reasonable. Avoid writing (and be wary of reading) posts that are inflammatory, divisive, absolute, or otherwise unreasonable.

READING ARGUMENT

Examining Online News and Blogs

The following article appeared on ChristandPopCulture.com. Analyze both the article and the comments that the author received in response to his blog posting on July 8, 2016, and then answer the questions that follow.

Summer Shootings, *Pokémon Go*: Rebuilding Community in the Wake of Destruction
LUKE T. HARRINGTON

The morning of Friday, July 8th, was like a punch in the gut. I'm an early riser—three in the morning is usually prime writing time for me. Most nights, I go to bed before nine, so if something important happens in the evening, I often don't hear about it until I pick up my phone the next day. I'm sure you're familiar with the drill—your alarm goes off, you grab your phone, you see you have 128 Facebook notifications.

A humor writer, Luke T. Harrington contributes a regular column to *Christianity Today* and manages social media for *Christ and Pop Culture*, an online magazine established "to edify the Church, glorify God, and witness to the world by encouraging and modeling a biblical presence within culture that is characterized by nuance and appreciation while resisting the extremes of thoughtless condemnation and uncritical embrace." This piece was posted on christandpopculture.com on July 21, 2016.

And some days, you're met with something horrific. That Friday, as I'm sure you're aware, was one of those days. There it was, all over my feed:

Dallas shooting. Five dead. Worst terrorist attack since 9/11. Peaceful #BlackLivesMatter protest interrupted by sniper cop-killer.

Obviously, the killings by cops that had preceded this latest tragedy—one in Minneapolis and one in Baton Rouge—were no less horrifying. But this one felt different: a peaceful protest deliberately foiled. A cold and calculated assassination, apparently performed by someone looking to ensure that anger and hatred would continue to burn white-hot. This was one of the fabled Men Who Want to Watch the World Burn.

It's difficult to encapsulate the anger and fear I felt in the moment, though I'm sure many share in both. Truth be told, I just wanted to stay in bed that day.

But life goes on. I run social media for CaPC, and I had to post *something*. So I posted this:

Walk out your front door. Meet your neighbor. Build a real community. Do it now, before it's too late.

Maybe the words were feeble, but it was all I could conjure at the moment. As Jake Meador recently put it over at Mere Orthodoxy, we're currently "experiencing a crisis of neighborliness in America today." While we are obviously dealing with systemic problems regarding race and policing, in a sense both the failure to obey the law and the failure to police with restraint are rooted in the same cause: the failure of community. Many of us don't share our lives with those who live around us. We're not invested in each other. We don't know each other, we don't care about each other, and we don't trust each other. And lately, our estrangement has been leading us to suspicion, fear, and hatred. In extreme cases, it's led us to murder.

It's not for nothing, I suspect, that one in ten Americans is on antidepressants.

It's not for nothing, I suspect, that one in ten Americans is on antidepressants—our dominant cultural scripts constitute the world's most efficient depression factory. The American norm is to avoid interacting with other people (witness the proliferation of online shopping and automated kiosks) and even to avoid basic physical activity (see: automobiles, online culture, home entertainment systems, etc.). We actively discourage the things that research has shown make people feel fulfilled—community, family, religious experience—in favor of largely sedentary entertainment. Plenty of us have active online social lives, but no investment whatsoever in our physical communities.

Of course, it doesn't have to be this way. I said earlier that Friday's social media feed was full of the Dallas shooting; but as the day went on, it became clear that there were actually two kinds of posts filling my online purview. On the one hand, there was the anger, sorrow and hatred stemming from the events in Baton Rouge, Minneapolis, and Dallas—and they were all palpable. But there was another type of post as well, breaking through like a green shoot of life pushing aside the concrete: posts inspired by *Pokémon Go*.

You might think that's a joke. I promise you, it isn't.

If you don't know the new game, you probably at least know the Pokémon franchise, which has been a staple on Nintendo's handheld systems for almost 20 years, and which challenges players to capture, train, and battle the titular monsters. While each Pokémon iteration has always had a social aspect to it (you could trade and battle pokémon via local console networking, for instance), the latest release—a mobile phone game—takes this to the next level, using the player's hometown as the game's playing field. *Pokémon Go* unfolds as a GPS-driven augmented reality game in which pokémon appear on screen as if in the real world through the magic of cell phone cameras, with landmarks like Pokémon gyms and hospitals located at real-life community hubs like churches, schools, and businesses.

The game was released on Wednesday the 6th, right in the middle of the spate of shootings. By Friday, it seemed like everyone was playing it. My social media feeds were quickly filling up with posts like this:

> *At union square collecting Pokemon, a guy turns to me and asks, "What team are you?"*
> — sarah jeong (@sarahjeon) July 9, 2016

and this:

> *@sarahjeong I have spoken to more strangers in the last 48 hrs than I usually do in a week, thanks to Pokemon*
> — Big Fat Iguana (@fossilfriendly) July 9, 2016

and this:

> *I wonder how many people are meeting their future significant others while playing pokemon go right now*
> — Jen Bartel (@heyjenbartel) July 13, 2016

It was kind of amazing. People were going outside. Meeting each other. Playing together. Engaging with their communities. Visiting important places they might never have given a second thought to, even if they lived just down the street from them. And—maybe just as important—they were getting some fresh air and exercise in the process.

In light of the murder and mayhem that was taking place in the streets, *Pokémon Go*'s popularity might seem like a small and frivolous thing. But to dismiss it on those grounds would be to miss the point. *Pokémon Go* is important entirely *because* it's a small and frivolous thing. What holds communities together, after all, isn't lofty ideals or strict law enforcement—it's their shared stories, their rituals, their songs. You may doubt this, but in the case of *Pokémon Go*, the results are hard to argue with: neighbors who previously had no reason to interact are now greeting each other and working together to turn up nests of Squirtles and Charizards across the nation.

Trends like this, by the way, are why we care so much about pop culture here at CaPC. Lofty ideals are important, but people can't strive after them 24/7. We get tired—and when we do, the culture we fall back on matters. Like liturgy, our art and entertainment shape our lives and our communities from the outside in, and the best of it teaches us to love our neighbors, serve God, and pursue whatever is good and true and beautiful.

It's taken me a while to realize this. When I was in high school, I thought I was too cool to participate in "school spirit" activities. I knew our school wasn't *really* the best—if it ever *became* great, I thought, *then* I would celebrate it. (Imagine if people took the same approach to, say, their marriages.) Later in life, though, when I found myself teaching at yet another not-the-best-in-the-world high school, I realized something: the students working to build "school spirit" weren't deluded. They didn't think their school was the best, either. Rather, they were simply determined to make the school environment as pleasant and beneficial as possible. They understood—perhaps not even consciously—that the sort of trust and camaraderie necessary for a thriving community is built on sharing experiences and traditions together.

Of course, it remains to be seen what sort of lasting impact *Pokémon Go* will have on our culture. (I myself have barely gotten to play it, due to software bugs and servers that are perpetually down.) For the moment, though, it appears to be exactly the sort of balm America needs—a bit of common grace sprinkled on the horror blazing around us; a small reminder to love our neighbors as ourselves.

In a summer like this one, that's a welcome reminder indeed.

Reading and Discussion Questions

1. On the morning of July 8, what event hit Harrington "like a punch in the gut"? What other recent events were background for that event?
2. What did he post on social media once he got up and going?

3. He discovered two subjects were monopolizing posts on social media. What were the two, and how does Harrington link the two?

4. What do the posts from others that he quotes suggest about the effects of *Pokemon Go*? Have you or those you know had any similar experiences? Explain.

Visual Lectures

Another source of online information comprises visual lectures, lectures delivered by means of Web technology. As with most of the resources available on the Internet, the quality can vary, but the idea is for a person or a group with expertise in a specific area to share it with anyone interested. The most common source of visual lectures is YouTube.

RESEARCH SKILL | Evaluating Online Sources

In your search for reliable online information, you may not always find it easy to determine who is responsible for a source. A good first step is to check the domain name. Next, ask yourself some questions about the domain as well as the author of the material. Be aware that nonprofit sites are not necessarily free of bias, commercial sites may offer plenty of useful information, and sites with an *.edu* extension are not always approved by the institution.

- **.com:** A commercial site, including corporate-sponsored sites such as nike.com, as well as news sites, such as cnn.com, and personal sites. Do you recognize the name as a brand, news source, or other corporate entity? If not, do a search on the site's name to see if you can find any information about it (keeping in mind, of course, that those sites must also be evaluated). If the site is personal, what can you find out about the author?

- **.gov:** A government-sponsored site, maintained by one of the many government agencies, such as whitehouse.gov, supremecourt.gov, and dol.gov (Department of Labor). Although most

government agencies should provide unbiased information, elected officials — from the White House to your local town government — may be selective or biased in the information they provide. What do you know about the party affiliation or political agenda of the source of your information?

- **.edu:** A site sponsored by an educational institution, such as clemson.edu. Although an educational institution may be hosting the Web site, schools often allow professors and students to put up personal pages that may or may not be scholarly or trustworthy. Who is the author of the information, and what do you know about this person?

- **.org:** A site sponsored by a nonprofit group, such as heart.org (American Heart Association) or sierraclub.org. Nonprofit organizations often have a particular focus to promote: consumer protection, civil liberties, health, environment, and the like. In addition, they may be sponsored or supported by groups that have particular agendas (check the "About Us" section). Is it possible that the information provided on the site is biased in favor of the sponsor's goals?

Interactive Web Sites

One of the most useful features of the Internet is the ability to find information about almost any subject in a matter of minutes — if not seconds. We'll discuss more fully in Chapter 12 how to evaluate Web sites; for now, we will focus only on how the interactive feature of Web sites plays into their attempt to make an argument.

READING ARGUMENT

Examining Interactive Web Sites

In the following example, we have applied our usual categories to a Web site — Prereading, Reading for Content, and Evaluation — but we have replaced the category Reading for Rhetorical Strategies with the category Online Interaction to explore the interactive features of the site.

embracerefugees.org
AD COUNCIL

Analysis

- **Prereading.** It is clear from the site's Web address that it is an organization's site. The name "embracerefugees.org" suggests that the site exists to aid refugees, eliciting the image of putting welcoming arms around them. We know from the news that refugees in the twenty-first century have not always been welcomed. The largest groups of refugees in recent years have been from Syria, Iraq, South Sudan, Burma, and, in the West, Colombia. Syrian refugees are feared in Eastern Europe and the United States because of the threat of terrorism. The copyright for the site is by the Ad Council, which produces public service advertising. A long list of resources suggests that embracerefugees.org has done substantial research into its subject.

- **Reading for Content.** The home page of the site immediately captures the eye with a picture of five children. One looks a bit uneasy, but four of them are smiling at the camera. The largest text tells us, "Refugees are no different from us." While our inclination might be to think, "Yes, they are!" the next sentence reminds us that all people are alike in that they don't want to live in fear. Next comes a definition of "refugee."

- **Online Interaction.** The image and words mentioned already are all that appear on the home page. How you proceed to read the site depends on how you move through it from here. There are two ways to maneuver through the site. A downward arrow and the words "Learn about the Refugee Experience" indicate that you can scroll down for more information, but dots along the right-hand margin also let you click to go to the same information in any order, if you prefer. Hovering over each reveals these topics: Refugee Journey, Their Stories, Investment, Watch Stories, Community, and Get Involved.

"Their Stories" presents a collage of photographs of different individuals and groups from all over the world. Hovering over each gives you a brief description and a link to go one level deeper into the site to read a longer description. Each has links to let you share via Facebook, Twitter, or LinkedIn.

"Investment" tries to dispel the myth that refugees are a burden on the countries they enter. Each of the circles at the bottom is a link with information about how refugees give back to the nations they enter: Are Eager to Work, Strive for Independence, Yield Dividends, Spark New Ideas, and Invigorate Our Economy. For each, as for each story above, a link to the source of the information is provided.

"Watch Stories" first reminds us that there are nearly 20 million refugees worldwide and that "59% of Americans believe that the US should do more to help refugees or should continue to offer assistance at the current level." Then comes a screen entitled "What's in Your Bag?" with four videos that you can move among by clicking on the arrows. The first shows four Americans who were told that they had five minutes to fill a bag with whatever they would take if that was all that they could take from their homes. The other three are stories by refugees who found themselves in similar positions when they had to flee their homes but who have succeeded in spite of those circumstances.

"Community" is another collage of individuals that reveals their success in America, with links to more information.

"Get Involved" is a call to action, and provides links that you can click on to find ways of contributing to the move to embrace refugees.

- **Evaluation.** The site is well designed for ease of movement from one level to another. It makes good use of hypertextuality. The color photographs are visually appealing, and you become an active reader whenever you click on a link to find more information. It moves from trying to establish common ground between you and the refugees to defining the term "refugee" to drawing you into the stories of refugees through photographs and additional text, plus videos. A range of types of appeal are designed to make you sympathize with the refugees, and at the end, there are opportunities to find out how to get involved in improving their plight.

Assignments for Critical Reading of Multimodal Arguments

Reading and Discussion Questions

1. Analyze the photograph on page 70. There is no caption other than a title. What caption would you write for it?

2. Find a picture that you believe makes a statement without words. Be prepared to explain your reading of it.

3. Locate a political cartoon, and be prepared to explain to your classmates the assumption or assumptions behind it.

4. Choose a television commercial, and analyze it like we analyzed the Toyota commercial.

5. Watch (and *listen to*) one of the afternoon television talk shows in which guests discuss a controversial social problem. (The *TV Guide*, daily newspapers, and online listings often list the subject. Past topics include when parents abduct their children, when children kill children, and when surgery changes patients' lives.) Analyze the discussion, considering the major claims, the most important evidence, and the declared or hidden assumptions. How much did the oral format contribute to the success or failure of the arguments?

6. Watch an episode of either *The Daily Show* with Trevor Noah or *Last Week Tonight* with John Oliver, and discuss how the show, successfully or not, tries to use humor to make serious points about political and/or social issues.

7. Locate an advertisement that you find visually and verbally interesting. Using as a model the analysis of embracerefugees.org (pp. 111–115), what sorts of observations can you make about your ad? Exchange ads with a classmate, and discuss whether the two of you respond in the same way to each ad.

Writing Suggestions

1. Choose a photograph, and write an essay explaining how content and structure work together to make an argument.

2. Choose a print ad to analyze, and present your observations in an essay. Be sure to organize your specific observations about the ad around a clear thesis statement.

3. Write an essay analyzing a television commercial.

4. Write a paragraph explaining any bias you see in a news report by CNN or Fox News.

5. Watch one of the television talk shows that features experts on social and political issues, such as *The O'Reilly Factor*. Write a review, telling how much you learned about the subject(s) of discussion. Be specific about the features of the show that were either helpful or not helpful to your understanding.

6. Read the speech by Nelson Mandela on p. 618. Write an essay in which you explain what Mandela's main points are about his trial and what support he offers for those main points.

RESEARCH ASSIGNMENT ▶ **Evaluating Online Sources**

Conduct an online search to answer the question "Is soda the leading cause of obesity?" Find one source each with domain extensions *.com*, *.gov*, *.edu*, and *.org*, for a total of four sources. For each source, answer the following questions:

1. Who is the sponsor of the Web site? What does the "About Us" section of the site reveal about the sponsor's mission? What else can you find out about the sponsor?

2. Who is the author of the material? Research this person to find any political or corporate affiliations he or she may have.

3. What is the main purpose of the site? Is the group looking for support or donations? Is it attempting to drive advertising? Is it trying to sell a product? Is it scholarly? Does it seem purely informational? How might its purpose affect its content?

Write a paragraph explaining which site you found to be the most reliable and which you determined to be the least reliable, based on the answers to your questions above.

---

bits

To see what you are learning about argumentation applied to the latest world and national news, read our *Bits* blog, "Argument and the Headlines," at **blogs.bedfordstmartins.com/bits.**

Writing Argument Analysis

Chapter 5 will discuss how to write your own arguments, including how to write arguments to fulfill course assignments. Before we move on to discuss the writing of arguments, consider in what academic contexts you might be called upon to write argument analysis.

The ability to write argument analysis is considered so predictive of success in college that if you took the SAT after March 2016, the optional essay assigned was argument analysis. The topic would have been like one of these essay topics released by the College Board, followed by a short passage to analyze:

- Write an essay in which you explain how Jimmy Carter builds an argument to persuade his audience that the Arctic National Wildlife Refuge should not be developed for industry.
- Write an essay in which you explain how Martin Luther King Jr. builds an argument to persuade his audience that American involvement in the Vietnam War is unjust.
- Write an essay in which you explain how Eliana Dockterman builds an argument to persuade her audience that there are benefits to early exposure to technology.

This is one example of how the College Board explains what students are expected to write:

As you read the passage below, consider how Paul Bogard uses

- evidence, such as facts or examples, to support claims.
- reasoning to develop ideas and to connect claims and evidence.
- stylistic or persuasive elements, such as word choice or appeals to emotion, to add power to the ideas expressed.

Write an essay in which you explain how Paul Bogard builds an argument to persuade his audience that natural darkness should be preserved. In your essay, analyze how Bogard uses one or more of the features in the directions that precede the passage (or features of your own choice) to strengthen the logic and persuasiveness of his argument. Be sure that your analysis focuses on the most relevant features of the passage.

Your essay should not explain whether you agree with Bogard's claims, but rather explain how Bogard builds an argument to persuade his audience.

This is how the College Board explains what the essay measures:

- Reading: A successful essay shows that you understood the passage, including the interplay of central ideas and important details. It also shows an effective use of textual evidence.
- Analysis: A successful essay shows your understanding of how the author builds an argument by:

    Examining the author's use of evidence, reasoning, and other stylistic and persuasive techniques
    Supporting and developing claims with well-chosen evidence from the passage

- Writing: A successful essay is focused, organized, and precise, with an appropriate style and tone that varies sentence structure and follows the conventions of standard written English.[1]

In your classes, any time you are asked to write on similar topics, you will be writing argument analysis. You will also be writing argument analysis any time you read a similar passage and are asked to evaluate its argument. Sometimes the source to be analyzed will be longer than the short passages provided on the SAT. At other times, the arguments may not be written, but may be oral, like a political speech, or visual, like an art work.

When you approach the end of your college career, some of you will be taking the Graduate Record Exam (GRE) for admission to graduate school. A part of the General Test of the GRE is the Analytical Writing Measure, which is made up of two writing tasks. One of these tasks requires you to write your own argument, which is the focus of our next chapter. The other is an evaluative analysis. This is a portion of the Educational Testing Service's description of the writing assignments:

The Analytical Writing measure consists of two separately timed analytical writing tasks:

- a 30-minute "Analyze an Issue" task
- a 30-minute "Analyze an Argument" task

The Issue task presents an opinion on an issue of general interest followed by specific instructions on how to respond to that issue. You are required to evaluate the issue, consider its complexities and develop an argument with reasons and examples to support your views.

The Argument task requires you to evaluate a given argument according to specific instructions. You will need to consider the logical

---

[1] collegereadiness.collegeboard.org.

soundness of the argument rather than agree or disagree with the position it presents.

The two tasks are complementary in that one requires you to construct your own argument by taking a position and providing evidence supporting your views on an issue, and the other requires you to evaluate someone else's argument by assessing its claims and evaluating the evidence it provides.[2]

One more example: If you take the GMAT exam in preparation for pursuing an MBA or similar degree, this is the type of essay required on the exam:

In this section, you will be asked to write a critique of the argument presented. You are NOT being asked to present your own views on the subject.

Question

The following appeared in the editorial section of a monthly business news magazine:

"Most companies would agree that as the risk of physical injury occurring on the job increases, the wages paid to employees should also increase. Hence it makes financial sense for employers to make the workplace safer: they could thus reduce their payroll expenses and save money."

Discuss how well reasoned you find this argument. In your discussion, be sure to analyze the line of reasoning and the use of evidence in the argument. For example, you may need to consider what questionable assumptions underlie the thinking and what alternative explanations or counterexamples might weaken the conclusion.

You can also discuss what sort of evidence would strengthen or refute the argument, what changes in the argument would make it more logically sound, and what, if anything, would help you better evaluate its conclusion.[3]

It should be more than clear by now how seriously educational institutions take the ability to analyze arguments. In your classes, you may be required to write formal analysis essays, or you may write impromptu essay responses on tests or exams. In theory, there are two parts of argument analysis: content analysis and rhetorical analysis. In practice, the two are virtually inseparable. Content analysis is the study of ideas, of what an author says. Rhetorical analysis is the study of strategy, of how the author presents the argument. Writing an analysis of an argument almost inevitably requires considering rhetorical strategies in the context of the ideas being discussed.

---

[2] ets.org.

[3] mba.com.

ARGUMENT ESSENTIALS
Argument Analysis

- Any time you are asked to read a statement or a longer passage taking a stand on any issue and told to explain the author's strategies, your response will be argument analysis.

- Any time you are asked to read or listen to a political speech and told to explain the author's strategies, your response will be argument analysis.

- Any time you are asked to examine a multimodal argument and told to explain the author's strategies, your response will be an argument analysis.

- Any time you are asked to examine an argument and evaluate its effectiveness, you will also be writing argument analysis.

Writing the Claim

When you write an analysis of an argument that you have read, listened to, or seen, you have two major options for your claim. You may choose to make a factual, nonjudgmental statement about the argument, or you may choose to evaluate it. If you examined the most recent McDonald's commercial and wrote an essay explaining what tactics were used to try to persuade consumers to eat at McDonald's or to try McDonald's newest sandwich, you would be supporting a factual claim, or a **claim of fact**. In contrast, if you evaluated the ad's effectiveness in attracting adult consumers, you would be supporting an evaluative claim, or a **claim of value**. It's the difference between *explaining* Geico's use of a talking gecko in its ads and *praising* that marketing decision. What this means, of course, is that an analysis of a commercial or any other type of argument that you see or read will itself have a claim of fact or a claim of value as its thesis.

What about a **claim of policy**, the third type of claim introduced in Chapter 1? In analyzing an argument, it would be rare to have a thesis that expressed what should or should not be done. Claims of policy are future oriented. They do not look back and express what should have been done in the past, but instead look forward to what should be done in the future. You might write an essay about what McDonald's should do in its future ads, but you would not really be writing an analysis.

Think how claims of fact and claims of value might serve as thesis statements for essays *about* arguments. For our examples, we have drawn on two famous historical arguments. Abraham Lincoln's Gettysburg Address is the subject of Charles Adams's essay "Lincoln's Logic," which supports a claim of value:

> Lincoln's address did not fit the world of his day. It reflected his logic, which was based on a number of errors and falsehoods.

ARGUMENT ESSENTIALS
Writing the Claim

	CLAIM OF FACT	CLAIM OF VALUE
Analyzing one argument	Analyze it objectively.	Evaluate it.
Analyzing two or more arguments	Compare and contrast objectively.	Evaluate them in relation to each other.

An objective analysis of the speech, based on a claim of fact, might explain the oration in the context of its time or Lincoln's use of poetic language.

Consider how your thesis looks different when you are making a *statement* about a document than when you are making a *judgment*:

Claims of fact: (statement)

The Declaration of Independence bases its claim on two kinds of support: factual evidence and appeals to the values of its audience.

As a logical pattern of argument, the Declaration of Independence is largely deductive.

Claims of value: (judgment)

Jefferson's clear, elegant, formal prose remains a master piece of English prose and persuades us that we are reading an important document.

The document's impact is lessened for modern readers because several significant terms are not defined.

In these examples based on the Gettysburg Address and the Declaration of Independence, we have been looking at one document at a time and thus at a single argument. At times, you will want to compare two (or more) arguments, synthesizing their ideas. Again, there are two basic types of thesis that you might choose to support: those that *objectively analyze* the points of comparison or contrast between the two, and those that *evaluate* the two in relationship to each other. If you wrote claims about how the two pieces compare, they might look like these:

Claims of fact:

Where Jefferson based his argument primarily on logical appeal, Lincoln depended primarily on emotional appeal.

Because Lincoln's purpose was to dedicate a cemetery, he left implicit most of his references to the political situation that was on the minds of his listeners. Because Jefferson knew he was justifying rebellion for King George III but also for the future, he spelled out explicitly why the colonies were breaking with England.

Claims of value:

Lincoln's address is a period piece that recalls a dark chapter in American history, but Jefferson's Declaration has had a much greater impact as an inspiration for other reform movements worldwide.

Different as the two historical documents are, both the Gettysburg Address and the Declaration of Independence were effective in achieving their respective purposes.

Planning the Structure

When your purpose in writing argument analysis is to support a factual claim, you will most likely use a very simple and direct form of organization called *defending the main idea*. In all forms of organization, you need to defend your main idea, or claim, with support; in this case, the support will come from the argument or arguments you are writing about.

At times, your claim may set up the organization of your essay, as was the case with the first example about the Declaration of Independence:

> The Declaration of Independence bases its claim on two kinds of support: factual evidence and appeals to the values of its audience.

The body of an essay with this thesis would most likely have two main divisions: one about factual evidence, providing examples, and the other about appeals to values, also providing examples. The other thesis about the Declaration of Independence does not suggest such an obvious structure. An essay based on that thesis would need to explain how the Declaration is an example of deductive reasoning, most likely by first establishing what generalization the document is based on and then what specifics Jefferson uses to prove that the colonists' situation fits that generalization.

Remember that when you compare or contrast two arguments, there will be two basic patterns to choose from for structuring the essay. One, often called **point-by-point comparison**, discusses each point about Subject A and Subject B together before moving on to the second point, where again both subjects are discussed:

I. Introduction
II. Context
   A. Jefferson
   B. Lincoln
III. Implicitness/explicitness
   A. Jefferson
   B. Lincoln
IV. Language
   A. Jefferson
   B. Lincoln
V. Conclusion

The second, often called **parallel order comparison**, focuses roughly half the essay on Subject A and then the other half on Subject B. The points made in each half should be parallel and should be presented in the same order.

I. Introduction
II. Jefferson
   A. Context
   B. Implicitness/explicitness
   C. Language

III. Lincoln
    A. Context
    B. Implicitness/explicitness
    C. Language
IV. Conclusion

ARGUMENT ESSENTIALS
Planning the Structure

- **Analyzing one argument:** Organize essay according to supporting points.
- **Analyzing two or more arguments:** Organize essay according to a point-by-point comparison pattern or by a parallel order comparison pattern.

Providing Support

In analyzing any argument, you will need to understand the argument and to make it clear to your readers that you do. You cannot write a clear explanation or a fair evaluation if you do not have a clear understanding of your subject. You will need to look closely at the piece to recall what specific words or ideas led you to the thesis statement that you have chosen to support.

Your support for your thesis will come from the text or texts you are writing about in the form of summary, paraphrase, or quotations. The ability to summarize, paraphrase, and quote material from your source is necessary in writing about arguments, but it is also essential in writing your own arguments, especially those that require research.

Summarizing

A summary involves shortening the original passage as well as putting it into your own words. It gives the gist of the passage, including the important points, while leaving out details. What makes summarizing difficult is that it requires you to capture often long and complex texts in just a few lines or a short paragraph. To summarize well, you need to imagine yourself as the author of the piece you are summarizing and be true to the ideas the author is expressing, even when those ideas conflict with your personal point of view. You must then move smoothly from being a careful reader to being a writer who, in your own words, re-creates another's thoughts.

We summarize for many reasons: to let our boss know the basics of what we have been doing or to tell a friend why she should or should not see a movie. In your classes, you are often asked to summarize articles or books, and even when this is not an explicit part of an assignment, the ability to summarize is usually expected. That is, when you are instructed to analyze an essay or to compare and contrast two novels, central to this work is the ability to carefully comprehend and re-create authors' ideas. See pages 51–53 in Chapter 2 for a more detailed treatment of summarizing.

Paraphrasing

Paraphrasing involves restating the content of an original source in your own words. It differs from summarizing in that a paraphrase is roughly the same length as the passage it paraphrases instead of a condensation of a longer passage. You will use paraphrasing when you want to capture the idea but there is nothing about the wording that makes repeating it necessary. You may also use it when the idea can be made clearer by rephrasing it or when the style is markedly different from your own. Here is an example drawn from a student paper:

> Randolph Warren, a victim of the thalidomide disaster himself and founder and executive director of the Thalidomide Victims Association of Canada, reports that it is estimated 10,000 to 12,000 deformed babies were born to mothers who took thalidomide. (40)

There is no single sentence on page 40 of the Warren article that both provides the estimate of the number of affected babies and identifies Warren as one of them. Both the ideas were important, but neither of them was worded in such a unique way that a direct quote was needed. Therefore, a paraphrase was the logical choice. In this case, the writer correctly documents the paraphrase using Modern Language Association (MLA) style.

Quoting

You may want to quote passages or phrases from your sources if they express an idea in words more effective than your own. In reading a source, you may come across a statement that provides succinct, irrefutable evidence for an issue you wish to support. If the author of this statement is a professional in his or her field, someone with a great deal of authority on the subject, it would be appropriate to quote that author. Consider the student research paper in Chapter 14 by Angela Mathers about women in combat. Suppose, during the course of Angela's research for her paper, she found several sources that agree that women in the military who are denied combat experience are, as a result, essentially being denied a chance at promotion to the highest ranks. Others argue that such considerations should not be a deciding factor in assigning women to combat. To represent the latter of these two positions, Angela chose to use a quotation from an authority in the field, using APA style:

ARGUMENT ESSENTIALS
Providing Support

Support your claim with information from your source(s) in the form of

- **Summary** — a shortened version of the original, in your own words
- **Paraphrase** — a version of the original in your own words that is about the same length as the original
- **Quotation** — exact words from the original, placed in quotation marks

Provide documentation, usually the author and page number, whenever you use someone else's words or ideas.

Elaine Donnelly, president of the Center for Military Readiness, says, "Equal opportunity is important, but the armed forces exist to defend the country. If there is a conflict between career opportunities and military necessity, the needs of the military must come first" (as qtd. in "Women in the Military," 2000).

It is especially important in argumentative writing to establish a source's authority on the subject under discussion. The most common way of doing this is to use that person's name and position of authority to introduce the quotation, as in the previous example. It is correct in both MLA and APA styles to provide the author's name in parentheses at the end of the quoted material, but that type of documentation precludes lending to the quote the weight of its having come from an authority. It is likely that those readers not in the military — and even some who are — will not know who Donnelly is just by seeing her name in parentheses. Your writing will always have more power if you establish the authority of each author from whose work you quote, paraphrase, or summarize. To establish authority, you may refer to the person's position, institutional affiliation, publications, or some other similar "claim to fame."

RESEARCH SKILL ▶ Incorporating Quotations into Your Text

There are three primary means of linking a supporting quotation to your own text. Remember that in each case, the full citation for the source will be listed alphabetically by the author's name in the list of works cited at the end of the paper, or by title if no author is given. The number in parentheses is the page of that source on which the quotation appears. The details of what appears in parentheses are covered in Chapter 14 in the discussion of APA (American Psychological Association) and MLA (Modern Language Association) documentation styles.

■ You may choose to make a brief quotation a grammatical part of your own sentence. In that case, you do not separate the quotation from your sentence with a comma, unless there is another reason for the comma, and you do not capitalize the first word of the quotation, unless there is another reason for doing so. In this sort of situation, there may be times when you have

to change the tense of a verb, in brackets, to make the quotation fit smoothly into your text or when you need to make other small changes, always in brackets.

Examples:
APA style
James Rachels (1976), University Professor of Philosophy at the University of Alabama at Birmingham and author of several books on moral philosophy, explains that animals' right to liberty derives from "a more basic right not to have one's interests needlessly harmed" (p. 210).

MLA style
James Rachels, University Professor of Philosophy at the University of Alabama at Birmingham and author of several books on moral philosophy, explains that animals' right to liberty derives from "a more basic right not to have one's interests needlessly harmed" (210).

continued

- You may use a traditional speech tag such as "he says" or "she writes." This is the most common way of introducing a quotation. Be sure to put a comma after the tag and to begin the quotation with a capital letter. At the end of the quotation, close the quotation, add the page number and any other necessary information in parentheses, and then add the period.

argues	implores
asks	insists
asserts	proclaims
concludes	questions
continues	replies
counters	responds
declares	states
explains	suggests

Examples:
APA style

James Rachels (1976), University Professor of Philosophy at the University of Alabama at Birmingham and author of several books on moral philosophy, writes, "The right to liberty — the right to be free of external constraints on one's actions — may then be seen as derived from a more basic right not to have one's interests needlessly harmed" (p. 210).

MLA style

James Rachels, University Professor of Philosophy at the University of Alabama at Birmingham and author of several books on moral philosophy, writes, "The right to liberty — the right to be free of external constraints on one's actions — may then be seen as derived from a more basic right not to have one's interests needlessly harmed" (210).

Students are sometimes at a loss as to what sorts of verbs to use in these tag statements. Try using different terms from this list or others like them. Remember that in writing about a printed or electronic text, it is customary to write in present tense unless there is a compelling reason to use past tense.

- You may vary the way you introduce quotations by at times using a colon to separate the quotation from a *complete sentence* that introduces it.

Examples:
APA style

For example, the Zurich Zoo's Dr. Heini Hediger (1985) protests that it is absurd to attribute human qualities to animals at all, but he nevertheless resorts to a human analogy: "Wild animals in the zoo rather resemble estate owners. Far from desiring to escape and regain their freedom, they are only bent on defending the space they inhabit and keeping it safe from invasion" (p. 9).

MLA style

The late Ulysses S. Seal III, founder of the Conservation Breeding Specialist Group and of a "computer dating service" for mateless animals, acknowledges the subordinate position species preservation plays in budgeting decisions: "Zoos have been established primarily as recreational institutions and are only secondarily developing programs in conservation, education, and research" (74).

Here is another example, also using APA style:

According to the late Ulysses S. Seal III (1982), founder of the Conservation Breeding Specialist Group and of a "computer dating service" for mateless animals, "None of these [zoo] budgets is allocated specifically for species preservation. Zoos have been established primarily as recreational institutions and are only secondarily programs in conservation, education, and research" (p. 74).

Notice that once the name of the author being cited has been mentioned in the writer's own text, it does not have to be repeated in the parentheses.

Documenting Your Sources

Chapter 14 will provide additional information about documenting sources, but you should start now documenting your use of others' work, even when the only sources you use are essays from this textbook. The single most important thing to remember is why you need to inform your reader about your use of sources. Once it is clear from your writing that an idea or some language came from a source and thus is not your own original thought or language, full documentation provides the reader with a means of identifying and, if necessary, locating your source. If you do not indicate your source, your reader will naturally assume that the ideas and the language are yours. It is careless to forget to give credit to your sources. It is dishonest to intentionally take credit for what is not your own intellectual property. Note, though, that the convention is for authors of magazine articles not to provide page numbers for their sources in the way that you will be expected to do.

The following Writer's Guide provides the general guidelines for documenting your use of sources.

WRITER'S GUIDE
Documenting Use of Summary, Paraphrase, and Quotation

---

1. **Give credit for any ideas you get from others**, not only for wording you get from them.
2. **Identify the author and the location of ideas that you summarize.** A *summary* is the condensing of a longer passage into a shorter one, using your own words.
3. **Identify the author and the location of ideas that you paraphrase.** A *paraphrase* is a rewording of another author's idea into your own words. A paraphrased passage is roughly the same length as the original.
4. **Identify the author and the location of language that you quote.** A *quotation* is the copying of the exact wording of your source and is placed in quotation marks. You cannot change anything inside quotation marks, with these exceptions: (a) If there is a portion of the quotation that is not relevant to the point that you are making and *that can be omitted without distorting the author's meaning*, you may indicate an omission of a portion of the quotation with an ellipsis (. . .). If there is a sentence break within the portion you are omitting, add a fourth period to the ellipsis to so indicate; (b) If you need to make a very slight change in the quote to make the quote fit grammatically into your own text or

to avoid confusion and if the change does not distort the author's meaning, you may make that slight change and place the changed portion in square brackets ([ ]). This method is used primarily to change the tense of a quoted passage to match that of your text or to identify a person identified in the quotation only by a pronoun.

5. **Make use of in-text or parenthetical documentation.** While a complete bibliographical listing for each work summarized, paraphrased, or quoted in your text is included in a Works Cited or References list at the end of your paper, each is also identified exactly at the point in the text where you use the source. If you are using the MLA system of documentation, the system most commonly used in the humanities, immediately following the sentence in which you use material from a source, you need to add in parentheses the author's name and the page number on which the material you are using appeared in the original source. However, since the credibility of your sources is critical in argumentative writing, it is even better to name the source in your own sentence and to identify the position or experience that makes that person a reliable source for the subject being discussed. In that case, you do not need to repeat the author's name in the parentheses. In fact, anytime the author's name is clear from the context, you do not need to repeat it in the parentheses.

Acceptable: The mall has been called "a common experience for the majority of American youth" (Kowinski 3).

Better: According to William Severini Kowinski, author of *The Malling of America*, "The mall is a common experience for the majority of American youth" (3).

In the APA system, the system most commonly used in the social sciences, in-text or parenthetical documentation is handled a bit differently because the citation includes the year of publication. The most basic forms are these:

The mall has been called "a common experience for the majority of American youth" (Kowinski, 1985, p. 3).

Kowinski (1985) writes, "The mall is a common experience for the majority of American youth" (p. 3).

6. **These examples show only the most basic forms for documenting your sources.** Some works will have more than one author. Sometimes you will be using more than one work by the same author. Usually Web sites do not have page numbers. Long quotations need to be handled differently than short ones. For all questions about documenting your use of sources not covered here, see Chapter 14.

Note: Unless your instructor indicates otherwise, use the page numbers on which your source appears **in this textbook** when summarizing, paraphrasing, or quoting from it instead of going back to the page numbers of the original. Also, unless your instructor indicates otherwise, use this model for listing in your Works Cited page a work reprinted here:

Isikoff, Michael. "The Snitch in Your Pocket." *Newsweek,* 18 Feb. 2010, pp. 40–41. Reprinted in *Elements of Argument: A Text and Reader*, edited by Annette T. Rottenberg and Donna Haisty Winchell, 12th ed., Bedford/St. Martin's, 2018, pp. 130–132.

READING ARGUMENT

Seeing a Claim of Fact Analysis

Michael Isikoff's *Newsweek* article "The Snitch in Your Pocket" is followed by a response by student Ray Chong. Chong's analysis supports a claim of fact, using a variety of examples to show how Isikoff appeals to his readers' need for security.

The Snitch in Your Pocket
MICHAEL ISIKOFF

Amid all the furor over the Bush administration's warrantless wiretapping program a few years ago, a mini-revolt was brewing over another type of federal snooping that was getting no public attention at all. Federal prosecutors were seeking what seemed to be unusually sensitive records: internal data from telecommunications companies that showed the locations of their customers' cell phones — sometimes in real time, sometimes after the fact. The prosecutors said they needed the records to trace the movements of suspected drug traffickers, human smugglers, even corrupt public officials. But many federal magistrates — whose job is to sign off on search warrants and handle other routine court duties — were spooked by the requests. Some in New York, Pennsylvania, and Texas balked. Prosecutors "were using the cell phone as a surreptitious tracking device," said Stephen W. Smith, a federal magistrate in Houston. "And I started asking the U.S. Attorney's Office, 'What is the legal authority for this? What is the legal standard for getting this information?'"

Those questions are now at the core of a constitutional clash between President Obama's Justice Department and civil libertarians alarmed by what they see as the government's relentless intrusion into the private lives of citizens.

There are numerous other fronts in the privacy wars — about the content of e-mails, for instance, and access to bank records and credit-card transactions. The Feds now can quietly get all that information. But cell-phone tracking is among the more unsettling forms of government surveillance, conjuring up Orwellian images of Big Brother secretly following your movements through the small device in your pocket.

How many of the owners of the country's 277 million cell phones even know that companies like AT&T, Verizon, and Sprint can track their devices in real time? Most "don't have a clue," says privacy advocate James X. Dempsey. The tracking is possible because either the phones have tiny GPS units inside or each phone call is routed through towers that can be used to pinpoint a phone's location to areas as small as a city block. This capability to trace ever more precise cell-phone locations has been spurred by a Federal Communications Commission rule designed to help police and other emergency officers during 911 calls. But the FBI and other law-enforcement outfits have been obtaining

---

Michael Isikoff is chief investigative correspondent with Yahoo News, formerly with *Newsweek* and NBC News. This essay was published in *Newsweek* on March 1, 2010.

more and more records of cell-phone locations — without notifying the targets or getting judicial warrants establishing "probable cause," according to law-enforcement officials, court records, and telecommunication executives. (The Justice Department draws a distinction between cell-tower data and GPS information, according to a spokeswoman, and will often get warrants for the latter.)

The Justice Department doesn't keep statistics on requests for cell-phone data, according to the spokeswoman. So it's hard to gauge just how often these records are retrieved. But Al Gidari, a telecommunications lawyer who represents several wireless providers, tells *Newsweek* that the companies are now getting "thousands of these requests per month," and the amount has grown "exponentially" over the past few years. Sprint Nextel has even set up a dedicated Web site so that law-enforcement agents can access the records from their desks — a fact divulged by the company's "manager of electronic surveillance" at a private Washington security conference last October. "The tool has just really caught on fire with law enforcement," said the Sprint executive, according to a tape made by a privacy activist who sneaked into the event. (A Sprint spokesman acknowledged the company has created the Web "portal" but says that law-enforcement agents must be "authenticated" before they are given passwords to log on, and even then still must provide valid court orders for all nonemergency requests.)

5   There is little doubt that such records can be a powerful weapon for law enforcement. Jack Killorin, who directs a federal task force in Atlanta combating the drug trade, says cell-phone records have helped his agents crack many cases, such as the brutal slaying of a DeKalb County sheriff: agents got the cell-phone records of key

suspects — and then showed that they were all within a one-mile area of the murder at the time it occurred, he said. In the fall of 2008, Killorin says, his agents were able to follow a Mexican drug-cartel truck carrying 2,200 kilograms of cocaine by watching in real time as the driver's cell phone "shook hands" with each cell-phone tower it passed on the highway. "It's a tremendous investigative tool," says Killorin. And not that unusual: "This is pretty workaday stuff for us."

But there is also plenty of reason to worry. Some abuse has already occurred at the local level, according to telecom lawyer Gidari. One of his clients, he says, was aghast a few years ago when an agitated Alabama sheriff called the company's employees. After shouting that his daughter had been kidnapped, the sheriff demanded they ping her cell phone every few minutes to identify her location. In fact, there was no kidnapping: the daughter had been out on the town all night. A potentially more sinister request came from some Michigan cops who, purportedly concerned about a possible "riot," pressed another telecom for information on all the cell phones that were congregating in an area where a labor-union protest was expected. "We haven't even begun to scratch the surface of abuse on this," says Gidari.

That was precisely what Smith and his fellow magistrates were worried about when they started refusing requests for cell-phone tracking data. (Smith balked only at requests for real-time information, while other magistrates have also objected to requests for historical data on cell-phone locations.) The grounds for such requests, says Smith, were often flimsy: almost all were being submitted as "2703(d)" orders — a reference to an obscure provision of a 1986 law called the Stored Communications Act, in which prosecutors only need to assert that records are "relevant" to an ongoing criminal investigation. That's the lowest possible standard in federal criminal law, and one that, as a practical matter, magistrates can't really verify. But when Smith started turning down government requests, prosecutors went around him (or "judge shopping," in the jargon of lawyers), finding other magistrates in Texas who signed off with no questions asked, he told *Newsweek*. Still, his stand — and that of another magistrate on Long Island — started getting noticed in the legal community. Facing a request for historical cell-phone tracking records in a drug-smuggling case, U.S. magistrate Lisa Pupo Lenihan in Pittsburgh wrote a 56-page opinion two years ago that turned prosecutors down, noting that the data they were seeking could easily be misused to collect information about sexual liaisons and other matters of an "extremely personal" nature. In an unusual show of solidarity — and to prevent judge shopping — Lenihan's opinion was signed by every other magistrate in western Pennsylvania.

The issue came to a head this month in a federal courtroom in Philadelphia. A Justice Department lawyer, Mark Eckenwiler, asked a panel of appeals-court judges to overturn Lenihan's ruling, arguing that the Feds were only asking for what amounted to "routine business records." But he faced stiff questioning from one of the judges, Dolores Sloviter, who noted that there are some governments, like Iran's, that would like to use such records to identify political protesters. "Now, can the government assure us," she pressed Eckenwiler, that Justice would never use the provisions in the communications law to collect cell-phone data for such a purpose in the United States? Eckenwiler tried to deflect the question, saying he couldn't speak to "future hypotheticals," but finally acknowledged, "Yes, your honor. It can be used constitutionally for that purpose." For those concerned about what the government might do with the data in your pocket, that was not a comforting answer.

Misuse of Cell-Phone Tracking
RAY CHONG

Ray Chong

English 103

A. Pollard

October 12, 2017

Misuse of Cell-Phone Tracking

Opening draws in reader with familiar example.

If you have watched many action films or police dramas at the theater or on television recently, you have probably seen law enforcement officials and others save the day by tracing the location of a cell phone as it "pings" off of towers it passes. Thousands held their breath as Halle Berry in *The Call*, for example, tried to save the life of a kidnap victim locked in the trunk of a serial killer's car by keeping in touch with her via cell phone. In "The Snitch in Your Pocket," Michael Isikoff acknowledges that the ability to track cell phones has helped law enforcement crack cases and respond to emergencies, but questions the FBI and other law enforcement agencies' using cell phones more and more to track their owners, often without the benefit of a search warrant. Isikoff warns that "cell-phone tracking is among the more unsettling forms of government surveillance, conjuring up Orwellian images of Big Brother secretly following your movements through the small device in your pocket" (130).

Isikoff cites instances in which cell-phone tracking has helped crack cases. In one case, cell-phone records put the suspects in the vicinity of the murder of a county sheriff at the time it occurred. In another, officers were able to track a truckload of cocaine because the driver's cell phone was tracked in real time (131). These examples appeal to readers' need for security since any reasonable person would like to know that cell-phone tracking would be used if it could solve crime committed against them or their loved ones—or to prevent one--or even that it can be used for crime-solving in general.

Isikoff immediately, however, undermines that sense of security by pointing out that the ability to track a cell phone can also be abused. In one case, an Alabama sheriff claimed his daughter had been kidnapped in order to locate her cell phone when the truth was that she had simply stayed out all night. In Michigan, police asked for information on cell phones at a certain location, claiming that they feared a riot, when what they really wanted was information on labor-union protesters (131). These cases remind readers that they could just as easily be victimized by cell-tracking as saved by it.

Isikoff goes on to build his case that a few magistrates are justified in finally saying no to requests for cell-phone information, which he feels are an intrusion into the privacy of individuals that those individuals often are not even aware of. Tracking one's location is, according to Isikoff, one of the "more unsettling" invasions of privacy because having someone track your movements is even more invasive than having someone track your money (130).

The number of requests for cell phone information has increased so much, backed by so little proof of need, that magistrates are

Claim of Fact

MLA-style quotation introduced with author's name and followed by page number in parentheses

Supporting detail paraphrased and identified by page number

Supporting detail, paraphrased with only two words quoted directly.

Supporting detail, paraphrased

beginning to question the constitutionality of letting law enforcement seek such information. Federal magistrates in New York, Pennsylvania, and Texas have questioned the legality of the requests. Stephen W. Smith in Texas and some colleagues are among those who have refused requests for cell-phone information (130). U.S. magistrate Lisa Pupo Lenihan wrote a fifty-six-page opinion explaining why she turned down a request for cell-phone records in a drug-smuggling case, and all of the other magistrates in western Pennsylvania joined her in signing it. When the Justice Department asked a federal court to overturn Lenihan's ruling, one judge "noted that there are some governments, like Iran's, that would like to use such records to identify political protesters." Isikoff concludes that it was not very reassuring that the Justice Department lawyer could not deny that there is nothing in our Constitution that prevents our government's doing exactly that (132).

Work Cited

Isikoff, Michael. "The Snitch in Your Pocket." *Newsweek*, 18 Feb. 2010, pp. 40–41. Reprinted in *Elements of Argument: A Text and Reader*, 12th ed., edited by Annette T. Rottenberg and Donna Haisty Winchell, Bedford/St. Martin's, 2018, pp. 130–132.

Seeing a Claim of Fact Analysis of Two Related Arguments

Isikoff's "The Snitch in Your Pocket" (p. 130) and Bruce Schneier's "The Internet Is a Surveillance State" (p. 63) both address the loss of privacy we suffer as a result of the technological devices that have become a part of our daily lives. This student essay, written by Clemson University student DeRon Williamson, compares the two. It supports a claim of fact.

How Our Technology Is Used against Us
DERON WILLIAMSON

DeRon Williamson

English 103

Mrs. Brantley

September 23, 2017

How Our Technology Is Used against Us

In today's world, cell phones and computers are not just nice to have. They are necessities, or at least we have come to feel that they are. Cell phones and the Internet have replaced land lines and letters as ways of keeping in touch with family and friends. We want to be in touch instantly. However, two authors, Michael Isikoff and Bruce Schneier, explain how we are giving up our privacy in order to have that instantaneous communication and convenience.

> Claim of fact

In his article "The Snitch in Your Pocket," Isikoff explains how law enforcement agencies at all levels are increasingly using cell phones to track their owners in real time and cell-phone records to track where they were at a particular time in the past. Most cellphone owners don't even realize that their phone either has a tiny GPS or can be located as its calls are routed through specific towers. It is good that these tracking systems can be used to locate the owner in an emergency, but they can also be used to locate an owner who doesn't want his or her location to be known. More and more, law enforcement officers are tracking cell phones or attaining cell-phone records without a warrant. Only recently have a few magistrates decided to say no to requests for phone records and real time tracking (Isikoff 131–32).

> Objective analysis of one argument

> Parenthetical citation at end of paragraph indicates para-phrased ideas.

In his article "The Internet Is a Surveillance State," from cnn.com, Bruce Schneier uses a variety of examples to explain how Internet users are tracked. Users are tracked by Facebook, by Google, and, via their iPads and iPhones, by Apple. Data about their online activity is even correlated with their offline activity, such as purchases, to get more detail about their lives. Schneier explains how even CIA director David Petraeus could not keep his private life private. His affair with Paula Broadwell became public because she used hotel and other public networks to e-mail him, and when the hotel records were correlated, the common name was hers. The government

> Objective analysis of second argument

Because the author's name is in the sentence, it does not have to be repeated in the parentheses.

works with corporations, corporations work with the government, and as Schneier concludes, "So, we're done. . . . Welcome to an Internet without privacy, and we've ended up here with hardly a fight" (57).

Schneier ends on this pessimistic note. Although Isikoff finds it far from comforting that it is constitutional to use cell-phone locations and cell-phone records to track users' whereabouts, at least some magistrates are starting to look a bit more closely at the numerous requests for cell-phone information and to sometimes just say no (132). Until we can say no to our cell phones and the Internet, we will just to have accept the lack of privacy.

Conclusion mentions both authors again.

Work Cited

Isikoff, Michael. "The Snitch in Your Pocket." *Newsweek*, 18 Feb. 2010, pp. 40–41. Reprinted in *Elements of Argument: A Text and Reader*, 12th ed., edited by Annette T. Rottenberg and Donna Haisty Winchell, Bedford/St. Martin's, 2018, pp. 130–132.

Schneier, Bruce. "The Internet Is a Surveillance State." *CNN.com*, 16 Mar. 2013, http://www.cnn.com/2013/03/16/opinion/ schneier-internet-surveillance/index.html. Reprinted in *Elements of Argument: A Text and Reader*, 12th ed., edited by Annette T. Rottenberg and Donna Haisty Winchell, Bedford/St. Martin's, 2018, pp. 63–65.

Practice: Analyzing a Multimodal Argument

Read the captioned graphics on pages 137–138, and answer the questions that appear at the end.

The Science Facts about Autism and Vaccines
HEALTHCARE MANAGEMENT

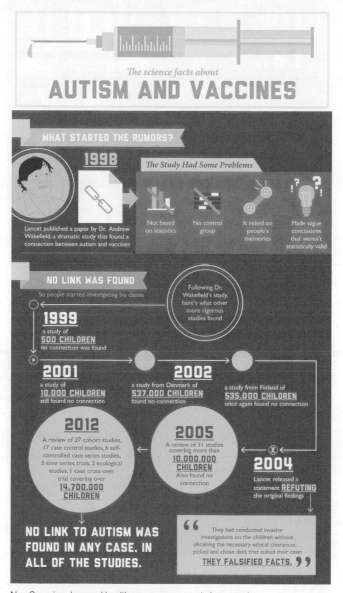

NowSourcing, Inc. and healthcare-management-degree.net

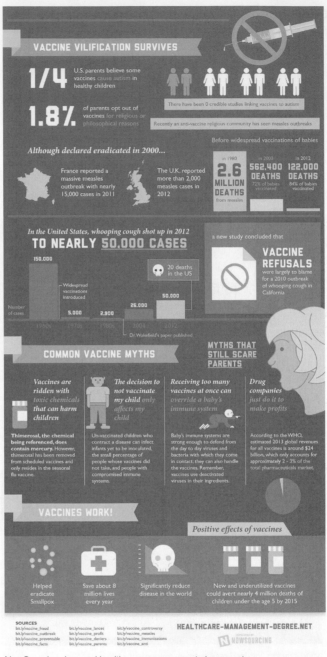

NowSourcing, Inc. and healthcare-management-degree.net

Reading and Discussion Questions

1. What were the problems with the research reported in *Lancet* by Dr. Andrew Wakefield in 1998? What have subsequent studies found?
2. What are some of the consequences of the belief that some people have that vaccines cause autism?
3. Do you find the arguments against the vaccine myths convincing? Why or why not?
4. Do you find the overall argument being made in this infographic convincing? Why or why not?

Writing Assignments

1. Write a paragraph in which you support one conclusion you can draw based on the evidence presented in the infographic and use specifics from it to support your topic sentence.
2. Write an essay in which you analyze the argument that is being made in the infographic.
3. Write an essay in which you evaluate the effectiveness of the infographic in making its argument.

Practice: Analyzing a Written Argument

Read the following essay and answer the questions that appear at the end.

Electoral College is Best Way to Choose U.S. President
JAMES W. INGRAM III

The Electoral College is once again under siege. Critics arguing that it is obsolete and undemocratic have greatly overestimated the benefits of electing presidents by popular vote plurality.

One key reason the founders of the United States of America created the Electoral College was the possibility that once George Washington retired or died, no other candidate could garner majority support from such a diverse nation. Their concern was well-founded.

Of the 49 presidential elections the United States has held since 1824, when many states began allowing the public to choose electors, a full 18 contests have not given any candidate a popular vote majority.

James Ingram teaches political science at San Diego State University and helped reform the mayoral systems of Los Angeles and San Diego. His article appeared in the *San Diego Union Tribune* on 13 January 2017.

The electoral vote has only reversed a popular vote majority once, in 1876, an election called into question by vote fraud. In 1888, when the person who won the electoral vote had a smaller share of the popular vote, no candidate won a popular majority.

Likewise in 2000 and 2016, the most recent elections in which crit- 5 ics claim the Electoral College subverted the people's will, neither Hillary Clinton nor Al Gore won popular vote majorities. Clinton won 48 percent compared to Donald Trump's 46 percent; Gore won 48.4 percent to George W. Bush's 47.9 percent. Clinton and Gore outpolled their opponents, but the majority supported someone else for president.

The Electoral College usually amplifies the people's voice, electing the candidate who wins most states and votes. This allows the winner to claim a mandate and lead the country.

Had the founders required presidents to gain a majority of the popular vote rather than of the Electoral College, over 30 percent of our presidential elections would have been decided by the U.S. House. In both 2000 and 2016, the Republican House majorities surely would have chosen the Republican candidate, the same one who won the electoral vote.

The problem with House selection is that this raises questions of legitimacy. In 1824, no one won an Electoral College or a popular vote majority. When the House chose John Quincy Adams over plurality winner Andrew Jackson, the latter denounced the "corrupt bargain," undermining Adams' presidency.

Every presidential election which lacked a popular majority featured significant thirdparty candidates. Gary Johnson in 2016, Ralph Nader in 2000, and Ross Perot in 1992 and 1996 are prominent examples.

Third-party candidates highlight neglected issues, but increase the probability 10 nobody wins a majority. The problem with electing the candidate who achieves only a popular vote plurality is that someone supported by a small minority of people and states could win, provided everyone else has even fewer votes.

By mandating an Electoral College majority rather than a popular vote plurality, the Constitution requires a presidential candidate to win more states. Since over half of the U.S.'s population lives in the nine largest states, plurality rules would instead allow presidents to win with only a small minority of states.

But since the nine most populous states have only 240 of the needed 270 electoral votes, the current system requires candidates to be competitive in more states. Clinton won almost 3 million more votes than Trump, but she won merely 19.75 states and D.C., while Trump won 30.25 states (they split Maine).

Alexander Hamilton defended the Electoral College in Federalist Paper No. 68, stating it was intended to ensure presidents would have "the esteem and confidence of the whole Union, or of so considerable a portion of it as would be necessary." Hamilton called it "unsafe to permit less than a majority" of the states' electors to select the president.

Our present system has only elected the candidate who won fewer states thrice, in 1824, 1960 and 1976. The two main candidates tied in the number of states won in 1848 and 1880, but both times the contestant with more popular support won the electoral vote. In every other presidential plebiscite, the winner carried a majority of states.

15   If presidents only needed plurality support, the victor might regularly be the candidate who won fewer states. This would weaken presidential leadership.

The Electoral College prevents smaller states from being ignored in presidential elections. The states' diversity should be just as fully represented as other dimensions of diversity in our multicultural republic.

Electing presidents by popular vote is a bad idea. The only big countries using this method are France, Mexico and Russia. Russia selected Vladimir Putin through popular vote majority. Are these three countries really better governed than America?

If our Electoral College mechanism for choosing presidents is imperfect, it is because human beings have never devised a perfect system. But in 11 score and 7 years we have chosen 45 presidents to lead our country. What isn't broken doesn't need fixing.

Reading and Discussion Questions

1. What is the difference between a plurality and a majority? Why are the definitions of those two terms critical to Ingram's argument?

2. Reread the second sentence of the essay. What *is* the benefit of electing the President by popular vote plurality?

3. In paragraph 5, Ingram writes that in the elections of 2000 and 2016, "in which critics claim the Electoral College subverted the people's will, neither Hillary Clinton nor Al Gore won popular vote majorities." Do you agree with the critics who felt the Electoral College subverted the people's will in those elections? Why or why not?

4. In that same paragraph, Ingram states that in those elections, "Clinton and Gore outpolled their opponents, but the majority supported someone else for president." Is that statement true or false? Explain.

5. In paragraph 7, Ingram writes, "Had the founders required presidents to gain a majority of the popular vote rather than of the Electoral College, over 30 percent of our presidential elections would have been decided by the U.S. House." Why is this an either/or fallacy?

6. How significant, in your opinion, is the number of states a presidential candidate wins? Explain.

7. Do you agree with Ingram's belief that "[e]lecting presidents by popular vote is a bad idea"? Why or why not? Does it matter in your reasoning that the only large countries doing so are France, Mexico, and Russia?

Writing Assignments

1. Write an essay explaining how Ingram builds his argument in his essay.

2. Write an essay in which you explain why you agree or disagree with Ingram's argument.

Assignments for Writing Argument Analysis

Reading and Discussion Questions

1. Choose an editorial from your campus or local newspaper and evaluate it. How successful an argument does it make?

2. Which essay do you find more effective, Schneier's or Isikoff's? Why?

3. Think of some television commercials that have caught your eye. What tactics are used to try to convince you to buy a product or service?

4. Locate another essay or article expressing an opinion about the Electoral College and explain why you think it does or does not present an effective argument.

Writing Suggestions

1. Choose an editorial from your campus or local newspaper, and write an objective analysis of it. Your thesis statement will be a claim of fact.

2. Locate two editorials or two articles that take different stands on the same controversial issue. Write an analysis in which you objectively compare the two as examples of argumentation.

3. Locate two editorials or two articles that take different stands on the same controversial issue. Write an essay in which you argue which of the two is a more effective argument and why.

4. Choose a print advertisement to analyze or evaluate in an essay.

5. Choose a political speech to analyze or evaluate in an essay.

RESEARCH ASSIGNMENT ▶ **Incorporating Quotations**

Read each of the following passages. Then for each, write one or two sentences incorporating a quotation. Also incorporate in your sentence(s) the author's name and the title of the work. Choose a different way of incorporating the quote each time so that all three ways are represented: (1) as a grammatical part of your own sentence, (2) with a speech tag such as "he says" or "she writes," and (3) with a complete sentence and a colon.

Put the page number in parentheses, and punctuate correctly according to MLA style.

Passage 1

The school district [in Washington, DC] Michelle Rhee inherited in 2007 was in freefall. Not only had student enrollment plummeted and test scores scraped the bottom of any national rankings, but also many principals had lost control of their schools. Rhee's response to the latter was to eject (or offer voluntary retirement to) nearly fifty principals who had tolerated those conditions.

Her yardstick for progress was basic. In the first year, a principal entering an out-of-control school must succeed in "locking down" the school: seize control of the hallways, bathrooms, lunchrooms, and the nearby city blocks during school dismissal and ensure calm and respect in the classrooms. If principals succeed with that first-year lockdown but test scores still look miserable, they generally got a pass. The second and third years, however, measurable "teaching and learning" was supposed to kick in. If that didn't happen, the principal was "non-reappointed," the district's euphemism for getting fired. Not surprisingly, a lot of principals stumbled along that path, which means a lot of non-reappointments — and a lot of interviews for new principals.
Source: Richard Whitmire, *The Bee-Eater* (San Francisco: Jossey-Bass, 2011): pp. 131–32.

Passage 2

Back in the 1970s, organic food had no such positive image. Many dismissed it as a fringy fad served cold with an eat-your-spinach sermon. How could organic taste good? Indeed, taste was the key challenge. Organic advocates couldn't popularize a cuisine simply by declaring it spiritually and ecologically superior. The world, like my mother, was not waiting for or willing to eat inedible soul food. To win acceptance, it had to be truly delectable.

But that would take a while. Many of us got involved in the organic movement for political reasons — to protest industrial agriculture. Some of us were back-to-the-land rebels with a strong passion for eating locally grown food. Others were food purists, excited by the opportunity to propagate and preserve heirloom varieties of produce and seed stocks. Still others came to the cause simply for the joy of growing our own food, talented amateurs at best who cared more about its appeal to a diner's political conscience than to his or her taste buds.

Luckily, what began as a philosophical fondness for dishes like brown rice and seaweed eventually matured into a tasty cuisine that attracted talented chefs, notably my friend Alice Waters, who called organics "the delicious revolution."

Source: Gary Hirshberg, "Organics — Healthy Food, and So Much More," in Karl Weber, ed., *Food, Inc.: How Industrial Food Is Making Us Sicker, Fatter and Poorer — And What We Can Do about It* (New York: Participant Media, 2009), p. 49.

To see what you are learning about argumentation applied to the latest world and national news, read our *Bits* blog, "Argument and the Headlines," at **blogs.bedfordstmartins.com/bits.**

Writing Arguments

As a citizen of the world, and of a particular country, city or town, and neighborhood, you have probably already found yourself at times drawn into controversy. By virtue of your membership in certain ethnic, religious, or political groups, you often have to take a position on a controversial issue. At times you may feel conflicted because of the pull of different allegiances that you have, to family or party or church. The presidential election of 2016 tested allegiances like they had not been tested since perhaps the Civil Rights era. Families were divided; friendships ended. People who had never taken part in a protest march were in the streets. If you spent any time at all on Facebook or Twitter, if you watched or read the news at all, you could not remain oblivious to the arguments spawned by the election and the following transfer of power. You may have been surprised to find yourself on opposite sides of some issues from people you have known all of your life — or thought you knew.

Some of the learning that goes on in college comes indirectly from being introduced to unfamiliar people with unfamiliar ideas. The more insular the community in which you grew up, the more jarring will be your first encounters with new ideas. That doesn't mean that you will give up your old values, but it may mean that you have to be able to explain them to yourself and others. Presenting a reasoned argument for what you believe is a skill that you will use dependent throughout your life, as a parent, a follower of a particular religion, a Democrat, Republican, or Independent, an employee. Your college classes are a place to practice reasoned argument.

Some of what you learn in college will come through memorization of facts or mastering of procedures. More of it will require **synthesis**, the bringing together and analyzing of ideas and the formulation of opinions. Any time you are asked to express an opinion and support it, you are being asked to write an argument, even if your **purpose** for writing will differ from one situation to another. In Chapters 12 through 14, we will discuss how to write an argument based on independent research. For now, we want to talk about writing an argument based on course material, as on an exam or in an assigned essay.

Think of the types of assignments that require a response in the form of an argument. You may not think of literary analysis, for example, as argumentation, but if you are defending an opinion you have about the literary work, you are writing an argument. Your **thesis** will be a claim of fact or a claim of value. Consider these other types of assignments that call for an argumentative response supporting a claim of fact, value, or policy.

Political Science: Do you support the National Popular Vote Interstate Compact as a replacement for the winner-take-all way of allocating electoral votes currently used in forty-eight states? Why or why not?

Biology: Can environmental factors affect DNA? Explain.

Education: How would you respond to parents who argue that having children with special needs mainstreamed into regular classes takes the teacher's time and attention away from other students?

Sociology: Should sports teams continue to use Native American imagery and names? Why or why not?

Chemistry: What threats are there to the continued effectiveness of antibiotics?

Media Studies: Why is there such a discrepancy between the financial success of a film and its critical success?

The topic will usually dictate the type of claim you will support in writing an argument. The audience for your writing is a bit artificial in that you are writing to an instructor or professor who knows more about the subject than you do. There is the temptation to think, "I don't need to say that. He knows it already!" Remember, though, that your goal is to build a case for your claim. You need to draw in any information from your textbooks or lectures that will help you do that. The more specific your support, the more convincing your argument will be.

Organizing the Argument

The first point to establish in organizing your argument is your purpose. Is your intention to make readers aware of some problem? to offer a solution to the problem? to defend a position? to refute a position held by others? The way you organize your material will depend to a great extent on your goal.

Let's look at various ways of organizing an argumentative paper. Here are four possibilities:

- Defending the thesis
- Refuting an opposing view
- Finding the middle ground
- Presenting the stock issues

Defending the Thesis

All forms of organization will require you to defend your thesis, or main idea, but one way of doing this is simple and direct. Early in the paper, state the thesis that you will defend throughout your argument. You can also indicate here the two or three points you intend to develop in support of your claim, or you can raise these later as they come up. Suppose your thesis is that widespread vegetarianism would solve a number of problems. You could phrase it this way: *If the majority of people in this country adopted a vegetarian diet, we would see improvements in the economy, in the health of our people, and in moral sensitivity.* You would then develop each of the improvements in your list with appropriate data. However, if you find that listing your two or three main ideas in the claim leads to too much repetition later in the paper, you can introduce each one as it arises in your discussion of the topic. Your claim would remain more general: *If the majority of people in this country adopted a vegetarian diet, there would be noticeable improvement.*

Defending the thesis is effective for factual claims as well as policy claims, in which you urge the adoption of a certain policy and give the reasons for its adoption. It is most appropriate when your claim is straightforward and can be readily supported by direct statements. DeRon Williamson's essay "How Our Technology Is Used Against Us" in Chapter 4 is an example of defending the main idea.

Defending the Thesis

Introduction

Thesis (Main Idea)

Evidence

Conclusion

Refuting an Opposing View

Refuting an opposing view means attacking it in order to weaken, invalidate, or make it less credible to a reader. Since all arguments are dialogues or debates — even when the opponent is only imaginary — refutation of another point of view is always implicit in your arguments. As you write, keep in mind the issues that an opponent may raise. You will be looking at your own argument as an unsympathetic reader may look at it, asking yourself the same kinds of critical questions and trying to find its weaknesses in order to correct them. In this way, every argument you write becomes a form of refutation.

A claim for this type of essay might take this form:

On the topic of _____, X claims that _____. However, _____.

Refuting an Opposing View

Introduction

Summary of Opposing View

Refutation of Opposing View

Conclusion

Strategies for Refuting an Opposing View

1. **Read the argument carefully,** noting the points with which you disagree. You must be familiar with your opponent's argument in order to refute it.

2. **Summarize an opposing view at the beginning of your paper** if you think your audience may be sympathetic to it or unfamiliar with it. Give readers enough information to understand what you plan to refute. Be respectful of the opposition's views. You do not want to alienate readers who might not agree with you at first.

3. **If your argument is long and complex, choose only the most important points to refute.** Otherwise, the reader who does not have the original argument on hand may find a detailed refutation hard to follow. If the argument is short and relatively simple — a claim supported by only two or three points — you may decide to refute them all, devoting more space to the most important ones.

4. **Attack the principal elements in the argument of your opponent.**

    a. Question the evidence. (See Chapter 7.) Question whether your opponent has proved that a problem exists.

    b. Attack the warrants or assumptions that underlie the claim. (See Chapter 8.)

    c. Attack the logic or reasoning of the opposing view. (Refer to the discussion of fallacious reasoning in Chapter 11.)

    d. Attack the proposed solution to a problem, pointing out that it will not work.

5. **Be prepared to do more than attack the opposing view.** Supply evidence and good reasons in support of your own claim.

READING ARGUMENT

Seeing Opposing Views

The following essay is an example of an argument that refutes opposing views.

The Rich Get Richer, the Poor Go Hungry
SHARON ASTYK AND AARON NEWTON

What is the most common cause of hunger in the world? Is it drought? Flood? Locusts? Crop diseases? Nope. Most hunger in the world has absolutely nothing to do with food shortages. Most people who go to bed hungry, both in rich and in poor countries, do so in places where markets are filled with food that they cannot have.

Despite this fact, much of the discourse about reforming our food system has focused on the necessity of raising yields. Though it is true that we might need more food in coming years, it is also true that the world produces more food calories than are needed to sustain its entire population. The problem is unequal access to food, land, and wealth, and any discussion must begin not

Sharon Astyk is a former academic, a writer, and a farmer in upstate New York. She is the author of *Depletion and Abundance: Life on the New Home Front* (2008) and coauthor, with Aaron Newton, of *A Nation of Farmers: Defeating the Food Crisis on American Soil* (2009). Newton is a sustainable systems land planner in North Carolina and director of environmental programs at Outdoor Living, a design firm. This excerpt is from *A Nation of Farmers*.

from fantasies of massive yield increases, but from the truth that the hunger of the poor is in part a choice of the rich.

Inequity and politics, not food shortages, were at the root of almost all famines in the twentieth century. Brazil, for example, exported $20 billion worth of food in 2002, while millions of its people went hungry. During Ethiopian famines in the 1980s, the country also exported food. Many of even the poorest nations can feed themselves—or *could* in a society with fairer allocation of resources.

It can be hard to grasp the degree to which the Western lifestyle is implicated. We don't realize that when we buy imported shrimp or coffee we are often literally taking food from poor people. We don't realize that our economic system is doing harm; in fact, the system conspires to make it nearly impossible to figure out whether what we're doing is destructive or regenerative.

5   We have been assured that "a rising tide lifts all boats," that it is necessary for us to make rich people richer, because that will, in turn, enrich the poor. The consequences have been disastrous—for the planet and for the people whose food systems have been disrupted, who never had a chance to be lifted by any tide.

Journalist Jeremy Seabrook, in his book *The No-Nonsense Guide to World Poverty*, describes First World efforts to eliminate poverty and hunger this way:

> It is now taken for granted that relief of poverty is the chief objective of all politicians, international institutions, donors, and charities. This dedication is revealed most clearly in a determination to preserve [the poor]. Like all great historical monuments, there should be a Society for the Preservation of the Poor;

only, since it is written into the very structures of the global economy, no special arrangements are required. There is not the remotest chance that poverty will be abolished, but every chance that the poor themselves might perish.

It is hard for many of us to recognize that the society we live in helps create poverty and insecurity, but it is true. Our economy is based on endless growth. We're told that if the rich get richer, it makes other people less poor. Think about it for a moment—about how crazy that is. Wouldn't it make much more sense to enrich the poor directly, to help them get land and access to resources?

Historically, rural people have been quite poor, but often, despite their poverty, could grow enough food to feed themselves. Over recent decades, however, industrial agriculture and widespread industrialization have moved large chunks of the human population into cities, promising more wealth. But rising food and energy prices (rising because of this move and this urban population's new demands for energy and meat) have left people unable to feed their families.

Multinational food companies have also worked their way into the food budgets of the poor. Faith D'Aluisio and Peter Menzel are the authors of *Hungry Planet*. "Few of the families we met [in the developing world] could afford a week's worth of a processed food item at one time," they report in the *Washington Post*, "so the global food companies make their wares more affordable by offering them in single-serving packets."

Around the world, industrial agriculture has   10 consolidated land ownership into the hands of smaller and smaller populations. Rich nations dumped cheap subsidized grain on poor nations. Local self-sufficiency was destroyed. Now, as the price of food has risen dramatically, those created dependencies on cheap grain, which doesn't exist anymore, mean that millions are in danger of starvation.

Real alleviation of poverty and hunger means reallocating the resources of our world into the hands of people who need them most. This is not only ethically the right thing to do, it is necessary. There is no hope that newly industrializing nations will help us fight climate change if it means a great inequity between their people and those of the United States. Russia, India, and China have all said so explicitly. The only alternative to the death of millions in a game of global chicken is for everyone to accept that the world cannot afford rich people — in any nation.

What is the best strategy of reallocation? One — that is, for those of us who live in nations where there is plenty of land and food so that we don't have to rely on the exports of poor nations — would be to enable the world's farmers to eat what they grow and to have sufficient land to feed themselves and their neighbors.

Most of the world's poorest people are urban slum dwellers (often displaced farmers) or land-poor farmers, agroecologist Peter Rosset notes. Both groups are increasing, in large degree because of economic policies that favor food for export and allow large quantities of land to be held in the hands of the richest.

"The expansion of agricultural production for export, controlled by wealthy elites who own the best lands, continually displaces the poor to ever more marginal areas for farming," Rosset writes in *Food Is Different*. "They are forced . . . to try to eke out a living on desert margins and in rainforests. As they fall deeper into poverty . . . they are often accused of contributing to environmental degradation."

In this system, poor people who depend on the land, and who best understand the urgency of preserving it, are forced by necessity to degrade and destroy it — and they, rather than we, are held responsible. But a large part of the responsibility rests on the way we eat. This is an important point, because it acknowledges that there are things that we in wealthy nations can do to enable poorer people to eat better — or even to eat at all.

One way to do this is simply to grow our own food, to rely not on foods grown thousands of miles away but on foods grown at local farms and gardens. We also can concentrate on creating food sovereignty in poor nations. We can cut back on global food trade, importing primarily high-value, fair-traded dry goods that take little energy to transport, and place limits on food speculation, which drives up prices so that multinational corporations can get richer at the expense of the poor.

Most of all, we can recognize that selfsufficiency is as urgent in the rich world as in the poor. Globalization's demise is coming. The rising costs of transportation and the trade deficit in the United States make it inevitable that we will increasingly be looking to meet our basic needs locally.

When we grow our own food, or buy it directly from local farmers, we take power away from multinationals. We make it harder for them to extract wealth and the best land of other nations — and if they don't need that land, local farmers may be able to use it for their own needs.

We also put power in the hands of our neighbors, many of whom are also victims of globalization. There are 49 million people in the

United States who can't consistently afford a basic nutritious diet. It turns out that the things that make us poor—lack of education, lack of access to land and home, and the industrial economy—are precisely the things that make other people poor. By creating local food systems, we can enrich our immediate neighbors as we stop impoverishing our distant ones.

Finding the Middle Ground

Although an argument, by definition, assumes a difference of opinion, we know that opposing sides frequently find accommodation somewhere in the middle. As you mount your own argument about a controversial issue, you need not confine yourself to support of any of the differing positions. You may want to acknowledge that there is some justice on all sides and that you understand the difficulty of resolving the issue.

A claim for this type of essay might take this form:

On the topic of _____, X claims that _____.

In contrast, Y argues that _____. They agree that _____, a view that deserves consideration.

Finding the Middle Ground

Introduction

Presentation of Various Viewpoints

Proposal of Middle Ground

Conclusion

Strategies for Finding the Middle Ground

Consider these guidelines for an argument that offers a compromise between or among competing positions:

1. **Explain the differing positions** early in your essay. Make clear the major differences separating the two (or more) sides.

2. **Point out, whenever possible, that the differing sides already agree** to some exceptions to their stated positions. Such evidence may prove that the differences are not so extreme as their advocates insist.

3. **Make clear your own moderation and sympathy,** your own willingness to negotiate.

4. **Acknowledge that opposing views deserve to be considered,** if you favor one side of the controversy.

5. **Provide evidence that accepting a middle ground can offer marked advantages** for the whole society. Whenever possible, show that continued polarization can result in violence, injustice, and suffering.

6. **Be as specific as possible** in offering a solution that finds a common ground, emphasizing the part that you are willing to play in reaching a settlement.

READING ARGUMENT

Seeing the Middle Ground

The following essay is an example of an argument that seeks to find the middle ground on a topic.

Finding the Moral, Sensible Middle Ground on Abortion
DAMON LINKER

Did you know that in the contemporary United States a woman who has a miscarriage after falling down a flight of stairs can be arrested for "attempted fetal homicide"?

Or that a judge can order a critically ill pregnant woman to undergo a cesarean section even though he knows it might kill her? (In at least one case, the woman and baby both ended up dead.)

Or that a pregnant woman who loses the pregnancy in the process of trying (and failing) to kill herself can be charged with the crime of "homicide by child abuse"?

I didn't know all this either—at least before reading "Pregnant, and No Civil Rights," an explosive Nov. 8 *New York Times* op-ed by Lynn M. Paltrow and Jeanne Flavin. Liberals and feminists might be consoling themselves about the defeat of proposed "personhood" amendments in North Dakota and Colorado last Tuesday. But as Paltrow and Flavin so powerfully show, moves to embed fetal rights in the law have made enormous strides over the past several years—and nothing about the results of the 2014 election is going to change that.

I find the trend deeply disturbing—and not because I'm an abortion-rights absolutist. On the contrary, I think that abortion raises extremely difficult moral questions on all sides. For that reason, it's an issue tailor-made to serve as a test case for liberal politics. And it's a test that too many of us, on all sides, are failing.

Liberal democratic government requires a citizenry capable of understanding and acting on two fundamental truths about the human condition: people often disagree about the highest good (or moral truth); and not all things deemed morally wrong ought to be outlawed and prosecuted by the government. Liberalism stands or falls by these distinctions—and the capacity of the citizenry to make them.

And that's where we're failing.

Consider the manifold complexities surrounding abortion. To begin with, it pits two absolute moral claims—the fetus's right to life and the woman's right to individual liberty (including control of her own body)—against each other in such a way that there is sometimes no outcome in which the rights of both parties can be upheld.

Then there's the fact that not everyone accepts that there is any such trade-off—because they reject the rights-claims of one or the other of the parties. Some advocates of abortion rights deny the humanity and thus dignity of the fetus, for example, while some anti-abortion advocates seem to think the woman's right to bodily freedom ends as soon as she becomes pregnant, because another life is at stake.

Damon Linker is a senior correspondent at *TheWeek.com*, where this article originally appeared on November 11, 2014.

10   Many others, meanwhile, building on their muddled (but quite possibly accurate) moral intuitions, believe that while the fetus is a matter of relative moral indifference at the start of a pregnancy (in the first trimester), by sometime in the second trimester, and certainly by the age of viability (which is constantly being pushed back by advances in medical expertise and technology), it develops into a being possessing full dignity and rights.

    This wide range of moral opinions would seem to point liberal politics in the direction of a messy political compromise. Rhetorically, such a compromise was nicely captured by Bill Clinton's line about the importance of making abortion "safe, legal, and rare." Policy-wise, it gestures toward easy availability of abortion in the early stages of pregnancy, severe restrictions close to viability, and a range of regulations in the middle, differing somewhat from state to state (because of the American federalist system).

    This (minus the federalism) is precisely what prevails throughout most of Europe today. Despite the absence of an organized religious right, abortions across much of the continent are extremely difficult to procure after 20 weeks of pregnancy. But during the first trimester? They're easily and safely available nearly everywhere, often at taxpayer expense.

    That makes no sense to the extremists on both sides of the American abortion debate—even though it's precisely what liberalism demands when an issue is shot through with tragic moral conflicts and deep fundamental disagreements.

    Don't tell that to Katha Pollitt, whose new book is just the latest in a series of attempts on the part of a certain style of feminist to de-moralize the act of aborting a fetus—to assert that women who terminate a pregnancy should feel no regrets or moral qualms, and that they should perhaps even embrace it as a positive good that involves no significant moral compromises at all.

15   An equal and opposite form of moral simplification—and one with far more political clout behind it at the present moment—can be seen in the personhood movement that, as Paltrow and Flavin so chillingly show, is changing the way the law treats pregnant women. If the movement gets its way, a pregnant woman will become, in the eyes of the law, a vessel that exists entirely for the sake of carrying fetal life to term. She will be transformed, in other words, from a woman possessing her own dignity, freedom, and rights into a mother expected and even required by law to sacrifice her own good for the good of her child.

    Those committed to a genuinely liberal politics—as Americans of every party or ideology ought to be—should actively seek to avoid either extreme. Whatever our personal moral convictions, we need to resist the temptation to adopt a politics of purity—to treat either fetal life or women's liberty as politically worthless.

    Both have value.

    No matter how many of our inveterate moral simplifiers and political mischief makers seek to deny it.

Presenting the Stock Issues

Presenting the stock issues, or stating the problem before the solution, is a type of organization borrowed from traditional debate format. It works for policy claims when an audience must be convinced that a need exists for changing the status quo (present conditions) and for introducing plans to solve the problem. You begin by establishing that a problem exists (need). You then propose a solution (plan), which is your thesis. Finally, you show reasons for adopting the plan (advantages). These three elements — need, plan, and advantages — are called the *stock issues.*

For example, suppose you wanted to argue that measures for reducing acid rain should be introduced at once. You would first have to establish a need for such measures by defining the problem and providing evidence of damage. Then you would present your claim, a means for improving conditions. Finally, you would suggest the benefits that would follow from implementation of your plan. Notice that in this organization your claim usually appears toward the middle of your paper, although it may also appear at the beginning.

A sentence form such as the following can guide you in writing an appropriate thesis:

_____ is a problem, but _____ can help resolve it.

A sample claim might look like this:

Traffic congestion around the stadium on game days is a problem, but temporarily limiting University Avenue to eastbound traffic would allow for a smoother and faster flow of traffic.

Presenting the Stock Issues

Introduction

Establishment of Problem (Need)

Proposal of Solution (Plan)

Explanation of Advantages

Conclusion

READING ARGUMENT

Seeing the Stock Issues

The following essay is an example of an argument that presents the stock issues on a topic.

States Can Reform Electoral College—Here's How to Empower Popular Vote

JOHN R. KOZA

Hillary Clinton and President-elect Donald Trump rarely agree, but in 2001 Clinton called for a bill for a national popular vote for president, while Trump referred to the current system of electing the President in 2012 as "a disaster for a democracy … a total sham and a travesty."

The reason why five of our nation's 45 incoming presidents have entered office after losing the national popular vote (while winning the Electoral-College vote) is that most states have winner-take-all laws that award all the state's electoral votes to the candidate receiving the most popular votes in that state. Given that there have now been eight consecutive presidential elections with an average national-popular-vote margin of less than 5 percent, it is safe to predict that the nation will continue to experience elections ending in this unhealthy way.

These state winner-take-all laws are also the reason why the 2016 presidential candidates concentrated 94 percent of their campaign events in just 12 closely divided "battleground" states, while giving little or no attention to states with 70 percent of the nation's population. Candidates have no reason to pay attention to the concerns of states where they are safely ahead or hopelessly behind (and therefore have nothing to gain and nothing to lose). The result of presidential candidates focusing on a mere 12 states is not just

that babies don't get kissed in the spectator states. There are real consequences to the current system and they are not trivial. Presidential candidates and sitting first-term presidents shape important policies with an eye to winning the 12 critical states that decide the election.

The 2016 candidates, for example, catered to Michigan, Wisconsin, Ohio, and Pennsylvania in fashioning their positions on trade treaties. In 2001, President George W. Bush imposed steel quotas, despite his party's long-standing preference for free trade. President Barack Obama bragged that the Small Business Administration gave its largest grant in history to a ricotta cheese factory in—you guessed it—Ohio.

Recent books such as "Presidential Pork; Presidential Swing States: Why Only Ten Matter;" "The Two Million Voters Who Will Elect the Next President;" "The Particularistic President;" and "The Rise of the President's Permanent Campaign" provide innumerable examples of battleground states receiving a wide variety of presidentially-controlled benefits, including grants, disaster declarations, and various exemptions.

5

John R. Koza is a computer scientist and a former consulting professor at Stanford University. This article originally appeared on TheHill.com on November 20, 2016 — two days after Donald Trump had been elected President of the United States.

Fortunately, the Founding Fathers provided us with a way to change the current method of electing the president so that the candidate receiving the most popular vote in all 50 states always wins the White House.

This makes every vote, in every state, politically relevant in every presidential election.

The U.S. Constitution empowers each state to choose the method of awarding its electoral votes ("Each State shall appoint, in such Manner as the Legislature thereof may direct, a Number of Electors...").

Despite attempts by defenders of the current system to suggest that the Founders designed or preferred the current state-by-state winner-take-all method of awarding electoral votes, winner-take-all is not in the U.S. Constitution, was not debated by the Constitutional Convention, was never mentioned in the Federalist Papers, and was used in only three states in the nation's first presidential election in 1789.

10 The National Popular Vote interstate compact provides a way to guarantee the presidency to the candidate who receives the most popular votes in all 50 states and the District of Columbia. The compact will go into effect after being enacted by states possessing a majority of the electoral votes—that is, enough to elect a president (270 of 538).

Under the compact, when the Electoral College meets in mid-December, the candidate who received the most popular votes in all 50 states (and the District of Columbia) would receive all the electoral votes from all the enacting states (and thereby become president).

So far, 11 states possessing 165 electoral votes have enacted the National Popular Vote bill into law. Enactment by states possessing an additional 105 electoral votes is necessary to bring the compact into effect. The bill has made significant progress in this direction by already passing one legislative chamber in 12 additional states with 96 electoral votes.

The bill was most recently approved by a bipartisan 40–16 vote in the Republican-controlled Arizona House, 28–18 in the Republican-controlled Oklahoma Senate, 37–21 in the Democratic-controlled Oregon House, and unanimously by legislative committees in Georgia and Missouri. A total of 2,794 state legislators have endorsed it.

When the state legislatures convene in 2017, they should enact the National Popular Vote compact in order to ensure that we have a 50-state campaign for President in 2020 and that the president is the candidate receiving the most popular votes in all 50 states and the District of Columbia.

Writing

Writing the Introduction

Having found a claim you can defend and an organizational pattern, you must now think about how to begin. An introduction to your subject should consist of more than just the claim. It should invite the reader to give attention to what you have to say. It should also point you in the direction you will take in developing your argument.

Consider the kind of argument you intend to present. Does your paper make a factual claim? Does it address values? Does it recommend a policy or action? Is it a rebuttal of some current policy or belief? The answers to those questions will influence the way you introduce the subject.

If your thesis makes a factual claim, you may be able to summarize it in one or two opening sentences. *Whether we like it or not, money is obsolete. The currency of today is not paper or coin, but plastic.* Refutations are easy to introduce in a brief statement: *Contrary to popular views on the subject, America is not as competitive in the cyber world as its citizens would like to believe.*

A claim that defends a value is usually best preceded by an explanatory introduction. *Sending troops to Iraq was the best decision Bush could have made at the time* is a thesis that can be stated as a simple declarative opening sentence. However, readers who disagree may not read any further than the first line. Someone defending this type of claim is likely to be more persuasive if he or she presents the thesis less directly.

> "When 9/11 happened I thought I'm not hearing from Muslims like ourselves," she says, meaning liberal and moderate *Saturday Evening Post* types. "I'd only hear from the old men and the conservative women. So I started writing opinion pieces. I wanted to get another voice out there to show that, look, 9/11 doesn't represent all Islam."[1]

One way to keep a thesis from alienating the audience is to phrase it as a question.

> How do you know you can trust what you read? Start by recognizing that there is no such thing as completely unbiased news. No one can report any news story without encapsulating complicated events, deciding what's really important, leaving out what the reporter thinks are insignificant details, and adopting a point of view that makes it possible to stitch together all the elements and tell a story. Therefore no two people will ever report any news story the same way. So there is no such thing as a single objective telling of a news event.[2]

For any subject that is highly controversial or emotionally charged, especially one that strongly condemns an existing situation or belief, you may sometimes want to express your indignation directly. Of course, you must be sure that your indignation can be justified. The author of the following introduction, a physician and writer, openly admits that he is about to make a case that may offend readers.

> Is there any polite way to introduce today's subject? I'm afraid not.
> It must be said plainly that the media have done about as sorry and

---

[1] Mona Eltahawy, qtd. in Ron Rosenbaum, "The Next Revolution," *Smithsonian*, May 2013, p. 30.
[2] Post Editors, "Balancing Act," *Saturday Evening Post*, May/June 2013, p. 46.

dishonest a job of covering health news as is humanly possible, and that when the media do not fail from bias and mendacity, they fail from ignorance and laziness.[3]

If your claim advocates a policy or makes a recommendation, it may be a good idea, as in a value claim, to provide a short background.

Competitive foods in schools are the soft drinks, sugary snacks, and chips that we were not allowed to buy in the school cafeteria but that today's public school students are. These foods that are largely lacking in nutrition contribute to the overall problem of obesity among children and youth. We may not be able to control what young children eat at home or what teenagers eat when they are out with their friends, but we can control what they eat while at school. For the good of the next generation, all competitive foods should be banned from the public schools.

There are also other ways to introduce your subject. One is to begin with an appropriate quotation or indirect quotation.

"Land is the only thing in the world that amounts to anything, for 'tis the only thing in this world that lasts. . . . 'Tis the only thing worth working for," says Gerald O'Hara to daughter Scarlett in *Gone with the Wind*.
    Wise words. Real estate was on an upward surge for decades. It seemed unstoppable. Then, along came the disastrous collapse of the housing bubble in 2007. Six years later, we're seeing a good rebound in real estate prices, and that has many, perhaps you, wondering if land is once again, if not worth fighting and dying for, at least worth investing in.[4]

Or you may begin with an anecdote:

As a child, Kamala accompanied her parents to civil rights marches in Oakland. She's been making strides for justice—and breaking down barriers—ever since.[5]

Or you may begin with a statement meant to capture your readers' attention—maybe even shock them a bit—in order to make them read on.

North Korea's Supreme Leader Kim Jong Un is the world's youngest head of state—and behaves like it.[6]

---

[3] Michael Halberstam, "TV's Unhealthy Approach to Health News," *TV Guide*, September 20–26, 1980, p. 24.

[4] Russell Wild, "Land Ho!," *Saturday Evening Post*, May/June 2013, p. 36.

[5] Nancy Pelosi, "Kamala Harris: California's Triple Threat," *Time*, April 29–May 6, 2013, p. 64.

[6] Barbara Demick, "Kim Jong Un: Asia's Nuclear Bully," *Time*, April 29–May 6, 2013, p. 68.

Writing the Conclusion

You may have heard the advice to tell your readers in the introduction what you are going to say, then say it in the body of your paper, and then in your conclusion tell them what you have said. That doesn't mean to repeat your thesis statement word for word, although you will want to return to your thesis idea.

Here are a few other don'ts for conclusions:

- Don't begin with "In conclusion," "In summary," "To conclude," or some other similar but unnecessary transition.
- Don't switch into first person with "I think," "I feel," or another similar personalization.
- Unless your paper is over ten pages long, your instructor requires it, or the conventions of your field require it, don't summarize your main points.
- Don't start a new topic.
- Don't let a concluding quotation replace your own concluding thoughts.
- Don't have a one-sentence conclusion.
- Don't use vague platitudes such as "Only time will tell" or "History will be the judge."

Here are some strategies to consider as you conclude your paper:

- Answer the question "So what?" What is the significance of your argument? Point out how the future may be affected or what other implications there might be.
- Issue a call for action. Make clear to your readers what they can do about the situation.
- Generalize about your subject's broader applications or what the next step might be.
- Bring all of your ideas into a coherent whole. Make clear how all of the pieces fit together.
- Use a relevant quotation in conjunction with, but not in place of, your own concluding ideas.

In any case, you will want to return to your thesis idea and be sure your conclusion encompasses the whole essay, not just part of it. The conclusion establishes the impression that your readers are left with, and you want it to be a good one.

Assignments for Writing Arguments

Reading and Discussion Questions

1. Consider the classes you are taking and think of controversial subjects you have encountered in any of them. What are some of the topics about which you could write an argument?

2. What are some of the controversial topics in your major area or in an area in which you might major?

3. Every week there are controversial issues being discussed in the news. What are some current ones?

Writing Suggestions

1. Look back at the sample topics listed by subject on page 146. Think of other examples in those or other subject areas.

2. It may seem ironic that in America, obesity is a problem among the poor. Write an essay in which you explain that seeming paradox.

3. Write an essay in which you explain why Planned Parenthood was such a controversial issue during the earliest days of President Trump's term in office.

4. Write an essay in which you defend your position on federal funding for Planned Parenthood.

5. Write an essay in which you explain candidate Trump's appeal to one particular segment of voters—evangelicals, for example, or blue-collar Southerners.

6. Write an essay in which you defend your position on the Electoral College as the means of selecting the American president.

7. Choose one of the topics you came up with in #1 or #2 in Reading and Discussion Questions and write an argument expressing and defending your opinion on the topic.

8. Choose an issue that is currently causing controversy on your campus or in your community and write an essay in which you take a stand on the issue.

Analyzing the ELEMENTS

Claims

What are you trying to prove? Your claim, or proposition, represents your answer to this question. A claim is the statement that a writer makes about a subject and thus is most closely aligned with the writer-subject leg of the communications triangle.

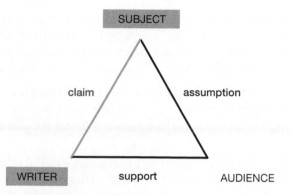

Your **claim** is a conclusion you reach when you are trying to decide what to say about a subject; it becomes your **thesis** when you write about that subject. Claims can be classified as claims of fact, claims of value, and claims of policy, although at times there is a fine line between one type of claim and another.

Claim of fact	States that a condition exists, has existed, or will exist, based on factual evidence.	■ *Excess sun exposure causes skin cancer.* ■ *Environmental policies have slowed the depletion of the Earth's ozone layer.*
Claim of value	Desirable or undesirable based on moral or aesthetic principles.	■ *The most relaxing vacations are spent on the beach.* ■ *Bathing suits have gotten too skimpy.*
Claim of policy	States that a specific course of action should be implemented.	■ *Sunscreen products should be more closely regulated.* ■ *Stricter emissions policies are needed for trucks.*

Claims of Fact

A fact, for the most part, is not a matter for argument — it is an undisputed truth. Many facts can be confirmed by our own senses: *The sun sets in the West. Water freezes at 32 degrees Fahrenheit.* For facts that we cannot confirm for ourselves, we must rely on other sources — reference works, scientific reports, media outlets — for information: *Salmon is rich in omega 3 fatty acids. The United States spent $528 billion on military expenditures in 2011.*

Unlike a simple fact, a **claim of fact** *asserts* that something is true — that a condition has existed, exists, or will exist. An argument built around a claim of fact must convince the reader that the statement is true, usually with the support of factual information such as statistics, examples, and testimony that most responsible observers assume can be verified. (For detailed discussion of support, see Chapter 7.)

Why, you may wonder, would a claim of fact need to be proven, if we all agree on facts? There are several reasons.

Different Interpretations.   Facts, while indisputable at their most basic level, may not always be interpreted the same way. Different interpretations lead to different points of view on a subject. Scientists, for example, may look at the same data yet disagree about whether the data indicate a warming of the planet.

> **Claim:** Based on the available evidence, the earth has been undeniably growing warmer for the past fifty years.
>
> **Claim:** The earth's temperatures have remained flat for the past twenty years.

Causal Relationships.   A claim of fact may assert a causal relationship based on facts. For example, some researchers may claim that soda consumption is responsible for the rise in the nation's obesity rates, while others may blame the higher obesity rates on Americans' increasingly sedentary lifestyles. Just as different interpretations of facts can lead to different perspectives, a different understanding of cause can lead to a different claim.

> **Claim:** Soda and other sugary drinks are the leading cause of obesity in the United States.
>
> **Claim:** Americans are overweight because they eat too much and exercise too little.

Predictions.   A prediction uses known facts to make a claim about the future. Based on available evidence, an analyst may predict that holding teachers accountable for their students' standardized test scores will improve our educational system. This prediction may be disputed by others, who assert that the available evidence indicates the opposite outcome is likely. A prediction can be tested in the future to determine its validity. But even in the future, the results will be subject to interpretation and potential disputes about cause.

Claim: An increased emphasis on standardized testing will lead to higher graduation rates among high school students.

Claim: Too much emphasis on standardized testing will decrease student and teacher morale, leading to higher dropout rates among high school students.

New Data. Scientists and scholars in all fields are constantly working not only to interpret existing data, but also to uncover new data. Such new data may change our understanding of history, physics, or biology and cause us to reevaluate our conclusions. In the health field in particular, researchers regularly uncover new information that may complicate or contradict earlier findings. When new data emerge in a field, the public may require some convincing to accept a new theory over the prevailing viewpoint, such as when the Environmental Protection Agency listed secondhand smoke as a major carcinogen in 1992.

Claim: Although it was once generally believed that cigarette smoke was harmful only to the smoker, researchers now conclude that second-hand smoke poses serious health hazards for nonsmokers as well.

Not all claims are so neatly stated or make such unambiguous assertions. Because we recognize that there are exceptions to most generalizations, we often qualify our claims with words such as *generally, usually, probably,* and *as a rule*. It would not be true to state flatly, for example, *College graduates earn more than high school graduates.* This statement is generally true, but we know that some high school graduates who are electricians or city bus drivers or sanitation workers earn more than college graduates who are schoolteachers or nurses or social workers. In making such a claim, therefore, the writer should qualify it with a word that limits the claim — a **qualifier**. However, watch out for words that overstate your claim. Words like *always, every, all,* and *never* allow for no exceptions.

Remember: Labeling a statement a claim of fact does not make it true. The label simply means that it is worded as though it were a true statement. It is up to the writer to provide support to prove that the statement is indeed true.

ARGUMENT ESSENTIALS
Claims of Fact

- Claims of fact assert that a condition has existed, exists, or will exist.
- Claims of fact are supported by factual information such as statistics, examples, and testimony.
- Claims of fact may take one of several forms:
  — a statement in favor of a particular interpretation of data.
  — a suggestion of a causal relationship.
  — a prediction.
  — a case for the acceptance of new evidence.
- Claims of fact may be limited by words such as *generally* and *probably*.

- Identify the source of any material that you quote, summarize, or paraphrase.
- At a minimum, give the author's last name and the page number in parentheses after the information taken from the source. (There will often not be a page number for online sources.)

- Better: Give the author's full name in your sentence the first time you use that source, and give only the page number in parentheses.
- Briefly identify who the source is, focusing on his or her expertise on the subject at hand.

READING ARGUMENT

Seeing a Claim of Fact

The following essay has been annotated to highlight claims of fact.

Loaded Language Poisons Gun Debate

JOSH LEVS

It's the biggest, fiercest debate taking place across America. But it's poisoned from the get-go by a Tower of Babel predicament.

Opening metaphor: gun debate = Tower of Babel

In disputes over the future of gun laws, people espousing different positions often literally don't understand each other.

Source identified by his claim to authority

"The sides are speaking different languages," says Harry Wilson, author of "Guns, Gun Control, and Elections: The Politics and Policy of Firearms."

Levs's claim of fact and thus his thesis

Many of the most frequently used words and phrases in this debate mean different things to different people — or, in some cases, don't have clear meanings to anyone. From terms like "assault weapons" to the battle between "gun control" and "gun rights," the language in the national conversation is making it tougher to find common ground.

Another source identified by her claim to authority

"What language does is frame the issue in one way that includes some things and excludes others," says Deborah Tannen, a Georgetown University linguistics professor and author of "The Argument Culture: Stopping America's War of Words."

5

Examples

It's a phenomenon that America sees all the time: "pro-life" vs. "pro-choice" in the abortion debate; "marriage equality" vs. "protecting marriage" in the battle over same-sex marriage. Those who oppose the estate tax have termed it a "death tax."

Josh Levs is a CNN journalist. This piece appeared on cnn.com on January 31, 2013.

"The gun control debate is catching up to this now," says Wilson, director of the Institute for Policy and Opinion Research at Roanoke College in Salem, Virginia.

The massacre at an elementary school in Newtown, Connecticut, "was a game changer. It changed the political landscape overnight."

As the debate rages in Washington and throughout the country, here's a look at some of the flashpoint lingo muddying the waters:

Gun Control vs. Gun Rights

10   When President Obama recently announced plans to sign 23 executive orders on the issue, he avoided the phrase "gun control." Instead, he emphasized the need "to reduce the broader epidemic of gun violence in this country."

"We've seen this transformation from use of the term 'gun control' to 'gun violence,'" says Wilson, "because no one can be in favor of gun violence. That's universal."

"Gun control," to many Americans, is not a positive term, Tannen adds.

The key is "the set of associations people have with a word" — and Americans don't like the idea of the government "controlling" many of their decisions.

That's why "gun rights" works well for the National Rifle Association in pushing against new gun laws. "For Americans, the word 'rights' is always a positive thing. That's not necessarily true in other cultures, but it is for Americans," Tannen says.

15   Wayne LaPierre, executive vice president of the NRA, spoke to those associations this week during his testimony before Congress.

"We believe in our freedom," he said, speaking for gun owners who are NRA members. "We're the millions of Americans from all walks of life who take responsibility for our own safety and protection as a God-given, fundamental right."

While the current debate has its own tenor, the focus on language has been around for decades. It's embodied in the title of one of the best-known gun control groups.

The Brady Campaign to Prevent Gun Violence grew out of an organization called the National Council to Control Handguns.

Common Sense

Listen to any leading voice on this issue, and you're likely to hear that term repeatedly.

Example

Sets up further examples

Headings identify examples developed more fully

President Obama used it to describe the steps he's calling for, including   20
universal background checks for gun owners and legislation prohibiting "further manufacture of military-style assault weapons."

Examples from both sides of
the debate

The NRA, meanwhile, announced in December that LaPierre would offer
"common sense solutions." He then pushed for armed guards in American
schools. Many Americans were angry and argued that was the opposite of
common sense. The NRA later said it believes each school should decide for
itself.

Former U.S. Rep. Gabby Giffords and her husband, Mark Kelly, have
begun a political action committee to take on the gun lobby's influence. In an
op-ed in *USA Today*, they said LaPierre's initial remarks showed that "winning
even the most common-sense reforms will require a fight."

Wilson says the term seems to be playing well for those pushing for new
gun regulations. "It makes people say, 'these are common-sense ideas,'" he says.

Assault Weapons

But what exactly are those ideas? When it comes to the most controversial one
being discussed—banning "assault weapons"—it's unclear. That's because the
term itself is abstract. There is no clear definition of an "assault weapon."

Definition of a key term is
unclear

The 10-year so-called assault weapons ban enacted in 1994 named 19   25
semiautomatic firearms, as well as semiautomatic rifles, pistols, and shotguns
with specific features.

"In general, assault weapons are semiautomatic firearms with a large magazine of ammunition that were designed and configured for rapid fire and combat use," the Justice Department said at the time.

That may be the closest thing to a simple explanation the government ever
gave, but if you want to see how incredibly complicated the official definition
is in the law itself, check out the language.

"I wrote a book on gun control. I don't know what an assault weapon is,"
Wilson says.

The National Shooting Sports Foundation and other gun enthusiasts
complain that what ultimately separated an "assault weapon" from a "non-as-
sault weapon" under the 1994 law was cosmetic.

Some Second Amendment groups and gun retailers prefer the terms "tac-   30
tical rifle" or "modern sporting rifle."

The term "assault rifle" was first used by Germany during World War II,
the *New York Times* notes. Later, U.S. manufacturers adopted the words as they
began to sell firearms modeled after new military rifles.

In today's parlance, adding "military-style" doesn't draw a clear line either.

Sen. Dianne Feinstein, D-California, who has submitted legislation for a new "assault weapons ban," says it would include, among other things, "all semiautomatic rifles that can accept a detachable magazine and have at least one military feature: pistol grip; forward grip; folding, telescoping, or detachable stock; grenade launcher or rocket launcher; barrel shroud; or threaded barrel."

Some very specific definitions

The previous ban included semiautomatic pistols with at least two features, including a detachable magazine, threaded barrel, a shroud allowing the shooter to "hold the firearm with the nontrigger hand without being burned," a weight of 50 ounces or more unloaded, or what was described as "a semiautomatic version of an automatic firearm."

Semiautomatic

35 An automatic weapon, as the Justice Department put it, is a machine gun that allows you to fire bullets in succession by holding in the trigger. Fully automatic weapons are severely restricted under existing law, but in some cases they are still legal to own, as the *Los Angeles Times* notes.

They're commonly used in the military but rarely owned by civilians.

A semiautomatic weapon can load bullets automatically, but it fires only once each time you pull the trigger.

In the effort to prevent mass killings, those pushing for a new assault weapons ban want to halt the production and sale of certain semiautomatic weapons and high-capacity "feeding devices"—such as magazines—that allow for a large number of rounds of ammunition.

Feinstein's bill would ban selling, transferring, importing, or manufacturing 120 named firearms, certain semiautomatic rifles, handguns, "shotguns that can accept a detachable magazine and have one military characteristic," and "semiautomatic rifles and handguns with a fixed magazine that can accept more than 10 rounds."

40 During the previous ban, gun manufacturers were able to make cosmetic changes to evade the law. One chief question now is how a piece of legislation could avoid the same happening again.

Can Words Help Bridge the Gap?

"If you get new words, there's a better chance of moving beyond the polarization," says Tannen, who is spending this year at Stanford's Center for Advanced Study in the Behavioral Sciences. But, she warns: "Words don't stay neutral for long—because they quickly get associated with the people that use them."

New words might help establish common ground.

When asked for a case in which more neutral language may have helped the government reach a consensus on a controversial topic, Tannen said "nothing comes to mind."

Instead, the race is on to control the semantics, which are "crucial," says Wilson.

"In American politics, the person who gets to define the issue wins."

Practice: Claim of Fact

Review the print advertisement on page 171, and answer the questions that follow.

Paper Because
DOMTAR PAPER

Domtar Paper Company

Reading and Discussion Questions

1. How is the claim qualified?
2. How does this ad use text and picture to reinforce each other?
3. How valid do you feel the text is? (Have you observed scenes like the one depicted in the ad, or perhaps been part of such a scene?)
4. How clear is the connection between what the ad says about social media and what is being advertised? What *is* being advertised?

Claims of Value

Unlike claims of fact, which state that something is true and can be validated by reference to the data, claims of value make a judgment. They express approval or disapproval. They attempt to prove that some action, belief, or condition is right or wrong, good or bad, beautiful or ugly, worthwhile or undesirable.

> **Claim:** Democracy is superior to any other form of government.
>
> **Claim:** Killing animals for sport is wrong.
>
> **Claim:** The Sam Rayburn Building in Washington is an aesthetic failure.

Some claims of value are simply expressions of taste, likes and dislikes, or preferences and prejudices. The Latin proverb *De gustibus non est disputandum* means that we cannot dispute taste. If you love the musical *Wicked*, there is no way for anyone to prove you wrong.

Many claims of value, however, can be defended or attacked on the basis of standards that measure the worth of an action, a belief, a performance, or an object. As far as possible, our personal likes and dislikes should be supported by reference to these standards. Value judgments occur in any area of human experience, but whatever the area, the analysis will be the same. We ask the arguer who is defending a claim of value: *What are the standards or criteria for deciding that this action, this belief, this performance, or this object is good or bad, beautiful or ugly, desirable or undesirable? Does the thing you are defending fulfill these criteria?*

There are two general areas in which people often disagree about matters of value: aesthetics and morality.

Aesthetics

Aesthetics is the study of beauty and the fine arts. Controversies over works of art — the aesthetic value of books, paintings, sculpture, architecture, dance, drama, and movies — rage fiercely among experts and laypeople alike. They may disagree on the standards for judging or, even if they agree about standards, may disagree about how successfully the art object under discussion has met these standards. The Rogerian approach to conflict resolution can be particularly useful in resolving disagreements over the standards for judging. Agreeing on those standards is the first step toward resolving the conflict and is a necessary step before seeking agreement on how well the standards have been met.

Consider a discussion about popular music. Hearing someone praise the singing of Manu Chao, a hugely popular European singer now playing to American crowds, you might ask why he is so highly regarded. You expect Chao's fans to say more than "I like him" or "He's great." You expect them to give reasons to support their claims. They might show you a short review from a respected newspaper that says, "Mr. Chao's gift is simplicity. His music owes a considerable amount to Bob Marley . . . but Mr. Chao has a nasal, regular-guy voice, and instead of the Wailers' brooding, bass-heavy undertow, Mr. Chao's band delivers a lighter bounce. His tunes have the singing directness of nursery rhymes."[1] Chao's fans accept these criteria for judging a singer's appeal.

You may not agree that simplicity, directness, and a regular-guy voice are the most important qualities in a popular singer. But the establishment of standards itself offers material for a discussion or an argument. You may argue about the relevance of the criteria, or you may agree with the criteria but argue about the success of the singer in meeting them. Perhaps you prefer complexity to simplicity. Or even if you choose simplicity, you may not think that Chao has exhibited this quality to good effect.

It is probably not surprising, then, that despite wide differences in taste, professional critics more often than not agree on criteria and whether an art object has met the criteria. For example, almost all movie critics agree that *Citizen Kane* and *Gone with the Wind* are superior films. They also agree that *Plan 9 from Outer Space*, a horror film, is terrible.

Morality

Value claims about morality express judgments about the rightness or wrongness of conduct or belief. Here disagreements are as wide and deep as in the arts — and more significant. The first two examples on page 172 reveal how controversial such claims can be. Although a writer and reader may share many values — among them a belief in democracy, a respect for learning, and a desire for peace — they may also disagree, even profoundly, about other values. The subject of divorce, for example, despite its prevalence in our society, can produce a conflict between people who have differing moral standards. Some people may insist on adherence to absolute standards, arguing that the values they hold are based on immutable religious precepts derived from God and biblical scripture. Since marriage is sacred, divorce is always wrong, they say, whether or not the conditions of society change. Other people may argue that values are relative, based on the changing needs of societies in different places and at different times. Since marriage is an institution created by human beings at a particular time in history to serve particular social needs, they may say, it can

---

[1] Jon Pareles, *New York Times*, July 10, 2001, p. B1.

ARGUMENT ESSENTIALS
Claims of Value

- Claims of value make a judgment.
- Claims of value should be supported by reference to standards that measure the worth of an action, belief, performance, or object.
- Claims of value most often are about aesthetics or morality.

also be dissolved when other social needs arise. The same conflicts between moral values might occur in discussions of abortion or suicide.

Nevertheless, even where people agree about standards for measuring behavior, a majority preference is not enough to confer moral value. If in a certain neighborhood a majority of heterosexual men decide to harass a few gay men and lesbians, that consensus does not make their action right. In formulating value claims, an arguer should be prepared to ask and answer questions about the way in which those value claims, as well as those of others, have been determined. Lionel Ruby, an American philosopher, sums it up in these words: "The law of rationality tells us that we ought to justify our beliefs by evidence and reasons, instead of asserting them dogmatically."[2]

READING ARGUMENT

Seeing a Claim of Value

The following essay has been annotated to highlight claims of value.

The NFL's Protest Crisis
SAMUEL CHI

A catchy opening

The National Football League has a real crisis on its hands.

Not these other things, but the national anthem is the crisis.

No, this isn't about concussions, domestic violence or even the ridiculously infamous "Deflategate." This is about the national anthem—whether to stand, kneel or raise a fist while giant American flags are being unfurled from end zone to end zone.

The crisis may turn out to be the response of the NFL's customers.

The anthem crisis maybe isn't an existential one—yet—to the NFL, but it has the potential to mushroom into something much bigger than being merely about Colin Kaepernick and a few other protesters. This crisis threatens to pit the league against its very own paying customers.

You see, strangely, a league that has no compunction about fining players for wearing the wrong socks, shoes or twerking after a touchdown is suddenly

---

Samuel Chi is a sports journalist: a college football analyst, proprietor of BCSGuru.com, senior editor at *RealClearPolitics* and managing editor at *RealClearSports*. His article was posted on cnn.com on 9 September 2016.

[2] Lionel Ruby, *The Art of Making Sense* (New York: Lippincott, 1968), p. 271.

silent about whether its employees must stand during the playing of the national anthem. "The Shield" that would not allow players to commemorate slain police officers in Dallas has no firm policy on whether it's OK or not if someone in an NFL uniform decides to chill during the singing of the Star-Spangled Banner.

Contrast with things that ARE deemed inappropriate

5   The NBA, generally considered the most player-friendly and progressive of the North American pro sports leagues, actually has a rule about the anthem (and it's pretty unequivocal): "Players, coaches and trainers are to stand and line up in a dignified posture along the sidelines or on the foul line during the playing of the National Anthem." And that goes for both the U.S. and Canadian anthems, since it has a team based in Toronto.

Contrast with how the NBA responds to the national anthem

But when Kaepernick, the San Francisco 49ers' backup quarterback, decided that he would no longer honor the flag, NFL Commissioner Roger Goodell limply made a statement saying the league merely "encourages" players to be "respectful" during the anthem, but there was no mention of requiring players to stand. If Kaepernick's protest left the door ajar, Goodell's response served to blow it from the hinges as a stampede of players decided to use the occasion to demonstrate whatever grievances they have against their own country.

Chi's disapproval is clear in his use of the word "limply." He is making a value judgment.

Kaepernick's stated reason for his protest is that minorities in the U.S. are being oppressed. But more specifically, he claimed that he could not stand for the flag while the police are murdering civilians and getting away with it. He also displayed his disdain for law enforcement by wearing socks featuring pigs in police hats during practice (and so far appears to have received no discipline from the league for impermissible gear).

Chi establishes that he understands why Kaepernick has done what Chi disapproves of. He also provides another instance of Kaepernick's ignoring the rules.

Whether anyone agrees with Kaepernick's sentiments, however, should be irrelevant to the NFL. This isn't a free speech issue as many sympathetic to Kaepernick's cause have claimed it to be. If Kaepernick made disparaging remarks toward gays, minorities or any ethnic group, he would've been fined and/or suspended. In fact, he was docked over $5,000 by the league in 2014 for allegedly uttering the N-word during a game toward Lamarr Houston of the Chicago Bears (although he was later judged not to have used the slur).

This is not a free speech issue, but a matter of breaking the rules.

This isn't about the First Amendment. While Congress shall make no law infringing on your freedom of expression, your employer damn well can impose what kind of conduct it expects when you're on company time while wearing company gear. The NFL—just like the NBA—has every right to demand that its players stand erect and make no fuss while the national anthem is playing.

If Congress does not have a law against Kaepernick's type of disrespect, the league can have rules.

By being derelict on this matter, though, Goodell risks his league alienating a healthy chunk of its paying customers—the fans and sponsors. The commissioner, already with an antagonistic relationship with the players and their union over what many see as his disciplinarian overreach, probably decided that he didn't want to pick another fight. Maybe he wished that this whole anthem business would go away quickly, especially had the shaky Kaepernick been cut by the 49ers.   10

But by suggesting that there are no rules, Goodell guaranteed that this issue would engulf his league—for the entire season and possibly beyond. And make no mistake, there's already a strong racial undercurrent in this chasm—so far, the protesting football players are black, and the most visceral reaction toward the protesters has come from the league's majority white fan base. The NFL has unwittingly allowed itself to become the biggest platform in America's summer of discontent, pitting certain minority groups against the police and their supporters.

What Goodell has done is not even condoned by some of the owners, who are ostensibly his bosses. And it is simply bad business. The NFL, already beset by problems with player safety and discipline, risks further erosion of its fan base, as reflected both in attendance and especially television ratings.

What the all-powerful commissioner should have told his players is this: Protest all you want, but do it on your own time and dime.

> By not enforcing rules, Goodell has made the matter worse.

> Chi's clearest statement of the problem

> Chi's claim of value: this is simply bad business.

Practice: Claim of Value

Movie reviews by definition support claims of value. Analyze the following review, focusing on its claim and support for that claim.

Grace Shines Past the Emotional Manipulations of "The Light between Oceans"
JUSTIN CHANG

There's an early scene in Derek Cianfrance's "The Light Between Oceans" that precisely captures the movie's tempestuous emotional undercurrents in miniature. It's the early 1920s, and Isabel Sherbourne, who has recently suffered a miscarriage, rebukes her husband, Tom, for having sent for a doctor to examine her—an assumption based on a misunderstanding that is soon resolved.

Yet that brief, violent collision of feeling—his quiet calm cushioning her fierce, implacable anger—echoes and reverberates through

Justin Chang is a film critic for the *Los Angeles Times* and a regular contributor to NPR's *Fresh Air Weekend* and *FilmWeek*, formerly chief film critic at *Variety*, and author of the book *FilmCraft: Editing* (2011).

the picture, meticulously foreshadowing the wrenching human dilemmas that loom on the horizon.

And what a horizon it is. The primary setting of this handsome, halfway-effective prestige weepie—adapted by Cianfrance from M.L. Stedman's 2012 debut novel—is the fictitious Janus Rock, a small island off the Australian coast. As lusciously photographed in a hundred different golden-pink sunset hues by the cinematographer Adam Arkapaw, the place is an almost unseemly repository of cinematic beauty, alive with the natural poetry—and at times, the inevitable kitsch—of windswept coastal vistas and gold-dappled waves lapping at the shore.

Tom and Isabel are very much of a piece with the movie's radiance, which is another way of saying that they are played by Michael Fassbender and Alicia Vikander, whose much-publicized off-screen relationship provides this somber movie with both a core of emotional truth and a juicy potential distraction. In this case, at least, truth largely wins out. The actors hurl themselves into their roles with sufficient commitment and feeling that you believe in Tom and Isabel completely, even when the creaky narrative machinery around them begins to trigger your skepticism.

5   It begins persuasively enough. The horrors of World War I are still fresh when Tom, a gentle, taciturn soul forever haunted by his memories of the Western Front, agrees to take a position as lighthouse keeper on Janus Rock. It's a job that suits his desire for a life of total isolation—that is, until he falls for Isabel, a spirited young woman from the mainland who renews his sense of joy and purpose. The two soon marry, and their life together on the island is one of blissful simplicity and simple bliss, marred only by a pair of pregnancies that are cut tragically short.

What follows is the story's most glaring (but not only) contrivance, one that calls forth much agitated camera movement and some churning, Philip Glass-like arpeggios from Alexandre Desplat's score: A dinghy washes ashore, carrying a man and an infant girl. The man is dead, but the baby lives, and Isabel, her grief abating in the presence of this divine miracle, persuades Tom to leave the discovery unreported in the lighthouse ledgers, so that they can raise the child as their own.

These fateful developments—a startling discovery, a criminal conspiracy hatched in the name of love—serve as a reminder that Cianfrance has a particular affinity for the big, dramatic turning point. His best-known earlier film, "Blue Valentine" (2010), arguably consisted of nothing but turning points as it shuttled back and forth through time, tracing the convulsive arc of a couple's difficult, doomed relationship.

The director's underappreciated follow-up, "The Place Beyond the Pines" (2012), adopted a more linear approach that nevertheless still found him pushing against the usual three-act strictures (befitting a student of the legendary avant-garde filmmakers Stan Brakhage and Phil Solomon).

"The Light Between Oceans" is both Cianfrance's first foray into a non-American period setting and his most traditionally constructed narrative, though he retains his interest in strategically placed flashbacks and shifting perspectives. As the foundling child, Lucy, grows into an adorable girl of 4 (at which point she is played by Florence Clery, a born scene-stealer), another major character emerges in the form of Hannah Potts (a fine Rachel Weisz), a grief-stricken widow who, like the Sherbournes, has her own unique set of war scars. Her mysterious connection to Tom, Isabel and Lucy is easy enough to figure out, even though it will take years—including one nearly three-decade leap into the future—for the characters' entwined fates to find their proper resolution.

10   Tom's function as keeper of the lighthouse flame is both literal and highly symbolic. He is more cursed than blessed by a level of superior knowledge that eludes the others, and in a drama that pivots on its characters' sudden triumphs and failures of conscience, Tom is the one who will ultimately guide the others to shore, no matter how much it may cost him, or how many fresh tears it may harvest from the audience. How effectively "The Light Between Oceans" earns your own tears—I misted up a little, almost out of a sense of duty—will likely depend on your susceptibility to the story's manifold manipulations, which are no less transparent for being so skillfully handled.

No movie lover, of course, can rightly claim to hate manipulation; even the purest, most spontaneous emotions are the product of a filmmaker's successful calculation, and "The Light Between Oceans," rooted somewhere between the grand tradition of classic melodrama and the seaside tearjerkers of Nicholas Sparks, need not apologize for lingering on Vikander's flurries of maternal anguish, Weisz's dignified sniffles and Fassbender's bravely choked-back sobs.

The deeper problem is that, in its overly insistent visual and musical touches, the film doesn't amplify so much as thwart the emotional integrity of what it's showing us.

Although he's stronger at realizing big moments than finding the connective tissue between those moments, Cianfrance tries to bridge the gaps as gracefully as possible, with an abundance of elegiac voice-over and tenderly observed scenes of a family dwelling together at the very edge of the world. These shots, with their natural lighting and fluttery camerawork, bespeak the subtle influence of the director Terrence Malick—as does the use of John Tavener's "Funeral Canticle," a magisterial choral piece that has been in heavy soundtrack rotation since it appeared in Malick's "The Tree of Life."

That film pointedly differentiated between the way of nature and the way of grace, between personal gratification and selfless compassion—a human struggle that "The Light Between Oceans" also embodies. Its most powerful moments are predicated less on the characters' sudden reversals of fortune than on their desperate, flailing attempts to do the right thing under impossible circumstances, and above all to show one another a decency they don't always deserve. In these fugitive moments, a movie that can seem hard to trust becomes surprisingly easy to forgive.

Reading and Discussion Questions

1. Notice Chang's use of plot summary. Explain how he uses plot summary instead of simply summarizing plot. Does he reveal too much of the plot or just enough?

2. This review would be classified as a mixed review because it comments on both strengths and weaknesses of the film. According to Chang, what are the film's good and bad points? Be specific. Look for specific sentences in the review that support your ideas.

3. Do the good points in the movie seem, for this reviewer, to outweigh the bad, or vice versa?

4. Can you find a single sentence that seems to summarize Chang's thesis? If not, formulate your own.

5. Consider how the review illustrates some of the conventions of film reviews:

   ■ In what verb tense is it written?

   ■ How does Chang work in information about the stars? the source of the story?

   ■ What different elements of filmmaking does Chang draw upon? He discusses plot, for instance. What else?

   ■ Is his thesis a claim of value, as it should be?

   ■ Has he supported his opinion about the film with specific references to it? Explain.

Claims of Policy

Claims of policy argue that certain conditions should exist. As the name suggests, they advocate adoption of policies or courses of action because problems have arisen that call for solution. Almost always, *should* or *ought to* or *must* is expressed or implied in the claim.

Claim: Voluntary prayer should be permitted in public schools.

Claim: A dress code ought to be introduced for all public high schools.

Claim: A law should permit sixteen-year-olds and parents to "divorce" each other in cases of extreme incompatibility.

Claim: Mandatory jail terms must be imposed for drunk driving violations.

Claim-of-policy arguments often begin by attempting to convince the audience that a problem exists. This will require a factual claim that offers data proving that present conditions are unsatisfactory. Claims of value may also be necessary to support the claim of fact. The policy itself is usually introduced after the problem is established; the policy is presented as a viable solution to the problem.

Consider this policy claim: *The time required for an undergraduate degree should be extended to five years.* Immediate agreement with this policy among student readers would certainly not be universal. Some students would not recognize a problem. They would say, "The college curriculum we have now is fine. There's no need for a change. Besides, we don't want to spend more time in school." First, then, the arguer would have to persuade a skeptical audience that there is a problem — that four years of college is no longer enough because the stock of knowledge in almost all fields of study continues to increase. The arguer would provide data to show that students today have many more choices in history, literature, and science than students had in those fields a generation ago and would also emphasize the value of greater knowledge and more schooling compared to the value of other goods the audience cherishes, such as earlier independence. Finally, the arguer would offer a plan for implementing

---

ARGUMENT ESSENTIALS

Claims of Policy

- Claims of policy argue for an action or a change in thinking.
- Claims of policy express or imply that something should or must be done.
- Claims of policy usually depend on a factual claim that establishes that present conditions are unacceptable.

---

the policy. The plan would have to consider initial psychological resistance, revision of the curriculum, costs of more instruction, and costs of lost production in the workforce. Most important, this policy would point out the benefits for both individuals and society if it were adopted.

In this example, we assumed that the reader would disagree that a problem existed. In many cases, however, the reader may agree that there is a problem but disagree with the arguer about the way to solve it. Most of us, no doubt, agree that we want to reduce or eliminate the following problems: misbehavior and vandalism in schools, drunk driving, crime on the streets, child abuse, pornography, pollution. But how should we go about solving those problems? What public policy will give us well-behaved, diligent students who never destroy school property? safe streets where no one is ever robbed or assaulted? loving homes where no child is ever mistreated? Some members of society would choose to introduce rules or laws that punish infractions so severely that wrongdoers would be unwilling or unable to repeat their offenses. Other members of society would prefer policies that attempt to rehabilitate or reeducate offenders through training, therapy, counseling, and new opportunities.

READING ARGUMENT

Seeing a Claim of Policy

The following essay has been annotated to highlight claims of policy.

College Life versus My Moral Code

ELISHA DOV HACK

Many people envy my status as a freshman at Yale College. My classmates and I made it through some fierce competition, and we are excited to have been accepted to one of the best academic and extracurricular programs in American higher education. I have an older brother who attended Yale, and I've heard from him what life at Yale is like.

Background that reveals his respect for Yale and his connection to it through his brother

He spent all his college years living at home because our parents are New Haven residents, and Yale's rules then did not require him to live in the dorms.

Elisha Dov Hack was a member of the Yale College freshman class of 1997. This article appeared on September 9, 1997, in the *New York Times*. The case brought by Hack and four other Jewish students remained in court until all but Hack had graduated. Hack went on to marry — and live off campus — before his 2003 graduation in engineering sciences.

But Yale's new regulations demand that I spend my freshman and sophomore years living in the college dormitories.

How residency rules have changed

I, two other freshmen, and two sophomores have refused to do this because life in the dorms, even on the floors Yale calls "single sex," is contrary to the fundamental principles we have been taught as long as we can remember — the principles of Judaism lived according to the Torah and 3,000-year-old rabbinic teachings. Unless Yale waives its residence requirement, we may have no choice but to sue the university to protect our religious way of life.

Establishes the problem

Bingham Hall, on the Yale quadrangle known as the Old Campus, is one of the dorms for incoming students. When I entered it two weeks ago during an orientation tour, I literally saw the handwriting on the wall. A sign titled "Safe Sex" told me where to pick up condoms on campus. Another sign touted 100 ways to make love without having sex, like "take a nap together" and "take a steamy shower together."

Examples of affronts to his religious beliefs

5   That, I am told, is real life in the dorms. The "freshperson" issue of the *Yale Daily News* sent to entering students contained a "Yale lexicon" defining *sexile* as "banishment from your dorm room because your roommate is having more fun than you." If you live in the dorms, you're expected to be part of the crowd, to accept these standards as the framework for your life.

Another example of accepted dorm standards

Can we stand up to classmates whose sexual morality differs from ours? We've had years of rigorous religious teaching, and we've watched and learned from our parents. We can hold our own in the intellectual debate that flows naturally from exchanges during and after class. But I'm upset and hurt by this requirement that I live in the dorms. Why is Yale — an institution that professes to be so tolerant and open-minded — making it particularly hard for students like us to maintain our moral standards through difficult college years?

Challenges whether Yale should make it difficult for students to maintain their morals outside of class

We are not trying to impose our moral standards on our classmates or on Yale. Our parents tell us that things were very different in college dormitories in their day and that in most colleges in the 1950s students who allowed guests of the opposite sex into their dorm rooms were subject to expulsion. We acknowledge that today's morality is not that of the 1950s. We are asking only that Yale give us the same permission to live off campus that it gives any lower classman who is married or at least twenty-one years old.

Tries to achieve middle ground by acknowledging that morality has changed, but argues that exceptions to the policy are already made

Claim of policy

Yale is proud of the fact that it has no "parietal rules" and that sexual morality is a student's own business. Maybe this is what Dean Richard H. Brodhead meant when he said that "Yale's residential colleges carry . . . a moral meaning." That moral meaning is, basically, "Anything goes." This morality is Yale's own residential religion, which it is proselytizing by force of its regulations.

Attacks the opposition by defining immorality as Yale's religion

We cannot, in good conscience, live in a place where women are permitted to stay overnight in men's rooms, and where visiting men can traipse through

Floors designated by gender
are not the solution.

the common halls on the women's floors — in various stages of undress — in the middle of the night. The dormitories on Yale's Old Campus have floors designated by gender, but there is easy access through open stairwells from one floor to the next.

The source of conflict

The moral message Yale's residences convey today is not one that our religion accepts. Nor is it a moral environment in which the five of us can spend our nights, or a moral surrounding that we can call home.   10

Uses Yale's own advertising
against it

Yale sent me a glossy brochure when it welcomed me as an entering student. It said, "Yale retains a deep respect for its early history and for the continuity that its history provides — a continuity based on constant reflection and reappraisal." Yale ought to reflect on and reappraise a policy that compels us to compromise our religious principles.

Follow Up

What happened to the lawsuit to which Hack refers? It was tied up in court until 2001, when all of the students involved except Hack had graduated. The students lost the legal battle at all levels, primarily because their case depended on their proving that having to live in a residence hall constituted discrimination based on religion. The university successfully argued that the residence requirement was not discriminatory. Hack graduated from Yale in 2003. All five students chose to live in apartments during their first two years while paying full housing fees for dorm rooms they never occupied.

Practice: Claim of Policy

Read the following essay, and answer the questions at the end.

Your Toxic Beauty Regime
KIARA VENTURA

As I flipped through *Seventeen* magazine, I stopped to look at an ad for Neutrogena's Pink Grapefruit Oil-Free Acne Wash. I'd been getting annoyed at having random pimples on my face, so I was instantly gripped by it. I smelled the scratch-and-stiff that came with the advertisement and agreed that it was an "uplifting blast of naturally derived grapefruit." As added bonuses, two actresses I like, Hayden Panettiere and Miranda Cosgrove, are the brand spokespeople,

and when you purchase the product, Neutrogena will donate $1 to something called Global Giving.

When she wrote this article, Kiara Ventura was a participant in a special writing program offered by Youth Communication. She is now a student at New York University, studying Art History, Criticism, and Conservation, and Journalism. The article was posted in the September/October 2012 issue of *YCteen* at youthcomm.org.

So when I buy this product my skin will be as clear as Miranda's and I will help out a charity? "Wow!" I thought, "that sounds like a plan!" But then I thought a little more, and one thing stopped me from running to my local Rite-Aid and buying a magical bottle of this stuff—the worry that some of the ingredients in it could be harmful.

I had just read a book called *No More Dirty Looks*, which takes a critical look at the beauty products industry, and I'd interviewed one of the authors, Siobhan O'Connor. During the interview, my friends and I brought in some personal care products like hand lotion, styling gel, deodorant, and shampoo for her to evaluate.

When she started reading the labels on our products, she showed us that many of the ingredients were chemicals that are carcinogens (which means they can cause cancer), neurotoxins (poisons that can mess up your nervous system), and endocrine disrupters (which can screw up how your body regulates hormones). It was hard to believe that we use products every day that could potentially damage our health.

Serious Risks

5   Health problems linked to ingredients in common products include everything from acne and rashes to brain damage, cancer, and nervous system damage. Young people and pregnant women should be especially wary because the harmful ingredients can hurt developing bodies. For example, "scientists are finding that women with high levels of certain chemicals in their blood and urine—BPAs and phthalates are the two big ones—are having babies with genital birth defects in baby boys at much higher rates than people who have low levels of these chemicals," O'Connor said.

So why would companies knowingly put harmful stuff in their products? Well, apparently it's just good for business. These chemicals are generally cheaper and less likely to spoil than natural ingredients, and they give products that feeling, smell, and quality that we consumers love. Certain chemicals make our shampoo lather up nicely, give our perfume that wonderful smell, and make our lotion smooth enough that it absorbs into our skin in seconds. But the truth is that some of the chemicals that improve our consumer experience can hurt our health.

Companies say that the dose of bad chemicals is so tiny that they're not dangerous, which is a convincing argument until you think about how many different products we use—each with its own trace amount of bad chemicals. Most people use about twelve to twenty products a day, including toothpaste, face wash, lotion, perfume, deodorant, ChapStick, soap, shampoo, conditioner, shaving cream, nail polish—and let's not even get started with makeup.

Just imagine how many chemicals our skin absorbs and our noses inhale each and every day of our lives. One product might not be so bad, but some would argue that the cumulative effect of all those chemicals—which is called "bioaccumulation"—is not worth the risk. In addition, no one really knows what constitutes a safe level of many of these chemicals, or how all the chemicals we use interact with each other. Unfortunately, this is something we don't usually think about—until something bad happens.

A Bad Reaction

The authors of *No More Dirty Looks*, best friends Siobhan O'Connor and Alexandra Spunt, first came up with the idea for the book after they got a popular keratin hair-straightening treatment at a salon. O'Connor recalled, "Our eyes were watering, we were coughing, I ended up getting a weird, red rash on my scalp and the back of my neck that has come and gone since then. And it was a reaction, we found out after the fact, to formaldehyde, which is one of the ingredients used to straighten our hair."

10 Formaldehyde (yes, the same stuff used to embalm dead people) is typically used as a preservative in things like nail polish, antiperspirant, makeup, bubble bath, shampoo, baby lotions, and hair dyes. It's also a known carcinogen. It's not that once you use these products you will definitely get cancer. Rather, they add up over a long period, which can increase risk.

After their reaction to the hair straightening treatment, the authors began researching how beauty products are regulated by the FDA (Food and Drug Administration). Their book provides a little history lesson that will not make you snooze. "The laws that govern cosmetics were written in 1938, and it is 2011 and they've barely changed," even though tons of new chemicals and products are being produced every year, O'Connor said.

Scary Secret Ingredients

Because there aren't many laws regulating what companies put into their products, the government has very little power to ensure that the stuff you see on the shelves is safe.

"Let's say we're all using lotion on our bodies and our skin's turning red, or we're getting rashes, or maybe our kids are having asthma reactions, getting really sick when they smell [a certain product] — the FDA cannot tell the company [that makes the product], 'You're not allowed to sell that.' It's not within their rights to do that, which is crazy," O'Connor said. The U.S. is clearly lagging behind in this area: Europe has banned more than 1,000 ingredients for use in personal care products while the United States has only banned nine.

One of the major issues that O'Connor warned us about is a sneaky ingredient called "fragrance." In the book, the authors tell us the story of Betty Bridges, who couldn't breathe when she came in contact with a mysterious substance that seemed to be in several products she used. When she called up the manufacturers to try to figure out what, exactly, she was allergic to, they wouldn't reveal what chemicals were in the fragrances they used in their products.

You see, "fragrance" isn't one particular chemi- 15 cal. It is just a word representing many chemicals. Companies don't list the specific ingredients they use to make their products smell good, because they consider this their secret formula (like SpongeBob's "krabby patty formula"). They don't want other companies to steal the recipe and make the same scent.

To protect companies' competitive advantages, the FDA allows them to hide the ingredients in "fragrance," so we basically don't know what chemicals we're using on ourselves. And unfortunately, "fragrance" is in almost everything — even in my friend's Purell Hand Sanitizer. Knowing this made me want to go "all natural" and stop buying products full of chemicals—but figuring out which products are healthy was harder than I thought.

Natural—or Nasty?

In the beauty section of any pharmacy, you see bottles of hair care products decorated with pictures of plants, fruits, and natural scenery. They may claim to be "natural" or "clean," which would make you think that they are safe, or free of synthetic chemicals, right?

Well, the authors warn us that even if a product says "organic" or "sulfate free," it doesn't mean that it is completely innocent. For example, while evaluating a green tea-scented Dove soap my friend brought to the interview, O'Connor pointed out, "There's no green tea anywhere in the whole thing!" In fact, it contained "fragrance" and something called propylene glycol, which animal studies have shown can affect the brain and nervous system and cause endocrine disruption.

"The illusion of something natural sells," said O'Connor. "They're trading on the idea that we don't know any better, because we don't."

20   To help us out, the book lists some dangerous ingredients to look out for (as does our story "Buyer Beware!"), and provides information about alternatives that are made from safer ingredients. O'Connor admitted that natural products can be less appealing in some ways: "Sometimes the packaging looks a little hippy-dippy; it's not as pretty, not as appealing — but it's loaded with ingredients that are ultra-great for your skin and body."

Even if a natural product doesn't feel as good as an artificial one — for example, some natural lotions will be a bit greasier than conventional ones, and natural shampoos will not create that satisfying lather because they don't contain the chemicals that create suds — just know that it is still doing its job and not exposing you to harmful chemicals.

Beauty Background Check

There are also a lot of online resources to help you investigate your beauty products. For example, the fantastically useful Web site ewg.org/skindeep gives products a rating from 1 to 10, and provides information about potential health hazards associated with the product's ingredients. If you are concerned about your products and your health, I recommend the site. You may be surprised by what you find.

In fact, when I looked up that awesome-looking grapefruit-scented Neutrogena face wash, I found out that it had some pretty toxic stuff in it. According to the Web site, it was a "high health concern," mostly because of two ingredients: fragrance and something called PEG-80 sorbitan laurate, which it said could possibly cause "organ system toxicity."

The advertisement for this face wash made it seem so positive, clean, and fresh, but I guess there is an ugly side to most products these days. So, the next time I go to my local pharmacy looking for a new face wash, I will have my glasses on and the bad ingredient list in hand!

Reading and Discussion Questions

1. Remember that a claim of policy may build on claims of fact and of value. What is Ventura's claim of policy? How does she use factual information and evaluation to build toward that claim?

2. One of the strengths of Ventura's article is its specific support. What are some of the most convincing supporting details that she provides?

3. Ventura makes good use of an authority on her subject whom she had interviewed. She also makes use of her own experience. In what sense is she also an "authority" on her subject? Do you find the first person portions of the article effective? Why, or why not?

WRITER'S GUIDE
Stating Your Claim

Whether you are making a claim of fact, a claim of value, or a claim of policy, your claim is the **thesis** of your argument. Here are some tips for writing an effective claim.

All Types of Claims

- Keep your audience and purpose in mind. Whom you are writing for, and why? What are you trying to convince them of? What do you want them to do? To gain your readers' interest, be sure to let them know how the issue pertains to them.

Claims of Fact

- Be sure you will be able to find sufficient supporting evidence to back up your claim.
- Use qualifiers such as *generally, usually,* and *probably* to limit a claim; avoid using words such as *always, every, all,* and *never,* which do not allow for exceptions.
- Be aware of opposing viewpoints, and be prepared to refute them.

Claims of Value

- When writing about an aesthetic issue, be sure you understand the criteria used to measure standards in the field you are writing about: sports, dance, music, photography, and so on.
- When writing about a moral issue, be careful not to alienate or offend readers who may espouse opposing views on the subject.
- As much as possible, provide strong evidence and good reasons for your claims of value, and avoid dogma.

Claims of Policy

- Begin by proving that the problem exists by employing a claim of fact with supporting evidence. (You may also need to include a claim of value to convince readers that something must be done.)
- Use special care to frame your claim of policy in a way that readers will not immediately reject. Depending on your topic, readers may have a high level of emotional involvement on the matter.
- Be aware that alternative solutions to the problem may exist, and be prepared to explain why your proposal is superior.
- Have realistic expectations about what you hope to achieve — what your audience can actually do about the situation. Sometimes you may argue for people to vote a certain way, sign a petition, or write letters to officials. At other times, the most you might hope to accomplish is to get your audience to consider the situation from your perspective.

Assignments for Claims

Reading and Discussion Questions

1. Find several recent print ads, and explain what their claims are.

2. Notice that Josh Levs's essay "Loaded Language Poisons Gun Debate" does not take a side in the debate. Choose a current controversial issue, and write a claim of fact about it.

3. Locate a movie review online or in hard copy that has a clear claim and is based on clear evaluative criteria. Choose a review that is an essay, not just a single paragraph. Bring it to class, and share it with your class or group. By looking at a range of different reviews, come to some conclusions about the sort of criteria used in making judgment calls about movies and what sort of claims provide good thesis statements for reviews. What are some other characteristics that all or most good movie reviews share?

4. Consider one or more of your school's policies that you would like to see changed. In your opinion, what is wrong with the policy as it currently stands? What exactly would you recommend be done to improve the situation?

Writing Suggestions

1. Choose a controversial issue in the field in which you are majoring or one in which you might major. Practice differentiating among the three types of claims by writing a claim of fact, a claim of value, and a claim of policy on that issue.

2. Choose one of the claims of fact you wrote for #2 above, and write an essay supporting it.

3. Choose a recent print ad, and write an essay explaining how text and pictures work together in it to support a claim.

4. Write a review of a recent movie. Your thesis will be a claim of value.

5. Write a review of a recent play, concert, art exhibit, or similar cultural event. Your thesis will be a claim of value.

6. Using Elisha Dov Hack's essay as a model, write an essay suggesting a change at your school. Write it in the form of a letter to your school's newspaper.

RESEARCH ASSIGNMENT **Acknowledging Reliable Authorities**

The next page includes a list of quotations and the names of those who are quoted. Do some research to find out what gives the person quoted the authority to speak knowledgeably on the subject of the quotation. Then work the information you found into a lead-in to the quotation, as in the example.

Example

"We are promoting human rights by building homes for people who don't have them."—Jimmy Carter

"We are promoting human rights by building homes for people who don't have them," explains former president Jimmy Carter, who has been involved with Habitat for Humanity International since 1984 and who, with his wife, leads its Jimmy and Rosalynn Carter Work Project one week each year.

1. "Innovation has nothing to do with how many R&D dollars you have. When Apple came up with the Mac, IBM was spending at least 100 times more on R&D. It's not about money. It's about the people you have, how you're led, and how much you get it."—Steve Jobs

2. "If gun laws in fact worked, the sponsors of this type of legislation should have no difficulties drawing upon long lists of crime rates reduced by such legislation. That they cannot do so after a century and a half of trying—that they must sweep under the rug the southern attempts at gun control in the 1870–1910 period, the northeastern attempts in the 1920–1939 period, the attempts at both Federal and State levels in 1965–1976—establishes the repeated, complete, and inevitable failure of gun laws to control serious crime."—Orrin G. Hatch

3. "The old argument that the networks and other 'media elites' have a liberal bias is so blatantly true that it's hardly worth discussing anymore. No, we don't sit around in dark corners and plan strategies on how we're going to slant the news. We don't have to. It comes naturally to most reporters."—Bernard Goldberg

4. "You built a factory and it turned into something terrific or a great idea—God bless! Keep a hunk of it. But part of the underlying social contract is you take a hunk of that and pay forward for the next kid who comes along."—Elizabeth Warren

5. "It takes more courage to send men into battle than to fight the battle yourself."—Colin Powell

6. "I want to state upfront, unequivocally and without doubt: I do not believe that any racial, ethnic, or gender group has an advantage in sound judging. I do believe that every person has an equal opportunity to be a good and wise judge, regardless of their background or life experiences."—Sonia Sotomayor

bits

To see what you are learning about argumentation applied to the latest world and national news, read our *Bits* blog, "Argument and the Headlines," at **blogs.bedfordstmartins.com/bits.**

Support

S upport for a claim represents the answer to the question "What have you got to go on?"[1] All claims in an argument — whether of fact, of value, or of policy — must be supported. Sometimes an author will use his or her own experience as support for a claim. At other times, authors may conduct interviews, field research, lab experiments, or surveys to obtain support for their position. As a student, you will most likely turn primarily to print and electronic sources for your support. (See Chapter 12 for a full discussion of finding sources.)

The emphasis in providing support is on the relationship between writer and audience — the rhetorical leg of the communications triangle:

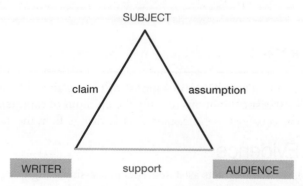

You are presenting **evidence** to an audience in hopes of convincing that audience to see the subject in the same way you do. You may remember from the discussion of Aristotelian rhetoric in Chapter 1 that arguments rely on *ethos, logos,* and *pathos* for their effectiveness. You must present your evidence and yourself in such a way that your audience finds you trustworthy (*ethos*). You also have to consider what evidence your audience will find convincing — what

---

[1] Stephen Toulmin, *The Uses of Argument* (Cambridge: Cambridge University Press, 1958), p. 98.

examples, statistics, and opinions will appeal to them logically (*logos*). You are using emotional appeal (*pathos*) in conjunction with other types of appeal when you appeal to your audience's needs and values.

WRITER'S GUIDE
Using Support

1. In deciding how much support you need for your claim, it is always a good idea to assume that you are addressing an audience that may be at least slightly hostile to that claim. Those who already agree with you do not need convincing.

2. Keep a mental, if not a written, list of the different types of support you use in an essay. Few essays will use all of the different types of support, but being aware of all the possibilities will prevent you from forgetting to draw on one or more types of support that may advance your argument.

3. In that checklist of types of support, don't forget that there are two main categories: evidence and appeals to needs and values. Appeals to needs and values will generally need the reinforcement that comes from more objective forms of evidence, but the two in combination can often provide the strongest case for your claim.

4. Remember that you will usually need to give credit to your source(s) for information you use as support. See Chapter 14 for complete treatment of how to document sources.

Evidence

When authors provide evidence in support of their claim, they primarily use facts, examples, statistics, opinions (usually the opinions of experts), and images.

Factual Evidence

In Chapter 6, we defined facts as statements possessing a high degree of public acceptance. Some facts can be verified by experience alone.

- Eating too much will make us sick.
- We can get from Hopkinton to Boston in a half hour by car.
- In the Northern Hemisphere, it is colder in December than in July.

The experience of any individual is limited in both time and space, so we must accept as fact thousands of assertions about the world that we ourselves can never verify. Thus we accept the report that human beings landed on the moon in 1969 because we trust those who can verify it.

Facts can provide important support for a claim, as shown in the example here. The claim has been underlined.

<u>Nuclear energy has a wide-ranging value proposition.</u> Nuclear energy

- produces large amounts of electricity at industry-leading reliability and efficiency levels
- is affordable and has forward price stability that will be important as our economy continues to bounce back
- provides nearly two-thirds of all carbon-free electricity
- maintains grid stability through voltage support
- contributes to the fuel and technology diversity that is one of the bedrock characteristics of a reliable and resilient electric sector
- is an economic driver through high-paying jobs and taxes in the communities and states where they are located.[2]

Factual evidence appears most frequently as examples and statistics, which are a numerical form of examples.

Examples

Examples are the most familiar kind of factual evidence. In addition to providing support for the truth of a generalization, examples can enliven otherwise dense or monotonous prose. In the following paragraph, the writer supports the claim (underlined in the topic sentence) by offering a series of specific examples.

> <u>You can hardly go anywhere these days and not see or hear an advertisement for college.</u> Throughout Concourse B at Denver International Airport, nearly every other advertisement greeting passengers is for a higher-education institution: Colorado State University, the University of Wyoming, Colorado Mesa College, and the University of Northern Colorado. Airline magazines are filled with promotions for executive MBA programs. At least once an hour on the all-news radio station in Washington, DC, listeners hear about the degree in cybersecurity offered by a University of Maryland campus. Sunday newspapers are filled with details on certificate programs in the latest hot job fields, such as social media and sustainability. Anyone checking e-mail on Google will see ads pop up for the creative writing program at Southern New Hampshire University or the political management degree at George Washington University.[3]

---

[2] Marvin S. Fertel, "United States Energy Association Briefing," Nuclear Energy Institute. nei. org, 16 Jan. 2014. Web.

[3] Jeffrey J. Selingo, *College (Un)Bound: The Future of Higher Education and What It Means for Students* (New York: New Harvest, 2013), p. 6.

Hypothetical examples, which create imaginary situations for the audience and encourage them to visualize what might happen under certain circumstances, can also be effective. The following paragraph illustrates the use of hypothetical examples. (The author is describing megaschools, high schools with more than two thousand students, and her claim is underlined.)

> And in schools that big there is inevitably a critical mass of kids who are neither jocks nor artists nor even nerds, kids who are nothing at all, nonentities in their own lives. . . . The creditable ballplayer who might have made the team in a smaller school is edged out by better athletes. The artist who might have had work hung in a smaller school is supplanted by abler talents. And the disaffected and depressed boy who might have found a niche, or a friend, or a teacher who noticed, falls between the cracks. Sometimes he quietly drops out. Sometimes he quietly passes through. And sometimes he comes to school with a gun.[4]

All claims about vague or abstract terms would be boring or unintelligible without examples to illuminate them. For example, if you claim that a movie contains "unusual sound effects," you will certainly have to describe some of the effects to convince the reader that your generalization can be trusted.

Statistics

Statistics express information in numbers. In the following example, statistics have been used to support the authors' claim, which has been underlined.

> To the kids growing up in a housing project on Chicago's south side, crack dealing was a glamour profession. For many of them, the job of gang boss — highly visible and highly lucrative — was easily the best job they thought they had access to. Had they grown up under different circumstances, they might have thought about becoming economists or writers. But in the neighborhood where J. T.'s gang operated, the path to a decent legitimate job was practically invisible. Fifty-six percent of the neighborhood's children lived below the poverty line (compared to a national average of 18 percent). Seventy-eight percent came from single-parent homes. Fewer than 5 percent of the neighborhood's adults had a college degree; barely one in three adult men worked at all. The neighborhood's median income was about $15,000 a year, well less than half the U.S. average. During the years that Venkatesh lived with J. T.'s gang, foot soldiers often asked his help in landing what they called "a good job": working as a janitor at the University of Chicago.[5]

---

[4] Anna Quindlen, "The Problem of the Megaschool," *Newsweek*, March 26, 2001, p. 68.
[5] Steven D. Levitt and Stephen J. Dubner, *Freakonomics: A Rogue Economist Explores the Hidden Side of Everything* (New York: William Morrow, 2005), p. 105.

Statistics are more effective in comparisons that indicate whether a quantity is relatively large or small and sometimes even whether a reader should interpret the result as gratifying or disappointing. For example, if a novice gambler were told that for every dollar wagered in a state lottery, 50 percent goes back to the players as prizes, would the gambler be able to conclude that the percentage is high or low? Would he be able to choose between playing the state lottery and playing a casino game? Unless he had more information, probably not. But if he were informed that in casino games, the return to the players is over 90 percent and in slot machines and racetracks the return is around 80 percent, the comparison would enable him to evaluate the meaning of the 50 percent return in the state lottery and even to make a decision about where to gamble his money.[6]

Comparative statistics are also useful for measurements over time. For instance, the following statistics show what comparisons based on BMI, or body mass index, reveal about how Miss America contestants have changed over the years.

> Miss America contestants have become increasingly thinner over the past 75 years. In the 1920s, contestants had BMIs in the normal range of 20–25. Since then, pageant winners' body weights have decreased steadily to a level about 12 percent below levels from the mid-1900s. Since 1970, nearly all of the winners have had BMIs below the healthy range, with some as low as 16.9, a BMI that would meet part of the diagnostic criteria for anorexia nervosa.[7]

Diagrams, tables, charts, and graphs can make clear the relations among many sets of numbers. Such charts and diagrams enable readers to grasp the information more easily than if it were presented in paragraph form. For example, Figure 7.1 shows bar graphs used by the Census Bureau to explore the issue of high school education attainment among selected groups. Figure 7.2 is a type of pie chart compiled by the Congressional Budget Office to show the 2011 U.S. Federal Budget.

Expert Opinion

Based on their reading of the facts, experts express opinions on a variety of controversial subjects: whether capital punishment is a deterrent to crime; whether legalization of marijuana will lead to an increase in its use; whether children, if left untaught, will grow up honest and cooperative; whether sex education courses will result in less sexual activity and fewer illegitimate births. The interpretations of the data are often profoundly important because they influence social policy and affect our lives directly and indirectly.

---

[6] Curt Suphee, "Lotto Baloney," *Harper's*, July 1983, p. 201.

[7] S. Rubenstein and B. Caballero, "Is Miss America an Undernourished Role Model?" *JAMA* (2000), p. 1569. Qtd. in Jillian Croll, "Body Image and Adolescents," *Guidelines for Adolescent Nutrition Services*, J. Stang and M. Story, eds. (2005). June 9, 2007. http://www.epi.umn.edu/let/pubs/adol_book.shtm.

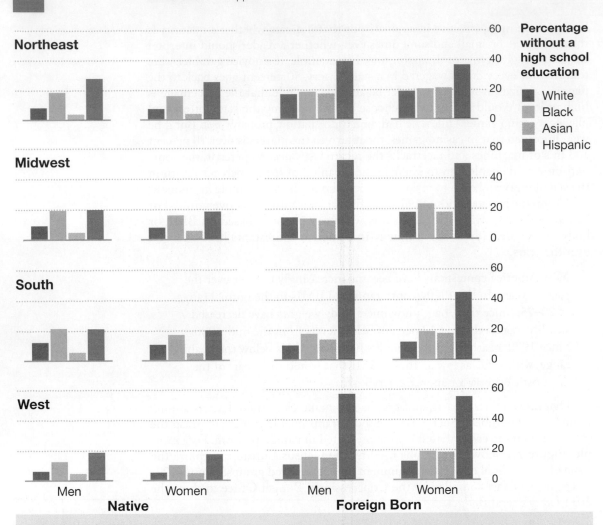

FIGURE 7.1 Without a High School Education. U.S. Census Bureau (census.gov/dataviz/visualizations/035)

For the problems mentioned above, the opinions of people recognized as authorities are more reliable than those of people who have neither thought about nor done research on the subject. But opinions may also be offered by student writers in areas in which they are knowledgeable. If you were asked, for example, to defend or refute the statement that work has advantages for teenagers, you could call on your own experience and that of your friends to support your claim. You can also draw on your experience to write convincingly about your special interests.

One opinion, however, is not always as good as another. The value of any opinion depends on the quality of the evidence and the trustworthiness of the person offering it. Clayton M. Christensen and Henry J. Eyring are both experts on the subject of education. Christensen holds a named professorship

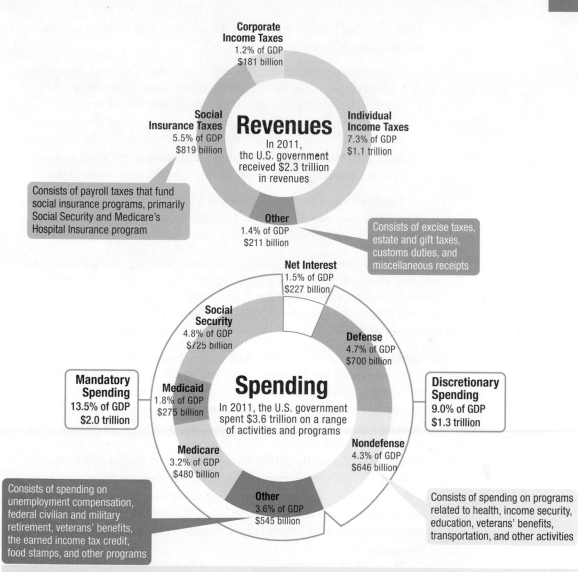

Corporate Income Taxes
1.2% of GDP
$181 billion

Social Insurance Taxes
5.5% of GDP
$819 billion

Revenues
In 2011, the U.S. government received $2.3 trillion in revenues

Individual Income Taxes
7.3% of GDP
$1.1 trillion

Consists of payroll taxes that fund social insurance programs, primarily Social Security and Medicare's Hospital Insurance program

Other
1.4% of GDP
$211 billion

Consists of excise taxes, estate and gift taxes, customs duties, and miscellaneous receipts

Net Interest
1.5% of GDP
$227 billion

Social Security
4.8% of GDP
$725 billion

Defense
4.7% of GDP
$700 billion

Mandatory Spending
13.5% of GDP
$2.0 trillion

Medicaid
1.8% of GDP
$275 billion

Spending
In 2011, the U.S. government spent $3.6 trillion on a range of activities and programs

Discretionary Spending
9.0% of GDP
$1.3 trillion

Medicare
3.2% of GDP
$480 billion

Nondefense
4.3% of GDP
$646 billion

Consists of spending on unemployment compensation, federal civilian and military retirement, veterans' benefits, the earned income tax credit, food stamps, and other programs

Other
3.6% of GDP
$545 billion

Consists of spending on programs related to health, income security, education, veterans' benefits, transportation, and other activities

FIGURE 7.2 The U.S. Federal Budget. Congressional Budget Office (cbo.gov/publication/42636)

in Business Administration at the Harvard Business School, and Eyring has been director of Brigham Young University's MBA program and is currently an administrator at BYU–Idaho. In spite of their own credentials, when they wrote their book *The Innovative University: Changing the DNA of Higher Education from the Inside Out* (2011), they were careful to establish the expertise of those whose ideas they drew upon:

No one could doubt that U. S. Education Secretary Margaret Spellings meant business. In upbraiding the nation's universities and colleges, the

2006 report of her commission on the future of higher education used the language of business:

> What we have learned over the last year makes clear that American higher education has become what, in the business world, would be called a mature enterprise: increasingly risk-averse, at times self-satisfied, and unduly expensive. It is an enterprise that has yet to successfully confront the impact of globalization, rapidly evolving technologies, an increasingly diverse and aging population, and an evolving marketplace characterized by new needs and paradigms. . . .

The Spellings Commission was not a lone voice of criticism in 2006. That same year two distinguished academics, Derek Bok and Harry Lewis, both of Harvard, published books critical of higher education.[8]

What happens when authoritative sources disagree? Such disagreement is probably most common in the social sciences. They are called the "soft" sciences precisely because a consensus about conclusions in these areas is more difficult to reach than in the natural and physical sciences. The following two paragraphs show experts disagreeing over the reason for rises in college tuition costs.

Suppose we asked the president of a public university to explain what he or she sees. Very likely that president would point out the fact that tuition and fees tend to rise very rapidly after decreases in growth in the overall economy. Your attention would be drawn to the rapid tuition increases following the episodes of negative GDP growth in 1982 and 1991 and the very slow GDP growth in 2001. Even the decade of falling tuition in the 1970s was interrupted by the oil shock years around 1974. The university president would say something like this: "When the overall economy slows down, state tax collections fall, and states cut appropriations for universities. As a result public universities have to resort to large tuition increases to make up for lost public funding."

If we asked Representatives Boehner and McKeon to comment on the data, they would focus on an entirely different phenomenon. In *The College Cost Crisis* they say "the facts show tuition increases have persisted regardless of the circumstances such as the economy or state funding, and have far outpaced inflation year after year, regardless of whether the economy has been stumbling or thriving." Essentially, they are looking at the fact that after 1980 the "real" growth in college tuition and fees always has been positive. This means that tuition and fees always have grown more rapidly than the CPI (Consumer Price Index).

---

[8] Clayton M. Christensen and Henry J. Eyring, *The Innovative University: Changing the DNA of Higher Education from the Inside Out* (Hoboken, NJ: Jossie-Bass, 2011), pp. 4-5.

Representatives Boehner and McKeon also claim they know why this has happened. They place the blame squarely on "wasteful spending by college and university management."[9]

But even in the natural and physical sciences, where the results of observation and experiment are more conclusive, we encounter heated differences of opinion. A popular argument concerns the extinction of the dinosaurs. Was it the effect of an asteroid striking the earth? or widespread volcanic activity? or a cooling of the planet? All these theories have their champions among the experts. A debate of more immediate relevance concerns the possible dangers of genetically modified foods, as distinguished from foods modified by traditional breeding practices. Jeffrey M. Smith, director of the Institute for Responsible Technology and author of *Seeds of Deception: Exposing Industry and Government Lies about the Safety of the Genetically Engineered Foods You're Eating* (2003) and *Genetic Roulette: The Documented Health Risks of Genetically Engineered Foods* (2007), presents a different perspective on the issue:

> In addition to unintended changes in the DNA, there are health risks from other aspects of GM crops. When a transgene starts to function in the new cell, for example, it may produce proteins that are different from the one intended. The amino acid sequence may be wrong, the protein's shape may be different, and molecular attachments may make the protein harmful. The fact that proteins act differently in new plant environments was made painfully clear to developers of GM peas in Australia. They cancelled their ten-year, $2 million project after their GM protein, supposedly identical to the harmless natural version, caused inflammatory responses in mice. Subtle, unpredicted changes in molecular attachments might have similarly triggered deadly allergic reactions in people if the peas were put on the market.[10]

In 2000, at a hearing before the U.S. Senate Committee on Foreign Relations, Subcommittee on International Economic Policy, Export and Trade Promotion, Roger N. Beachy made the following statement. Beachy produced the world's first genetically modified tomato and in 2009–2011 was President Obama's director of the National Institute for Food and Agriculture.

> Agricultural producers in the U.S. have a growing awareness of their duties as keepers of the environment; many are actively reducing the use of harmful agrichemicals while maintaining highly efficient production of safe foods. Plant scientists and agriculturists have developed better crops and improved production methods that have

---

[9] Robert B. Archibald and David H. Feldman, *Why Does College Cost So Much?* (New York: Oxford UP, 2010), p. 9.

[10] Jeffrey M. Smith, *Genetic Roulette: The Documented Health Risks of Genetically Engineered Foods* (St. Louis: Yes!, 2007). Web.

enabled farmers to reduce the use of insecticides and chemicals that control certain diseases. Methods such as integrated pest management, no-till or low-till agriculture have been tremendously important in this regard. Some of the success has come through the judicious application of biotechnology to develop new varieties of crops that resist insects and that tolerate certain herbicides. For example, biotechnology was used to develop varieties of cotton and corn that are resistant to attack by cotton bollworm and corn borer. These varieties have allowed farmers to reduce the use of chemical insecticides by between 1.5 and 2 mil gallons, while retaining or increasing crop yields. Crops that are tolerant to certain "friendly" herbicides have increased no-till and low-till agriculture, reducing soil erosion and building valuable topsoil to ensure the continued productivity of our valuable agricultural lands.[11]

How can you choose between authorities who disagree? If you have applied the tests discussed so far and discovered that one source is less qualified by training and experience or makes claims with little support or appears to be biased in favor of one interpretation, you will have no difficulty in rejecting that person's opinion. If conflicting sources prove to be equally reliable in all respects, then you should continue reading other authorities to determine whether a greater number of experts support one opinion rather than another. Although numbers alone, even of experts, don't guarantee the truth, nonexperts have little choice but to accept the authority of the greater number until evidence to the contrary is forthcoming. Finally, if you are unable to decide between competing sources of evidence, you may conclude that the argument must remain unsettled. Such an admission is not a failure; after all, such questions are considered controversial because even the experts cannot agree, and such questions are often the most interesting to consider and argue about.

Images

Evidence does not always have to be verbal. Images can also provide support for an argument. Before there were photographs, paintings and even crude cave drawings provided evidence of the cultures that produced them. A man named Mathew Brady captured the reality of war through his photos of the Civil War and thus earned the title, the Father of Photojournalism. Crime scene photos and video surveillance tapes provide evidence on screen and in real life. In April 2013, the Boston Marathon bombers were identified

---

[11] "World Renowned Plant Scientist Dr. Roger N. Beachy Testifies before U.S. Senate Committee to Explain the Role of Agricultural Biotechnology in the Battle against Poverty and Hunger in Developing Countries," agbioworld.org, 12 Jul. 2000.

FIGURE 7.3 A police shooting. Tulsa Police Department via AP

through photos from more than one source, some of them first circulated via reddit.com and Facebook.

Figure 7.3 is a picture released by the Tulsa Police Department. It is from a police video taken from a helicopter Sept. 16, 2016, of Terence Crutcher, left, with his arms up as he walked next to his stalled SUV before he was shot and killed by one of the police officers. The video has brought into question whether the officer was justified. Videos such as the one this still is taken from and those taken routinely now by dash-cams can be critical support in such a situation.

Images are also critical as evidence in scientific research. Proof of a hypothesis often takes the form of plants and animals viewed in the wild or in the lab, of cells viewed through a microscope, or of distant objects viewed through a telescope. The photo shown in Figure 7.4 was released by NASA in December 2013, as possible evidence of liquid water active on Mars.

50 m

FIGURE 7.4 Martian surface. NASA/JPL-Caltech/ University of Arizona.

RESEARCH SKILL ▶ Evaluating Evidence

Before you begin to write, you must determine whether the evidence you have chosen to support your claim is sound. Can it convince your readers?

Evaluation of Factual Evidence

- **Are the facts up to date?** The importance of up-to-date information depends on the subject. For many of the subjects you write about, recent research and scholarship will be important, even decisive, in proving the sound-ness of your data. "New" does not always mean "best," but in fields where research is ongoing — education, psychology, technology, medicine, and all the natural and physical sci-ences — you should be sensitive to the dates of the research.

- **Is the factual evidence sufficient?** The amount of factual evidence you need depends on the complexity of the subject and the length of your paper. Given the relative brevity of most of your assignments, you will need to be selective. For the claim that indoor pollu-tion is a serious problem, one supporting fact would obviously not be enough. For a 750- to 1,000-word paper, three or four supporting facts would probably be sufficient. The choice of evidence should reflect different aspects of the problem: in this case, different sources of indoor pollution — gas stoves, fireplaces, kerosene heaters, insulation — and the conse-quences for health.

- **Are the facts relevant?** All the factual evi-dence should, of course, contribute to the development of your argument. Also keep in mind that not all readers will agree on what is relevant. Is the unsavory private life of a politi-cian relevant to his or her performance in office? If you want to prove that a politician is unfit to serve because of his or her private activities, you may first have to convince some members of the audience that private activities are rele-vant to public service.

Examples

- **Are the examples representative?** This question emphasizes your responsibility to choose examples that are typical of all the examples you do not use. If you were trying to build a case about the economic impact of illegal immigrants in the United States but took your statistics from Maine, Vermont, Montana, North Dakota, and West Virginia, your sample would not be representative because these states have the smallest numbers of illegal immigrants, estimated to be less than 0.5 percent of the population for each of the five states.

- **Are the examples consistent with the experience of the audience?** The members of your audience use their own experiences to judge the soundness of your evidence. If your examples are unfamiliar or extreme, they will probably reject your conclusion. If most mem-bers of the audience find that your examples don't reflect their own attitudes, they may ques-tion the validity of the claim.

Statistics

- **Do the statistics come from trustworthy sources?** You should ask whether the reporter of the statistics is qualified and likely to be free of bias. Among the generally reliable sources are polling organizations such as Gallup, Roper, and Louis Harris and agencies of the U.S. government such as the Census Bureau and the Bureau of Labor Statistics. Other qualified sources are well-known research foundations, university centers, and insurance companies that prepare actuarial tables.

- **Are the terms clearly defined?** The more abstract or controversial the term, the greater the necessity for clear definition. *Unemployment* is an example of a term for which statistics will be difficult to read if the definition varies from one user to another. For example, are seasonal workers employed or unemployed during the off-season? Are part-time workers employed?

- **Are the comparisons between comparable things?** Folk wisdom warns us that we cannot compare apples and oranges. Population statistics for the world's largest city, for example, should indicate the units being compared. Greater London is defined in one way, greater New York in another, and greater Tokyo in still another. The population numbers will mean little unless you can be sure that the same geographical units are being compared.

- **Has any significant information been omitted?** In July 2013, Lifestyle Lift's Web site included this history of the company:

The Origin of a Revolutionary Approach
In 2001, Lifestyle Lift Founder, Dr. David Kent, was determined to find a safer and more affordable approach to facial rejuvenation. He knew there had to be a better alternative to traditional facelift, necklift, minilift, and eyelift procedures — one that eliminated the dangers of general anesthesia, shortened the long recovery times, and substantially reduced the cost. Working closely with his wife, Linda Kent, R.N., Lifestyle Lift was born and together they grew the idea into a nationwide company across the United States. The groundbreaking Lifestyle Lift approach yields amazing, lasting results that

- are customized for each person
- address face, eye, and neck aging
- leave you with a natural, refreshed appearance
- allow for quicker recovery.

What the Web site does not mention is that as a result of a probe in Florida, the company was ordered by Florida's attorney general in June 2013 to stop calling its procedures revolutionary and that a similar probe in New York "found evidence that company employees were posing as satisfied customers." Florida's attorney general ordered the company to make clear whether its satisfied customers were compensated for their testimonials. The Lifestyle Lift company still advertises its procedures as groundbreaking in spite of the fact that they are tried and true plastic surgery methods done with local instead of general anesthesia.

Expert Opinion

- **Is the source of the opinion qualified to give an opinion on the subject?** The discussion of credibility in Chapter 1 (p. 7) pointed out that certain achievements by the interpreter of the data — publications, acceptance by colleagues — can tell us something about his or her competence. The answers to questions you must ask are not hard to find: Is the source qualified by education? Is the source associated with a reputable institution — a university or a research organization? Is the source credited with having made contributions to the field — books, articles, research studies? If the source is not clearly identified, you should treat the data with caution.

  In addition, you should question the identity of any source listed as "spokesperson" or "reliable source" or "an unidentified authority." Even when the identification is clear and genuine, you should ask if the credentials are relevant to the field in which the authority claims expertise. All citizens have the right to express their views, but this does not mean that all views are equally credible or worthy of attention.

- **Is the source biased for or against his or her interpretation?** Even authorities who satisfy the criteria for expertise may be guilty of bias. Bias arises as a result of economic reward, religious affiliation, political loyalty, and other interests. The expert may not be aware of the bias; even an expert can fall into the trap of ignoring evidence that contradicts his or her own intellectual preferences. Before accepting the interpretation of an expert, you should ask: Is there some reason why I should suspect the motives of this particular source?

  This is not to say that all partisan claims lack support. They may, in fact, be based on the best available support. But whenever special interest is apparent, there is always the danger that an argument will reflect this bias.

■ **Has the source bolstered the claim with sufficient and appropriate evidence?** An author might claim, "Statistics show that watching violence on television leads to violent behavior in children." But if the author gave no further information — neither statistics nor proof that a cause-effect relation exists between televised violence and violence in children, the critical reader would ask, "What are the numbers? Who compiled them?"

Even those who are reputed to be experts in the subjects they discuss must do more than simply allege that a claim is valid or that the data exist. They must provide facts to support their interpretations.

Images

■ **Is the image relevant?** The photograph or other image should advance your argument. If it doesn't, it is not effective support. If it does, it must deserve the trust put in it as legitimate support. In the 2012 movie *Promised Land*,

unscrupulous businessmen posing as environmental activists try to prove that fracking is killing livestock in the surrounding area by showing the locals a photograph of dead cows. They lose local support, however, when a closer look at the photo reveals that it was taken in a completely different part of the country.

■ **Are you confident the photograph has not been altered?** It is so easy these days to PhotoShop or otherwise alter images that we can hardly trust what our eyes tell us.

■ **Does the image depend too much on emotional appeal?** Emotional appeal is a legitimate form of appeal if it complements, instead of replaces, logic. We have all seen pictures of starving children and abused animals used to move us to donate money to alleviate their suffering. That is a legitimate use of emotional appeal as long as the money really goes to help the suffering children or animals. A little research can reveal what percentage of money donated to a given charity actually reaches those in need.

ARGUMENT ESSENTIALS
Evidence

- Evidence can take the form of facts, or statements possessing a high degree of public acceptance.

- Evidence can take the form of examples, which provide specific support for a generalization and enliven prose.

- Evidence can take the form of statistics, or information expressed in numbers.

- Evidence can take the form of expert opinion, or the interpretations of facts by people recognized as authorities on or at least knowledgeable about the subject.

- Evidence can take the form of images, or nonverbal support for an assertion.

READING ARGUMENT

Seeing Evidence

The following professional essay on sports fans and student essay on organic food have been annotated to highlight the use of evidence. Read each essay, and answer the questions that follow.

Are Sports Fans Happier?

SID KIRCHHEIMER

Let the madness begin!

March is the time when vasectomies increase by 50 percent thanks to the much-anticipated opportunity for patients to "recover" in front of their TVs.

Some opening statistics

March is also the time when workplaces do some real number-crunching: on the expected loss in employee productivity (estimated at 8.4 million hours and $192 million last year); on money bet on office pools (a hefty chunk of the $2.5 billion in total sports wagering each year); and even on the number of times workers hit the so-called "Boss Button" (computer software that instantly hides live video of games with a phony business spreadsheet), which was activated more than 3.3 million times during the first four days of last year's tournament.

But mostly, the NCAA Basketball Championship — better known as "March Madness" or "The Big Dance" — is a time that gives us something to cheer about beyond the game itself. If history and science hold true, no matter the outcome of the three-week tournament that begins in March, most of the millions who will follow its hard-court action will emerge as winners. "That's because in the long run it's really not the games that matter," says Daniel Wann, PhD, a professor of psychology at Murray State University in Kentucky and author of *Sports Fans: The Psychology and Social Impact of Spectators*. "Being a fan gives us something to talk about, to share and bond with others. And for the vast majority of people, it's psychologically healthier when you can increase social connections with others."

His thesis: Fans are winners.

Expert opinion

Thesis: Being a fan leads to social connections, which lead to psychological health.

5   After conducting some 200 studies over the past two decades, Wann, a leading researcher on "sports fandom," finds consistent results: people who identify themselves as sports fans tend to have lower rates of depression and higher self-esteem than those who don't. Blame it on our primal nature.

Sid Kirchheimer is a health and medical writer and editor who has written for AARP since 2000. This article appeared in the March 13, 2012, edition of the *Saturday Evening Post*.

Opinion: causal connection

"Sports fandom is really a tribal thing," says Wann, a phenomenon that can help fulfill our psychological need to belong — providing similar benefits to the social support achieved through religious, professional, or other affiliations. "We've known for decades that social support — our tribal network — is largely responsible for keeping people mentally sound. We really do have a need to connect with others in some way."

A different expert's opinion

But when it comes to opportunities to connect, the Big Dance may have a foothold over other sporting events. "The beauty of March Madness is that it attracts people of all levels of sports fandom — and for different reasons," says Edward Hirt, Ph.D., a professor of psychology at Indiana University who researches how fanship affects social identity.

Examples of reasons people watch

Some watch, whether or not they usually follow sports, because they are alumni or have another previous affiliation to these "tribal networks" — the 60-plus participating college teams. Others connect on the spot, perhaps because it's easier to form emotional allegiances with gutsy amateur athletes who compete with heart and soul (and while juggling mid-term exams) rather than for the paychecks collected by millionaire pros.

Also consider the unique nature of the tournament itself — a series of back-to-back games over the course of several weeks with little to no idle time in between during which a casual fan might lose interest. "I have not seen any empirical evidence to support that March Madness is necessarily better than other sports events" for promoting mood and mindset enhancements. "But theoretically I expect it could be," says Wann.

"There are only a couple of events — the Super Bowl also comes to mind — that seem to transcend typical fandom into being akin to a national holiday . . . a reason for people to get together. But with the Super Bowl, everything leads to one game — and most of the time it's an anticlimactic one that's over by half-time."

With March Madness, however, Wann notes, "there's a longer, more drawn   10 out event that provides more opportunities to engage in social opportunities and connections. And bonds tend to be stronger with a longer passage of time."

Examples

Do the math: More games + more time = more opportunities to share for better bonding. "Because upsets are a normal occurrence, and you get runs by Cinderella teams knocking off the perennial favorites, there's enough uncertainty and unpredictability in this tournament to get people excited — and keep them excited," adds Hirt. "Early games affect later decisions; there's a cascading effect, as opposed to a one-time pick . . . and that allows for the pride that comes with someone with no sports expertise being able to win the office pool."

Maybe that's why despite a short-term productivity loss many experts believe that March Madness actually benefits the workplace in the long term. Bonds formed in office pools and post-game water-cooler chatter build morale and inspire teamwork. At afterwork get-togethers in front of the tube, buddies can share chicken wings — and their emotions. "You have guys hugging each other, cursing at the ref, and bonding by sharing a sense of commonality," says Hirt. "Where else can guys express their emotions like that?"

And those other relationships? Although studies show that two to four percent of marriages are negatively affected when one spouse is an ardent fan (think of the so-called "football widow"), sports fandom has a positive or neutral effect on nearly half of relationships, says Wann. "It gives many couples something to do together or allows one to have time to go off and do their own thing."

Even if you watch in solitude, March Madness and other sporting events provide a diversion from the woes of everyday life — if only for a few hours. "Older people, especially when widowed or physically incapacitated, are more likely than others to relate to televised events," says Stuart Fischoff, Ph.D., senior editor of the *Journal of Media Psychology* and a California State University, Los Angeles, professor emeritus of psychology. "Watching sports helps us get outside ourselves."

15   With the thrill of victory, many fans experience bona fide joy — complete with hormonal and other physiological changes such as increased pulse and feelings of elation. And with defeat, the overwhelming majority may initially feel sadness and disappointment, but usually rebound within a day or two, studies show.

However, lest we present too rosy a picture, it must be said that sports fandom can also be a health hazard. In a 2008 study published in the *New England Journal of Medicine*, researchers found that on days when Germany's soccer team played in the World Cup, cardiac emergencies more than tripled for German men and nearly doubled for women. Of course, European soccer fans are an extreme bunch; but even in the U.S., although visits to hospital emergency rooms tend to decrease during a much-anticipated sports game, there's a higher-than-usual surge immediately after the game ends. The explanation: To see a game's final outcome, some die-hard fans delay making that trip to the ER.

And, of course, no story about March Madness would be complete without mention of gambling. The odds of predicting all game winners are about 9.2 quintillion to one. Yet when it comes to sports betting, nothing turns John Q. Fan into Jimmy the Greek more than the NCAA tournament. Workplace camaraderie is one reason. But there's another important factor.

Bragging rights.

Margin notes:

Expert opinion: causal connection

Examples

Expert opinion

Opinion: causal connection

Examples of health hazards

Expert opinion

With Super Bowl pools there's just a series of boxes with different scores. If you're lucky enough to pick the right one, you win. "But it's a more complex task in filling out all the March Madness brackets, and a seductive pleasure in trying to predict the upsets," says psychologist Edward Hirt.

Another reason why nearly twice as much money is wagered on March Madness than the Super Bowl: More than in other events, NCAA tournament fans simultaneously root for more than one team, triggering a greater likelihood of making multiple bets.

20

With other sports championships you have to wait a week or at least several days between games, but this sports soap opera — with its David versus Goliath battles — continues night and day, providing a stronger hook.

Returns to thesis idea

So let the games begin. Whatever the final outcome, odds are good that the overall advantage — for mind, body, and spirit — is definitely in your court.

Reading and Discussion Questions

1. As you look back over the annotations, what are the types of support used most often by Kirchheimer?

2. If you were going to write an essay analyzing Kirchheimer's use of support, what would your thesis be?

3. Do you find Kirchheimer's essay effective? Why, or why not? If you were going to write an evaluative essay about "Are Sports Fans Happier?" what would its thesis be?

Safer? Tastier? More Nutritious? The Dubious Merits of Organic Foods
KRISTEN WEINACKER

Kristen Weinacker
ENGL 203
Dr. Winchell
October 23, 2017

Safer? Tastier? More Nutritious? The Dubious

Merits of Organic Foods

Causal connections

Organic foods are attractive to some consumers because of the principles behind them and the farming techniques used to produce them. There is a special respect for organic farmers who strive to

At the time she wrote this essay, Kristen Weinacker was an undergraduate at Clemson University.

maintain the ecological balance and harmony that exist among living things. As these farmers work in partnership with nature, some consumers too feel a certain attachment to the earth (Wolf 1–2). They feel happier knowing that these foods are produced without chemical fertilizers, pesticides, and additives to extend their shelf life (Pickrell; Agricultural Extension Service 5). They feel that they have returned to nature by eating organic foods that are advertised as being healthy for maintaining a vigorous lifestyle. Unfortunately, research has not provided statistical evidence that organic foods are more nutritious than conventionally grown ones.

The debate over the nutritional benefits has raged for decades. Defenders of the nutritional value of organic foods have employed excellent marketing and sales strategies. First, they freely share the philosophy behind their farming and follow up with detailed descriptions of their management techniques. Second, organic farmers skillfully appeal to our common sense. It seems reasonable to believe that organic foods are more nutritious since they are grown without chemical fertilizers and pesticides. Third, since the soil in which these crops are grown is so rich and healthy, it seems plausible that these crops have absorbed and developed better nutrients. As Lynda Brown asserts in her book *Living Organic,* "Organic farmers believe that growing crops organically provides the best possible way to produce healthy food" (26). Brown provides beautifully illustrated and enlarged microscopic photographs to show the more developed structure of organic foods compared to conventional products to convince the consumer to believe that organic foods are more nutritious (27). Fourth, many consumers view the higher price tags on organic foods and assume that they must be more nutritious. Generalizations permeate the whole world of organic foods. These marketing strategies persuade the consumer that organic foods are healthier than conventional foods without providing any factual comparisons.

In their book *Is Our Food Safe?* Warren Leon and Caroline Smith DeWaal compare organic and conventionally produced foods. They strongly suggest that consumers buy organic foods to help the environment (68). They believe that organic foods are healthier than conventional ones. However, statistics supporting this belief are not provided. The authors even warn consumers that they need to read product labels because some organic foods may be as unhealthy as conventional ones (68–69). An interesting poll involving 1,041 adults was conducted by ABC News asking, "Why do people buy organic?" Analyst Daniel Merkle concluded that 45 percent of the

Claim of fact

Expert opinion

Causal connection: Consumers believe organic foods are healthier because of these marketing strategies.
Expert opinion

Statistics

American public *believes* that organic products are more nutritious than conventionally grown ones. Also, 57 percent of the population maintains that organic farming is beneficial for the environment. According to the pollsters, the primary reason why people bought organic foods is the belief that they are healthier because they have less pesticide residue. However, there has never been any link established between the nutritional value of organic foods and the residue found on them. Clever marketing strategies have made the need for concrete data really not of prime importance for the consumer to join the bandwagon promoting organic foods.

Expert opinion

This pervasive belief among the American public that organic foods are probably healthier than conventionally grown foods was reiterated in my telephone interview with Mr. Joseph Williamson, an agricultural county extension agent working with Clemson University. When asked if organically grown foods are more nutritious than those grown conventionally, he replied that they probably were for two reasons. First, organic crops tend to grow more slowly. Therefore, the nutrients have more time to build up in the plants. Second, organic plants are usually grown locally. The fruits and vegetables are allowed to stay on the plants for a longer period of time. They ripen more than those picked green and transported across miles. He contends that these conditions promote a better nutrient buildup. Unfortunately, the extension agent acknowledges that statistical evidence is not available to support the claim that organic products are more nutritious.

Suspected causal connections, but not supported by statistical evidence

Expert opinion

An article entitled "Effect of Agricultural Methods in Nutritional Quality: A Comparison of Organic with Conventional Crops" reports on conclusions drawn by Dr. Virginia Worthington, a certified nutrition specialist. Worthington examines why it is so difficult to ascertain if organic foods are more nutritious. First, "the difference in terms of health effects is not large enough to be readily apparent." There is no concrete evidence that people are healthier eating organic foods or, conversely, that people become more ill eating conventionally grown produce. Second, Dr. Worthington notes that variables such as sunlight, temperature, and amount of rain are so inconsistent that the nutrients in crops vary yearly. Third, she points out that the nutrient value of products can be changed by the way products are stored and shipped. After reviewing at least thirty studies dealing with the question if organic foods are more nutritious than conventionally grown ones, Dr. Worthington concludes that there is too little data available to substantiate the claim

Causal connections cannot be drawn.

of higher nutritional value in organic foods. She also believes that it is an impossible task to make a direct connection between organic foods and the health of those people who consume them.

After being asked for thirty years about organic foods by her readers and associates, Joan Dye Gussow, writer for *Eating Well* magazine, firmly concludes that there is "little hard proof that organically grown produce is reliably more nutritious." Reviewing seventy years' worth of studies on the subject, Gussow has no doubt that organic foods should be healthier because of the way they are produced and cultivated. Gussow brings up an interesting point about chemical and pesticide residue. She believes that the fact that organic foods have been found to have fewer residues does not make them automatically more nutritious and healthier for the consumer. As scientific technologies advance, Gussow predicts that research will someday discover statistical data that will prove that organic foods have a higher nutritional value compared to conventionally grown ones.

In order to provide the public with more information about the nature of organic foods, the well-known and highly regarded magazine *Consumer Reports* decided to take a closer look at organic foods in their January 1998 magazine, in an article entitled "Organic Foods: Safer? Tastier? More nutritious?" By conducting comparison tests, their researchers discovered that organic foods have less pesticide residue, and that their flavors are just about the same as conventionally grown foods. These scientists came to the conclusion that the "variability within a given crop is greater than the variability between one cropping system and another." *Consumer Reports* contacted Professor Willie Lockeretz from the Tufts University School of Nutrition Science and Policy. He told researchers that "the growing system you use probably does affect nutrition. . . . But it does it in ways so complex you might be studying the problem forever." Keeping in mind these comments made by Dr. Lockeretz, *Consumer Reports* believes it would be an impossible task to compare the nutritional values of organic and conventional foods. Therefore, researchers at *Consumer Reports* decided not to carry out that part of their comparison testing.

Although statistical evidence is not available at this time to support the claim that organic foods are more nutritious than conventionally grown ones, there is a very strong feeling shared by a majority of the general public that they are. We are called back to nature as we observe the love that organic farmers have for the soil and

Another expert opinion that causal connections cannot be drawn

Expert opinion

their desire to work in partnership with nature. We are easily lured to the attractive displays of organic foods in the grocery stores. However, we must keep in mind the successful marketing techniques that have been used to convince us that organic foods are more nutritious than conventionally grown ones. <u>Although common sense tells us that organic foods should be more nutritious, research has not provided us with any statistical data to prove this claim.</u>

Restatement of thesis

Works Cited

Agricultural Extension Service. *Organic Vegetable Gardening.* University of Tennessee, PB 1391.

Brown, Lynda. *Organic Living.* Dorling Kindersley, 2000.

Gussow, Joan Dye. "Is Organic Food More Nutritious?" *Eating Well,* May/June 1997, 27 Mar. 2003, www.prnac.net/rodmap-nutrition.html.

"Effect of Agricultural Methods on Nutritional Quality: A Comparison of Organic with Conventional Crops." *Alternative Therapies* 4, 1998, pp. 58–69, 18 Feb. 2003, www.purefood.org/healthier101101.cfm.

Leon, Warren, and Caroline Smith DeWaal. *Is Our Food Safe?* Three Rivers, 2002.

Merkle, Daniel. "Why Do People Buy Organic?" *ABC News* Polls, 3 Feb. 2000, abcnews.go.com/onair/DailyNews/poll_2000203.html.

"Organic Foods: Safer? Tastier? More Nutritious?" *Consumer Reports,* Jan. 1998, www.consumerreports.org/main/detailsv2.jsp?content%3%ecnt_id+18959&f.

Pickrell, John. "Federal Government Launches Organic Standards." *Science News,* vol. 162. no. 17, www.sciencenews.org/blog/food-thought/federal-government-launches-organic-standards.

Williamson, Joseph. Telephone interview. 28 Feb. 2013.

Wolf, Ray, ed. *Organic Farming: Yesterday's and Tomorrow's Agriculture.* Rodale, 1977.

Reading and Discussion Questions

1. Looking back over the annotations, what types of support did you find noted most often?
2. What is unusual about the use of causal connections in this particular piece? How does that contribute to Weinacker's thesis?

Practice: Evidence
Read the following essay, and answer the questions at the end.

I'm Sorry, Steve Jobs: We Could Have Saved You
SIDDHARTHA MUKHERJEE

On October 5, the night that Steve Jobs died, I ascended 30,000 feet into the thin air above New York on a flight to California. On my lap was a stash of scientific papers. I was reading and taking notes — where else? — on an iPad.

Jobs's death — like a generational Rorschach test — had provoked complex reactions within each of us. There was grief in abundance, of course, admixed with a sense of loss, with desolation and nostalgia. Outside the Apple store in SoHo, New York, that evening, there were bouquets of white gerberas and red roses. Someone had left a bushel of apples by the doorstep and a sign that read "I-miss . . ."

I missed Jobs, too — but I also felt a personal embarrassment in his death. I am an oncologist and a cancer researcher. I felt as if my profession, my discipline, and my generation had let him down. Steve Jobs had promised — and then delivered — life-altering technologies. Had we, in all honesty, given him any such life-altering technologies back?

I ask the question in all earnestness. Jobs's life ended because of a form of pancreatic cancer called pancreatic neuroendocrine tumor, or PNET. These tumors are fleetingly rare: about five in every million men and women are diagnosed with PNETs each year. Deciphering the biology of rare cancers is often challenging. But the past five years have revealed extraordinary insights into the biology of some rare cancers — and PNETs, coincidentally enough, have led part of that charge. By comparing several such tumors, scientists are beginning to understand the biology of these peculiar tumors.

But understanding biology is an abstract activity. Steve Jobs needed more than "biology." He needed medicines. And despite our efforts, we were unable to transform our knowledge about PNETs into medical realities during his lifetime. The question is, are we ready to achieve this transformation sometime in the near future?

Let's take PNETs as a case in point. In 2008 a team of scientists from Johns Hopkins University set out to document all the gene mutations in PNETs — creating a systematic genetic "anatomy" of these tumors. Cancer, of course, is ultimately a disease of mutations in genes. Human cells possess about 23,000 genes in total. In cancer cells some of these genes are changed — mutated — and begin to function abnormally.

Many of the genes that are mutated in various cancers, predictably, control cellular growth. Genes regulate the growth of cells like invisible puppeteers tugging and pushing opposing strings behind curtains. There are genes that command a cell to grow and those that tell a cell to stop growing. Cancer occurs when these

5

Siddhartha Mukherjee is an Indian-born American oncologist and hematologist who won the 2011 Pulitzer Prize for General Nonfiction for his book *The Emperor of All Maladies: A Biography of Cancer* (2010). Currently he teaches at Columbia University and practices at Columbia University Medical Center. This article appeared in *Newsweek* on October 8, 2012.

growth-control genes are mutated, resulting in the dysregulated growth of a cell.

But the genes most frequently mutated in PNETs are odd. They don't seem to control growth directly; rather they seem to affect the way cells regulate genes. Take a moment to understand this by considering normal development. A cell in the retina possesses the same 23,000 genes as a cell in the skin, yet these two cells barely resemble each other in shape, size, or behavior. How does a cell, then, "know" how to become a retinal cell versus a skin cell? How can the same set of 23,000 genes be used to specify such radically diverse behaviors, functions, and forms?

Part of the answer lies in the way genes are controlled, or regulated. Although a skin cell and a retinal cell inherit the same set of 23,000 genes, a skin cell activates or suppresses a unique subset of the total—say 5,000 of the 23,000—while a retinal cell activates another subset. It's like an elaborate mix-and-match game: each cell dips into the same box of genes and chooses a unique spectrum of genes for itself, thereby attaining its form, function, and behavior.

10   To use an analogy that Jobs might have used: every human cell contains the same "hardware" of genes. But every individual cell type activates a particular "software"—a program (involving a particular combination of genes) that is unique unto itself to achieve its particular function.

But the answer raises a question: how does the skin cell know how to activate such software? In part through master regulatory genes that accomplish this task. These master-control genes exercise exquisite control on the growth, shape, size, and identity of a cell. They activate entire programs of gene expression; they toggle hundreds of molecular switches to turn "on" and turn "off" programs.

There are many such families of master-control genes, and one such family acts

by modifying DNA—the stuff that all genes are made of. And PNETs appear to possess frequent mutations in these DNA-modifying genes. The phenomenon is not unique to PNETs. In my own laboratory we have discovered that leukemias and other blood disorders also possess frequent changes in such DNA-modifying genes. Others have found mutations in DNA-modifying genes in lymphomas and brain tumors, and in colon and stomach cancers.

There is, in short, a novel principle of cancer unfolding here: that DNA-modifying genes can be mutated in certain tumors. But what connects these DNA-modifying genes to the ultimate growth behavior of a cancer cell? Might these genes become targets for new drugs? Might one such medicine be used to treat—or even cure—PNETs?

Indeed, DNA-modifying genes aren't the only new and unusual targets unfolding as we learn more about cancer. There are genes that affect the way cancer cells use glucose or other building blocks, such as amino acids, during their metabolism.

This knowledge—gleaned over the past five   15 years—should have accelerated an effort to find medicines that affect these new pathways that seem to control cancer. And indeed, to an extent, it has. Many of these new pathways have become reasonable targets for anti-cancer drugs. Medicines that attack a specific family of genes termed "kinases"—genes dysregulated in blood and lung cancers and melanoma—have made their way into human use. Nearly all of these originated with the discovery of specific gene mutations in particular variants of cancer.

But there are vast gaps in knowledge still, and even larger chasms in drug development. Targeting an errant gene in a cancer cell might sound like a simple, well-defined task, but in fact it is mind-bogglingly complex. Cancer cells arise out of normal cells—and they resemble normal cells so closely that it can be difficult, at times, to tell them apart at a genetic level (of the 23,000 genes in a normal cell, a cancer cell may share 22,962 and have only 38 that are altered).

I wonder whether Jobs himself might have enjoyed the strange challenge of creating anti-cancer drugs: it is, after all, the ultimate design problem. Molecules have to be made to "fit" exactly into unique clefts and pockets of a cell's machinery in order to logjam malignant growth. Extraneous bits and pieces have to be shaved off so that the drug can bind to its intended target with a neat, satisfying click. The human testing and clinical trials that follow drug discovery present peculiar operational challenges. And there's production and safety monitoring that come after. The popular press has adopted the term "designer drugs" for the new generation of molecules that can target cancer cells with exquisite specificity. I like to think that the ultimate designer of our generation might have had something to add to this most profound frontier of design.

Certainly he could have added a plea for adequate resources. The National Cancer Institute (NCI) is the nation's preeminent institution tasked with leading cancer scientists toward new means to prevent, treat, and cure cancers. Its annual budget of about $5 billion is stagnating and threatened. The Food and Drug Administration, charged with ensuring that new cancer medicines are brought effectively and safely to the public, operates on a budget of about $4 billion. If these amounts sound impressive, consider the fact that in 2008 the United States was spending about $12 billion every month on conflict in the Middle East—more than the annual NCI and FDA budgets combined.

If we are truly committed to creating medicines to prevent and treat cancer, we seem to be doing a rather lax job in funding this effort. We cannot continue to develop medicines under these circumstances. The postdoctoral researcher who identified the alterations in DNA-modifying genes in leukemia in my lab is debating whether to continue his research. His bench mate, a talented chemist I hired out of graduate school, is teaching biology at a local night school to supplement her income. Next year, when she runs out of grant funds, she is thinking of returning to Florida to work in a tattoo parlor.

The Japanese people speak of a "Lost Decade"—the *Ushinawareta Junen*—a period between 1990 and 2000 when banks collapsed, the economy stagnated, and culture lost its effervescence. Emblematic of this decade was a "lost generation" of Japanese men and women who were unable to contribute to critical problems affecting their generation. My fear is that we too will face a lost generation—of molecules.

Cancer, meanwhile, marches onward. The statistics are stark: in the United States, one in two men and one in three women will encounter it. One in four will die from it. It's important—given the complexity of the problem—not to oversell the speed or effectiveness of cancer research. Creating new medicines for cancer is slow, painstaking, time-consuming work. But that's precisely why we need federal support to keep this process intact. It is exactly why—when Congress chooses to ax the NCI budget—we should take that decision with utmost seriousness. If we don't generate enough political support for cancer research, we will not bring to life the kinds of medicines we need to treat our own cancers in the future—including the kind that killed Jobs. The vast gene-decoding efforts of the last decade will remain abstract, academic exercises—biology without medicine.

On my way back from the airport two days after his death, the signs and the apples were still outside the Apple store. I felt as if I should have added my own: "I'm sorry, Steve. I wish we had done better."

Reading and Discussion Questions

1. How does Mukherjee make use of Steve Jobs's death to advance the point he is trying to make? How did Jobs's death make him feel?
2. What parallels does Mukherjee make between Jobs's career and his own in the article?
3. Because Mukherjee is an oncologist and cancer researcher, he is expressing an expert's opinion. What other types of evidence does he offer?
4. What is Mukherjee's claim?
5. How effective do you find Mukherjee's argument? Does the use of Jobs's death add to its effectiveness? Explain your response.

Appeals to Needs and Values

Good factual evidence is usually enough to convince an audience that your factual claim is sound. Using examples, statistics, and expert opinion, you can prove, for example, that women do not earn as much as men for the same work. But even good evidence may not be enough to convince your audience that unequal pay is wrong or that something should be done about it. In making value and policy claims, an **appeal to the needs and values** of your audience is absolutely essential to the success of your argument. If you want to persuade the audience to change their minds or adopt a course of action — in this case, to demand legislation guaranteeing equal pay for equal work — you will have to show that assent to your claim will bring about what they want and care deeply about.

If the audience concludes that the things you care about are very different from what they care about, if they cannot identify with your goals and principles, they may treat your argument with indifference, even hostility, and finally reject it. But you can hope that decent and reasonable people will share many of the needs and values that underlie your claims. Finding these shared needs and values is what Carl Rogers was advocating when he said that the way to improved communication is to try to express your audience's position fairly and to look for common ground between their position and yours. The appeal to these needs and values was what Aristotle called *pathos*.

Appeals to Needs

The most familiar classification of needs was developed by the psychologist Abraham H. Maslow in 1954.[12] These needs, said Maslow, motivate human thought and action. In satisfying our needs, we attain both long- and short-term goals. Because Maslow believed that some needs are more important than others, he arranged them in hierarchical order from the most urgent biological needs to the psychological needs that are related to our roles as members of a society.

---

[12] Abraham H. Maslow, *Motivation and Personality* (New York: Harper and Row, 1954), pp. 80–92.

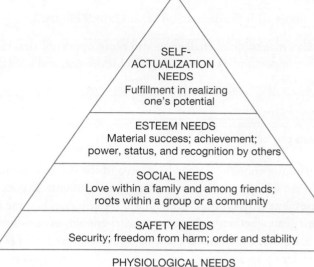

SELF-ACTUALIZATION NEEDS
Fulfillment in realizing one's potential

ESTEEM NEEDS
Material success; achievement;
power, status, and recognition by others

SOCIAL NEEDS
Love within a family and among friends;
roots within a group or a community

SAFETY NEEDS
Security; freedom from harm; order and stability

PHYSIOLOGICAL NEEDS
Basic bodily requirements: food and drink; health; sex

For most of your arguments, you won't have to address the audience's basic physiological needs for nourishment or shelter. The desire for health, however, now receives extraordinary attention. Appeals to buy health foods, vitamin supplements, drugs, exercise and diet courses, and health books are all around us. Many of the claims are supported by little or no evidence, but readers are so eager to satisfy the need for good health that they often overlook the lack of facts or authoritative opinion. The desire for physical well-being, however, is not so simple as it seems; it is strongly related to our need for self-esteem and love.

Appeals to our needs to feel safe from harm, to be assured of order and stability in our lives, are also common. Insurance companies, politicians who promise to rid our streets of crime, and companies that offer security services all appeal to this profound and nearly universal need. (We say "nearly" because some people are apparently attracted to risk and danger.) At the time of this writing, those who monitor terrorist activity are attempting both to arouse fear for our safety and to suggest ways of reducing the dangers that make us fearful.

The last three needs in Maslow's hierarchy are the ones you will find most challenging to appeal to in your arguments. It is clear that these needs arise out of human relationships and participation in society. Advertisers make much use of appeals to these needs.

Social Needs

"Whether you are young or old, the need for companionship is universal." (ad for dating service)

"Share the Fun of High School with Your Little Girl!" (ad for a Barbie doll)

Esteem Needs

"Enrich your home with the distinction of an Oxford library."

"Apply your expertise to more challenges and more opportunities. Here are outstanding opportunities for challenge, achievement, and growth." (Perkin-Elmer Co.)

Self-Actualization Needs

"Be all that you can be." (former U.S. Army slogan)

"Are you demanding enough? Somewhere beyond the cortex is a small voice whose mere whisper can silence an army of arguments. It goes by many names: integrity, excellence, standards. And it stands alone in final judgment as to whether we have demanded enough of ourselves and, by that example, have inspired the best in those around us." (*New York Times*)

Of course, it is not only advertisers who use these appeals. We hear them from family and friends, from teachers, from employers, from editorials and letters to the editor, from people in public life.

Appeals to Values

Needs give rise to values. If we feel the need to belong to a group, we learn to value commitment, sacrifice, and sharing. And we then respond to arguments that promise to protect our values. It is hardly surprising that values, the principles by which we judge what is good or bad, beautiful or ugly, worthwhile or undesirable, should exercise a profound influence on our behavior. Virtually all claims, even those that seem to be purely factual, contain expressed or unexpressed judgments.

For our study of argument, we will speak of groups or systems of values because any single value is usually related to others. People and institutions are often defined by such systems of values.

Values, like needs, are arranged in a hierarchy; that is, some are clearly more important than others to the people who hold them. Moreover, the arrangement may shift over time or as a result of new experiences. In 1962, for example, two speech teachers prepared a list of what they called "Relatively Unchanging Values Shared by Most Americans."[13] Included were "puritan and pioneer standards of morality" and "perennial optimism about the future." More than fifty years later, an appeal to these values might fall on a number of deaf ears.

---

[13] Edward Steele and W. Charles Redding, "The American Value System: Premises for Persuasion," *Western Speech*, 26 (Spring 1962), pp. 83–91.

You should also be aware of not only changes over time but also different or competing value systems that reflect a multitude of subcultures in the United States. Differences in age, sex, race, ethnic background, social environment, religion, even in the personalities and characters of its members, define the groups we belong to. Such terms as *honor, loyalty, justice, patriotism, duty, responsibility, equality, freedom,* and *courage* will be interpreted very differently by different groups.

All of us belong to more than one group, and the values of the several groups may be in conflict. If one group to which you belong — say, peers of your own age and class — is generally uninterested in and even scornful of religion, you may nevertheless hold to the values of your family and continue to place a high value on religious belief.

How can a knowledge of your readers' values enable you to make a more effective appeal? Suppose you want to argue in favor of a sex education program in the middle school you attended. The program you support would not only give students information about contraception and venereal disease but also teach them about the pleasures of sex, the importance of small families, and alternatives to heterosexuality. If the readers of your argument are your classmates or your peers, you can be fairly sure that their agreement will be easier to obtain than that of their parents, especially if their parents think of themselves as conservative. Your peers are more likely to value experimentation, tolerance of alternative sexual practices, freedom, and novelty. Their parents are more likely to value restraint, conformity to conventional sexual practices, obedience to family rules, and foresight in planning for the future.

Knowing that your peers share your values and your goals will mean that you need not spell out the values supporting your claim; they are understood by your readers. Convincing their parents, however, who think that freedom, tolerance, and experimentation have been abused by their children, will be a far more challenging task. In one written piece you have little chance of changing their values, a result that might be achieved only over a longer period of time. So you might first attempt to reduce their hostility by suggesting that even if a community-wide program were adopted, students would need parental permission to enroll. This might convince some parents that you share their values regarding parental authority and primacy of the family. Second, you might look for other values to which the parents subscribe and to which you can make an appeal. Do they prize maturity, self-reliance, responsibility in their children? If so, you could attempt to prove, with authoritative evidence, that the sex education program would promote these qualities in students who took the course.

But familiarity with the value systems of prospective readers may also lead you to conclude that winning assent to your argument will be impossible. It would probably be fruitless to attempt to persuade a group of lifelong pacifists to endorse the use of nuclear weapons. The beliefs, attitudes, and habits that support their value systems are too fundamental to yield to one or two attempts at persuasion.

RESEARCH SKILL ▶ Evaluating Appeals to Needs and Values

If your argument is based on an appeal to the needs and values of your audience, the following questions will help you evaluate the soundness of your appeal.

■ **Have the values been clearly defined?** Because value terms are abstractions, you must make their meaning explicit by placing them in context and providing examples. If a person values his Second Amendment rights, does that mean he is opposed to any restrictions on gun ownership? Does another's opposition to abortion extend to cases of rape and incest?

■ **Are the needs and values to which you appeal prominent in the reader's hierarchy at the time you are writing?** Gun control becomes a focus in the media and on people's minds whenever a mass shooting occurs. The need for election reform is a hot topic every four years but fades from memory in between.

■ **Is the evidence in your argument clearly related to the needs and values to which you appeal?** Remember that readers must see some connection between your evidence and their goals. Statistics can be impressive, for example, but your audience must see their relevance.

ARGUMENT ESSENTIALS
Appeals to Needs and Values

■ In making value and policy claims, it is essential to appeal to the needs and values of your audience, but first you must identify what those needs and values are.

■ Needs can be viewed on a hierarchy developed by psychologist Abraham Maslow.

■ Values are the principles by which we judge what is good or bad, beautiful or ugly, worthwhile or undesirable.

READING ARGUMENT

Seeing Appeals to Needs and Values

The following essay on genetics has been annotated to highlight appeals to needs and values. Read the selection, and answer the questions that follow. The numbered annotations in paragraphs 5–9 point out threats to human needs and values posed by reprogenetics. The second set of numbered annotations sum up the author's response.

Building Baby from the Genes Up

RONALD M. GREEN

The two British couples no doubt thought that their appeal for medical help in conceiving a child was entirely reasonable. Over several generations, many female members of their families had died of breast cancer. One or both spouses in each couple had probably inherited the genetic mutations for the disease, and they wanted to use in-vitro fertilization and preimplantation genetic diagnosis (PGD) to select only the healthy embryos for implantation. Their goal was to eradicate breast cancer from their family lines once and for all.

Appeal to physiological need for health

In the United States, this combination of reproductive and genetic medicine — what one scientist has dubbed "reprogenetics" — remains largely unregulated, but Britain has a formal agency, the Human Fertilization and Embryology Authority (HFEA), that must approve all requests for PGD. In July 2007, after considerable deliberation, the HFEA approved the procedure for both families. The concern was not about the use of PGD to avoid genetic disease, since embryo screening for serious disorders is commonplace now on both sides of the Atlantic. What troubled the HFEA was the fact that an embryo carrying the cancer mutation could go on to live for 40 or 50 years before ever developing cancer, and there was a chance it might never develop. Did this warrant selecting and discarding embryos? To its critics, the HFEA, in approving this request, crossed a bright line separating legitimate medical genetics from the quest for "the perfect baby."

Appeal to values: Was it right to reject an embryo that would develop into a person who might never get the disease or live 40 to 50 years without it?

Like it or not, that decision is a sign of things to come — and not necessarily a bad sign. Since the completion of the Human Genome Project in 2003, our understanding of the genetic bases of human disease and non-disease traits has been growing almost exponentially. The National Institutes of Health has initiated a quest for the "$1,000 genome," a 10-year program to develop machines that could identify all the genetic letters in anyone's genome at low cost (it took more than $3 billion to sequence the first human genome). With this technology, which some believe may be just four or five years away, we could not only scan an individual's — or embryo's — genome, we could also rapidly compare thousands of people and pinpoint those DNA sequences or

Ronald M. Green is a professor emeritus of religion and the Eunice and Julian Cohen Professor Emeritus for the Study of Ethics and Human Values at Dartmouth College, a member of the Department of Community and Family Medicine at Dartmouth's Geisel School of Medicine, the author of *Babies by Design: The Ethics of Genetic Choice* (2007) and *Kant and Kierkegaard on Time and Eternity* (2011), and co-editor of *Suffering and Bioethics* (2014). This article was published in the *Washington Post*.

combinations that underlie the variations that contribute to our biological differences.

With knowledge comes power. If we understand the genetic causes of obesity, for example, we can intervene by means of embryo selection to produce a child with a reduced genetic likelihood of getting fat. Eventually, without discarding embryos at all, we could use gene-targeting techniques to tweak fetal DNA sequences. No child would have to face a lifetime of dieting or experience the health and cosmetic problems associated with obesity. The same is true for cognitive problems such as dyslexia. Geneticists have already identified some of the mutations that contribute to this disorder. Why should a child struggle with reading difficulties when we could alter the genes responsible for the problem?

Many people are horrified at the thought of such uses of genetics, seeing echoes of the 1997 science-fiction film *Gattaca*, which depicted a world where parents choose their children's traits. Human weakness has been eliminated through genetic engineering, and the few parents who opt for a "natural" conception run the risk of producing offspring — "invalids" or "degenerates" — who become members of a despised underclass. *Gattaca*'s world is clean and efficient, but its eugenic obsessions have all but extinguished human love and compassion.

These fears aren't limited to fiction. Over the past few years, many bioethicists have spoken out against genetic manipulations. The critics tend to voice at least four major concerns. First, they worry about the effect of genetic selection on parenting. Will our ability to choose our children's biological inheritance lead parents to replace unconditional love with a consumerist mentality that seeks perfection?

Second, they ask whether gene manipulations will diminish our freedom by making us creatures of our genes or our parents' whims. In his book *Enough*, the techno-critic Bill McKibben asks: If I am a world-class runner, but my parents inserted the "Sweatworks2010 GenePack" in my genome, can I really feel pride in my accomplishments? Worse, if I refuse to use my costly genetic endowments, will I face relentless pressure to live up to my parents' expectations?

Third, many critics fear that reproductive genetics will widen our social divisions as the affluent "buy" more competitive abilities for their offspring. Will we eventually see "speciation," the emergence of two or more human populations so different that they no longer even breed with one another? Will we re-create the horrors of eugenics that led, in Europe, Asia and the United States, to the sterilization of tens of thousands of people declared to be "unfit" and that in Nazi Germany paved the way for the Holocaust?

Finally, some worry about the religious implications of this technology. Does it amount to a forbidden and prideful "playing God"?

5

Marginal annotations:

Appeal to need for health, physical and cognitive

1. Appeal to need for love and community

2. Appeal to need for self-actualization

3. Appeal to values — threat of increased social division and a return to the horrors of the Holocaust

4. Appeal to religious values

10   To many, the answers to these questions are clear. Not long ago, when I asked a large class at Dartmouth Medical School whether they thought that we should move in the direction of human genetic engineering, more than 80 percent said no. This squares with public opinion polls that show a similar degree of opposition. Nevertheless, "babies by design" are probably in our future — but I think that the critics' concerns may be less troublesome than they first appear.

Will critical scrutiny replace parental love? Not likely. Even today, parents who hope for a healthy child but have one born with disabilities tend to love that child ferociously. The very intensity of parental love is the best protection against its erosion by genetic technologies. Will a child somehow feel less free because parents have helped select his or her traits? The fact is that a child is already remarkably influenced by the genes she inherits. The difference is that we haven't taken control of the process. Yet.

> 1. Author responds with faith in parental love.

Knowing more about our genes may actually increase our freedom by helping us understand the biological obstacles — and opportunities — we have to work with. Take the case of Tiger Woods. His father, Earl, is said to have handed him a golf club when he was still in the playpen. Earl probably also gave Tiger the genes for some of the traits that help make him a champion golfer. Genes and upbringing worked together to inspire excellence. Does Tiger feel less free because of his inherited abilities? Did he feel pressured by his parents? I doubt it. Of course, his story could have gone the other way, with overbearing parents forcing a child into their mold. But the problem in that case wouldn't be genetics, but bad parenting.

> 2. Author responds that there will be no threat to self-actualization.

Granted, the social effects of reproductive genetics are worrisome. The risks of producing a "genobility," genetic overlords ruling a vast genetic underclass, are real. But genetics could also become a tool for reducing the class divide. Will we see the day when perhaps all youngsters are genetically vaccinated against dyslexia? And how might this contribute to everyone's social betterment?

> 3. Author responds that some divisions could be reduced.

As for the question of intruding on God's domain, the answer is less clear than the critics believe. The use of genetic medicine to cure or prevent disease is widely accepted by religious traditions, even those that oppose discarding embryos. Speaking in 1982 at the Pontifical Academy of Sciences, Pope John Paul II observed that modern biological research "can ameliorate the condition of those who are affected by chromosomic diseases," and he lauded this as helping to cure "the smallest and weakest of human beings . . . during their intrauterine life or in the period immediately after birth." For Catholicism and some other traditions, it is one thing to cure disease, but another to create children who are faster runners, longer-lived, or smarter.

> 4. Author responds that religions tend to accept modification for disease cures or prevention but not for other reasons.

15   But why should we think that the human genome is a once-and-for-all-finished, untamperable product? All of the biblically derived faiths permit

Human genetic improvement is *not* a bad thing.

human beings to improve on nature using technology, from agriculture to aviation. Why not improve our genome? I have no doubt that most people considering these questions for the first time are certain that human genetic improvement is a bad idea, but I'd like to shake up that certainty.

Genomic science is racing toward a future in which foreseeable improvements include reduced susceptibility to a host of diseases, increased life span, better cognitive functioning, and maybe even cosmetic enhancements such as whiter, straighter teeth. Yes, genetic orthodontics may be in our future. The challenge is to see that we don't also unleash the demons of discrimination

Claim

and oppression. Although I acknowledge the risks, I believe that we can and will incorporate gene technology into the ongoing human adventure.

Reading and Discussion Questions

1. Remember that the annotations here focus only on appeals to needs and values because that is the focus of this portion of the chapter. That does not mean that those are the only types of support in the essay. What other types of support did you notice? To begin with, what type of support does the first paragraph provide?

2. The annotations make the organization of most of the essay fairly obvious. Explain the organizational pattern.

3. If you were going to write an essay analyzing Green's use of support, what would your thesis be?

Practice: Appeals to Needs and Values

In the following opinion piece, Jeremy Markel takes an insightful look at marketing aimed at "tweens." Read the essay, and answer the questions that follow it.

Marketing to "Tweens" Objectifies Women
JEREMY MARKEL

Last November Victoria's Secret showcased its new "tween" lingerie line at its annual fashion show. The showcase was part of Pink's new marketing campaign intended for what the industry calls "tweens": girls and teens.

Pink, Victoria's Secret's "teen friendly" clothing store, and others like it such as Hot Topic and American Eagle, have created their own lingerie lines and have begun marketing them toward young women. Even Justice, a store that is intended for girls ages 7–12, has begun selling flowered underwear and tie-dye bras online.

When he wrote this piece, Jeremy Markel was a junior majoring in communication studies at the University of Georgia. He now lives in San Jose, California. The opinion piece was published on March 24, 2013, in the campus newspaper, *Red and Black*.

In 2011, Walmart launched its makeup line, geoGirl, which is marketed to 8–12 year-old girls. The line has 69 cosmetic products including blush, mascara, and exfoliants.

These marketing trends target younger and younger girls and women; they manipulate them by standardizing certain behaviors and styles of dress, impress upon them the idea that being sexy is necessary, engender an arbitrary and unrealistic idea of what being "sexy" is, and distort their self-concepts.

5 Stuart Burgdoerfer, the chief financial officer of Limited Brands, the parent company of Victoria's Secret, stated that "when somebody's 15 or 16 years old, what do they want to be? They want to be older, and they want to be cool like the girl in college, and that's part of the magic of what we do at Pink."

By "magic," Stuart essentially meant that Pink is manipulating younger generations based upon their ideas of what being older is like and is exploiting a need that it, as well as other clothing and cosmetics stores, helps create.

Victoria's Secret uses college-age models, and defines "sexiness" as being extremely thin, having flawless skin, wearing make-up, and having unnaturally white teeth. It then provides young women with the tools — lingerie, makeup, and perfume — that will help them achieve the unrealistic and arbitrary standard of appearance that it helps create.

The fact that teen heartthrob Justin Bieber was hired to perform during the showcasing of Pink's "tween" lingerie line during the Victoria's Secret fashion show last November clearly illustrates Limited Brands's intention to persuade girls and teens that they need to use Pink's products in order to be appealing.

Even though Hot Topic and American Eagle have not stated that they are targeting the same 15–16 age group as Pink, Marcie Merriman, founder of PrimalGrowth, stated stores are "all going to say they're targeting 18–22 year-olds, but the reality is you're going to get the younger customer."

10 This is especially true in stores that are "teen friendly." Placing clothing that is marketed to 18–22 year-olds alongside clothing intended for younger audiences will attract younger girls and women who, in Burgdoerfer's words, "want to be cool like the girl in college."

In addition to standardizing behaviors and constructing beauty, the increasing number of images that women and girls see of super-thin models have been linked to body image issues in women and girls. Researchers have stated that, "having unrealistic expectation[s] for one's body image creates a greater chance for body dissatisfaction. The media may influence one's body image in such a way through constant portrayal of the 'thin ideal.'"

15 Walmart's makeup line is a perfect example of the creation of unrealistic and arbitrary ideals of beauty for girls. Marketing cosmetics to any age group implies that one's current appearance needs adjusting, but one striking fact about geoGirl is that it includes exfoliators. "The line's creators claim it's formulated for fresh young skin, with ingredients like willow bark to exfoliate and chamomile to calm, as well as anti-oxidants, which reportedly prevent aging."

Preventing aging is impossible, however. Entropy cannot be stopped no matter how much willow bark or chamomile one uses. What is even more ridiculous is that we are talking about 8–12 year-olds whose skin is probably in the best condition it will ever be in. Other than "early bloomers" who experience acne at young ages and other similar cases, rarely do cosmetics problems exist for this age group.

Regardless, geoGirl is creating cosmetics problems for 8–12 year-olds, and then providing them with the tools to fix those problems.

What Walmart, Pink, and similar clothing stores are doing is detrimental to the self-esteem, body image, and general well-being of girls and women. Their marketing campaigns and lingerie and cosmetics lines create unrealistic standards by which women and girls are intended to live. Moreover, they objectify and sexualize their own consumers.

Reading and Discussion Questions

1. What is the author's claim?
2. Who is the author's audience? How does the author appeal to that audience's needs and values?

Assignments for Support

Reading and Discussion Questions

1. Consider what types of evidence you find most convincing in an argument. Is the best type of evidence dependent on the topic and the context? Explain.

2. Look for examples in the media of the misuse of evidence. Explain why the evidence is misleading.

3. Use examples to explain which news shows depend on factual evidence and which depend largely on opinion. Do both have a useful role to play in our society? Explain.

4. In the aftermath of the massacre at Sandy Hook Elementary, there was talk of passing laws requiring teachers to carry weapons on school and college campuses. What needs of the people were those who proposed the law appealing to? How could opponents of such laws have used similar types of appeal to argue their case?

5. Consider presidential debates you have seen or other televised coverage of candidates during the months leading up to an election. What are some specific examples of how the candidates try to appeal to the voters' needs and values?

6. The average American citizen is usually ignorant of much of the reality of what goes on in the Islamic world. When Americans take a stand on issues such as U.S. involvement in Afghanistan, to what extent do you believe they are basing that stand on solid supporting evidence?

Writing Suggestions

1. Analyze different television commercials for the same product or similar products. Write an essay supporting a conclusion you are able to draw about the types of appeal used in the commercials.

2. Write a letter about a problem on your campus to the person who is in a position to correct the problem. Provide convincing evidence that a problem exists, and in suggesting a solution to the problem, keep in mind the needs and values of your audience as well as those of others on campus.

3. Write an essay in which you explain the types of support that Sid Kirchheimer makes use of the most in his essay "Are Sports Fans Happier?" You will need to provide examples of the types of support that he uses.

4. Write an essay explaining how effective you think Siddhartha Mukherjee is in supporting the claim that he makes in the title of his essay — that Steve Jobs could have been saved. Use specific evidence from the essay to support your claim.

5. Write an essay explaining whether or not you believe that it was acceptable for the HFEA to approve the request made by two British couples in Ronald M. Green's "Building Baby from the Genes Up." Use specific evidence from the essay to support your opinion.

RESEARCH ASSIGNMENT

1. Do some preliminary research on the following topics:
   - The link between autism and vaccines
   - The link between cell phones and cancer
   - The movement to drop the SAT as a requirement for college admissions
   - The environmental impact of plastic water bottles

2. For each of the topics above, track down one or more sources that use each type of evidence and emotional appeal discussed in the chapter:
   - an example
   - a statistic
   - an expert opinion
   - an image
   - an appeal to a need
   - an appeal to a value

3. Evaluate the sources you have found, using the Research Skill boxes on pages 200 to 218.

---

bits

To see what you are learning about argumentation applied to the latest world and national news, read our *Bits* blog, "Argument and the Headlines," at **blogs.bedfordstmartins.com/bits.**

Assumptions

We now come to the third element in the structure of the argument—the warrant, or underlying assumption. Claim and support, the other major elements we have discussed, are more familiar in ordinary discourse, but there is nothing mysterious or unusual about the idea of an underlying assumption. All our claims, both formal and informal, are grounded in assumptions that the audience must share with us if our claims are to prove to be acceptable.

The arrows in the following diagram illustrate that writer and audience must be looking at the subject with the same underlying beliefs in order for the argument to be persuasive.

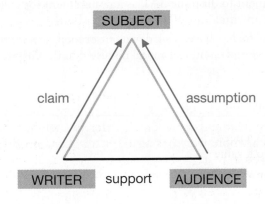

General Principles

The following exercise provides a good starting point for this chapter. Do the assigned task by yourself or in a small group.

Practice: Assumptions

A series of environmental catastrophic events has virtually wiped out human life on Earth. The only known survivors in your vicinity are the eleven listed below. There are resources to sustain only seven. Choose seven of the following people to survive. List them in the order in which you would choose them, and be prepared to explain the reasons for your selection: that is, why you chose these particular persons and why you placed them in this certain order.

- Dr. D. — thirty-seven, PhD in history, college professor, in good health (jogs daily), hobby is botany, enjoys politics, married with one child (Bobby).
- Mrs. D. — thirty-eight, rather obese, diabetic, MA in psychology, counselor in a mental health clinic, married to Dr. D., has one child.
- Bobby D. — ten, cognitively deficient with IQ of 70, healthy and strong for his age.
- Mrs. G. — twenty-three, ninth-grade education, cocktail waitress, worked as a prostitute, married at age sixteen, divorced at age eighteen, one son (Joseph).
- Joseph G. — three months old, healthy.
- Mary E. — eighteen, trade school education, wears glasses, artistic.
- Mr. N. — twenty-five, starting last year of medical school, music as a hobby, physical fitness buff.
- Mrs. C. — twenty-eight, daughter of a minister, college graduate, electronics engineer, single now after a brief marriage, member of Zero Population Growth.
- Mr. B. — fifty-one, BS in mechanics, married with four children, enjoys outdoors, much experience in construction, quite handy.
- Father Frans — thirty-seven, Catholic priest, active in civil rights, former college athlete, farming background, often criticized for liberal views.
- Dr. L. — sixty-six, doctor in general practice, two heart attacks in the past five years, loves literature and quotes extensively.

There may have been a great deal of disagreement over which survivors in the above scenario to select. If so, the reason for that disagreement was that in making their choices, different members of your group or of your class as a whole were basing their decisions on different assumptions. Some of you may have chosen not to let Mrs. G. survive because she seemed to have nothing particularly vital to offer to the survival of the group as a whole. If you analyzed your claim, support, and assumption in that case, they would look something like the following. Notice the assumption in particular.

Claim: Mrs. G. should not be allowed to survive.

Support: She has no skills vital to the survival of the group.

Assumption: Those chosen to survive must have skills vital to the survival of the group.

Another way of looking at the assumption is to ask yourself this question: **What would I have to believe in order to accept that claim, given the support I have to go on?**

Others may have felt that Mrs. G. should be allowed to survive along with her child, the infant in the group. The reasoning would look like this:

Claim: Mrs. G. should be allowed to survive.

Support: She has an infant son.

Assumption: Those with infants should be allowed to survive.

That assumes, of course, choosing to allow the infant, Jospeh G., to survive. If that was not the case, the assumption behind letting Mrs. G. survive would be invalid.

Did you decide to let Baby Joseph survive? If so, what was your reasoning? How would you fill in the blanks?

Claim: Joseph G. should be allowed to survive.

Support: _____

Assumption: _____

Or if you thought the opposite — that the infant should not be one of the seven allowed to survive — what was your reasoning?

Claim: Joseph G. should not be allowed to survive.

Support: _____

Assumption: _____

You may have felt that an infant had very little chance of survival and therefore his spot should be given to someone more likely to survive. Or you may have thought that the future of the civilization depended on the survival of the young. Or you may just not have liked the thought of killing an infant.

There are few easy answers in this exercise, but behind each choice is an underlying assumption. If you chose to kill off Dr. L., it was probably because he had had two heart attacks and was less likely than others to survive. You might have decided that the young Mr. N., a physical fitness buff and a medical student, would be more vital to the survival of the others. Out of compassion, you might have wanted to save Bobby D., or you might have concluded that a cognitively deficient ten-year-old with an IQ of 70 had the least to offer the rest of the group.

Obviously, this is an exercise with no right answer. What it can teach us, however, is to consider the assumptions on which our beliefs are based. There are reasons you might have chosen certain individuals to survive that could be stated as general principles:

Those who are in the best physical condition should be allowed to survive.

Those with the most useful skills should be allowed to survive.

Those who are mentally deficient should not be allowed to survive.

Those who are most likely to reproduce should be allowed to survive.

Fortunately, this is merely an intellectual exercise. Whenever you take a stand in a real-life situation, though, you do so on the basis of certain general principles that guide your choices. Those general principles that you feel most strongly about exist as part of your intellectual and moral being because of what you have experienced in your life thus far. They have been shaped by your observations, your personal experience, and your participation in a culture. Some of the general principles behind your thoughts and actions may be these:

> Cheating is always wrong.
>
> I have a right to express my opinion.
>
> Premarital sex is wrong.
>
> Morality changes with the times.
>
> Killing under any circumstances is wrong.
>
> Killing is wrong except in self-defense.
>
> Killing is wrong except in war.
>
> Cruelty to animals is wrong.
>
> Government intrudes too much in my daily life.

All of these are broad statements that could apply in any number of different circumstances. That's why we refer to them as general principles. Your stated assumptions may not always be this broad, but at times they will be. Because the observations, experiences, and cultural associations on which these principles are based vary from one individual to another, your audience may not always agree with your assumptions. The success of Rogerian argument depends on identifying at least one assumption, or warrant, that opposing sides share. The success of any argument depends on at least understanding your own assumptions and those of your audience.

Widely Held Assumptions

Some assumptions are so widely accepted that they do not need to be stated or require any proof of their validity. If an argument claims that every new dorm on campus should have a sprinkler system, it probably does not even need to state that assumption. If it did, it would be something like this: *Measures that would increase the likelihood that dorm residents would survive a fire should be implemented in all dorms.*

If your house catches on fire, you call 911. If your car is stolen, you call the police (or 911). You may have never used the term *warrant* in such cases because these assumptions are so widely agreed on that they don't have to be stated. We teach these responses even to young children, who in some cases have saved their own lives and those of others by knowing what to do.

> **Claim:** I should call 911.
>
> **Support:** I just saw a stranger sneaking around my neighbor's house.
>
> **Assumption:** If you see a stranger sneaking around the neighborhood, you should call 911.

Other widely held assumptions:

Claim: Michael should get a smoke detector.

Support: His new apartment doesn't have a working smoke detector.

Assumption: Every apartment needs a working smoke detector.

Claim: I should drive you home.

Support: You've been drinking, and I haven't.

Assumption: The one who hasn't been drinking should do the driving.

Claim: Ping's mother won't let him visit at Daniel's house.

Support: Daniel's parents keep guns that are not locked up in their home.

Assumption: People shouldn't let their children visit where guns are not kept locked up.

Notice that an assumption is a broad generalization that can apply to a number of different situations, while the claim is about a specific place and time. It should be added that in other arguments the assumption may not be stated in such general terms. However, even in arguments in which the assumption makes a more specific reference to the claim, the reader can infer an extension of the assumption to other similar arguments. In the sprinkler system example on page 229, the assumption mentions dorms in particular. But it is clear that such warrants can be generalized to apply to other arguments in which we accept a claim based on an appeal to our very human need to feel secure.

What about claims that are more controversial? Why is it so difficult for those who oppose abortion, for example, to communicate with those who favor it, and vice versa? Anyone who believes that abortion is the murder of an unborn child is basing that argument on the assumption that a fetus is a child from conception. Many on the other side of the debate do not accept that assumption and thus do not accept the claim. Obviously, disagreements on such emotionally charged issues are very difficult to resolve because the underlying assumptions are based on firmly held beliefs that are resistant to change. It is always better to be aware of your opponent's assumptions, however, than to simply dismiss them as irrelevant.

The British philosopher Stephen Toulmin, who developed the concept of warrants, dismissed more traditional forms of logical reasoning in favor of a more audience-based, courtroom-derived approach to argumentation. He refers to warrants as "general, hypothetical statements, which can act as bridges" and "entitle one to draw conclusions or make claims."[1] The word *bridges* to denote the action of the warrant, or assumption, is crucial. We use the word *assumption* to emphasize that in an argument it guarantees a connecting link — a bridge — between the claim and the support. This means that even if a reader agrees that the support is sound, the support cannot prove the validity of the claim unless the reader also agrees with the underlying assumption.

---

[1] Stephen Toulmin, *The Uses of Argument* (Cambridge: Cambridge University Press, 1958), p. 98.

The following dialogue offers another example of the relationship between the assumption and the other elements of the argument.

"Stop talking on the phone, and concentrate on driving!"
"Aw, I always talk on my cell when I'm driving."
"Well, you shouldn't. It's not safe."
"So what?"
"You shouldn't do unsafe things while driving."

If we put this into outline form, the assumption in the argument is clear.

Claim: You shouldn't talk on your cell phone while you are driving.

Support: Talking on a cell phone while driving is not safe.

Assumption: You shouldn't do unsafe things while driving.

We can also represent an argument in diagram form, which shows the assumption as a bridge between the claim and the support.

SUPPORT ─────────────→ CLAIM

ASSUMPTION
(expressed or unexpressed)

The argument above can then be written like this:

SUPPORT ─────────────→ CLAIM

Talking on a cell phone while   You shouldn't talk on your
driving is not safe.   cell phone while driving.

ASSUMPTION
You shouldn't do unsafe
things while driving.

Claim and support (or lack of support) are relatively easy to uncover in most arguments. One thing that makes the assumption different is that it is often unexpressed and therefore unexamined by both writer and reader because they take it for granted. In the argument about using a cell phone while driving, the assumption was stated. Consider another example where the assumption is implied, not stated. What is the implied assumption in the following?

The technological revolution in how information is distributed and consumed holds the promise to scale higher education to serve more students and cut costs. At the same time, the rush to embrace technology as a solution to every problem has created tension on campuses over whether the critical role higher education plays in preparing the whole person to be a productive citizen in a democratic society is at risk. Indeed, in an increasingly complex world, the foundation of learning — a liberal arts education — is more important than ever.[2]

The claim is that traditional higher education has the potential to be transformed by technology. The implied assumption — the implied warrant — is that increasing the number of students receiving a quality liberal arts education in a cost-effective way will lead to a better society.

Recognizing and Analyzing Assumptions

There is no simple formula for locating assumptions. And, yes, there can be more than one assumption in a single text because different portions of the text may be based on separate assumptions. Once you have read a selection, it is a good idea to locate the thesis statement or try to put the thesis into your own words. Then look at the evidence the author offers in support of that thesis. The assumption will be a statement that shows the connection between the claim and support.

Unstated Assumptions

We have already noted that sometimes the assumption is unstated. Arguers might neglect to state their assumptions for one of two reasons: (1) as in our earlier examples, they may believe that the assumption is obvious and need not be expressed; (2) they may want to conceal the assumption in the hope that the reader will overlook its weakness.

Here are a few more examples of assumptions that are so obvious that they need not be expressed:

Mothers love their children.
A good harvest will result in lower prices for produce.
Killing innocent children is wrong.
First come, first served.

These statements seem to embody beliefs that most of us would share and that might be unnecessary to make explicit in an argument. The last statement, for example, is taken as axiomatic, an article of faith that we

---

[2] Jeffrey J. Selingo, *College (Un)Bound: The Future of Higher Education and What It Means for Students* (New York: New Harvest, 2013), p. xvii.

seldom question in ordinary circumstances. Suppose you hear someone make the claim, *I deserve to get the last ticket to the concert.* If you ask why he is entitled to a ticket that you also would like to have, he may answer in support of his claim, "Because I was here first." No doubt you accept his claim without further argument because you understand and agree with the assumption that is not expressed: *If you arrive first, you deserve to be served before those who come later.*

But even those assumptions that seem to express universal truths invite analysis if we can think of claims for which these assumptions might not, after all, be relevant. "First in line," for example, may justify the claim of a person who wants a concert ticket, but it cannot in itself justify the claim of someone who wants a vital medication that is in short supply.

Moreover, offering a rebuttal to a long-held but unexamined assumption can often produce an interesting and original argument. If someone exclaims, "All this buying of gifts! I think people have forgotten that Christmas celebrates the birth of Christ," she need not express the assumption — that the buying of gifts violates what ought to be a religious celebration. It goes

unstated by the speaker because it has been uttered so often that she knows the hearer will supply it. But one writer, in an essay titled "God's Gift: A Commercial Christmas," argued that contrary to popular belief, the purchase of gifts — which means the expenditure of time, money, and thought on others rather than oneself — is not a violation but an affirmation of the Christmas spirit.[3]

The second reason for refusal to state the assumption lies in the arguer's intention to disarm or deceive the reader, although the arguer may not be aware of this. For instance, failure to state the assumption is common in advertising and politics, where the desire to sell a product or an idea may outweigh the responsibility to argue explicitly. The advertisement on the previous page was famous not only for what it said but for what it did not say.

What is the unstated assumption in the ad? The manufacturer of Virginia Slims hoped we would agree that being permitted to smoke cigarettes was a significant sign of female liberation. But many readers would insist that proving "You've come a long way, baby" requires more evidence than women's freedom to smoke (or "serve" the business world). The shaky assumption weakened the claim.

Strategies for Recognizing Assumptions

1. In written arguments, locate the one sentence that best states the author's claim. If the argument is unwritten (such as a print advertisement), or if there is no single sentence that sums up the claim, try to express the claim in a single sentence of your own.

2. Think about what audience the author was targeting. How is that audience likely to respond to the claim? The most important question to ask about the audience regarding assumptions is this one: What assumption or assumptions must the audience make to be able to accept the claim? The answer to that question will be the assumption or assumptions on which the piece is based.

3. Most written arguments include support to strengthen the author's claim. Remember that the assumption is the link between claim and support. It may help to use the formula used in this chapter to think systematically through the argument. Ask yourself what the claim is, what support the author is offering, and what assumption connects the two. Do that for each of the author's major supporting statements.

4. The author may not need to state his or her assumption directly if it is a universally accepted truth that most reasonable readers would agree with. It should be clear to you as a reader, however, what the assumption is.

---

[3] Robert A. Sirico, *Wall Street Journal*, December 21, 1993, sec. A, p. 12.

READING ARGUMENT

Recognizing Unstated Assumptions

The following essay was written in August 2013 and examines a judge's ruling concerning the "stop, question, and frisk" policy that the New York Police Department claims has cut down on crime in the city over the last two decades. This is a more complex argument than others we have looked at in this chapter, but it will help if you approach it considering what Terry Eastland's claim of policy is and why.

Don't Stop Frisking
TERRY EASTLAND

Since the early 1990s the New York Police Department has used a crime-prevention strategy that it calls "stop, question, and frisk." Accordingly, officers stop and question a person based on reasonable suspicion and sometimes pat down the clothing of the individual to ensure that he is not armed. The department credits the strategy in large part for the huge declines in murder and major crimes over two decades in what is now the nation's safest big city. But the liberal opposition to stop-question-and-frisk has been fighting back, and last week federal district judge Shira A. Scheindlin declared the NYPD's use of the strategy unconstitutional and ordered a set of remedies whose implementation is to be overseen by an independent monitor she has appointed.

> The police claim the policy has reduced crime, but Scheindlin has declared it unconstitutional.

During the trial, which ended three weeks ago, a *New Yorker* writer sympathetic to Scheindlin's view of the case observed that the litigation was "rooted in the hope that a single judge can diagnose a complex problem and reform a huge organization like the New York Police Department based on the imperfect medium of trial testimony," and that while the judge's "dedication to protecting citizens' rights is beyond question . . . it is less clear that she has the wisdom, or even the ability, to impose her vision in the real world of New York."

> Even her sympathizers question Scheindlin's ability to make and enforce the decision alone.

Before the world discovers whether Judge Scheindlin can indeed impose her vision, and with what consequences, it would be good to know

---

Terry Eastland is an executive editor for the *Weekly Standard*, where this article appeared on August 26, 2013. During the Reagan era, Eastland was Director of Public Affairs for the Justice Department and later was a resident scholar at the Ethics and Public Policy Center. Among his works is *Freedom of Expression in the Supreme Court* (2000).

Mayor plans to appeal.

whether her decision in the class-action case of *Floyd* v. *New York City* can stand. Fortunately, Mayor Michael Bloomberg has declared that he will appeal. The mayor has said the judge was biased against the city, and on so important an issue as stop-question-and-frisk — public safety long being a top concern of New Yorkers — a fresh set of judicial eyes could help ensure public confidence in the process and what it ultimately yields in this case.

Details of ruling

In her decision, Judge Scheindlin did not strike down stop-question-and-frisk as such, which the Supreme Court upheld against constitutional challenge in the 1968 case of *Terry* v. *Ohio*, but instead ruled against the tool "as applied" in the city. The nineteen *Floyd* plaintiffs — each of them black or Hispanic — contended that stop-question-and-frisk violated their constitutional rights in two ways. First, they said they were stopped without a legal basis — that is, without "reasonable suspicion"— in violation of the Fourth Amendment's prohibition against unreasonable searches and seizures. And second, they said they were targeted for stops because of their race and ethnicity in violation of the Fourteenth Amendment's equal protection guarantee.

Judging the plaintiffs' "Terry-stop" claims under the Fourth Amendment, Scheindlin concluded that "nine of the stops and frisks were unconstitutional — that is, they were not based on reasonable suspicion." In five others she said the stops were based on reasonable suspicion but the frisks were not and on that account were unconstitutional. And in the remaining five, she said those stopped or frisked failed to prove their claims. By the way, there could have been hundreds of plaintiffs, but the nineteen were apparently all the *Floyd* lawyers could find, or were willing to find, and they had mixed results in trying to persuade a sympathetic judge of their claims.

More details

5

Statistics put ruling in larger context.

The nineteen stops of the named plaintiffs were a tiny subset of the more than 4.4 million stops made by the NYPD between 2004 and 2012, more than 80 percent of them stops of blacks or Hispanics, with slightly more than 50 percent of them resulting in a frisk, weapons being found in 1.5 percent of the frisks, and some 6 percent of the stops resulting in arrests. It is hard to see how much could be reliably inferred from those numbers about the 4.4 million stops.

Scheindlin recognized as much when she wrote that *Floyd* was "not primarily about the nineteen individual stops that were the subject of testimony at trial." Nor was the case about an actual stop-question-and-frisk law or regulation that the judge found in violation of the Fourth Amendment, for there were no such instruments. What the case was about, the judge wrote, was "whether the City has a *policy* or *custom* [the judge's emphasis] of violating the Constitution by making unlawful stops and conducting unlawful frisks." Weighing "extensive expert submissions and testimony" on various aspects of the department's use of the strategy, she concluded there was. But her assessment of the relevant law and how she looked for it, in a case of such importance to not just New York City but in municipalities across the country, merits appellate review.

Claim: Scheindlin's ruling should be reviewed.

As for the plaintiffs' claims about being targeted by race and ethnicity for stops, here there is an oddity. For while none of the nineteen plaintiffs were able to prove equal protection claims against actual police officers, Scheindlin, using statistics and anecdotal evidence, decided that the class the plaintiffs represented (and which included them) had been discriminated against. As with stop-and-frisk, she said, there was no stated policy that endorsed racial targeting but an unwritten one, which relied in part upon how crime victims had described those they say committed the crimes against them, descriptions that include the race and ethnicity of the alleged perpetrators.

Scheindlin ruled that racial profiling is an unwritten policy.

In concluding that the NYPD was guilty of "indirect racial profiling," Scheindlin made much of one police chief's testimony that officers are to focus their reasonable-suspicion-based stops on "the right people," citing it more than a dozen times, but whether she used those words in context could interest the appeals court. So could her analysis of competing statistical models, especially since she seems at times to embrace the dubious notion that the racial Terry-stop rates in a given community should be comparable to the percentages by race of the people who live in that community.

Author questions Scheindlin's reasoning.

10   Judge Scheindlin emphasized throughout *Floyd* that her mandate was to judge the constitutionality of the policy as carried out, not its effectiveness. Evidently constitutionality in the context at hand may not, ever, take into account the first imperative of government, which is to ensure the safety of its citizens. The judge's determination to regulate the NYPD, through ambitious reforms and a monitor reporting to her, may result in less safe streets in the poor and minority communities where crime once thrived and where stop-question-and-frisk has most often been employed. That is why an appeal is necessary — to determine, with so much weighing in the balance, whether the judge's decision is correct or not.

Amazing, is it not, that the best hope for continuing one of the most successful anticrime strategies in modern times lies in the U.S. Court of Appeals for the Second Circuit, not exactly a tribunal dominated by judicial conservatives.

Analysis

Using Toulmin's terms, Eastland's argument could be outlined like this.

Claim: Scheindlin's ruling — that the "stop, question, and frisk" policy as applied in New York is unconstitutional — should be appealed.

Support: The current policy is effective at keeping citizens safe.

Implied assumption: The effectiveness of the policy is more important than its constitutionality.

RESEARCH SKILL   Finding and Narrowing a Research Topic

When you have a research assignment, you might start with a topic idea that is too broad for the length of the paper you have been assigned. That does not mean that you have to abandon the idea completely. Instead, you can narrow the topic to one that is more manageable, given the length of the paper you will be writing.

1. Try using some of these approaches to identify a part of your broad topic that might be appropriate:

	Instead of	Try
Narrow according to **time**:	The U.S. space program	The U.S. space program in the twenty-first century
Narrow according to **place**:	Same-sex marriage	Same-sex marriage in California
Narrow to one **aspect**:	Abortion	Late-term abortion
Narrow to one **part**:	Obamacare	Insurance for businesses with fewer than fifty employees
Narrow to one **group**:	Immigration reform	Immigration reform and college students
Narrow to a single **problem**:	Standardized testing	Cultural bias in standardized testing

2. You may get some additional ideas by applying to your broad topic the traditional reporter's questions: *who, what, where, when,* and *why.*

3. You may get still different information if you look at your broad subject in terms of *relationships*: How do parts *compare* and *contrast*? What can you discover about *causes* and *effects*? How is the *definition* of your key term different from that of similar terms?

Once you narrow your topic, you can start working toward a thesis. As you do, you will want to consider your purpose and your audience. Part of analyzing your audience should involve trying to understand what their view of the subject is and what warrants underlie their beliefs about it.

READING ARGUMENT

Analyzing Assumptions

The following essay has been annotated to highlight claims, supports, and assumptions.

The Case for Torture

MICHAEL LEVIN

It is generally assumed that torture is impermissible, a throwback to a more brutal age. Enlightened societies reject it outright, and regimes suspected of using it risk the wrath of the United States.

Introduction: statement of opposing view

I believe this attitude is unwise. There are situations in which torture is not merely permissible but morally mandatory. Moreover, these situations are moving from the realm of imagination to fact.

Claim of policy: rebuttal of opposing view

Suppose a terrorist has hidden an atomic bomb on Manhattan Island which will detonate at noon on July 4 unless . . . (here follow the usual demands for money and release of his friends from jail). Suppose, further, that he is caught at 10 A.M. of the fateful day, but — preferring death to failure — won't disclose where the bomb is. What do we do? If we follow due process — wait for his lawyer, arraign him — millions of people will die. If the only way to save those lives is to subject the terrorist to the most excruciating possible pain, what grounds can there be for not doing so? I suggest there are none. In any case, I ask you to face the question with an open mind.

Support: hypothetical example to test the reader's belief

Torturing the terrorist is unconstitutional? Probably. But millions of lives surely outweigh constitutionality. Torture is barbaric? Mass murder is far more barbaric. Indeed, letting millions of innocents die in deference to one who flaunts his guilt is moral cowardice, an unwillingness to dirty one's hands. If *you* caught the terrorist, could you sleep nights knowing that millions died because you couldn't bring yourself to apply the electrodes?

These questions are assumptions that he rejects. His responses are assumptions he can accept.

5   Once you concede that torture is justified in extreme cases, you have admitted that the decision to use torture is a matter of balancing innocent lives against the means needed to save them. You must now face more realistic cases involving more modest numbers. Someone plants a bomb on a jumbo jet. He alone can disarm it, and his demands cannot be met (or if they can, we refuse to set a precedent by yielding to his threats). Surely we can, we must, do anything to the extortionist to save the passengers. How can we tell three

The assumptions on which the essay is based

Support: hypothetical example

Michael Levin is a professor of philosophy at the City University of New York. This essay is reprinted from the June 7, 1982, issue of *Newsweek*.

hundred, or one hundred, or ten people who never asked to be put in danger, "I'm sorry, you'll have to die in agony, we just couldn't bring ourselves to . . ."

Here are the results of an informal poll about a third, hypothetical, case. Suppose a terrorist group kidnapped a newborn baby from a hospital. I asked four mothers if they would approve of torturing kidnappers if that were necessary to get their own newborns back. All said yes, the most "liberal" adding that she would administer it herself.

I am not advocating torture as punishment. Punishment is addressed to deeds irrevocably past. Rather, I am advocating torture as an acceptable measure for preventing future evils. So understood, it is far less objectionable than many extant punishments. Opponents of the death penalty, for example, are forever insisting that executing a murderer will not bring back his victim (as if the purpose of capital punishment were supposed to be resurrection, not deterrence or retribution). But torture, in the cases described, is intended not to bring anyone back but to keep innocents from being dispatched. The most powerful argument against using torture as a punishment or to secure confessions is that such practices disregard the rights of the individual. Well, if the individual is all that important — and he is — it is correspondingly important to protect the rights of individuals threatened by terrorists. If life is so valuable that it must never be taken, the lives of the innocents must be saved even at the price of hurting the one who endangers them.

Better precedents for torture are assassination and preemptive attack. No Allied leader would have flinched at assassinating Hitler, had that been possible. (The Allies did assassinate Heydrich.) Americans would be angered to learn that Roosevelt could have had Hitler killed in 1943 — thereby shortening the war and saving millions of lives — but refused on moral grounds. Similarly, if nation A learns that nation B is about to launch an unprovoked attack, A has a right to save itself by destroying B's military capability first. In the same way, if the police can by torture save those who would otherwise die at the hands of kidnappers or terrorists, they must.

There is an important difference between terrorists and their victims that should mute talk of the terrorists' "rights." The terrorist's victims are at risk unintentionally, not having asked to be endangered. But the terrorist knowingly initiated his actions. Unlike his victims, he volunteered for the risks of his deed. By threatening to kill for profit or idealism, he renounces civilized standards, and he can have no complaint if civilization tries to thwart him by whatever means necessary.

Just as torture is justified only to save lives (not extort confessions or recantations), it is justifiably administered only to those *known* to hold innocent lives

10

in their hands. Ah, but how can the authorities ever be sure they have the right malefactor? Isn't there a danger of error and abuse? Won't we turn into Them?

Questions like these are disingenuous in a world in which terrorists proclaim themselves and perform for television. The name of their game is public recognition. After all, you can't very well intimidate a government into releasing your freedom fighters unless you announce that it is your group that has seized its embassy. "Clear guilt" is difficult to define, but when 40 million people see a group of masked gunmen seize an airplane on the evening news, there is not much question about who the perpetrators are. There will be hard cases where the situation is murkier. Nonetheless, a line demarcating the legitimate use of torture can be drawn. Torture only the obviously guilty, and only for the sake of saving innocents, and the line between Us and Them will remain clear.

d) Easy identification of terrorists

There is little danger that the Western democracies will lose their way if they choose to inflict pain as one way of preserving order. Paralysis in the face of evil is the greater danger. Some day soon a terrorist will threaten tens of thousands of lives, and torture will be the only way to save them. We had better start thinking about this.

Conclusion assumption: "Paralysis in the face of evil is the greater danger."

Practice: Recognizing and Analyzing Warrants

Read the following argument by Robert A. Sirico. Then summarize the argument in a paragraph. Next, explain what the claim is, what types of support are used, and what the underlying assumption is. Is the assumption one that you agree with? Explain.

An Unjust Sacrifice
ROBERT A. SIRICO

An appeals court in London has made a Solomonic ruling, deciding that eight-week-old twins joined at the pelvis must be separated. In effect, one twin, known as Mary, is to be sacrificed to save the other, known as Jodie, in an operation the babies' parents oppose.

The judges invoked a utilitarian rationale, justified on the basis of medical testimony. The specialists agreed that there is an 80 to 90 percent chance that the strong and alert Jodie could not survive more than a few months if she continued to support the weak heart and lungs of Mary, whose brain is underdeveloped.

This is a heartbreaking case, and the decision of the court was not arrived at lightly. But even the best of intentions, on the part of the state or the parents, is no substitute for sound moral reasoning. Utilitarian considerations like Mary's quality of life are not the issue. Nor should doctors' expert testimony, which is subject to error, be considered decisive.

Robert A. Sirico, a Roman Catholic priest, is founder of the Action Institute for the Study of Religion and Liberty in Grand Rapids, Michigan. This article appeared in the September 28, 2000, *New York Times*.

Here, as in the case of abortion, one simple principle applies: There is no justification for deliberately destroying innocent life. In this case, the court has turned its back on a tenet that the West has stood by: Life, no matter how limited, should be protected.

5   While this case is so far unique, there are guidelines that must be followed. No human being, for instance, can be coerced into donating an organ — even if the individual donating the organ is unlikely to be harmed and the individual receiving the organ could be saved. In principle, no person should ever be forced to volunteer his own body to save another's life, even if that individual is a newborn baby.

To understand the gravity of the court's error, consider the parents' point of view. They are from Gozo, an island in Malta. After being told of their daughters' condition, while the twins were in utero, they went to Manchester, England, seeking out the best possible medical care. Yet, after the birth on August 8, the parents were told that they needed to separate the twins, which would be fatal for Mary.

They protested, telling the court: "We cannot begin to accept or contemplate that one of our children should die to enable the other one to survive. That is not God's will. Everyone has a right to life, so why should we kill one of our daughters to enable the other one to survive?"

And yet, a court in a country in which they sought refuge has overruled their wishes. This is a clear evil: coercion against the parents and coercion against their child, justified in the name of a speculative medical calculus.

The parents' phrase "God's will" is easily caricatured, as if they believed divine revelation were guiding them to ignore science. In fact, they believe in the merit of science, or they would not have gone to Britain for help in the first place.

But utilitarian rationality has overtaken   10 their case. The lawyer appointed by the court to represent Jodie insisted that Mary's was "a futile life." That is a dangerous statement — sending us down a slippery slope where lives can be measured for their supposed value and discarded if deemed not useful enough.

Some might argue that in thinking about the twins, we should apply the philosophical principle known as "double effect," which, in some circumstances, permits the loss of a life when it is an unintended consequence of saving another. But in this case, ending Mary's life would be a deliberate decision, not an unintended effect.

Can we ever take one life in favor of another? No, not even in this case, however fateful the consequences.

Assignments for Assumptions

Reading and Discussion Questions

1. Should students be given a direct voice in the hiring of faculty members? On what assumptions about education do you base your answer?

2. Discuss the validity of the assumption in this statement from the *Watch Tower* (a publication of the Jehovah's Witnesses) about genital herpes: "The sexually loose are indeed 'receiving in themselves the full recompense, which was their due for their error' (Romans 1:27)."

3. In 2010, a judge in Saudi Arabia had to make the decision whether or not a man could be intentionally paralyzed as punishment for having paralyzed another man in a fight. His victim had requested this punishment. What would the judge's assumption be if he chose to order the punishment? What would it be if he decided not to honor the victim's request?

4. In view of the increasing interest in health in general, and nutrition and exercise in particular, do you think that universities and colleges should impose physical education requirements? If so, what form should they take? If not, why not? What assumption underlies your position?

5. What are some of the assumptions underlying the preference for natural foods and medicines? Can *natural* be clearly defined? Is this preference part of a broader philosophy? Try to evaluate the validity of the assumption.

6. The author of the following passage, Katherine Butler Hathaway, became a hunchback as a result of a childhood illness. Here she writes about the relationship between love and beauty from the point of view of someone who is deformed. Discuss the assumptions on which the author bases her conclusions.

> I could secretly pretend that I had a lover . . . but I could never risk showing that I thought such a thing was possible for me . . . with any man. Because of my repeated encounters with the mirror and my irrepressible tendency to forget what I had seen, I had begun to force myself to believe and to remember, and especially to remember, that I would never be chosen for what I imagined to be the supreme and most intimate of all experience. I thought of sexual love as an honor that was too great and too beautiful for the body in which I was doomed to live.

Writing Suggestions

1. Diagram three of the decisions you made about survivors of the imaginary catastrophe in the opening assignment. Show claim, support, and assumption.

2. In "An Unjust Sacrifice," Robert A. Sirico presents a case in which he finds no justification for letting one twin die in order to save the other. His belief in the sanctity of human life appears to be absolute, even when it will most likely lead to the death of both twins. Write an essay in which you give examples of how your value system underlies your political views.

3. Both state and federal governments have been embroiled in controversies concerning the rights of citizens to engage in harmful practices. In Massachusetts, for example, a mandatory seat-belt law was repealed by voters who considered the law an infringement of their freedom. (It was later reinstated.) Write an essay in which you explain what principles you believe should guide government regulation of dangerous practices.

4. Henry David Thoreau writes, "Unjust laws exist: Shall we be content to obey them, or shall we endeavor to amend them, and obey them until we have succeeded, or shall we transgress them at once?" Write an essay in which you explain under what circumstances you would feel compelled to break the law, or why you feel that you would never do so.

RESEARCH ASSIGNMENT ▶ **Narrowing a Research Topic**

1. Think of three different ways to narrow each of the following broad topics:
   - The effects of stress
   - Eating disorders
   - Presidential elections
   - Genetic engineering
   - Athletes and drugs
   - College admissions tests
   - Suicide in the military
   - Social networking

2. For each broad topic, select one of the narrower topics you came up with. For that narrower topic, identify some widely held assumptions. Then explain what underlying assumptions that are not so widely held might make it difficult to reach agreement.

---

bits

To see what you are learning about argumentation applied to the latest world and national news, read our *Bits* blog, "Argument and the Headlines," at **blogs.bedfordstmartins.com/bits.**

Using the
ELEMENTS

Definition: Clarifying Key Terms

The Purposes of Definition

Before we examine the other elements of argument, we need to consider definition, a component you may have to deal with early in writing an essay.

Arguments often revolve around definitions of crucial terms. Consider the following examples. In the gun control debate, there is disagreement over what an assault weapon is. In the debate over euthanasia, it makes a difference whether the issue is passive or active euthanasia. When planning the prosecution of an alleged criminal, whether the accused is defined as an enemy combatant or not determines how he will be tried. In the publicity surrounding the death of Trayvon Martin, it made a difference whether George Zimmerman was viewed as a neighborhood watch leader or as a vigilante. Likewise, it made a difference whether the attack on the U.S. consulate in Benghazi in 2012 was seen as a protest gone wrong or a terrorist attack.

A corrupt use of definition can be used to distort reality. But even where there is no intention to deceive, the snares of definition are difficult to avoid. How do you define *abortion*? Is it "termination of pregnancy"? Or is it "murder of an unborn child"? During a celebrated trial of a physician who performed an abortion and was accused of manslaughter, the prosecution often used the word *baby* to refer to the fetus, but the defense referred to "the products of conception." These definitions of *fetus* reflected the differing judgments of those on opposite sides. Not only do judgments create definitions, but definitions also influence judgments.

Definitions can indeed change the nature of an event or a "fact." How many farms are there in the United States? The answer to the question depends on the definition of *farm*. For example, read the following excerpt:

> Because of a change in the official definition of the word *farm*, New York lost 20 percent of its farms on January 1, with numbers dropping from 56,000 to 45,000. . . .
>
> The U.S. Department of Agriculture (USDA) defines *farm* broadly as any operation with the potential to produce at least $1,000 worth of agricultural goods in a given year. Based on 2006 prices, an operation

could be considered a farm for growing 4 acres of corn, a tenth of an acre of berries, or for owning one milk cow. Consequently, most U.S. establishments classified as a farm produce very little, while most agricultural production occurs on a small number of much larger operations. . . .

USDA's farm definition has remained unchanged since 1975. However, the increasing concentration of agricultural production on large farms and the proliferation of small "rural residence" farms with little or no production have led to proposals to narrow the definition of a farm to more closely target "actively engaged" farmers.

Any change in the farm definition could have far-reaching consequences since the characteristics of farms vary from place to place. For example, changing the annual farm sales threshold to $10,000 would result in a redistribution of the share of farms located in each state. Under this scenario, almost two-thirds of all states would experience changes in their share of farms of less than 0.5 percent (in either direction).[1]

A change in the definition of *poverty* can have similar results. An article in the *New York Times,* under the headline "A Revised Definition of Poverty May Raise Number of U.S. Poor," makes this clear:

> The official definition of *poverty* used by the Federal Government for three decades is based simply on cash income before taxes. But in a report to be issued on Wednesday, a panel of experts convened by the [National] Academy of Sciences three years ago at the behest of Congress says the Government should move toward a concept of poverty based on disposable income, the amount left after a family pays taxes and essential expenses.[2]

The differences are wholly a matter of definition. But such differences can have serious consequences for those being defined, most of all in the disposition of billions of federal dollars in aid of various kinds.

In fact, local and federal courts almost every day redefine traditional concepts that can have a direct impact on our lives. The definition of *family*, for example, has undergone significant changes that acknowledge the existence of new relationships. In January 1990, the New Jersey Supreme Court ruled that a family may be defined as "one or more persons occupying a dwelling unit as a single nonprofit housekeeping unit, who are living together as a stable and permanent living unit, being a traditional family unit or the *functional*

---

[1] Erik O'Donoghue, "Changing the Definition of a 'Farm' Can Affect Federal Funding," *Amber Waves,* Dec. 2009, p. 7.

[2] *New York Times,* April 10, 1995, sec. A, p. 1.

equivalent thereof" (italics for emphasis added). This meant that ten Glassboro State College students, unrelated by blood, could continue to occupy a single-family house despite the objection of the borough of Glassboro.[3] Even the legal definition of *maternity* has shifted. Who is the mother — the woman who contributes the egg or the woman (the surrogate) who bears the child? Several states, acknowledging the changes brought by medical technology, now recognize a difference between the birth mother and the legal mother.

ARGUMENT ESSENTIALS
Purposes of Definition

- Controversy often revolves around definitions of crucial terms.
- Effective communication between writer and reader is not possible if they do not have in mind the same definition of a key term.
- Negotiating a definition that all parties can agree on is the starting point to resolving conflict.

READING ARGUMENT

Seeing Definition

The following essay illustrates how definition can aid argumentation.

The True Meaning of the Word "Cisgender"
SUNNIVIE BRYDUM

Let's get one thing straight: The Oxford English Dictionary describes the word "cisgender" as an adjective and defines it as "Denoting or relating to a person whose self-identity conforms with the gender that corresponds to their biological sex; not transgender."

Beginning a feature with the "dictionary definition" of a subject goes against every lesson drilled into a prospective journalist's head in J-school, but in this instance, it's necessary. Because alongside the stratospheric rise in media visibility for transgender people comes the all-too-predictable pushback from those who are uncomfortable with change or those who claim the term is yet another unnecessary label

that only serves to divide us, spotlighting our differences.

With such phenomena as angry hashtags on the fringes of social media proclaiming #DieCisScum and passionate op-eds defiantly declaring "I Am NOT Cisgendered," the cisgender population seems to be having an identity crisis. Perhaps that's because for many of us, "cisgender" is a new identity, a new label, that many people may not have even realized has applied to our lived experience all along.

Sunnivie Brydum is the managing editor of *The Advocate* and a journalist who enjoys covering the politics of equality. Her essay was posted on advocate.com on July 31, 2015.

[3] *New York Times*, February 1, 1990, sec. B, p. 5.

But it has existed all along. Or at least since the mid-1990s, explains K.J. Rawson, a transgender scholar and assistant professor of English and women's and gender studies at College of the Holy Cross, who earned his Ph.D. in composition and cultural rhetoric from Syracuse University.

5   "The term is typically credited to biologist Dana Leland Defosse, who used 'cisgender' in 1994," explains Rawson. "Like most subcultural terms, I would guess that it was being used informally with increasing frequency, but the print literature we have available is slightly behind in representing that."

From an epistemological standpoint, the word is essentially a straightforward antonym of "transgender." Both words share Latin roots, with "trans" meaning "across, beyond, or on the other side of" and "cis" meaning "on this side of." Add the suffix "gender" onto either word, and both terms emerge as strictly descriptive adjectives.

"It's not meant to be dismissive, but rather descriptive," Rawson says.

Last month the word "cisgender" was officially added to the Oxford English Dictionary. It was added along with 499 other new words, including some more recently popularized, such as "meh," "Twitterati," and "twerk." Other news sites have reestablished a practice of highlighting the most unusual new OED inductees, with Time pointing out "fo' shizzle," "Masshole," and "hot mess."

The OED is currently undergoing a full revision, organized by alphabetical ranges, says Katherine Connor Martin, head of U.S. Dictionaries at Oxford University Press. While many of the latest additions are a direct result of that revision process, Martin does acknowledge that the road bringing "cisgender" to the OED's pages was paved by those advocating for its inclusion.

"In the past few years, 'cisgender' has gone   10 from being a relatively specialized word to one which is commonly used in mainstream publications without any comment, and is a notable addition to the general vocabulary of English," Martin explains to *The Advocate*, noting that she was a member of the editing team that finalized the additions.

The word first appeared on the editor's radar in 2010, when it was flagged by a reader participating in the OED's reading program, which asks "people around the world [to] read books and periodicals and gather citations from them for emerging vocabulary," Martin says.

"One of our readers submitted a citation for 'cisgender' in 2010, so it has officially been in our files since then. ... An entry was added to our online dictionary of current English ... in May 2013," she explains. "The historical OED typically waits until words have been established for some time before adding them, but by this year it was clear that 'cisgender' had entered the general vocabulary of English."

Asked whether she or other OED editors have faced pushback on the word's inclusion in the ever-expanding lexicography reference, Martin is blunt. "No," she says. "We add and define words based on the evidence of their use, and 'cisgender' easily met our criteria for inclusion."

It's worth noting that the word "transgender" was officially added to the OED in 2003.

To help dispel myths that adding new   15 words to the dictionary "involves intense debate amongst a cabal of ancient, bearded lexicographers, with winners and losers for the honor of being included," Martin offers the following summary of the OED's formal process for consideration of new terminology:

> Once a word comes to our attention, it is added to an in-house database of potential entries. We look at how much evidence there is for the word and over how long a period of time, in a number of in-house and external databases. If there is sufficient evidence of it being used (in a variety of texts, without explanation, over a period of time), then it can be added to the dictionary. … There is always room for more words — the last print edition of the OED ran to 20 volumes, and the online edition has no space limitations at all.

But for such a simple adjective, the word certainly incites a good deal of strife.

"For me, 'cis' reifies something that is mostly a fiction," University of Southern California gender studies professor Chris Freeman, Ph.D. tells *The Advocate*. "It creates — or re-creates — a gender binary, which is exactly what many scholars and activists have been fighting against for decades."

"To me, 'cisgender' is a clunky, unhelpful, and maybe even regressive term," Freeman concludes. "It does not move the gender conversation forward in a constructive way. Or in a productive way."

The word is part of the "gender conversation," however. As a testament to the phrase's seeping influence in pop culture (from Urban Dictionary to Stephen Colbert), Facebook's myriad gender-identity options now include "cisgender woman," "cisgender man," and simply "cis." Full disclosure:

This writer has her Facebook profile set to identify her as a queer cisgender woman.

Even among LGBT people, the word is hotly debated. Advocate contributor and transgender Navy veteran Brynn Tannehill argues in a piece at *The Huffington Post* that when used by LGBT people, "the C word" often has a negative connotation. 20

> "When someone is referred to as a 'cisgender lesbian' or 'cis gay man' by a transgender person, it is often in a negative way," Tannehill posits. "The addition of 'cis' or 'cisgender' is used to imply a certain level of contempt and a desire that they leave discussions on transgender issues. It also implies that they don't, can't, or won't ever understand transgender issues."

But others who embrace the word argue that it's in fact a necessary part of an honest conversation about gender, giving language to a privilege that many Americans may never have closely examined. It's for that reason that *The Advocate* uses the word in its reporting, followed by a parenthetical explanation of "nontrans" on the first reference.

"The term 'cisgender' is a means of accounting for privilege and trying to counteract the tendency to only name that which is different," explains Rawson, lamenting that even some gay, lesbian, and bisexual people are struggling to comprehend the damage that can be done by othering language that declares one type of experience normal. "Referring to someone as 'cis-' or 'cisgender' is no different than referring to someone as 'straight' — it's a way to distinguish people's experiences and identities."

Rawson, who says he has never heard the word "cis" used in a derogatory way, stresses that he views the word's growing popularity and cultural usage as a step toward meaningful allyship to a population that, despite glamorous magazine covers and documentaries, experiences violence, discrimination, and poverty at staggering rates.

"If LGB people want to be genuine allies and advocates for trans people, they need to come to recognize the privileges of being cisgender," says Rawson. "What advantages do they have? What things do they never need to worry about? How can they leverage their own relative privilege?"

25   "Of course, LGB people can be genuine advocates for trans issues without identifying as 'cisgender,'" Rawson adds, "but for most, such critical self-reflection is an important step leading to more meaningful engagement."

As for those who argue that labeling them "cisgender" is forcing an unwelcome label on their own, hard-fought identity, Rawson has a powerful parallel:

> Is 'heterosexual' a slur? No. It describes an identity and experience. Because straight folks don't typically experience their heterosexuality as an identity, many don't identify as heterosexual — they don't need to, because culture has already done that for them. Similarly, cisgender people don't generally identify as cisgender because societal expectations already presume that they are. . . .

It's an incredible and invisible power to not need to name yourself because the norms have already done that for you. You don't need to come out as heterosexual or cisgender because it is already expected. Since it isn't a derogatory term, those who take exception to it may be uncomfortable with trans issues or perhaps they are unwilling to confront their own privilege.

Practice: Definition

Consider what Charles's purpose is in using definition. Read the essay, and answer the questions that follow it. Earlier in January of 2010, Haiti had been hit by a 7.0 magnitude earthquake, followed closely by two aftershocks that were almost as strong. More than 160,000 people were killed, and almost 1.5 million were displaced.

Stop Calling Quake Victims Looters
GUY-URIEL CHARLES

To define someone as a looter is not simply to describe him, or her, through an act, it is to make a moral judgment. It is to characterize the person as lawless and criminal. It connotes someone who is without self-restraint; an animal; wanton and depraved.

It is a description that is void of empathy for someone who is consciously or subconsciously viewed as "the other." Tragically, it fits into the stereotype that many have about people of African descent, be they African Americans or Haitian Americans.

Guy-Uriel Charles is a law professor at Duke Law School and founder of Duke's Center on Law, Race, and Politics. He is Haitian American. The article appeared on cnn.com on January 21, 2010.

The news media have to stop describing starving Haitians who are simply trying to survive the earthquake and aftershocks that took their homes, their loved ones, and all their possessions by this highly derogatory term.

It's a lesson they should have learned covering the devastation wrought by Hurricane Katrina. I remember the news accounts then that described black residents of New Orleans as "looters," but used benign words to describe white residents engaged in the same action: "taking things."

5 Academics have found repeated instances of this in media content analyses after disasters. One example, widely disseminated on the Web post-Katrina, juxtaposed an Associated Press photo that showed a young black man wading through chest-high water "after looting a grocery store" (said the caption), with an AFP/Getty photo of a white woman in the same position, although the caption this time described her "finding" food "from a local grocery store."

It is time to put this practice to rest.

Put yourself in the position of the average Haitian in Port-au-Prince. One minute you were going about your business, the next minute the earth shook and literally your world crumbled all around you. But you were one of the lucky ones, you survived the earthquake. Injured? Yes. But alive.

Your first thought is to cry out for your family, especially your kids. But most of your family is buried under a rubble pile somewhere. You had four children but only one survived the earthquake. You have spent the last few days, along with your fellow survivors, digging through the rubble trying to find them.

It is now a week after the earthquake, and you have eaten little or nothing. You are hungry and thirsty, and while you hear rumors of aid coming, you have not seen any evidence of it.

You have not heard from the president and 10 indeed you've heard rumors that his wife is dead. Perhaps he left the country; you would too, if you could. There is no police presence at all. No governmental authority to provide support. There are no markets.

The only money you have are the few gourdes (Haitian dollars) that you have in your pockets. The rest of your money is in the safe place you always kept it — but it is now buried with your food. The banks are not open. There is no one to borrow from; they are all in the same boat as you. There are no functioning institutions.

You have family in the United States and they are desperately trying to get you some help. They have contacted all of the big aid agencies, but those agencies have issues of their own. Some have lost staff members. They are doing the best they can, but they have no idea that you exist and you have no way of finding them. The roads are impassable, and they can't get clearance from whoever is in charge of the airport to land their planes, which bring much needed supplies.

They're afraid to go anywhere without security because they've heard that the people are becoming restless. Indeed, though you do not know this, the U.S. military is also worried that citizens will get violent and start stealing. The United Nations is waiting for more troops, and the doctors have stopped treating patients because of those same fears: violence, looting.

Under normal circumstances you would not think of taking food without paying for it. You are what other Haitians would call "bien eleve" not "mal eleve." By that they mean you were well-raised, with manners and dignity.

15   Haitians put a strong premium on dignity. To take something for which you have not paid does not only offend your sense of legality but also your sense of personhood. It is undignified. But not only are you starving, so is your only surviving child. You would prefer to pay, but whom? What would you pay with? You'd prefer to wait, but for whom? How long can you afford to wait?

You feel that your desperate state is evidence that you have been abandoned by your family, your country, the international community, and Bondié (God). (The Creole word for God literally means "good God.")

So you take. You take just enough for a couple of days and a couple of family members. You take and you run to feed those for whom the only measure of fortune is survival in Haiti, post-earthquake. You take and you run.

Are you a looter? Try as we might to prevent it, the answer to that question is inevitably racialized. We cannot separate the word looting from its racial implications or the supposed crime of looting from its racial origins. In the throes of the civil rights movement in the United States, many states made looting a crime. Almost all of these states were southern states that had a history of criminalizing behavior that they associated more with African Americans than with whites.

Even so, the criminal law, for all of its shortcomings, is often more sophisticated than we are. It recognizes that context matters. It has been developed with concepts — such as necessity and justification — to identify the circumstances under which a person who would normally be held culpable can be held either less culpable or not at all culpable. Taking food is different than taking a television.

20   It is past time for our news media to develop similar sophistication. It is time to stop characterizing black people trying to survive in dire circumstances as looters. Are they takers? Yes. Are they looters? Let's wait for a criminal conviction first.

This photo was taken on March 18, 2010, in Port-au-Prince, Haiti, in the aftermath of a devastating earthquake. STEVE LINDRIDGE / Alamy

Reading and Discussion Questions

1. What is Charles's claim in the article?
2. How is what happened in Haiti after the earthquake similar to what happened in New Orleans after Hurricane Katrina?
3. What support does Charles offer for his contention that the answer to the question of whether or not a person is considered a looter "is inevitably racialized" (para. 18)?
4. Why is *looter* not an appropriate term to use to describe those in Haiti who took food and other goods without paying?
5. What does Charles mean when he says that criminal law "is often more sophisticated than we are" (para. 19)?

Defining the Terms in Your Argument

In some of your arguments, you will introduce terms that require definition. We've pointed out that a definition of *poverty* is crucial to any debate on the existence of poverty in the United States. The same may be true in a debate about the legality of euthanasia, or mercy killing. Are the arguers referring to passive euthanasia (the withdrawal of life-support systems) or to active euthanasia (the direct administration of drugs to hasten death)? It is not uncommon, in fact, for arguments about controversial questions to turn into arguments about the definition of terms.

An argument can end almost before it begins if writer and reader cannot agree on definitions of key terms. While clear definitions do not guarantee agreement, they do ensure that all parties understand the nature of the argument. In the Rogerian approach to argumentation, negotiating a definition that all parties can accept is the starting point to resolving conflict.

The Limitations of Dictionary Definitions

Reading a dictionary definition is the simplest and most obvious way to learn the basic definition of a term. An unabridged dictionary is the best source because it usually gives examples of the way a word can be used in a sentence; that is, it furnishes the proper context.

In many cases, the dictionary definition alone is not sufficient. It may be too broad or too narrow for your purpose. Suppose, in an argument about pornography, you want to define the word *obscene. Webster's New International Dictionary* (3rd edition, unabridged) gives the definition of *obscene* as "offensive to taste; foul; loathsome; disgusting." But these synonyms do not tell you what qualities make an object or an event or an action "foul," "loathsome," and "disgusting." In 1973 the Supreme Court, attempting to narrow the definition of *obscenity*, ruled that obscenity was to be determined by the community in accordance with local standards. One person's obscenity, as numerous cases have demonstrated, may be another person's art. The celebrated trials in the early twentieth century about the distribution of novels regarded as pornographic — D. H. Lawrence's *Lady Chatterley's Lover* and James Joyce's *Ulysses* — emphasized the problems of defining obscenity.

Another dictionary definition may strike you as too narrow. *Patriotism,* for example, is defined in one dictionary as "love and loyal or zealous support of one's country, especially in all matters involving other countries." Some readers may want to include an unwillingness to support government policies they consider wrong.

These limitations illustrate why opening an essay with a dictionary definition is often not a very effective strategy, although many beginning writers use it. In order to initiate the effective discussion of a key term, you should be able to define it in your own words.

Stipulation and Negation: Stating What a Term *Is* and *Is Not*

Since definitions can vary so much and well-meaning writers want their readers to understand their arguments, it is often necessary to establish from the beginning what definition a writer is using for the purposes of a particular argument. That means writers may **stipulate** the definition that they are using, knowing that other people in other contexts may define the term differently. In some cases, one way to clarify how a term is being used is to stipulate what it is not. This is called **negation**.

In stipulating the meaning of a term, the writer asks the reader to accept a definition that may be different from the conventional one. The writer does this to limit or control the argument. A term like *national security* can be defined by a nation's leaders in such a way as to sanction persecution of citizens and reckless military actions. Likewise, a term such as *liberation* can be appropriated by terrorist groups whose activities often lead to oppression rather than liberation.

Even the word *violence,* which the dictionary defines as "physical force used so as to injure or damage" and whose meaning seems utterly clear and uncompromising, can be manipulated to produce a definition different from the one that most people normally understand. Some pacifists refer to conditions in which "people are deprived of choices in a systematic way" as "institutionalized quiet violence." Even where no physical force is employed, this lack of choice in schools, in the workplace, in black neighborhoods is defined as violence.[4]

A writer and an audience cannot agree on a solution to a problem if they cannot even agree on what they are talking about. Carl Rogers's advice applies

---

[4] Newton Garver, "What Violence Is," in James Rachels, ed., *Moral Choices* (New York: Harper & Row, 1971), pp. 248–49.

here: Listen to how your audience defines a key term. Make clear how you define it. Then work from there toward a definition that you can stipulate as the agreed-upon definition that you will use as you move toward resolution.

In *Through the Looking-Glass*, Alice asked Humpty Dumpty "whether you can make words mean so many different things."

"When *I* use a word," Humpty Dumpty said scornfully, "it means just what I choose it to mean — neither more nor less."[5]

A writer, however, is not free to invent definitions that no one will recognize or that create rather than solve problems between writer and reader.

To avoid confusion, it is sometimes helpful to tell the reader what a term is *not*. In discussing euthanasia, a writer might say, "By euthanasia I do not mean active intervention to hasten the death of the patient." Another example: "Patients are diagnosed with PDD-NOS (Pervasive Developmental Disorder- Not Otherwise Specified) if they have some behaviors seen in autism but do not meet the full criteria for having an autistic disorder." A negative definition may be more extensive, depending on the complexity of the term and the writer's ingenuity.

Defining Vague and Ambiguous Terms

You will need to define other terms in addition to those in your claim. If you use words and phrases that have two or more meanings, they may appear vague and ambiguous to your reader. In arguments of value and policy, abstract terms such as *freedom of speech, justice,* and *equality* require clarification. Despite their abstract nature, however, they are among the most important in the language because they represent the ideals that shape our laws. When conflicts arise, the courts must define these terms to establish the legality of certain practices. Is the Ku Klux Klan permitted to make disparaging public statements about ethnic and racial groups? That depends on the court's definition of *free speech.* Can execution for some crimes be considered cruel and unusual punishment? That, too, depends on the court's definition of *cruel and unusual punishment.*

Consider the definition of *race,* around which so much of U.S. history has revolved, often with tragic consequences. Until recently, the only categories listed in the census were white, black, Asian-Pacific, and Native American, "with the Hispanic population straddling them all." But rapidly increasing intermarriage and ethnic identity caused a number of political and ethnic groups to demand changes in the classifications of the Census Bureau. Some Arab Americans, for example, prefer to be counted as "Middle Eastern" rather than white. Children of black-white unions are defined as black 60 percent of the time, while children of Asian-white unions are described as Asian 42 percent of the time. Research has been conducted to discover how people feel about the terms that are used

---

[5] Lewis Carroll, *Alice in Wonderland* and *Through the Looking-Glass* (New York: Grosset & Dunlap, 1948), p. 238.

to define them. As one anthropologist pointed out, "Socially and politically assigned attributes have a lot to do with access to economic resources."[6]

"Socially and politically assigned attributes" can also be the basis for judging others. The definition of *success*, for example, varies among social groups as well as among individuals within the group. So difficult is the formulation of a universally accepted measure for success that some scholars regard the concept as meaningless. Nevertheless, we continue to use the word as if it represents a definable concept because the idea of success, however defined, is important for the identity and development of the individual and the group. It is clear, however, that when crossing subcultural boundaries, even within a small group, we need to be aware of differences in the use of the word. If contentment — that is, the satisfaction of achieving a small personal goal — is enough, then a person making a minimal salary but doing work that he or she loves may be a success. But you should not expect all your readers to agree that these criteria are enough to define *success*.

Abstract terms can be one source of vagueness in writing. Concrete examples usually help to define an abstraction. Abstract and concrete terms are treated more fully in the Language chapter on pages 285–286.

RESEARCH SKILL ▶ Using Encyclopedias

When there is disagreement about the definition of a term, you may need more than a dictionary definition to clarify the points on which the disagreement occurs. Often an encyclopedia can give a much fuller discussion of the complexities of defining terms that defy simple, clear-cut definitions. The more specialized the encyclopedia, the more useful the information — unless it uses so much jargon that it is useful only to specialists.

For example, *abortion* is defined in the *Encyclopedia Britannica Online* like this:

> **Abortion** — the expulsion of a fetus from the uterus before it has reached the stage of viability (in human beings, usually about the 20th week of gestation). An abortion may occur spontaneously, in which case it is also called a miscarriage, or it may be brought on purposefully, in which case it is often called an induced abortion.

A specialized encyclopedia may provide more detailed information by discussing different positions in the debate for or against abortion. What follows is only a portion of an article from the *Encyclopedia of Philosophy*, which also includes a list of works cited that leads to other possible sources:

> The claims to which partisans on both sides of the "abortion" issue appeal seem, if one is not thinking of the abortion issue, close to self-evident, or they appear to be easily defensible. The case against abortion (Beckwith 1993) rests on the proposition that there is a very strong presumption that ending another human life is seriously wrong. Almost everyone who is not thinking about the abortion issue would agree. There are good arguments for the view that fetuses are both living and human. ("Fetus" is generally used in the philosophical literature on abortion to refer to a human organism from

---

[6] *Wall Street Journal*, September 9, 1995, sec. B, p. 1.

the time of conception to the time of birth.) Thus, it is easy for those opposed to abortion to think that only the morally depraved or the seriously confused could disagree with them. Standard pro-choice views appeal either to the proposition that women have the right to make decisions concerning their own bodies or to the proposition that fetuses are not yet persons. Both of these propositions seem either to be platitudes or to be straightforwardly defensible. Thus, it is easy for pro-choicers to believe that only religious fanatics or dogmatic conservatives could disagree. This explains, at least in part, why the abortion issue has created so much controversy. The philosophical debate regarding abortion has been concerned largely with subjecting these apparently obvious claims to the analytical scrutiny philosophers ought to give to them.

Consider first the standard argument against abortion. One frequent objection to the claim that fetuses are both human and alive is that we do not know when life begins. The reply to this objection is. . . .

You may find that your library has a database — such as Gale Virtual Reference Library — that lets you search a number of different encyclopedias at the same time. Just the first six entries from the list generated by that database lead to a range of encyclopedias you can investigate:

1. Abortion: I. Medical Perspectives. Allan Rosenfield, Sara Iden, and Anne Drapkin Lyerly. *Encyclopedia of Bioethics*. Ed. Stephen G. Post. Vol. 1. 3rd ed. New York: Macmillan Reference USA, 2004. p. 1–7.

2. Abortion. Menachem Elon. *Encyclopaedia Judaica.* Ed. Michael Berenbaum and Fred Skolnik. Vol. 1. 2nd ed. Detroit: Macmillan Reference USA, 2007. p. 270–273.

3. Abortion. Don Marquis. *Encyclopedia of Philosophy*. Ed. Donald M. Borchert. Vol. 1. 2nd ed. Detroit: Macmillan Reference USA, 2006. p. 8–10.

4. Abortion. *National Survey of State Laws*. Ed. Richard A. Leiter. 6th ed. Detroit: Gale, 2008. p. 339–371.

5. Abortion. *West's Encyclopedia of American Law*. Ed. Shirelle Phelps and Jeffrey Lehman. Vol. 1. 2nd ed. Detroit: Gale, 2005. p. 13–26.

6. Abortion. Mark R. Wicclair and Gabriella Gosman. *Encyclopedia of Science, Technology, and Ethics*. Ed. Carl Mitcham. Vol. 1. Detroit: Macmillan Reference USA, 2005. p. 1–6.

Note: Wikipedia is a convenient source that often appears as the first source listed in the results from an online search, but it should be used with caution, if at all, for serious research. The information it contains can be written by anyone, no matter what their credentials may be. However, it may serve as a good source of references and links to more reputable sources.

Definition by Example

One of the most effective ways of defining terms in an argument is to use examples. Both real and hypothetical examples can bring life to abstract and ambiguous terms. The writer in the following passage defines *cognate* in the first two sentences through negation and then by means of examples:

At some colleges and universities, a cognate is a personalized alternative to a minor. Where a minor is a cluster of courses from one department that a student takes in addition to a major as a secondary emphasis area, a cognate lets a student, with the approval of an advisor,

ARGUMENT ESSENTIALS
Defining the Terms in Your Argument

- You and your reader must agree on definitions of key terms if your argument is to be effective.
- In most cases, a dictionary definition is not sufficient.
- Stipulate the definition of key terms that you are using because other people in other contexts may define the term differently.
- In some cases, you may clarify a term by stipulating what it is not, or by negation.
- Avoid vague and ambiguous terms, or take the time to explain which of two or more possible meanings is the one you intend.

choose a cluster of courses from different departments that serve as a secondary emphasis area to complement his or her minor. For example, a film studies major might take a course in the Foreign Languages department about how foreign cultures are represented through film, a course in the anthropology department focusing on anthropology in film, a course in the English department about film adaptation of novels, and a course in the psychology department on the representation of abnormal psychology in film. A student interested in the environment might major in biology and put together a cognate from courses in law, economics, geography, and history.

Writing Extended Definitions

When we speak of an extended definition, we usually refer not only to length but also to the variety of methods for developing the definition. The argumentative essay can take the form of an extended definition. This type of definition essay is appropriate when the idea under consideration is so controversial or so heavy with historical connotations that even a paragraph or two cannot make clear exactly what the arguer wants his or her readers to understand. For example, if you were preparing a definition of *patriotism,* you would probably use a number of methods to develop your definition: personal narrative, examples, stipulation, comparison and contrast, and cause-and-effect analysis.

WRITER'S GUIDE
Writing a Definition Essay

The following are important steps to take when you write an essay of definition.

1. **Choose a term that needs definition** because it is controversial or ambiguous, or because you want to offer a personal definition that differs from the accepted interpretation. Explain why an extended definition is necessary. Or choose an experience that lends itself to treatment in an extended definition. One student defined *culture shock* as she had experienced it while studying abroad in Hawaii among students of a different ethnic background.

2. **Decide on the thesis** — the point of view you wish to develop about the term you are defining. If you want to define *heroism*, for example, you may choose to develop the idea that this quality depends on motivation and awareness of danger rather than on the specific act performed by the hero.

3. **Distinguish wherever possible between the term you are defining and other terms with which it might be confused.** If you are defining *love*, can you make a clear distinction between the different kinds of emotional attachments that the word conveys?

4. **Try to think of several methods of developing the definition** — using examples, comparison and contrast, analogy, cause-and-effect analysis. However, you may discover that one method alone — say, use of examples — will suffice to narrow and refine your definition.

5. **Arrange your supporting material** in an order that gives emphasis to the most important ideas.

READING ARGUMENT

Seeing an Extended Definition

In the United States, terrorism has received unprecedented attention since the tragic events of September 11, 2001. You may be surprised to learn that the essay that follows was written in May of that year, before planes crashing into the World Trade Center, the Pentagon, and a field in Pennsylvania gave the term new meaning for Americans forever. Just as the problem of terrorism has not yet been solved, the problem of defining terrorism remains unsolved as well. The essay has been annotated to highlight the use of definition.

The Definition of Terrorism
BRIAN WHITAKER

Decide for yourself whether to believe this, but according to a new report there were only 16 cases of international terrorism in the Middle East last year.

That is the lowest number for any region in the world apart from North America (where there were none at all). Europe had 30 cases — almost twice as many as the Middle East — and Latin America came top with 193.

This article was published May 7, 2001, in *Guardian Unlimited*, the daily online version of the British newspaper the *Guardian*. Whitaker is a former editor on Comment Is Free, the *Guardian's* Web expansion.

Statistics on terrorism from before 9/11

The figures come from the U.S. State Department's annual review of global terrorism, which has just been published on the Internet. Worldwide, the report says confidently, "there were 423 international terrorist attacks in 2000, an increase of 8% from the 392 attacks recorded during 1999."

Problems with attempts to define terrorism

No doubt a lot of painstaking effort went into counting them, but the statistics are fundamentally meaningless because, as the report points out, "no one definition of terrorism has gained universal acceptance."

That is an understatement. While most people agree that terrorism exists, few can agree on what it is. A recent book discussing attempts by the UN and other international bodies to define terrorism runs to three volumes and 1,866 pages without reaching any firm conclusion.

5

U.S. State Department's definition

Using the definition preferred by the state department, terrorism is: "Premeditated, politically motivated violence perpetrated against noncombatant* targets by subnational groups or clandestine agents, usually intended to influence an audience." (The asterisk is important, as we shall see later.)

Definition of "international" terrorism

"International" terrorism — the subject of the American report — is defined as "terrorism involving citizens or the territory of more than one country."

Main point of agreement is motivation.

The key point about terrorism, on which almost everyone agrees, is that it's politically motivated. This is what distinguishes it from, say, murder or football hooliganism. But this also causes a problem for those who compile statistics because the motive is not always clear — especially if no one has claimed responsibility.

Example of incidents with no known motivation

So the American report states — correctly — that there were no confirmed terrorist incidents in Saudi Arabia last year. There were, nevertheless, three unexplained bombings and one shooting incident, all directed against foreigners.

Another part of the definition

Another essential ingredient (you might think) is that terrorism is calculated to terrorize the public or a particular section of it. The American definition does not mention spreading terror at all, because that would exclude attacks against property. It is, after all, impossible to frighten an inanimate object.

10

Among last year's attacks, 152 were directed against a pipeline in Colombia which is owned by multinational oil companies. Such attacks are of concern to the United States and so a definition is required which allows them to be counted.

Questions about which examples meet the criteria

For those who accept that terrorism is about terrorizing people, other questions arise. Does it include threats, as well as actual violence? A few years ago, for example, the Islamic Army in Yemen warned foreigners to leave the country if they valued their lives but did not actually carry out its threat.

More recently, a group of Israeli peace activists were arrested for driving around in a loudspeaker van, announcing a curfew of the kind that is imposed on Palestinians. Terrifying for any Israelis who believed it, but was it terrorism?

Another characteristic

Another characteristic of terrorism, according to some people, is that targets must be random — the intention being to make everyone fear they might be the next victim. Some of the Hamas suicide bombings appear to follow this principle but when attacks are aimed at predictable targets (such as the military) they are less likely to terrorize the public at large.

15   Definitions usually try to distinguish between terrorism and warfare. In general this means that attacks on soldiers are warfare and those against civilians are terrorism, but the dividing lines quickly become blurred.

What terrorism is not

The state department regards attacks against "noncombatant* targets" as terrorism. But follow the asterisk to the small print and you find that "noncombatants" includes both civilians and military personnel who are unarmed or off duty at the time. Several examples are given, such as the 1986 disco bombing in Berlin, which killed two servicemen.

Examples

The most lethal bombing in the Middle East last year was the suicide attack on USS *Cole* in Aden harbor which killed 17 American sailors and injured 39 more.

As the ship was armed and its crew on duty at the time, why is this classified as terrorism? Look again at the small print, which adds: "We also consider as acts of terrorism attacks on military installations or on armed military personnel when a state of military hostilities does not exist at the site, such as bombings against U.S. bases."

Unanswered question

A similar question arises with Palestinian attacks on quasi-military targets such as Israeli settlements. Many settlers are armed (with weapons supplied by the army) and the settlements themselves — though they contain civilians — might be considered military targets because they are there to consolidate a military occupation.

20   If, under the state department rules, Palestinian mortar attacks on settlements count as terrorism, it would be reasonable to expect Israeli rocket attacks on Palestinian communities to be treated in the same way — but they are not. In the American definition, terrorism can never be inflicted by a state.

Limitations of American definition

Israeli treatment of the Palestinians is classified as a human rights issue (for which the Israelis get a rap over the knuckles) in a separate state department report.

Denying that states can commit terrorism is generally useful, because it gets the U.S. and its allies off the hook in a variety of situations. The disadvantage is that it might also get hostile states off the hook — which is why there has to be a list of states that are said to "sponsor" terrorism while not actually committing it themselves.

The term's original meaning

Interestingly, the American definition of terrorism is a reversal of the word's original meaning, given in the *Oxford English Dictionary* as "government by intimidation." Today it usually refers to intimidation of governments.

Its history

The first recorded use of "terrorism" and "terrorist" was in 1795, relating to the Reign of Terror instituted by the French government. Of course, the Jacobins, who led the government at the time, were also revolutionaries and gradually "terrorism" came to be applied to violent revolutionary activity in general. But the use of "terrorist" in an anti-government sense is not recorded until 1866 (referring to Ireland) and 1883 (referring to Russia).

The difficulty of making laws against terrorism

In the absence of an agreed meaning, making laws against terrorism is especially difficult. The latest British anti-terrorism law gets round the problem by listing 21 international terrorist organizations by name. Membership of these is illegal in the UK.

25

There are six Islamic groups, four anti-Israel groups, eight separatist groups, and three opposition groups. The list includes Hizbullah, which though armed, is a legal political party in Lebanon, with elected members of parliament.

Among the separatist groups, the Kurdistan Workers Party — active in Turkey — is banned, but not the KDP or PUK, which are Kurdish organizations active in Iraq. Among opposition groups, the Iranian People's Mujahedeen is banned, but not its Iraqi equivalent, the INC, which happens to be financed by the United States.

This author's stipulated definition

Issuing such a list does at least highlight the anomalies and inconsistencies behind anti-terrorism laws. It also points toward a simpler — and perhaps more honest — definition: terrorism is violence committed by those we disapprove of.

Practice: Extended Definition

Like most extended definitions, the definition of "conscientious objection" in the essay beginning on page 265 uses several of the means of defining a term that this chapter has covered. Which of them do you see, and where? Read the essay, and answer the questions that follow it.

Conscientious Objection in Medicine: A Moral Dilemma
ISHMEAL BRADLEY

Consider this: what would you do if a patient with terminal pancreatic cancer told you, his primary care doctor of twenty years, that he wanted your help to end his life? Or, what if a woman in her first trimester who contracted an infection that threatened the health of her fetus asked you, her obstetrician, to perform an abortion? Ethical questions like these are encountered not infrequently today. However, they can pose a moral dilemma for the physician. Where are the boundaries between professional obligations and personal morality? Can personal morality override professional duty when it comes to patient care?

Conscientious objection in medicine is the notion that a health care provider can abstain from offering certain types of medical care with which he/she does not personally agree. This includes care that would otherwise be considered medically appropriate. An example would be a pro-life obstetrician who refuses to perform abortions or sterilizations. On the one hand, there is the argument that physicians have a duty to uphold the wishes of their patients, as long as those wishes are reasonable. On the other is the thought that physicians themselves are moral beings and that their morality should not be infringed upon by dictates from the legislatures, medical community or patient interests.

Several states in the last few years have passed laws that protect health care providers from retribution if those providers, who invoke their conscience, refuse to provide medical care. One example is the Michigan Conscientious Objector Policy Act of 2004 which allows providers to decline offering care if that care compromises the provider's beliefs, except in the event of an emergency.[1] Furthermore, a state law in Georgia extends conscientious objection to pharmacists by allowing them to refuse to fill a prescription for emergency contraception, even to a victim of sexual assault.[2]

This issue was reignited in December 2008 by the passage of the Medical Conscience Rule by the Department of Health and Human Services in the closing weeks of the Bush administration. Then-Secretary Michael Leavitt sought to expand the scope of several laws passed by Congress in the 1970s, 1990s, and 2000s.[3] Those previous laws were designed to protect health care entities — individual providers, insurance companies, hospitals, charitable organizations providing medical care — who received any form of federal funding from reprisal if they chose not to provide certain medical services that violated their conscience, most notably abortion services.

Specifically, the goal of the new law is to "prohibit recipients of certain federal funds from coercing individuals in the health care field into participating in actions they find religiously or morally objectionable" and to "prohibit discrimination on the basis of one's objection to, participation in, or refusal to participate in,

5

Ishmeal Bradley is a doctor of internal medicine in New York. His article was posted on May 28, 2009, on *Clinical Correlations: The NYU Langone Online Journal of Medicine*.

specific medical procedures, including abortion and sterilization."[4] Also, the new regulation aims to educate the health care community about the protections afforded by federal law, ensure compliance with current federal law, hear grievances brought to the Department's attention by plaintiffs, and to "take an active role in promoting open communication within the health care field [in order to foster] a more inclusive, tolerant environment . . . than [what] may currently exist."[4] Any health care entity found to be in violation of the new law would be subject to a termination of federal support and repayment of funds already received.

In a statement released on the DHHS website, Secretary Leavitt expressed that "health care providers should not be forced to choose between good professional standing and violating their conscience." Critics say that there are already federal and state laws on this issue, and that the Secretary was acting more out of ideology than for concern for the actual dilemma. Also, the language of the Medical Conscience Rule is so broad that it could seriously hinder patient access to health care. Opposing the new law are the American Hospital Association and the American Medical Association, while faith-based organizations, like the Catholic Health Association, support it. Although the AMA's guidelines do say that a physician can choose whom to serve in non-emergent situations, they also emphasized that the "responsibility to the patient is paramount." In a letter to the DHHS last fall, the AMA expressed concern about the wording of the new law, feeling that it was "overly broad and could lead to differing interpretations causing unnecessary confusion and disruption among health care institutions and professionals," thereby hindering patient access to care.[5] Despite

opposition from several prominent professional organizations, the new law went into effect on January 20, 2009. Responding to pressure from the new Obama administration and patient advocacy groups, the new DHHS is currently taking steps to rescind the law.[6,7]

Since the 1970s, Congress has passed several laws to protect health care entities from perceived discrimination. In 1973 Congress passed the Church Amendments in response to Roe v. Wade. The first amendment stated that any entity that received federal support from the DHHS could not compel employees to perform sterilization or abortion procedures, make their facilities available for such procedures, or provide personnel for such procedures if doing so would be contrary to the entity's religious beliefs.[4] The second and third amendments outlawed job discrimination on the basis of personal convictions regarding these reproductive matters.

Then came the Public Health Service Act of 1996, which was both more specific and expansive about reproductive rights than the earlier Church Amendments. It explicitly forbade federal, state, and local agencies that received federal funding from discriminating against any health care entity that refused to provide abortion services, training for such services, or referrals for patients to other agencies that did perform those services, and outlawed health care organizations from requiring their physicians from being trained in abortions.[4] Similarly, the Weldon Amendment, a rider on the 2005 appropriations bill for the DHHS, reiterated that no funds from the Department would be provided to an agency if that agency subjected a "health care entity to discrimination on the basis that the health care entity [did] not provide, pay for, provide coverage of, or refer for abortions."[4]

Against this backdrop of the Medical Conscience Rule, the question remains, is there a place for conscientious objection in medicine? Is it acceptable for a health care provider to deny appropriate and legal medical care to a patient when asked to do so? Critics cite the supremacy of patient autonomy and the professional duty of a physician as reasons to oppose conscientious objection. On the other side, those in favor stress that the morality of the physician is an integral part in the doctor–patient relationship and should not be ignored.

10   In a controversial article published in 2006, Julian Savulescu, a medical ethicist from Oxford, wrote that the "primary goal of a health service is to protect the health of its recipients."[8] Furthermore, he wrote that doctors should not be able to "offer partial medical services or partially discharge their obligations to care for their patients" because they are not ready to offer legal and beneficial, but controversial, care. He argues that the personal beliefs and morality of the physician should not enter into medical decision-making. The only thing that matters is what is "best" for the patient as both the patient and the law see fit.

This paradigm is unabashedly absolutist. Critics of his have mentioned that in his reasoning, physicians would be forced to perform procedures or services that they may view as immoral. According to Savulescu, what some of his critics may not fully appreciate is that there is no question of personal morality in this model. To appreciate this, one has to accept a priori several fundamental premises. One, that patients can make reasonable decisions when presented with all the data. Two, that the duty of a physician is to honor a patient's wishes, if those wishes are within reason. And three, that patient autonomy and the right to guide one's own medical care are universal truths. Conscientious objection inherently takes the decision-making power away from the patient and places it in the hands of the physician.

The professional duty of the physician is a subject of debate, too. Whereas Savulescu argues that duty is absolute and unwavering, those in favor of conscientious objection feel that duty is malleable and can change depending on the situation at hand.

Proponents of this case-specific model argue that conscientious objection does have a place in medicine and that the individual health care provider can decide what he or she will or will not offer to a patient. The patient's requests are only one part of the decision-making process, the other part being the will of the health care provider. They contend that every controversial situation should be viewed uniquely and judged on its own singular status. Along these lines, Plato once said that "prudence is not concerned with universals only; it must also take cognizance of particulars." However, disregard for "universals" can introduce an element of caprice into the health care community, which would only create more confusion and inconsistencies.[6]

One potential solution for conscientious objection is the so-called "physician-referral policy." If a patient requests something that the physician feels uncomfortable providing, the physician can refer the patient to someone else who will honor that request. However, for this system to function, there must be enough providers available to perform those services. If there are not, then patients are needlessly harmed by not having access to appropriate medical care.

The Medical Conscience Rule complicates   15
this policy because it exempts physicians from the requirement of referring patients to other

providers. The patient, who relies on the physician for his or her expert advice and referrals to other providers, is left without recourse. Furthermore, the physician referral policy can damage the notion of informed consent. The physician may not present the patient with all the available options, especially if some of those options are not in line with the physician's beliefs, like abortion or withdrawing life support.[9] Or, the physician may present or withhold the data in such a way as to push the patient towards one course of action that may be more acceptable to the physician but not in the interest of the patient.

Unfortunately, difficult decisions will always arise in the practice of medicine, and when they do, doctors should work with patients to determine the best option specific to that patient and his or her circumstance. We must all remember, patients and doctors together, that no pro-choice physician is pro-abortion, that no doctor is pro-death. But sometimes, physicians must perform certain tasks for the ultimate good of their patient, even if one has to take the plunge and place one's personal convictions aside.

On a personal note, I believe myself to be a moral and religious man. I use those values to guide my own personal decision-making, but I try to stop short of imposing those rules on another person — including a patient — who may have a very different set of values. Furthermore, I took an oath on the day that I graduated from medical school that obligated me to offer, to the best of my abilities, appropriate, uncompromised medical care without bias. There will certainly be times when I will be faced with a request from a patient or patient's representative that I will personally find morally difficult, but one that is still legally and ethically acceptable. I hope that those instances are few and far between;

when they do arrive, I expect that I will be able to take a step back and fully take on the mantle of the physician and act for the good of my patients, respecting their values as well as medical evidence, never putting my own interests before those of my patients.

Notes

1. Michigan Conscientious Objector Policy Act of 2004, HB-5006. 11 Mar. www.legislature. mi.gov/documents/2003-2004/billengrossed/ house/htm/2003-HEBH-5006.htm.
2. National Women's Law Center, "Pharmacy Refusals: State Laws, Regulations, and Policies," 6 Apr. 2009. www.nwlc.org/pdf/ pharmacyrefusalpoliciesapril2009.pdf.
3. David Stout, "Medical 'Conscience Rule' Is Issued," *New York Times,* 19 Dec. 2008.
4. United States Dept. of Health and Human Services, "Ensuring That Department of Health and Human Services Funds Do Not Support Coercive or Discriminatory Policies or Practices in Violation of Federal Law," 45 CFR Part 88. Federal Register, 19 Dec. 2008, Vol. 73, no. 245, 78071–78101. http:// edocket.access.gpo.gov/2008/E8-30134.htm.
5. Amy Lynn Sorrel, "Revised Language in Proposed HHS Rule Still Bolsters Abortion Conscience Laws," *American Medical News*, 22.29, Sept. 2008.
6. Julie D. Cantor, "Conscientious Objection Gone Awry — Restoring Selfless Professionalism in Medicine," *NEJM* 360.15 (2009): 1484–85.
7. Most parts of the Medical Conscience Rule were rescinded in 2011.— Eds.
8. Julian Savulescu, "Conscientious Objection in Medicine," *BMJ* 332 (2006): 294–97.
9. Karen E. Adams, "Moral Diversity among Physicians and Conscientious Refusal of Care in the Provision of Abortion Services," *J Am Med Womens Assoc,* 58 (2003): 223–26.

Reading and Discussion Questions

1. Where does Bradley most concisely state his definition of conscientious objection in medicine?

2. Why is conscientious objection in medicine so controversial?

3. What was the goal of the Medical Conscience Rule? What were some of the different reactions to that law?

4. What is Bradley's personal opinion regarding conscientious objection in medicine? Do you agree? Why, or why not?

Assignments for Definition: Clarifying Key Terms

Reading and Discussion Questions

1. Why is definition such a crucial element in argumentation? In what ways can it help resolve issues? How can it lead to problems?

2. Who has the power to stipulate how a term is defined? The government? The media? Society in a broader sense? Where have you seen examples of each in the readings in this chapter?

Writing Suggestions

1. Narrate an experience you have had in which you felt either aided or hindered by being defined as a member of a specific group. It could be a group defined by gender, race, religious affiliation, or membership on a team or in a club.

2. Would adoption at the state level of a policy prohibiting classifying people by race, color, ethnicity, or national origin be beneficial or pernicious for the individual and for society? In other words, what is good or bad about classifying people?

3. Find a subject for which definition is critical to how statistics are interpreted and for which you can make a successful argument in a 750- to 1,000-word paper. Your essay should provide proof for a claim.

4. Write about an important or widely used term whose meaning has changed since you first learned it. Such terms often come from the slang of particular groups: drug users, rock music fans, musicians, athletes, computer programmers, or software developers.

5. Write an essay in which you provide specific examples of how government officials sometimes use euphemisms and other careful word choices to disguise the truth.

RESEARCH ASSIGNMENT ▶ **Using Encyclopedias**

1. Find out what encyclopedias your library has to offer. A librarian may be able to give you a list. Some may be in print and others online. If there is no list, you can search under "encyclopedia" and scan the list for relevant titles.

2. Now choose one of the controversial subjects listed below, and investigate what you can learn about it from three different encyclopedias. Do not use more than one general encyclopedia. Cut, paste, and print; photocopy; or take notes on the three sources and be prepared to discuss what you found. One question you should consider is how useful each encyclopedia would be to a researcher.

   ■ Solar power
   ■ Undocumented workers
   ■ Current legal status of gender-neutral bathroom bills
   ■ Sexual harassment

bits   To see what you are learning about argumentation applied to the latest world and national news, read our *Bits* blog, "Argument and the Headlines," at **blogs.bedfordstmartins.com/bits**.

Language: Using Words with Care

The Power of Words

Words play such a critical role in argument that they deserve special treatment. An important part of successful writers' equipment is a large and active vocabulary, but no single chapter in a book can give this to you; only reading and study can widen your range of word choices. Even in a brief chapter, however, we can point out how words influence the feelings and attitudes of an audience, both favorably and unfavorably.

One kind of language responsible for shaping attitudes and feelings is **emotive language**, language that expresses and arouses emotions. Understanding it and using it effectively are indispensable to the arguer who wants to move an audience to accept a point of view or undertake an action.

Nowhere is the power of words more obvious and more familiar than in advertising, where the success of a product may depend on the feelings that certain words produce in the prospective buyer. Even the names of products may have emotive significance. Although most manufacturers agree that a good name won't save a poor product, they also recognize that the right name can catch the attention of the public and persuade people to buy a product at least once. According to an article in the *Wall Street Journal,* a product name not only should be memorable but also should "remind people of emotional or physical experiences."[1]

Practice

Careful thought and extensive research go into the naming of automobiles, a "big ticket" item for most consumers. What reasoning might have gone into the naming of the models, old and new, listed on page 272? What response do the names Mercedes-Benz and Rolls-Royce evoke?

---

[1] *Wall Street Journal,* August 5, 1982, p. 19.

Eclipse	Jaguar	Odyssey	Trailblazer
Fusion	Land Rover	Patriot	Trophy
Grand Prix	Malibu	Phantom	Vanquish
Grand Safari	Matrix	Quest	Versailles
Impala	Mustang	Rendezvous	Tundra
Infinity	Nova	Sequoia	Vixen

Even scientists recognize the power of words to attract the attention of other scientists and the public to discoveries and theories that might otherwise remain obscure. A good name can even enable the scientist to visualize a new concept. One scientist says that "a good name," such as "quark," "black hole," "big bang," "chaos," or "great attractor," "helps in communicating a theory and can have a substantial impact on financing." Certainly the subatomic particle that gives mass to matter attracts more attention when called the "God particle" than when referred to as the "Higgs boson."

It is not hard to see the connection between the use of words in conversation and advertising and the use of emotive language in the more formal arguments you will be writing. Emotive language reveals your approval or disapproval, assigns praise or blame — in other words, makes a judgment about the subject. Keep in mind that unless you are writing purely factual statements, such as scientists write, you will find it hard to avoid expressing judgments. Neutrality does not come easily, even where it may be desirable, as in news stories or reports of historical events. For this reason, you need to attend carefully to the statements in your argument, making sure that you have not disguised judgments as statements of fact. In Rogerian argument, you need to remain neutral as you summarize your opponent's argument as well as your own.

Of course, in attempting to prove a claim, you will not be neutral. You will be revealing your judgment about the subject — first in the selection of facts and opinions and the emphasis you give to them, and second in the selection of words.

Like the choice of facts and opinions, the choice of words can be effective or ineffective in advancing your argument, moral or immoral in the honesty with which you exercise it. This chapter offers some insights into recognizing and evaluating the use of emotive language in the arguments you read, as well as into using such language in your own arguments where it is appropriate and avoiding it where it is not. Your decisions about language determine the voice you project in your writing. You do not use the same voice in everything you write, but in formal written arguments you will want to be especially mindful of using a voice appropriate for your intended audience.

READING ARGUMENT

Practice: The Power of Words
Analyze the use of language in this Stihl ad.

Consumer Confidence
STIHL

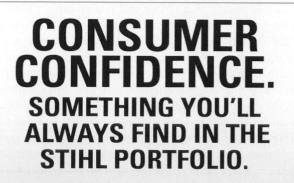

CONSUMER CONFIDENCE.
SOMETHING YOU'LL ALWAYS FIND IN THE STIHL PORTFOLIO.

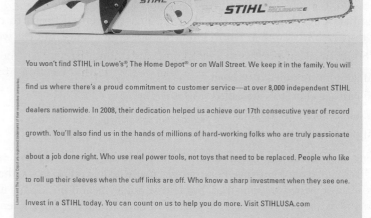

You won't find STIHL in Lowe's®, The Home Depot® or on Wall Street. We keep it in the family. You will find us where there's a proud commitment to customer service—at over 8,000 independent STIHL dealers nationwide. In 2008, their dedication helped us achieve our 17th consecutive year of record growth. You'll also find us in the hands of millions of hard-working folks who are truly passionate about a job done right. Who use real power tools, not toys that need to be replaced. People who like to roll up their sleeves when the cuff links are off. Who know a sharp investment when they see one. Invest in a STIHL today. You can count on us to help you do more. Visit STIHLUSA.com

Number 1 Worldwide

Connotation

The **connotations** of a word are the meanings we attach to it apart from its explicit definition. Because these added meanings derive from our feelings, connotations are one form of emotive language. For example, the word *rat* denotes or points to a kind of rodent, but the attached meanings of "selfish person," "evil-doer," "betrayer," and "traitor" reflect the feelings that have accumulated around the word.

In Chapter 9, we observed that definitions of controversial terms, such as *poverty*, may vary so widely that writer and reader cannot always be sure that they are thinking of the same thing. A similar problem arises when a writer assumes that the reader shares his or her emotional response to a word. Emotive meanings originate partly in personal experience. The word *home*, defined merely as "a family's place of residence," may suggest love, warmth, and security to one person; it may suggest friction, violence, and alienation to another. The values of the groups to which we belong also influence meaning. Writers and speakers count on cultural associations when they refer to our country, our flag, and heroes and enemies we have never seen. The arguer must also be aware that some apparently neutral words trigger different responses from different groups — words such as *cult, revolution, police,* and *beauty contest*.

Various reform movements have recognized that words with unfavorable connotations have the power not only to reflect but also to shape our perceptions of things. In 2007, the NAACP went so far as to hold a "funeral for the N—word." The women's liberation movement also insisted on changes that would bring about improved attitudes toward women. The movement condemned the use of *girl* for a female over the age of eighteen and the use in news stories of descriptive adjectives that emphasize the physical appearance of women. And the homosexual community succeeded in reintroducing the word *gay*, a word current centuries ago, as a substitute for words they considered offensive.

Members of certain occupational groups have invented terms to confer greater respectability on their work. The work does not change, but the workers hope that public perceptions will change

— if janitors are called *custodians*.
— if garbage collectors are called *sanitation engineers*.
— if undertakers are called *morticians*.
— if people who sell makeup are called *cosmetologists*.

Events considered unpleasant or unmentionable are sometimes disguised by polite terms, called **euphemisms**. For example, many people refuse to use the word *died* and choose *passed away* instead. Some psychologists and physicians use the phrase *negative patient care outcome* for what most of us would call *death*. Even when referring to their pets, some people cannot bring themselves to say *put to death* but substitute *put to sleep* or *put down*. In place of a term to describe an act of sexual intercourse, some people use *slept together* or *went to bed together* or *had an affair*.

Polite words are not always so harmless. If a euphemism disguises a shameful event or condition, it is morally irresponsible to use it to mislead the reader into believing that the shameful condition does not exist. An example of such usage was cited by a member of Amnesty International, a group monitoring human rights violations throughout the world. He objected to a news report describing camps in which the Chinese government was promoting "reeducation through labor." This term, he wrote, "makes these institutions seem like a cross between Police Athletic League and Civilian Conservation Corps camps." On the contrary, he went on, the reality of "reeducation through labor" was that the victims were confined to "rather unpleasant prison camps." The details he offered about the conditions under which people lived and worked gave substance to his claim.[2]

Perhaps the most striking examples of the way that connotations influence our perceptions of reality occur when people respond to questions posed by poll-takers. Sociologists and students of poll-taking know that the phrasing of a question, or the choice of words, can affect the answers and even undermine the validity of the poll. In one case, poll-takers first asked a selected group of people if they favored continuing the welfare system. The majority answered no. But when the poll-takers asked if they favored government aid to the poor, the majority answered yes. Although the terms *welfare* and *government aid to the poor* refer to essentially the same forms of government assistance, *welfare* has acquired for many people negative connotations of corruption and shiftless recipients.

In 2013, Michael Dimock, director of the Pew Research Center for the People & the Press, provided an excellent example of how much difference the wording of a survey question can make. It had just been made public that the Department of Justice had subpoenaed the phone records of AP journalists. The following bar graphs show how three different polling organizations worded their questions about the action by the Justice Department — and the responses. Dimock called his report "a case study in the challenges pollsters face in a breaking news environment when public attention and information is relatively limited."[3]

Three Questions on the Department of Justice/AP Issue

Do you approve or disapprove of the Justice Department's decision to subpoena the phone records of AP journalists as part of an investigation into the disclosure of classified information? (Data from Pew Research)

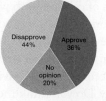

The AP reported classified information about U.S. anti-terrorism efforts and prosecutors have obtained AP's phone records through a

---

[2] Letter to the *New York Times*, August 30, 1982, p. 25.
[3] Michael Dimock, "Polling When Public Attention Is Limited: Different Questions, Different Results," pewresearch.org. Original charts provided by Pew Research Center.

court order. Do you think this action by federal prosecutors is or is not justified? (Data from *Washington Post*/ABC News)

As you may know, after the AP ran news stories that included classified information about U.S. anti-terrorism efforts, the Justice Department secretly collected phone records for reporters and editors who work there. Do you think that the actions of the Justice Department were acceptable or unacceptable? (Data from CNN/ORC)

Fox News began its own survey two days later and concluded it one day later than the other polling organizations. The slight delay in timing raises the possibility that opinions in this fourth poll had shifted over time—even just a few days.

Fox News Question and Context

Does it feel like the federal government has gotten out of control and is threatening the basic civil liberties of Americans, or doesn't it feel this way to you? (Data from Fox News)

As you may have heard, the U.S. Justice Department secretly seized extensive telephone records of calls on both work and personal phones for reporters and editors working for the Associated Press in the spring of 2012. At the time, the news organization, using government leaks, had broken a story about an international terrorist plot. The government obtained the phone records without giving the news organization prior notice, as is customary. Do you think the government was probably justified in taking these actions or does this sound more like the government went too far? (Data from Fox News)

Polls concerning rape address another highly charged subject. Dr. Neil Malamuth, a psychologist at the University of California at Los Angeles, says, "When men are asked if there is any likelihood they would force a woman to have sex against her will if they could get away with it, about half say they would. But if you ask them if they would rape a woman if they knew they could get away with it, only about 15 percent say they would." The men who change their answers aren't aware that "the only difference is in the words used to describe the same act."[4]

The wording of an argument is crucial. Because readers may interpret the words you use on the basis of feelings different from your own, you must support your word choices with definitions and with evidence that enables readers to determine how and why you made them.

READING ARGUMENT

Practice: Connotation

Read and analyze the following commentary. Pick out specific words and phrases that have negative connotations.

Why Keep Athletes Eligible but Uneducated?
FRANK DEFORD

So much about big-time college sports is criticized. But the worst scandal is almost never mentioned; the academic fraud wherein the student-athletes, so-called, are admitted without even remotely adequate credentials and then aren't educated so much as they are just kept eligible.

The reason this shameful practice seldom surfaces is because all the major conference schools are guilty and everybody — presidents, trustees, coaches, media, fans — everybody accepts the corruption. Only occasionally does the truth bubble up. Enter Mary Willingham at the University of North Carolina. She was a learning specialist, working with the Tar Heel athletes who needed study help. And invariably, almost all of the most unqualified were from the revenue sports, football and basketball. She was

so appalled at the academic inability of so many players that she began to speak out about the terrible hypocrisy.

Meanwhile, the university removed her from working with athletes, reduced her title and, she says, "doubled my workload. They're trying to get rid of me," she told me. Fans of the Tar Heel teams treat her unkindly. This invariably happens to college sports whistleblowers who dare reveal what is called a dirty little secret, wink-wink; but which is, in fact, a filthy, big lie.

Frank Deford was a commentator for NPR's *Morning Edition*, senior correspondent on HBO's *RealSports with Bryant Gumbel*, and senior contributing editor at *Sports Illustrated*. His peers have voted him the U.S. Sportswriter of the Year six times. These comments aired on *Morning Edition* on September 4, 2013.

---

[4] *New York Times*, August 29, 1989, sec. C, p. 1.

Imagine, showing up at college, Ms. Willingham says, with reading, writing, and vocabulary skills so below your classmates that nothing makes sense. She found some athletes admitted to Chapel Hill, one of the most elite public universities in the country, with fourth-grade reading skills. Worse, some are, simply, non-readers. More upsetting, she found cheating rampant. It troubles her, she admits, that she herself lied about that, filling out boilerplate NCAA forms that affirmed that there was no cheating. But everybody does it. Just tell the NCAA what it wants, and sell more tickets.

5   What is so sad, Ms. Willingham says, is that almost all the academically deficient players whom she worked with wanted to learn, wanted an education. But their time and energy were eaten up by their sport. There wasn't enough time left over for the student-athletes to try to become students.

But understand, as another college year begins — or, more visibly, as another college football season begins — that what goes on at Chapel Hill is substantially no different than the way athletic programs are run across the country. It's the only way to win. As Ms. Willingham says she's been told so often: Athletics is in charge of the university. She doesn't want to believe that because among other things, she says that she loves the University of North Carolina. She loves that place of learning.

Practice: Connotation

The following passage comes from the January 2007 issue of the *International Journal of Inclusive Democracy*. Read the passage, underlining any words that have negative connotations. Then rewrite the passage using neutral language.

Dispatches from a Police State: Animal Rights in the Crosshairs of State Repression
STEVEN BEST

Welcome to the post-constitutional America, where defense of animal rights and the earth is a terrorist crime.

In the wake of 9/11, and in the midst [of] the neoliberal attack on social democracies, efforts to grab dwindling resources, and [to] crush dissent of any kind, the U.S. has entered a neo-McCarthyist period rooted in witch-hunts and political persecution. The terms and players have changed, but the situation is much the same as the 1950s: The terrorist threat has replaced the communist threat, Attorney General Alfred [sic] Gonzalez dons the garb of Sen. Joseph McCarthy, and the Congressional Meetings on Eco-Terrorism stand in for the House Un-American Activities Committee. The Red Scare of communism has morphed into the Green Scare of ecoterrorism, where the bad guy today is not a commie but an animal, environmental, or peace activist. In a nightmare replay of the 1950s, activists of all

Steven Best is an associate professor of humanities and philosophy at the University of Texas at El Paso. His books include (with Anthony J. Nocella II) *Terrorists or Freedom Fighters? Reflections on the Liberation of Animals* (2004). This article appeared in the January 2007 issue of the *International Journal of Inclusive Democracy*.

kinds today are surveilled, hassled, threatened, jailed, and stripped of their rights. As before, the state conjures up dangerous enemies in our midst and instills fear in the public, so that people willingly forfeit liberties for an alleged security that demands secrecy, nonaccountability, and centralized power. . . .

The bogus "war on terror" has served as a highly effective propaganda and bullying device to ram through Congress and the courts a pro-corporate, anti-environmental, authoritarian agenda. Using vague, catch-all phrases such as "enemy combatants" and "domestic terrorists," the Bush administration has rounded up and tortured thousands of non-citizens (detaining them indefinitely in military tribunals without right to a fair trial) and surveilled, harassed, and imprisoned citizens who dare to challenge the government or corporate system it protects and represents.

Slanting

Slanting, says one dictionary, is "interpreting or presenting in line with a special interest." The term is almost always used in a negative sense. It means that the arguer has selected facts and words with favorable or unfavorable connotations to create the impression that no alternative view exists or can be defended. For some questions, it is true that no alternative view is worthy of presentation, and emotionally charged language to defend or attack a position that is clearly right or wrong would be entirely appropriate. We aren't neutral, nor should we be, about the tragic abuse of human rights anywhere in the world or even about infractions of the law such as drunk driving or vandalism, and we should use strong language to express our disapproval of these practices.

Most of your arguments, however, will concern controversial questions about which people of goodwill can argue on both sides. In such cases, your own judgments should be restrained. Slanting will suggest a prejudice — that is, a judgment made without regard to all the facts. Unfortunately, you may not always be aware of your bias or special interest; you may believe that your position is the only correct one. You may also feel the need to communicate a passionate belief about a serious problem. But if you are interested in persuading a reader to accept your belief and to act on it, you must also ask: If the reader is not sympathetic, how will he or she respond? Will he or she perceive my words as "loaded" — one-sided and prejudicial — and my view as slanted?

R. D. Laing, a Scottish psychiatrist, defined *prayer* in this way: "Someone is gibbering away on his knees, talking to someone who is not there."[5] This description probably reflects a sincerely held belief. Laing also clearly intended it for an audience that already agreed with him. But the phrases "gibbering away" and "someone who is not there" would be offensive to people for whom prayer is sacred. Consider the effect on an audience of such statements as these:

---

[5] "The Obvious," in David Cooper, ed., *The Dialectics of Liberation* (Harmondsworth, U.K./ Baltimore, MD: Penguin Books, 1968), p. 17.

- Any senator who would vote for this bill is ignoring the most basic rights of humanity.
- It is selfish for gun owners to think only of their own desires.
- The children had the misfortune of being raised by a single mother.
- Drug company executives who refuse dying children the compassionate use of experimental drugs have no conscience.
- The current level of airport security is an insult to the law-abiding citizens who are delayed by it.
- No one who values human life would text while driving.

You can slant an argument by means of the facts you choose to include or leave out as well as by means of word choice.

- During the search for Malaysia Airlines Flight 370, one reporter made headlines with the report that one of the pilots had been having marital difficulties. What he did not offer was any proof whatsoever that the pilot's personal life had any bearing on the plane's disappearance.
- A defense sometimes offered when a young person is accused of a crime is that he is a straight-A student, a fact that is irrelevant to his guilt or innocence.
- The fact that a defendant does not testify in her own defense is often assumed to be a sign of guilt when there may be a number of reasons why she does not take the stand. That fact may override, for some, other facts that are clearly in evidence.
- An argument might be made that a man has never been indicted for abusing his wife. Other records may reveal, however, that the police have been called to the home on numerous occasions to investigate domestic violence but no charges have been filed.
- In the movie *The Hunt*, a kindergarten teacher is accused of molesting a little girl because she describes the teacher's anatomy in language it is assumed she would not know otherwise. What the viewers know is that she has heard her older brother and his friends using such language while looking at sexually explicit pictures.

RESEARCH SKILL Evaluating Language in Sources

The sources you use are in a sense "witnesses" on behalf of your argument. Some sources are believable and trustworthy, just as some witnesses are. However, your argument is weakened by any hint that your sources are unreliable. Be sure that your sources do not weaken your argument by

- using so many words with negative connotations that there seems to be a clear and unfair bias.

- using such inflammatory language that ideas get lost in the emotion.
- using language that builds on hidden assumptions.
- using language that would be offensive to your intended audience.

Practice

Locate specific examples of slanted language in the first of these two excerpts. What effect does the word choice have in the first piece? How does it compare to the word choice in the second passage, on the same topic?

1. Grandstanding politicians love to rail against the gun. Inanimate objects are good targets to beat up on. That way, politicians do not have to address the real problems in our society. We pay a price for this craven misdirection, though, in thousands of murders, muggings, rapes, robberies, and burglaries.

   Yet that is not the greatest danger we face. The Founding Fathers knew that *governments* could turn criminal. That is the principal reason they wanted every man armed: An armed citizenry militates against the development of tyranny. The Founding Fathers did not want every man armed in order to shoot a burglar, although they had nothing against doing so. The Founding Fathers did not want every man armed in order to shoot Bambi or Thumper, although they had nothing against doing so. The Founding Fathers wanted every man armed in order to shoot soldiers or police of tyrannical regimes who suppress the rights of free men.[6]

2. Americans also have a right to defend their homes, and we need not challenge that. Nor does anyone seriously question that the Constitution protects the right of hunters to own and keep sporting guns for hunting game any more than anyone would challenge the right to own and keep fishing rods and other equipment for fishing — or to own automobiles. To "keep and bear arms" for hunting today is essentially a recreational activity and not an imperative of survival, as it was 200 years ago; "Saturday night specials" and machine guns are not recreational weapons and surely are as much in need of regulation as motor vehicles.

   Americans should ask themselves a few questions. The Constitution does not mention automobiles or motorboats, but the right to keep and own an automobile is beyond question; equally beyond question is the power of the state to regulate the purchase or the transfer of such vehicle and the right to license the vehicle and the driver with reasonable standards. In some places, even a bicycle must be registered, as must some household dogs.[7]

Figurative Language

Figurative language consists of words that produce images in the mind of the reader. Students sometimes assume that vivid picture-making language is the exclusive instrument of novelists and poets, but writers of arguments can also avail themselves of such devices to heighten the impact of their messages.

Figurative language can do more than render a scene. It shares with other kinds of emotive language the power to express and arouse deep feelings.

---

[6] Roger McGrath, "A God-Given Natural Right," *Chronicles,* October, 2003, p. 425.
[7] Warren Burger, "The Right to Bear Arms," *Parade,* January 14, 1990, p. 419.

Like a fine painting or photograph, it can draw readers into the picture where they partake of the writer's experience as if they were also present. Such power may be used to delight, to instruct, or to horrify. In 1741, the Puritan preacher Jonathan Edwards delivered his sermon "Sinners in the Hands of an Angry God," in which people were likened to repulsive spiders hanging over the flames of Hell to be dropped into the fire whenever a wrathful God was pleased to release them. The congregation's reaction to Edwards's picture of the everlasting horrors to be suffered in the netherworld included panic, fainting, hysteria, and convulsions. Subsequently Edwards lost his pulpit in Massachusetts, in part as a consequence of his success at provoking such uncontrollable terror among his congregation.

Language as intense and vivid as Edwards's emerges from very strong emotion about a deeply felt cause. In the following paragraphs from his 1963 "Letter from Birmingham Jail," Martin Luther King Jr. uses figurative language to express his disappointment with the attitude of America's churches toward the treatment of black Americans.

> I have traveled the length and breadth of Alabama, Mississippi and all the other southern states. On sweltering summer days and crisp autumn mornings I have looked at the South's beautiful churches with their lofty spires pointing heavenward. I have beheld the impressive outlines of her massive religious education buildings. Over and over I have found myself asking: "What kind of people worship here? Who is their God? Where were their voices when the lips of Governor Barnett dripped with words of interposition and nullification? Where were they when Governor Wallace gave a clarion call for defiance and hatred? Where were their voices of support when bruised and weary Negro men and women decided to rise from the dark dungeons of complacency to the bright hills of creative protest?" . . .
>
> There was a time when the church was very powerful — in the time when the early Christians rejoiced at being deemed worthy to suffer for what they believed. In those days the church was not merely a thermometer that recorded the ideas and principles of popular opinion; it was a thermostat that transformed the mores of society. Whenever the early Christians entered a town, the people in power became disturbed and immediately sought to convict the Christians for being "disturbers of the peace" and "outside agitators." But the Christians pressed on, in the conviction that they were "a colony of heaven," called to obey God rather than man. Small in number, they were big in commitment. They were too God-intoxicated to be "astronomically intimidated." By their effort and example they brought an end to such ancient evils as infanticide and gladiatorial contests. Things are different now. So often the contemporary church is a weak, ineffectual voice with an uncertain sound. So often it is an archdefender of the status quo. Far from being disturbed by the presence of the church, the power structure of the

average community is consoled by the church's silent — and often even vocal — sanction of things as they are.[8]

You are familiar with some of the most common figures of speech. You know that you can occasionally add creativity and sensory appeal to your writing by means of metaphors and similes. A famous **simile** — a comparison using *like* or *as* — comes from the acceptance speech that George H. W. Bush gave before the Republican convention in 1988:

> For we are a nation of communities, of thousands and tens of thousands of ethnic, religious, social, business, labor union, neighborhood, regional and other organizations, all of them varied, voluntary, and unique.
>
> This is America: the Knights of Columbus, the Grange, Hadassah, the Disabled American Veterans, the Order of Ahepa, the Business and Professional Women of America, the union hall, the Bible study group, LULAC, "Holy Name" — a brilliant diversity spread like stars, like a thousand points of light in a broad and peaceful sky.

Had Bush simply left out the word *like* in the last sentence, he would have been using a **metaphor**.

Another quote from the same speech illustrates another use of language that comes in handy at times in writing an argument: the analogy. An **analogy** is like a metaphor or simile in that it compares; but it is generally more complex, drawing parallels between two things that are similar in some ways but dissimilar in others. At times, an analogy is useful in explaining something unknown or less well known in terms of something else the audience is more familiar with.

In this particular analogy, Bush was comparing the economy to a patient. In comparing the economy to a human being, he was also making use of **personification**:

> My friends, eight years ago this economy was flat on its back — intensive care. We came in and gave it emergency treatment: Got the temperature down by lowering regulation, got the blood pressure down when we lowered taxes. Pretty soon the patient was up, back on his feet, and stronger than ever.
>
> And now who do we hear knocking on the door but the doctors who made him sick. And they're telling us to put them in charge of the case again. My friends, they're lucky we don't hit them with a malpractice suit!

The rules governing the use of figurative language are the same as those governing other kinds of emotive language. Is the language appropriate? Is it too strong, too colorful for the purpose of the message? Does it result in slanting or distortion? What will its impact be on a hostile or indifferent audience? Will they be angered, repelled? Will they cease to read or listen if the imagery is too disturbing?

---

[8] April 16, 1963.

READING ARGUMENT

Practice: Figurative Language

Read the following excerpt from W. E. B. Du Bois's treatise *The Souls of Black Folk*. Analyze the figurative language used in the essay, and answer the questions that follow.

Of Our Spiritual Strivings

W. E. B. Du BOIS

Between me and the other world there is ever an unasked question: unasked by some through feelings of delicacy; by others through the difficulty of rightly framing it. All, nevertheless, flutter round it. They approach me in a half-hesitant sort of way, eye me curiously or compassionately, and then, instead of saying directly, How does it feel to be a problem? they say, I know an excellent colored man in my town; or, I fought at Mechanicsville; or, Do not these Southern outrages make your blood boil? At these I smile, or am interested, or reduce the boiling to a simmer, as the occasion may require. To the real question, How does it feel to be a problem? I answer seldom a word.

And yet, being a problem is a strange experience,—peculiar even for one who has never been anything else, save perhaps in babyhood and in Europe. It is in the early days of rollicking boyhood that the revelation first bursts upon one, all in a day, as it were. I remember well when the shadow swept across me. I was a little thing, away up in the hills of New England, where the dark Housatonic winds between Hoosac and Taghkanic to the sea. In a wee wooden schoolhouse, something put it into the boys' and girls' heads to buy gorgeous visiting-cards—ten cents a package—and exchange. The exchange was merry, till one girl,

a tall newcomer, refused my card,—refused it peremptorily, with a glance. Then it dawned upon me with a certain suddenness that I was different from the others; or like, mayhap, in heart and life and longing, but shut out from their world by a vast veil. I had thereafter no desire to tear down that veil, to creep through; I held all beyond it in common contempt, and lived above it in a region of blue sky and great wandering shadows. That sky was bluest when I could beat my mates at examination-time, or beat them at a foot-race, or even beat their stringy heads. Alas, with the years all this fine contempt began to fade; for the words I longed for, and all their dazzling opportunities, were theirs, not mine. But they should not keep these prizes, I said; some, all, I would wrest from them. Just how I would do it I could never decide: by reading law, by healing the sick, by telling the wonderful tales that swam in my head,—some way. With other black boys the strife was not so fiercely sunny: their youth shrunk into tasteless sycophancy, or into silent hatred of the pale world about them and mocking distrust of everything white; or wasted itself in a bitter cry, Why did God make me an

W. E. B. Du Bois was an American sociologist, historian, civil rights activist, and author. This excerpt is taken from his 1903 work *The Souls of Black Folk*.

outcast and a stranger in mine own house? The shades of the prison-house closed round about us all: walls strait and stubborn to the whitest, but relentlessly narrow, tall, and unscalable to sons of night who must plod darkly on in resignation, or beat unavailing palms against the stone, or steadily, half hopelessly, watch the streak of blue above.

After the Egyptian and Indian, the Greek and Roman, the Teuton and Mongolian, the Negro is a sort of seventh son, born with a veil, and gifted with second-sight in this American world,—a world which yields him no true self-consciousness, but only lets him see himself through the revelation of the other world. It is a peculiar sensation, this double-consciousness, this sense of always looking at one's self through the eyes of others, of measuring one's soul by the tape of a world that looks on in amused contempt and pity. One ever feels his twoness,—an American, a Negro; two souls, two thoughts, two unreconciled strivings; two warring ideals in one dark body, whose dogged strength alone keeps it from being torn asunder.

Reading and Discussion Questions

1. What kind of figurative language does Du Bois use in his opening paragraph? What tone does his language set?
2. Analyze the language in paragraph 2. How does Du Bois use personification to talk about the strife that he and other black boys felt?
3. What metaphor does Du Bois introduce in paragraph 3? Is the metaphor effective?

Concrete and Abstract Language

Unlike **concrete words**, which point to real objects and real experiences, **abstract words** express qualities apart from particular things and events.

Concrete	*Abstract*
Velvety, dark red roses	Beauty
Returning money found in the street to the owner, although no one has seen the discovery	Honesty

Although they also rely on the vividness of concrete language, arguments use abstract terms far more extensively than other kinds of writing. Using abstractions effectively, especially in arguments of value and policy, is important for two reasons:

1. Abstractions represent the qualities, characteristics, and values that the writer is explaining, defending, or attacking.
2. Abstractions enable the writer to make generalizations about his or her data.

Abstractions tell us what conclusions we have arrived at; details tell us how we got there. Look at the following paragraph by Michael Pollan.

> Domestication is an evolutionary, rather than a political, development. It is certainly not a regime humans somehow imposed on animals some ten thousand years ago. Rather, domestication took place when a handful of especially opportunistic species discovered, through Darwinian trial and error, that they were more likely to survive and prosper in an alliance with humans than on their own. Humans provided the animals with food and protection in exchange for which the animals provided the humans their milk, eggs, and — yes — their flesh. Both parties were transformed by the new relationship: The animals grew tame and lost their ability to fend for themselves in the wild (natural selection tends to dispense with unneeded traits) and the humans traded their hunter-gatherer ways for the settled lives of agriculturists. (Humans changed biologically, too, evolving such new traits as the ability to digest lactose as adults.)[9]

Taken by itself, Pollan's first sentence (or topic sentence) is a bit general, relying heavily on the abstract word *evolutionary* to describe *domestication*. The rest of the paragraph, however, supports the first sentence with concrete details. Just as definitions are needed for vague or ambiguous terms (see Chapter 9), an arguer must use concrete language to provide readers with a clear understanding of an abstract concept.

A common problem in using abstractions is omission of details. Either the writer is not a skilled observer and cannot provide the details, or the writer believes that such details are too small and quiet compared to the grand sounds made by abstract terms. These grand sounds, unfortunately, cannot compensate for the lack of clarity and liveliness. Lacking detailed support, abstract words may be misinterpreted. They may also represent ideas that are so vague as to be meaningless.

Practice

Write three to five specific details to support one of these topic sentences that use abstract language.

1. High school students often live with a lot of stress.
2. Much of the coursework in high school is not relevant to students' future plans.
3. Bipartisanship has hampered the passage of legislation that would improve the quality of life of the average American.
4. Our campus should work toward sustainability.
5. Social networking encourages relationships that are very superficial.
6. Shoppers have to admit that healthy food choices are available if they take the time to look for them.

---

[9] Michael Pollan, *The Omnivore's Dilemma* (New York: Penguin, 2006), p. 320.

Shortcuts

Shortcuts are abbreviated substitutes for argument that avoid the hard work necessary to provide facts, expert opinion, and analysis of warrants. Even experts, however, can be guilty of using shortcuts, and the writer who consults an authority should be alert to that authority's use of language. Two of the most common uses of shortcuts are clichés and slogans.

Clichés

A cliché is an expression or idea grown stale through overuse. Clichés in language are tired expressions that have faded like old photographs; readers no longer see anything when clichés are placed before them. Some phrases are so obviously clichés and so old-fashioned that you are not likely to use them in your writing:

Thick as thieves	As old as the hills
Opposites attract	Time heals all wounds
Read between the lines	Live and learn
Age before beauty	Avoid like the plague
Dry as a bone	Fit as a fiddle
All bets are off	All bent out of shape
Caught me off guard	Clean bill of health
Take it from me	Takes its toll on you
Par for the course	Pass the buck
Fall through the cracks	Make a federal case of it
First things first	Made of money
More than meets the eye	A half-baked idea

Others are a bit more likely to slip into your writing because they are almost filler in sentences, empty words:

All in due time	A bad call
Back against the wall	The bottom fell out
Boils down to	By the book
Business as usual	Call the shots
Call it a day	Cut your losses
Close rank	From day one
Go downhill	Raise the bar
In this day and time	

Another category of phrases has been labeled *thought-terminating clichés*. These clichés represent ready-made answers to questions, stereotyped solutions to problems, "knee-jerk" reactions:

God moves in mysterious ways.
You don't always get what you want.
To each his own.

We will have to agree to disagree.
Because that is our policy.
I'm the parent, that's why.
There's no silver bullet.
You're either with us or against us.

Certain cultural attitudes encourage the use of clichés. The liberal American tradition has been governed by hopeful assumptions about our ability to solve problems. A professor of communications says that "we tell our students that for every problem there must be a solution."[10] But real solutions are hard to come by. In our haste to provide them, to prove that we can be decisive, we may be tempted to produce familiar responses that resemble solutions. All reasonable solutions are worthy of consideration, but they must be defined and supported if they are to be used in a thoughtful, well-constructed argument.

Attitudes toward certain cultures also encourage the use of clichéd language and thought. When we accept a worn-out and overused perception of an ethnicity, nationality, or any other group, we are viewing individuals as **stereotypes**. Avoid stereotypes in your writing, and be wary of other writers who employ them to further an argument.

Slogans

Slogans, like clichés, are short, undeveloped arguments. They represent abbreviated responses to often complex questions. As a reader, you need to be aware that slogans merely call attention to a problem; they cannot offer persuasive proof for a claim in a dozen words or less. As a writer you should avoid the use of slogans that evoke an emotional response but do not provide a reason for that response.

Advertising slogans are the most familiar. These may give us interesting and valuable information about products, but most advertisements give us slogans that ignore proof—shortcuts substituting for argument.

Walmart: Save money. Live better.
FedEx: When there is no tomorrow.
Red Cross: The greatest tragedy is indifference.
PlayStation: Live in your world. Play in ours.
Disneyland: The happiest place on earth.
Ajax: Stronger than dirt.
IBM: Solutions for a small planet.
McDonald's: i'm lovin' it.
Hallmark: When you care enough to send the very best.
DeBeers: A diamond is forever.
Levi's: Quality never goes out of style.
Subway: Eat fresh.

---

[10] Malcolm O. Sillars, "The New Conservatism and the Teacher of Speech," *Southern Speech Journal* 21 (1956), p. 240.

The persuasive appeal of advertising slogans heavily depends on the connotations associated with products. In Chapter 7, we discussed the way in which advertisements promise to satisfy our needs and protect our values (see p. 214, "Appeals to Needs and Values"). Wherever evidence is scarce or nonexistent, the advertiser must persuade us through skillful choice of words and phrases (as well as pictures), especially those that produce pleasurable feelings. "Let it inspire you" is the slogan of a popular liqueur. It suggests a desirable state of being but remains suitably vague about the nature of the inspiration. Another familiar slogan — "Noxzema, clean makeup"— also emphasizes a quality that we approve of, but what is "clean" makeup? Since the advertisers are silent, we are left with warm feelings about the word and not much more. What feelings are evoked by the slogans listed on the previous page?

Advertising slogans are persuasive because their witty phrasing and punchy rhythms produce an automatic *yes* response. We react to them as we might react to the lyrics of popular songs, and we treat them far less critically than we treat more straightforward and elaborate arguments. Still, the consequences of failing to analyze the slogans of advertisers are usually not serious. You may be tempted to buy a product because you were fascinated by a brilliant slogan, but if the product doesn't satisfy, you can abandon it without much loss. However, ignoring ideological slogans coined by political parties or special-interest groups may carry an enormous price, and the results are not so easily undone.

Ideological slogans, like advertising slogans, depend on the power of connotation, the emotional associations aroused by a word or phrase. American political history is, in fact, a repository of slogans:

1864	Abraham Lincoln	Don't Swap Horses in the Middle of the Stream
1900	William McKinley	A Full Dinner Pail
1916	Woodrow Wilson	He Kept Us Out of War
1924	Calvin Coolidge	Keep Cool with Coolidge
1928	Herbert Hoover	A Chicken in Every Pot and a Car in Every Garage
1964	Lyndon B. Johnson	The Stakes Are Too High for You to Stay at Home
1980	Ronald Reagan	Are You Better Off Than You Were Four Years Ago?
1988	George Bush	A Kinder, Gentler Nation
1992	Bill Clinton	Putting People First
2000	George W. Bush	Leave No Child Behind
2008	Barack Obama	Change We Can Believe In
2016	Donald Trump	Make America Great Again

Over time, slogans, like clichés, can acquire a life of their own and, if they are repeated often enough, come to represent an unchanging truth we no longer need to examine. "Dangerously," says Anthony Smith, "policy makers become prisoners of the slogans they popularize."[11]

WRITER'S GUIDE
Choosing Your Words Carefully

---

1. **Strive for a voice that is appropriate for your intended audience.** Following the rest of these suggestions will help you achieve that goal. Think about the type of *ethos* you want to present to your readers by means of the language you use.

2. **Avoid language with connotations that might produce a negative reaction in your audience.** Even if you do not agree with your audience, you want your case to be heard. Let your ideas speak for you, and don't let your word choice alienate your audience.

3. **If you have used slanted language, consider whether it will advance or weaken your argument.** Your argument will be an opinion. You don't want to seem so opinionated that no one will listen.

4. **Use figurative language where appropriate for your purposes.** It can produce images in the minds of audience members and can arouse emotion when doing so is appropriate.

5. **Support abstract language with concrete language.** Concrete details can convey to your readers exactly what you have in mind much more precisely than abstract language.

6. **Edit out any clichés or slogans from your early drafts.** Clichés and slogans are stale, unoriginal language or catchphrases that are too brief to convey complex ideas.

Slogans also have numerous shortcomings as substitutes for the development of an argument. **First, their brevity presents serious disadvantages.** Slogans necessarily ignore exceptions or negative instances that might qualify a claim. They usually speak in absolute terms without describing the circumstances in which a principle or idea might not work. Their claims therefore seem shrill and exaggerated. In addition, brevity prevents the sloganeer from revealing how he or she arrived at conclusions.

Second, slogans may conceal unexamined assumptions. When Japanese cars were beginning to compete with American cars, the slogan

---

[11] "Nuclear Power — Why Not?" *The Listener*, October 22, 1981, p. 463.

"Made in America by Americans" appeared on the bumpers of thousands of American-made cars. A thoughtful reader would have discovered in this slogan several implied assumptions: *American cars are better than Japanese cars; the American economy will improve if we buy American; patriotism can be expressed by buying American goods.* If the reader were to ask a few probing questions, he or she might find these warrants unconvincing.

Silent assumptions that express values hide in other popular and influential slogans. "Pro-life," the slogan of those who oppose abortion, assumes that the fetus is a living being entitled to the same rights as individuals already born. "Pro-choice," the slogan of those who favor abortion, suggests that the freedom of the pregnant woman to choose is the foremost or only consideration. The words *life* and *choice* have been carefully selected to reflect desirable qualities, but the words are only the beginning of the argument.

Third, although slogans may express admirable sentiments, they often fail to tell us how to achieve their objectives. They often address us in the imperative mode, ordering us to take an action or refrain from it. But the means of achieving the objectives may be nonexistent or very costly. If sloganeers cannot offer workable means for implementing their goals, they risk alienating the audience. Sloganeering is one of the recognizable attributes of propaganda. Propaganda for both good and bad purposes is a form of slanting, of selecting language and facts to persuade an audience to take a certain action. Even a good cause may be weakened by an unsatisfactory slogan. If you assume that your audience is sophisticated and alert, you will probably write your strongest arguments devoid of clichés and slogans.

ARGUMENT ESSENTIALS
Evaluating Language

- The writer's choice of words should advance the writer's argument.

- Emotive language may be used appropriately to express and arouse emotions.

- Words with positive and negative connotations should be used with care.

- Avoid using one-sided and prejudicial language.

- Words that produce images in the mind of the reader can heighten the impact of the message.

- Use concrete language to support abstract language.

- Clichés and slogans are no substitutes for facts, expert opinion, and analysis.

READING ARGUMENT

Seeing Language

The following selection incorporates all of the aspects of language discussed in this chapter. As you read it, consider connotation, slanting, figurative language, concrete versus abstract language, and shortcuts. After reading the article and the accompanying annotations, answer the questions that follow.

Food for Thought (and for Credit)

JENNIFER GROSSMAN

Humorous tone; speaks directly to audience with *you* and *we*

Want to combat the epidemic of obesity? Bring back home economics. Before you choke on your 300-calorie, trans-fat-laden Krispy Kreme, consider: Teaching basic nutrition and food preparation is a far less radical remedy than gastric bypass surgery or fast-food lawsuits. And probably far more effective. Obesity tends to invite such drastic solutions because it is so frustratingly difficult to treat. This intractability, coupled with the sad fact that obese children commonly grow up to be obese adults, argues for a preventative approach. As the new school year begins, we need to equip kids with the skills and practical knowledge to take control of their dietary destinies.

Starts with slang (*rep*); moves into more formal language

Despite its bad rep as Wife Ed 101, home economics has progressive roots. At the turn of the century it "helped transform domesticity into a vehicle to expand women's political power," according to Sarah Stage in *Rethinking Home Economics: Women and the History of a Profession.* In time, focus shifted from social reform to the practical priorities of sanitation and electrification, and then again to an emphasis on homemaking after World War II — giving ammunition to later critics like Betty Friedan who charged home ec with having helped foster the "feminine mystique."

Loaded language

Concrete data back up abstractions.

Banished by feminists, Becky Home-ecky was left to wander backwater school districts. For a while it seemed that mandating male participation might salvage the discipline while satisfying political correctness. By the late 1970s one-third of male high school graduates had some home-ec training, whereas they comprised a mere 3.5 percent of home-ec students in

Jennifer Grossman is CEO of the Atlas Society and former senior vice president of the Dole Food Company, which distributes health information to the public through lectures and publications. Formerly, she was director of Education Policy at the Cato Institute and a speechwriter for President George H. W. Bush. She has written editorials for the *New York Times*, where this column appeared on September 2, 2003; the *Wall Street Journal*; the *Los Angeles Times*; the *New York Post*; the *Weekly Standard*; the *National Review*; and the *Women's Quarterly*.

1962. Since then, "home economics has moved from the mainstream to the margins of American high school," according to the United States Department of Education, with even female participation—near universal in the 1950s—plummeting by 67 percent.

What has happened since? Ronald McDonald and Colonel Sanders stepped in as the new mascots of American food culture, while the number of meals consumed outside the home has doubled—from a quarter in 1970 to nearly half today. As a result, market economics has increasingly determined ingredients, nutrient content, and portion size. Agricultural surpluses and technological breakthroughs supplied the cheap sweeteners and hydrogenated oils necessary for food to survive indefinitely on store shelves or under fast-food heat lamps.

5   Unsurprisingly, the caloric density of such foods soared relative to those consumed at home. Good value no longer meant taste, presentation, and proper nutrition—but merely more-for-less. Thus, the serving of   *Concrete example* McDonald's French fries that contained 200 calories in 1960 contains 610 today. The lure of large was not limited to fast-food, inflating everything from snack foods to cereal boxes.

But the hunger for home economics didn't die with its academic exile. Martha Stewart made millions filling the void, vexing home-ec haters like Erica Jong for having "earned her freedom by glorifying the slavery of home." Home and Garden TV, the Food Network, and countless publications thrive on topics once taught by home ec.

All of which begs the question: If the free market has done such a good job   *Shortcuts* of picking up the slack, why bring home ec back? Because much of the D.I.Y. (do-it-yourself) culture is divorced from the exigencies of everyday life. It's more like home rec: catering to pampered chefs with maids to clean up the kitchen.

The new home economics should be both pragmatic and egalitarian. Traditional topics—food and nutrition, family studies, home management—should be retooled for the twenty-first century. Children should be   *Concrete suggestions* able to decipher headlines about the dangers of dioxin or the benefits of antioxidants. Subjects like home finance might include domestic problem-solving: How would you spend $100 to feed a family of four, including a diabetic, a nursing mother, and infant, for one week?

While this kind of training might most benefit those low-income minority children at highest risk of obesity, all children will be better equipped to make smart choices in the face of the more than $33 billion that food companies spend annually to promote their products. And consumer education is just part of the larger purpose: to teach kids to think, make, fix, and generally fend for themselves.

Some detractors will doubtless smell a plot to turn women back into stitching, stirring Stepford Wives. Others will argue that schools should focus on the basics. But what could be more basic than life, food, home, and hearth? A generation has grown up since we swept home ec into the dust heap of history and hung up our brooms. It's time to reevaluate the domestic discipline, and recapture lost skills.

Figurative language

Reading and Discussion Questions

1. How would the students at the high school you attended have responded to a course such as the one Grossman describes?
2. Do you think that offering such a course would be a good idea? Why, or why not?
3. How convincing is Grossman's argument that there is a need for consumer education?
4. How does Grossman's use of language add or detract from her argument?

Practice: Examining Language

Use the questions following this speech by President Barack Obama to guide your analysis of its author's use of language.

Remarks by the President at Memorial Service for Fallen Dallas Police Officers, July 12, 2016
BARACK OBAMA

THE PRESIDENT: Mr. President and Mrs. Bush; my friend, the Vice President, and Dr. Biden; Mayor Rawlings; Chief Spiller; clergy; members of Congress; Chief Brown—I'm so glad I met Michelle first, because she loves Stevie Wonder—(laughter and applause)—but most of all, to the families and friends and colleagues and fellow officers.

Scripture tells us that in our sufferings there is glory, because we know that suffering produces perseverance; perseverance, character; and character, hope. Sometimes the truths of these words are hard to see. Right now, those words test us. Because the people of Dallas, people across the country, are suffering.

We're here to honor the memory, and mourn the loss, of five fellow Americans—to grieve with their loved ones, to support this community, to pray for the wounded, and to try and find some meaning amidst our sorrow.

For the men and women who protect and serve the people of Dallas, last Thursday began like any other day. Like most Americans each day, you get up, probably have too quick a breakfast, kiss your family goodbye, and you head to work. But your

Barack Obama served as President of the United States 2009–2017. He made this speech at a memorial service for five Dallas police officers gunned down during a protest of the shooting of black men by police officers.

work, and the work of police officers across the country, is like no other. For the moment you put on that uniform, you have answered a call that at any moment, even in the briefest interaction, may put your life in harm's way.

5   Lorne Ahrens, he answered that call. So did his wife, Katrina—not only because she was the spouse of a police officer, but because she's a detective on the force. They have two kids. And Lorne took them fishing, and used to proudly go to their school in uniform. And the night before he died, he bought dinner for a homeless man. And the next night, Katrina had to tell their children that their dad was gone. "They don't get it yet," their grandma said. "They don't know what to do quite yet."

Michael Krol answered that call. His mother said, "He knew the dangers of the job, but he never shied away from his duty." He came a thousand miles from his home state of Michigan to be a cop in Dallas, telling his family, "This is something I wanted to do." Last year, he brought his girlfriend back to Detroit for Thanksgiving, and it was the last time he'd see his family.

Michael Smith answered that call—in the Army, and over almost 30 years working for the Dallas Police Association, which gave him the appropriately named "Cops Cop" award. A man of deep faith, when he was off duty, he could be found at church or playing softball with his two girls. Today, his girls have lost their dad, for God has called Michael home.

Patrick Zamarripa, he answered that call. Just 32, a former altar boy who served in the Navy and dreamed of being a cop. He liked to post videos of himself and his kids on social media. And on Thursday night, while Patrick went to work, his partner Kristy posted a photo of her and their daughter at a Texas Rangers game, and tagged her partner so that he could see it while on duty.

Brent Thompson answered that call. He served his country as a Marine. And years later, as a contractor, he spent time in some of the most dangerous parts of Iraq and Afghanistan. And then a few years ago, he settled down here in Dallas for a new life of service as a transit cop. And just about two weeks ago, he married a fellow officer, their whole life together waiting before them.

10   Like police officers across the country, these men and their families shared a commitment to something larger than themselves. They weren't looking for their names to be up in lights. They'd tell you the pay was decent but wouldn't make you rich. They could have told you about the stress and long shifts, and they'd probably agree with Chief Brown when he said that cops don't expect to hear the words "thank you" very often, especially from those who need them the most.

No, the reward comes in knowing that our entire way of life in America depends on the rule of law; that the maintenance of that law is a hard and daily labor; that in this country, we don't have soldiers in the streets or militias setting the rules. Instead, we have public servants—police officers—like the men who were taken away from us.

And that's what these five were doing last Thursday when they were assigned to protect and keep orderly a peaceful protest in response to the killing of Alton Sterling of Baton Rouge and Philando Castile of Minnesota. They were upholding the constitutional rights of this country.

For a while, the protest went on without incident. And despite the fact that police conduct was the subject of the protest, despite the fact that there must have been signs or slogans or chants with which they profoundly disagreed, these men and this department did their jobs like the professionals that they were. In fact, the police had been part of the protest's planning. Dallas PD even posted photos on their Twitter feeds of their own officers standing among the protesters. Two officers, black and white, smiled next to a man with a sign that read, "No Justice, No Peace."

And then, around nine o'clock, the gunfire came. Another community torn apart. More hearts broken. More questions about what caused, and what might prevent, another such tragedy.

15   I know that Americans are struggling right now with what we've witnessed over the past week. First, the shootings in Minnesota and Baton Rouge, and the protests, then the targeting of police by the shooter here—an act not just of demented violence but of racial hatred. All of it has left us wounded, and angry, and hurt. It's as if the deepest fault lines of our democracy have suddenly been exposed, perhaps even widened. And although we know that such divisions are not new—though they have surely been worse in even the recent past—that offers us little comfort.

Faced with this violence, we wonder if the divides of race in America can ever be bridged. We wonder if an African-American community that feels unfairly targeted by police, and police departments that feel unfairly maligned for doing their jobs, can ever understand each other's experience. We turn on the TV or surf the Internet, and we can watch positions harden and lines drawn, and people retreat to their respective corners, and politicians calculate how to grab attention or avoid the fallout. We see all this, and it's hard not to think sometimes that the center won't hold and that things might get worse.

I understand. I understand how Americans are feeling. But, Dallas, I'm here to say we must reject such despair. I'm here to insist that we are not as divided as we seem. And I know that because I know America. I know how far we've come against impossible odds. (Applause.) I know we'll make it because of what I've experienced in my own life, what I've seen of this country and its people—their goodness and decency—as President of the United States. And I know it because of what we've seen here in Dallas—how all of you, out of great suffering, have shown us the meaning of perseverance and character, and hope.

When the bullets started flying, the men and women of the Dallas police, they did not flinch and they did not react recklessly. They showed incredible restraint. Helped in some cases by protesters, they evacuated the injured, isolated the shooter, and saved more lives than we will ever know. (Applause.) We mourn fewer people today because of your brave actions. (Applause.) "Everyone was helping each other," one witness said. "It wasn't about black or white. Everyone was picking each other up and moving them away." See, that's the America I know.

The police helped Shetamia Taylor as she was shot trying to shield her four sons. She said she wanted her boys to join her to protest the incidents of black men being killed. She also said to the Dallas PD, "Thank you for being heroes." And today, her 12-year old son wants to be a cop when he grows up. That's the America I know. (Applause.)

20   In the aftermath of the shooting, we've seen Mayor Rawlings and Chief Brown, a white man and a black man with different backgrounds, working not just to restore order and support a shaken city, a shaken department, but

working together to unify a city with strength and grace and wisdom. (Applause.) And in the process, we've been reminded that the Dallas Police Department has been at the forefront of improving relations between police and the community. (Applause.) The murder rate here has fallen. Complaints of excessive force have been cut by 64 percent. The Dallas Police Department has been doing it the right way. (Applause.) And so, Mayor Rawlings and Chief Brown, on behalf of the American people, thank you for your steady leadership, thank you for your powerful example. We could not be prouder of you. (Applause.)

These men, this department—this is the America I know. And today, in this audience, I see people who have protested on behalf of criminal justice reform grieving alongside police officers. I see people who mourn for the five officers we lost but also weep for the families of Alton Sterling and Philando Castile. In this audience, I see what's possible—(applause)—I see what's possible when we recognize that we are one American family, all deserving of equal treatment, all deserving of equal respect, all children of God. That's the America that I know.

Now, I'm not naïve. I have spoken at too many memorials during the course of this presidency. I've hugged too many families who have lost a loved one to senseless violence. And I've seen how a spirit of unity, born of tragedy, can gradually dissipate, overtaken by the return to business as usual, by inertia and old habits and expediency. I see how easily we slip back into our old notions, because they're comfortable, we're used to them. I've seen how inadequate words can be in bringing about lasting change. I've seen how inadequate my own words have been. And so I'm reminded of a passage in John's Gospel [First John]: Let us love not with words or speech, but with actions and in truth. If we're to sustain the unity we need to get through these difficult times, if we are to honor these five outstanding officers who we've lost, then we will need to act on the truths that we know. And that's not easy. It makes us uncomfortable. But we're going to have to be honest with each other and ourselves.

We know that the overwhelming majority of police officers do an incredibly hard and dangerous job fairly and professionally. They are deserving of our respect and not our scorn. (Applause.) And when anyone, no matter how good their intentions may be, paints all police as biased or bigoted, we undermine those officers we depend on for our safety. And as for those who use rhetoric suggesting harm to police, even if they don't act on it themselves—well, they not only make the jobs of police officers even more dangerous, but they do a disservice to the very cause of justice that they claim to promote. (Applause.)

We also know that centuries of racial discrimination—of slavery, and subjugation, and Jim Crow—they didn't simply vanish with the end of lawful segregation. They didn't just stop when Dr. King made a speech, or the Voting Rights Act and the Civil Rights Act were signed. Race relations have improved dramatically in my lifetime. Those who deny it are dishonoring the struggles that helped us achieve that progress. (Applause.)

But we know—but, America, we know that bias remains. We know it. Whether you are black or white or Hispanic or Asian or Native American or of Middle Eastern descent, we have all seen this bigotry in our own lives at some point. We've heard it at times in our own homes. If we're honest, perhaps we've heard

25

prejudice in our own heads and felt it in our own hearts. We know that. And while some suffer far more under racism's burden, some feel to a far greater extent discrimination's sting. Although most of us do our best to guard against it and teach our children better, none of us is entirely innocent. No institution is entirely immune. And that includes our police departments. We know this.

And so when African Americans from all walks of life, from different communities across the country, voice a growing despair over what they perceive to be unequal treatment; when study after study shows that whites and people of color experience the criminal justice system differently, so that if you're black you're more likely to be pulled over or searched or arrested, more likely to get longer sentences, more likely to get the death penalty for the same crime; when mothers and fathers raise their kids right and have "the talk" about how to respond if stopped by a police officer—"yes, sir," "no, sir"—but still fear that something terrible may happen when their child walks out the door, still fear that kids being stupid and not quite doing things right might end in tragedy—when all this takes place more than 50 years after the passage of the Civil Rights Act, we cannot simply turn away and dismiss those in peaceful protest as troublemakers or paranoid. (Applause.) We can't simply dismiss it as a symptom of political correctness or reverse racism. To have your experience denied like that, dismissed by those in authority, dismissed perhaps even by your white friends and coworkers and fellow church members again and again and again—it hurts. Surely we can see that, all of us.

We also know what Chief Brown has said is true: That so much of the tensions between police departments and minority communities that they serve is because we ask the police to do too much and we ask too little of ourselves. (Applause.) As a society, we choose to underinvest in decent schools. We allow poverty to fester so that entire neighborhoods offer no prospect for gainful employment. (Applause.) We refuse to fund drug treatment and mental health programs. (Applause.) We flood communities with so many guns that it is easier for a teenager to buy a Glock than get his hands on a computer or even a book—(applause)—and then we tell the police "you're a social worker, you're the parent, you're the teacher, you're the drug counselor." We tell them to keep those neighborhoods in check at all costs, and do so without causing any political blowback or inconvenience. Don't make a mistake that might disturb our own peace of mind. And then we feign surprise when, periodically, the tensions boil over.

We know these things to be true. They've been true for a long time. We know it. Police, you know it. Protestors, you know it. You know how dangerous some of the communities where these police officers serve are, and you pretend as if there's no context. These things we know to be true. And if we cannot even talk about these things—if we cannot talk honestly and openly not just in the comfort of our own circles, but with those who look different than us or bring a different perspective, then we will never break this dangerous cycle.

In the end, it's not about finding policies that work; it's about forging consensus, and fighting cynicism, and finding the will to make change.

Can we do this? Can we find the character, as Americans, to open our hearts to each other? Can we see in each other a common humanity and a shared dignity, and recognize how our different experiences have shaped us? And it doesn't make anybody perfectly good or perfectly bad, it just makes us human. I don't know. I confess that sometimes I, too, experience doubt. I've been to too many of these things. I've seen too many families go through this. But then I am reminded of what the Lord tells Ezekiel: I will give you a new heart, the Lord says, and put a new spirit in you. I will remove from you your heart of stone and give you a heart of flesh.

That's what we must pray for, each of us: a new heart. Not a heart of stone, but a heart open to the fears and hopes and challenges of our fellow citizens. That's what we've seen in Dallas these past few days. That's what we must sustain.

Because with an open heart, we can learn to stand in each other's shoes and look at the world through each other's eyes, so that maybe the police officer sees his own son in that teenager with a hoodie who's kind of goofing off but not dangerous—(applause)—and the teenager—maybe the teenager will see in the police officer the same words and values and authority of his parents. (Applause.)

With an open heart, we can abandon the overheated rhetoric and the oversimplification that reduces whole categories of our fellow Americans not just to opponents, but to enemies.

With an open heart, those protesting for change will guard against reckless language going forward, look at the model set by the five officers we mourn today, acknowledge the progress brought about by the sincere efforts of police departments like this one in Dallas, and embark on the hard but necessary work of negotiation, the pursuit of reconciliation.

35   With an open heart, police departments will acknowledge that, just like the rest of us, they are not perfect; that insisting we do better to root out racial bias is not an attack on cops, but an effort to live up to our highest ideals. (Applause.) And I understand these protests—I see them, they can be messy. Sometimes they can be hijacked by an irresponsible few. Police can get hurt. Protestors can get hurt. They can be frustrating.

But even those who dislike the phrase "Black Lives Matter," surely we should be able to hear the pain of Alton Sterling's family. (Applause.) We should—when we hear a friend describe him by saying that "Whatever he cooked, he cooked enough for everybody," that should sound familiar to us, that maybe he wasn't so different than us, so that we can, yes, insist that his life matters. Just as we should hear the students and coworkers describe their affection for Philando Castile as a gentle soul—"Mr. Rogers with dreadlocks," they called him—and know that his life mattered to a whole lot of people of all races, of all ages, and that we have to do what we can, without putting officers' lives at risk, but do better to prevent another life like his from being lost.

With an open heart, we can worry less about which side has been wronged, and worry more about joining sides to do right. (Applause.) Because the vicious killer of these police officers, they won't be the last person who tries to make us turn on one other. The killer in Orlando wasn't, nor was the killer in Charleston. We know there is evil in this world. That's why we need police departments. (Applause.) But as Americans, we can decide that people like this killer will ultimately fail. They will not drive us apart. We can decide to come together and make our country reflect the good inside us, the hopes and simple dreams we share.

"We also glory in our sufferings, because we know that suffering produces perseverance; perseverance, character; and character, hope."

For all of us, life presents challenges and suffering—accidents, illnesses, the loss of loved ones. There are times when we are overwhelmed by sudden calamity, natural or manmade. All of us, we make mistakes. And at times we are lost. And as we get older, we learn we don't always have control of things—not even a President does. But we do have control over how we respond to the world. We do have control over how we treat one another.

40   America does not ask us to be perfect. Precisely because of our individual imperfections, our founders gave us institutions to guard against tyranny and ensure no one is above the law; a democracy that gives us the space to work through our differences and debate them peacefully, to make things better, even if it doesn't always happen as fast as we'd like. America gives us the capacity to change.

But as the men we mourn today—these five heroes—knew better than most, we cannot take the blessings of this nation for granted. Only by working together can we preserve those institutions of family and community, rights and responsibilities, law and self-government that is the hallmark of this nation. For, it turns out, we do not persevere alone. Our character is not found in isolation. Hope does not arise by putting our fellow man down; it is found by lifting others up. (Applause.)

And that's what I take away from the lives of these outstanding men. The pain we feel may not soon pass, but my faith tells me that they did not die in vain. I believe our sorrow can make us a better country. I believe our righteous anger can be transformed into more justice and more peace. Weeping may endure for a night, but I'm convinced joy comes in the morning. (Applause.) We cannot match the sacrifices made by Officers Zamarripa and Ahrens, Krol, Smith, and Thompson, but surely we can try to match their sense of service. We cannot match their courage, but we can strive to match their devotion.

May God bless their memory. May God bless this country that we love.

Reading and Discussion Questions

1. One powerful way to use language effectively is through the careful use of repetition. Where in his speech does President Obama make use of repetition, and for what purpose?

2. In paragraph 15, Obama makes use of the term "fault line." How is that term an example of figurative language?

3. What examples of figurative language do you see in paragraph 21?

4. When Obama says that each of us must pray for a new heart, he is not being literal. What point is he trying to make in his use of heart imagery?

5. How would you summarize some of the main points that Obama is trying to make?

6. How effective do you feel that Obama was in his choice of language to make his points, considering the context in which he spoke? Do you find many words with either positive or negative connotations? What sort of tone does the language create? Is that tone appropriate for the situation?

Assignments for Language: Using Words with Care

Reading and Discussion Questions

1. Listen to or read the "I Have a Dream" speech by Martin Luther King Jr., noting its uses of figurative language.

2. Look back at the company slogans on page 288, and explain what each means.

3. Examine a few periodicals from fifty or more years ago. Select either an advertising or a political slogan in one of them, and relate it to beliefs or events of the period. Alternatively, tell why the slogan is no longer relevant.

4. Make up a slogan for a cause that you support. Explain and defend your slogan.

5. In watching television dramas about law, medicine, or criminal or medical investigation, do you find that the professional language, some of which you may not fully understand, plays a positive or negative role in your enjoyment of the show? Explain your answer.

Writing Suggestions

1. Analyze a print ad of your choosing, explaining how text and visuals work together to support a claim. Your essay can be analytical or evaluative.

2. Write two paragraphs about your roommate, a family member, or a former teacher, making one balanced and the other either negatively slanted or positively slanted. Make the two distinctive through the facts you choose to include or omit, not the words you choose.

3. Write two paragraphs, one a positive and one a negative description of either a fictional person or someone you know. The facts should be essentially the same, but you will use charged words to make the difference.

4. Locate a speech by Martin Luther King Jr. such as "I Have a Dream" (choose a short one), and write an essay analyzing its use of figurative language. You'll need a thesis that holds your examples together.

5. Choose a popular slogan from advertising or politics. Write a paragraph explaining how it appeals to needs and/or values.

6. Explain in an essay why shortcuts are a natural result of our technological age.

7. Analyze a presidential or other debate using some of the terms discussed in this chapter.

8. Locate a copy of President Bush's first speech after the attacks of 9/11, and compare it to President Roosevelt's after the bombing of Pearl Harbor.

> **RESEARCH ASSIGNMENT** ▶ **Evaluating Language**

In the following passages, locate words with negative connotations, inflammatory language, language that builds on hidden assumptions, or offensive language.

Passage 1

Until we have universal background checks, better reporting from the states, and more — just more safety across the board, maybe a presence in schools is worth considering. I know that there is a police presence in the new location of the Sandy Hook school, and it certainly does reassure me when I drop my daughters off to see that there is that level of protection.

　　— Veronique Pozner, mother of one of the children killed at Sandy Hook Elementary

(Source: *Anderson Cooper 360 Degrees*, "Guns under Fire Town Hall." CNN, 31 Jan. 2013.)

Passage 2

The Three Percent movement I founded has been denounced by that paragon of moral virtue, Bill Clinton, and I am a perennial "honorable mention" on the Southern Poverty Law Center's list of dangerous folks. I have even been the subject of an eighteen and a half minute rant by Rachel Madcow on MSNBC, and the current attorney general of the United States knows — and despises — me by name because of the Fast and Furious scandal that, with my friend David Codrea, I broke the news of on the Internet. Eric Holder would not be surprised to know that the feeling is mutual.

　　— Speech at a Hartford firearm rights rally, April 20, 2013

(Source: Mike Vanderboegh, "My Name Is Mike Vanderboegh & I Am an Arms Smuggler." Sipseystreetirregulars.blogspot.com, 20 Apr. 2013.)

Passage 3

The rapidity of change and the speed with which new situations are created follow the impetuous and heedless pace of man rather than the deliberate pace of nature. Radiation is no longer merely the background radiation of cosmic rays, the ultraviolet of the sun that have existed before there was any life on earth; radiation is now the unnatural creation of man's tampering with the atom. The chemicals to which life is asked to make its adjustment are no longer merely the calcium and silica and copper and all the rest of the minerals washed out of the rocks and carried in rivers to the sea; they are the synthetic creations of man's inventive mind, brewed in his laboratories, and having no counterparts in nature.

(Source: Rachel Carson, "The Obligation to Endure," *Silent Spring*. New York: Houghton Mifflin, 1962, p. 7.)

> **bits** To see what you are learning about argumentation applied to the latest world and national news, read our *Bits* blog, "Argument and the Headlines," at **blogs.bedfordstmartins.com/bits.**

Logic: Understanding Reasoning

Throughout the book, we have pointed out the weaknesses that cause arguments to break down. In the vast majority of cases, these weaknesses represent breakdowns in logic or the reasoning process. We call such weaknesses **fallacies**, a term derived from Latin. Sometimes these false or erroneous arguments are deliberate; in fact, the Latin word *fallere* means "to deceive." But more often these arguments are either carelessly constructed or unintentionally flawed. Thoughtful readers learn to recognize them; thoughtful writers learn to avoid them.

As discussed in Chapter 1, the reasoning process was first given formal expression by Aristotle. In his famous treatises, he described the way we try to discover the truth — observing the world, selecting impressions, making inferences, generalizing. In this process, Aristotle identified two forms of reasoning: induction and deduction. Both forms, he realized, are subject to error. Our observations may be incorrect or insufficient, and our conclusions may be faulty because they have violated the rules governing the relationship between statements. Induction and deduction are not reserved only for formal arguments about important problems; they also represent our everyday thinking about the most ordinary matters. As for the fallacies, they, too, unfortunately, may crop up anywhere, whenever we are careless in our use of the reasoning process.

In this chapter, we examine some of the most common fallacies. First, however, a closer look at induction and deduction will make clear what happens when fallacies occur.

Induction

Induction is the form of reasoning in which we come to conclusions about the whole on the basis of observations of particular instances. For example, two friends decided to do some price comparisons.[1] They went to four popular stores, and at each one they checked the prices of the same four items: Sunbeam Giant Bread, Charmin Ultra Strong 9 Pack MegaRoll toilet paper, a gallon of store-brand whole milk, and a 12-pack of Cherry Coke Zero.

These shoppers were using the inductive method to determine which store is the least expensive. They studied the prices of individual items at individual stores and used that information to arrive at a generalization. They were moving from specifics — the prices of specific items at specific stores — to general observations. They compared the prices at the four stores and concluded that Walmart is the least expensive.

They were using induction, but how accurate was their conclusion? In inductive reasoning, the reliability of your conclusion depends on the quantity and quality of your observations. Were four items out of the thousands available at these four stores a sufficiently large sample? Would the friends' conclusion have been the same if they had chosen fifty items? One hundred? Even without pricing every item in all four stores, you would be more confident of your generalization as the quality and quantity of your samples increased.

Bloomberg Industries did a study of prices at Walmart and Target that made headlines in *Time* magazine.[2] The headline read, "Target Battles Walmart for Low-Price Supremacy." Who won the battle? Target did, but by only 0.46 percent. That means that for every $100 spent at Target, shoppers save $0.46 over Walmart for the same items. In this study, researchers compared prices on 150 similar items at the two stores, a much more convincing sample size than in our previous example. In this case, there were far more specific pieces of information to put together in reaching a generalization. Again, the process represents inductive reasoning because the researchers moved from specifics to generalizations. Later in the chapter, we will discuss a fallacy called "hasty generalization" that occurs when a generalization is based on too little evidence.

In some cases, you can observe all the instances in a particular situation. For example, by acquiring information about the religious beliefs of all the residents of a dormitory, you can arrive at an accurate assessment of the number of Buddhists. But since our ability to make definitive observations about everything is limited, we must make an inductive leap about categories of things that we ourselves can never encounter in their entirety. We make a leap when we have to accept less than absolute certainty or complete data and conclude that we have enough information on which to generalize. It is too much of a leap to conclude from a study of four items that one store is less expensive than another. It is less of a leap to conclude on the basis of 150 items.

---

[1] Amanda Miller, "Shop-o-nomics: 'Which Grocery Store Has the Lowest Prices?'" getoutofdebt.org. 20 Sept. 2010.
[2] Brad Tuttle, "Target Battles Walmart for Low-Price Supremacy." business.time.com. 27 Aug. 2012.

Generalizations can also be complicated by other factors. Walmart recently aired television commercials citing specific items to prove that its prices on groceries are better than those at Publix. A blogger on Iheartpublix.com responded with her own list of prices on 53 items, showing that Publix prices are better.[3] How can both be true? The blogger acknowledges that her prices were drawn from Publix's weekly ads. In other words, she compared Publix's sale prices with Walmart's everyday prices. (Her argument was that at least some of the Walmart items in the commercial were on sale and that smart shoppers buy when an item is on sale.)

In other cases, we may rely on a principle known in science as "the uniformity of nature." We assume that certain conclusions about oak trees in the temperate zone of North America, for example, will also be true for oak trees growing elsewhere under similar climatic conditions. We also use this principle in attempting to explain the causes of behavior in human beings. If we discover that the institutionalization of some children from infancy results in severe developmental delay, we think it safe to conclude that under the same circumstances all children would suffer the same consequences. As in the previous example, we are aware that certainty about every case of institutionalization is impossible. With rare exceptions, the process of induction can offer only probability, not certain truth.

Keep in mind that induction is a reasoning process, not an organizational pattern for academic essays. An author may make use of inductive reasoning to arrive at a generalization that then becomes the thesis of an essay. It may not always be obvious that the author used induction to arrive at his or her thesis. In the essay that follows, however, the author discloses how he arrived at his thinking about big businesses and their attitude toward the environment. Jared Diamond did not start out thinking that big businesses are active in preserving the environment. A number of specific instances of actions by these companies changed his thinking; thus by the process of inductive reasoning he arrived at his thesis. He provides detailed examples of the environmentally responsible acts by big businesses that shaped his opinion.

> **ARGUMENT ESSENTIALS**
> ## Induction
>
> - Induction is the process of arriving at a generalization based on the observation of a number of particular instances.
> - The accuracy of the generalization depends on the quantity and quality of the particular instances observed.
> - In most cases, the generalization will be a probability, not a certainty.
> - Arriving at a generalization based on too few particular instances is a logical fallacy called "hasty generalization."

---

[3] Michelle, "See the Real Difference — Publix vs. Walmart Shopping." iheartpublix.com. 16 July 2012.

READING ARGUMENT

Seeing Induction

The following excerpted essay has been annotated to show inductive reasoning.
Read the essay, and answer the questions that follow.

Will Big Business Save the Earth?
JARED DIAMOND

There is a widespread view, particularly among environmentalists and liberals,
that big businesses are environmentally destructive, greedy, evil, and driven by
short-term profits. I know — because I used to share that view.

But today I have more nuanced feelings. Over the years I've joined
the boards of two environmental groups, the World Wildlife Fund and
Conservation International, serving alongside many business executives.

As part of my board work, I have been asked to assess the environments
in oil fields, and have had frank discussions with oil company employees at all
levels. I've also worked with executives of mining, retail, logging, and financial
services companies. I've discovered that while some businesses are indeed as
destructive as many suspect, others are among the world's strongest positive
forces for environmental sustainability.

The embrace of environmental concerns by chief executives has accelerated
recently for several reasons. Lower consumption of environmental resources
saves money in the short run. Maintaining sustainable resource levels and not
polluting saves money in the long run. And a clean image — one attained by,
say, avoiding oil spills and other environmental disasters — reduces criticism
from employees, consumers, and government.

What's my evidence for this? Here are a few examples involving three   5
corporations — Walmart, Coca-Cola, and Chevron — that many critics of
business love to hate, in my opinion, unjustly.

Let's start with Walmart. Obviously, a business can save money by
finding ways to spend less while maintaining sales. This is what Walmart did
with fuel costs, which the company reduced by $26 million per year simply
by changing the way it managed its enormous truck fleet. Instead of running
a truck's engine all night to heat or cool the cab during mandatory 10-hour

---

Claim: the generalization he arrived at over time

Reasons CEOs are embracing environmental concerns

He will use three companies to illustrate the evidence that led him (inductively) to his generalization.
First example: Walmart
Four paragraphs of specifics on how Walmart shows concern for the environment

---

Jared Diamond is a professor of geography at the University of California, Los Angeles, and
winner of the 1998 Pulitzer Prize for general nonfiction for his book *Guns, Germs, and Steel*.
His most recent book is *The World until Yesterday* (2012). This piece appeared in the *New York
Times* on December 6, 2009.

rest stops, the company installed small auxiliary power units to do the job. In addition to lowering fuel costs, the move eliminated the carbon dioxide emissions equivalent to taking 18,300 passenger vehicles off the road.

Walmart is also working to double the fuel efficiency of its truck fleet by 2015, thereby saving more than $200 million a year at the pump. Among the efficient prototypes now being tested are trucks that burn biofuels generated from waste grease at Walmart's delis. Similarly, as the country's biggest private user of electricity, Walmart is saving money by decreasing store energy use.

Another Walmart example involves lowering costs associated with packaging materials. Walmart now sells only concentrated liquid laundry detergents in North America, which has reduced the size of packaging by up to 50 percent. Walmart stores also have machines called bailers that recycle plastics that once would have been discarded. Walmart's eventual goal is to end up with no packaging waste.

One last Walmart example shows how a company can save money in the long run by buying from sustainably managed sources. Because most wild fisheries are managed unsustainably, prices for Chilean sea bass and Atlantic tuna have been soaring. To my pleasant astonishment, in 2006 Walmart decided to switch, within five years, all its purchases of wild-caught seafood to fisheries certified as sustainable.

10   Coca-Cola's problems are different from Walmart's in that they are largely long-term. The key ingredient in Coke products is water. The company produces its beverages in about 200 countries through local franchises, all of which require a reliable local supply of clean fresh water.

But water supplies are under severe pressure around the world, with most already allocated for human use. The little remaining unallocated fresh water is in remote areas unsuitable for beverage factories, like Arctic Russia and northwestern Australia.

Coca-Cola can't meet its water needs just by desalinizing seawater, because that requires energy, which is also increasingly expensive. Global climate change is making water scarcer, especially in the densely populated temperate-zone countries, like the United States, that are Coca-Cola's main customers. Most competing water use around the world is for agriculture, which presents sustainability problems of its own.

Hence Coca-Cola's survival compels it to be deeply concerned with problems of water scarcity, energy, climate change, and agriculture. One company goal is to make its plants water-neutral, returning to the environment water in quantities equal to the amount used in beverages and their production. Another goal is to work on the conservation of seven

Second example: Coca-Cola

Five paragraphs of specifics about Coca-Cola

of the world's river basins, including the Rio Grande, Yangtze, Mekong, and Danube — all of them sites of major environmental concerns besides supplying water for Coca-Cola.

These long-term goals are in addition to Coca-Cola's short-term cost-saving environmental practices, like recycling plastic bottles, replacing petroleum-based plastic in bottles with organic material, reducing energy consumption, and increasing sales volume while decreasing water use.

Third example: Chevron — three paragraphs

The third company is Chevron. Not even in any national park have I seen   15 such rigorous environmental protection as I encountered in five visits to new Chevron-managed oil fields in Papua New Guinea. (Chevron has since sold its stake in these properties to a New Guinea–based oil company.) When I asked how a publicly traded company could justify to its shareholders its expenditures on the environment, Chevron employees and executives gave me at least five reasons.

First, oil spills can be horribly expensive: it is far cheaper to prevent them than to clean them up. Second, clean practices reduce the risk that New Guinean landowners become angry, sue for damages, and close the fields. (The company has been sued for problems in Ecuador that Chevron inherited when it merged with Texaco in 2001.) Next, environmental standards are becoming stricter around the world, so building clean facilities now minimizes having to do expensive retrofitting later.

Also, clean operations in one country give a company an advantage in bidding on leases in other countries. Finally, environmental practices of which employees are proud improve morale, help with recruitment, and increase the length of time employees are likely to remain at the company.

Reading and Discussion Questions

1. Diamond has changed his mind about big businesses. What has changed his mind?

2. What is his belief now about big businesses and the environment, which is also his thesis?

3. If that thesis is Diamond's major premise, explain how the essay is based on the inductive process. What are the specifics from which this generalization was drawn?

4. Considering Walmart as an example, are you convinced by the details Diamond presents to prove that the company is sincere about the environment? Identify a couple of examples showing the difference that a single large company can make when it takes the protection of the environment seriously.

Deduction

It is useful to think of deduction as working in the opposite direction from induction. With deductive reasoning, an arguer essentially starts with a general statement that would apply to a number of specific situations. Then the arguer applies that generalization to one specific instance. Unlike the conclusions from induction, which are only probable, the conclusions from **deduction** are certain. The simplest deductive argument consists of two premises and a conclusion. In outline form, such an argument looks like this:

> **Major premise:** All students with 3.5 averages and above for three years are invited to become members of Kappa Gamma Pi, the honor society.
>
> **Minor premise:** George has had a 3.8 average for over three years.
>
> **Conclusion:** Therefore, he will be invited to join Kappa Gamma Pi.

This deductive conclusion is *valid,* or logically consistent, because it follows necessarily from the premises. No other conclusion is possible. **Validity**, however, refers only to the form of the argument. The argument itself may not be satisfactory if the premises are not true — if Kappa Gamma Pi has imposed other conditions or if George has only a 3.4 average. The difference between truth and validity is important because it alerts us to the necessity for examining the truth of the premises before we decide that the conclusion is sound.

One way of discovering how the deductive process works is to look at the methods used by Sherlock Holmes, that most famous of literary detectives, in solving his mysteries. On one occasion, Holmes observed that a man sitting opposite him on a train had chalk dust on his fingers. From this observation, Holmes deduced that the man was a schoolteacher. If his thinking were outlined, it would take the form of a **syllogism**, the classic form of deductive reasoning:

> **Major premise:** All men with chalk dust on their fingers are schoolteachers.
>
> **Minor premise:** This man has chalk dust on his fingers.
>
> **Conclusion:** Therefore, this man is a schoolteacher.

The major premise offers a generalization about a large group or class. This generalization has been arrived at through inductive reasoning, or observation of particulars. The minor premise makes a statement about a specific member of that group or class. The third proposition is the conclusion, which links the other two propositions, in much the same way that an assumption links support and a claim.

But although the argument may be logical, it is faulty. A deductive argument is only as strong as its premises. In this case, the major premise, the generalization that all men with chalk dust on their fingers are schoolteachers, is not true. Perhaps all the men with dusty fingers whom Holmes had so far observed had turned out to be schoolteachers, but his sample was not

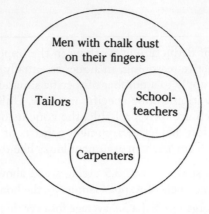

sufficiently large to enable him to conclude that all dust-fingered men are teachers. In Holmes's day, draftsmen or carpenters or tailors might have had fingers just as white as those of schoolteachers. Sometimes it is helpful to draw a Venn diagram, circles representing the various groups in their relation to the whole.

If the large circle above represents all those who have chalk dust on their fingers, we see that several different groups may be contained in this universe. To be safe, Holmes should have deduced that the man on the train *might have been* a schoolteacher; he was not safe in deducing more than that. Obviously, if the inductive generalization or major premise is false, the conclusion of the particular deductive argument is also false or invalid.

The deductive argument may also go wrong elsewhere. What if the *minor* premise is untrue? Could Holmes have mistaken the source of the white powder on the man's fingers? Suppose it was not chalk dust but flour or confectioner's sugar or talcum or heroin. Any of these possibilities would weaken or invalidate Holmes's conclusion.

Another example, closer to the kinds of arguments you will examine in your academic work, reveals the flaw in the deductive process.

Major premise: All Communists oppose organized religion.

Minor premise: Robert Roe opposes organized religion.

Conclusion: Therefore, Robert Roe is a Communist.

The fact that two things share an attribute does not mean that they are the same thing. The following diagram makes clear that Robert Roe and Communists do not necessarily share all attributes. Remembering that Holmes may have misinterpreted the signs of chalk on the traveler's fingers, we may also want to question whether Robert Roe's opposition to organized religion has been misinterpreted.

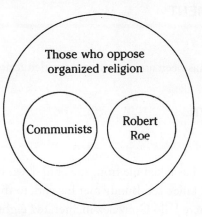

Some deductive arguments give us trouble because one of the premises, usually the major premise, is omitted. As in the assumptions we examined in Chapter 8, a failure to evaluate the truth of an unexpressed premise may lead to an invalid conclusion. When only two parts of a syllogism appear, we call the resulting form an **enthymeme**. Suppose we overhear the following bit of conversation:

> "Did you hear about Jean's father? He had a heart attack last week."
> "That's too bad. But I'm not surprised. I know he always refused to go for his annual physical checkups."

The second speaker has used an unexpressed major premise, the cause-and-effect assumption *If you have annual physical checkups, you can avoid heart attacks.* He does not express it because he assumes that it is unnecessary to do so. The first speaker recognizes the unspoken assumption and may agree with it. Or the first speaker may produce evidence from reputable sources that such a generalization is by no means universally true, in which case the conclusion of the second speaker is suspect.

A knowledge of the deductive process can help guide you toward an evaluation of the soundness of your reasoning in an argument you are constructing. A syllogism is often clearer than an outline in establishing the relations between the different parts of an argument.

Setting down your own or someone else's argument in this form will not necessarily give you the answers to questions about how to support your claim, but it should clearly indicate what your claims are and, above all, what logical connections exist between your statements.

ARGUMENT ESSENTIALS
Deduction

- Deduction is the process of applying a generalization to a particular instance.
- The simplest deductive argument consists of two premises and a conclusion — a syllogism.
- The conclusions from deduction are certain if both premises are true.

READING ARGUMENT

Seeing Deduction

The following essay has been annotated to show deduction.

It's All about Him

DAVID von DREHLE

The author establishes his knowledge of mass murders, his "claim to authority."

My reporter's odyssey has taken me from the chill dawn outside the Florida prison in which serial killer Ted Bundy met his end, to the charred façade of a Bronx nightclub where Julio Gonzalez incinerated eighty-seven people, to a muddy Colorado hillside overlooking the Columbine High School library, in which Eric Harris and Dylan Klebold wrought their mayhem. Along the way, I've come to believe that we're looking for why in all the wrong places.

Thesis statement (and major premise): Mass murderers are narcissists.

I've lost interest in the cracks, chips, holes, and broken places in the lives of men like Cho Seung-Hui, the mass murderer of Virginia Tech. The pain, grievances, and self-pity of mass killers are only symptoms of the real explanation. Those who do these things share one common trait. They are raging narcissists. "I died — like Jesus Christ," Cho said in a video sent to NBC.

The traits of the narcissist

Psychologists from South Africa to Chicago have begun to recognize that extreme self-centeredness is the forest in these stories, and all the other things — guns, games, lyrics, pornography — are just trees. To list the traits of the narcissist is enough to prove the point: grandiosity, numbness to the needs and pain of others, emotional isolation, resentment, and envy.

Major premise applied to Ted Bundy

In interviews with Ted Bundy taped a quarter-century ago, journalists Stephen Michaud and Hugh Aynesworth captured the essence of homicidal narcissism. Through hour after tedious hour, a man who killed 30 or more young women and girls preened for his audience. He spoke of himself as an actor, of life as a series of roles, and of other people as props and scenery. His desires were simple: "control" and "mastery." He took whatever he wanted, from shoplifted tube socks to human lives, because nothing mattered beyond his desires. Bundy said he was always surprised that anyone noticed his victims had vanished. "I mean, there are so many people," he explained. The only death he regretted was his own.

Criminologists distinguish between serial killers like Bundy, whose crimes occur one at a time and who try hard to avoid capture, and mass killers   5

David von Drehle is editor-at-large for *Time* magazine. His most recent book is *Abraham Lincoln and America's Most Perilous Year* (2012). This article appeared in *Time* on April 30, 2007.

like Cho. But the central role of narcissism plainly connects them. Only a narcissist could decide that his alienation should be underlined in the blood of strangers. The flamboyant nature of these crimes is like a neon sign pointing to the truth. Charles Whitman playing God in his Texas clock tower, James Huberty spraying lead in a California restaurant, Harris and Klebold in their theatrical trench coats—they're all stars in the cinema of their self-absorbed minds.

Other examples of narcissistic mass murderers

Freud explained narcissism as a failure to grow up. All infants are narcissists, he pointed out, but as we grow, we ought to learn that other people have lives independent of our own. It's not their job to please us, applaud for us, or even notice us—let alone die because we're unhappy.

Freud said narcissists never grow up. They put their happiness over others' lives.

A generation ago, the social critic Christopher Lasch diagnosed narcissism as the signal disorder of contemporary American culture. The cult of celebrity, the marketing of instant gratification, skepticism toward moral codes, and the politics of victimhood were signs of a society regressing toward the infant stage. You don't have to buy Freud's explanation or Lasch's indictment, however, to see an immediate danger in the way we examine the lives of mass killers. Earnestly and honestly, detectives and journalists dig up apparent clues and weave them into a sort of explanation. In the days after Columbine, for example, Harris and Klebold emerged as alienated misfits in the jock culture of their suburban high school. We learned about their morbid taste in music and their violent video games. Largely missing, though, was the proper frame around the picture: the extreme narcissism that licensed these boys, in their minds, to murder their teachers and classmates.

Investigators have failed to recognize narcissism as the real motivation in mass murder cases.

Something similar is now going on with Cho, whose florid writings and videos were an almanac of gripes. "I'm so lonely," he moped to a teacher, failing to mention that he often refused to answer even when people said hello. Of course he was lonely.

Major premise applied to Cho

In Holocaust studies, there is a school of thought that says to explain is to forgive. I won't go that far. But we must stop explaining killers on their terms. Minus the clear context of narcissism, the biographical details of these men can begin to look like a plausible chain of cause and effect—especially to other narcissists. And they don't need any more encouragement.

Outside the context of narcissism, the murderers' actions can seem too logical.

10   There's a telling moment in Michael Moore's film *Bowling for Columbine*, in which singer Marilyn Manson dismisses the idea that listening to his lyrics contributed to the disintegration of Harris and Klebold. What the Columbine killers needed, Manson suggests, was for someone to listen to them. This is the narcissist's view of narcissism: Everything would be fine if only he received more attention. The real problem can be found in the killer's mirror.

The author reiterates that the killer's problem is not lack of attention but how the killer sees himself.

Analysis

Von Drehle wrote "It's All about Him" shortly after the 2007 massacre at Virginia Tech. Although we cannot know exactly how he arrived at the thesis, we can reasonably assume he went through something of an inductive process on the way to writing this deductive essay. Perhaps he read and watched enough about Cho, the shooter at Virginia Tech, to hypothesize about Cho's motivation. His earlier observations of other mass murderers led him to notice similarities among them. Once he arrived at a theory about what they had in common, he had the major premise for a deductive argument that he could test out on other mass murderers. He was able to construct an argument that could be summarized in syllogistic form:

> **Major premise:** Mass murderers are narcissistic.
> **Minor premise:** Cho was a mass murderer.
> **Conclusion:** Cho was narcissistic.

In his essay, he presents his major premise early and then applies it to other U.S. mass murderers: Ted Bundy, Charles Whitman, James Huberty, Eric Harris, and Dylan Klebold.

If von Drehle's major and minor premises are true, then the conclusion, of necessity, must be true. That Cho was a mass murderer is an indisputable fact; thus the minor premise is true. But what of the major premise? If we applied the deduction that mass murderers are narcissistic to mass murderers not mentioned by von Drehle, would the conclusion be the same in each case? In other words, is it true that all mass murderers are narcissistic?

Because it would be virtually impossible to apply von Drehle's deduction to all mass murderers, he would have built a more convincing case had he restricted his thesis statement with a word like *most* or *many*. That, however, would have invalidated the deductive logic that tells us that a syllogism's conclusion must be true. As it is, the examples he offers are not enough to convince all readers that his theory of narcissism is valid. Still, he offers a unique look at the motivation of mass murderers and one that makes it impossible for anyone else to be blamed for the crimes that these men and boys have committed. Behind his argument are his many years of journalistic experience and his opening revelation that he has been on the scene during the aftermath of many of the crimes to which he refers.

Practice: Deduction

The excerpt below exemplifies former Secretary of State Hillary Clinton's frequent use of deduction. Read the excerpt, and answer the questions that follow it.

Excerpt from Remarks at the Asia Pacific Economic Cooperation Women and the Economy Summit
HILLARY CLINTON

Integrating women more effectively into the way businesses invest, market, and recruit also yields benefits in terms of profitability and corporate governance. In a McKinsey survey, a third of executives reported increased profits as a result of investments in empowering women in emerging markets. Research also demonstrates a strong correlation between higher degrees of gender diversity in the leadership ranks of business and organizational performance. The World Bank finds that by eliminating discrimination against female workers and managers, managers could significantly increase productivity per worker by 25 to 40 percent. Reducing barriers preventing women from working in certain sectors would lower the productivity gap between male and female workers by a third to one half across a range of countries.

Hillary Clinton served as Secretary of State for President Barack Obama from 2009 to 2013. The speech was given in September 2011.

Reading and Discussion Questions

1. What is the major premise in this passage from Clinton's speech?
2. What is the relationship between the first sentence and the rest of the paragraph?

Common Fallacies

In this necessarily brief review it would be impossible to discuss all the fallacies listed by logicians, but we can examine the ones most likely to be found in the arguments you will read and write. Fallacies are difficult to classify, first, because there are literally dozens of systems for classifying, and second, because under any system there is always a good deal of overlap. It's helpful to remember that even if you cannot name the particular fallacy, you can learn to recognize it and not only refute it in the arguments of others but avoid it in your own as well.

RESEARCH SKILL ▶ Identifying Reliable Authorities

We all like to think that if information is in print, it is reliable. Unfortunately, that is not always the case. People with unjust biases and even those who want to sow hatred often find a way to get their opinions into print. In general, works that appear in print go through a much more extensive vetting process than what appears online, but there are so-called vanity presses that will publish pretty much anything if the author will pay the cost. There are also all sorts of periodicals that express slanted — and often conflicting — points of view, some of them offensive to many of us. That's what comes of freedom of the press. Whether in print, online, or in audiovisual sources, you should always look for well-known, credentialed authors and speakers who employ logical reasoning and avoid inflammatory language.

Hasty Generalization

Many of our prejudices are a result of **hasty generalization**. A prejudice is literally a judgment made before the facts are in. On the basis of experience with two or three members of an ethnic group, for example, we may form the prejudice that all members of the group share the characteristics that we have attributed to the two or three in our experience.

Superstitions are also based in part on hasty generalization. As a result of a very small number of experiences with black cats, broken mirrors, Friday the thirteenth, or spilled salt, some people will assume a cause-and-effect relation between these signs and misfortunes. *Superstition* has been defined as "a notion maintained despite evidence to the contrary." The evidence would certainly show that contrary to the superstitious belief, in a lifetime hundreds of such "unlucky" signs are not followed by unfortunate events. To generalize about a connection is therefore unjustified.

Any generalization based on too few particular instances is a hasty generalization. Since we seldom have the chance to observe every possible instance before arriving at a generalization, we have to interpret what "too few" means in a particular context.

- I got a parking ticket for parking on the street before I got my permit and another ticket for parking facing the wrong way on the street. These police in Columbia are just out to make money off of college students!
- That driver who cut me off was an old lady. Old people shouldn't be allowed to drive.
- I studied for my first two statistics tests and still failed. I'm not going to even bother to study for the final because I'm going to fail it anyway.
- I've got to wear my lucky Clemson shirt! We never lose when I wear it!
- It made me really nervous having that family of Muslims on my flight.

Faulty Use of Authority

The use of authority — the attempt to bolster claims by citing the opinions of experts — was discussed in Chapter 7. Experts are a valuable source of information on subjects we have no personal experience with or specialized knowledge about. Properly identified, they can provide essential support. The **faulty use of authority** occurs when individuals are presented as authorities in fields in which they are not. An actor who plays a doctor on television may be hired to advertise the latest sleep medicine but actually has

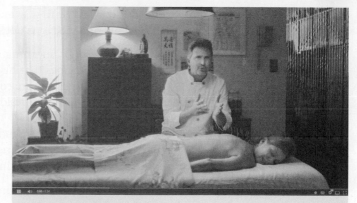

FIGURE 11.1 Holiday Inn Express commercial.

no more expertise with medications than the average consumer. The role that he plays may make him appear to be an authority but does not make him one. No matter how impressive credentials sound, they are largely meaningless unless they establish relevant authority.

Vintage ads are a rich source of false use of authority:

- More doctors smoke Camels than any other cigarettes. (1949)
- For Sun Giant Raisins: Horror film star Vincent Price says, "Around my kitchen this is raisin time of year . . . because raisins are good, and good for you." (1974)
- The Soda Pop Board of America claimed that laboratory tests have proven that babies who start drinking soda early have a much higher chance of gaining acceptance and "fitting in" during the preteen years. (2002 parody)

In a series of popular television commercials for Holiday Inn Express that ran for eleven years starting in 1998 and then were started again in 2013, ordinary people step in to perform the role of professionals. When it is discovered that they are not professionals as others assumed, the retort is always the same: "But I stayed at a Holiday Inn Express last night." In one of the ads a woman relaxes under what she assumes to be the talented hands of a skilled acupuncturist, only to find that his sole claim to authority is what hotel he stayed at the night before. (See Figure 11.1)

Post Hoc or Doubtful Cause

The entire Latin term for this fallacy is *post hoc, ergo propter hoc*, meaning, "After this, therefore because of this." The arguer infers that because one event follows another event, the first event must be the cause of the second. But proximity of events or conditions does not guarantee a causal relation.

- The rooster crows every morning at 5:00 and, seeing the sun rise immediately after, decides that his crowing has caused the sun to rise.
- A month after A-bomb tests are concluded, tornadoes damage the area where the tests were held, and residents decide that the tests caused the tornadoes.
- After the school principal suspends daily prayers in the classroom, acts of vandalism increase, and some parents are convinced that failure to conduct prayer is responsible for the rise in vandalism.

In each of these cases, the fact that one event follows another does not prove a causal connection. The two events may be coincidental, or the first event may be only one — and an insignificant one — of many causes that have produced the second event. The reader or writer of causal arguments must determine whether another more plausible explanation exists and whether several causes have combined to produce the effect. Perhaps the suspension of prayer was only one of a number of related causes: a decline in disciplinary action, a relaxation of academic standards, a change in school administration, and changes in family structure in the school community.

In the social sciences, cause-and-effect relations are especially susceptible to challenge. Human experiences can seldom be subjected to laboratory conditions. In addition, the complexity of the social environment makes it difficult, even impossible, to extract one cause from among the many that influence human behavior.

False Analogy

Many analogies are merely descriptive and offer no proof of the connection between the two things being compared. An analogy is called a **false analogy** when two things are compared to each other on the basis of superficial similarities while significant dissimilarities are ignored.

- Bill Clinton had no experience of serving in the military. To have Bill Clinton become president, and thus commander-in-chief of the armed forces of the United States, was like electing some passerby on the street to fly the space shuttle.
- Students should be allowed to look at their textbooks during examinations. After all, surgeons have X-rays to guide them during an operation; lawyers have briefs to guide them during a trial; carpenters have blueprints to guide them when building a house. Why, then, shouldn't students be allowed to look at their textbooks during an examination?
- Education cannot prepare men and women for marriage. Trying to educate them for marriage is like trying to teach them to swim without allowing them to go into the water. It can't be done.
- People are like dogs. They respond best to clear discipline.

Ad Hominem

The Latin term *ad hominem* means "against the man" and refers to an attack on the person rather than on the argument or the issue. The assumption in such a fallacy is that if the speaker proves to be unacceptable in some way, his or her statements must also be judged unacceptable. Attacking the author of the statement is a strategy of diversion that prevents the reader from giving attention where it is due — to the issue under discussion.

You might hear someone complain, "What can the priest tell us about marriage? He's never been married himself." This ad hominem accusation ignores the validity of the advice the priest might offer. In the same way, an overweight patient might reject advice on diet by an overweight physician. In politics, it is not uncommon for antagonists to attack each other for personal characteristics that may not be relevant to the tasks they will be elected to perform. They may be criticized for infidelity to their partners, homosexuality, atheism, or a flamboyant social life. Even if certain assertions should be proved true, voters should not ignore the substance of what politicians do and say in their public offices.

- I wouldn't vote for Higgins because he left his wife and three kids to run off with his secretary.
- The CEO of that company is gay, so I wouldn't buy its products.
- She shouldn't serve on the school board; she had her first child before she was married!

Ad hominem accusations against the person do *not* constitute a fallacy if the characteristics under attack are relevant to the argument. If the politician is irresponsible and dishonest in the conduct of his or her personal life, we may be justified in thinking that the person will also behave irresponsibly and dishonestly in public office.

False Dilemma

As the name tells us, the **false dilemma**, sometimes called the "black-white fallacy," poses an either-or situation. The arguer suggests that only two alternatives exist, although there may be other explanations of or solutions to the problem under discussion. The false dilemma reflects the simplification of a complex problem. Sometimes it is offered out of ignorance or laziness, sometimes to divert attention from the real explanation or solution that the arguer rejects for doubtful reasons.

You may encounter the either-or situation in dilemmas about personal choices. "At the University of Georgia," says one writer, "the measure of a man was football. You either played it or worshipped those who did, and there was no middle ground."[4] Clearly, this dilemma — playing football or worshiping those who do — ignores other measures of manhood.

---

[4] Phil Gailey, "A Nonsports Fan," *New York Times Magazine,* December 18, 1983, sec. 6, p. 96.

David Frent/Getty Images

Politics and government offer a wealth of examples.

- U.S.A.: Love it or leave it.
- If we don't end our dependence on oil, we will destroy our children's future.
- Either you are with us, or you are with the terrorists.

In an interview with the *New York Times* in 1975, the Shah of Iran was asked why he could not introduce into his authoritarian regime greater freedom for his subjects. His reply was, "What's wrong with authority? Is anarchy better?"

Slippery Slope

If an arguer predicts that taking a first step will lead inevitably to a second, usually undesirable step, he or she must provide evidence that this will happen. Otherwise, the arguer is guilty of a **slippery-slope** fallacy.

Predictions based on the danger inherent in taking the first step are commonplace. In a speech to Congress on October 27, 1999, Independent presidential candidate Ron Paul said, "I am strongly pro-life. I think one of the most disastrous rulings of this century was *Roe versus Wade*. I do believe in the slippery-slope theory. I believe that if people are careless and casual about life at the beginning of life, we will be careless and casual about life at the end. Abortion leads to euthanasia. I believe that."[5] Here are other examples:

- The Connecticut law allowing sixteen-year-olds and their parents to divorce each other will mean the death of the family.
- If we ban handguns, we will end up banning rifles and other hunting weapons.

---

[5] Quoted in "Protect All Human Life." ronpaul.com.

Slippery-slope predictions are simplistic. They ignore not only the dissimilarities between first and last steps but also the complexity of the developments in any long chain of events.

Begging the Question

If the writer makes a statement that assumes that the very question being argued has already been proved, the writer is guilty of **begging the question**. In a letter to the editor of a college newspaper protesting the failure of the majority of students to meet the writing requirement because they had failed an exemption test, the writer said, "Not exempting all students who honestly qualify for exemption is an insult." But whether the students are honestly qualified is precisely the question that the exemption test was supposed to resolve. The writer has not proved that the students who failed the writing test were qualified for exemption. She has only made an assertion *as if* she had already proved it.

Circular reasoning is an extreme example of begging the question: "Women should not be permitted to join men's clubs because the clubs are for men only." The question to be resolved first, of course, is whether clubs for men only should continue to exist.

Other examples:

- I hate soccer because it's a sport I just don't like.
- The reason these clubs are in such demand is that everyone wants to get in them.
- Freedom of speech is important because people should be able to speak freely.

Straw Man

The **straw-man** fallacy consists of an attack on a view similar to but not the same as the one your opponent holds. It is a familiar diversionary tactic. The name probably derives from an old game in which a straw man was set up to divert attention from the real target that a contestant was supposed to knock down.

Notice how in the following passage about New York mayor Michael Bloomberg's proposed ban on the sale of sugary drinks larger than sixteen ounces, conservative pundit George Will shifts the focus from that proposed restriction to global warming:

> "That's modern liberalism: They delight in bossing people around,"
> Will complained to ABC's George Stephanopoulos. "What
> Bloomberg is saying [is] the government helps with your health care,
> the government's implicated in your health. Therefore, we own you.
> Therefore, the government can fine tune all the decisions you make
> pertinent to your health."

"This is one of the reasons liberals are so enamored over the issue of climate change," Will continued. "They say all our behaviors in some way affect the climate, therefore, the government — meaning, we liberals, the party of government — can fine tune all your behavior right down to the light bulbs you use."[6]

Red Herring

Another diversionary tactic is the **red herring**. The straw man is an attempt to draw an opponent's attention to an issue similar to but not exactly what the opponent was talking about that the speaker or writer can better address. A red herring is an attempt to divert attention away from the subject at hand to *any* other subject, not just one related to the original subject.

An outstanding example of the red herring fallacy occurred in the famous Checkers speech of Senator Richard Nixon. In 1952, during his vice-presidential campaign, Nixon was accused of having appropriated $18,000 in campaign funds for his personal use. At one point in the radio and television speech in which he defended his reputation, he said:

> One other thing I probably should tell you, because if I don't they will probably be saying this about me, too. We did get something, a gift, after the election.
>
> A man down in Texas heard Pat on the radio mention the fact that our two youngsters would like to have a dog, and, believe it or not, the day before we left on this campaign trip we got a message from Union Station in Baltimore saying they had a package for us. We went down to get it. You know what it was?
>
> It was a little cocker spaniel dog, in a crate that he had sent all the way from Texas, black and white, spotted, and our little girl, Tricia, the six-year-old, named it Checkers.
>
> And, you know, the kids, like all kids, loved the dog, and I just want to say this, right now, that regardless of what they say about it, we are going to keep it.[7]

Of course, Nixon knew that the issue was the alleged misappropriation of funds, not the ownership of the dog, which no one had asked him to return.

Two Wrongs Make a Right

The **two-wrongs-make-a-right** fallacy is another example of the way in which attention may be diverted from the question at issue.

---

[6] David Edwards, "George Will Uses Bloomberg's Soda Ban to Blast Climate Change Laws," rawstory.com, 3 June 2012.

[7] Radio and television address of Senator Nixon from Los Angeles on September 23, 1952.

After President Jimmy Carter in March 1977 attacked the human rights record of the Soviet Union, Russian officials responded:

> As for the present state of human rights in the United States, it is characterized by the following facts: millions of unemployed, racial discrimination, social inequality of women, infringement of citizens' personal freedom, the growth of crime, and so on.[8]

The Russians made no attempt to deny the failure of *their* human rights record; instead they attacked by pointing out that the Americans are not blameless either.

Other examples:

- Anyone who killed those innocent children deserves the death penalty.
- It's ok to use chemical weapons against the U.S. since the U.S. used them against Viet Nam.
- I had every right to take his Blu-ray player. He broke mine!

Non Sequitur

The Latin term **non sequitur**, which means "it does not follow," is another fallacy of irrelevance. An advertisement for a book, *Worlds in Collision*, whose

JOEL PETT
LEXINGTON HERALD-LEADER

Joel Pett Editorial Cartoon used with the permission of Joel Pett and the Cartoonist Group. All rights reserved.

---

[8] Joel Pett/The Cartoonist Group

theories about the origin of the earth and evolutionary development have been challenged by almost all reputable scientists, states:

> Once rejected as "preposterous"! Critics called it an outrage! It aroused incredible antagonism in scientific and literary circles. Yet half a million copies were sold and for twenty-seven years it remained an outstanding bestseller.

We know, of course, that the popularity of a book does not bestow scientific respectability. The number of sales, therefore, is irrelevant to proof of the book's theoretical soundness — a non sequitur.

Other examples sometimes appear in comments by politicians and political candidates. In June 2010, President Obama said, "After all, oil is a finite resource. We consume more than 20 percent of the world's oil, but have less than 2 percent of the world's oil reserves."[9] This is a non sequitur because the relevant relationship would be between the U.S. percentage of world *population* (not oil reserves) and the U.S. percentage of world oil consumption.

Ad Populum

Arguers guilty of the **ad populum** fallacy make an appeal to the prejudices of the people (*populum* in Latin). They assume that their claim can be adequately defended without further support if they emphasize a belief or attitude that the audience shares with them. One common form of ad populum is an appeal to patriotism, which may enable arguers to omit evidence that the audience needs for proper evaluation of the claim. In the following advertisement, the makers of Zippo lighters made such an appeal in urging readers to buy their product:

> It's a grand old lighter. Zippo — the grand old lighter that's made right here in the good old U.S.A.
>
> We truly make an all-American product. The raw materials used in making a Zippo lighter are all right from this great land of ours.
>
> Zippo windproof lighters are proud to be Americans.

Other examples:

- But you have to let me go to the party! *Everyone* will be there!
- Everybody drives a little over the speed limit. If I drove the speed limit, I would get rear-ended!
- Lipton Ice Tea. Join the Dance.

[9] Glen Kessler, "U.S. Oil Resources: President Obama's 'Non Sequitur Facts,'" Washington Post Online, washingtonpost.com, 15 Mar. 2012.

Strategies for Uncovering Logical Fallacies

1. If your source is making use of induction — that is, drawing a conclusion based on a number of individual examples — does it have enough examples with variety to justify the conclusion? In other words, will your readers be able to make the inductive leap from examples to the conclusion you are asking them to make?

2. If your source is making use of deduction, is its conclusion a logical one based on the premises underlying it? To be sure, write out its argument in the form of a syllogism, and confirm that both the major and the minor premises are true.

3. Avoid sources that word their thesis statements in absolute terms like *all, every, everyone, everybody,* and *always.*

4. Use the list of fallacies in this chapter as a checklist while you read each of your sources with a critical eye, looking for any breakdown in logic.

Appeal to Tradition

In making an **appeal to tradition**, the arguer assumes that what has existed for a long time and has therefore become a tradition should continue to exist *because* it is a tradition. If the arguer avoids telling his or her reader *why* the tradition should be preserved, he or she may be accused of failing to meet the real issue.

The following statement appeared in a letter defending the membership policy of the Century Club, an all-male club established in New York City in 1847 that was under pressure to admit women. The writer was a Presbyterian minister who opposed the admission of women.

> I am totally opposed to a proposal which would radically change the nature of the Century. . . . A club creates an ethos of its own over the years, and I would deeply deplore a step that would inevitably create an entirely different kind of place.
>
> A club like the Century should surely be unaffected by fashionable whims. . . .[10]

Numerous activities continue "because it's always been done that way." They range from debutante balls that may seem out of sync with modern times to football traditions. Texas A&M students were so devoted to the massive bonfire that marked the approach of their game with rival University of Texas that it was continued off campus, unsanctioned by the school, even after eleven students and one former student died during a collapse of the stacked wood in 1999. Tradition in and of itself is not a bad thing, but discrimination, injustice, and unsafe behaviors have often been prolonged in the name of tradition.

---

[10] David H. C. Read, letter to the *New York Times,* January 13, 1983, p. 14.

Practice

Decide whether the reasoning in the following examples is faulty. Use the common fallacies presented in the previous pages to explain your answers.

1. The presiding judge of a revolutionary tribunal, being asked why people are being executed without trial, replies, "Why should we put them on trial when we know that they're guilty?"

2. The government has the right to require the wearing of helmets while operating or riding on a motorcycle because of the high rate of head injuries incurred in motorcycle accidents.

3. Children who watch game shows rather than situation comedies receive higher grades in school. So it must be true that game shows are more educational than situation comedies.

4. The meteorologist predicted the wrong amount of rain for May. Obviously, the meteorologist is unreliable.

5. Women ought to be permitted to serve in combat. Why should men be the only ones to face death and danger?

6. If Lady Gaga uses Truvia, it must taste better than Splenda.

7. People will gamble anyway, so why not legalize gambling in this state?

8. Because so much money was spent on public education in the last decade while educational achievement declined, more money to improve education can't be the answer to reversing the decline.

9. He's a columnist for a campus newspaper, so he must be a pretty good writer.

10. We tend to exaggerate the need for Standard English. You don't need much Standard English for most jobs in this country.

11. It's discriminatory to mandate that police officers must conform to a certain height and weight.

12. A doctor can charge for a missed appointment, so patients should be charged less when a doctor keeps them waiting.

13. Because this soft drink contains so many chemicals, it must be unsafe.

14. Core requirements should be eliminated. After all, students are paying for their education, so they should be able to earn a diploma by choosing the courses they want.

15. We should encourage a return to arranged marriages in this country since marriages based on romantic love haven't been very successful.

16. I know three redheads who have terrible tempers, and since Annabel has red hair, I'll bet she has a terrible temper, too.

17. Supreme Court Justice Byron White was an all-American football player while in college, so how can you say that athletes are dumb?

18. Benjamin H. Sasway, a student at Humboldt State University in California, was indicted for failure to register for possible conscription. Barry Lynn, president of Draft Action, an antidraft group, said, "It is disgraceful that

this administration is embarking on an effort to fill the prisons with men of conscience and moral commitment."

19. James A. Harris, former president of the National Education Association: "Twenty-three percent of schoolchildren are failing to graduate and another large segment graduates as functional illiterates. If 23 percent of anything else failed — 23 percent of automobiles didn't run, 23 percent of the buildings fell down, 23 percent of stuffed ham spoiled — we'd look at the producer."

20. A professor at Rutgers University: "The arrest rate for women is rising three times as fast as that of men. Women, inflamed by the doctrines of feminism, are pursuing criminal careers with the same zeal as business and the professions."

21. Physical education should be required because physical activity is healthful.

22. George Meany, former president of the AFL-CIO, in 1968: "To these people who constantly say you have got to listen to these younger people, they have got something to say, I just don't buy that at all. They smoke more pot than we do and if the younger generation are the hundred thousand kids that lay around a field up in Woodstock, New York, I am not going to trust the destiny of the country to that group."

23. That candidate was poor as a child, so he will certainly be sympathetic to the poor if he's elected.

24. When the federal government sent troops into Little Rock, Arkansas, to enforce integration of the public school system, the governor of Arkansas attacked the action, saying that it was as brutal an act of intervention as Russia's sending troops into Hungary to squelch the Hungarians' rebellion. In both cases, the governor said, the rights of a freedom-loving, independent people were being violated.

25. Governor Jones was elected two years ago. Since that time, constant examples of corruption and subversion have been unearthed. It is time to get rid of the man responsible for this kind of corrupt government.

26. Are we going to vote a pay increase for our teachers, or are we going to allow our schools to deteriorate into substandard custodial institutions?

27. You see, the priests were right. After we threw those virgins into the volcano, it quit erupting.

28. The people of Rome lost their vitality and desire for freedom when their emperors decided that the way to keep them happy was to provide them with bread and circuses. What can we expect of our own country now that the government gives people free food and there is a constant round of entertainment provided by television?

29. From Mark Clifton, "The Dread Tomato Affliction" (proving that eating tomatoes is dangerous and even deadly): "Ninety-two point four percent of juvenile delinquents have eaten tomatoes. Fifty-seven point one percent of the adult criminals in penitentiaries throughout the United States have eaten tomatoes. Eighty-four percent of all people killed in automobile accidents during the year have eaten tomatoes."

30. From Galileo, *Dialogues Concerning Two New Sciences*: "But can you doubt that air has weight when you have the clear testimony of Aristotle affirming that all elements have weight, including air, and excepting only fire?"

31. Robert Brustein, artistic director of the American Repertory Theater, commenting on a threat by Congress in 1989 to withhold funding from an offensive art show: "Once we allow lawmakers to become art critics, we take the first step into the world of Ayatollah Khomeini, whose murderous review of *The Satanic Verses* still chills the heart of everyone committed to free expression." (The Ayatollah Khomeini called for the death of the author Salman Rushdie because Rushdie had allegedly committed blasphemy against Islam in his novel.)

READING ARGUMENT

Seeing Logical Fallacies

The following essay has been annotated to point out places where the author finds logical fallacies with cyclists' demands for road privileges. Annotations also note logical problems with the author's argument.

Drivers Get Rolled
CHRISTOPHER CALDWELL

Late last August, along the coast of New Hampshire, Kevin Walsh, police chief in the town of Rye, got a lecture on law enforcement from a bunch of grown-up bicyclists. Local law requires bikers to ride single-file when there is traffic. But this day, a pack of a dozen or so bikers were racing down Ocean Boulevard, at high speed, up to five abreast, according to an interview the chief later gave. Walsh decided to flag them down and tell them what they were doing was unsafe, "out of control," and "an accident waiting to happen." He stood in the middle of Ocean Boulevard and signaled them to stop. The bikers blew past him in a whoosh! of Lycra, sweat, and profanity. Walsh got in his cruiser and cut off the bikers four miles up the road. When he stopped them, they began to chew him out. "You almost killed somebody back there, standing in the middle of the road," one of them screamed at the cop. "Do you understand we can't stop? Do you understand we can't stop like a car?"

> The bikers are setting up a straw man to divert blame from themselves.

Like many episodes in the world of adult recreational cycling, this one breaks new ground in the annals of chutzpah. Few non-cyclists would think to scold a law enforcement official for having nearly been run over by them.

> Shows the false analogy: If they can't stop like a car, they shouldn't expect the rights of drivers.

Christopher Caldwell is a senior editor at the *Weekly Standard*. His article appeared on weeklystandard.com on November 18, 2013.

Fewer still would release to the news media a video of the incident—which came from a camera mounted on the handlebars of one of the bikers—in the almost demented belief that it constituted a vindication rather than an incrimination. And yet you can see it online.

Incidents like this now happen every day. Laws governing bikes on roads have never been crystal-clear, and have always been marked by a degree of common sense and compromise. An increase in racing and commuting bikers has altered what passes for common sense. Cyclists like the ones in New Hampshire, whose reckless riding and self-righteousness have earned rolled eyes nationwide and the nickname of "Lycra louts" in England, have tested the public's willingness for compromise. As bicyclists become an ever more powerful lobby, ever more confident in the good they are doing for the environment and public health, they are discovering—to their sincere surprise—that they are provoking mistrust and even hostility among the public.

Transported

When there are more bicyclists on the road, when most bicyclists are no longer children and teens, and when well-built bikes can easily descend a hill at 50 miles an hour, new questions come up. The first is how we are to think of bikes. Are they like really fast pedestrians? Or like cars with a lower maximum speed? The law's general view is that they are vehicles. But what the law really means is not that bikes are exactly like cars but that they are analogous. You don't need to get a license to ride a bike, you don't need your vehicle inspected to put it on the road, and you aren't charged tax for the upkeep of highways. There is considerable ambiguity here, and activist bikers, with lawyerly sophistication, almost unfailingly claim the best of both worlds. Consider the guy we mentioned above who insisted police chief Walsh give him all the rights of the road for a vehicle he claimed to be unable to stop. Bicyclists are exactly like cars when it suits them—as when they occupy the middle of a lane in rush hour. But they are different when it suits them—going 18 mph in that very same lane even though the posted speed is 45, riding two abreast, running red lights if there's nothing coming either way, passing vehicles on the right when there's a right turn coming up. This makes bikes a source of unpredictability, frustration, and danger.

Shows why the analogy between cars and bikes works only part of the time

5   This should not alarm us unduly. Bicyclists sometimes do require the middle of the roadway, and do need special consideration. The rightmost part of the road is often punctuated with old-fashioned sewer grates that will swallow a tire whole and fling you over the handlebars. There are broken bottles, dropped hypodermic needles, oil slicks that have drained off the road's

crown, and places where the road is frittered away. The right side of the road is also where passenger doors get flung open, sometimes suddenly, and one piece of bad timing will send you to kingdom come. Almost 700 cyclists died on the road in the United States in 2011. Let us not forget the environmental, aesthetic, and health benefits of cycling over driving, which are obvious and undeniable.

The problem is that our transportation network, built at the cost of trillions over the decades, is already over capacity, as the Obama administration was fond of reminding us when arguing for the 2009 stimulus package. It is not so easily rejiggered. Unquestionably we have misbuilt our transport grid. It makes us car-dependent. It should better accommodate bikers and walkers. But for now it can't. Unless you want to cover much more of the country in asphalt — which is far from the professed wishes of bikers — lane space is finite. There are few places in America where public transportation can serve as a serious alternative to driving. In only five metropolitan areas — Boston, New York, Washington, Chicago, and San Francisco — do as many as 10 percent of commuters take public transportation.

So, except in a few spots where roads were built too wide and can now accommodate bike paths, adding bicycles to the mix means squeezing cars. Bike-riders don't "share" the road so much as take it over. Their wish is generally that the right-hand lane of any major or medium-sized road be turned into a bike lane or, at best, a shared-use lane. This would place drivers in a position of second-class citizenship on roads that were purpose-built for them. There are simply not enough cyclists to make that a reasonable idea. What is going on is the attempt of an organized private interest to claim a public good. Cyclists remind one of those residents in exurban subdivisions who, over years, allow grass and shrubbery to encroach on dirt public sidewalk until it becomes indistinguishable from their yards, and then sneakily fence it in.

Our numbers about how many people bike and how often are relatively imprecise. The best estimates come from counting commutes and accidents. According to the U.S. census, 120 million people drive to work every weekday, and 750,000 bike. In other words, there are 160 drivers for every biker. Bike use is growing — but even at 40 times the present level it would still not be sensible public policy to squander a quarter, a third, or half of the lane space on a busy rush-hour artery for a bike lane.

Bike riding could be the wave of the future, or it could be a sports fad, the way tennis was in the 1970s or skateboarding in the 1980s or golf in the 1990s. It is hard to tell, since bike riding is now the beneficiary of vast public and private subsidies and massive infrastructure projects, from Indianapolis's $100 million

A reminder of the dangers of bicycling

A simple if unfortunate fact: Our transportation network was not built to accommodate bicycles.

False dilemma: Private interest and public good do not have to be mutually exclusive.

plan to add bike lanes and other nonauto byways to Citibank's underwriting of the New York City bike-share program. "Subsidize it and they will come," could be the motto. Drivers are being taxed to subsidize their own eviction.

High Rollers

10   There are a number of internationally recognized signals through which bicyclists convey their intentions to drivers. The raised left hand means a right turn, the dropped left hand means slowing down, and so on. I have never seen either of these gestures used. Instead, cyclists tend to communicate with motorists through a simpler, all-purpose gesture, the raised middle finger. The self-righteousness, the aplomb, of bicyclists is their stereotypical vice and quirk, like the madness of hatters, the drunkenness of poets, and the communism of furriers.

> Hasty generalization: Not all bikers are rude.

The attitude was nicely captured in a pro-biking letter to the editor in the *Brookline TAB*, the community paper for Boston's richest neighborhoods: "Whenever someone bikes or walks to the store or to work," the writer began, "he or she is taking one automobile off the road and making a significant contribution both to Brookline's safety and to reducing the carbons so dangerous to life on earth." You see? It only looks like I'm having a midlife crisis — I'm actually on a rescue mission! The question of what courtesy the cyclist owes the community is immediately taken off the table, replaced by the question of what the community can possibly do to repay its debt to the cyclist.

> The virtues of biking are irrelevant to the issue of biking safely.

All of us who care about the environment have a sense — even a conviction — that biking is more virtuous than driving. What distinguishes the biking enthusiast is that he is just as convinced that biking is more virtuous than walking: "While riding," another *TAB* correspondent wrote, "I have encountered pedestrians who are texting. They are a danger to themselves and others, because they sometimes make erratic movements and often ignore requests to step to the side so a bicycle can pass." By "request," the writer probably means a barked command of "On your right!" or "On your left!" made by a cyclist approaching from behind at 30 mph.

If bicyclists have a more highly developed sense that they can boss others around, this is because they disproportionately belong to the classes from which bosses come. They are, to judge from their blogs, more aggrieved by delivery trucks parked in bike lanes than drivers are by delivery trucks parked in car lanes. This may be because proportionately fewer of them have ever met a person who drives a delivery truck. The 2011 accident data of the National Highway Traffic Safety Administration give us a hint that ardent bicycling is not, for the most part, a youthful avocation, as those whose biking days ended in the 1970s or '80s might assume. The average age of those killed cycling — presumably a rough proxy for those doing the most grueling road riding — has been rising by close to a year annually. In 2003 it was 36; in 2011 it was 43. Cyclists are heavily weighted towards the baby boom generation. The group involved in the most fatal accidents in 2011 is ages 45–54, followed by ages 55–64. The two cohorts make up those born between 1947 and 1966.

This generation is at the height of its earning power, and bikers are drawn from the very richest part of it. Shortly after Birmingham, England, got almost $30 million from the government to make itself more bike-friendly, the *Birmingham Post* researched who was building bike spaces in London. Topping the list were the Gherkin, the ghastly Norman Foster–designed skyscraper in the financial district that houses a lot of London's financial-services industry; Goldman Sachs's Fleet Street headquarters; and London Wall Place, a high-end office building slated for construction in the City. This helps explain why Portland, Oregon, is so proud of its status as the country's most "bicycle-friendly" city, and why Las Vegas, Louisville, and other places are vying to outdo it. City officials want to be "bicycle-friendly" for the same reason they want to be "gay-friendly" or "Internet-friendly," and for the same reason they built opera houses in the nineteenth century and art museums in the twentieth — it is a way of telling investors: "Rich people live here."

Doubtful cause: Is that why cities want to be bicycle friendly?

Once you understand that bicycling is a rich person's hobby, you can understand the fallacy that *Slate* editor David Plotz, an ardent bicyclist, committed when he asked why such a large number of dangerous drivers he encountered while cycling to work drove the same make of car. Of the twenty scares he's had in his life, ten came from BMWs. "In other words," Plotz wrote, "the BMW, a car that has less than 2 percent market share in the United States, was responsible for 50 percent of the menacing." Why, he wondered? Was it a sense of entitlement, or were BMW-drivers just "assholes"? Probably neither — it is that luxury-car-driving and bike-commuting are heavily concentrated in the same very top sliver of the American class hierarchy. The percentage of BMWs driving between where the average cyclist lives to where the average cyclist works is a heck of a lot higher than 2 percent. It may not be 50 percent — the Help, after all, needs to use these roads, too — but it is high.

False dilemma: Feeling entitled and being assholes are not the only alternatives.

15

Wheel Estate

If bike-friendly areas are rich neighborhoods, they are a particular kind of rich neighborhood. They are college towns, or at least "latte towns," to use the term David Brooks coined in these pages. The top cities for cycling commuters, according to the U.S. census, are Corvallis and Eugene in Oregon,

Fort Collins and Boulder in Colorado, and Missoula, Montana. The census notes that Portland, Oregon, is the only metropolitan area in which at least 2 percent of commutes are by bike.

Its concentration in cultural hubs has consequences. Bicycling's apostles have behind them not just the economic and lobbying power of the "One Percent," but also the cultural and intellectual power of its most sophisticated members. The idea that there might be alternative social goods competing with cycling, or any reason not to offer cyclists as much leeway and indulgence as they might demand, seems scarcely to have occurred to anybody who discusses it in public. That, surely, is why a cyclist might think that posting a video of a cyclist scolding a well-meaning New Hampshire police chief might help the cycling cause. The promotion of cycling is open to discussion as to means, but not as to ends. The question is how, not whether, to build more bike infrastructure; and how, not whether, to educate motorists about their responsibilities to bikers. It is never about educating bicyclists on how to find alternative modes of transport.

Bicyclists expect privileges.

Leaders of the biking community, though, most often try to cast themselves as an underprivileged minority. Ian Walker, a "traffic psychologist" from the University of Bath, describes cyclists as a "minority outgroup"—they suffer in a society that "views cycling as anti-conventional and possibly even infantile." In an August editorial calling for an end to "anti-cyclist bias," the *San Francisco Bay Guardian* opined: "To focus exclusively on the behavior of cyclists is like blaming a rape victim for wearing a short skirt."

False analogy

As is not uncommon when progressive utopias are being constructed, there are a number of informal activist groups for enforcing opinion. The Twitter feed CycleHatred was founded in Britain to expose those who wrote negative things about cyclists, although recent press reports have implicitly questioned whether such exposure might do the anti-cycling cause more good than harm. The cycling journalist Peter Walker of the *Guardian* commented on a Tweet (probably good-humored) attacking Britain's Olympic gold medalist Bradley Wiggins for having made cycling popular ("If Wiggins came in here, I'd give him a piece of my mind"). Ian Walker responded:

> This is a fantastic example of what is sometimes called the "cyclists should get their house in order" argument—that people who have nothing in common except choosing cycling as one of their several regular forms of transport are nonetheless necessarily defined by it, and are somehow responsible for the worst actions by others on bikes.

Walker points out the hasty generalization.

20   But this is a category error. That our road system cannot provide the resources to support cyclists in the style to which they would like to become

accustomed is a matter of policy and limited resources, not of civil rights and prejudice. An action that is ignorable at the individual level — such as cycling down the middle of the street at high speed — can become a problem when the masses do it. That is why, for instance, people have been forbidden to burn leaves in their backyard for the past half-century. One pile of leaves is a beautiful smell. Several are a pollution problem, or so they tell us. Right or wrong, those who consider leaf burning a problem are not making a bigoted assessment of the personalities of the individual leaf-burners.

Bikers' unmet needs, in terms of both infrastructure and law, are limitless. A common trope is to compare America's spending on bikes with that of the Netherlands. Amsterdam spends $39 per resident on bike trails, laments the *Boston Globe*, while Boston spends under $2. Until we shell out as much as the Dutch, there can be no such thing as misspent money. Pointing to areas, mostly poor, in which Washington, D.C.'s Capital Bikeshare program has failed to win a following, the director of the program assured the *Washington Post* that "those areas where the bike community is not yet self-sustaining" are "precisely where the District Department of Transportation needs to double its efforts."

The analogy is incomplete unless the number of bikers is also compared.

The bicycle agenda is coming to resemble the feminist agenda from the 1970s, when previously all-male universities went co-ed. Everything that was ever off-limits to the aggrieved minority must be opened up, while sancta established for the minority in the old days must be preserved, and new ones founded. So bikers must have access to roads and hiking trails, but also get their own new "bike boulevards." Having a special bike-friendly highway, such as Route 9W, west of the Hudson River, does not mean that certain other highways will ever be closed off to bikes in the interest of efficiency or fairness.

The analogy is not clear.

While it is wrong to call bicyclists a downtrodden minority, they are a minority in one sense. They are one of those compact, issue-oriented small groups that, as the economist Mancur Olson warned in his classic *The Logic of Collective Action* (1965), generally take unmotivated majorities to the cleaners. There are probably a million dedicated cyclists in this country, bent on taking over a quarter or a third of the nation's road space, built at the price of, let us repeat, trillions. They are ranged against the 200 million drivers who have a vague sense they are being duped. But this sense is only vague, and because motorists, like other American voters, have developed the habit of being talked into giving up what is theirs, any wise person would bet on the bicyclists' winning all they ask for. A small collection of elite hobbyists will continue, as Tacitus might have put it, to make a traffic jam and call it peace.

Reading and Discussion Questions

1. Explain why the anecdote in the first paragraph is an example of the straw man fallacy.

2. Explain one or more of the examples of false analogy in the article.

3. How convincing is Caldwell's argument that bicyclists are among our richest citizens? Does your experience seem to support that claim? Explain.

4. Have you experienced or witnessed the sorts of problems between bikers and drivers that Caldwell describes? If so, give an example.

5. In spite of the focus in the annotations on logical fallacies, what strengths does the article have?

Practice: Uncovering Logical Fallacies

Read the essay below, and answer the questions that follow.

"Gender Neutral" Bathrooms Are Dangerous
ELIZABETH LEE VLIET, M.D.

Federal and state governments have opened a new Pandora's box of dangers to the public, especially for women and girls, with the new push for "gender neutral" public bathrooms and locker rooms, allowing people to choose such facilities based on self-perceived gender, rather than biological sex.

Consequence of such absurd ideas are predictable.... Just recently, a Seattle man began undressing at a public swimming pool women's locker room when a group of young girls were changing for a swim team practice. He was not arrested, as a result of Washington's new law allowing "transgender" men to use women's restrooms. I use quotes around the term transgender because this man had no outward identifying statements or attire to suggest he thought of himself as a woman.

Bathroom equality or "gender neutral" locker rooms is just the latest absurdity in the move by "progressives" to "progress" the United States right out of common sense and public safety. It continues the liberal expansion of "rights" for a minority few against safety and privacy rights of the majority.

To put the tyranny of the minority in perspective here: There are approximately 700,000 transgender people in the U.S., representing about 0.3 percent of the entire population. That means the safety, privacy and common decency concerns for 99.7 percent of the

Elizabeth Lee Vliet, MD, is the founder and Medical Director of HER Place®: Health Enhancement and Renewal for Women, Inc.®, where hormonal changes in women are studied and evaluated. She also speaks on women's health issues and teaches courses on women's health to physicians and other health professionals. Her books include *It's My Ovaries, Stupid!* (2003), *Screaming to Be Heard: Hormone Connections Women Suspect... and Doctors Still Ignore* (1995), and *Women, Weight and Hormones* (2001).

American population are sacrificed on the altar of political correctness and "feel good" policies for a tiny fraction of the public.

5   Indecent exposure (males exposing genitals to women in public is the most common occurrence), sexual battery, assault, molestation, sex with minors and rape are all crimes in almost all jurisdictions. It shouldn't take a rocket scientist to see that telling men they can suddenly decide they "feel" like a woman and thereby use women's bathrooms is a slippery slope to more of all types of these sexual crimes. How does the "feeling" of a gender dysphoric man take priority over the safety of your wife, daughter, girlfriend, mother, sister or friend?

The Association of American Physicians and Surgeons released a statement about the importance of separate facilities for men and women to protect public safety: "Attempts by activist groups to force businesses or government facilities to harm, threaten, demean, or offend women and girls who do not want to share facilities with biological males are to be resisted and condemned as immoral, irrational, oppressive, and contrary to public order, human rights, public health, and our founding principles."

Let's look at real-life issues. I am a practicing physician with specialty training from the Johns Hopkins Sexual Medicine Consultation team. I have treated people seeking help for many sex and gender issues: gay/lesbian, pedophilia, transvestism, gender dysphoria, voyeurism and serial rapists. At the time transgender patients have undergone surgery to become their new gender, it is then appropriate to use the bathroom facilities for their gender reassignment. Until then, common sense and public safety should require those with male genitalia (regardless of self-perception) use men's bathrooms, and those with female genitalia should use women's bathrooms.

Several striking common denominators emerged from many years of treating patients in this area of medicine:

- The unpredictability, and at times uncontrollability, of sexual drives to engage in behaviors potentially harmful physically and/or psychologically to others.
- The complete lack of empathy for the victim shown by sexual predators, whether "mild" predation of voyeurism or the obviously serious and criminal acts of rape and assault.
- We cannot predict who will engage in sexual assault, or when they will do it.
- Statistics show that women and girls are overwhelmingly the victims in such cases of sexual predator actions.

Speaking as a physician, separate bathroom and locker facilities for men and women helps provide physical and psychological safety, particularly for women and girls, from those who would do harm by giving into their sudden urge to rape or molest others. While such safety issues may apply to men as well, it is far less probable that a female enters a men's restroom and starts molesting males, who are typically bigger and stronger and better able to defend themselves.

As James Arlandson wrote in the *American Thinker* April 12: "Mankind is stronger than womankind. There are simply too many differences between the sexes. Yet our society in its 'infinite wisdom' seems to be smashing those differences. Further, since mankind is stronger than womankind, women need to feel safe. And breaking down the safe space for a woman at her most vulnerable — while she is changing and dressing and showering outside the home — is insane. Her zone of safety, her right to privacy, needs to be protected at all costs."

10

America really does seem to be entering the Twilight Zone of Absurdity with assaults on morals, decency and safety coming from all directions. The election of 2016 is becoming about far more than "politics" as usual: It is about restoring common sense in the public arena, public safety and enforcing laws that are designed to maintain civil order and civility for ALL, not just a favored few in the minority group du jour.

Reading and Discussion Questions

1. Vliet states her claim very clearly in her first sentence. Under what circumstances does she believe a transgender person should be allowed to use a bathroom other than the one of his or her birth gender?
2. What problem or problems with logic do you see in paragraph 2?
3. Where does Vliet's use of slanted language or language with negative connotations reveal her bias?
4. Why is paragraph 4 an example of begging the question?
5. What exactly is the slippery slope in paragraph 5? Do you agree with the point Vliet is making? Why or why not?
6. Does the last sentence in paragraph 5 represent an either/or fallacy? Why or why not?
7. In paragraph 7, Vliet lists a number of "sex and gender issues" for which she says she has treated people who have asked for help. What problems do you see with that list?
8. Do you see any problems with the logic in paragraphs 8-9? Explain.
9. What is your response to the quote from James Arlandson in the next-to-last paragraph?
10. What is your response to the closing term of the essay: "minority group du jour"?

Assignments for Logic: Understanding Reasoning

Reading and Discussion Questions

1. How do the inductive and deductive reasoning processes relate to the scientific method?
2. Look at an issue of *Consumer Reports* or at the *Consumer Reports* Web site. Pick a general category like laptop computers, SUVs, or digital cameras. Explore how the researchers arrive at their recommendations. Do they use induction or deduction?

3. Why is it difficult to read an essay and tell whether the writer approached the topic through induction or deduction?

4. Do you feel that Jared Diamond's essay "Will Big Business Save the Earth?" is effective? Why, or why not?

5. Locate print ads to illustrate some of the fallacies covered in this chapter.

Writing Suggestions

1. Do some research on the other side of the issue that Diamond addresses. Choose a company that is not doing its part environmentally, and write an essay similar to Diamond's treatment of one company in his essay.

2. Using David von Drehle's essay as a model, write an essay supporting one of these thesis statements or a similar one:

   Those who do these things share one common trait. They are eternal optimists.
   Those who do these things share one common trait. They are eternal pessimists.
   Those who do these things share one common trait. They are tireless workers.
   Those who do these things share one common trait. They are selfless givers.

3. Write an essay in which you analyze one or more fallacies in a single print ad or use several ads to illustrate logical fallacies.

RESEARCH ASSIGNMENT

1. Go to *Google* or another general search engine that you are familiar with. Do a search for either "autism and vaccines" or "cell phones and cancer." (You may have used one of these subjects for an earlier exercise.) Before you click on a link, examine the first ten to fifteen entries in the resulting list. Look at each URL, and see what you can learn from it. Also notice any other information that might affect your opinion of the source's reliability or objectivity.

   - Are there sources that you immediately trust as reliable? Which ones, and why?
   - Are there any that you immediately assume will present a biased perspective? Which ones, and why?
   - Are there any that are completely unfamiliar to you? If so, choose two or three, and speculate what type of source each might be.

2. Now click on a couple of the sources that you trusted as being reliable. Identify exactly who wrote the document that you have accessed. If you cannot find an author, what does that suggest? If there is an author, search that person's name. See if you find convincing credentials that support the assumption that he or she is qualified to write on the subject at hand.

3. Do the same with at least two sources that you predicted would be biased. Does further investigation support your assumption? If so, how?

4. Go to at least one of the sources that were unfamiliar to you. Once you look more closely at the source, do you find any evidence of its reliability or lack thereof? Explain.

bits

To see what you are learning about argumentation applied to the latest world and national news, read our *Bits* blog, "Argument and the Headlines," at **blogs.bedfordstmartins.com/bits**.

Researching and Crafting ARGUMENTS

Planning and Research

By now, you should be fairly adept at supporting claims. The next step is to apply your skills to writing an argument of your own on a subject of your choice or one assigned to you that requires research.

In this chapter, we move through the various stages involved in preparing to write a researched argument: choosing a topic, locating and evaluating sources, and taking notes.

Finding an Appropriate Topic

To write an argument, you first must identify your topic. This is a relatively easy task for someone writing an argument as part of his or her job — a lawyer defending a client, for example, or an advertising executive presenting a campaign. For a student, however, it can be daunting. Which of the many ideas in the world worth debating would make a good subject?

Several guidelines can help you evaluate the possibilities. Perhaps your assignment limits your choices. If you have been asked to write a research paper, you obviously must find a topic on which research is available. You need a topic that is worth the time and effort you expect to invest in it, and your subject should be one that interests you. Don't feel you have to write about what you know — very often, finding out what you don't know will turn out to be more satisfying. You should, however, choose a subject that is familiar enough for you to argue about without fearing you're in over your head.

In this chapter, we will follow a student, Katie, who has been assigned a research paper for her first-year English class. In preparation for the assignment, the class has viewed the movie *Food, Inc.* This is the assignment that Katie must complete:

> The movie *Food, Inc.* raises a multitude of questions about food: the
> link between the corporate world and our food supply, organic foods,
> world hunger, alternative fuels, farm workers, childhood obesity. These

are just a sampling of the issues raised. For your research essay, choose an argumentative topic related in some way to the issues discussed in the film. Your thesis should be either a claim of value or a claim of policy. Your essay should be 6–8 double-spaced pages and must use at least six sources. There should be some variety in type of sources — books, articles, electronic journals, etc. Use MLA guidelines for documentation.

Invention Strategies

As a starting point, think of conversations you've had in the past few days or weeks that have involved defending a position. Is there some current political issue you're concerned about? some dispute with friends that would make a valid paper topic? One of the best sources is controversies in the media. Keep your project in mind as you watch TV, read print or online sources, or listen to the radio. You may even run into a potential subject in your course reading assignments or classroom discussions. Fortunately for the would-be writer, nearly every human activity includes its share of disagreement.

As you consider possible topics, write them down. One that looks unlikely at first glance may suggest others or may have more appeal when you come back to it later. Further, simply putting words on paper has a way of stimulating the thought processes involved in writing. Even if your ideas are tentative, the act of converting them into phrases or sentences can often help in developing them.

When student researcher Katie began thinking about her research assignment, she made the following entry in her journal:

I have started thinking about a topic related to food. I knew that there is also a book called *Food, Inc.*, so I went to the library's Web site and looked it up. It is a collection of essays edited by Karl Weber. It looked like a source worth investigating, so I checked it out.

The subtitle of the book is *How Industrial Food Is Making Us Sicker, Fatter, and Poorer—And What We Can Do about It*. That's what the film was about too. I don't have time to read the whole book for this assignment, but I looked at the preface and table of contents to get ideas about how to find a narrow enough subject. One subject that I thought might be interesting is today's epidemic of childhood obesity. There is one chapter in the part of the book that suggests solutions that's called "Improving Kids' Nutrition: An Action Tool Kit for Parents." There is also another essay paired with that one entitled "Childhood Obesity: The Challenge."

When I skimmed the second one, I could tell immediately that it has some good statistics about how bad the problem of childhood obesity is. I know that childhood obesity is too large a subject, and I have to come up with a thesis that is either a claim of value or a claim of policy. I don't think there is much controversy that a problem exists, and that would be a claim of fact. In the first essay I read about something I had never heard of—competitive foods. I found out that competitive foods are the "extras" sold to students in addition to or instead of the nutritious food served in the cafeteria. That has to be a controversial subject.

Evaluating Possible Topics

As you consider possible topics, you must, of course, follow any guidelines provided by your instructor. Not every topic is appropriate for an argumentative essay. Some would be difficult or impossible to find support for; others would make your job as a researcher more difficult than it has to be. The Writer's Guide below describes some characteristics of effective research paper topics.

WRITER'S GUIDE
Effective Research Paper Topics

Keep the following points in mind when settling on a topic for your research paper.

- **Interesting.** Your topic must interest your audience. Who is the audience? For a lawyer, it is usually a judge or jury; for a columnist, anyone who reads the newspaper in which his or her column appears. For the student writer, the audience is to some extent hypothetical. You should assume that your paper is directed at readers who are reasonably intelligent and well informed, but who have no specific knowledge of the subject. It may be useful to imagine you are writing for a local or school publication.

Less Interesting	More Interesting
Nice places to go bird watching	The effect of increasing feral cat population on native song birds
Which college has the best basketball team	The debate over whether schools should drop their intercollegiate sports program in favor of improved health and wellness for all students

- **Debatable.** The purpose of an argument is to defend or refute a thesis, so you should choose a topic that can be seen from more than one perspective. In evaluating a subject that looks promising, ask yourself: Can a case be made for other views? If not, you have no workable ground for building your own case.

Less Debatable	*More Debatable*
Shoplifting (Nobody would disagree that it is wrong.)	The increased use of security cameras in public spaces
Popularity of electronic tablets (Nobody would disagree that these have become enormously popular.)	The inability to share e-books, which cost just as much as print books

- **Not Too Broad.** Consider how long your paper will be and whether you can do justice to your topic in that amount of space. Your essay will not be very effective if you are able to cover your subject in only a general way with no specifics. As a general rule, the more specific your topic, the better the resulting essay.

- **Not Too Narrow.** In contrast, if you can cover your subject in a paragraph or even in a single page, it clearly is too narrow to be the subject for an argumentative essay.

Too Broad	*Too Narrow*	*Appropriate*
Nuclear energy around the world	Why a hybrid car made sense to me	Why the United States should invest in solar energy

- **Not Too Unconventional.** When offering an explanation, especially one that is complicated or extraordinary, look first for a cause that is not too difficult to accept — one that doesn't strain credibility. A reasonable person interested in the truth would search for more conventional explanations before accepting the bizarre or the incredible. Looking for a supernatural explanation for the disappearance of ships in the Bermuda Triangle or a new conspiracy theory to explain the assassination of John F. Kennedy is probably not the best use of your research time and would lead to a claim that would be difficult if not impossible to support.

Even if you start out with a topic that does not meet these criteria, you can use that as a starting point and move toward one that does, as in the examples above. Don't discard a topic that you are interested in until you have tried reworking and improving it. A topic that is too broad can be narrowed down; one that is too narrow can become part of a larger argument. A shift in focus can sometimes make a topic that is not debatable or interesting into one that is.

At this preliminary stage, don't worry if you don't know exactly how to word your thesis. It's useful to write down a few possible phrasings to be sure your topic is one you can work with, but you need not be precise. The information you unearth as you do research will help you to formulate your ideas. Also, stating a thesis in final terms is premature until you know the organization and tone of your paper. Student researcher Katie focused her initial topic idea like this:

> I narrowed my topic first to childhood obesity and then to competitive foods in schools. I think that I would like my claim to be that competitive foods should not be allowed in schools, but I will have to see if I can find enough good sources to support that claim.

Initiating Research

The success of any argument, short or long, depends in large part on the quantity and quality of the support behind it. Research, therefore, can be crucial for any argument outside your own experience.

Keeping Research on Track

You should prepare for research by identifying potential resources and learning how they work. Make sure you know how to use the library's catalog and other databases available either in the library or through the campus network. For each database that looks useful, explore how to execute a subject search, how to refine a search, and how to print out or download results. Make sure you know how to find books, relevant reference materials, and journals. Find out whether interlibrary loan is an option and how long it takes. If you plan to use government publications, find out if your library is a depository for federal documents. Identify relevant organizations using the *Encyclopedia of Associations*, and visit their Web sites. Finally, discuss your topic with a librarian at the reference desk to make sure you haven't overlooked anything.

WRITER'S GUIDE
Keeping Your Research on Track

---

1. **Focus your investigation on building your argument,** not merely on collecting information about the topic. Do follow any promising leads that turn up from the sources you consult, but don't be diverted into general reading that has no direct bearing on your thesis.

2. **Look for at least two pieces of evidence to support each point you want to make.** If you cannot find sufficient evidence, you may need to revise or abandon the point.

3. **Use a variety of sources.** Seek evidence from different kinds of sources (books, magazines, Web sites, government reports, even personal interviews with experts) and from different fields.

4. **Be sure your sources are authoritative.** Articles and essays in scholarly journals are more authoritative than articles in college newspapers or in magazines. Authors whose credentials include many publications and years of study at rep-

utable institutions are probably more reliable than newspaper columnists and the so-called man in the street. However, you can judge reliability much more easily if you are dealing with facts and inferences than with values and emotions.

5. **Don't let your sources' opinions outweigh your own.** Your paper should demonstrate that the thesis and ideas you present are yours, arrived at after careful reflection and supported by research. The thesis need not be original, but your paper should be more than a collection of quotations or a report of the facts and opinions you have been reading.

6. **Don't ignore information that opposes the position you plan to support.** Your argument is not strengthened by pretending such information does not exist. You may find that you must revise or qualify your position based on what your research reveals. Your readers may be aware of other positions on the issue and may judge you to be unreliable, careless, or dishonest if you do not acknowledge them. It is far better to fairly summarize opposing arguments and refute them than to ignore them.

7. **Be sure to use the right number of sources.** Review your assignment to see if the instructor has provided guidelines. Eight sources is about right for a 1,500-word paper, unless your assignment states otherwise. That means sources that you actually use, not ones that you examine but never use ideas or wording from. You want to have enough sources, but not too many. Don't place so much weight on any single source that your paper seems to be mostly a rehash of one author's ideas.

RESEARCH SKILL What Is Common Knowledge?

Common knowledge is information so widely known that you do not need to identify a source. How do you decide?

- One rule that some writers follow is to classify information as common knowledge if at least three to five general reference works such as dictionaries or encyclopedias provide the same information. A more general guideline is to

consider it common knowledge if the average reader would be familiar with it.

- It is not necessary to document common knowledge because it is readily available information.

- If you are in doubt as to whether certain information is common knowledge, it is better to identify your source.

Sketching a Preliminary Outline

An outline is usually not written in complete sentences, but some instructors prefer complete sentences, so check your assignment. If your outline is written in sentence form, it will pretty closely match the topic sentences in your paper. If not, the ideas in the outline will provide the organization of the ideas in your paper. Ideas represented by Roman numerals are parallel in significance;

the same is true for items represented by *A, B, C,* and so on. You would never have a *I* without a *II.* The same is true at the next level: You wouldn't have an *A* without a *B.* The logic behind that guideline is that there is no reason for breaking a category into only one subordinate category. If your outline needs to be more detailed, *A*-level heads are broken down using *1, 2, 3,* and so on. Those heads can be further broken down into *a, b, c* heads if necessary. You will most likely not need that level of specificity in your outline unless your instructor requires it.

Save the Roman numeral heads for the major divisions of your paper. Use the *A*-level heads for paragraph-level ideas. Make the wording of each level as nearly parallel as possible, as in the following preliminary outline:

Thalidomide: Changing a Drug's Reputation

I. Thalidomide's history: a promising drug but a medical nightmare
  A. Explain how drug was developed
  B. Explain the medical disaster it caused
II. New look at thalidomide: its potential to effectively treat cancer and other diseases
  A. Discuss how it first worked to treat leprosy
  B. Support how it can treat cancer
  C. Support how it can treat other diseases
III. Conclusion

Now you are ready to begin the search for material that will support the argument you have outlined. Remember that your plan for your paper may change depending on what your research reveals. Be prepared to change your outline as necessary so that the outline you turn in with your final draft matches the paper you eventually write.

Student researcher Katie's preliminary outline looked like this:

At this point, I can sketch only a very rough outline of the shape my essay may take. My thesis and my outline may have to change as I continue my research.

Competitive Food in Schools

I. The history of competitive food in schools
  A. Explain what competitive food is
  B. Explain why competitive food is allowed
II. The dangers of competitive food in schools
  A. Explain the immediate effect on school performance
  B. Explain the long-term health effects
III. Suggested solutions
IV. Conclusion

Types of Sources

There are two principal ways of gathering supporting evidence for your argument — primary research and secondary research.

Primary Research

Primary sources are firsthand information. By *firsthand* we mean information taken directly from the original source, including field research (interviews, surveys, personal observations, or experiments). If your topic relates to a local issue involving your school or community, or if it focuses on a story that has never been reported by others, field research may be more valuable than anything available in the library. However, the library can be a source of firsthand information. Memoirs and letters written by witnesses to past events, photographs, contemporary news reports of historical events, or expert testimony presented at congressional hearings are all primary sources that may be available in your library. The Internet, too, can be a source of primary data. A discussion list, newsgroup, or chat room focused on your topic may give you a means to converse with activists and contact experts. Web sites of certain organizations provide documentation of their views, unfiltered by others' opinions. The text of laws, court opinions, bills, debates in Congress, environmental impact statements, and even selected declassified FBI files can be found through government-sponsored Web sites. Other sites present statistical data or the text of historical or political documents. Be aware that primary sources do not have to be print sources. Photographs, posters, advertisements, and other visuals can also serve as raw material to be interpreted. Student researcher Katie came up with the following list of possible primary sources:

> I want to find at least two good primary sources on my topic. Here is a list of possibilities:
>
> Interview with parents of school-age children
>
> Interview with students
>
> Interview with school cafeteria workers/manager
>
> Printed regulations governing school lunches
>
> Statistics about school nutrition
>
> Statistics about competitive foods
>
> School menus
>
> Poster advertising competitive foods
>
> Letter to the editor

One of the rewards of primary research is that it often generates new information, which in turn produces new interpretations of familiar conditions. It is a favored method for anthropologists and sociologists, and most physical and natural scientists use observation and experiment at some point as essential tools in their research.

The information gleaned from primary research can be used directly to support your claim, or it can provide a starting point for secondary research.

Secondary Research

Secondary sources provide commentary on and analysis of a topic. In addition to raw evidence found in primary sources, secondary sources provide a sense of how others are examining the issues and can yield useful information and analysis. Secondary sources may be written for a popular audience, ranging from news coverage, to popular explanations of research findings, to social analysis, to opinion pieces. Or they may be scholarly publications — journals in which experts present their research and theories to other researchers. (For more on popular and scholarly sources, see the Research Skill box below.) These sources might also take the form of analytical reports written to untangle possible courses of action, such as a report written by staff members for a congressional committee or an analysis of an issue by a think tank that wants to use the evidence it has gathered to influence public opinion.

You can find both primary and secondary sources in your school library and online. For example, you can find journal articles in a library database and statistics on a government Web site.

RESEARCH SKILL ▶ Popular vs. Scholarly Articles

Popular Articles (Magazines)

- Are often written by journalists or professional writers for a general audience
- Use language easily understood by the general public
- Rarely give full citations for sources
- Tend to be shorter than journal articles

Scholarly Articles (Journals)

- Are written by and for faculty, researchers, or scholars (chemists, historians, doctors, artists, etc.)
- Use scholarly or technical language
- Tend to be longer articles about research
- Include full citations for sources
- Are often refereed or peer-reviewed (articles are reviewed by an editor and other specialists before being accepted for publication)
- Book reviews and editorials are not considered scholarly articles, even when found in scholarly journals.

Popular magazines. RICHARD B. LEVINE/Newscom/Levine Roberts Photography/NEW YORK/NY/USA

Some Points to Remember

- Both magazine and journal articles can be good sources for your work.

- When selecting articles, think about how you intend to use the information:

  - Do you want background on a topic that is new to you? **(use magazines)**

  - Did your instructor say to cite scholarly resources? **(use journals)**

- Often a combination of the two will be most appropriate for undergraduate research.

  Source: Adapted from the University of Arizona Library Web site, www.library.arizona.edu/help /tutorials/scholarly/guide.html. Copyright Arizona Board of Regents for the University of Arizona.

The American Economic Review

ARTICLES

JAMES HECKMAN, RODRIGO PINTO, AND PETER SAVELYEV
　Understanding the Mechanisms Through Which an Influential Early Childhood
　Program Boosted Adult Outcomes

DAMON CLARK AND HEATHER ROYER
　The Effect of Education on Adult Mortality and Health: Evidence from Britain

DAVID H. AUTOR, DAVID DORN, AND GORDON H. HANSON
　The China Syndrome: Local Labor Market Effects of Import Competition in the
　United States

AMIT K. KHANDELWAL, PETER K. SCHOTT, AND SHANG-JIN WEI
　Trade Liberalization and Embedded Institutional Reform: Evidence from Chinese
　Exporters

ERICA FIELD, ROHINI PANDE, JOHN PAPP, AND NATALIA RIGOL
　Does the Classic Microfinance Model Discourage Entrepreneurship Among the Poor?
　Experimental Evidence from India

NICO VOIGTLÄNDER AND HANS-JOACHIM VOTH
　How the West "Invented" Fertility Restriction

MICHAEL J. ROBERTS AND WOLFRAM SCHLENKER
　Identifying Supply and Demand Elasticities of Agricultural Commodities:
　Implications for the US Ethanol Mandate

KLAUS DESMET AND ESTEBAN ROSSI-HANSBERG
　Urban Accounting and Welfare

JIN LI AND NIKO MATOUSCHEK
　Managing Conflicts in Relational Contracts

PHILIPPE GAGNEPAIN, MARC IVALDI, AND DAVID MARTIMORT
　The Cost of Contract Renegotiation: Evidence from the Local Public Sector

GIACOMO CALZOLARI AND VINCENZO DENICOLÒ
　Competition with Exclusive Contracts and Market-Share Discounts

MARCIN PĘSKI AND BALÁZS SZENTES
　Spontaneous Discrimination

PAOLO BUONANNO AND STEVEN RAPHAEL
　Incarceration and Incapacitation: Evidence from the 2006 Italian Collective Pardon

ARTHUR CAMPBELL
　Word-of-Mouth Communication and Percolation in Social Networks

LEVON BARSEGHYAN, FRANCESCA MOLINARI, TED O'DONOGHUE,
AND JOSHUA C. TEITELBAUM
　The Nature of Risk Preferences: Evidence from Insurance Choices

SHORTER PAPERS: J. A. Parker, N. S. Souleles, D. S. Johnson, and R. McClelland; S. Dhingra; E. E. Schlee;
A. Kurmann and C. Otrok; A. Ziegelmeyer, C. March, and S. Krügel

OCTOBER 2013

Scholarly journal. American Economic Association

Finding Sources

The nature of your topic will determine which route you follow to find good sources. If the topic is current, you may find it more important to use articles than books and might bypass the library catalog altogether. If the topic has to do with social policy or politics, government publications may be particularly useful, though they would be unhelpful for a literary paper. If the topic relates to popular culture, the Internet may provide more information than more traditional publications. Consider what kinds of sources will be most useful as you choose your strategy. If you aren't certain which approaches fit your topic best, consult with a librarian at the reference desk.

Databases

You will most likely use one or more databases (online catalogs of reference materials) to locate books and articles on your topic. The library catalog is a database of books and materials owned by the library; other databases may cover articles in popular or specialized journals and may even provide the full text of articles. Some databases may be available only in the library; others may be accessible all over campus.

To search for books, videos, or periodical publications, use the library catalog. For every book in the library, there is an entry in the catalog that gives the book's author, title, publisher, date, length, and subject headings and perhaps some notes about its contents. The catalog entry also gives the call number or location on the shelf and may offer some indication as to the book's availability. Remember when searching the catalog, though, that entries are for whole books and not specific parts of them. If you use search terms that are too narrow, you may not find a book that has a chapter on exactly what you are looking for. Plan to browse the shelves and examine the tables of contents of the books that you find through the catalog to see which ones, in fact, are most helpful for your topic. Student researcher Katie's catalog search is described and illustrated on pages 353 to 355.

When I did a keyword search of the university library catalog for *competitive foods*, I got 22 results, but most of them had nothing to do with competitive foods in schools. I tried putting the term in quotation marks, and the number was reduced to 8:

This is a listing from the library catalog for a publication that looks promising. I can access the whole publication online by way of the link in the listing:

Clemson University, https://libraries.clemson.edu

To search for articles, use a generalized database of periodicals. Online indexes such as *EBSCOhost*, *Infotrac*, *Searchbank*, *Readers' Guide Abstracts*, and *ProQuest* may include citations, citations with abstracts (brief summaries), or the entire text of articles. Ask the librarian what is available in your school's library. Student researcher Katie's database search is included on page 355.

I used *Academic OneFile* to search for articles about competitive foods in schools. When I searched *competitive foods,* I got 2,200 results! When I put *competitive foods* in quotation marks, that number was reduced to 50. When I added the search word *school,* the number was still 49. When I clicked the options for peer-reviewed only and full text only, and subject "school food services," I ended up with a more manageable list of 8, including these 3 that look promising:

1. The National School Lunch and competitive food offerings and purchasing behaviors of high school students. Alyvia Burkey, Casey Korba, and Anastasia M. Snelling. *Journal of School Health.* 77.10 (Dec. 2007) p701. Word Count: 3101. BACKGROUND: Across the nation, schools have become actively involved in developing obesity prevention strategies both in classrooms and in cafeterias. We sought to determine the type of foods being offered during lunch ...

2. Food fight: the battle over redefining competitive foods. Sheila Fleischhacker. *Journal of School Health.* 77.3 (Mar. 2007) p147. Word Count: 4543. BACKGROUND: Environmental and policy influences are potentially the most powerful—and yet the least understood—strategies for reversing the current childhood obesity epidemic. METHODS: This essay focuses on the school ...

3. The effects of competitive foods promoted in schools. Donald Siegel. JOPERD—*The Journal of Physical Education, Recreation & Dance.* 77.9 (November–December 2006) p12. Word Count: 717. What Was the Question? Recently there has been a great deal of concern about childhood obesity and the role of foods consumed during and after school in mediating a child's weight. While noting that federal guidelines ...

In addition to these general databases, you may find you need to delve deeper into a particular subject area. **Every academic discipline has some sort of in-depth index to research in that field**, and though the materials these indexes cover tend to be highly specialized, they can provide more substantial support for your claims because they usually include sources written by experts in their fields. These resources may be available in electronic or print form. Here are some examples:

Art Index

Biological Abstracts (the online version is known as *Biosis*)

Business Periodicals Index

ERIC (focused on education research)

Index Medicus (*Medline* or *PubMed* online)

Modern Language Association International Bibliography
   (*MLA Bibliography* online)

Psychological Abstracts (*PsychInfo* or *PsychLit* online)

Sociological Abstracts (*Sociofile* online)

Check with a librarian to find out which specialized databases or indexes that relate to your topic are available in your school's library.

Here are some common features that appear in many databases.

Keyword or Subject Searching. You might have the option of searching a database by *keyword*— using the words that you think are most relevant to your search — or by subject. Typically, a keyword search will search for any occurrence of your search term in titles, notes, or the descriptive headings provided by database catalogers or indexers. The advantage to keyword searching is that you can use terms that come naturally to mind so that you cast your net as widely as possible. The disadvantage is that there may be more than one way to express your topic and you may not capture all the relevant materials unless you use the right keywords.

With *subject searching,* you use search terms from a list of subject headings (sometimes called "descriptors") established by the creators of the database. To make searching as efficient as possible, they choose one word or phrase to express a subject. Every time a new source is entered into the database, the indexers describe it using words from the list of subject headings: When you use the list to search the database, you retrieve every relevant source. You might find that a database lists these subject headings through a thesaurus feature. The sophisticated researcher will always pay attention to the subject headings or descriptors generally listed at the bottom of a record for clues to terms that might work best and for related terms that might be worth trying.

Searching for More Than One Concept. Most database searches allow you to combine terms using the connectors *and, or,* and *not.* These connectors (also known as *Boolean operators*) group search terms in different ways. If you search for "zoos *and* animal rights," for example, the resulting list of sources will include only those that deal with both zoos and animal rights, leaving out any that deal with only one subject and not the other. If you connect terms with *or,* your list will contain sources that deal with either concept: A search for "dogs *or* cats" will create a list of sources that cover either animal. *Not* excludes concepts from a search. A search for "animal rights *not* furs" will search for the concept animal rights and then cut out any sources that deal with furs.

Limiting a Search. Most databases have options for limiting a search by a number of variables:

- Publication date
- Language
- Format

- Peer-reviewed (scholarly works chosen for publication by other scholars)
- Full-text (instead of simply a brief abstract)
- Includes images

Truncating Search Terms with Wild Cards. At times, you will search for a word that has many possible endings. A wild card is a symbol that, placed at the end of a word root, allows for any possible ending for a word. For example, *animal** will allow a search for *animal* or *animals.*

Options for Saving Records. You may have the opportunity to print, download, or e-mail to yourself the citations you find in a database. Many databases have a feature for marking just the records you want so you save only those of interest.

Encyclopedias

General and specialized encyclopedias offer quick overviews of topics and easy access to factual information. They also tend to have excellent selective bibliographies, pointing you toward useful sources. You will find a wide variety of encyclopedias in your library's reference collection; you may also have an online encyclopedia, such as *Britannica Online,* available through the Web anywhere on campus. Some specialized encyclopedias include the following:

Encyclopedia of African American History and Culture
Encyclopedia of American Social History
Encyclopedia of Bioethics
Encyclopedia of Educational Research
Encyclopedia of Hispanic Culture in the United States
Encyclopedia of International Relations
Encyclopedia of Philosophy
Encyclopedia of Sociology
Encyclopedia of the United States in the Twentieth Century
Encyclopedia of World Cultures
International Encyclopedia of Communications
McGraw-Hill Encyclopedia of Science and Technology

Statistical Resources

Often statistics are used as evidence in an argument. If your argument depends on establishing that one category is bigger than another, that the majority of people hold a certain opinion, or that one group is more affected by something than another group, statistics can provide the evidence you need. Of course, as with any other source, you need to be sure that your statistics are as reliable as possible and that you are reporting them responsibly.

It isn't always easy to find things counted the way you want. If you embark on a search for numbers to support your argument, be prepared to spend some time locating and interpreting data. Always read the fine print that explains how and when the data were gathered. Some sources for statistics include these:

U.S. Bureau of the Census. This government agency produces a wealth of statistical data, much of it available on the Web at www.census.gov. A handy compilation of the agency's most useful tables is found in the one-volume annual handbook *Statistical Abstract of the United States*, which also includes statistics from other government sources.

Other Federal Agencies. Numerous federal agencies gather statistical data. Among these are the National Center for Education Statistics, the National Center for Health Statistics, the National Bureau of Labor Statistics, and the Federal Bureau of Investigation, which annually compiles national crime statistics. One handy place to find a wide variety of federal statistics is the Web site *FedStats* at www.fedstats.gov.

United Nations. Compilations of international data published by the United Nations include the *Demographic Yearbook and Statistical Yearbook*. Some statistics are also published by U.N. agencies such as the Food and Health Organization. Some are available from the U.N. Web site at www.un.org.

Opinion Polls. Several companies conduct opinion polls, and some of these are available in libraries. One such compilation is the Gallup Poll series, which summarizes public opinion polling from 1935 to the present. Other poll results are reported by the press. Search a database that covers news publications by using your topic and "polls" as keywords to locate some summaries of results.

Government Resources

Beyond statistics, government agencies compile and publish a wealth of information. For topics that concern public welfare, health, education, politics, foreign relations, earth sciences, the environment, or the economy, government documents may provide just the information you need.

The U.S. federal government is the largest publisher in the world. Its publications are distributed free to libraries designated as document depositories across the country. If your library is not a depository, chances are there is a regional depository somewhere nearby. Local, state, and foreign governments are also potential sources of information.

Federal documents distributed to depository libraries are indexed in *The Monthly Catalog of U.S. Government Documents*, available in many libraries as an electronic database. These include congressional documents such as hearings and committee reports, presidential papers, studies conducted by the Education Department or the Centers for Disease Control, and so on. Many government documents are available through the Internet. If you learn about a government publication through the news media, chances are you will be able to obtain a copy at the Web site of the sponsoring agency or congressional body. In fact, government publications are among the most valuable of resources available on the Web because they are rigorously controlled for content. You know you are looking at a U.S. federal government site when you see the domain suffix *.gov* in the URL.

Web-Based Sources

The World Wide Web is an important resource for researchers. It is particularly helpful if you are looking for information about organizations, current events, political debates, popular culture, or government-sponsored research and activities. It is not an especially good place to look for literary criticism, historical analysis, or scholarly research articles, which are still more likely to be published in traditional ways. Biologists reporting on an important experiment, for example, are more likely to submit an article about it to a prestigious journal in the field than simply post their results on the Web.

Because anyone can publish whatever they like on the Web, searching for good information can be frustrating. Search engines operate by means of automated programs that gather information about sites and match search terms to whatever is out there, regardless of quality. A search engine may locate thousands of Web documents on a topic, but most are of little relevance and dubious quality. The key is to know in advance what information you need and who might have produced it. For example, if your topic has to do with some aspect of free speech and you know that the American Civil Liberties Union is involved in the issue, a trip to the ACLU home page may provide you with a wealth of information, albeit from a particular perspective. If your state's pollution control agency just issued a report on water quality in the area, you may find the report published at the agency's Web site or the e-mail address of someone who could send it to you. The more you know about your topic before you sit down to surf, the more likely you will use your time productively.

If you have a fairly broad topic and no specific clues about where it might be covered, you may want to start your search by using a selective guide to good sites. For example, the University of Texas maintains an excellent directory to sites relating to Latin America. Subject guides that selectively list valuable sites can be found at the University of California's *Infomine* at http://infomine.ucr .edu and the *World Wide Web Virtual Library* project at www.vlib.org/Home .html. Reference librarians will also be able to point you to quality sites that relate to your topic.

If you have a fairly specific topic in mind or are looking for a particular organization or document on the Web, a search engine can help you find it. *Google* is one of the best. No matter what search engine you choose, find out how it works, how it ranks results, and how deeply it indexes Web pages. Some search engines will retrieve more results than others simply because of the way the program gathers information from sites. As with databases, there are usually ways to refine a search and improve your results. Many search engines offer an advanced search option that may provide some useful options for refining and limiting a search.

It is important to know what will not be retrieved by a search engine. Because publishing and transmitting texts on the Web are relatively easy, it is becoming more common for libraries to subscribe to databases and electronic journals that are accessed through a Web browser. You may have *Britannica Online* and *LexisNexis* as options on your library's home page. However, the contents of those subscriptions will be available only to your campus community and will not be searched by general Web search engines.

Student researcher Katie's Web search on "school nutrition" produced the following results.

I clicked on the fourth site, "Child Nutrition Programs/Food and Nutrition Service." This looked good because it had a *.gov* domain. The link took me here:

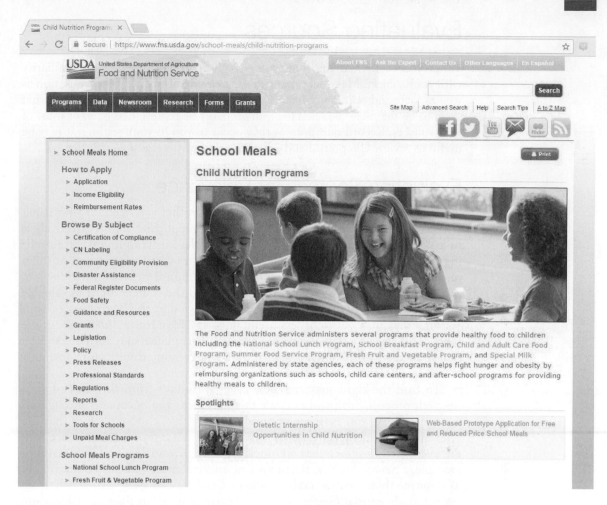

Multimodal Sources

Since the Internet is a world of images as well as words, it may give you ideas for livening up your own work with all sorts of visuals — if your instructor allows it. You may also find useful visuals in the books and articles that you read. Don't forget, though, that you are obligated to give credit to the source of your visuals along with the ideas and words that you use. A graph or chart may provide just the sort of statistical support that will make a key point in your argument, and it can be easily cut and pasted into your electronic text, but you must document that graph or chart as you would text. You should acknowledge the location where you found the visual and as much information as is provided about who produced it. You must seek permission to use visuals that you intend to publish in print or electronic form.

Evaluating Sources

When you begin studying your sources, read first to acquire general familiarity with your subject. Make sure that you are covering both sides of the question as well as facts and opinions from a variety of sources. As you read, look for what seem to be the major issues. They will probably be represented in all or most of your sources. Record questions as they occur to you in your reading. It may be useful to review Chapters 2 and 3 for more help with reading critically.

Evaluating Sources for Relevance

The sources you find provide useful information that you need for your paper and help you support your claims. One key to supporting claims effectively is to make sure you have the best evidence available. It is tempting when searching a database or the Web to take the first sources that look good, print them or copy them, and not give them another thought until you are sitting down to compose your argument — only to discover that the sources aren't as valuable as they could be. Sources that looked pretty good at the beginning of your research may turn out to be less useful once you have learned more about the topic. And a source that seems interesting at first glance may turn out to be a rehash or digest of a much more valuable source, something you realize only when you sit down and look at it carefully.

To find the right material, be a critical thinker from the start of your research process. Scan and evaluate the references you encounter throughout your search. As you examine options in a database, choose sources that use relevant terms in their titles, seem directed to an appropriate audience, and are published in places that will look credible in your Works Cited list. For example, a Senate Foreign Relations Committee report will carry more weight as a source than a comparable article in *Good Housekeeping*. An article from the scholarly journal *Foreign Affairs* will carry more clout than an article from *Reader's Digest,* even if they are on the same subject. (For more on popular versus scholarly sources, see the Research Skill box on page 351.)

Skim and quickly evaluate each source that looks valuable.

- Is it relevant to your topic?
- Does it provide information you haven't found elsewhere?
- Can you learn anything about the author, and does what you learn inspire confidence?

As you begin to learn more about your topic and revise your outline as necessary, you can use sources to help direct your search. If a source mentions an organization, for example, you may use that clue to run a search on the Web for that organization's home page. If a newspaper story refers to a study published in a scientific journal, you may want to seek out that study to see the results of the research firsthand. And if you have a source that includes references to other publications, scan through them to see which ones might also prove helpful to you. When you first started your research, chances are you weren't quite sure what you were looking for. Once you are familiar with your topic, you need to concentrate on finding sources that will best support the claims you want to make, and your increasing familiarity with the issue will make it easier to identify the best sources. That may mean a return trip to the library.

Practice: Evaluate Sources for Relevance

Look at the entries in the list from *LexisNexis*, an academic database. The topic being researched was competitive foods in schools. (Competitive foods are those sold in schools other than foods provided through the federally funded school lunch program.) The search terms were *competitive foods* and *school*.

LexisNexis

1. You can tell immediately that some entries are clearly not relevant to the topic competitive foods in school. Which ones?
2. Which ones seem most directly relevant to the topic?
3. Item #6 seems unrelated at first, perhaps, but how might it be relevant?
4. Are there any articles that might be too narrow in their focus? Why?

Evaluating Sources for Reliability

Once you have selected some useful sources to support your claims, it is time to make a more in-depth evaluation to be sure you have the best evidence available.

- Is it current enough? Have circumstances changed since this text was published?
- Is the author someone you would want to call on as an expert witness? Does the author have the experience or credentials to make a solid argument that will carry weight with your readers?

- Is it reliable information for your purposes? It may be highly opinionated, but are the basic facts it presents confirmed in other sources? Is the evidence presented in the text convincing?

These questions are not always easy to answer. In some cases, articles will include some information about the author, such as where he or she works. In other cases, no information or even an author's name is given. In that case, it may help to evaluate the publication and its reputation. If you aren't familiar with a publication and don't feel confident making your own judgment, see if it is described in Katz's *Magazines for Libraries*, which evaluates the reputation and quality of periodicals.

Web sites pose challenges and offer unique opportunities for researchers, for one reason because they are part of a developing genre of writing. When evaluating a Web site, first examine what kind of site you are reading.

- Is the Web page selling or advertising goods or services (a business site)?
- Is it advocating a point of view (an advocacy site) or providing relatively neutral information, such as that found in the yellow pages (an informative or educational site)?
- Is the Web site addressing the interests of people in a particular organization or with common interests (an information-sharing site)?
- Is it reporting up-to-the-minute news (a news site) or appealing to some aspect of an individual's life and interests (a personal site)?

Useful information for a research paper may be obtained from any of these kinds of Web pages, but it is helpful to know what the main purpose of the site is — and who its primary audience is — when determining how productive it will be for your research.

RESEARCH SKILL Evaluating Web-Based Sources

- **Authority.** Is the author an expert in the field or otherwise qualified through experience to write about the subject? Be wary of a source if no author is listed.

- **Accuracy.** Does the support the author offers for his or her ideas convince you that the major ideas expressed are valid and accurate? Factual information can often be checked by finding another source that provides the same information.

- **Objectivity.** Does the author reveal bias that could keep the content from being reliable? You do not want to build your case on someone else's unsupported opinion.

- **Currency.** Is the information recent unless there is a reason for using a source from an earlier period? You do not want to build your case on information that has been superseded by more recent sources.

- **Coverage.** Does the author provide enough information about the subject, in enough detail, to be useful for your purposes? If not, you might find other sources to be more useful.

Source: Adapted from Wolfgram Memorial Library (Widener University, Chester, PA) Web site, www .widener.edu/about/campus_resources/wolfgram _library/evaluate/info.aspx. Copyright Jan Alexander and Marsha Ann Tate, 1996–2005.

As you weigh the main purpose of the site, evaluate its original context. Does the site originate in a traditional medium, such as a print journal or an encyclopedia? Is the site part of an online journal, in which case its material had to go through a screening process? Or is the site the product of one individual's or organization's desire to create a Web page, which means the work may not have been screened or evaluated by any outside agency? In that case, the information may still be valuable, but you must be even more careful when evaluating it.

To find answers to many of the questions in the Research Skill box, make a brief overview of the site itself by looking, for example, at the clues contained in the Web address. That is, *.com* in the address means a business or commercial site; *.edu* is a site sponsored by a university or college; *.k12* is a site associated with a primary or secondary school; *.gov* indicates that the federal government sponsored the site; and *.org* suggests that the site is part of a nonprofit or noncommercial group. Sites originating outside the United States have URLs that end with a two-letter country abbreviation, such as *.uk* for United Kingdom. Although these address clues can reveal a great deal about the origins and purposes of a Web site, remember that personal Web sites may also contain some of these abbreviations. Institutions such as schools and businesses sometimes sponsor individuals' personal Web sites (which are often unscreened by the institution) as well as official institutional sites. One possible key to determining whether a Web site is a personal page, however, is to look for a tilde (~) plus a name or part of a name in the address. Finally, if you are unsure of the sponsoring organization of a page, try erasing all the information in the URL after the first slash (/) and pressing the "Enter" key. Doing so often brings you to the main page of the organization sponsoring the Web site. For more help with evaluating online sources, see page 364.

Most Web sites include a way to contact the author or sponsoring organization of the site, usually through e-mail. This is often a quick and easy way to get answers to the preliminary questions. If the site contains an address or phone number as part of its contact information, this means the organization or individual is available and probably willing to stand behind the site's content.

RESEARCH SKILL ▶ Evaluating Multimodal Sources

Whether you find them in print or online, sources that include a mix of images, audio, video, and even text require special attention. Keep the following questions in mind.

- **Audio.** How does the sound affect what is being shown or spoken? Is there a speaker? Does the speaker shout or use any specific style or tone? Is there music or noise? How does the noise or music affect the mood? Do you think this was intentional?

- **Images.** How does color (or lack of color) affect the presentation of the image? What effect does image size and quality have on the message? What effect does the composition as a whole have (cropping, focus, angle, etc.)?

- **Film/Video.** Is the production quality slick or rough? Do you think the quality reflects the limitations of the filmmaker or an intentional creative choice? What is the perspective of the film? Do you feel like a participant in the action or a viewer? How does the use of close-ups, long shots, color, lighting, and other visual effects affect the mood? How does sound affect the mood?

- **Other Multimodal Sources.** Consider the mood or tone that the creator is trying to achieve through sound, pictures, and video. Think about pace, volume, and imaging. Do they play on emotions with fear, humor, guilt, or sadness? How do these factors influence the content?

ARGUMENT ESSENTIALS

Evaluating Sources

Check All Sources for Relevance

- Be critical of your sources from the beginning of your research. Look for the best sources, not the first ones you can locate.
- Look for sources that use relevant terms in their titles, are directed to an appropriate audience, and are published in reputable places.
- Skim possible sources for relevance, usefulness (not information you already have), and informative value.
- Let your sources lead you to other possible sources.

Check All Sources for Reliability

- Check each source for currency.
- Check the authority of the author(s).
- Check whether the information is reliable for your purposes.

Use Special Care with Web-Based Sources

- Consider what type of site it is. Is it trying to sell something, advocating a point of view, providing information, reporting the news?
- Consider its original context. Is it, for example, a journal article available through a database? A site created and maintained by a single person?
- Is it a *.gov, .com, .edu,* or *.org* site? What does that tell you?

Special Considerations for Multimodal Sources

- Consider livening up your work with visuals if your instructor allows it.
- Be sure to give your source for information in modes other than text just as conscientiously as you would for text.

Practice: Evaluating Web-Based Search Results

Look at the entries from a *Google* search of the terms *competitive foods* and *school*. Use the questions that follow to consider how reliable these potential sources might be.

1. The first entry is a publication of the CDC and has a *.gov* URL. What is the CDC, and what does that suggest to you about how reliable the source might be?
2. The fourth entry is also a .gov source. What do the acronyms *FNS* and *USDA* stand for? What does that suggest about the reliability of the sources?
3. There are two sources here that are from organizations' sites. Go to the articles, and see what you can determine about the organizations that would suggest they are trustworthy sources.

READING ARGUMENT

Seeing Evaluation of a Web-Based Source

The annotations here show how student researcher Katie evaluated a Web-based source using the five characteristics listed in the Research Skill box on page 364: authority, accuracy, objectivity, currency, and coverage.

Child Nutrition Programs
UNITED STATES DEPARTMENT OF AGRICULTURE

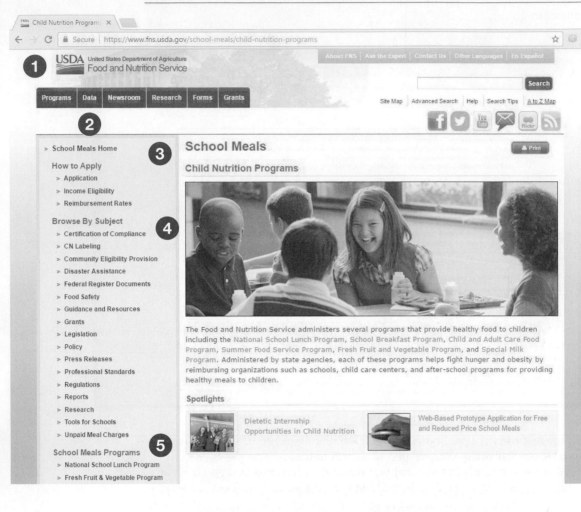

1 Authority: This should be a trustworthy site because it is maintained by the Food and Nutrition Service of the U.S. Department of Agriculture.

2 Objectivity: This tab provides links to data and research regarding USDA Nutrition Assistance programs.

3 Accuracy: This and the data tab link to evidence-based analysis and rigorous evaluation, "critical tools to promote effective policies and strong management in the Federal nutrition assistance programs."

4 Currency: Links provide information about the subjects listed. Information is usually listed in reverse chronological order and is current to at least the last six months.

5 Coverage: The site provides links to each of the school nutrition programs funded by the federal government.

Taking Notes

While everyone has methods of taking notes, here are a few suggestions that should be useful to research writers who need to read materials quickly, comprehend and evaluate the sources, use them as part of a research paper assignment, and manage their time carefully. If you need more detailed help with quoting, paraphrasing, and summarizing, review pages 124–28 in Chapter 4.

When taking notes from a source, summarize instead of quoting long passages. Summarizing as you read saves time. If you feel that a direct quote is more effective than anything you could write and provides crucial support for your argument, copy the material word for word. Leave all punctuation exactly as it appears, and insert ellipsis points (. . .) if you delete material. Enclose all quotations in quotation marks, and copy complete information about your source, including the author's name, the title of the book or article, the journal name if appropriate, page numbers, and publishing information. If you quote an article that appears in an anthology, record complete information about the book itself.

If you aren't sure whether you will use a piece of information later, don't copy the whole passage. Instead, make a note of its bibliographic information so that you can find it again if you need it. Taking too many notes, however, is preferable to taking too few, a problem that will force you to go back to the source for missing information.

One of the most effective ways to save yourself time and trouble when you are ready to write your research paper is to document your research as you go along. That way, when the time comes to create your Works Cited page, you will be ready to put the works you used in alphabetical order — or let your computer do it for you — and provide a list of those works at the end of your paper. Some instructors may require a bibliography, or a list of all of the works you consulted (sometimes titled simply Works Consulted), but at a minimum you will need a Works Cited page. As that title indicates, the list will include only those works that you quote, paraphrase, or summarize in your paper.

Once you are fairly certain that you will use a certain source, go ahead and put it in proper bibliographic form. That way, if the citation form is complicated, you can look it up or ask your instructor before the last minute. Also, you will realize immediately if you are missing information required by the citation and can record it while the source is still at hand. See Chapter 14 for complete details about what information you will need and the proper form for it.

Note Taking and Prewriting

Use the note-taking process as a prewriting activity. Often when you summarize an author's ideas or write down direct quotes, you see or understand the material in new ways. Freewrite about the importance of these quotes, paraphrases, or summaries, or at least about those that seem especially important. If nothing else, take a minute to justify in writing why you chose to record the notes. Doing so will help you clarify and develop your thoughts about your argument.

Taking this prewriting step seriously will help you analyze the ideas you record from outside sources. You will then be better prepared for the more formal (and inevitable) work of summarizing, paraphrasing, and composing involved in thinking critically about your topic and writing a research paper. Maybe most important, such work will help with that moment all writers face when they realize they "know what they want to say but can't find the words to say it." Overcoming such moments does not depend on finding inspiration while writing the final draft of a paper. Instead, successfully working through this common form of writer's block depends more on the amount of prewriting and thoughtful consideration of the notes done early in the research process.

Working with Your Outline

As you take notes, also remember to refer to your outline to ensure that you are acquiring sufficient data to support all the points you intend to raise. Of course, you will be revising your outline during the course of your research as issues are clarified and new ideas emerge, but the outline will serve as a rough guide throughout the writing process. Keeping close track of your outline will also prevent you from recording material that is interesting but not relevant. It may help to label your notes with the heading from the outline to which they are most relevant.

Relying on the knowledge of others is an important part of doing research; expert opinions and eloquent arguments help support your claims when your own expertise is limited. But remember, this is *your* paper. Your ideas and insights into other people's ideas are just as important as the information you uncover at the library or through reputable online sources. When writing an argument, do not simply regurgitate the words and thoughts of others in your essay. Work to achieve a balance between providing solid information from expert sources and offering your own interpretation of the argument and the evidence that supports it.

Managing and Documenting Sources

Using word-processing software can invigorate the processes of note taking and of outlining. Taking notes using a computer gives you more flexibility than using pen and paper alone. For example, you can save your computer-generated notes and your comments on them in numerous places (at home, school, or work, or on a disk); you can cut and paste the text into various documents; you can add to the notes or modify them and still revert to the originals with ease.

You can also link notes to background material on the Web that may be useful once you begin writing drafts of your paper. For example, you could create links to an author's Web page or to any of his or her other works published on the Web. You could create a link to a study or an additional source cited in your notes, or you could link to the work of other researchers who support or argue against the information you recorded.

Because you can record information in any number of ways on your computer, your notes act as tools in the writing process. One of the best ways to start is to open a file for each source; enter the bibliographic information; directly type into the file a series of potentially useful quotations, paraphrases, and summaries; and add your initial ideas about the source. (For each entry, note the correct page references as you go along, and indicate clearly whether you are quoting, paraphrasing, or summarizing.) You can then use the capabilities of your computer to aid you in the later stages of the writing process. For example, you can collect all your research notes into one large file in which you group similar sources, evaluate whether you have too much information about one issue or one side of an argument, or examine sources that conflict with one another. You can imagine various organizational schemes for your paper based on the central themes and issues of the notes you have taken, and you can more clearly determine which quotes and summaries are essential to your paper and which ones may not be needed.

When you're ready to begin your first draft, the computer enables you to readily integrate material from your source notes into your research paper by cutting and pasting, thus eliminating the need to retype and reducing the chance of error. Be sure, though, that cutting and pasting do not lead you to plagiarize inadvertently. Any wording taken from your sources that you use in your paper must be placed in quotation marks and attributed to the source. You can also combine all the bibliographic materials you have saved in separate files and then use the computer to alphabetize your sources for your final draft.

Although taking notes on the computer does not dramatically change the research process, it does highlight the fact that taking notes, prewriting, drafting a paper, and creating a Works Cited page are integrated activities that should build from one another. When you take notes from a journal, book, or Web site, you develop your note-taking abilities so that they help with the entire writing process.

ARGUMENT ESSENTIALS
Taking Notes

- Summarize instead of quoting long passages.

- If you do quote a passage, copy it word for word in quotation marks, using ellipsis points (. . .) to indicate any words that you left out (but only if the omission does not change the essential meaning of the passage).

- Write down all the bibliographic information (in proper form) that you will need for your Works Cited page. (See Chapter 13 for details.)

- Jot down a few notes to yourself about why these notes are important.

- Label notes according to the part of your rough outline they support.

- When taking notes on your computer, start a new file for each potential source.

- When cutting and pasting information from a source, be sure not to plagiarize unintentionally.

READING ARGUMENT

Seeing How to Take Notes

Read the following essay, and then read student researcher Katie's notes following it as an example of how to take notes on your reading. Katie's notes (p. 373) begin with the label "IIB — Long-term health effects." This label is referencing her outline, shown on page 349. Katie's notes also include page references to the original source.

Childhood Obesity: The Challenge
THE ROBERT WOOD JOHNSON FOUNDATION

Childhood obesity is a serious public health problem in the United States. Over the past three decades, obesity rates have soared among all age groups, increasing more than four times among children ages six to eleven. Today, more than twenty-three million children and teenagers are overweight or obese. That's nearly one in three young people. Even among ages two to five, a quarter of children are now overweight or obese. Among certain racial and ethnic groups, the rates are still higher.

The ramifications are alarming. If we don't succeed in reversing this epidemic, we are in danger of raising the first generation of American children who will live sicker and die younger than their parents' generation.

Preventing obesity during childhood is critical because habits formed during youth frequently continue well into adulthood:

- Research shows that obese adolescents have up to an eighty percent chance of becoming obese adults. Overweight and obese children are at higher risk for a host of serious illnesses, including heart disease, stroke, asthma, and certain types of cancer.
- Increasing numbers of children are being diagnosed with health problems once considered to be adult ailments, including high blood pressure, type 2 diabetes, and gallstones.

- Obesity poses a tremendous financial threat to our economy and our health-care system. It's estimated that the obesity epidemic costs our nation $117 billion annually in direct medical expenses and indirect costs, including lost productivity. Childhood obesity alone carries a huge price tag — up to $14 billion annually in direct health-care costs.

How did we get to this point? There's a simple explanation for the childhood obesity epidemic: our children are consuming far more calories than they burn. Today's obese teenagers consume between 700 and 1,000 more calories per day than what's needed for the growth, physical activity, and body function of a normal-weight teen. Over the course of ten years, that "energy gap" is enough to pack an average of fifty-eight extra pounds on an obese adolescent.

As a society, we've dramatically altered the way we live, eat, work, and play — creating an environment that fuels obesity:

5

The Robert Wood Johnson Foundation is the largest philanthropic organization in the country devoted exclusively to improving the health and health care of all Americans. The group spearheaded the establishment of 911 emergency telephone service throughout the United States. Now it is focusing much of its efforts on the childhood obesity epidemic. This essay appeared in *Food, Inc.: How Industrial Food Is Making Us Sicker, Fatter, and Poorer — And What You Can Do about It* (2009).

- On average, today's young people spend more than four hours per day using electronic media, including television, DVDs, and video games.
- A generation ago, about half of all school-aged children walked or biked to school. Today, nearly nine out of ten are driven to school. And once they get there, there aren't many opportunities for exercise—fewer than four percent of elementary schools provide daily physical education.
- At the same time, children are eating more unhealthy foods in ever-larger sizes. In recent decades, the typical calorie content of menu items like French fries and sodas has increased approximately fifty percent.

Children consume these high-calorie, low-nutrient foods not only in restaurants, but also in their homes and schools.

- In communities hardest hit by obesity, families frequently have little access to affordable healthy foods. There often are no grocery stores, only convenience marts that rarely stock fresh fruits and vegetables. There aren't enough safe places for kids to play or programs to help them be physically active every day.

To reverse the childhood obesity epidemic, we must remove these barriers by creating policies and environments that provide families with better access to healthy foods and opportunities for physical activity.

IIB — Long-term health effects

Robert Wood Johnson Foundation. "Childhood Obesity: The Challenge." *Food, Inc.: How Industrial Food Is Making Us Sicker, Fatter and Poorer—and What You Can Do about It*, edited by Karl Weber, PublicAffairs, 2009, pp. 259–61.

Link to Foundation: www.rwjf.org

Might need to lead in to quotes: The Foundation is "the nation's largest philanthropy devoted exclusively to improving the health and health care of all Americans." 259

In three decades, the obesity rate has quadrupled for those age 6–11. 259

"If we don't succeed in reversing this epidemic, we are in danger of raising the first generation of American children who will live sicker and die younger than their parents' generation." 259

Because of the difference between calorie intake and the physical activity needed to burn those calories, in ten years an adolescent could gain 58 pounds. 260

50% of children a generation ago walked to school. Now 90% ride. 260

"fewer than four percent of elementary schools provide daily physical education" 260

In some places where obesity is worst, the people can't afford healthy foods, there are convenience stores instead of grocery stores, and it is not safe for children to play outside. 261

Practice: Taking Notes

Using Katie's notes as a model, take notes on the following essay.

To Curb School Lunch Waste, Ease the Fruit and Vegetable Rules

LOS ANGELES TIMES EDITORIAL BOARD

No one should have expected that putting more vegetables in front of elementary school students would instantly turn them into an army of broccoli fans. Plenty of food has been thrown out since new federal rules took effect in 2011 requiring students in the subsidized school lunch program to choose a fruit or vegetable each day. Nevertheless, studies find that continued exposure to produce is resulting in more children eating at least some of it.

That's worth a certain amount of wasted food. The new lunch rules, pushed by the Obama administration and passed by Congress, provide better nutrition and introduce more students to healthful eating habits that they will, it's hoped, carry into adulthood.

Still, the program is afflicted by rigid, overreaching regulations that defy common sense. Schools must provide items from five food groups, including a fruit and a vegetable, every day. Students must choose three items, even if they're not hungry enough for all of them, and at least one must be produce. But fruits and vegetables rank as the least popular items, so requiring

schools to offer one of each for each student practically guarantees that an enormous amount of fruits and vegetables will go to waste.

Even worse are the rules about what kinds of produce must be offered and in what form. They make it nearly impossible, for example, to hide the vegetables in soups or lasagna, where they might be more palatable to students. It took a long, intense lobbying effort for schools to get permission to serve smoothies; even though cafeterias are encouraged to serve yogurt and fruit, they weren't allowed until just recently to combine them into a healthful drink.

The federal rules even prohibit students from taking food out of the cafeteria to eat later.   5

No wonder so much ends up in garbage cans. In the Los Angeles Unified School District, as the *Times* recently reported, it adds up to $100,000 in wasted food each day.

Congress is supposed to reauthorize the school lunch bill in 2015, and there are many

---

This editorial appeared in the *Los Angeles Times* on April 8, 2014.

changes it should make. Though the law should continue to require all students to take a fruit or vegetable, it should allow them to take only as much food as they want. Children should be able to pick two fruits or two vegetables in a day, which they can't do now, and eat their leftovers later. Schools should be free to mix vegetables together in appealing and healthful dishes. Lawmakers need to think more like budget-conscious parents and less like detail-obsessed regulators.

bits

To see what you are learning about argumentation applied to the latest world and national news, read our *Bits* blog, "Argument and the Headlines," at **blogs.bedfordstmartins.com/bits.**

CHAPTER 13

Drafting, Revising, and Presenting Arguments

Chapter 12 discusses the planning of an argumentative paper and the process involved in researching topics that require support beyond what the writer knows firsthand. This chapter discusses moving from the planning and researching stage into the actual writing of the paper or presentation.

Reviewing Your Research

Making a preliminary outline before you conduct any needed research gives direction to your research and helps you to organize your own thoughts on the subject. Preliminary outlines can change, however, in the process of researching and writing the paper. As you begin drafting the paper, be sure you have a solid thesis and strong and plentiful evidence for each topic in your preliminary or revised outline.

Once you are satisfied that you have identified all the issues that will appear in your paper, you should begin to determine what kind of organization will be most effective for your argument. Now is the time to organize the results of your thinking into a logical and persuasive form. If you have read about your topic, answered questions, and acquired some evidence, you may already have decided on ways to approach your subject. If not, you should look closely at your outline now, recalling your purposes when you began your investigation, and develop a strategy for using the information you have gathered to achieve those purposes.

As you did in Chapter 5 in writing arguments not based on independent research, be mindful of the context in which the argument is taking place, and try this procedure for tackling the issues in any controversial problem.

1. Raise the relevant issues, and omit those that would distract you from your purpose. Plan to devote more time and space to issues you regard as crucial.
2. Produce the strongest evidence you can to support your factual claims, knowing that the opposing side or critical readers may try to produce conflicting evidence.

3. Defend your value claims by finding support in the fundamental principles with which most people in your audience would agree.
4. Explain as specifically as possible what you want your audience to think or do when you are arguing a policy claim.
5. Argue with yourself. Try to foresee what kinds of refutation are possible. Try to anticipate and meet the opposing arguments.
6. Consider the context in which your argument will be read, and be sensitive to the concerns of your audience.

RESEARCH SKILL ▸ Reviewing Your Research

- Is your thesis the right scope — not too broad or too narrow?

- Does your working outline show any gaps in your argument?

- Does your research show enough counterarguments? If not, your thesis may not be debatable and may need to be changed.

- Does your research show strong counterarguments that might make you want to change your thesis or shift the perspective of your argument?

- Have you identified the assumptions linking your claim with data and ensured that these assumptions, too, are adequately documented?

- Have you found sufficient data to support your claim?

- Is your research varied enough and not too reliant on one source or source type? Have you met your instructor's guidelines for number and type of sources?

- Do your notes include exact copies of all statements you may want to quote and paraphrased or summarized versions of material that does not need to be quoted directly? Do your notes include complete references?

- Have you answered all the relevant questions that have come up during your research?

- Do you have enough information about your sources to document your paper?

Student researcher Katie applied the six steps in the review process to her topic like this:

1. The relevant issue for my thesis is that competitive foods should not be in schools. I need to establish that there is an obesity epidemic, which is a factual claim, but that is not my main focus. Competitive foods are one thing that contributes to the obesity epidemic, and it is one that something could be done about. I need to spend most of my time focusing on what is wrong with competitive foods and what should be done about the problem.

2. My thesis will be a claim of policy, but along the way I will establish that competitive foods are one factor that leads to childhood obesity. I think I have enough evidence to support that.

3. I am not supporting a values claim, but behind my thesis, anyone should agree that we should do what we can to stop the increase in childhood obesity. Everyone should be in favor of good health for children.

4. What I want to happen is for all competitive foods to be removed from schools.

5. Some people would argue that the competitive foods are what the kids want to eat, or they would already be eating the cafeteria food. I have also discovered that some people think there are economic reasons for letting these vendors sell their products in the schools. I will have to argue that that is not as important as the children's health.

6. People who have children in school or will have should be concerned. One thing that makes my argument stronger is that people are already starting to read and hear more and more about healthy eating. It's in the news a lot.

Avoiding Plagiarism

Plagiarism is the use of someone else's words or ideas without adequate acknowledgment — that is, presenting such words or ideas as your own. Putting something into your own words is not in itself a defense against plagiarism; the source of the ideas must be identified as well. Giving credit to the sources you use serves three important purposes:

1. It reflects your own honesty and seriousness as a researcher.
2. It enables the reader to find the source of the reference and read further, sometimes to verify that the source has been correctly used.
3. It adds the authority of experts to your argument.

Plagiarism is nothing less than cheating, and it is an offense that deserves serious punishment. You can avoid accidentally slipping into plagiarism if you are careful in researching and writing your papers.

Taking care to document sources is an obvious way to avoid plagiarism. You should also be careful in taking notes and, when writing your paper, indicating where your ideas end and someone else's begin. When taking notes, make sure either to quote word for word or to paraphrase — one or the other, not both. If you quote, enclose any language that you borrow from other sources in quotation marks. That way, when you look back at your notes days or weeks later, you won't mistakenly assume that the language is your own. If you know that you aren't going to use a particular writer's exact words, then take the time to summarize that person's ideas right away. That will save you time and trouble later.

When using someone else's ideas in your paper, always let the reader know where that person's ideas begin and end. Here is an example from a student paper that uses APA style:

When zoo animals do mate successfully, the offspring is often weakened by inbreeding. According to geneticists, this is because a population of 150 breeder animals is necessary in order to "assure the more or less permanent survival of a species in captivity" (Ehrlich & Ehrlich, 1981, p. 211).

The phrase "according to geneticists" indicates that the material to follow comes from another source, cited parenthetically at the end of the borrowed material. If the student had not included the phrase "according to geneticists," it might look as if she only borrowed the passage in quotation marks, and not the information that precedes that passage.

ARGUMENT ESSENTIALS Avoiding Plagiarism

- Take notes with care.
- Be clear in your writing where another person's words and ideas begin and end.
- Either quote word for word or paraphrase, not a mixture of both.
- Document your use of sources, whether you are quoting, paraphrasing, or summarizing.

Using Sentence Forms to Write Arguments

You need to be respectful of what others say and write, and you need to account for their positions accurately. You'll want to be sure to clearly summarize other authors' ideas when you write about them.

When you present a negative evaluation of an argument, it is important to clearly explain how the previous writer approached the topic, and then explain how your view differs. Sometimes the points of difference are large, sometimes small. But in writing for college, it is crucial that you explain your own understanding of a situation *and* that you express your own point of view.

It is easier to think about how you might summarize the argument of others and present your own if you have a model from which to work. This kind of model is called a *sentence form*, and we showed you a few examples in Chapter 5. Sentence forms can help you to organize the presentation of others' views and your own responses to them. Here are some basic sentence forms for this kind of work.

Presenting Another's View

In _____, X claims that _____.

X's conclusion is that _____.

On the topic of _____, X attempts to make the case that

_____.

These sentence forms are useful for presenting a brief summary of another's views on an issue. Note that the final sentence form implies that the writer has failed to make a convincing argument. (You would then go on to explain X's failure.)

Presenting Another's View Using Direct Quotations

In _____, X writes, "_____."

After discussing the topic of _____, X's conclusion is that

"_____."

X attempts to make the case that "_____."

Quotations are a powerful way to present another's views when the language is particularly striking, clear, and succinct. (For more on using quotations, including a list of alternatives to the verb "writes," see Research Skill: "Incorporating Quotations into Your Text" on p. 126.) These templates help you to employ a key skill in making an argument: showing the work others have done on the issue. The next step is to introduce your own voice.

Presenting Another's View and Responding to It

She claims _____. It is actually true that _____.

In his essay _____, X writes that _____. However,

_____.

X attempts to make the case that "_____."

In her essay, X implies _____. However, careful consideration

shows that _____.

The formula for this kind of template introduces what the author has to say and then has you take your turn with your own view of the matter.

When you agree with some of what a writer says, but not all of it, you must distinguish between the parts you think are correct and those parts that are not. Sentence forms for this kind of response include the following.

Agreeing in Part

Although most of what X writes about _____ is true, it is not

true that _____.

X is correct that _____. But because of _____ it is actually

true that _____.

X argues that _____. While it is true that _____ and

_____ are valid points, _____ is not. Instead, _____.

These sentence templates ask you to identify those parts of the argument that are valid. Keep in mind that it is rare to disagree totally with every view expressed in an argument. A careful arguer will separate out what is correct and what is not. The writer can then focus energy on showing why these parts are not correct.

At times, you'll need to correct a distortion or misstatement of fact. Statistics, for instance, can be and often are manipulated to present the arguer's viewpoint in the best light. You may wish to propose an alternative interpretation or set the statistics in a different context, one more accurate and favorable to your own point of view. Of course, you'll want to be certain that you do not distort statistics. (For more on the importance of using statistics fairly, see the full discussion on pp. 192–93.) Here's a sentence form for correcting factual information in an argument.

Correcting a Factual Mistake

While X claims _____, it is actually true that _____.

Although X states _____, a careful examination of _____

and _____ indicates that _____.

These templates allow you to identify a mistaken claim of fact in an argument and present evidence opposing it.

More often, rather than correcting clear mistakes of fact, you'll need to refine the argument of a writer. You may find that much of the argument makes sense to you, but that the writer does not sufficiently anticipate important objections. In those cases, a sentence form such as one of the following can help you refine the argument to make a stronger conclusion.

Refining Another's Argument

Although it is true, as X shows, that _____, the actual result is

closer to _____ because _____.

While X claims _____ and _____, he fails to consider the

important point _____. Therefore, a more accurate conclusion is

_____.

Such sentence forms enable you to clarify and amplify an argument.

At times, you'll need to distinguish between the views of two different writers and then weigh in with your own assessment of the situation. When two authors write on the same topic, they will most likely share similar views on some of the points. They will, however, disagree on other points. Similarly, you may find that you agree with some of what each writer has to say, but disagree with some other parts. Your job is to identify the points of contrast between the two authors and then explain how your own position differs from one or both. In those cases, you may find the following sentence forms helpful.

Explaining Contrasting Views and Adding Your Position

X says _____. Y says _____. However, _____.

On the topic of _____, X claims that _____. In contrast,

Y argues that _____. However, _____.

A careful writer makes sure the reader understands fine distinctions. The forms above help make those distinctions clear.

While sentence forms may be rather simple — perhaps even simplistic — good writers use them all the time. Once you have tried them out a few times, you'll begin to use them automatically, perhaps without even realizing it. They are powerful tools for incorporating others' views into your own work and then helping you to make careful distinctions about various parts of arguments.

ARGUMENT ESSENTIALS
Using Sentence Forms

Before you analyze or evaluate another's argument, you must first be sure that you understand it. Then you can use some of the sentence forms in this section to show where it is weak and how your view is different.

- Presenting another's view
- Presenting another's view using direct quotations
- Presenting another's view and responding to it
- Agreeing in part
- Correcting a factual mistake
- Refining another's argument
- Explaining contrasting views and adding your position

Building an Effective Argument

In general, the writer of an argument follows the same rules that govern any form of expository writing. Your organization should be logical, your style clear and readable, your ideas connected by transitional phrases and sentences, your paragraphs coherent. The main difference between an argument and expository writing is the need to persuade an audience to adopt a belief or take an action. You should assume your readers will be critical rather than neutral or sympathetic. Therefore, you must be equally critical of your own work. Any apparent gap in reasoning or ambiguity in presentation is likely to weaken the argument.

For help with your organization, look back at the organizational patterns discussed in Chapter 5 on pages 146–56:

- Defining the thesis
- Refuting an opposing view
- Finding the middle ground
- Presenting the stock issues

You may also want to review what Chapter 5 says about writing introductions and conclusions. The style and tone you choose depend not only on the nature of the subject but also on how you can best convince readers that you are a credible source. **Style** in this context refers to the elements of your prose — simple versus complex sentences, active versus passive verbs, metaphors, analogies, and other literary devices. It is usually appropriate in a short paper to choose an expository style, which emphasizes the elements of your argument rather than your personality. You can discover some helpful pointers on essay style by reading the editorials in newspapers such as the *New York Times,* the *Washington Post,* and the *Wall Street Journal.* The authors are typically addressing a mixed audience comparable to the hypothetical readers of your own paper. Though their approaches vary, each writer is attempting to portray himself or herself as an objective analyst whose argument deserves careful attention. **Tone** is the approach you take to your topic — solemn or humorous, detached or sympathetic. Style and tone together compose your **voice** as a writer.

Remember too that part of establishing your credibility as a writer is to document your sources with care. You will need to use a combination of quotations, paraphrases, and summaries to support your points. See Chapter 4 for guidance on how to incorporate these elements into your paper. See Chapter 14 for advice on how to cite these sources.

Revising

The final stage in writing an argument is revising. The first step is to read through what you have written to be sure your paper is complete and well organized. Have you omitted any of the issues, warrants, or supporting evidence on your outline? Is each paragraph coherent in itself? Do your paragraphs work together to create a coherent paper? All the elements of the argument — the issues raised, the underlying assumptions, and the supporting material — should contribute to the development of the claim in your thesis statement. Any material that is interesting but irrelevant to that claim should be cut.

Next, be sure that the style and tone of your paper are appropriate for the topic and the audience. Remember that people choose to read an argument because they want the answer to a troubling question or the solution to a recurrent problem. Besides stating your thesis in a way that invites the reader to join you in your investigation, you must retain your audience's interest through a discussion that may be unfamiliar or contrary to their convictions. The outstanding qualities of argumentative prose style, therefore, are clarity and readability. In addition, your paper should reach a clear conclusion that reinforces your thesis.

Style is obviously harder to evaluate in your own writing than organization. Your outline provides a map against which to check the structure of your paper. Clarity and readability, by comparison, are somewhat abstract qualities. Two procedures may be helpful. The first is to read two or three (or more) essays by authors whose style you admire and then turn back to your own writing. Awkward spots in your prose are sometimes easier to see if you get away from it and respond to someone else's perspective than if you simply keep rereading your own writing.

The second method is to read aloud. If you have never tried it, you are likely to be surprised at how valuable this can be. Again, start with someone else's work that you feel is clearly written, and practice until you achieve a smooth, rhythmic delivery that satisfies you. And listen to what you are reading. Your objective is to absorb the patterns of English structure that characterize

ARGUMENT ESSENTIALS
Checklist for Effective Arguments

- Interesting and debatable thesis
- All claims supported with documented evidence
- No unsupported controversial warrants
- Appropriate organization
- Opposing arguments refuted

the clearest, most readable prose. Then read your paper aloud, and listen to the construction of your sentences. Are they also clear and readable? Do they say what you want them to say? How would they sound to a reader? According to one theory, you can learn the rhythm and phrasing of a language just as you learn the rhythm and phrasing of a melody. And you will often *hear* a mistake or a clumsy construction in your writing that has escaped your eye in proofreading.

Use the spell-check and grammar-check functions of your word-processing program, but keep in mind that correctness depends on context. A spell-check program will not flag a real word that is used incorrectly, such as the word *it's* used where the word *its* is needed. Also, a grammar-check function lacks the sophistication to interpret the meaning of a sentence and may flag as incorrect a group of words that is indeed correct while missing actual errors. It is ultimately up to you to proofread the paper carefully for other mistakes. Correct the errors, and reprint the pages in question.

Oral Arguments

You will often be asked to make oral presentations in your college classes. Many jobs, both professional and nonprofessional, will call for speeches to groups of fellow employees or prospective customers, to community groups, and even to government officials. Wherever you live, there will be controversies and public meetings about schooling and political candidates, about budgets for libraries and road repairs and pet control. The ability to rise and make your case before an audience is one that you will want to cultivate as a citizen of a democracy.

Some of your objectives as a writer will also be relevant to you as a speaker: making the appropriate appeal to an audience, establishing your credibility, finding adequate support for your claim. But other elements of argument will be different: language, organization, and the use of visual and other aids.

The Audience

Most speakers who confront a live audience already know something about the members of that audience. They may know why the audience is assembled to hear the particular speaker, their vocations, their level of education, and their familiarity with the subject. They may know whether the audience is friendly, hostile, or neutral to the views that the speaker will express. Analyzing the audience is an essential part of speech preparation.

In college classes, students who make assigned speeches on controversial topics are often encouraged to first survey the class. Questionnaires and interviews can give the speaker important clues to the things he should emphasize or avoid: They will tell him whether he should give both sides of a debatable question, introduce humor, use simpler language, and bring in visual or other aids.

If you know something about your audience, ask yourself what impression your clothing, gestures and bodily movements, voice, and general demeanor might convey. Make sure, too, that you understand the nature of the occasion — is it too solemn for humor? too formal for personal anecdotes? — and the purpose of the meeting, which can influence your choice of language and the most effective appeal.

Credibility

Credibility, as you learned in Chapter 1, is another name for *ethos* (the Greek word from which the English word *ethics* is derived) and refers to the honesty, moral character, and intellectual competence of the speaker.

Public figures, whose speeches and actions are reported in the media, can acquire (or fail to acquire) reputations for being endowed with those characteristics. And there is little doubt that a reputation for competence and honesty can incline an audience to accept an argument that would be rejected if offered by a speaker who lacks such a reputation.

How, then, do speakers who are unknown to the audience or who boast only modest credentials convince listeners that they are responsible advocates? From the moment the speaker appears before them, members of the audience begin to make an evaluation based on external signs such as clothing, mannerisms, and body language. But the most significant impression of the speaker's credibility will be based on what the speaker says — and how. Does the speaker give evidence of knowing the subject? of being aware of the needs and values of the audience? Especially if arguing an unpopular claim, does the speaker seem modest and conciliatory?

Unknown speakers are often advised to establish their credentials in the introduction to their speech, to summarize their background and experience as proof of their right to argue the subject they have chosen.

Speakers often use an admission of modesty as proof of an honest and unassuming character, presenting themselves not as experts but as speakers well aware of their limitations. Such an appeal can generate sympathy in the audience (if they believe the speaker) and a sense of identification with the speaker.

Organization

A well-planned speech has a clearly defined beginning, middle, and end. The beginning, which offers the introduction, can take a number of forms, depending on the kind of speech and its subject. Above all, the introduction must win the attention of the audience, especially if they have been required to attend, and encourage them to look forward to the rest of the speech. The authors of *Principles of Speech Communication* suggest seven basic attention-getters:

- referring to the subject or occasion
- using a personal reference
- asking a rhetorical question

- making a startling statement of fact or opinion
- using a quotation
- telling a humorous anecdote
- using an illustration[1]

The middle or body of the speech is, of course, the longest part. It is devoted to development of the claim that appears at the beginning. The length of the speech and the complexity of the subject determine how much support you provide. Some points are more important than others and should therefore receive more extended treatment. Unless the order is chronological, it makes sense for the speaker to arrange the supporting points in emphatic order, that is, the most important at the end because this may be the one that listeners will remember.

The conclusion should be brief; some rhetoricians suggest that the ending should constitute 5 percent of the total length of the speech. For speeches that contain several main points with supporting data, you may need to summarize. Or you may return to one of the attention-getters mentioned earlier. One writer recommends this as "the most obvious method" of concluding speeches, "particularly appropriate when the introduction has included a quotation, an interesting anecdote, a reference to an occasion or a place, an appeal to the self-interest of the audience, or a reference to a recent incident."[2]

The speaker must also ensure the smooth flow of argument throughout. Coherence, or the orderly connections between ideas, is even more important in speech than in writing because the listener cannot go back to uncover these connections. The audience listens for expressions that serve as guideposts — words, phrases, and sentences to indicate which direction the argument will take. Words such as *next, then, finally, here, first of all, whereas, in addition, second, in fact, now,* and *in conclusion* can help the listener to follow the argument's development.

Language

> It should be observed that each kind of rhetoric has its own appropriate style. That of written prose is not the same as that of spoken oratory.
>
> — Aristotle

In the end, your speech depends on the language you use. No matter how accurate your analysis of the audience, how appealing your presentation of self, how deep your grasp of the material, if the language does not clearly and emphatically convey your argument, the speech will probably fail. Fortunately, the effectiveness of language does not depend on long words or complex sentence

---

[1] Bruce E. Gronbeck et al., *Principles of Speech Communication*, 13th brief ed. (New York: Longman, 1998), pp. 243–47.

[2] James C. McCroskey, *An Introduction to Rhetorical Communication* (Englewood Cliffs, NJ: Prentice-Hall, 1968), p. 204.

structure — quite the contrary. Most speeches, especially those given by beginners to small audiences, are distinguished by an oral style that respects the rhythms of ordinary speech and sounds spontaneous.

- Use words that both you and your listeners are familiar with, language that convinces the audience you are sharing your knowledge and opinions, neither speaking down to them nor talking over their heads. You never want to use language that makes the audience appear ignorant or unreasonable.
- Make sure that the words you use will not be considered offensive by some members of your audience. Today we are all sensitive, sometimes hypersensitive, to terms that were once used freely if not wisely. One word, improperly used, can cause some listeners to reject the whole speech. This is particularly true of terms that suggest bias based on gender, race, or sexual orientation.
- Consider whether the subject is one that the particular audience you are addressing is not likely to be familiar with. If this is the case, then explain even the basic terms. In one class, a student who had chosen to discuss a subject about which he was extremely knowledgeable, betting on horse races, neglected to define clearly the words *exacta, subfecta, trifecta, parimutuel,* and others, leaving his audience fairly befuddled.
- Wherever it is appropriate, use concrete language with details and examples that create images and cause the listener to feel as well as think. One student speaker used strong words to good effect in providing some unappetizing facts about hot dogs: "In fact, the hot dog is so adulterated with chemicals, so contaminated with bacteria, so puffy with gristle, fat, water, and lacking in protein, that it is nutritionally worthless."[3]
- Because the audience must grasp the grammatical construction without the visual clues of punctuation available on the printed page, use short, direct sentences. Use subject-verb constructions without a string of phrases or clauses preceding the subject or interrupting the natural flow of the sentence. Use the active voice frequently.
- Consider a popular stylistic device — repetition and balance, or parallel structure — to emphasize and enrich parts of your message. Almost all inspirational speeches, including religious exhortation and political oratory, take advantage of such constructions, whose rhythms evoke an immediate emotional response. It is one of the strengths of Martin Luther King Jr.'s "I Have a Dream" speech, which you can read and listen to online. Keep in mind that the ideas in parallel structures must be similar and that, for maximum effectiveness, they should be used sparingly in a short speech. Not least, the subject should be weighty enough to carry this imposing construction.

---

[3] Donovan Ochs and Anthony Winkler, *A Brief Introduction to Speech* (New York: Harcourt, Brace, Jovanovich, 1979), p. 74.

Support

The support for a claim is essentially the same for both spoken and written arguments. Factual evidence, including statistics and expert opinion, as well as appeals to needs and values, is equally important in oral presentations. But time constraints will make a difference. In a speech, the amount of support that you provide will be limited to the capacity of listeners to digest and remember information that they cannot review. This means that you must choose subjects that can be supported adequately in the time allotted.

While both speakers and writers use logical, ethical, and emotional appeals in support of their arguments, the forms of presentation can make a significant difference. The reasoning process demanded of listeners must be relatively brief and straightforward, and the supporting evidence readily assimilated. The ethical appeal or credibility of the speaker is affected not only by what is said but also by the speaker's appearance, bodily movements, and vocal expressions. And the appeal to the sympathy of the audience can be greatly enhanced by the presence of the speaker. Take the example of former U.S. congresswoman Gabrielle Giffords, shot in the head in 2012 and slowly recovering movement and speech. Written descriptions of pain and heartbreak are very moving, but place yourself in an audience, looking at Giffords and imagining her suffering. No doubt the effect would be deep and long-lasting, perhaps more memorable even than the written word.

Because the human instrument is so powerful, it must be used with care. You have probably listened to speakers who used gestures and voice inflections that had been dutifully rehearsed but were obviously contrived and worked, unfortunately, to undermine rather than support the speaker's message and credibility. If you are not a gifted actor, you should avoid gestures, body language, and vocal expressions that are not truly authentic.

Some speeches, though not all, can be enhanced by visual and other aids: charts, graphs, maps, models, objects, handouts, recordings, and computerized images. These aids, however, no matter how visually or aurally exciting, should not overwhelm your own oral presentation. The objects are not the stars of the show. They exist to make your spoken argument more persuasive.

Presentation Aids

Charts, Graphs, Handouts

Charts and graphs, large enough and clear enough to be seen and understood, can illuminate speeches that contain numbers of any kind, especially statistical comparisons. You can make a simple chart yourself, on paper for use with an easel or on a computer to be projected or to be printed for presentation to an audience. Enlarged illustrations or a model of a complicated machine — say, the space shuttle — would help a speaker to explain its function. You already know that photographs or videos are powerful instruments of persuasion, above all in support of appeals for humanitarian aid, for both people and animals.

The use of a handout also requires planning. It's probably unwise to put your speech on hold while the audience reads or studies a handout that requires time and concentration. Confine the subject matter of handouts to material that can be easily grasped as you discuss or explain it.

Audio

Audio aids may also enliven a speech or even be indispensable to its success. One student played a recording of a scene from *Romeo and Juliet,* spoken by a cast of professional actors, to make a point about the relationship between the two lovers. Another student chose to define several types of popular music, including rap, goth, heavy metal, and techno. But he used only words, and the lack of any musical demonstration meant that the distinctions remained unclear.

Video

With sight, sound, and movement, a video can illustrate or reinforce the main points of a speech. A speech warning people not to text while driving will have a much greater effect if enhanced by a video showing the tragic and often grue-some outcome of car accidents caused by distracted driving. Schools that teach driver's education frequently rely on these bone-chilling videos to show their students that getting behind the wheel is a serious responsibility, not a game. If you want to use video, check to make sure that a computer, Blu-ray, or DVD player and television are available to you. Most schools have an audio-visual department that manages the delivery, setup, and return of all equipment.

Multimedia

Multimedia presentation software programs enable you to combine several different media such as text, charts, sound, and still or moving pictures into one unit. In the business world, multimedia presentations are commonly used in situations where there is a limited amount of time to persuade or teach a fairly large audience.

Though effective when done well, technically complicated presentations require careful planning. First you need to familiarize yourself with the program. Most presentation software programs come equipped with helpful tutorials. If the task of creating your own presentation from scratch seems overwhelming, you can use one of the many preformatted presentation templates: You will simply need to customize the content.

You also need to make sure the equipment you need (computer, projector, connection cords, etc.) will be available. Robert Stephens, founder of the Geek Squad, a Minneapolis-based business that provides on-site emergency response to computer problems, gives the following tips for multimedia presentations:

1. In case of equipment failure, always bring two of everything.
2. Back up your presentation on a second device.
3. Avoid live visits to the Internet. Because connections can fail or be pain-fully slow, and sites can move or disappear, if you must visit the Internet

in your presentation, download the appropriate pages onto your hard drive ahead of time. It will still look like a live visit.

4. In the end, technology cannot replace creativity. Make sure that you are using multimedia to reinforce, not replace, your main points.[4]

If you have never used the devices you need for your presentation, practice using them before the speech. Few things are more disconcerting for the speechmaker and the audience than a speaker who is fumbling with his or her materials, unable to find the right picture or to make a machine work.

READING ARGUMENT

Examining a Speech

Read the following excerpts from a speech by Anna Maria Chávez, the CEO of the Girl Scouts of the USA, to get a better understanding of audience, credibility, organization, language, and support. The first two paragraphs (in italic) provide background on Chávez and the speech.

Address to the National Council Session/52nd Convention of the Girl Scouts of the USA
ANNA MARIA CHÁVEZ

The following speech was presented by Girl Scouts of the USA national CEO Anna Maria Chávez to delegates of the organization's 2011 National Council Session/52nd Convention in Houston, Texas. The speech served to introduce Ms. Chávez as the nineteenth CEO of the national organization of the Girl Scout Movement, and the first Latina to lead the organization. Chávez was addressing more than 15,000 members of the 112 local Girl Scout councils across the country, in addition to Girl Scout alumnae, current and prospective donors, and active girl members of the Movement.

The triennial convention also celebrated the 100th Anniversary of the Girl Scouts, and Ms. Chávez used her address to talk about how far the Movement had come in its first 100 years and the opportunities and challenges it faced as it stood

---

In 2011, the Girl Scouts of the USA welcomed Anna Maria Chávez as the organization's CEO. The excerpts are from the speech Chávez gave at its National Council Session/52nd Convention in Houston, in November 2011. Address courtesy of the Girl Scouts of the USA.

---

[4] Robert Stephens as paraphrased in Eric Matson, "When Your Presentation Crashes . . . Who You Gonna Call?," *Fast Company,* February/March 1997, p. 130.

on the doorstep of its second century. In her remarks, Ms. Chávez suggests that Girl Scouts are at a pivotal and transitional moment in its history and positions herself as a change-agent who would bring a new kind of dynamism and leadership to bear in propelling the Girl Scouts into their second century of service to girls.

. . . One day my parents took me on a picnic, and I found this cave and it had really important Native American hieroglyphics, and these kids had graffitied all over it. And I was mad. So I stomped back down that hill with my little science kit. And I ran up to my mother and I said, "Mother, this isn't fair! They destroyed this wonderful cave and the environment, and the Girl Scouts taught me that we need to cherish the environment. This has to stop." And she looked at me very calmly and said, "Well, Anna Maria, what do we do in these instances?" And she said to me, and I repeated to her, "Well, I've got to do something. I've got to change this." And she said, "Okay, how are you going to do that? Who does these things?" I said, "Well, people who make laws and change the world, and lawyers." And she goes, "Okay, so what happens next?" "Well, if I want to be a lawyer, I must go to law school," so as a Girl Scout, by then the age of twelve, I was headed to law school.

And that courage kept me well, because I went to Yale because they invited me. They sent me a brochure, so I'd assumed they wanted me. So I went. I hadn't even gone, and my parents go, "Do you want us to take you?" "No, I got this." I get there, and I discovered a whole new environment. I was a kid from a small town on scholarship, and I worked two jobs to scrape by. And I remember one December my scholarship was running out, and I had one dollar left, so I went and I took that dollar and I taped it to the wall above my desk where I studied every night, and I stared at it. And it had to last me about four weeks because if I missed dinner, because of my second job, I had to pay for it. So every night I would run home from work to get to that dining hall. But it taught me, as we are taught in Girl Scouts, to use our resources wisely. So I saved that dollar, and I thought, you know, I can do this. And I went on to law school and after that I went to Washington, and that is where this Girl Scout learned how to take a few hard knocks. But that was okay, because I eventually got to advise a U.S. president, a vice president, two cabinet secretaries, three federal administrators, two governors, and a husband. And that's when the Girl Scouts of Southwest Texas called. And they said, "You know, we would really be interested for you to come work with us."

And I took that leap of chance, and I went out there, and I took that opportunity—who wouldn't?—to take the opportunity to champion such a

Support: Personal example of how scouting influenced her

Audience: Identifies with Girl Scouts and leaders who are her audience

Support: Another personal example of a helpful lesson learned through scouting

Credibility: Establishes that she is well educated and resourceful

Support/credibility: Uses herself as an example of leadership

noble cause, to play a role in changing lives and through their lives change a nation. So in just two years, our team in Southwest Texas established unprecedented partnerships with school districts and leading businesses to serve more girls than ever. And that really shows the success we can have in building strategic partnerships to offer the Girl Scout leadership experience to as many girls as we can. I love working for girls. They make our job fun, and they keep us real, and the exuberance they bring to their daily work really energizes me, which is my secret of energy. And they motivate me every day to jump out of bed. . . .

Audience: Praises her audience

Support: Other examples of Girl Scouts as leaders

[These girls] need encouragement. They need someone to tell them that anything is possible. Because they can. All of you, I know, can share a story of Girl Scouts who are doing great things. Maybe your story is about a group of ten Brownies from Worcester, Massachusetts, who, through examples in *The Wild Journey*, worked through their local TV station to produce and air PSAs that educated their community on water conservation. Or maybe your story can be taken from the amazing girls we have seen this week here in Houston. They are leading the nation in making the world a better place, one project at a time.

5   But I want to tell you about a young lady I met in San Antonio because the teens in our council came to me and said, ". . . You need to help us bring more teenaged girls into our system, and you need to retain us as well." So they created a program, a new pathway called Gamma Sigma girls, and it was targeted toward high school girls that didn't have an opportunity to be Girl Scouts in their younger years. And in that program, Irene saw things she had never seen before. She was so energized, and even though she was a senior, she felt that she could give back to her community, and she was a positive force in her school. She did everything she could to help her Girl Scout sisters. Irene is a bright girl who has unfortunately faced some challenges. And at the end of the year — the Girl Scout year — I learned that through all of this, Irene, since the age of nine, had been homeless, and since the age of fourteen had been in twelve schools. Now, even with all of this going against her, she felt she had found a home with Girl Scouts. She felt she was in a safe environment with other girls to help other people change the world.

Support: One specific extended example

As a Girl Scout, Irene has blossomed. She is doing amazing things in her community, she graduated in the top ten of her graduating class, and she now goes across the country to talk to other teens and children about the ability to express your views, to live through barriers, and make a difference to others. She's created a close-knit friend group at school, and I don't think we can ever underestimate the importance of what our program and Girl Scouts meant to her and to other girls. She used to wake up every day at 5:00 a.m. to get to school, ride an hour and a half on the bus just to see her Girl Scout sisters. Today Irene is a freshman at Texas State University in San Marcos. She is the first in her family to graduate from [high school], and she is here with us today. . . I am in awe of her and the thousands of girls she represents. She is really an important part of our history.

Now, forever, we will have a lifelong circle of friends. There are ten thousand of us here today in this room alone. What breaks my heart and keeps me moving forward is that Irene was almost never a Girl Scout. Because of limited funds, she almost was unable to become a member of our organization. And there are millions of girls outside our movement just like Irene, because of lack of funding, not enough volunteer support, [who] have yet to join our movement. Those girls are the ones I worry about the most, the ones who need us. These are the girls that literally keep me up late at night but motivate me to wake up in the morning to keep going. That is why I took on this important yet daunting role. Like Irene, I too faced obstacles, but Girl Scouts gave me the hope to push through them, and I wanted to make sure our important work continued.

> Organization: She generalizes from one example to the thousands in attendance, but also to the millions not yet reached by her organization.

Right now, Girl Scouts reaches about ten percent of the girls in our country, and that is not enough. Today there is a girl out there who is searching for a place where she feels at home. Do you see her? Somewhere in this country there is a teenager who really needs the guidance and confidence that she can gain through Girl Scouts. Can you hear her?

We need to reach out to these girls. We need to let them know we're here for them. To do that, we need to turn ourselves outward and address the world about our movement. In the next hundred years — because we are experts at mobilizing and grassroots organization — we can unite our members to make a difference. Now, let's ask the world to imagine their communities without Girl Scouts. Imagine the thousands of food drives, clothing and toy collections that would never take place were it not for Girl Scouts. Imagine the hundreds of thousands of hours spent on take-action projects, to plant trees, adopt pets, and build gardens, projects that would have never happened if not for Girl Scouts. And the most terrifying of all, imagine this world without Girl Scout cookies.

> Organization: She starts to address the solution to the problem.

> Language: She uses everyday language throughout and occasional humor.

We need to step forward and shout from the rooftops: the time is now, the time is right. The question of female leadership has moved onto the front pages. There is enormous and growing understanding of what it can mean for women to really play a role in leading our society. And there is greater and greater awareness of the benefit of teaching girls to lead, so that they can be the leaders in their lives no matter what they do.

> Organization: She generalizes about the increased awareness of women as leaders.

10

Now, I'm not just talking about executives or judges or scientists. I'm also talking about the women that go out and get their degrees so they can stay home and raise their children. Any girl deserves a chance to be what she wants to be because that is her choice. That's something you give girls, and they know it. Why do you think Irene woke up at 5:00 a.m. so she could tolerate a long bus ride to go to a Girl Scout meeting. Because, my friends, we have something precious, we are something precious. The world is waiting for a leader to step forward in the name of girls and women. We are that leader. With three million members in the United States, ten million sisters worldwide, and fifty million alumnae, we are bigger than we recognize. We are turning a hundred years old, and the eyes of the world are upon us. So let's show them what we've got. Let's tell **everybody** about it. We're going to stand up and say, "This is who we are, and this is who we are not." This is what we are going to say to the country and the world: "Girl Scouts is developing the female leaders of tomorrow with the courage, confidence, and character they will need to help make this world a better place."

This is what we are going to say to parents: "Girl Scouts will open the doors of possibilities for your daughter — or your niece — that life has to offer, and we will provide them the leadership skills that they will need to navigate their own paths to success.

And this is what we are going to say to the girls: "We are proud to renew our promise to you. The recognition you receive for making things better in your school, in your place of worship, in your community all contribute to the lifting up of your voices to signal a brand new day for an impatient world waiting for the goodness you bring. We know that you are capable, you are strong, you are smart, you are beautiful, you are bold. Your family recognized your greatness as soon as they called you by your name for the very first time. Juliette[5] recognized it as soon as she called you by your name. She called you Girl Scout. You must know that your time is now."

Our time is now, so here's what I want from everybody in this room here today. Will you help me? Will **you** be the force that propels this movement further than even Juliette could imagine? Will you? Will you tell your stories so that we are no longer the best kept secret? Will you raise your voices so that all girls can raise theirs? Well, to paraphrase Juliette Gordon Low, we've got something for the girls of Houston and all of America and all of the world, and we are going to start today. Thank you.

---

[5] Juliette Gordon Low founded the Girl Scouts in 1912.

Margin notes:

Organization: Her claim

Organization/language: Parallel order, repeated language

Audience: She draws in her audience by asking questions to which they shout answers.

Practice: Examining a Speech

Read the following speech given at Georgetown University on May 18, 2012, by U.S. Department of Health and Human Services secretary Kathleen Sebelius, and answer the questions that follow it.

Remarks to Georgetown University's Public Policy Institute
KATHLEEN SEBELIUS

Dean Montgomery, members of the faculty, family, friends, and graduates: It's an honor to be with you this morning. And let me start with some well-earned congratulations. Last weekend, on Mother's Day, I was at the University of Kansas when my younger son received his Master's degree. So I know the hard work and effort that got you here today.

I married a Georgetown law graduate and am a Hoya Mom — the mother of a double Georgetown graduate. So in my family, Hoya Saxa comes second only to Rock Chalk Jayhawk.

And I was especially pleased to be invited to speak to you, the public policy graduates. Having spent my entire life in public service, I believe you've chosen the most challenging, frustrating, exciting, consequential, and rewarding career there is. And today, I want to share a few lessons from my career that I hope will be useful as you begin yours.

I started out as an "unpaid volunteer." My dad got into politics when I was five, so for most of my childhood, I spent my fall days putting up yard signs and going door to door.

Actually, the more accurate term might be forced labor. There wasn't a lot of choice in the matter. (It was only later that I discovered that other families were going to football games
5 and picnics while I was attending political rallies.)

But what I got from those fall outings, and from our conversations around our dinner table, was a deep belief in the value of public service. And throughout my career, it's been that unwavering belief that's carried me to my highest points — and gotten me through my lowest.

I know you share that belief. If you didn't, you wouldn't be here today. You wouldn't have suffered through regression analysis. You wouldn't have passed up bigger salary possibilities in other fields.

So my first hope for you today is that you always hold on to your commitment to work for the common good. If you let that focus guide you, you will never go off course.

I learned the second lesson when I came to Washington in the late 60s to attend Trinity College. Those were tumultuous times in our nation's history, and DC was right in the middle of it. During my college years, the draft was reinstated, as the government ramped up the war in Vietnam. Racial tensions, that had been smoldering, erupted after the assassination of Martin Luther King Jr., and neighborhoods in DC were burned to the ground.

Kathleen Sebelius served as governor of Kansas from 2003 to 2009, when she became the secretary of the U.S. Department of Health and Human Services.

10 What was striking at the time is how young people were driving these national debates. There was a feeling not just that young people could change the world — but that we had to.

Robert Kennedy spoke about those times in a famous speech. He said: "This world demands the qualities of youth. Not a time of life, but a state of mind, a temper of the will, a quality of the imagination, a predominance of courage over timidity, of the appetite for adventure over the life of ease."

As you set out on your careers, you may find yourselves tempted to defer to those who are older or have more experience. And on behalf of the parents in the audience, I want to be clear that even though we may not know who Kim Kardashian is, or why everyone is always so angry about her, we do still have some wisdom to share. You still need to call your mom! (In fact, after this ceremony ends, the first thing you should do is thank the parents, teachers, mentors, and friends who supported your journey to this graduation day.)

But the truth is, wisdom isn't the only thing that comes with age. Growing older can also bring complacency and cautiousness.

I know Georgetown hasn't trained you to sit on the sidelines. You've studied under leading policy-makers. You've proven your skills, not just on tests and papers, but in the real world through programs like Project Honduras.

15 So my second piece of advice is: Don't wait. Go ahead and do it yourself — because if you don't, it might never happen.

Now, I wish I could give you a roadmap for exactly how to do that. But the truth is that career paths are usually only visible looking backwards, like the tracks we make in the snow.

I'm an accidental feminist who learned that girls can do anything by attending an all-girls school where we had to do everything. I ended up in Kansas because that's where my husband grew up. I began my political career because our part-time legislature was a better fit for me, as a mother with two young children, than the 60-hour-a-week job I had.

As I moved along, I sought out opportunities to learn new skills and new subject areas. I started out working in corrections. Later, I worked on everything from education, to children and family issues, to the budget, to jobs and economic development, to rural challenges.

One of the issues I kept coming back to was health care, culminating in my current position. And now, I have the extraordinary opportunity to help implement legislation that is finally, after seven decades of failed debate, ensuring that all Americans have access to affordable health coverage.

20 But I never would have been here if I hadn't taken some chances. For me, the biggest risk was running for Kansas Insurance Commissioner. The indicators were not promising. The statewide office had never been held by a woman or a Democrat. The previous three commissioners had close ties to the insurance industry and had served nearly fifty years combined. And it was 1994, when running for office as a Democrat was the basic equivalent of wearing a Georgetown jersey in the Syracuse student section.

But I went for it and won. And I ended up not just getting an incredible opportunity to make a difference, but also gaining invaluable experience for the job I have now. (Who knew?)

All of you are going to face similar choices in your careers. It might be taking a more senior position at a much smaller organization. It might be moving abroad to work. It might be going from running a campaign to becoming a candidate.

And when you do encounter these opportunities, I encourage you take a deep breath and seize them.

And that brings me to the final lesson I want to leave with you today, which is that no matter what path you choose, it's going to be hard.

25 Ultimately, public policy is about making difficult choices. Today, there are serious debates under way about the direction of our country—debates about the size and role of government, about America's role as a global economic and military leader, about the moral and economic imperative of providing health care to all our citizens. People have deeply held beliefs on all sides of these discussions, and you, as public policy leaders, will be called on to help move these debates forward.

These are not questions with quick and easy answers. When I was in junior high, John Fitzgerald Kennedy was running for president. I wasn't old enough to vote, but it was the first national campaign I really remember. Some of then-Senator Kennedy's opponents attacked him for his religion, suggesting that electing the first Catholic president would undermine the separation of church and state, a fundamental principle of our democracy. The furor grew so loud that Kennedy chose to deliver a speech about his beliefs just seven weeks before the election.

In that talk to Protestant ministers, Kennedy talked about his vision of religion and the public square, and said he believed in an America, and I quote, "where no religious body seeks to impose its will directly or indirectly upon the general populace or the public acts of its officials—and where religious liberty is so indivisible that an act against one church is treated as an act against us all."

Kennedy was elected president on November 8, 1960. And more than fifty years later, that conversation, about the intersection of our nation's long tradition of religious freedom with policy decisions that affect the general public, continues.

Contributing to these debates will require more than just the quantitative skills you have learned at Georgetown. It will also require the ethical skills you have honed—the ability to weigh different views, see issues from other points of view, and in the end, follow your own moral compass.

These debates can also be contentious. But 30 this is a strength of our country, not a weakness. In some countries around the world, it is much easier to make policy. The leader delivers an edict and it goes into effect. There's no debate, no criticism, no second guessing.

Our system is messier, slower, more frustrating, and far better. It requires conversations that can be painful, and it almost always ends in compromise. But it's through this process of conversation and compromise that we move forward, together, step by step, toward a "more perfect union."

Looking out on you this morning, I feel very optimistic about the future of that union. If you hold on to your idealism, resist complacency, take chances, and engage thoughtfully with the difficult challenges of our time, you will succeed. And I can't wait to see what you will accomplish.

Congratulations and good luck!

Reading and Discussion Questions

1. How does Sebelius attempt to relate to audience members and thus draw them into her speech?

2. What did Sebelius learn from her early involvement in her father's campaigns? How does that relate to her audience on this occasion?

3. What advice does she offer the graduates?

4. Why does she feel that the jobs the graduates will enter will require ethical skills? Does she come across as an ethical person herself? Why, or why not?

 To see what you are learning about argumentation applied to the latest world and national news, read our *Bits* blog, "Argument and the Headlines," at **blogs.bedfordstmartins.com/bits.**

Documenting Sources

As you write your paper, anytime that you make use of the wording or ideas of one of your sources, you must document that use. Two of the most common methods of crediting sources are the Modern Language Association (MLA) and American Psychological Association (APA) systems. The MLA system consists of two main components: the in-text citations (explained below) and the list of Works Cited (shown on pages 402–10).

MLA In-Text Citations

In the text of your paper, immediately after any quotation, paraphrase, or idea you need to document, simply insert a parenthetical mention of the author's last name and the page number(s) on which the material appears. You don't need a comma after the author's name or an abbreviation of the word *page* or *p.* For example, the following sentence appears in the sample MLA paper later in this chapter:

> Although there are nutritious competitive options, those do not sell as well as the ones high in sugar, salt, and calories (Hartline-Grafton 2–3).

The parenthetical reference tells the reader that the information in this sentence came from pages of the book or article that appears in the Works Cited at the end of the paper. The complete reference on the Works Cited page provides all of the information readers need to locate the source:

> Hartline-Grafton, Heather. "How Competitive Foods in Schools Impact Student Health, School Meal Programs, and Students from Low-Income Families." *Issue Briefs for Child Nutrition Reauthorization*, no.5, Food Research and Action Center, 2010, pp. 1–3, www.frac.org/pdf/CNR05_competitivefoods.pdf.

If the author's name is mentioned in the same sentence, it is also acceptable to place only the page numbers in parentheses; it is not necessary to repeat the author's name. For example:

According to Heather Hartline-Grafton, although there are nutritious competitive options, those do not sell as well as the ones high in sugar, salt, and calories (2–3).

Remember, though, that a major reason for using qualified sources is that they lend authority to the ideas expressed. The first time an author is mentioned in the paper, he or she — or they — should be identified by full name and by claim to authority:

> Parke Wilde and Mary Kennedy, both researchers in the Friedman School of Nutrition Science and Policy at Tufts University in Boston, explain some of the complexities in an article entitled "The Economics of a Healthy School Meal."

A last name and page number in parentheses do not carry nearly the same weight as a full name and credentials. You should save the former for subsequent citations once the author has been fully identified. If more than one sentence comes from the same source, you do not need to put parentheses after each sentence. One parenthetical citation at the end of the material from a source is enough if it is clear from the way you introduce the material where your ideas end and the source's begin.

> According to the Robert Wood Johnson Foundation, a charitable organization whose goal is to improve the health of all Americans, the rate of obesity for those between the ages of six and eleven has quadrupled in three decades. Children are being diagnosed with what used to be considered adult diseases, like high blood pressure, adult-onset diabetes, and gallstones. The Foundation reports, "If we don't succeed in reversing this epidemic, we are in danger of raising the first generation of American children who will live sicker and die younger than their parents' generation" (259–60).

If you are using more than one work by the same author, you will need to provide in the parentheses the title or a recognizable shortened form of the title of the particular work being cited. If the author's name is not mentioned in the sentence, you should include in parentheses the author's last name, the title, and the page number, with a comma between the author's name and the title. If both the author's name and the title of any work being cited are mentioned in the sentence, the parentheses will include only the page number. Had two works by Hartline-Grafton been listed in the Works Cited in the sample paper, the first example on page 399 would have looked like this:

> Although there are nutritious competitive options, those do not sell as well as the ones high in sugar, salt, and calories (Hartline-Grafton, "How Competitive Foods" 2–3).

If there is more than one author, don't forget to give credit to all. Two authors are acknowledged by name in the parentheses if not in your own sentence: (Hacker and Sommers 23). With three or more authors, use *et al.,* the Latin term for *and others*: (Braithwaite et al. 137).

Some sources do not name an author. To cite a work with an unknown author, give the title, or a recognizable shortened form, in the text of your paper. If the work does not have numbered pages, which is often the case in Web pages or nonprint sources, do not include page numbers. For example:

> In some cases Sephardic Jews, "converted" under duress, practiced Christianity openly and Judaism in secret until recently ("Search for the Buried Past").

Direct quotations should always be introduced or worked into the grammatical structure of your own sentences. If you need help introducing quotations, refer to the Writer's Guide in Chapter 4 (pp. 126–27). Remember, however, that you need to provide parenthetical documentation not only for every direct quotation but also for every paraphrase or summary. Document any words or ideas that are not your own.

As a general rule, you cannot make any changes in a quotation. Two exceptions must be clearly marked when they occur. At times, you may use brackets to make a slight change that does not alter the meaning of the quotation. For example, a pronoun may need to be replaced by a noun in brackets to make its reference clear. Or a verb tense may be changed and bracketed to make the quotation fit more smoothly into your sentence. An ellipsis (. . .) is used when you omit a portion of the quotation that does not change the essential meaning of the quote. You do not need to use ellipses at the beginning or end of a direct quotation. If the omitted portion included the end of one sentence and the beginning of another, there should be a fourth period (. . . .).

If a quotation is more than four typed lines long, it needs to be handled as a block quotation. A block quotation is usually introduced by a sentence followed by a colon. The quotation itself is indented one inch or ten spaces from the left margin. No quotation marks are necessary since the placement on the page informs the reader that it is a quotation. The only quotation marks in a block quotation would be ones copied from the original, as in dialogue. A paragraph break within a block quotation is indented an additional 1/4". The parenthetical citation is the same as with a quotation run into your text, but the period appears before the parenthesis.

With print sources in particular, you will often need to cite one work that is quoted in another or a work from an anthology. For the former, the parenthetical documentation provides the name and page number of the source you actually used, preceded by the words "qtd. in":

> The National School Lunch Program has been in existence since 1946 "as a measure of national security, to safeguard the health and well-being of the Nation's children and to encourage the domestic consumption of nutritious agricultural commodities and other food" (qtd. in Center for Science 230).

A work in an anthology is cited parenthetically by the name of the author of the work, not the editor of the anthology: (Simkovich 3).

The list of Works Cited includes all material you have used to write your research paper. This list appears at the end of your paper and always starts on a new page. Center the title Works Cited, double-space between the title and the first entry, and begin your list, which should be arranged alphabetically by author. Each entry should start at the left margin; indent all subsequent lines of the entry five spaces or one-half inch. Number each page, and double-space throughout.

One more point: *Content notes,* which provide additional information not readily worked into a research paper, are indicated by superscript numbers. Content notes are included on a Notes page before the list of Works Cited.

MLA Works Cited Entries

Following are examples of the citation forms you are most likely to need as you document your research. In general, for both books and magazines, information should appear in the following order: author, title, and publication information. Each item should be followed by a period. When using as a source an essay that appears in this book, follow the citation model for "Material Reprinted from Another Source," unless your instructor indicates otherwise. Consult the *MLA Handbook*, Eighth Edition (2016), for other documentation models.

Directory of MLA Works Cited Entries

Print Sources

1. A Book by a Single Author

Edsel, Robert M. *Saving Italy: The Race to Rescue a Nation's Treasures from the Nazis.* W. W. Norton, 2013.

2. Two or More Works by the Same Author or Authors

Rashid, Ahmed. *Pakistan on the Brink: The Future of America, Pakistan, and Afghanistan.* Penguin Books, 2012.

---. *Taliban: The Power of Militant Islam in Afghanistan and Beyond.* 2nd ed., Yale UP, 2008.

For the second and subsequent books by the same author, replace the author's name with three hyphens, followed by a period and the title.

3. A Work with Two Authors

Alderman, Ellen, and Caroline Kennedy. *The Right to Privacy.* Vintage Books, 1997.

NOTE: This form is followed even for two authors with the same last name.

Ehrlich, Paul, and Anne Ehrlich. *Extinction: The Causes and Consequences of the Disappearance of Species.* Random House, 1981.

4. A Work with Three or More Authors

Fry, Tony, et al. *Design and the Question of History.* Bloomsbury Academic Press, 2015.

If there are more than two authors, name only the first and add "et al." (meaning "and others").

5. A Work with a Corporate Author

Cracked.com. *The De-Textbook: The Stuff You Didn't Know about the Stuff You Thought You Knew.* Plume-Penguin, 2013.

6. An Anthology or a Compilation

Dark, Larry, editor. *Prize Stories 1997: The O. Henry Awards.* Anchor, 1997.

7. A Work in an Anthology

Sayrafiezadeh, Saïd. "Paranoia." *New American Stories,* edited by Ben Marcus, Vintage Books, 2015, pp. 3–29.

The Elements of Citation

BOOK (MLA)

When you cite a book using MLA style, include the following:

1 Author

2 Title and subtitle

3 Publisher

4 Date of publication

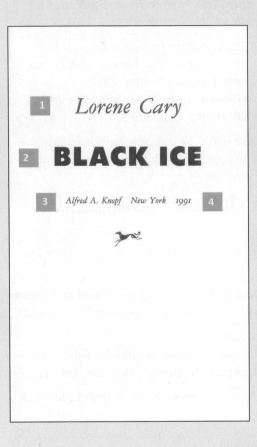

Works Cited entry for a book in MLA style

```
  ┌───1────┐ ┌──2──┐ ┌────3────┐ ┌─4─┐
```
Cary, Lorene. *Black Ice.* Alfred A. Knopf, 1991.

8. **An Introduction, Preface, Foreword, or Afterword**

Buatta, Mario. Foreword. *George Stacey and the Creation of American Chic*, by Maureen Footer, Rizzoli Press, 2014.

9. **A Multivolume Work**

Corcoran, Kevin, and Joel Fischer, editors. *Measures for Clinical Practice and Research: A Sourcebook*. Vol 1., Oxford UP, 2013. 2 vols.

10. **An Edition Other Than the First**

Charters, Ann, editor. *The Story and Its Writer: An Introduction to Short Fiction*. 9th ed., Bedford/St. Martin's, 2015.

11. **A Translation**

Modi, Narendra. *A Journey: Poems by Narendra Modi*. Translated by Ravi Mantha, Rupa Publications, 2014.

12. **A Republished Book**

Bellamy, Edward. *Looking Backward*. 1888. BiblioBazaar, 2008.

NOTE: The only information about original publication you need to provide is the publication date, which appears immediately after the title.

13. **A Book in a Series**

Sutton, Matthew Avery. *Jerry Falwell and the Rise of the Religious Right: A Brief History with Documents*. Bedford/St. Martin's, 2013. The Bedford Series in History and Culture.

The series title goes after the publication information.

14. **An Article from a Journal**

Manzi, Jim. "The New American System." *National Affairs*, vol. 1, no. 19, Spring 2014, pp. 3–24.

15. **An Article from a Daily Newspaper**

Doctorow, E. L. "Quick Cuts: The Novel Follows Film into a World of Fewer Words." *New York Times*, 15 Mar. 1999, p. B 1+.

16. **An Article from a Magazine**

Sanneh, Kelefa. "Skin in the Game." *The New Yorker*, 24 Mar. 2014, pp. 48–55.

17. **Anonymous Works**

Keep Walking, This Doesn't Concern You: The Internet's Favourite Memes. Ebury Press, 2016.

"The March Almanac." *Atlantic Monthly*, Mar. 1995, p. 20.

18. **A Review**

    Jackson, Lawrence. "The Vampire: The Fickle Career of Carl Van Vechten." Review of *The Tastemaker: Carl Van Vechten and the Birth of Modern America*, by Edward White. *Harper's Magazine*, Apr. 2014, pp. 89–94.

19. **An Article in a Reference Work**

    "Child Abuse." *Mosby's Medical Dictionary*, 10th ed., Elsevier, 2017.

20. **A Government Publication**

    United States. Congress. Committees on Foreign Relations of the U.S. Senate and the International Relations of the U.S. House of Representatives. *Annual Report on International Religious Freedom: 2000*. Government Printing Office, 2000.

21. **An Unpublished Manuscript**

    Leahy, Ellen. "An Investigation of the Computerization of Information Systems in a Family Planning Program." MS thesis, University of Massachusetts Amherst, 2010.

22. **A Letter to the Editor**

    Starr, Evva. "Local Reporting Thrives in High Schools." *The Washington Post*, 4 Apr. 2014. Letter.

23. **Personal Correspondence**

    Bennett, David. Letter to the author. 3 Mar. 2017.

24. **A Cartoon or a Comic Strip**

    Ziegler, Jack. "Tai Chi vs. Chai Tea." *The New Yorker*, 14 Apr. 2014, p. 51. Cartoon.

    Henley, Marian. "Maxine." *Valley Advocate*, 25 Feb. 2010, p. 39. Comic strip.

Online Sources

25. **A Web Site**

    Glazier, Loss Pequeño, director. *Electronic Poetry Center*. State U of New York at Buffalo, 2017, epc.buffalo.edu/.

Include the name of the author or editor of the Web site when this information is available; otherwise, begin the entry with the name of the Web site in italics, followed by a period; the name of the Web site, followed by a comma; and the date of publication or last update. Then list the URL, without http://. If the Web site does not have an update date or publication date, include your date of access at the end (see the second example in item 26).

26. **A Short Work from a Web Site**

Enzinna, Wes. "Syria's Unknown Revolution." *Pulitzer Center on Crisis Reporting*, 24 Nov. 2015, pulitzercenter.org/projects/middle-east-syria-enzinna-war-rojava.

Bali, Karan. "Kishore Kumar." *Upperstall.com*, upperstall.com/profile/kishore-kumar/. Accessed 10 Oct. 2017.

27. **An Online Book**

Euripides. *The Trojan Women*. Translated by Gilbert Murray, Oxford UP, 1915. *Internet Sacred Text Archive*, 2011, www.sacred-texts.com/cla/eurip/troj_w.htm.

In this case, the book had been previously published, and information about its original publication was included at the site.

28. **An Article from an Online Journal**

Bryson, Devin. "The Rise of a New Senegalese Cultural Philosophy?" *African Studies Quarterly*, vol. 14, no. 3, Mar. 2014, pp. 33–56, asq.africa.ufl.edu/files/Volume-14-Issue-3-Bryson.pdf.

29. **An Article from a Database**

Coles, Kimberly Anne. "The Matter of Belief in John Donne's Holy Sonnets." *Renaissance Quarterly*, vol. 68, no. 3, Fall 2015, pp. 899–931. *JSTOR*, doi:10.1086/683855.

30. **A Personal E-mail Communication**

Franz, Kenneth. "Re: Species Reintroduction." Received by Selena Anderson, 18 Sept. 2017.

31. **A Posting to a Social Media Site**

kevincannon. "Portrait of Norris Hall in #Savannah, GA—home (for a few more months, anyway) of #SCAD's sequential art department." *Instagram*, Mar. 2014, www.instagram.com/p/lgmqk4i6DC/.

@grammarphobia (Patricia T. O'Conner and Steward Kellerman). "Is 'if you will,' like, a verbal tic? http://goo.gl/oYrTYP #English #language #grammar #etymology #usage #linguistics #WOTD." *Twitter*, 14 Mar. 2016, 9:12 a.m., twitter.com/grammarphobia.

Treat these as short works from a Web site. List the poster's handle as the author name, and include the poster's real name in parentheses, if available. Use the text accompanying the post as the title, in quotation marks, if such text is available. If the post has no title or text, use the label *Post*.

The Elements of Citation

ARTICLE FROM A WEB SITE (MLA)

When you cite a brief article from a Web site using MLA style, include the following:

1 Author

2 Title of work

3 Title of Web site

4 Date of publication or latest update

5 URL

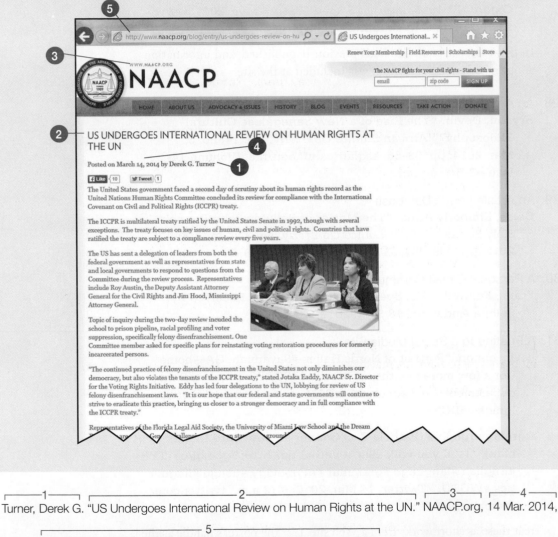

```
┌──1──┐  ┌──────────────────────────2─────────────────────────────┐  ┌──3──┐  ┌──4──┐
Turner, Derek G. "US Undergoes International Review on Human Rights at the UN." NAACP.org, 14 Mar. 2014,

        ┌────────────────────5────────────────────┐
        www.naacp.org/blog/entry/us-undergoes-review-on-human-rights.
```

Other Sources

32. A Lecture

   Grant, Adam. 92Y Talks. "Giving: The Secret of Getting
   Ahead." 92nd Street Y, New York, NY, 16 Apr. 2014.

33. A Film or Video

   Bale, Christian, performer. *The Big Short*. Directed by Adam
   McKay, Paramount Pictures, 2015.

   Jenkins, Barry, director. *Moonlight*. Performances by Trevante
   Rhodes, André Holland, Naomie Harris, Janelle Monáe, and
   Mahershala Ali, A24, 2016.

34. A Television or Radio Program

   "The London Season." *Downton Abbey*, performances by Shir-
   ley MacLaine and Elizabeth McGovern, PBS, 23 Feb. 2014.

   "Obama's Failures Have Made Millennials Give Up
   Hope." *The Rush Limbaugh Show*, narrated by
   Rush Limbaugh, Premiere Radio Networks, 14 Apr.
   2014, www.rushlimbaugh.com/daily/2014/04/14/
   obama_s_failures_have_made_millennials_give_up_hope.

35. A Performance

   Piano Concerto no. 3. By Ludwig van Beethoven, conducted by
   Andris Nelsons, performances by Paul Lewis and Boston Symphony Orchestra, Symphony Hall, Boston, MA, 9 Oct. 2015.

36. An Interview

   Bacharach, Sam. "Where Money Meets Morale." Interview by
   Alexa Von Tobel. *Inc.*, Apr. 2014, pp. 48–49.

If the interviewer's name is not given or if there is no title to the
interview, these elements may be left out.

   Phillips, Adam. "The Art of Nonfiction No. 7." Interview. *The
   Paris Review*, Spring 2014, pp. 29–54.

An interview conducted by the author of the paper would be documented as follows:

   Hines, Gregory. Personal interview. 29 Mar. 1987.

A broadcast interview would be documented as follows:

   Hines, Gregory. Interview by Charlie Rose. *Charlie Rose*, PBS,
   30 Jan. 2001.

The Elements of Citation

ARTICLE FROM A WEB SITE (MLA)

When you cite a brief article from a database using MLA style, include the following:

1 Author

2 Title of article

3 Title of periodical, volume and issue numbers

4 Date of publication

5 Inclusive pages

6 Name of database

7 URL (or DOI, if available)

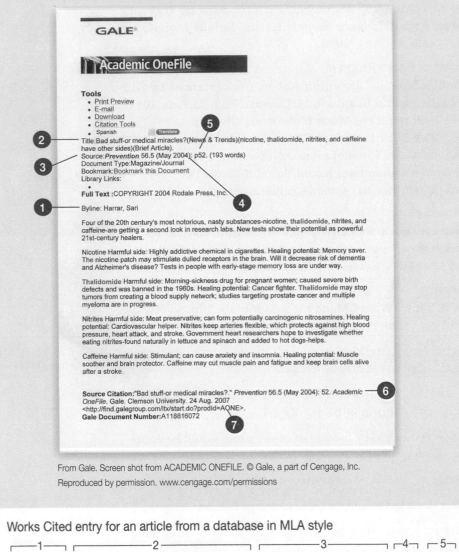

From Gale. Screen shot from ACADEMIC ONEFILE. © Gale, a part of Cengage, Inc.
Reproduced by permission. www.cengage.com/permissions

Works Cited entry for an article from a database in MLA style

┌──1──┐ ┌────────2────────┐ ┌────────3────────┐ ┌4┐ ┌5┐
Harrar, Sari. "Bad Stuff — or Medical Miracles?" *Prevention*, vol. 56, no. 5. 2004, p. 52.
      └────6────┘ ┌──────────────7──────────────┐
      Academic OneFile, find.galegroup.com/itx/start.do?prodID=AONE.

MLA-Style Annotated Bibliography

An annotated bibliography is a list of sources that includes the usual bibliographic information followed by a paragraph describing and evaluating each source. Its purpose is to provide information about each source in a bibliography so that the reader has an overview of the resources related to a given topic.

For each source in an annotated bibliography, the same bibliographic information included in a Works Cited or References list is provided, alphabetized by author. Each reference also has a short paragraph that describes the work, its main focus, and, if appropriate, the methodology used in or the style of the work. An annotation might note special features such as tables or illustrations. Usually an annotation evaluates the source by analyzing its usefulness, reliability, and overall significance for understanding the topic. An annotation might include some information on the credentials of the author or the organization that produced it.

A Sample Annotation Using the MLA Citation Style

Warner, Marina. "Pity the Stepmother." *New York Times*, 12 May 1991, www.nytimes.com/1991/05/12/opinion/pity-the-stepmother.html.

The author asserts that many fairy tales feature absent or cruel mothers, transformed by romantic editors such as the Grimm brothers into stepmothers because the idea of a wicked mother desecrated an ideal. Warner argues that figures in fairy tales should be viewed in their historical context and that social conditions often affected the way that motherhood figured in fairy tales. Warner, a novelist and author of books on the images of Joan of Arc and the Virgin Mary, writes persuasively about the social roots of a fairy-tale archetype.

APA style does not call for annotated citations. However, some instructors may require an annotated bibliography, so with either MLA or APA, follow your instructor's guidelines.

MLA Paper Format

Print your essay on one side of 8½-by-11-inch white computer paper, double-spacing throughout. Leave margins of 1 to 1½ inches on all sides, and indent each paragraph one-half inch or five spaces. Unless a formal outline is part of the paper, a separate title page is unnecessary. Instead, beginning about one inch from the top of the first page and flush with the left margin, type your name, the instructor's name, the course title, and the date, each on a separate line; then double-space and type the title, capitalizing the first letter of the words of the title except for articles, prepositions, and conjunctions. Double-space and type the body of the paper.

Number all pages at the top-right corner, typing your last name before each page number in case pages are mislaid. If an outline is included, number its pages with lowercase roman numerals.

MLA-Style Sample Research Paper

Hedden 1

Kathleen Hedden
Mrs. Swanson
English 102-14
October 29, 2010

Competitive Foods and the Obesity Epidemic

It is difficult these days to watch television or read a newspaper without hearing about the problem of childhood obesity in the United States. Opinions differ as to the best solution for dealing with this problem that threatens the health of a rising generation, but few would deny that it is a problem.

Thomas R. Frieden, head of the Centers for Disease Control and Prevention in Atlanta and thus one of the leading health officials in the country, is among those who have used the term *epidemic* to describe what is happening: "What has changed, in just the course of a generation, is that childhood obesity has become an epidemic," he says. "In the 1960s, 5 percent of children were overweight. Today, nearly 20 percent are" (Frieden, Dietz, and Collins). Concern about obesity is concern not just for how our children—and our future adults—look, but for their present and future health. According to the Robert Wood Johnson Foundation, a charitable organization whose goal is to improve the health of all Americans, the rate of obesity for those between the ages of six and eleven has quadrupled in three decades. Children are being diagnosed with what used to be considered adult diseases, like high blood pressure, adult-onset diabetes, and gallstones. The Foundation reports, "If we don't succeed in reversing this epidemic, we are in danger of raising the first generation of American children who will live sicker and die younger than their parents' generation" (259–60).

The problem of childhood obesity will have to be attacked on several fronts. Parents and other caregivers have to be

Hedden follows "presenting stock issues" approach.

Frieden's name and position lend authority to the quotation.

Defining the problem (presenting evidence)

Frieden is quoted, but all three authors need to be cited.

Establishing a need for a solution

Foundation as author, mentioned in text, so page number only needed in parentheses

Hedden 2

educated and motivated to control children's diet and physical
activity. Because of the number of hours that most children
spend in school five days a week for a large part of the year,
however, the CDC's *Morbidity and Mortality Weekly Report*
has stated that "schools are in a unique position to help improve youth dietary behaviors and prevent and reduce obesity"
(Centers for Disease Control).

The federal government has long subsidized the nation's
school lunch program. The National School Lunch Program has
been in existence since 1946 "as a measure of national security, to
safeguard the health and well-being of the Nation's children and
to encourage the domestic consumption of nutritious agricultural
commodities and other food" (qtd. in Center for Science 230).

One problem now is the sale of what are called competitive
foods, or those foods and beverages sold in schools but outside
of the meal program supported by the federal government.
They may be sold through vending machines, snack bars, school
stores, or in a la carte lines, but they do not have to meet the
nutrition standards that must be met by cafeteria food. They
are not supposed to be available in the food service area during
lunch, but they sometimes are and in other cases are close by.

Dr. Heather Hartline-Grafton, Senior Nutrition Policy Analyst for the Food Research and Action Center (FRAC), explains
how this competitive food contributes to the obesity epidemic:

> Competitive foods are often energy-dense, nutrient-poor
> items, and their availability at school undermines efforts
> to promote healthy diets and prevent obesity. Not only
> do the sales of competitive foods and beverages decrease
> participation in the school meal programs, but the sales
> are often subsidized by school meal reimbursements. (1)

Competitive foods are a widespread presence in schools: They are
available in 73% of elementary schools, 97% of middle schools, and
100% of high schools, most often in the form of vending machines
and a la carte lines. Although there are nutritious competitive
options, those do not sell as well as the ones high in sugar, salt, and
calories (Hartline-Grafton 2–3).

While the U.S. Department of Agriculture has the power to
regulate the food served in the school lunch program, it currently
has little power to regulate competitive foods. That power

The organization is
the author. No page
number because
accessed online.

Claim

Support

One work quoted
in another. The
citation is to the
work Katie actually
used.

Support

Support

Support

Author not men-
tioned in text,
so her name is
included with
page number
in parentheses.

Hedden 3

depends in part on what foods are defined as foods of minimal nutritional value (FMNVs). Hartline-Grafton explains:

Block quota-
tion. Notice
that the whole
quotation is
indented, there
are no quotation
marks, and the
period comes
before the
parenthesis.

> FMNVs are defined as foods providing less than five percent of recommended intakes for eight key nutrients. Examples include carbonated soda, gum, hard candies, and jelly beans. Other competitive foods, including candy bars, chips, and ice cream, are not considered FMNVs (and therefore not under USDA authority) and may be sold in the cafeteria during meal periods. In short, unlike the federal school lunch and breakfast programs, competitive foods are, for the most part, exempt from federal nutrition standards and regulation. (2)

If it is obvious that many competitive foods are a danger to our children's health and well-being and that they are beyond the control of even the USDA's regulations, why are these foods not removed from schools?

Explains why
problem exists

One simple answer is because students like them and buy them. Most students are in the habit of eating fast food away from school and see no problem eating it at school. They like the high-fat, high-sugar foods that do not conform to the regulations that school cafeterias must follow.

If students are not willing to monitor their own food intake and the USDA cannot, why do schools continue to allow these foods lacking in nutritional value to be sold? Part of the answer is that some school districts in some states have chosen to regulate the competitive foods sold in the district or to eliminate them entirely. The economics of school meals, however, are much more complicated than one might think. Parke Wilde and Mary Kennedy, both researchers in the Friedman School of Nutrition Science and Policy at Tufts University in Boston, explain some of the complexities in an article entitled "The Economics of a Healthy School Meal." Schools are reimbursed a set amount for each lunch subsidized by the federal government. Even when better-off students pay for their lunch, the federal government pays its part. Other students, depending on their parents' income, pay a reduced rate or nothing at all. Even that set formula, however, is affected by competitive foods. Students and their parents are pushing for more nutritious

Hedden 4

foods than are required by the federal government, and the districts must balance the money lost when students don't eat school lunches with that gained by selling competitive foods. Wilde and Kennedy write,

> Any successful business must understand the economic interactions across its product lines, but these interactions are particularly intense for a school food service. A child who consumes a reimbursable lunch and breakfast will have lower demand for *a la carte* items, while a child who skips a real meal may be hungrier for a snack. This interaction means that school food service decisions about competitive foods strongly affect the federal school meals program, and vice versa.

By that logic, if competitive foods were not available, students might opt for the healthier alternative of the school meal.

In September 2010, Congress passed the Healthy, Hunger-Free Kids Act of 2010, a huge step forward in schools' ability to control the foods served at school. The act was designed to "commit an additional $4.5 billion to child-nutrition programs over the next 10 years and implement the most sweeping changes to those programs in decades." In response to the problem of competitive foods, it "directs the U.S. Department of Agriculture to set new nutrition standards for all food served in schools, from lunchrooms to vending machines" (Eisler).

Ironically, it is not a foregone conclusion that all schools will benefit from this new legislation. They have to adopt the new nutrition standards, which the Institute of Medicine will recommend and the U.S. Department of Agriculture will write. Schools that adopt the new nutrition requirements will get an increase of six cents per meal in their federal reimbursement rate, the first increase since 1973 and one that has long been needed (Eisler). Stipends are also available for those schools that need to upgrade their kitchens to accommodate preparing the more nutritious meals (Wilde and Kennedy).

It seems obvious that all school districts across the country should adopt the new nutritional standards that are being presented to them with the additional incentive of getting more money per meal for school lunches and breakfasts than they currently get. The new standards will remove from schools

No page number because an electronic source.

Solution

Author not identified in text. No page number because electronic source.

Conclusion

Hedden 5

competitive foods that are particularly unhealthy and replace them with foods that fall under the nutrition guidelines of the new act. Students may not get all of the choices of foods that they would like, but parents, teachers, and school officials — and the students themselves — will know that schools are contributing less to the problem of childhood and adolescent obesity.

Hedden 6

Works Cited

Center for Science in the Public Interest. "Improving Kids' Nutrition: An Action Kit for Parents and Citizens." *Food, Inc.: How Industrial Food Is Making Us Sicker, Fatter and Poorer — And What You Can Do about It*, edited by Karl Weber, PublicAffairs, 2009, pp. 227–57.

Centers for Disease Control and Prevention. "Competitive Foods and Beverages Available for Purchase in Secondary Schools — Selected Sites, United States, 2006." *MMWR Weekly*, 29 Aug. 2008, pp. 935–38. *CDC*, www.cdc.gov/mmwr/preview/mmwrhtml/mm5734a2.htm.

Eisler, Peter. "Sweeping School Lunch Bill Clears Senate Panel." *USA Today*, 24 Mar. 2010, usatoday30.usatoday.com/news/education/2010-03-24-school-lunch-safety_N.htm.

Frieden, Thomas R., et al. "Reducing Childhood Obesity through Policy Change: Acting Now to Prevent Obesity." *Health Affairs*, vol. 29, no. 3, pp. 357–63. *ResearchGate,* www.researchgate.net/publication/41657054.

Hartline-Grafton, Heather. "How Competitive Foods in Schools Impact Student Health, School Meal Programs, and Students from Low-Income Families." *Issue Briefs for Child Nutrition Reauthorization*, no. 5, Food Research and Action Center, 2010, pp. 1–3, www.frac.org/pdf/CNR05_competitivefoods.pdf.

Robert Wood Johnson Foundation. "Childhood Obesity: The Challenge." *Food, Inc.: How Industrial Food Is Making Us Sicker, Fatter and Poorer — And What You Can Do about It*, edited by Karl Weber, PublicAffairs, 2009, pp. 259–61.

Wilde, Parke, and Mary Kennedy. "The Economics of a Healthy School Meal." *Choices*, vol. 24, no. 3. *ResearchGate*, www.researchgate.net/publication/227352555.

Margin notes:

Begin Works Cited on a new page.

A work in an anthology

A journal article accessed online

A newspaper article accessed online

A document accessed online

APA In-Text Citations

Instructors in the social sciences might prefer the citation system of the American Psychological Association (APA), which is used in the sample paper on women in the military (pp. 428–436). Like the MLA system, the APA system calls for a parenthetical citation in the text of the paper following any quotations from your sources. The APA only recommends that page numbers be included for paraphrases or summaries, but you should provide page numbers for these anyway unless your instructor advises you that they are not necessary. In the text of your paper, immediately after any quotation, paraphrase, or idea you need to document, insert a parenthetical mention of the author's last name and the page number on which the material appears. Unlike the MLA system, the APA system also includes the year of publication in the parenthetical reference, using a comma to separate the items within the citation and using "p." or "pp." before the page number(s). Even if the source has a month of publication, only the year is included in the parenthetical citation. Here is an example:

> As of now, women are restricted from 30% of Army assignments and 1% of Air Force assignments (Baer, 2003, p. 1A).

The parenthetical reference tells the reader that the information in this sentence comes from page 1A of the 2003 work by Baer that appears on the References page at the end of the paper. The complete publication information that a reader would need to locate Baer's work will appear on the References page:

> Baer, S. (2003, March 3). In Iraq war, women would serve closer to front lines than in past. *The Baltimore Sun*, p. 1A.

If the author's name is mentioned in the same sentence in your text, the year in which the work was published follows it, in parentheses, and the page number only is placed in parentheses at the end of the sentence.

> According to Baer (2003) of *The Baltimore Sun*, as of now, women are restricted from 30% of Army assignments and 1% of Air Force assignments (p. 1A).

In the APA system, it is appropriate to include only the last name of the author unless you have more than one author with the same name in your list of references, in which case you would include the first initial of the author.

If your list of references includes more than one work written by the same author in the same year, cite the first work as "a" and the second as "b." For example, Baer's second article of 2003 would be cited in your paper like this: (Baer, 2003b).

If a work has two authors, list both in your sentence or in the parentheses, using "and" between them. In these examples from the women in combat paper, there is no page number because the source is a short work from a Web site:

> The fall 2000 suggestion from DACOWITS included a possible recruiting slogan: "A gynecologist on every aircraft carrier!" (Yoest & Yoest, 2002).

> Yoest and Yoest (2002) recall the fall 2000 suggestion from DACOWITS for a possible recruiting slogan: "A gynecologist on every aircraft carrier!"

If there are three to five authors, list them all by last name the first time they are referred to, and after that, by the last name of the first author and the term "et al." (meaning "and others"): (Sommers, Mylroie, Donnelly, & Hill, 2001); (Sommers et al., 2001). Also use the last name of the first author and "et al." when there are more than five authors, which is often the case in the sciences and social sciences.

If no author is given, use the name of the work where you would normally use the author's name, placing the names of short works in quotation marks and italicizing those of book-length works.

When using electronic sources, follow as much as possible the rules for parenthetical documentation of print sources. If no author's name is given, cite by the title of the work. If no date is given, use the abbreviation "n.d." instead. For a long work, if there are no page numbers, as is often the case with electronic sources, give paragraph numbers if the work has numbered paragraphs, or, if the work is divided into sections, the paragraph number within that section:

> Jamison (1999) warned about the moral issues associated with stem cell research, particularly the guilt that some parents felt about letting their children's cells be used (Parental Guilt section, para. 2).

Remember that the purpose of parenthetical documentation is to help a reader locate the information that you are citing.

At times, you will need to cite one work that is quoted in another or a work from an anthology. For the former, the parenthetical documentation provides author's name, year of publication, and page number of the source you actually used, preceded by the words "as cited in":

> The female soldier "is, on the average, about five inches shorter than the male soldier, has half the upper body strength, lower aerobic capacity and 37 percent less muscle mass" (as cited in Owens, 1997, Anatomy section, para. 2).

A work in an anthology is cited parenthetically by the name of the author of the work, not the editor of the anthology.

APA List of References

Following are examples of the bibliographical forms you are most likely to employ if you are using the American Psychological Association (APA) system for documenting sources. If you need the format for a type of publication not listed here, consult the *Publication Manual of the American Psychological Association*, Sixth Edition (2010).

If you are used to the Modern Language Association (MLA) system for documenting sources, take a moment to notice some of the key differences. In APA style, authors and editors are listed by last name and initials only, and the year comes immediately after the author's or editor's name instead of at or near the end of the entry. Titles in general are not capitalized in the conventional way. The overall structure of each entry, however, will be familiar: author, title, publication information.

Directory of APA Reference Entries

Print Sources

1. A Book by a Single Author

Isreal, J. (2012). *Democratic enlightenment: Philosophy, revolution, and human rights, 1750–1790.* Oxford, England: Oxford University Press.

2. Multiple Works by the Same Author in the Same Year

Gardner, H. (1982a). *Art, mind, and brain: A cognitive approach to creativity.* New York, NY: Basic Books.

Gardner, H. (1982b). *Developmental psychology: An introduction* (2nd ed.). Boston, MA: Little, Brown.

3. A Work by Two to Seven Authors or Editors

Lester, D., & Rogers, J. R. (2012). *Crisis intervention and counseling by telephone and the Internet* (3rd ed.). Springfield, IL: Charles C. Thomas.

NOTE: List the names of *all* the authors or editors, with an ampersand before the last one. For eight or more authors, list the first six authors followed by an ellipsis (three dots), and then list the last author's name. In these citations, there is no ampersand before the last author.

4. A Work by a Corporate Author

Congressional Quarterly, Inc. (2014). *Issues for debate in American public policy: selections from* CQ Researcher (14th ed.). Los Angeles, CA: CQ Press.

5. An Anthology or Compilation

Strayed, C., & Atwan, R. (Eds.). (2013). *The best American essays 2013.* New York, NY: Houghton Mifflin Harcourt.

6. A Work in an Anthology

Yang, V. W. (2013). Field notes on hair. In J. C. Oates & R. Atwan (Eds.), *Best American essays 2013* (pp. 217–224). Boston, MA: Houghton Mifflin Harcourt.

7. An Introduction, Preface, Foreword, or Afterword

Atwan, R. (2013). Foreword. In J. C. Oates & R. Atwan (Eds.), *Best American essays 2013* (pp. ix–xiv). Boston, MA: Houghton Mifflin Harcourt.

8. An Edition Other Than the First

Litin, S. (Ed.). (2009). *Mayo Clinic family health book* (4th ed.). Des Moines, IA: Time Inc. Home Entertainment.

9. A Translation

Khalifa, K. (2008). *In praise of hatred* (L. Price, Trans.). New York, NY: Thomas Dunne Books-St. Martin's Press.

10. A Republished Book

Dickens, C. (2013). *Great expectations.* New York, NY: Penguin. (Original work published 1861)

The Elements of Citation

BOOK (APA)

When you cite a book using APA style, include the following:

1 Author

2 Date of publication

3 Title and subtitle

4 City and state of publication

5 Publisher

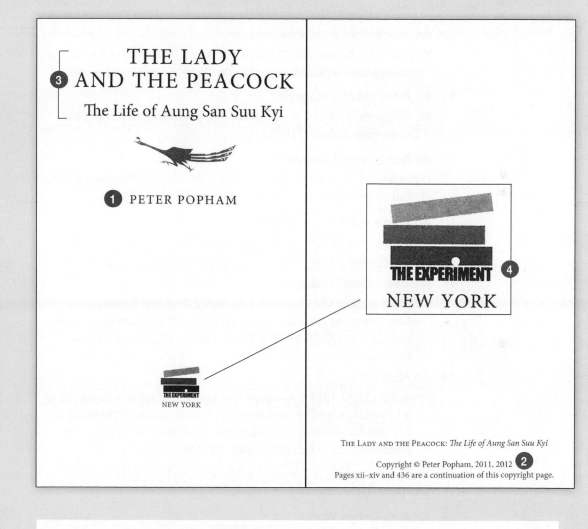

Reference list entry for a book in APA style

```
          ┌─────1─────┐  ┌──2──┐ ┌─────────────────3──────────────────┐
          Bordo, S Popham, P. (2012). The lady and the peacock: The life of Aung San Suu Kyi.
              ┌────4────┐ ┌───────────5───────────┐
              New York, NY: The Experiment. New York, NY
```

11. **A Book in a Series**

     Stone, M. (2013). *The Fascist revolution in Italy: A brief history with documents. The Bedford series in history and culture.* Boston, MA: Bedford/St. Martin's.

12. **A Multivolume Work**

     Helfgott, J. B. (Ed.). (2013). *Criminal psychology* (Vols. 1–4). Santa Barbara, CA: Praeger.

13. **An Article from a Daily Newspaper**

     Yeginsu, C., & Arango, T. (2014, 17 Apr.). Turkey greets Twitter delegation with list of demands. *New York Times*, p. A6.

14. **An Article from a Magazine**

     McWilliams, J. (2014, Spring). Loving animals to death. *The American Scholar*, 18–30.

15. **An Article from a Journal**

     Purchase, H. C. (2014). Twelve years of diagrams research. *Journal of Visual Languages & Computing, 25*(2), 57–75.

16. **An Article in a Reference Work**

     Chichinguane (2014). In P. Monaghan, *Encyclopedia of goddesses and heroines* (p. 6). Novato, CA: New World Library.

17. **A Government Publication**

     U.S. Department of Homeland Security, Federal Emergency Management Agency (2009, August). *Flood insurance claims handbook* (FEMA F-687). Washington, DC: Government Printing Office.

18. **An Abstract**

     Fritz, M. (1990/1991). A comparison of social interactions using a friendship awareness activity. *Education and Training in Mental Retardation, 25,* 352–359. Abstract retrieved from *Psychological Abstracts,* 1991, 78. (Abstract No. 11474)

     When the dates of the original publication and of the abstract differ, give both dates separated by a slash.

19. **An Anonymous Work**

     The status of women: Different but the same. (1992–1993). *Zontian, 73*(3), 5.

20. **A Review**

     Huff, T. E. (2013). Why some nations succeed. [Review of the book *Why nations fail: The origins of power, prosperity &*

poverty, by D. Acemoglu & J. A. Robinson]. *Contemporary Sociology, 42*(1), 55–59.

Start with the author of the review, followed by the year and the title (if any). Provide the title of the book or film being reviewed in brackets, along with the title of the book or the year of the film.

21. A Letter to the Editor

Pritchett, J. T., & Kellner, C. H. (1993). Comment on spontaneous seizure activity [Letter to the editor]. *Journal of Nervous and Mental Disease, 181,* 138–139.

22. Personal Correspondence

B. Ehrenreich (personal communication, August 7, 2010).
(B. Ehrenreich, personal communication, August 7, 2010.)

Cite all personal communications to you (such as letters, memos, e-mails, and telephone conversations) in text only, *without* listing them among the references. The phrasing of your sentences will determine which of the two above forms to use.

23. An Unpublished Manuscript

McIntosh, P. (2008). *White privilege and male privilege: A personal account of coming to see correspondences through work in women's studies.* Working Paper 189. Unpublished manuscript, Center for Research on Women, Wellesley College, Wellesley, MA.

24. Proceedings of a Meeting, Published

Guerrero, R. (1972/1973). Possible effects of the periodic abstinence method. In W. A. Uricchio & M. K. Williams (Eds.), *Proceedings of a Research Conference on Natural Family Planning* (pp. 96–105). Washington, DC: Human Life Foundation.

If the date of the symposium or conference is different from the date of publication, give both, separated by a slash. If the proceedings are published annually, treat the reference like a periodical article.

Electronic Sources

25. An Article from an Online Periodical with a DOI

Chattopadhyay, P. (2003). Can dissimilarity lead to positive outcomes? The influence of open versus closed minds. *Journal of Organizational Behavior, 24,* 295–312. doi:10.1002/job.118

If the article duplicates the version that appeared in a print periodical, use the same basic primary journal reference. See "An Article from a Periodical." Some online articles have a "digital object identifier" (DOI). Use the DOI at the end of the entry in place of the URL.

26. **An Article from an Online Periodical without a DOI**

    Riordan, V. (2001, January 1). Verbal-performance IQ discrepancies in children attending a child and adolescent psychiatry clinic. *Child and Adolescent Psychiatry On-Line.* Retrieved from http://www.priory.com/psych/iq.htm

    If an article does not have a DOI, after the publication information add the exact URL for the article or the URL of the home page of the journal.

27. **A Nonperiodical Web Document**

    Munro, K. (2001, February). *Changing your body image.* Retrieved from http://www.kalimunro.com/article_changing_body_image.html

    In general, follow this format: author's name, the date of publication (if no publication date is available, use "n.d."), the title of the document in italics, and the source's URL.

28. **A Chapter or Section in a Web Document**

    National Council of Welfare, Canada. (1998). Other issues related to poverty lines. In *A new poverty line: Yes, no or maybe?* (chap. 5). Retrieved from http://www.ncwcnbes.net/htmdocument/reportnewpovline/chap5.htm

29. **An E-mail**

    Do not include personal communications such as e-mails in your list of references. See "Personal Correspondence."

30. **A Message Posted to a Newsgroup**

    Isaacs, K. (2008, January 20). Re: Philosophical roots of psychology [Electronic newsgroup message]. Retrieved from news://sci.psychology.psychotherapy.moderated

    Include an online posting in your reference list only if the posting is archived and is retrievable. Otherwise, cite an online posting as a personal communication and do not include it in the list of references. Care should be taken when citing electronic discussions. In general, they are not scholarly sources.

The Elements of Citation

ARTICLE FROM A WEB SITE (APA)

When you cite an article from a Web site using APA style, include the following:

1 Author

2 Date of publication or most recent update

3 Title and subtitle

4 Title of section (if any)

5 Date of access (only if content is likely to change)

6 URL of document

Common Sense Media

Reference list entry for a brief article from a Web site in APA style

┌─────1─────┐ ┌──────2──────┐ ┌──────────────────────3──────────────────────┐
Mendoza, K. (2014, March 31). Webinar rewind: How to implement digital citizenship districtwide.

┌──────────4──────────┐   ┌────────────────6────────────────┐
In Common Sense Education. Retrieved from http://www.commonsensemedia.org

/education/blog/webinar-rewind-how-to-implement-digital-citizenship-districtwide

The Elements of Citation

ARTICLE FROM A DATABASE (APA)

When you cite an article from a database using APA style, include the following:

1 Author

2 Date of publication

3 Title of article

4 Name of periodical

5 Volume and issue numbers

6 Page numbers

7 DOI (if available)

8 URL for journal's home page (if no DOI)

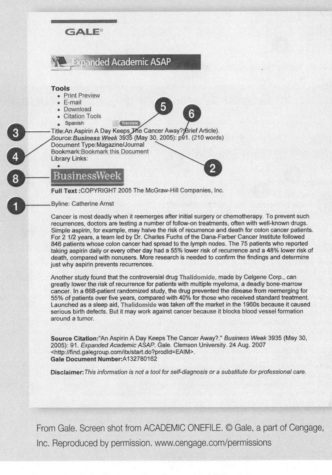

From Gale. Screen shot from ACADEMIC ONEFILE. © Gale, a part of Cengage, Inc. Reproduced by permission. www.cengage.com/permissions

---

Reference list entry for an article from a database in APA style

┌—1—┐ ┌——2——┐ ┌————————3————————┐ ┌———4———┐

Arnst, C. (2005, May 30). An aspirin a day keeps the cancer away? *Business Week*

┌5┐ ┌6┐ ┌————————8————————┐

3935, 91. Retrieved from http://businessweek.com/

31. **An Article from a Database**

Lopez, F. G., Melendez, M. C., Sauer, E. M., Berger, E., & Wyss-
mann, J. (1998). Internal working models, self-reported problems, and help-seeking attitudes among college students.
Journal of Counseling Psychology, 45, 79–83. Retrieved from
http://www.apa.org/journals/cou

To cite material retrieved from a database, follow the format appropriate to the work retrieved. If the article has a DOI, include this at the
end of the entry. If the article does not have a DOI, include the URL
of the periodical's home page at the end of the entry.

Other Sources

32. **A Film**

Wachowski, A., & Wachowski, L. (Writers/Directors), & Silver,
J. (Producer). (1999). *The matrix* [Motion picture]. United
States: Warner Bros.

Include the name and the function of the originator or primary contributor (director or producer). Identify the work as a motion picture,
or if you viewed a videocassette or DVD, include the appropriate label
in brackets. Include the country of origin and the studio. If the motion
picture is of limited circulation, provide the name and address of the
distributor in parentheses at the end of the reference.

33. **A Television Series**

Jones, R. (Producer). (1990). *Exploring consciousness* [Television
series]. Boston, MA: WGBH.

APA-Style Sample Research Paper

The following paper shows APA citations in the context of an actual text and
the format for several different entries on the References page. Angela has used
quotations sparingly and has instead made extensive use of summary and paraphrase. Often there is no page number in her parenthetical citations. That is
because she was drawing from short online sources in which the paragraphs are
not numbered but in which it is easy to find the material she refers to.

The format of the title page illustrates APA guidelines, as does the running
head that is on each page.

Notice that Angela's thesis appears as the last sentence in her first paragraph. She carefully documents the restrictions on women in the U.S. military
and argues why those restrictions are appropriate.

Women in Combat 1

The Controversy over Women in Combat

Angela Mathers
English 103-13
Ms. Carter
April 7, 2011

Women in Combat 2

Abstract

Women have served in the U.S. military since World War I. Although many barriers to their complete participation in all phases of military service have been broken, women are still appropriately restricted from direct ground combat assignments. Because women are held to a lower physical standard than men, men in their units cannot trust their ability to perform on the battlefield. One argument in favor of combat assignments for women has been that the lack of combat experience stands in the way of their progressing through the ranks. Such careerism, however, goes against a soldier's sworn duty, and there are ways to advance in the military other than through combat service. The social and logistical problems created are an argument against women's serving in close quarters with men. Pregnancy among some enlisted women is also highly likely and poses its own medical and logistical problems. Combat assignments for women would be a threat to the effectiveness and readiness of American troops.

The Controversy over Women in Combat

Throughout the history of the military, the role of women has changed and adapted as the needs of the country have. From Molly Pitcher to Rosie the Riveter, women have always held a place in making the military what it is today. Issues have surfaced in the modern military about the current role of female service members with regard to combat assignments. Positions on submarines, small destroyers, specialized combat teams, and a handful of other assignments are restricted to men-only clubs. The factors determining why women are restricted from these assignments include physical ability, deployability, the cost effectiveness of providing the facilities that women need, and the effect on the overall readiness of the military. Women who desire these assignments, and other opponents of these restrictions, have retorted with reasons that they should be included, the foremost being women's rights and their desire to advance up the ranks of the military. However, women are rightly restricted from direct ground combat assignments to ensure the readiness of the military and the effectiveness of these combat units.

Women were first recruited, and began serving, in the military during World War I because they were needed to fill the clerical, technical, and health care jobs that were left vacant as more men were drafted. All these women, however, were discharged as soon as the war ended. The Women's Army Corps (WAC) was founded during World War II and gave women their own branch of the military. They served in the same jobs as they did in World War I but with the addition of noncombatant pilot assignments. Women did not get their permanent place in the ranks until 1948 when the Women Armed Services Integration Act was passed through Congress, allowing them to serve under the conditions that they were not to hold any rank above colonel, were limited mostly to clerical or health-care jobs, and were not to make up more than 2% of the entire military. They were still limited to their own female-only corps until 1978, when the military was fully integrated and women were allowed to hold any assignment that their male counterparts could except for combat roles. The rules have been relaxed over the years as women have proven themselves in combat support missions, especially in the Persian Gulf War in 1991 ("Women," 2000). They continue to push to be allowed into every job that men hold, and the effect this is having on the military is a fiery issue. According to

Overview of the controversy

Opposing view

Thesis

A history of women in the military from a source accessed through a subscription service

The parenthetical citation shows where paraphrase ends and her ideas begin.

Women in Combat 4

Baer (2003) of *The Baltimore Sun,* as of now, women are restricted from 30% of Army assignments, 38% of Marine assignments, and 1% of Air Force assignments. From the Navy, women are excluded from the special operations SEAL groups. These exclusions are from Military Occupational Specialities (MOS) "whose primary mission is ground combat" as defined by the Pentagon. They are also excluded from Navy submarines and small battleships that do not have the facilities to accommodate women (p. 1A).

There have been many advancements for combat-seeking women since the Persian Gulf War. McDonough (2003), writing for the Associated Press, reports that females are now allowed to fly combat missions in fighter jets and bombers for the Air Force and Navy. They can serve in many combat support roles such as combat Military Police companies. They can also be assigned to chemical specialist units that clean up contaminated areas on the battlefield, and to engineering units that build and repair bridges and runways in high-risk areas. Women can also pilot the Army's Apache assault helicopters over the battlefield during high risk conditions, and pilot troop-carrying helicopters onto the battlefield to deliver troops for a rescue mission during an assault. However, none of these MOSs are in selective special operations units such as Marine Force Recon or Army Airborne Rangers, who serve as the "tip of the spear" in ground combat for missions like Operation Enduring Freedom in Afghanistan or Operation Iraqi Freedom.

The federal government and military have been under pressure from several sides on the issue of women serving in combat roles in the military. There are those that believe that all assignments, no matter how demanding of time, body, talent, and mind, should be open to women as well as men. According to Gerber (2002) of the James MacGregor Burns Academy of Leadership, this is the general consensus of the Defense Advisory Committee on Women in the Services (DACOWITS). It was established in 1951 by General George Marshall but was disbanded when Secretary of Defense Donald Rumsfeld let its charter run out when it came up for renewal in 2002. However, its motives could be called into question as to whether it is rallying for the good of the military and its purposes or pushing its own platform that women should be integrated in all parts just because they believe it is deserved. Former DACOWITS Chairperson Vickie McCall even told the U.S. Air Force in Europe News Service, "You have to understand. We don't report facts, we

Source and year included in text

Page only in parentheses

Author and year in text; no page number because electronic version

A Web site

One source
quoted in
another; source
with two
authors

report perception" (as qtd. in Yoest & Yoest, 2002). DACOWITS has often teamed up with other private women's rights activist groups that believe that the military should be an "equal opportunity employer" along with all other private and public employers.

One cause of concern over women's inclusion in combat units has been the rigorous physical standards these troops must meet in training and in turn on the battlefield. Many studies have been done to prove or disprove a distinction between men's and women's physical capabilities. In the quest for evidence, Col. Patrick Toffler, Director of the United States Military Office of Institutional Research, reported that it had identified 120 physical differences (Owens, 1997, p. 40). The female soldier "is, on the average, about five inches shorter than the male soldier, has half the upper body strength, lower aerobic capacity and 37 percent less muscle mass" (as qtd. in Owens, 1997, p. 38). Leo (1997) reports in *U.S. News and World Report* that the way that the military accommodates for these differences is called "gender norming" and works by lowering the standards that women have to reach to pass the physical fitness tests. For instance, in the Marines, men are required to climb the length of a rope and females are only required to climb to a point below that marked with a yellow line (p. 14). These standards are mostly for people to enlist in the services; so the bar is significantly raised for those that choose to compete for a MOS in special operations or combat units. Females enrolled in Army Jump School to be paratroopers are still not required to run as far or do as many push-ups or sit-ups as their male counterparts. When this double standard is employed in the military, it blurs the distinction as to which soldiers actually have the physical ability to perform on the battlefield.

When there is a question as to the physical abilities of a fellow soldier in a unit, there can be no guarantee that everyone can cover your back as well as you could for them. When there is no trust in a unit, it breaks down. Take, for example, the Marine ideology that no one is left behind on the battlefield. Imagine an officer trying to motivate his troops to jump out of a helicopter in the heat of battle. Some of the soldiers may doubt a female comrade's capability to carry them to safety should they be injured, because she does not have to meet the same physical standards as her male counterparts do. The training is not only meant to prepare the troops for war combat and to show the officers that they meet the physical requirements. It is also a time to begin to build the trust that binds

A journal paginated by issue

A magazine

Women in Combat 6

the troops' lives together and prove to each other they have the physical and mental toughness to accomplish the mission and bring each other back safely. How can this trust be established when male soldiers witness some female soldiers being excused from throwing live grenades in practice because they cannot throw the dummy ones far enough to keep from being blown to shreds? "The military should be the real world," said Jeanne Holm, retired two-star General of the Air Force. "The name of the game is putting together a team that fits and works together. That is the top priority, not social experimentation" (as qtd. in Yoest & Yoest, 2002). The military studies prove that a female body is not equipped to perform the same physical rigors as the male body; therefore, women should not be put in the position where impossible war-fighting demands are put on them.

One source quoted in another

When left out of selective combat positions, there is the possibility that women cannot advance up the ranks because they would not get ample opportunity to prove themselves on the battlefield and gain combat experience. This experience goes a long way because it stands to prove that an officer has the leadership ability to command troops under fire and accomplish the mission. Experience can be gained in many ways, though, since America is not always at war. All officer career fields are necessary to the overall success of the mission, and in order to be promoted every officer must pull his or her weight. Even though the proceedings of the promotion committees are supposed to be kept private, it is no secret that combat experience weighs heavily on promotion picks (Nath, 2002). In a military that is centered on the chain of command, seniority is the most valuable commodity for any member, especially officers. The practice of officers' jockeying for promotions to further their career, stature, and income is called "careerism" (Nath, 2002). This is supposedly prohibited under the Air Force's second core value of "Service Before Self," and similar pledges in the other branches. The argument lies in the conflict between the career ambition of female officers seeking a combat MOS and the needs of a ready military to support the mission.

No page number given

The truth is, however, that the United States Armed Forces is not an "equal opportunity employer" as many other public and private organizations are. The military is not out to make a profit or provide a ladder to corporate success. Instead, military officers swear to "support and defend the Constitution of the United States against all enemies, foreign and domestic; that I will bear the true faith and allegiance to the same" (Oath of Office, 2003). This oath states they are to uphold the best interest of the mission that the Commander in Chief charges them with. Careerism is not an option under this oath because it is only serving the individual's ambition, not the mission of the military. Elaine Donnelly, President of the Center for Military Readiness, says, "Equal opportunity is important, but the armed forces exist to defend the country. If there is a conflict between career opportunities and military necessity, the needs of the military must come first" (as qtd. in "Women," 2000).

Another concern with females in combat is their deployability, or their availability to be deployed. Because the very nature of combat units is being the "tip of the spear" in battle, they are deployed and away from home much of the year and are used for an indefinite period of time during the war. Donnelly explains that "if you have a pregnancy rate and it's constant, 10 or 15%, you know that out of 500 women on a carrier at least 50 are going to be unavailable before or during the six-month deployment" (Sommers, Mylroie, Donnelly, & Hill, 2001). This pregnancy issue is not just applicable for conception before the deployment, but during deployment, as is evident on Navy aircraft carriers and destroyers that house women. Even though fraternization, defined as "sexual relationships between service members" (Nath, 2002), is illegal, many ships such as the U.S.S. *Lincoln* "report a dozen [pregnancies] a month" (Layton, 2003). In a close-quarters environment, where combat units are together every hour of the day, this kind of problem distracts from the mission. Also, sailors on submarines sleep in what they call "hot beds," which are rotating shifts for sleep in the few available beds, and changing this system to accommodate separate quarters for females would not be cost effective. Also, pregnant females aboard aircraft carriers are being taken from their duty, and they must be replaced, which is a costly endeavor for the military and throws off the working relationship between service members.

When men and women are put in close quarters, it is just human nature that sexual relationships will begin to develop. This fact has been proven all around the military from the pregnancies on board naval ships all the way up to the Navy's "Tailhook Convention," where in Las Vegas in 1991 dozens of female officers reported being openly sexually assaulted by male officers, both married and

First reference to source with four authors

Different parts of the same sentence cited to different sources

Women in Combat 8

unmarried ("Women," 2000). If there were this kind of distraction within special operation ground combat units, the mission would suffer greatly because fraternization would become a huge issue, for favoritism would ensue. When the mission is not the first thing on these troops' minds, the morale, and most important, the trust breaks down.

Another very real barrier to the inclusion of women in these units and on small battleships and submarines is the medical needs of the female body. The fall 2000 suggestion from DACOWITS included as a possible recruiting slogan "A gynecologist on every aircraft carrier!" (Yoest & Yoest, 2002). This is a possibility on every base and possibly on huge aircraft carriers, but these needs of women cannot be met in the field hospitals in the deserts of Iraq and Afghanistan, where the only goal is to keep soldiers from dying long enough to get them to a base hospital. Another dilemma on forty- to fifty-person submarines is that if a woman were to get pregnant, as is the proven trend, the vessel would have to make a risky surface to get her off to be cared for and find a replacement for her job on board. DACOWITS also suggested to "ensure an adequate supply of hygiene products during deployment" (Yoest & Yoest, 2002), which is a far cry from reality when Marines who are currently in Iraq already march with a 130-pound rucksack holding their bare living necessities. The military certainly does not have the money to cover these hygiene and medical needs when in high-risk areas simply because the resources must go to fulfilling the mission.

As the way we do battle continues to change, so will the roles of males and females; and the military will always have to come up with the best solution to accommodate these differences. As for now, the restrictions that are placed on women's assignments are based in sound reasoning. For the military's purposes, women do not have the physical abilities to fill combat-oriented jobs, and the military does not have the resources to make these assignments available to them. The military needs to be aware of and most concerned with the effectiveness and readiness of its troops and figure out the best way to accomplish its mission and preserve America's freedom and sovereignty.

Conclusion

Women in Combat 9

References

Baer, S. (2003, March 3). In Iraq war, women would serve closer to front lines than in past. *The Baltimore Sun*, p. 1A. Retrieved from http://www.baltimoresun.com

Gerber, R. (2002, September 23). Don't send military women to the back of the troop train. *USA Today*. Retrieved from http://www.usatoday.com

Layton, L. (2003, March 15). Navy women finding ways to adapt to a man's world. *The Washington Post,* p. A15. Retrieved from http://www.washingtonpost.com

Leo, J. (1997, August 11). A kinder, gentler army. *U.S. News and World Report, 123*(6), 14.

McDonough, S. (2003, February 10). More U.S. military women edging closer to combat positions in preparation for Iraq war. *The Associated Press*. Retrieved from http://www.ap.org/

Nath, C. (2002). *United States Air Force Leadership Studies*. Washington, DC: Air Education and Training Command, United States Air Force.

Oath of office: U.S. federal and military oath of office. (2003). Retrieved from http://www.apfn.org/apfn/oathofoffice.htm

Owens, M. (1997, Spring). Mothers in combat boots: Feminists call for women in the military. *Human Life Review, 23*(2), 35–45.

Sommers, C., Mylroie, L., Donnelly, E., & Hill, M. (2001, October 17). IWF panel: Women facing war. *Independent Women's Forum*. Retrieved from RDS Contemporary Women's Issues.

Women in the military. (2000, September 1). *Issues and Controversies*. Retrieved from http://www.2facts.com

Yoest, C., & Yoest, J. (2002, Winter). Booby traps at the Pentagon. *Women's Quarterly*. Retrieved from http://www.bnet.com

DEBATING
the Issues

The chapters in Part Five contain pairs of articles on five controversial questions. These questions generate conflict among experts and laypeople alike for two principal reasons: First, even when the facts are not in dispute, they may be interpreted differently. Second, and more difficult to resolve, equally worthwhile values may be in conflict.

There are not always two diametrically opposed views of the same controversial issue. This will occur when there are only two options: A certain bill should or should not be passed. The president should or should not be impeached. This medical procedure should or should not be allowed. Often, however, there are more than two possible solutions to a problematic situation, or more than two possible views of an issue are worth considering. Here we have chosen to present only two opposing responses to each question.

Debating the Issues lends itself to classroom debates, both formal and informal. It can also serve as a useful source of informed opinions, which can lead to further research. For each of the topics that follow, read both articles and consider the following questions:

1. Are there two — and only two — possible points of view on the subject? Does each author make clear what he or she is trying to prove? What is each author's claim?

2. How important is the evidence in support of the claims? Does the support fulfill the appropriate criteria? If not, what are its weaknesses? Do the authorities have convincing credentials?

3. What stated or unstated assumptions (warrants) are the claims based on? Are the warrants widely accepted? If they need to be defended or qualified, have the authors done so?

4. How important is the definition of key terms? Does definition become a significant issue in the controversy?

5. Other than definition, what role does language play in the authors' arguments?

6. Do the arguments have any flaws in inductive or deductive reasoning? Do they contain any logical fallacies?

Rating Your Professors

Do Course Evaluations Matter?

CHAPTER 15

You may not have had the opportunity yet to evaluate your professors and instructors. You may welcome the chance to express your opinion about those who teach your classes in a more formal manner than talking about them with your classmates. After all, you may not have ever been asked to evaluate your teachers in high school. On the other hand, you may feel that student evaluations of faculty are a waste of time. Your school may make use of paper forms on which you bubble in your response and perhaps add written comments, but more likely, you will do your course evaluations online. How seriously should you take course evaluations? How seriously do faculty and administrators take them? In the following essays, Rebecca Schuman and Stephen Burt offer different opinions about the value of student evaluations of faculty.

Needs Improvement

REBECCA SCHUMAN

It's student evaluation time again—and I should be the last professor in the world to complain. With slight exceptions for "caring too much" and courses that meet "too early" (9:10 a.m.), my evaluations are quite good. And yet the student evaluations of teaching (SETs) I've received during my decade-long teaching career have meant absolutely nothing. This is because student evaluations are useless.

Ostensibly, SETs give us valuable feedback on our teaching effectiveness, factor importantly into our career trajectories, and provide accountability to the institution that employs us. None of this, however, is true.

First, evaluations promote sucking up to customers—I'm sorry, students—often at the expense of teaching effectiveness. A recent comprehensive study, for example, showed that professors get good evaluations by teaching to the test and being entertaining. Student learning hardly factors in, because (surprise) students are often poor judges of what will help them learn. (They are, instead, excellent judges of how to get an easy A.)

Rebecca Schuman is a columnist for *Slate* and the author of *Schadenfreude, A Love Story* and *Kafka and Wittgenstein*. She lives in St. Louis.

Indeed, some of the worst evaluations I ever got were for hands-down the best teaching I've ever done—which I measured by the revolutionary metric of "the students were way better at German walking out than they were walking in." Alas, this took work, and some of the Kinder attempted to stage a mutiny on evaluation day. Little did they know that a "too much work" dig is the #humblebrag of the academy—and, indeed, anything less on evals is seen as pandering at best, and out-and-out grade-bribery at worst.

Speaking of grade bribery: Evaluations impact career trajectories, all right, but only of the most vulnerable faculty in the university—yes, adjuncts, whose semester-long contracts are often renewed (or not) on the basis of student feedback alone. Meanwhile, only in the rarest and most politicized cases do even scathing evaluations harm tenured big shots—who, unsurprisingly, often care about undergraduate teaching the least. In short, asking students to evaluate their professors anonymously is basically like Trader Joe's soliciting Yelp reviews from a shoplifter.

5 I'm sorry—a bigoted shoplifter. Because student evaluations aren't just useless: They're biased. The other day I put a call out for notable evaluation stories, and the response was both overwhelmingly depressing and depressingly unsurprising:

> @pankisseskafka *"His [physical handicap] makes him bitter and a bad teacher." Thanks, I'll get right on that. :P*
>
> —jmatonak (@jmatonak)
> April 17, 2014

> @pankisseskafka *"She wasn't an angry black woman (surprise!), but she's wayyyy too liberal"*
>
> —Laurian Bowles (@drlaurian)
> April 17, 2014

> *Already gotten "great" stories of sexism, looksism and all-caps-ism in student evals. Anyone else had an -ism show up on a course eval?*
>
> —Rebecca Schuman (@pankisseskafka)
> April 16, 2014

> @pankisseskafka *I was told I graded too hard because I was on my period.*
>
> —Katie Krcmarik (@KatieKrcmarik)
> April 16, 2014

Indeed, many evaluations, no matter who the professors were, focused on hair (and beards!), clothes, general disdain for the subject matter ("Philosophy sucks!")—anything but constructive assessment of teaching. Seriously, though, anecdotal data notwithstanding: Bias in evaluations is widely accepted, so much so that some who use evals as assessment tools already control for it:

> @pankisseskafka *we discuss those things (compare women to average among women, not pure averages, for example). 1/2*
>
> —Tom Pepinsky (@TomPepinsky)
> April 17, 2014

Just what I wanted, to be "pretty smart, for a girl." Oh wait:

> *Schumaniacs: I want your best, worst, craziest, most depressing, most unbelievable student evaluation stories. Please?*
>
> —Rebecca Schuman (@pankisseskafka)
> April 16, 2014

> @pankisseskafka *One-sentence narrative eval: "Thinks she's pretty smart for a girl."*
>
> —Alyssa Picard (@ThatPicard)
> April 16, 2014

Because of all this—off-topic vitriol, irrelevance, bias—most tenure-track professors I know (who aren't hanging onto their evals for dear life) don't read their evaluations at all. This isn't to say that professors should be left solely to their own devices, a million poorly-dressed sovereign nations, left to declare "constructive" naptime during a Freud seminar, or emulate Wittgenstein's turn as a school-teacher and employ corporal punishment. Egad. Assessment of teaching is vitally important—but how can we actually do it so that it works?

Peer evaluations are a common suggestion (and, indeed, often common practice). But those only work if your peer actually cares about teaching in the first place—or doesn't want to sabotage you. Outside reviewers (from other departments) could solve for this, but only if you underestimate the academic's propensity toward petty vindictiveness: One bad review from English of a history professor, and we've got a permanent schism between two departments that should be clinging onto each other for survival.

All right, so what about "effectiveness measures" from the administration? Yes, let's create even more administrators—what today's universities need are more people who've never taught a day, highly invested in running departments on the cheap. All right, fine, how about we just test the students, and base professor effectiveness on the results? Sure, because that's worked out so fantastically for K–12.

10 Or, OK, we could measure performance in subsequent classes—but many of us teach general ed, and our departments will never see those kids again. Measuring "good teaching" is a touchy, complicated subject, and all solutions involve both massive compromises in pedagogical autonomy and substantial amounts of "service work"—two of professors' very favorite things.

I see two actual resolutions to the evaluation calamity. One of them is massively important and will never happen; the other is fairly trivial and could happen tomorrow.

The first: A complete cultural shift at doctoral-granting institutions about the importance and value of teaching. Damn near everyone with a doctorate learned to teach (or didn't!) in an environment where undergraduate teaching is, to paraphrase Nietzsche, an affair of the rabble: Graduate TAs and adjuncts.

In grad school, I was actively told "not to care too much" about teaching—advice that is standard practice:

@JoshDavisSays @pankisseskafka *Let your teaching slide & finish your degree. (undergrads' education doesn't matter?!)*

—Despicable G (@GracieG)
April 20, 2014

Woke up to a funny-sad thread about #badseniorfacultyadvice. Mine was 100% definitely "Take that adjunct job, it will help you." Yours?

—Rebecca Schuman (@pankisseskafka)
April 20, 2014

@pankisseskafka *'don't take that pedagogy fellowship. That won't help you get a job.' Good thing I didn't listen, eh?*

—missoularedhead (@missoularedhead)
April 20, 2014

@pankisseskafka *"Pedagogy isn't that important. It won't help you with your research."*

Ah yes, all that research I got paid to do…

—Josh Davis (@JoshDavisSays) April 20, 2014

So here's another solution, almost breath-taking in its simplicity. Combine peer evaluative measures (of lesson plans and assignments, not just classroom charisma or test scores) with student evaluations—but make the students leave their names on the evals.

The day the first yahoo on Yahoo wrote a comment was the day we should have stopped anonymous student evaluations dead. The "online disinhibition effect" both enables and encourages unethical, rash behavior, and today's digital native students see no difference between evaluations and the abusive nonsense they read (and perhaps create) every day.

15   Actual constructive criticism can be delivered as it ought to be: to our faces. Any legitimate, substantive complaints can go to the chair or dean. There is no reason for anonymity—after all, we have no way to retaliate against a student for a nasty evaluation, because we can't even see our evals until students' grades have been handed in to the registrar (and if you hated us that much, you won't take our class again). And besides, I hate to tell you this, but professors know handwriting; we recognize patterns of speech; we can glean the sources of grudges. We know who it was anyway.

Sure, this won't change the culture of academia, where getting a position at a so-called "teaching college"—and thus spending all of your time with undergrads, as I now do—is considered abject failure. But it will certainly de-Yelp-ify the evaluation process, cut down on some of the bigotry, and it might even (gasp) offer us some constructive feedback. That's a solution I evaluate at 4 out of 5 ("Agree"!)—which isn't bad at all, for a girl.

Why Not Get Rid of Student Evaluations?
STEPHEN BURT

Everybody has reasons to hate student evaluations. If they represented the judgments of one individual, rather than being a big heterogeneous data set, we would call that individual sexist. Women face double standards and, often, tougher expectations. Students in some experiments give higher scores to teachers who they think are men. Evaluations may also favor the white and the young, or punish the homely (when we find someone attractive, we tend to rate their other qualities more highly, in what psychologists call the halo effect). And better scores don't mean that students learned more—not if you go by subsequent performance in sequenced classes (e.g., Spanish 1 and Spanish 2) in which you can measure such things.

Based on such findings, and on her own experience as a language teacher, Rebecca Schuman called evaluations biased and worthless in *Slate* last year. They are biased. Everyone's biased. But they're far from worthless, and now that the end of the school year—the season of student evaluations—is upon us, it's worth looking again at what's wrong with them, and what's irreplaceably right.

The cases against them are hard to ignore. Student evaluations encourage pandering, given

Stephen Burt is a renowned poet, literary critic, and professor at Harvard University. Burt has written essays for the *Boston Review*, the *London Review of Books*, *The New York Times Book Review*, *The Times Literary Supplement*, the *Poetry Review*, *Slate*, and the *Yale Review*. The following essay originally appeared on slate.com on May 15, 2015.

that most people—most teachers—want to be liked. Some teachers *have* to be liked, and to prove they are liked in order to keep their jobs. Evaluations also encourage a consumer mentality—students are shopping for classes, as it were—and they create a perfect forum for trolling. (Schuman compared them to Yelp ratings.) My university recently decided to stop publishing the number that shows how hard students think a course is because students were using that number to pick easy courses. As with election polls and athletes' stats, quantitative evaluations can attract enthusiasts who lack statistical literacy, who then build castles from quantitative sand. ("Twentieth-Century Novel got consistently higher ratings than 18th-Century Novel—I guess we need to hire more modernists!") Careful studies by people soaked in statistical literacy, such as Philip Stark and Richard Freishtat at the University of California–Berkeley, conclude that effective teaching is quite hard to measure and that anonymous student evaluations cannot do that job.

So why not bid goodbye to commencement season by just getting rid of them? Why not replace them with nothing, if they're worse than nothing, or (as Schuman suggested) replace them with end-of-term comments to which students must sign their names?

5   The answer requires us to think about power. If you look hard at the structure of academia, you will see a lot of teachers who, in one way or another, lack power: adjuncts and term hires (a large population, and growing); untenured faculty (especially in universities like mine); faculty, even tenured faculty, in schools where budget cuts loom; graduate students, always and everywhere. You might see evaluations as instruments by which students, or administrators, exercise

power over those vulnerable employees. But if you are a student, and especially if you are a student who cares what grades you get or who needs recommendations, then teachers, for you—even adjuncts and graduate teaching assistants—hold power.

That means you might not tell them to their faces, nor over your signature, what they did wrong as your teacher. You're not going to tell them, for example, that you never finished Tennyson's *In Memoriam*, or that (as far as you know) nobody in the class finished *Red Mars*. (Both of them are great, by the way. Please do finish them.) And you're almost certainly not going to tell your professor that his English class was too easy, that it felt more like a book group than like the demanding seminar it was supposed to be.

All of the above examples come from classes I've taught; two of them were problems I discovered only through reading evaluations. The more stake your students have in your opinion of them—even when you're done grading their work—the less honest they can be when their name is attached. Some of those students have information you need, even if others are trolls.

As Stark and Freishtat also conclude, "students are ideally situated to comment *about their experience* of a course" as long as they don't think they're going to lose out by doing it. Conversely, because evaluations remain anonymous, we can take their praise as sincere. If anonymous student evaluators tell you they recommended your course to their friends, they aren't just saying so to get an A.

Teachers should not become simply entertainers. But we would like students to view our classes as time well spent; we would like them to regard what we teach as *dulce et utile*—sweet and useful, as Horace put it, or at least one out of the two. We believe that Goethe and Marianne Moore and Theocritus and Max Weber and W. E. B. Du Bois are worth the time it took students to learn how to read them, and we'd like to know whether they came to agree.

10   But don't all those numbers in student evals get misused? They do. So do all numbers in fields where the modern demand for data exceeds the useful supply (see also: K–12 education, where I'd love to see more attention to what students prefer). The worst cases of inappropriate quantification in higher ed these days come from Britain, where government demands for quantifiable research results, and enforced competition for funding, make it look like U.K. higher ed has been taken over by some combination of the Borg, Friedrich Hayek, and Ultron. There, too, more attention to what students think, or at least to what students *say* they think, might be a good thing.

        But student evaluations are racist! And sexist! And they punish things no instructor can control, such as class size! That's true, but if we use evals in the right ways, they become evidence that can help us mitigate the unfairness that they reflect. Small courses in a given topic almost always get better ratings than large ones—which shows that students prefer small courses, which is something that people making decisions about class size, section size, and requirements should know. The high satisfaction that comes with small class sizes also gives fields and disciplines that will never attract large numbers of majors a useful argument for their existence. (If a very small department has very dissatisfied students, someone should ask why.)

        As for the racism, sexism, ableism: These are problems not with anonymous student

evaluations in particular, but with any evaluation of anything performed by human beings, whose implicit bias ought to be noticed before it can be addressed. (Symphony orchestras alleviated sexism in hiring by conducting auditions behind a curtain, which isn't a solution those of us who value face-to-face teaching can use.) Yet numbers can show one teacher whether she's improving, or where a particular course went wrong. Bias that favors men over women, or tall teachers over short ones, won't affect evaluations that pertain to the same teacher's various courses, given that most teachers don't change height or gender between semesters. (Midterm evaluations can also help a teacher improve a course while there's still time.)

        Of course, some teachers *do* change gender; evaluations have helped at least one transgender professor consider how students saw him during and after transition. Evaluations identify both good and bad reactions to visible difference, telling us what to encourage and what should raise an alarm. Chairmen and deans should want to find out whether students respect teachers' gender transitions and whether teachers show respect for students. These forms are one way students can let us know.

        Chairmen and deans also need to know when classroom teaching fails: when a professor makes catastrophically wrong assumptions as to what students already know, for example, or when students find a professor incomprehensible thanks to her thick Scottish accent. Student evaluations are one of just a few venues through which that information can travel, short of a student's coming to visit a chairman in person or filing a formal complaint. Responsible registrars—my institution has one—also have ways to reduce the impact of trolls. When I got a long, jeering, negative evaluation some years back, stuck in among the positives (and lowering their average), I complained, and the registrar then discovered that this student had done the same thing in every course. (I've been told there's a note in the files to that effect, though I don't know if the tallied average changed.)

15   "O wad some Pow'r the giftie gie us/ To see oursels as others see us!" Robert Burns wrote, in a poem with a thick Scottish accent. "It wad frae manie a blunder free us." That power lies in student evaluations. They have obvious flaws, and all college teachers know how they can be misused—but colleges, and instructors, do better with them than without them. They can free teachers from blunders as well as flatter our self-regard, they remind us that if we care what our students learn, we ought to care about what they think; anonymous evaluations are one of the few ways that we can try to find out.

Discussion Questions

1. What reasons does Schuman give for believing that course evaluations are useless?

2. How convincing do you find her argument? Do you share her cynicism about students and faculty?

3. Why does Burt think that student course evaluations are valuable?

4. Does Burt see any potential weaknesses in student course evaluations? If so, what are they, and what does he say about them?

5. If you had a choice between a class taught by Schuman and one taught by Burt, which would you choose? Why?

6. Which of the two arguments do you find more convincing, and why?

CHAPTER 16

Public Restrooms
Should They Be Gender Neutral?

Men's Room/Ladies' Room. Men's Restroom/Women's Restroom. Boys/Girls. Blokes/Sheilas. A stick figure wearing pants/a stick figure wearing a dress. It all used to seem so simple and clear cut. In 2015, Axosoft started a brilliant campaign called, It Was Never a Dress. They took the universal sign for women's restrooms — the stick figure wearing a dress to differentiate it from the male stick figure wearing pants — and reimagined the woman wearing pants and a cape. It was a new way of empowering women, but it also came at a time when new ways of perceiving gender were needed. A number of states have already passed or considered laws that would dictate who uses which restroom. Why the need? Why the controversy?

With transgender individuals increasingly open about their sexuality and gender fluid individuals further blurring the lines among genders, some states have tried to force each person to use the public restroom assigned to the gender to which he or she was born. That has proved awkward for those in transition or those who identify with a gender other than that to which they were born. For many, it goes beyond a question of comfort to become a question of safety. In the essays that follow, Pamela Powers Hannley and Nico Lane present two opposing positions on the subject of gender-neutral restrooms.

Bathroom Politics: Preserving the Sanctity of the "Ladies' Room"
PAMELA POWERS HANNLEY

In the 1950s the Ladies' Room was a place of refuge, a wall-papered lounge with a couch, polished mirrors, fresh flowers, and often an attendant armed with fresh towels, perfume, and mints. As men have always suspected, we didn't go there just to use the facilities; the Ladies' Room was a safe gathering place.

We went there to talk, to primp, to smoke, to cry, to adjust a poor wardrobe choice, to sneak away from a bad dinner date, or just to sneak away. The Ladies' Room was a place where women could be women—a place with no men watching, commenting, judging.

The Politicization of Bathrooms

In the early 1970s, at the height of the feminist era, "Ladies" Rooms came under fire. We feminists were not "ladies" who needed fainting couches in restrooms because we didn't have the fortitude to work an 8-hour day without a nap or a good cry. "Ladies" were well-behaved women; we early feminists were anything but ladylike. As a result, "Ladies" Rooms became the Women's Rooms—or Womyn's Rooms—and the couches all but disappeared.

Further politicization of public bathrooms came later in the 1970s. I remember my first trip to a gay bar with a couple of gay guy friends, George and Henry. As professional photographers, the three of us worked together and played together. The Kismet, a legendary downtown Columbus gay bar, was hopping the night we were there—loud disco music, flashing lights, dancing, plenty of booze, and other adult entertainment and harder drugs, if you knew who to ask. Not long after our arrival, I realized that there were two types of women at

the bar (three types if you count me—the only openly straight woman). All of the real women (AKA people with vaginas) were wearing jeans and weren't wearing any make-up. All of the "women" who were decked out with slinky dresses, big hair, heels, and gobs of make-up were men… transvestites, as we called them back then. I noted my observation to George, and he validated it.

Then it dawned on me: If there are men dressed as women, which restroom do they use?

"They're men. They use the Men's Room," George answered matter-of-factly. That solution worked at the Kismet but not so much in mainstream Columbus, I'm sure.

Papers to Pee Laws

Fast forward to Arizona in 2013, the City of Phoenix passed an anti-discrimination law that extended "basic protections to transgender people in housing, the workplace, and places of public accommodation." Since "public accommodation" includes public restrooms, this got the attention of Arizona Representative John Kavanagh who proposed legislation stating that people should use the bathroom assigned to their sex—not what "they think in their head". In other words,

5

Pamela Powers Hannley describes herself as "a published author, photographer, videographer, clay artist, mother, nana, and wife." In November 2016, she won election to the Arizona House of Representatives from District 9. She is also managing editor for the *American Journal of Medicine*; with her husband co-directs Arizonans for a New Economy, Arizona's public banking initiative; and co-chairs the Arizona Democratic Progressive Caucus, the largest caucus of the Arizona Democratic Party. This entry was posted on 6 May 2014 on tucsonprogressive.com.

a person with a penis—even if it's covered by a dress—should use the Men's Room.

From *The Daily Beast*…

Going to the bathroom in a public venue can be a huge source of anxiety for transgender people, particularly those who are just transitioning and don't yet "pass" as their true gender. According to a recent study conducted by the National Gay and Lesbian Task Force, 53 percent of transpeople report being "harassed or disrespected in a place of public accommodation."

10 There was a huge outcry over Kavanagh's "papers to pee" bill, and it died in the Arizona Legislature.

The latest twist in Arizona bathroom politics comes after a Henry Elementary School girl who identifies as a boy used the Boys' Room at the school. Shortly after that, Tucson Unified School District's (TUSD) changed its nondiscrimination policy.

From the *Arizona Daily Star*…

TUSD amended its nondiscrimination policy in March [2014], adding "gender identity or expression" to a list that prohibits discrimination based on disability, race, color, religious beliefs, sex, sexual orientation, age or national origin. While the policy does not directly address bathroom use by transgender children, the discussion that led to the change stemmed from an incident at Henry Elementary School, 650 N. Igo Way, in which parents raised concerns about a transgender student using the boys' restroom…

Sanchez [TUSD Superintendent] said the policy revision is in line with case law that has gone all the way to the U.S.

Supreme Court and in line with other districts of TUSD's size that have dealt with such circumstances.

This story and a similar one from Colorado   15 about 5-year-old Coy Mathis, who is a boy self-identifying as a girl and who recently won a court case which allows him to attend school as a girl, or the little girl whose Christian school told her she looked too much like a boy because she self-identifies as a girl but prefers pants, t-shirts, and short hair.

The two stories about young children "self-identifying" as the opposite gender concern me. First of all, how can a 5-year-old know and express the belief that he feels more comfortable as a girl? I do believe that people can show signs of being gay when they are children, but in my opinion, the concept of gender identification is far more complex and beyond the intellectual capacity of an elementary school student. I wonder what role parents and psychologists have played in this "self-identification."

I've been a Mom and a Grandma for decades. Besides my two children, my two grandchildren, and now my two step-children, I've known many young people since they were little kids. Four of my children's friends grew up to be gay. The girl was a tomboy who liked sports, but she also wore make-up and dated guys all the way through high school. There was no indication (to me, anyway) that she would be a Lesbian later in life. The three boys were a different story. By the time they were 10–11 years old, my gaydar was picking up the signal; the one little boy showed signs of being gay much younger and enjoyed "playing dress-up" with my daughter's large collection of frilly dress-up clothes. I never said anything about my observations to the parents, to those children, to my children, or to anyone (except my husband in private). Then and now, these four young people were accepted by the neighborhood gang that played together and went to school together.

What about the Women?

Women have suffered a long history of discrimination and violence at the hands of men. The statistic above says, "53 percent of transpeople report being 'harassed or disrespected in a place of public accommodation.'" Welcome to our world.

How many times have women heard the establishment (i.e., straight men, including some elected politicians) say that rape victims "asked for it" with the way they dressed? How many times are women told, "If you don't want to be jeered at, harassed, fondled, or raped, don't dress that way." In other words, sexual violence can't be controlled, so potential victims must curb their actions. Don't walk alone at night. Don't go to those parts of town. Drive with your windows up and doors locked. Don't wear that. Don't wear shoes you can't run in. Carry a gun. Society's message for the "weaker sex": You are vulnerable. Get used to it.

20   Straight men are in power. Period.

Bringing this back to the bathroom question, there are lots of solutions floating around the Internet. There are stories like this one about the City of Philadelphia, which recently passed a law saying that all new or renovated city buildings should include unisex bathrooms, in addition to traditional men's and women's restrooms. This is a good solution, in my opinion, because it provides a safe space for everyone—including transgender people and families. (It bothers me when my son has to take my little granddaughter into the Men's Room because most restaurants don't have unisex or family bathrooms.) I also agree with converting all of the one-seaters out there to unisex bathrooms.

Others—primarily activists and academics aligned with the LGBTQQIA (Lesbian, Gay, Bisexual, Transgender, Queer, Questioning, Intersex, Androgynous, Allies) community—advocate for all public bathrooms to be gender neutral, no gender-specific restrooms.

From *The Ethics of Gender-Segregated Bathrooms…*

Avoids Marginalization

One of the most often-cited arguments in favor of gender neutral bathrooms is that on a societal level, adhering to a binary system with only two choices (male or female) "others" people who do not fit into or subscribe to this dichotomy, with consequences that extend beyond the immediate discomfort of having to choose which bathroom to use.

This group of marginalized people   25
includes people who identify as transgender, transsexual or intersex, and people who do not identify within the confines of these categories.

In "Coming Out of the Water Closet: The Case against Sex Segregated Bathrooms" (*Texas Journal of Women and the Law*), Alex More discusses the extent to which having male and female bathrooms excludes people. More writes, "Sex segregated restrooms force people to choose 'male' or 'female'—those who refuse to accept the dichotomy become defined out of existence. People who do not identify with their socially assigned sexual category represent the remainder of sexual division—the leftovers, sexuality's refuse…"

Safer

A concern for safety motivates people on both sides of this debate.

In the article "Embodiment, Elimination, and the Role of Toilets in Struggles for Social Justice," Judith Plaskow, a professor of religious studies at Manhattan College, raises the issue of how to reconcile the "need of transgender persons for safe and accessible restrooms" with some people, primarily women's, desire "for the privacy and safety they associate with women-only space." [Emphasis added.]

At Harvard, the Co-Chair of the Harvard College Queer Students and Allies wrote in an opinion piece titled "Safe Bathrooms for All" that a *Crimson* editorial arguing against gender-neutral bathrooms on safety and modesty grounds ignored "that gender-neutral bathrooms are a matter of dignity and safety for those in our community who don't conform to traditional gender norms," and "… treated unsubstantiated risks of sexual harassment and assault against women as though they were facts, without offering any evidence for their claims."

Why Not?

30   On the other side of the issue are people who believe that the creation of gender-neutral bathrooms would make bathrooms more dangerous, and make people feel uncomfortable in terms of privacy and modesty.

A Concern for Safety… But Safety for Whom?

One of the biggest concerns raised by people who are against the implementation of gender-neutral bathrooms is safety.

When Harvard University was considering building gender-neutral bathrooms, the editorial board of the *Harvard Crimson* student newspaper argued against the creation of gender-neutral bathrooms on-campus. Much of the editorial "Rethinking Privacy" focused on safety: "Gender-neutral bathrooms could provide opportunities for verbal harassment and even unwanted attention that perhaps could be avoided in gender-specific bathrooms. We understand that assault and harassment can occur anywhere; we simply believe that gender-neutral bathrooms would make it easier."

Privacy and Modesty Concerns

While the potential for increased danger for bathroom users is a major deterrent for people in favor of maintaining sex segregated bathrooms, The *Crimson* raises another issue in its editorial advocating against the addition of gender-neutral bathrooms, that of modesty, a concern often brought up by religious groups as well.

The *Crimson* asserts that although a small minority of students may feel discomfort at having to use sex segregated bathrooms, many students would also feel discomfort if forced to use gender-neutral bathrooms.

From "No More Women's Rooms: Why   35 Bathrooms Should All Be Gender Neutral," published by *Slate*…

The foremost reason for being anti-bathroom-neutralization involves the sensitive issue of sexual assault. Many people who believe gender-neutral bathrooms would benefit society in both providing for the needs of trans people and helping to alleviate severe separations between the genders don't want to be insensitive to the needs of sexual assault survivors. That said, conceding the fight for neutralization solely based on this concern ignores the fact that sexual assault can—and more importantly does—occur among members of every gender, and all survivors of assault deserve the same sensitivity. Choosing not to rid society of the bathroom divide because of an assumption that sexual assault survivors are all women who have been assaulted by men perpetuates a culture that embraces this as inevitable. This opposition also minimizes the existence of sexual assault that is not male-on-female.

On the grounds of safety, I completely disagree with the idea of making all public bathrooms—including those with multiple stalls—gender neutral, and thus allowing anyone to go anywhere. The *Slate* author misses the point. This may come as a news flash to some, but women don't trust men. It's not just about sensitivity to assault victims (although that is part of it) that I oppose "neutralizing" bathrooms. It's about common sense and safety for everyone—especially the vulnerable, which includes women, the young, the elderly, and, yes, transgender and transsexual people. Would I want my little granddaughter or my 90-year-old Mother to be forced to use a gender neutral bathroom with men? No.

A third "solution" is what TUSD and Sunnyside School District have adopted: Allow transgender students to choose any bathroom where they feel comfortable. I call this the capitalist or bureaucratic solution because it is the cheapest and easiest. No remodeling. No new construction. No new signage. Just force everyone to deal with the embarrassment, the lack of privacy, and the safety risks. There are definite privacy issues surrounding this solution—not the least of which is the deplorable conditions of many

public school bathrooms. Having attended many Democratic Party State Committee Meetings in high schools around the state, I can attest to the horrid conditions of many girls' bathrooms. Yes, they're basically clean, but broken or misaligned door locks and missing stall doors abound. At one high school, out of six stalls, only one or two had both a functioning door and lock. And the school districts want to allow transgender girls (boys who identify as girls) to use these facilities with the girls? I trust teenage boys less than I trust grown men. (Seriously, how hard is it to align a latch? Misaligned, broken, or missing bathroom stall latches are everywhere—even in swanky hotels.)

Is it wrong to long for the bygone days of the Ladies' Room? Is it wrong to long for a sanctuary where men are not allowed? A place where women can be women? A place where women can feel safe? No.

My opinion…

1. All one-seater public bathrooms should be unisex

40

This would help everyone whose life doesn't fit neatly into the "men go here" and "women go there" paradigm, including but not limited to transpeople. It will solve one problem women have everyday—standing in line outside of a women's room while the men's room is empty or at least has no waiting. This solution also helps family members who have to care for others of the opposite sex (i.e., a Mom with a son, a Dad with a daughter, a spouse who has to help his/her partner, a nurse and patient).

2. New construction should include building codes for family bathrooms, in addition to multi-stall men's and women's bathrooms

The Phoenix Convention Center is a good example of this. It has large multi-stall traditional men's and women's rooms but also has many family bathrooms throughout the facility.

3. Transpeople should be able to use the bathroom in which they are comfortable

I am not afraid of transwomen in the women's room. I totally get why they don't want to use the men's room; it's the same reason why I oppose full gender neutral bathrooms.

4. For safety and privacy reasons, I oppose multi-stall gender neutral bathrooms

Existing multi-stall bathrooms are sealed up for privacy, often with heavy doors. Putting men and women into the same bathrooms when they are designed in this way sets the vulnerable up for assault. This also goes back to my original concern: privacy and sanctuary for women.

Why All Public Bathrooms Should Be Gender Neutral
NICO LANG

When you're gender nonconforming, it's hard to know where you belong, especially when you're using the bathroom.

Alok Vaid-Menon, who works for the Audre Lorde Project and uses gender-neutral pronouns, explained that deciding whether to use the men's or women's restroom "depends on the day and the mood."

"In a given day, I can look like a lot of different things," Vaid-Menon told the *Daily Beast*. Their daily wardrobe is incredibly eclectic— ranging from plaid bow ties and vests to bright purple lipstick and long, flowing dresses.

According to Vaid-Menon, using the restroom is "a combination of assessing my safety and asking how much I want to push people's buttons... I try to be very responsive and aware of all the other people in the room," they said. "I'm thinking: 'Are other people staring at me too long? What do I do? What's going on?' I try to leave as quickly as possible."

5   Devin-Norelle, a genderfluid trans activist and writer who lives in New York, has a full beard and a man bun, which often looks like a women's hairstyle from behind. That combination doesn't make going to the bathroom in public an easy task.

"In general, I hate using the restroom because I'm such a feminine- or androgynous-looking person," Norelle told the *Daily Beast*. "I get a lot of looks. There was a time where I was very concerned about my own safety... I'm putting myself at risk when I'm walking into the men's restroom and I'm putting myself at risk when I'm walking into the women's restroom."

The 26-year-old has been repeatedly stopped, denied entry, and kicked out of both bathrooms. "As soon as someone can't read your gender, they are afraid of you," Norelle said. "People don't like it if they don't know if you're a man or a woman. There's no gray area for anybody."

Last week, 16-year-old Ny Richardson found that out the hard way. Richardson, who is a cisgender lesbian, was thrown out of a McDonald's in Hull, England, after using the women's room. This incident is very similar what transpired last year at a Fishbone's in

Nico Lang is a critic, an essayist, a reporter for the *Advocate*, and a contributor to the *Daily Dot, Salon, Rolling Stone, Vox,* the *Washington Post,* the *L.A. Times, BuzzFeed,* the *Huffington Post, Mic,* and the *Guardian*. He's also the author of *The Young People Who Traverse Dimensions* and the co-editor of the bestselling *Boys: An Anthology*.

Detroit, when a security guard mistook Cort-
ney Bogorad for a man and pulled her out of
a stall in the women's room. He proceeded to
bodyslam her against the wall. She's suing the
establishment.

These cases prove something that should be obvious by now: Gendered restrooms don't work.

10   For trans and gender nonconforming people,
they justify harassment and abuse. For restaurants
and private businesses, playing gender police
could open proprietors up to a costly lawsuit. For
everyone else, dividing bathrooms by gender is an
unnecessary vestige of the 19th century that leads
to longer lines and bigger headaches for everyone.
It's time to banish them back to the dark ages
where they belong.

Where do gender-segregated restrooms come
from? In "Unisex Toilets and the Sex-Elimina-
tion Linkage," Emory University professor Sheila
Cavanagh explains that the earliest instance of
this phenomenon dates back to 1739 at a Parisian
ball. Signs at the fete directed patrons to "Men
Toilet" and "Women Toilet."

Before this time, public bathrooms were commonly designated for men only, but as women
began to emerge in the workplace, reforms
increasingly became necessary. Nearly a century
and a half later, urinary segregation came to
the United States. "In 1887, Massachusetts was
the first state to pass a law mandating women's
restrooms in workplaces with female employees,"
Reason's Elizabeth Nolan Brown writes. "By the
1920s, most states had passed similar laws."

Since those states initially passed legislation
codifying public facility use, these laws have gone
virtually unchanged. According to *Slate*'s Ted
Trauman, neither have the politics behind them.

The advent of urinary segregation was part of
a push for total gender division in public life, as a
means of "[protecting] women from the full force
of the world outside their homes."

Trauman writes that this led to "ladies' reading   15
rooms at libraries, parlors at department stores,
separate entrances at post offices and banks, and
their own car on trains, intentionally placed at the
very end so that male passengers could chival-
rously bear the brunt in the event of a collision."

Since the Roaring Twenties, many of these
divides have been torn down. Today, men and
women share apartment buildings. They sit side by
side on public transportation and in church. The
sexes absolutely do not, however, pee together.

This is both a matter of social custom and the
laws themselves. Nolan Brown states that part of
the problem is that "businesses are legally prohibited from offering only gender-neutral restrooms"
in many states and many of those "potty parity"
codes mandate a certain ratio of women's to men's
restrooms, but that is slowly changing.

That effort is being led by cities like Berlin,
which has led a push toward unisex bathrooms
across the city, starting in government buildings.

"Initially we were laughed at for this, but now
that people are discovering that unisex toilets
are just normal bathrooms, we are experiencing
rather broad acceptance," Simon Kowalewski, a
German Member of Parliament, told the
Washington Post.

In the United States, New York,   20
Washington, D.C., Austin, Texas, and San
Francisco have all championed the desegregation
of public facilities. The nation's capital has long
led the way on the issue: Back in 2006, the D.C.
Office of Human Rights mandated that all
single-occupancy restrooms across the city be
accessible to all genders.

Philadelphia passed a similar law last year,
offering an online guide for those seeking a safe
space to use the restroom. According to Helen

Fitzpatrick, who serves as the director of the mayor's office of LGBT affairs, the resolution was meant to serve as a "teachable moment" about the need for inclusivity.

For Sofia Nelson, an attorney practicing in Detroit, Michigan, this legislation is common sense.

"I think if you are a business—or any place with public accommodation—that has single-stalled restrooms, they should be gender neutral," Nelson told The Daily Beast. "There's no reason that a one-person bathroom needs to be gendered. It's great to have the option of a gender neutral restroom and also gendered restrooms."

Many businesses, however, are even pushing to make multi-occupancy bathrooms open to everyone. At New York's MoMa PS1 in Long Island City, museum guests might notice long lines of men and women both waiting to use the same restroom.

25 Moss, an architecture firm in Chicago, believes that every public restroom can—and should—be gender neutral. In a 2015 design proposal, their answer to the problem of gendered bathrooms is similar to PS1's: clusters of single-occupancy stalls that look like closets and share a common sink space. You've likely used facilities like these before and not even realized it.

Such solutions might make those worried about the threat of sexual assault in a public restroom squirm. That's a more than understandable fear, but statistics show that most rapists aren't lurking in the bathroom. According to the National Institute for Justice, an estimated 6 in 10 "sexual assault victims… were assaulted by an intimate partner, relative, friend, or acquaintance." Many of these incidents take place at a private residence or at home.

This number is even higher for female college students: 9 in 10 survivors knew their assailant prior to the assault.

In Houston, Texas, critics of a nondiscrimination bill voted down last November attempted to brand trans people as "dangerous bathroom predators," ready to attack other restroom users if given the chance. That myth, however, has been thoroughly disproven. Currently, 190 cities around the country allow trans people equal access in public accommodations, and there has yet to be a surge in violence in any of those areas.

In fact, multiple independent studies have shown that there's never been a reported case of a transgender person attacking someone else in a public facility.

30 The opposite is true: Disproportionate numbers of trans people have been the victim of violence or harassment in public restrooms. According to UCLA's Williams Institute, 9 percent of transgender folks report being sexually assaulted in a bathroom.

States including North Carolina have put transgender people at greater risk for harm by passing laws denying affirming bathroom access to trans people. In March, Gov. Pat McCrory signed into law House Bill 2, which forces the state's transgender residents to use the facility that matches the sex they were assigned at birth.

South Carolina, Kentucky, Illinois, Minnesota, and Missouri are among the 14 states considering similar legislation.

But while we should be fighting for trans people to be able to use the bathroom that most closely corresponds with their gender identity, it's also about providing better, safer options for everyone. If legislation like HB 2 essentially outs transgender folks every time they go to the bathroom, some folks—including Devin-Norelle and Alok Vaid-Menon—have no choice but to be out whenever they use either facility.

This will prove especially true for Millennials: In a 2015 Fusion poll, the network found that half of young people no longer believe in a binary concept of gender. For a new generation radically rethinking gender boundaries, the status quo isn't enough.

35   Even for non-trans folks, there are a number of reasons to champion greater adoption of gender-neutral and inclusive restroom options. If you're tired of endless lines at the women's room, unisex facilities will help reduce your wait time.

For people with disabilities, single-occupancy bathrooms save the frustration of the only accessible stall being occupied by a mother changing her newborn.

According to Nelson, shifting nearly four centuries of societal norms might sound complicated, but it's actually not. She said, "We're just talking about people—who could be your child, your friend, or your co-worker—wanting to do something super basic that we all have to do: use the bathroom."

Discussion Questions

1. Lang quotes Devin-Norelle, who says, "As soon as someone can't read your gender, they are afraid of you." Do you feel this is a fair assessment of how people look at those of unclear gender? Why or why not?

2. Do you feel that Lang provides convincing evidence that gendered bathrooms don't work? Explain.

3. How practical are Lang's suggestions for changing bathroom culture?

4. Is safety a legitimate concern for those using public restrooms? Would Lang's suggestion change that? Explain.

5. Do you support laws that would require a person to use the restroom for the gender on his or her birth certificate unless he or she has undergone sex-change surgery? Why or why not?

6. What is Hannley's proposal for handling bathrooms and the issue of gender? Do you feel it is a valid proposal? Why or why not?

7. Who do you feel presents a more convincing argument, Lang or Hannley? Why?

Trigger Warnings
Have Some Schools Gone Too Far?

When Donald Trump unexpectedly won the presidential election in November 2016, some colleges and universities reacted as they have traditionally done in times of crisis and tragedy. They offered their students counseling and "safe spaces" and advice on how to cope. Trump supporters labeled the scared and "grieving" students whiners and spoiled brats and argued that federal funding should be taken away from schools that used that funding to support activities to help students recover from the fair election of an American president.

Colleges and universities have also been accused of coddling students when they require trigger warnings, warnings that subject matter in a class might be "triggering" to students who have experienced trauma. A short story about rape, for example, might trigger a PTSD episode in a rape survivor. There has been widespread disagreement about whether trigger warnings constitute coddling or a necessary concession to students' sensibilities. In the following essays, the members of a subcommittee of the American Association of University Professors and Professor Aaron Hanlon present different views on trigger warnings.

The Trigger Warning Myth
AARON R. HANLON

In *The Atlantic's* latest cover story, "The Coddling of the American Mind," Greg Lukianoff and Jonathan Haidt insinuate that trigger warnings and "vindictive protectiveness" are behind the college mental health crisis. "A movement is arising, undirected and driven largely by students, to scrub campuses clean of words, ideas, and subjects that might cause discomfort or give offense," they write, adding that a "campus culture devoted to

policing speech and punishing speakers is likely to engender patterns of thought that are surprisingly similar to those long identified by cognitive behavioral therapists as causes of depression and anxiety. The new protectiveness may be teaching

Aaron R. Hanlon is Assistant Professor of English at Colby College and advisor for Georgetown University's MLA/Mellon Foundation "Connected Academics" project. The article appeared on newrepublic.com on August 14, 2015.

students to think pathologically." Which is just an academic way of saying that politically correct students are driving themselves crazy.

How have trigger warnings, of all things, been elevated to explanatory value akin to academic and professional pressures, increased accessibility to college, familial and broader economic pressures, reduced sleep, sexual assault epidemics, social media image policing, and any number of other factors that experts have identified as serious contributors to mental health problems on college campuses? I don't doubt that emotional coddling can play a negative role in the mental health of college students, and so is worth investigating. But I also think Lukianoff, the head of the Foundation for Individual Rights in Education, and Haidt, a social psychologist at the NYU-Stern School of Business, are granting certain practices of care on college campuses outsized and in some cases misleading roles in the mental health crisis.

I write this as a professor well outside of Haidt's field, from a pedagogical standpoint; which is to say from one of several very different kinds of caregiving roles on a college campus, one concerned primarily with students' intellectual development (as opposed to their general mental health in a clinical context). Our national conversations about trigger warnings and political correctness evince a troubling lack of awareness about what it actually looks like in real life to express sensitivities to college students about their apparently increasing anxieties and traumas. We're still getting trigger warnings wrong.

I never imagined becoming a defender of trigger warnings. This is the first time I've written (or spoken) the word "microaggressions" in recent memory. I have been and continue to be a proponent of the idea that the best way to handle wrongheadedness and hate speech is to address

these with corrective speech, to present ideas, rationales, and evidence that overwhelm ignorance and bigotry with a blistering light. Accordingly, when vulgar or emotionally challenging material is part of the subject matter I'm responsible for teaching, or serves an otherwise specific pedagogical purpose, I'm not shy about it.

Here's a brief and by no means exhaustive list of things I've carefully selected for college syllabi and deliberately taught in college courses: a pair of poems about impotence and premature ejaculation; a satire about slaughtering human infants and feeding them to "persons of quality and fortune"; a poem that uses the c-word twice in a mere 33 lines, and describes King Charles II in coitus with his mistress with the phrase "his dull, graceless bollocks hang an arse"; a novel in which a wealthy man gets his maid to marry him by kidnapping her and continually cornering her with unwanted sexual advances; a graphic history of the torture methods and other cruelties done to African slaves leading up to the Haitian Revolution; a poem written in the voice of a male domestic servant and attempted rapist contacting his victim from prison.

The items on this list, and many others on my syllabi, could be censored by "social justice warriors" from the left, since many of them could be triggering for students suffering from post-traumatic stress. In another context, however, they could be censored from the right, by people who tell the sexual assault survivor balking at a literary rape scene to "grow up," then turn around and oppose the teaching of sexually explicit material because it's "trash."

In both cases, censoring this material is a bad idea, and providing context is the best avenue for explaining why. If you read the list above and wonder how or why any serious person would

5

teach such material at a prestigious (and expensive) college, consider the authors behind the list. It includes works by major, canonical authors from antiquity to the eighteenth century, such as Ovid, Aphra Behn, Jonathan Swift, John Wilmot, Samuel Richardson, and Lady Mary Wortley Montagu. It also includes the historian C.L.R. James's *The Black Jacobins*, one of the definitive histories of the Haitian Revolution. Simply put, leaving this stuff off the syllabus because it might be triggering is not an option.

As I've explained elsewhere, however, I use trigger warnings in the classroom as a way of preparing students who may be suffering from post-traumatic stress disorder while also easing the entire class into a discussion of the material. The thinking behind the idea that trigger warnings are a form of censorship is fundamentally illogical: those who offer warnings, at our professional discretion, about potentially triggering material are doing so precisely because we're about to teach it! If we used trigger warnings to say, effectively, "don't read this, it's scary," then there'd be no need to warn in the first place; we'd just leave the material off the syllabus.

10   It's true that giving a warning runs the risk of students avoiding or disengaging with the material out of fear of being triggered (in my three years of teaching, students have come to office hours to discuss sensitive material, but not one has left class or failed to turn in an assignment because of a trigger warning). If a student disengages, however, a professor still can (and should) follow up in a couple of ways. One is to have a private conversation with the student about the material, away from the pressures of the classroom; another is to take the student's response as an occasion to check in with the student and make sure they have access to campus mental health resources. Few of

the media voices catastrophizing trigger warnings seem to understand that professors' interactions with students in the classroom and during office hours are some of the most important ways of catching mental health (or time management, or substance abuse) issues in our students that may need further attention. While the purpose of trigger warnings is not to screen for mental health problems, being attuned to how students are reacting to material, and prompting them to react to the hard stuff, can help us catch problems before they become real catastrophes.

For those of you who are imagining scores of students using professors' trigger warnings disingenuously, as a way to get out of class or a reading assignment, this isn't (for most of us) our first rodeo. Students use deception all the time, but an office hours summons is really all we need to determine whether the student might need help from a mental health professional, or was just trying to game the system. In most cases, however, when you warn students that something might be emotionally challenging or explicit, most of them do exactly what we do when someone tells us to watch out for something lurid: they become even more curious.

Lukianoff and Haidt view trigger warnings as ways of assuming negative outcomes despite the facts of the situation, a form of what they describe as "fortune-telling": "'predicting the future negatively' or seeing potential danger in an everyday situation." Further, for Lukianoff and Haidt, trigger warnings are ways of enabling those who do suffer from PTSD to disengage, counterproductively, from the harsh realities of the world. They view trigger warnings, in other words, as not only a form of censoring what professors can teach, but of censoring students' experience of real life. But trigger warnings don't need to be the end of a difficult conversation; more often they're actually the beginning of one.

Lukianoff and Haidt define trigger warnings as "alerts that professors are expected to issue if something in a course might cause a strong emotional response." Note the syntax of this sentence, which presents trigger warnings not as something professors choose to do in environments that we control, but as something externally imposed upon us ("are expected to issue"). This way of describing trigger warnings is an example of a tactic we see used widely to critique trigger warnings while portraying college students as a bunch of paradoxically terrifying wimps.

Lukianoff and Haidt provide a series of such examples, from the viral *Vox* essay "I'm a Liberal Professor, and My Liberal Students Terrify Me" to the complaints of Jerry Seinfeld that young people are so threateningly soft that he won't play at college campuses. The implication here is that students are at once too thin-skinned to withstand discussions of Ovid or rape law or gay jokes, and powerful to the extent that their demands for trigger warnings must be heeded by professors, university administrations, and visiting comedians.

Between these two extremes—of teachers buckling under students' demands and of teachers coddling oversensitive students—there's the reality of teaching. While a miniscule number of colleges and universities have gone so far as to codify trigger warnings for professors, most trigger warnings exist as a pedagogical choice that professors make in situations over which we exercise considerable control. (And have existed as such for much longer than the present debate suggests: While "trigger warning" was not part of my vocabulary as an undergraduate, introductory comments like "we're going to spend some time

today on lynching images, so prepare yourselves for graphic and difficult material" were indeed.)

Professors give warnings of all sorts that, when not explicitly entangled in the national politics of political correctness, amount less to coddling than to minimizing chances of disengagement with material. "Block off more time this weekend than you usually do, since the reading for Monday is a particularly long one," for instance, is a reasonable way of reducing the number of students who show up unprepared by issuing a warning. "Today we're discussing a poem about rape, so be prepared for some graphic discussion, and come to office hours if you have things to say about the poem that you're not comfortable expressing in class," meanwhile, is a similarly reasonable way of relieving the immediate pressure to perform in class, which stresses out so many students.

Those of us who occasionally use trigger warnings are not as naïve as we're made out to be; we understand that there is no magical warning that will assuage all anxieties and protect students from all traumas, nor is there a boilerplate trigger warning or trigger warning policy that professors can be reasonably expected to follow formulaically. Rather, trigger warnings are, in practice, just one of a set of tools that professors use with varying degrees of formality to negotiate the give-and-take of classroom interactions. If you take away the media hysteria surrounding trigger warnings, you're left with a mode of conversational priming that we all use: "You might want to sit down for this"; "I'm not sure how to say this, but…" It's hardly anti-intellectual or emotionally damaging to anticipate that other people may react to traumatic material with negative emotions, particularly if they suffer from PTSD; it's human to engage others with empathy. It's also human to have emotional responses to life 15 and literature, responses that may come before, but in no way preclude, a dispassionate analysis of a text or situation.

I'm not blind to the problems with trigger warnings and hyperbolic political correctness. The examples Lukianoff and Haidt cite are alarming: Harvard law students asking professors not to use the word "violate"; Brandeis students calling even critical acknowledgment of racial stereotypes of Asian-Americans "microaggressions"; Northwestern professor Laura Kipnis being accused of Title IX violations for an article she wrote for *The Chronicle of Higher Education*. But I'm not convinced that we can lay these problems—and by extension, adverse developments in the mental health of college students—at the feet of trigger warnings.

The backlash against trigger warnings is part of a larger iteration of backlash against political correctness, which tells us something important about where the public thinks the power lies. People on the margins may get press for tweeting things like "kill all white men," and the occasional professor may be undeservedly shamed or ousted for running afoul of students with certain P.C. language expectations. In both scenarios, however, the heart of the matter is who holds the authority to choose the best (or worst) course of action. The P.C. backlash and the trigger-warning backlash hold a common fallacy: They see pushback from the margins and mistake it for threats to the most institutionally powerful.

20   "Kill all white people" is a despicable sentiment, but in practice it's not white people who face the gravest threats of being gunned down by those who wield the authority to do so. Similarly, students can demand trigger warnings or sensitivity trainings, but students remain more vulnerable to institutional power than the professors who assign their grades or the administrators

who adjudicate their missteps. And if there exist situations in which professors really are "terrified" by our students, and students are actually lapsing into mental distress because we're too afraid to cross them, then the problem is much bigger than trigger warnings. The problem is mistrusting the experience and authority of professors in our roles as teachers and intellectual caregivers. If we can lose our jobs either for teaching traumatic material or for failing to warn students adequately about it, what's really happening here isn't that we're ruining students by coddling them; we're losing the authority we rely on to be sensitive to students' anxieties without giving into them, to use techniques like trigger warnings judiciously without being forced to use them in some generalized and codified way.

The trigger warning problem isn't actually a trigger warning problem; it's what happens when the messy business of teaching and learning, and the complex challenges to students' mental well-being, become flashpoints in the culture wars. The effect of this entanglement is an exaggerated impression of trigger warnings that draws on the most extreme examples, a tactic that mirrors and plays into the very currents of partisan politics that Lukianoff and Haidt lament as a threat to American democracy. Of course, the authors consider trigger warnings to be "bad for American democracy," too, and call on universities to "officially and strongly discourage" them. Instead of seeking new sources of outrage around trigger warnings, though, we should understand more thoroughly why this particular pedagogical choice, one of so many, has become a national wedge issue. That trigger warnings are rare, and may be of occasional benefit to professors like me who employ them, is too inconvenient a reality for those who are busy waging war on political correctness.

On Trigger Warnings
AMERICAN ASSOCIATION OF UNIVERSITY PROFESSORS

A current threat to academic freedom in the classroom comes from a demand that teachers provide warnings in advance if assigned material contains anything that might trigger difficult emotional responses for students. This follows from earlier calls not to offend students' sensibilities by introducing material that challenges their values and beliefs. The specific call for "trigger warnings" began in the blogosphere as a caution about graphic descriptions of rape on feminist sites, and has now migrated to university campuses in the form of requirements or proposals that students be alerted to all manner of topics that some believe may deeply offend and even set off a post-traumatic stress disorder (PTSD) response in some individuals. Oberlin College's original policy (since tabled to allow for further debate in the face of faculty opposition) is an example of the range of possible trigger topics: "racism, classism, sexism, heterosexism, cissexism, ableism, and other issues of privilege and oppression." It went on to say that a novel like Chinua Achebe's *Things Fall Apart* might "trigger readers who have experienced racism, colonialism, religious persecution, violence, suicide and more." It further cautioned faculty to "[r]emove triggering material when it does not contribute directly to the course learning goals."

As one report noted, at Wellesley College students objected to "a sculpture of a man in his underwear because it might be a source of 'triggering thoughts regarding sexual assault.' While the [students'] petition acknowledged that the sculpture might not disturb everyone on campus, it insisted that we share a 'responsibility to pay attention to and attempt to answer the needs of

all of our community members.' Even after the artist explained that the figure was supposed to be sleepwalking, students continued to insist it be moved indoors."[1]

The presumption that students need to be protected rather than challenged in a classroom is at once infantilizing and anti-intellectual. It makes comfort a higher priority than intellectual engagement and—as the Oberlin list demonstrates—it singles out politically controversial topics like sex, race, class, capitalism, and colonialism for attention. Indeed, if such topics are associated with triggers, correctly or not, they are likely to be marginalized if not avoided altogether by faculty who fear complaints for offending or discomforting some of their students. Although all faculty are affected by potential charges of this kind, non-tenured and contingent faculty are particularly at risk. In this way the demand for trigger warnings creates a repressive, "chilly climate" for critical thinking in the classroom.

Our concern extends to academic libraries, the repositories of content spanning all cultures and types of expression. We think the statement of the American Library Association regarding "labeling and rating systems" applies to trigger

This report was drafted by a subcommittee of the Committee on Academic Freedom and Tenure of the American Association of University Professors in August 2014 and was approved by that Committee. The AAUP "defends academic freedom and tenure, advocates collegial governance, and develops policies ensuring due process." The article appeared on aaup.org.

[1] Jenny Jarvie, "Trigger Happy." *New Republic*, March 3, 2014, www.newrepublic.com/article/116842/trigger-warnings-have-spread-blogs-college-classes-thats-bad.

warnings. "Prejudicial labels are designed to restrict access, based on a value judgment that the content, language, or theme of the material, or the background or views of the creator(s) of the material, render it inappropriate or offensive for all or certain groups of users.... When labeling is an attempt to prejudice attitudes, it is a censor's tool."

5   Institutional requirements or even suggestions that faculty use trigger warnings interfere with faculty academic freedom in the choice of course materials and teaching methods. Faculty might feel pressured into notifying students about course content for fear that some students might find it disturbing. Of course there may be instances in which a teacher judges it necessary to alert students to potentially difficult material and that is his or her right. Administrative requirements are different from individual faculty decisions. Administration regulation constitutes interference with academic freedom; faculty judgment is a legitimate exercise of autonomy.

There are reasons, however, for concern that even voluntary use of trigger warnings included on syllabi may be counterproductive to the educational experience. Such trigger warnings conflate exceptional individual experience of trauma with the anticipation of trauma for an entire group, and assume that individuals will respond negatively to certain content. A trigger warning might lead a student to simply not read an assignment or it might elicit a response from students they otherwise would not have had, focusing them on one aspect of a text and thus precluding other reactions. If, for example, *The House of Mirth* or *Anna Karenina* carried a warning about suicide, students might overlook the other questions about wealth, love, deception, and existential

anxiety that are what those books are actually about. Trigger warnings thus run the risk of reducing complex literary, historical, sociological and political insights to a few negative characterizations. By calling attention to certain content in a given work, trigger warnings also signal an expected response to the content (e.g., dismay, distress, disapproval), and eliminate the element of surprise and spontaneity that can enrich the reading experience and provide critical insight.

Some discomfort is inevitable in classrooms if the goal is to expose students to new ideas, have them question beliefs they have taken for granted, grapple with ethical problems they have never considered, and, more generally, expand their horizons so as to become informed and responsible democratic citizens. Trigger warnings suggest that classrooms should offer protection and comfort rather than an intellectually challenging education. They reduce students to vulnerable victims rather than full participants in the intellectual process of education. The effect is to stifle thought on the part of both teachers and students who fear to raise questions that might make others "uncomfortable."

The classroom is not the appropriate venue to treat PTSD, which is a medical condition that requires serious medical treatment. Trigger warnings are an inadequate and diversionary response. Medical research suggests that triggers for individuals can be unpredictable, dependent on networks of association. So color, taste, smell, and sound may lead to flashbacks and panic attacks as often as the mention of actual forms of violence such as rape and war. The range of any student's sensitivity is thus impossible to anticipate. But if trigger warnings are required or expected, anything in a classroom that elicits a traumatic response could potentially expose teachers to all manner of discipline and punishment.

10   Instead of putting the onus for avoiding such responses on the teacher, cases of serious trauma should be referred to student health services. Faculty should, of course, be sensitive that such reactions may occur in their classrooms, but they should not be held responsible for them. Instead, as with other disabilities, a student diagnosed with PTSD should, in advance, agree on a plan for treatment with the relevant health advisors who, in some cases, may want to alert teachers to the presence of a trauma victim in their classroom. The Americans with Disabilities Act contains recommendations for reasonable accommodation to be made on an individual basis. This should be done without affecting other students' exposure to material that has educational value.

It is probably not coincidental that the call for trigger warnings comes at a time of increased attention to campus violence, especially to sexual assault that is often associated with the widespread abuse of alcohol. Trigger warnings are a way of displacing the problem, however, locating its solution in the classroom rather than in administrative attention to social behaviors that permit sexual violence to take place. Trigger warnings will not solve this problem, but only misdirect attention from it and, in the process, threaten the academic freedom of teachers and students whose classrooms should be open to difficult discussions, whatever form they take.

Reading and Discussion Questions

1. Why does the AAUP consider trigger warnings a threat to academic freedom?
2. Why are even voluntary warnings a threat?
3. Do you agree with the committee who drafted the report that "[s]ome discomfort is inevitable in classrooms"? Is such discomfort necessarily bad? Explain.
4. Why is Hanlon surprised to find himself defending trigger warnings?
5. What does he mean when he says, "We're still getting trigger warnings wrong"?
6. Part of the appeal of Hanlon's argument is that he puts a lot of faith in faculty members to act with integrity and compassion. What classroom experiences have you had or observed that suggest that his faith in teachers in not misplaced?
7. In what sense is Hanlon seeking a middle ground in his argument?
8. Which of the two arguments do you find more convincing and why?

Gender Stereotypes
Is the "Princess" Phenomenon Detrimental
to Girls' Self-Image?

Some parents make an effort not to box their children into stereotyped gender roles by choosing "boy toys" or "girl toys." Even some of those enlightened parents, though, find themselves with daughters who want to live in a world of tiaras, pink evening gowns, castles, and "happily ever after." Many of these little girls get their notion of being a princess from movies, and that notion is reinforced through multimillion-dollar marketing campaigns. It can be expensive for Mom and Dad, but is it truly harmful? That is the question debated in these articles by Calah Alexander and Crystal Liechty.

The Dangers of the Princess Culture
CALAH ALEXANDER

The other day my sister called. She, my mom and my grandma were shopping for my kids, born and unborn, and she wanted to know if they could buy Charlotte a Disney princess book that plays music. I said, probably a little too vehemently, "No! No princess stuff!"

Now, I realize that this call itself may seem weird to some of you readers, let alone my answer. But here's the deal with my husband and me: we are extremely particular when it comes to children's toys. And since the time when our oldest was still gestating in my womb, we've been very vocal about that. We don't allow toys that light up or make noise unless we have approved them first; we don't allow toys that mimic radios, cell phones,

computers, or televisions; we don't allow handheld video games of any type; and we don't allow either Barbies or anything that relates to princesses. And believe me, we are not above giving a toy back to the giver or even taking it away from our kids once it's been given. (Unless, of course, the giver doesn't know our rules. We're not ingrates.)

These aren't arbitrary rules; we really want our kids to grow up learning to use their imaginations. We also want them to be avid readers and to have attention spans that haven't been

Calah Alexander is a blogger who writes for patheos.com, a Web site dedicated to religion and spirituality. This piece originally appeared on patheos.com on August 2, 2010.

shortened by the in-your-face, at-your-fingertips technology so available to children today. And generally our families don't give us too much grief about those things. The princess rule, however, has been another matter entirely. That one has been as difficult to enforce as it has been to explain. I think a large part of that difficulty lies in the fact that it took me years to even understand the rule, much less agree with it and support my husband in it.

See, when I was pregnant with Sienna, my husband declared in tyrannical fashion that she would not be allowed to have any princess paraphernalia. No tiaras, no big poofy dresses, no princess dolls, no Disney princess merchandise, etc. Also, he decreed that no one was allowed to call her "princess."

5   At the time, I was not only outraged by this, but was actually a little hurt. I considered this to be a sign that he didn't love his daughter in a normal way, the way most fathers do. It didn't make sense to me. Didn't he think she was the most special, beautiful, wonderful thing ever to make its way into Creation? Didn't he want her to grow up knowing how much he loved her, knowing that she was the absolute center of his life? Didn't she deserve all this doting? Wouldn't she always feel undervalued and unloved when she alone of all the other little girls in America was not called "princess"? Wouldn't she always feel that her father just didn't love her enough?

I was so angry about the whole thing that, in a rare occasion in our marriage, my husband had to remind me that I had promised to obey him... which I had, and which I did, very grudgingly.

But as the years wore on he no longer had to serve as the sole enforcer of this rule. The more I met other little girls and the more familiar I became with the culture that surrounds them in our day and age, the more I myself became disgusted with the pampering and preening that is so encouraged by the princess culture.

It took some time for me to really understand what is behind this culture and what exactly is so dangerous to children: but once I did, I began to see its effects everywhere I looked. From strippers to trophy wives, the vast majority of women in our culture are suffering from the debilitating effects of the princess culture.

One of the most sinister aspects of raising little girls with the idea that they are princesses is that it is a heresy; that is, a half-truth. Every little girl is unique and special and wonderful, just like every little boy, just like every person on the face of our planet. But the problem with letting little children believe that they are Somebody is that they very often forget that everyone else is Somebody as well.

In his fairy tale "The Wise Woman, or the   10 Lost Princess," from *The Gifts of the Child Christ*, George MacDonald puts it this way:

> As she grew up, everybody about her did his best to convince her that she was Somebody; and the girl herself was so easily persuaded of it that she quite forgot that anybody had ever told her so, and took it for a fundamental, innate, primary, first-born, self-evident, necessary, and incontrovertible idea and principle that she was Somebody ... and the worst of it was that the princess never thought of there being more than one Somebody — and that was herself.

Consider the damage this does to a child in the long run. The most obvious effect is that the child risks growing up considering herself more important than anyone else. But more subtle and far more sinister is the fact that she will consider herself more important not through any virtue that she possesses, but simply by the very fact of her existence.

If a parent raises a little girl to believe that she is Somebody, i.e., a princess, simply because of who she is, some girls will never be motivated to be other than that. They will have no motivation to obtain an education; no motivation to perfect a skill; no motivation to improve their characters. Rather, they will believe that they do not need any of those things, because they already are . . . sorry for the repetition . . . a princess. Other little girls will make it their mission in life to prove to the world that they are what their parents have always assured them they are. They will seek to set themselves apart in whatever they attempt—athletics, business, music, art—for the sole purpose of showing the world that they are better than others. And that recognition, when and if it comes, will necessarily be hollow and unsatisfying.

Some little girls will grow to expect the same level of praise and devotion from others that they receive from their parents. When they don't get it, they will blame the person failing to give that praise for not understanding, not seeing their true value. Any teacher or coach today is intimately familiar with this. There is a veritable revolving door of students and parents laying blame at the teachers' feet for poor grades, accusing coaches of favoritism for playing athletes that deserve to be played for their talent as opposed to those who deserve to be played for their parents and their own high regard.

Eventually, every one of these little girls will become dissatisfied with everything she looks upon. With no desire to better herself or with that desire motivated only by the need for acclaim, she will never come to understand the joy of learning or the pleasure of work. She will spin her wheels in an endless cesspool of vanity and idleness, dissatisfied with everyone and everything for contributing to her own unhappiness. After all, her own unhappiness couldn't possibly be of her own creation, because she is a princess!

Take a look at the malaise that has afflicted the mothers of suburbia: prescription drug abuse, alcoholism, adultery, rampant depression . . . all of these are symptoms of deep and profound problems in the modern woman's relationship with the world. We (and I say we, because I battle it as much as the next woman) feel that the world owes us something, that every problem we have is due to some terrible injustice being done to us.

Popular culture has only contributed to this problem. Disney in particular reigns supreme in the encouragement of this culture. Take The Little Mermaid, one of the worst movies with the best soundtracks ever made. Consider the character of Ariel. A genuine princess, complete with a king for a father and a kingdom of doting mer-people, yet she wants to live on land. Why? Well, that doesn't really matter, does it? She just wants to. And that's a good enough reason to turn her back on everyone who loves her and resort to desperate measures with no thought for the consequences her actions will have on anyone else, including her poor little guardian who is nearly cooked in the process of trying to protect her! Outrageously, she suffers no consequences. Her father, selfless and loving father that he is, is willing to give his life in exchange for hers. Her prince, a typical lovestruck boy, is willing to risk drowning, shipwreck, and the wrath of a disgusting octopus-witch to save her life. Meanwhile, Ariel flails around in true damsel-in-distress fashion, horrified by the mean, wicked witch. There's

15

never an apology, never a moment when she realizes that this is all her own doing. Instead, by sheer luck, things turn out well. Ariel gets everything she wanted in the beginning without ever having to admit, or even realize, what her blind selfishness nearly did to all those she claimed to love. And her father and the mer-people wave her off into the sunset . . . because after all, she's a princess.

Well, I don't want my daughter to be that kind of a girl. First and foremost, she's simply not a princess. In point of fact, a princess is the daughter of a king, and Sienna is the daughter of a poor graduate student. Second, while she is certainly special to her family and to God, in the eyes of the world she's just another four year old. If she truly wants to become Somebody, to distinguish herself from the millions upon millions of other souls in the world, then she needs to work hard at it, and she needs to choose work that is worth doing for its own sake. She has no innate gift that makes her more, or better, and the sooner she realizes that, the better a person she will become. Third, I don't want her to grow up dissatisfied with the world. The world is a beautiful place, full of wonder and delight, but she will never be able to recognize the beauty of the world if she can't look past herself.

It may seem cruel to other parents, and it's certainly been hard to come to terms with this myself, much less explain to family, but I don't want my child treated as if she's any different than the billions of children who have come before her. The truth is, she isn't. And until she learns that, she'll never truly be at peace with herself or the world.

In Defense of Princess Culture
CRYSTAL LIECHTY

Let me preface this with the disclaimer that the following is my opinion and only my opinion and I realize sane, intelligent women can have other opinions on this topic. Yadda, yadda, yadda. Whatever. Here goes.

I was reading a blog the other day. In it, a mother talked about her daughter's love of princess culture — the movies, the dresses, the stories, and all that goes with it. To paraphrase her, this particular mom was pretty disappointed in this. She "hates" the princess stories. She "really, really" does.

But she was sucking it up and supporting her daughter, anyway (kudos for that). Though it killed her to do so, this mother allowed her daughter to tiptoe through the magical world of castles and happy endings.

But when she had to read the story of Cinderella to her daughter's Kindergarten class, she (and this is where she lost me) adjusted the story to suit herself: Cinderella's stepsisters? "Jealous and misunderstood." The stepmother: "lonely, rather than cruel." Cinderella's prince? A "like-minded partner."

Um . . .

SERIOUSLY!?!

My daughter also loves princess culture, as anyone who has met her is aware. She loves the dresses and the stories and the books and the PRINCES and the LOVE! It's all so wonderful and magical! The funny thing is, when she was

5

Crystal Liechty is a mom — and writer — from Utah. She published her novel *The First Year* in 2006. She posted these comments on the blog *The Unexceptional Mom* on February 7, 2013.

born, I had it in my mind she'd be a tomboy, following after her brother in dirty overalls and messy pigtails.

That is not how things played out. And at first I wasn't sure how I felt about it.

After seeing my daughter decked out in her princess best, someone asked me, "Were you into princesses when you were little, too?"

10   "I don't know," I said, realizing I really didn't know. "I was never given the chance."

I grew up with hand-me-downs and once-a-year trips to Walmart. I'd never really been presented with a princess dress. But thinking back, if I had been, I'm pretty sure I would've been STOKED.

Somewhere along the way, I'd come to believe princesses were a bad thing. Degrading to women; a symbol of being spoiled and superficial (thanks, Paris Hilton); a precursor to those sad little girls in beauty pageants.

But is any of that actually true?

Because, ladies, have you watched Disney's Snow White lately? That girl had someone try to KILL her, yo. And she got away and survived! And the whole time, she was really, really NICE about it.

15   And Cinderella? Talk about work ethic. Plus she had a good attitude, even when people were completely awful to her — she remained honest and sweet. And it was because of that goodness that she was rewarded with a happy ending.

So what's so offensive about this? We don't want our daughters learning that if you work hard and are good and sweet, even in the face of difficult circumstances, you'll find happiness?

I already know the rebuttal to this question: it's the idea that a woman needs a prince to rescue her in order for her to be happy that women find so offensive.

To which I have one question:
WHAT'S SO AWFUL ABOUT THAT?

Why is it offensive that a woman might need   20
a man to be happy? I can tell you, I wouldn't be happy without MY man. Does this make me weak? Or just honest with myself? I know, I know, there are a lot of women out there without men in their lives and they're doing just fine. Great. Good for them.

But why does that mean I should shield my daughter from the idea of finding love? I'm kind of hoping she finds a "prince" to take care of her one day. And these princess movies give me a great chance to talk to her about what kind of guy she should marry: namely someone who is courteous, gallant, willing to do anything for her; to protect her from the bad things in the world.

Which brings me to my next point: lonely stepmothers and misunderstood stepsisters?? I'm sorry but if you're bullying someone and treating them like a slave, I don't care WHY you're doing it — you're a bad guy.

And I want my daughter to understand that there are BAD people out there in the world. If someone hurts her or treats her badly, I don't want her to try understanding where they're coming from. I want her running in the other direction.

And my final point: as far as role models go, do you have any better ideas!?

Would you rather your daughter dress up as   25
and admire Bratz dolls?

Or Katy Perry and Ke$ha? I'm racking my brain, scanning popular culture, trying to find a better avenue to direct my daughter down. There are options — but not a lot.

If my daughter knows all the words to every song in *The Little Mermaid,* so what? It's better than her singing along with Rihanna's latest ode to promiscuity.

And if she hopes to someday find a gallant man to marry, awesome! I hope she finds him. And if she loves wearing princess dresses and crowns and jewels, guess what? Those dresses are pretty classy. She could do worse.

I have another daughter. She's just learning how to be alive right now (dude, getting a toy into your mouth with brand new hands is HARD WORK) but when she's old enough to care, will I steer her in the same direction? No, I won't. If she's into pirates or animals or ninja spies, I will totally support her in that. And use that culture to teach her the values I want her to learn.

But in the meantime, I ain't hating on the princesses and I don't think you should either.

Discussion Questions

1. Why is Calah Alexander initially angry about her husband's "no princess stuff" rule?

2. Alexander claims that telling little girls they are princesses is "heresy." What evidence does she provide to support this claim?

3. How is Crystal Liechty's style different from Alexander's? Is it an effective style for her purposes? Explain.

4. Why does Liechty feel different from Alexander about the princess way of life? Does she offer evidence for her position other than her personal feelings? Explain.

5. Which of the two articles do you find more convincing, and why?

6. Does either author's view of the princess phenomenon coincide with memories you have of children you grew up with — or of your own childhood? Explain.

Economics and College Sports

Should College Athletes Be Paid?

What once might have been dismissed as a ridiculous question is now the stuff of cover stories of leading periodicals. How have sports changed to the point that there is now serious discussion of paying college athletes? Revenue sports bring in millions of dollars. Star athletes are more likely to leave college for the pros before finishing their degrees, lured by the prospect of huge salaries. And many athletes who don't make it to the pros never graduate anyway, but instead play out their eligibility and drop out of sight. The best coaches make millions of dollars while strict rules prohibit their players from earning money signing autographs or from accepting even small gifts from donors. The discrepancy is being noted more and more by the athletes who bring in those millions of dollars and who also bring fame to their schools. Paul Marx and Warren Hartenstine look at two sides of the question.

Athlete's New Day

PAUL MARX

College football is heading for a new day. It won't be long before the players on the field are going to receive more than a pittance. The present structure governed by the rules of the National Collegiate Athletic Association is beginning to crack.

There is the O'Bannon suit against the NCAA challenging its right to prohibit college athletes from sharing in the profits from sales of their names and images. There is the new attention to concussions, often resulting in lifelong disabilities for which the athletes are meagerly compensated. There is the growing awareness that college football is not an amateur sport, as the NCAA insists that it is. And there is the players' growing resentment of the huge gap between their compensation and that of their coaches.

The four highest coaches' salaries for 2012 were $5.2 million for the University of Texas's Mack Brown, $4.2 million for Ohio State's Urban

Paul Marx is a retired English professor from Maryland. His article appeared in the *Baltimore Sun* on October 30, 2013.

Meyer, $3.8 million for the University of Iowa's Kirk Ferentz, and $3.7 million for Louisiana State University's Les Miles. It is rare for any head coach at a major football school to have a base salary of less than half a million. The compensation for the best college football players, on the other hand, is the traditional tuition and fees, room and board, and books. Never is there spending money.

Players are not happy about these disparities, and a protest movement is beginning. As things stand now players put in a full work week of games, practices, meetings, body-building sessions, and travel. There's not much time for, or interest in, school work.

5   But not everyone is cut out to be a student; most football players are not. Most do not meet their college's admission standards. Nevertheless, they are enrolled, as "special admits." At Georgia and Texas A&M, not untypically, 94 percent of freshman football players were special admits. Even with gut courses and special tutoring, barely 50 percent of college football players graduate.

Why can't these athletes play for a college without having to abide by anachronistic NCAA rules? On their recruiting trips, what do coaches tell high school stars? Most often the selling point is simply that playing at his school will enhance the player's chances of being noticed by an NFL team. At the football factories, most players are full-time students, as the NCAA requires, only on paper.

How would a pay-the-player system come about? The key is to get all the schools in one major conference to go ahead and make the change. Already, players at Georgia in the Southeastern Conference and Georgia Tech in the Atlantic Coast Conference have made protests on the field. The protests will spread to teams in other major conferences — the Big 10, the Big 12, the PAC-12.

With more player protests, students will begin to sympathize with the players, and they too will protest. College presidents will sympathize with their students, and they will bring the issue to their conference. The conference will realize that if its schools pay, the best players available will gravitate to that conference. Because their games will be played by the best players out there, broadcasters will pay the conference more to get their games. The necessity of football membership in the NCAA will be gone. To be competitive other major conferences will begin to pay their players.

Enrolling as a full-time student and working on a degree should be optional, not compulsory. Players' relationships to the schools they play for should be spelled out in an individualized pay-for-service contract rather than an NCAA-standardized letter of intent that impinges on basic freedoms. In any case, on game days, paid players would take the field in the school's traditional colors. The cheerleaders would perform, just as they do now. Stadiums would still ring with fight songs and the brass of marching band.

Every two weeks players would receive a   10
paycheck, the amount determined by the demand for a player's services. If players sold their autographs, there would be no penalty. If they wanted to accept free tattoos, they could do so without fear. If automobile dealers wanted to give them breaks on the purchase of new cars, they could accept the deal. Boosters who wanted to help players out financially could do so above board. The injustices of fake amateurism would be gone.

College Athletes Should Not Be Paid
WARREN HARTENSTINE

In ["Athlete's New Day"], Paul Marx demonstrates an embarrassing lack of knowledge and research about his subject. The graduation rate by 2011 for all freshmen entering all U.S. colleges and universities in 2005 was 59 percent, 61 percent for women, and 56 percent for men. Meanwhile, "[a]ccording to the most recent Graduation Success Rate data 82 percent of Division I freshmen scholarship student-athletes who entered college in 2004 earned a degree. In Division II, 73

5 percent of freshmen student-athletes who entered college in 2004 graduated. The graduation rate data are based on a six-year cohort prescribed by the U.S. Department of Education."

Yes, a small percentage of student athletes are admitted as "exceptional admits." But these numbers speak to the success of standards that indicate a high probability of success and the tutoring programs that exist in today's programs, not unlike programs in place for many high potential, non-athletes admitted to every institution.

While Mr. Marx was attending every home game at Michigan and Iowa, I was playing Division I football at one of the other Big Ten institutions with an annual graduation success rate in the top 10 percent nationally, at 85 percent. While he was teaching English, I spent the early years of my career as an assistant dean at a large East Coast state university. Of the 800 living football lettermen from my alma mater who listed a career, the most common professions indicated enormous success. Some 15 percent played professional football as a first career, but 15 percent were corporate executives, 13 percent were K–12 educators, 13 percent were corporate

sales executives, and 10 percent were professionals (doctors, lawyers, dentists, financial services, etc.).

I think contemporary college football players are still motivated by winning the game and earning opportunities to play at the next level. Like us, I seriously doubt that players in at least 100 of the Division I schools even know how much their coaches earn. And I would bet those who do see the high salaries as an institutional investment in their success as players.

In the 1960s when Mr. Marx was presumably warming a bleacher in the Big House, the NCAA scholarship cap provided for tuition, room, board, books and $15 per month "laundry money," period. Fifty years later, with 50-week football programs, no opportunities for summer employment and players predominantly from poorer families, the cap has not changed at $15, period. And scholarship student athletes do not qualify for any additional forms of aid, leaving their parents to sacrifice to subsidize their education.

For those of you who want to cheer for paid college athletes, contact Mr. Marx for more information on Michigan and Iowa. Or better yet, buy Orioles or Ravens tickets. For those of us who want to cheer for student athletes, 85 percent of whom graduate and two-thirds of whom become professional and community leaders, yes, speak up for fairer allowances but stay true to the principles of the self discipline and dual success of those who actually pay a huge price to represent and succeed in your favorite institution of higher education.

Warren Hartenstine is a Penn State graduate who played football for Coach Joe Paterno. The article appeared in the *Baltimore Sun* on November 2, 2013, in response to Marx's.

Discussion Questions

1. Do you find Marx's argument in favor of paying student athletes convincing? Why, or why not?

2. How do you respond to both writers' comments about the high salaries paid to college coaches?

3. Short of paying college football players a salary, what change does Hartenstine suggest in how athletes are compensated?

4. Critique Hartenstine's argument. Do you find it more or less effective than Marx's? Why?

5. Do you personally feel that college athletes should be paid? Why, or why not?

Acknowledgments

Calah Alexander, "The Dangers of the Princess Culture." Reprinted by permission of the author.

American Association of University Professors, "On Trigger Warnings." Reprinted with permission of the American Association of University Professors.

Sharon Astyk and Aaron Newton, "The Rich Get Richer, the Poor Go Hungry" from Sharon Astyk and Aaron Newton, *A Nation of Farmers*. (Originally published in *The Utne Reader*, September/October 2010). Reprinted by permission of New Society Publishers.

Julia Belluz and Steven J. Hoffman, "Katie Couric and the Celebrity Medicine Syndrome." Reprinted by permission of the authors.

Steven Best, "Dispatches from a Police State: Animal Rights in the Crosshairs of State Repression." Reprinted by permission of the author.

Ishmeal Bradley, "Conscientious Objection in Medicine: A Moral Dilemma." Reprinted by permission of Ishmeal Bradley, MD, MPH.

Sunnivie Brydum, "The True Meaning of 'Cisgender'." Courtesy of Advocate.com.

Stephen Burt, "Why Not Get Rid of Student Evaluations?" from *Slate*, May 2015. © 2015 The Slate Group. All rights reserved. Used by permission and protected by the Copyright Laws of the United States. The printing, copying, redistribution, or retransmission of this Content without express written permission is prohibited.

Christopher Caldwell, "Drivers Get Rolled" *The Weekly Standard*, November 8, 2013. ©The Weekly Standard. Reprinted with permission.

Justin Chang, "Grace Shines Past the Emotional Manipulations of 'The Light Between Oceans.'" From the *Los Angeles Times*, September 1, 2016. © 2016 Los Angeles Times. Reprinted with permission.

Guy-Uriel Charles, "Stop Calling Quake Victims Looters" from *CNN.com*, January 21, 2010. Courtesy CNN.

Anna Maria Chávez, "Address to the National Council Session/52nd Convention of the Girl Scouts of the USA (2014)." Copyright © GSUSA. Used with permission.

Samuel Chi, "The NFL's Protest Crisis" from *CNN.com*, September 16, 2016. Courtesy CNN.

CNN Correspondents, "Coverage of Obama's Announcement in Support of Gay Marriage" from *CNNStudentNews.CNN.com*, May 9, 2012. Courtesy CNN.

Richard J. Davis, "In Gun Control Debate, Logic Goes Out the Window" from *CNN.com*, January 25, 2013. Courtesy CNN.

Frank Deford, "Why Keep Athletes Eligible but Uneducated?" originally published in *NPR*, September 4, 2013. Reprinted by permission from the author.

Jared Diamond, "Will Big Business Save the Earth?" from *The New York Times*, December 6, 2009 © 2009 The New York Times. All rights reserved. Used by permission and protected by the Copyright Laws of the United States. The printing, copying, redistribution, or retransmission of this Content without express written permission is prohibited.

Terry Eastland, "Don't Stop Frisking," *The Weekly Standard,* August 26, 2013 © 2014 The Weekly Standard. Used with permission.

Editorial, "Warning: College Students, This Editorial May Upset You." From the *Los Angeles Times*, March 31, 2014. © 2014 Los Angeles Times. Reprinted with permission.

Christopher Elliott, "The Insider: A Tale of Two Airlines," *National Geographic Traveler,* December 2012/January 2013. Reprinted by permission.

Stephanie Fairyington. "Choice As Strategy: Homosexuality and the Politics of Pity," *Dissent* vol. 57, no 1 (Winter 2010), pp. 7-10. Reprinted with permission of the University of Pennsylvania Press.

Ronald Green, "Building Baby from the Genes Up." Reprinted by permission of the author.

Jennifer Grossman. "Food for Thought (and for Credit)." From *The New York Times*, Sept. 2, 2003, p. 23, col. 1. Copyright © 2003 by Jennifer Grossman. Reprinted by permission of the author.

Elisha Dov Hack. "College Life Versus My Moral Code." From *The New York Times*, September 9, 1997. Reprinted by permission of the author.

Aaron R. Hanlon, "The Trigger Warning Myth" from *The New Republic* August 14, 2015. Copyright © 2015 by The New Republic. All rights reserved. Used by permission and protected by the Copyright Laws of the United States. The printing, copying, redistribution, or retransmission of this Content without express written permission is prohibited.

Pamela Powers Hannley, "Bathroom Politics: Preserving the Sanctity of the 'Ladies' Room." Used with permission of the author.

Luke T. Harrington, "Summer Shootings, Pokemon Go: Rebuilding Community in the Wake of Destruction." Used with permission from the author.

Warren Hartenstine, "College Athletes Should Not Be Paid." Reprinted by permission of the author.

James W. Ingram III, Electoral College Is Best Way to Choose U. S. President. Used with permission from the author.

Michael Isikoff, "The Snitch in Your Pocket" from *Newsweek*, February 18, 2010 © 2010 Newsweek Media Group. All rights reserved. Used by permission and protected by the Copyright Laws of the United States. The printing, copying, redistribution, or retransmission of this content without express written permission is prohibited.

Glossary

Abstract language: language expressing a quality apart from a specific object or event; opposite of *concrete language*

Ad hominem: "against the man"; attacking the arguer rather than the *argument* or issue

Ad populum: "to the people"; playing on the prejudices of the *audience*

Analogy: a complex comparison between two things similar in some ways but dissimilar in others, often used to explain the less familiar in terms of the more familiar

Anecdotal evidence: stories or examples used to illustrate a *claim* but that do not prove it with scientific certainty

Appeal to needs and values: an attempt to gain assent to a *claim* by showing that it will bring about what your *audience* wants and cares deeply about

Appeal to tradition: a proposal that something should continue because it has traditionally existed or been done that way

Argument: a process of reasoning and advancing proof about issues on which conflicting views may be held; also, a statement or statements providing *support* for a *claim*

Aristotelian rhetoric: the approach to oral persuasion espoused by Aristotle (384 BCE–322 BCE) and used to shape school curricula well into the nineteenth century; a rhetorical theory based on using a combination of *logos*, *ethos*, and *pathos* to move an audience to a change in thought or action

Assumption: a general principle that establishes a connection between the *support* and the *claim*; see also *warrant*

Audience: those who will hear an *argument*; more generally, those to whom a communication is addressed

Backing: the assurances on which an *assumption* is based

Begging the question: making a statement that assumes that the issue being argued has already been decided

Charged words: words that present a subject favorably or unfavorably

Claim: the conclusion of an argument; what the arguer is trying to prove

Claim of fact: a *claim* that asserts something exists, has existed, or will exist, based on facts or data that the *audience* will accept as objectively verifiable

Claim of policy: a *claim* asserting that specific courses of action should be instituted as solutions to problems

Claim of value: a *claim* that asserts some things are more or less desirable than others

Cliché: a worn-out expression or idea, no longer capable of producing a visual image or provoking thought about a subject

Common ground: used in Rogerian argument to refer to any concept that two opposing parties agree on and that can thus be used as a starting point for negotiation

Concrete language: language that describes specific, generally observable, persons, places, or things; in contrast to *abstract language*

Connotation: the overtones that adhere to a word through long usage

Credibility: the audience's belief in the arguer's trustworthiness; see also *ethos*

Data: facts or figures from which a conclusion may be inferred; see *evidence*

Deduction: reasoning by which we establish that a conclusion must be true because the statements on which it is based are true; see also *syllogism*

Definition: an explanation of the meaning of a term, concept, or experience; may be used for clarification, especially of a *claim*, or as a means of developing an *argument*

Definition by negation: defining a thing by saying what it is not

Emotive language: language that expresses and arouses emotions

Empirical evidence: *support* verifiable by experience or experiment

Enthymeme: a *syllogism* in which one of the premises is implied

Ethos: the qualities of character, intelligence, and goodwill in a writer or speaker that contribute to an *audience's* acceptance of the *claim*

Euphemism: a pleasant or flattering expression used in place of one that is less agreeable but possibly more accurate

Evaluation: a reader's reaction to an argument

Evidence: *facts* or opinions that support an issue or *claim*; may consist of statistics, reports of personal experience, or views of experts

Extended definition: a *definition* that uses several different methods of development

Fact: something that is believed to have objective reality; a piece of information regarded as verifiable

Factual evidence: *support* consisting of *data* that are considered objectively verifiable by the *audience*

Fallacy: an error of reasoning based on faulty use of *evidence* or incorrect *inference*

False analogy: assuming without sufficient proof that if objects or processes are similar in some ways, then they are similar in other ways as well

False dilemma: simplifying a complex problem into an either/or dichotomy

Faulty emotional appeals: basing an argument on feelings, especially pity or fear — often to draw attention away from the real issues or conceal another purpose

Faulty use of authority: failing to acknowledge disagreement among experts or otherwise misrepresenting the trustworthiness of sources

Figurative language: words that produce images in the mind of the reader

Hasty generalization: drawing conclusions from insufficient evidence

Induction: reasoning by which a general statement is reached on the basis of particular examples

Inference: an interpretation of the *facts*

Logos: an argument based on reason

Major premise: see *syllogism*

Metaphor: a comparison that does not make use of *like* or *as*

Minor premise: see *syllogism*

MLA: the Modern Language Association, a professional organization for college teachers of English and foreign languages

Motivational appeal: an attempt to reach an *audience* by recognizing their *needs* and *values* and how these contribute to their decision making

Multimodal argument: words in combination with another medium or an argument in a mode other than the printed word: photographs, illustrations, audio, video, or digital media, for example

Need: in the hierarchy of Abraham Maslow, whatever is required, whether psychological or physiological, for the survival and welfare of a human being

Negation: classification of a term by stipulating what it is not

Non sequitur: "it does not follow"; using irrelevant proof to buttress a *claim*

Paraphrase: a restatement of the content of an original source in your own words

Pathos: appeal to the emotions

Personification: giving human attributes to the nonhuman

Persuasion: the use of a combination of *logos*, *ethos*, and *pathos* to move an *audience*

Picturesque language: words that produce images in the minds of the *audience*

Plagiarism: the use of someone else's words or ideas without adequate acknowledgment

Policy: a course of action recommended or taken to solve a problem or guide decisions

Positional relationship: an audience's ideas about or position on an issue, represented by the audience-subject leg of the communications triangle

Post hoc: mistakenly inferring that because one event follows another they have a causal relation; from *post hoc ergo propter hoc* ("after this, therefore because of this"); also called "doubtful cause"

Proposition: see *claim*

Qualifier: a restriction placed on the *claim* to indicate that it may not always be true as stated

Quote: to repeat exactly words from a printed, electronic, or spoken source

Red herring: an attempt to divert attention away from the subject at hand

Referential relationship: the relationship between writer and subject

Referential summary: a summary that focuses on the author's ideas rather than on the author's actions and decisions

Refutation: an attack on an opposing view to weaken it, invalidate it, or make it less credible

Reservation: a restriction placed on the *assumption* to indicate that unless certain conditions are met, the assumption may not establish a connection between the *support* and the *claim*

Rhetorical relationship: the relationship between writer and audience

Rhetorical summary: a condensation of a passage in the writer's own words that stresses the author's decisions as a writer

Rogerian argument: a rhetorical theory based on the counseling techniques of Carl Rogers (1902–1987) that emphasizes a search for common ground that would allow two opposing parties to start negotiations

Simile: a comparison using *like* or *as*

Slanting: selecting *facts* or words with *connotations* that favor the arguer's bias and discredit alternatives

Slippery slope: predicting without justification that one step in a process will lead unavoidably to a second, generally undesirable step

Slogan: an attention-getting expression used largely in politics or advertising to promote support of a cause or product

Stasis theory: a set of four questions for exploring argumentative topics, developed by the ancient Greek philosophers Aristotle and Hermagoras

Statistics: information expressed in numerical form

Stereotype: overgeneralized perception of an ethnic group, nationality, or any other group

Stipulative definition: a *definition* that makes clear that it will explore a particular area of meaning of a term or issue

Straw man: disputing a view similar to, but not the same as, that of the arguer's opponent

Style: choices in words and sentence structure that make a writer's language distinctive

Summary: a condensation of a passage into a shorter version in the writer's own words

Support: any material that serves to prove an issue or *claim*; in addition to *evidence*, it includes appeals to the *needs* and *values* of the *audience*

Syllogism: a formula of deductive *argument* consisting of three propositions: a major premise, a minor premise, and a logical conclusion

Thesis: the main idea of an essay

Toulmin model: a conceptual system of argument devised by the philosopher Stephen Toulmin; the terms *claim*, *support*, *assumption* (often called *warrant*), *backing*, *qualifier*, and *reservation* are adapted from this system

Two wrongs make a right: diverting attention from the issue by introducing a new point, e.g., by responding to an accusation with a counteraccusation that makes no attempt to refute the first accusation

Validity: logical consistency in a deductive conclusion that follows necessarily from the major and minor premises

Values: conceptions or ideas that act as standards for judging what is right or wrong, worthwhile or worthless, beautiful or ugly, good or bad

Warrant: see *assumption*

Index of Subjects

Index of Authors and Titles